For Social Peace in Brazil

BARBARA WEINSTEIN

FOR SOCIAL PEACE
IN BRAZIL

Industrialists
and the
Remaking
of the
Working
Class in
São Paulo,
1920–1964

The
University
of North
Carolina
Press

Chapel Hill
and
London

HD
8289
S282
W45
1996

© 1996 The University of North Carolina Press
All rights reserved
Manufactured in the United States of America

Library of Congress
Cataloging-in-Publication Data

Weinstein, Barbara.
For social peace in Brazil: industrialists and
the remaking of the working class in São Paulo,
1920–1964 / by Barbara Weinstein.
p.   cm.
Includes bibliographical references and index.
ISBN 0-8078-2297-3 (alk. paper)
ISBN 0-8078-4602-3 (pbk.: alk. paper)
1. Working class—Brazil—São Paulo (State)—History.
2. Industrialists—Brazil—São Paulo (State)—History.
3. Brazil. Serviço Nacional de Aprendizagem Industrial—History.
4. Serviço Social da Indústria—History.
5. Occupational training—Brazil—São Paulo (State)—History.
6. Industrial welfare—Brazil—São Paulo (State)—History.
I. Title.

HD8289.S282W45   1996
305.5'62'098161—dc20   96-10888
                                                          CIP

00 99 98 97 96   5 4 3 2 1

For Erich

Contents

Illustrations

Acknowledgments

For reasons both professional and personal, this book has taken many more years to complete than I originally expected—an admission that will hardly come as a shock to my fellow academics. This protracted process of research and writing has given me plenty of time to incur innumerable intellectual debts that I am happy, at last, to be in a position to acknowledge. I fear, however, that the lapse of time may lead me to omit inadvertently individuals who played an important role when the project was in its early stages. If I do so, I hope they will forgive me and chalk it up to the distortions and lacunae of memory.

I am particularly beholden to the officials and personnel of the Serviço Nacional de Aprendizagem Industrial, the Serviço Social da Indústria, and the Federação das Indústrias do Estado de São Paulo who helped me in the course of my research. Since SENAI, SESI, and FIESP operate as virtually private agencies, their staffs had no obligation to share their published and unpublished documentation with me. Moreover, when I initiated this project, neither SENAI nor SESI showed great interest in preserving historical material or institutional memory. Therefore, the staff members who aided me in my research did so not out of obligation but out of their own goodwill, often interrupting their regular work routines to ferret out sources or make space for me in cramped quarters that were never intended for academic research. Moreover, in some instances, staff members helped me despite the apparent reluctance of "higher-ups" to accommodate a historian whose motives seemed to them somewhat suspect.

Despite my deep gratitude to those in SENAI, SESI, and FIESP who helped me and without whose assistance this project would have been impossible, I feel compelled to note the institutional limits of personal kindness. On several occasions in the course of my research, I was denied access to documents I regarded as important by officials who apparently made their decisions arbitrarily since previous researchers had been granted access to some of these documents. In one instance, an official refused my request to examine records with the assurance that they contained little of interest to me; he will forgive me if I continue to believe that it would have been more appropriate for me to make such a judgment. Yet I had absolutely no recourse in these situations since the organizations claimed the rights of private entities even though their policies had profound implications for the Brazilian public. It is my hope that, over time, these agencies will come to view their documents as public records that should be made available to any serious researcher. Indeed, SENAI has already taken major steps in that direction with the creation of the Núcleo de Memória, which has published a series of important monographs and has gathered together published and unpublished material of a historical nature, transcripts of interviews with SENAI officials, and a wonderful collection of photographs. SESI, regrettably, has not followed suit—I recently discovered that an internal archive that had been an invaluable source for my study literally had been tossed into the dustbin of history due to "lack of space."

These experiences only reinforce my gratitude to those officials and staff members who were willing to make materials available to me. Particularly crucial to my research at SESI was the intervention of Hélvio M. Pinheiro Lima, then director of public relations for SESI–São Paulo; he and his staff generously provided me with material, work space, and encouragement. I am likewise grateful to the personnel of SESI's Divisão de Orientação Social, especially Ana Cristina Gasparini and the very gracious staff of SESI's (now defunct) internal archive.

It gives me great pleasure to acknowledge the assistance I received from the staff of the Núcleo de Memória at SENAI–São Paulo. I offer my heartfelt thanks to its coordinator, Vera Helena Farinas Tremel, and to Maria Helena Valente Senise and Odete Ernestina Pereira; a scholar could not ask for a more knowledgeable and supportive "nucleus" of researchers. The photographs in the text appear courtesy of the Núcleo de Memória. In the early stages of my research, most of SENAI's historical materials were housed in its library. My thanks to the head librarian, Wanda Lúcia Schmidt, and the other members of the library staff, who were unfailingly helpful and congenial. I also thank Naguiça Abe of the SENAI library in Rio de Janeiro for her help.

A considerable portion of my research took place in FIESP's Biblioteca e Arquivo Roberto Simonsen. I greatly appreciate the assistance I received from its resourceful staff, who always managed to locate materials I requested despite having to cope with the challenges posed by the library's relocation. Having done research at so many different locations, I cannot thank every librarian and archivist personally, but I would like to acknowledge the staff at the Departamento Intersindical de Estatísticas e Estudos Sócio-Econômicos, who managed to find a desk for me in an already crowded space and who provided me with good company and lively political commentary. I also thank the staff of the Patrimônio Histórico of São Paulo Light & Power, as well as the personnel of the administrative archive of Light. In Rio, the Centro de Pesquisa e Documentação at the Fundação Getúlio Vargas was a delightful place to work, especially for a researcher on a tight schedule.

Throughout this project, I have benefited from the unflagging support and intellectual inspiration of friends and colleagues both in Brazil and in the United States. I owe my deepest thanks to Maria Lígia Coelho Prado, who read the manuscript and discussed it with me on many occasions and shared with me her views on the difficult questions raised by the political developments of the past decade. I also had the good fortune of finding an intellectual home away from home at the History Department and Arquivo Edgard Leuenroth of the Universidade Estadual de Campinas. The intellectual atmosphere at Unicamp stimulated many of the ideas that informed this project. My thanks to my colleagues there, especially Stella Bresciani, Michael Hall, Edgar de Decca, Ítalo Tronca, Paulo Miceli, Paulo Sérgio Pinheiro, and Marco Aurélio Garcia. My various stays in São Paulo were also enlivened by my good friends Joaquim Alves de Aguiar, Jorge Schwartz, and Maria Helena Capelato.

Closer to home, I had the great advantage of being able to draw support from the unique scholarly environment created by the Latin American labor history conferences. I am indebted to all of the participants at these annual conferences for allowing me to share my work with them (and vice versa), but I am especially grateful to Danny James and John French, whose criticisms and suggestions were consistently helpful and challenging.

I offer special thanks to Robert J. Alexander for graciously making his collection of documents and interview transcripts available to me. His papers are a truly remarkable collection of materials on post–World War II Brazil. I am also grateful to Joel Wolfe, who made the ultimate gesture of scholarly solidarity by providing me with photocopies of his notes on collections to which I was denied access.

At the State University of New York at Stony Brook, I have had the benefit of working within a department that, despite the extreme scarcity of material resources, manages to provide the intellectual energy and personal encouragement that should be the norm in academic life. Many colleagues and graduate students at SUNY–Stony Brook have contributed either directly or indirectly to this project over the years. My thanks to Brooke Larson, Helen Cooper, Temma Kaplan, Gene Lebovics, Paul Gootenberg, and Nancy Tomes for their scholarly advice, constant encouragement, and good humor, which were especially helpful when I hit a rough spot.

I have received financial support from several different sources for the research and writing of this book. A postdoctoral fellowship from the National Endowment for the Humanities allowed me to begin my research, and an NEH summer stipend later made it possible for me to return to São Paulo to make a final round of archival visits. A Fulbright-CIES research fellowship funded another summer in Brazil, and a Fulbright-Hays postdoctoral training fellowship enabled me to spend an entire year in São Paulo and Rio during which I did the bulk of my research. I am exceedingly grateful for this support and therefore especially regret the fact that several of these awards are in danger of extinction. I also thank SUNY–Stony Brook for granting a sabbatical leave during which I wrote most of the first draft of this book; indeed, it is inconceivable to me that I could have completed this study if I had not been able to take that time off from teaching.

I thank David Perry of the University of North Carolina Press for his steadfast interest in this project and for his considerable enthusiasm for all things Brazilian.

When I first conceived this project, my entire family unit consisted of me, myself, and I. Since then, life has become a good deal more complicated and stressful but also far more exciting. It gives me great pleasure to acknowledge the unique "contribution" made by my children, Sarah and Danny, to the completion of this book. As one might expect, they have taken every opportunity to disrupt, distract, and divert me from my writing. I hope they will not be too disappointed that I managed to complete the book anyway.

Finally, this book is dedicated to my husband, Erich Goode, who has contributed to it in countless ways. He twice interrupted his own scholarly routine to accompany me to Brazil and along the way developed his own affection for Brazilian culture and cuisine. Over the years, he has read drafts of portions of the manuscript, cooked me many wonderful meals, and frequently contended single-handedly with two very challenging children. And he did it all with love and affection, even when family life became much tougher than we had ever expected.

Abbreviations

The following abbreviations are used in the text. For abbreviations used in the notes, see pp. 349–50.

ABNT   Associação Brasileira de Normas Técnicas (Brazilian Association for Technical Norms)

ASSESI   Associação dos Servidores do SESI (Association of SESI Employees)

CAD   Centro de Aprendizado Doméstico (Center for Domestic Instruction)

CAI   Curso de Aspirantes a Indústria (Course for Minors Seeking Industrial Employment)

CAO   Curso de Aprendizes de Ofício (Course for Craft Apprentices)

CBAI   Comissão Brasileira-Americana de Educação Industrial (Brazilian-American Commission for Industrial Education)

CFESP   Centro Ferroviário de Ensino e Seleção Profissional (Railway Center for Professional Education and Selection)

CGTB   Confederação Geral dos Trabalhadores do Brasil (General Confederation of Brazilian Workers)

CIESP   Centro das Indústrias do Estado de São Paulo (Center of Industry in the State of São Paulo)

CIFTSP   Centro dos Industriaes de Fiação e Tecelagem do Estado de São Paulo (Center for the Textile Industry in the State of São Paulo)

CIPA   Comissão Interna para a Prevenção de Acidentes (Internal Commission for Accident Prevention)

CLT   Consolidação das Leis do Trabalho (Consolidated Labor Laws)

CNI   Confederação Nacional da Indústria (National Confederation of Industry)

CO   Círculo Operário (Workers' Circle)

CSPI   Curso de Supervisão do Pessoal na Indústria (Course for Supervision of Personnel in Industry)

CTM   Curso de Trabalhadores Menores (Course for Working Minors)

DOPS   Departamento de Ordem Política e Social (Department for Political and Social Order)

DOS   Divisão de Orientação Social (Division of Social Orientation)

FGTS   Fundo de Garantia por Tempo de Serviço (Severance Pay Fund)

FIESP   Federação das Indústrias do Estado de São Paulo (Federation of Industries in the State of São Paulo)

GEIA   Grupo Executivo da Indústria Automobilística (Executive Group for the Automobile Industry)

IAPI   Instituto de Aposentadorias e Pensões dos Industriários (Retirement and Pension Institute for Industrial Employees)

IDORT   Instituto de Organização Racional do Trabalho (Institute for the Rational Organization of Work)

MOP   Movimento de Organização Profissional (Movement for Professional/Craft Organization)

MSD   Movimento Sindical Democrático (Democratic Union Movement)

MUT   Movimento Unificador dos Trabalhadores (Workers' Unifying Movement)

PCB   Partido Comunista do Brasil (Brazilian Communist Party)

PIPMOI Preparação Intensiva para Mão de Obra Industrial (Intensive Preparation for Industrial Labor)

PSD   Partido Social Democrático (Social Democratic Party)

PTB   Partido Trabalhista Brasileiro (Brazilian Labor Party)

PUI   Pacto de Unidade Intersindical (Interunion Unity Pact)

SAPS   Serviço de Alimentação da Previdência Social (Social Welfare Nutrition Service)

SENAC   Serviço Nacional de Aprendizagem Comercial (National Service for Commercial Training)

SENAFI Serviço Nacional de Seleção, Aperfeiçoamento e Formação de Industriários (National Service for the Selection, Improvement, and Training of Industrial Workers)

SENAI   Serviço Nacional de Aprendizagem Industrial (National Service for Industrial Training)

SESC   Serviço Social do Comércio (Commercial Social Service)

SESI   Serviço Social da Indústria (Industrial Social Service)

SESP   Serviço de Ensino e Seleção Profissional (Professional Education and Selection Service)

SIFT   Sindicato da Indústria de Fiação e Tecelagem (Textile Industry Employers' Syndicate)

STIMMMESP	Sindicato dos Trabalhadores nas Indústrias Metalúrgicas, Mecânicas e de Material Elétrico de São Paulo (Union for Workers in the Metallurgical, Mechanical, and Electrical Material Industries of São Paulo)
TWI	training within industry
UDN	União Democrática Nacional (National Democratic Union)

For Social Peace in Brazil

Introduction

On January 26, 1942, Getúlio Vargas, as dictator of Brazil's Estado Novo, created the National Service for Industrial Training (Serviço Nacional de Aprendizagem Industrial, or SENAI). Four and half years later, Vargas's successor, Eurico Dutra, still operating within the constitutional framework of the Estado Novo, created the Industrial Social Service (Serviço Social da Indústria, or SESI).[1] Neither event was attended by great drama or fanfare, but both represented important new developments in the area of Brazilian social policy. These developments were not just new but unusual, since both of these agencies were to be funded and operated by associations of industrialists rather than by the state that had decreed them into existence. And they were unusual not just in Brazil but in global terms as well, since it would have been difficult during the 1940s, when the role of the state in industrial relations and everyday life was expanding, to find another society where responsibility for vocational training and social services was being assigned to essentially private organizations.[2] By government decree, Brazilian industrialists had acquired jurisdiction over two agencies that would prove central to industrial relations and worker discipline.

This book is about the origins of SENAI and SESI and the roles they played in the industrialists' campaign for greater productivity and social peace. The actual founding of SENAI and SESI can be attributed to specific historical circumstances, but the forms and practices they assumed reflected a discourse of rationalization and scientific management that had been percolating among industrialists, engineers, social hygienists, and educators in São Paulo since the 1920s. These employers and professionals touted rational organization as a means to create a more productive, efficient, and modern Brazil, with a higher standard of living for all.

Several studies of labor and industrialization in Brazil during the 1920s highlight this new inclination within the industrial elite, viewing it through the lens of class conflict and seeking to unmask it as a thinly disguised strategy for social control.[3] From this perspective, rationalization is a dialectical and instrumental response to new challenges from workers and an assertion of employer authority against the power of skilled craftspeople. Inspired by accounts of struggles between craft-based production and scientific management in early industrializing nations, students of Latin American labor have scoured archives and memory banks for similar conflicts in Brazil.[4]

I began my research with these same assumptions, but I gradually came to the conclusion that those who were hunting for Brazilian versions of such struggles elsewhere were on the wrong track. For one thing, the evidence of either resistance by skilled workers or efforts by employers to reorganize the work process in the 1920s and 1930s proved rather sparse. In Brazil, as in most other industrializing nations, innovations associated with scientific management and rational organization were implemented erratically and unevenly. Yet the instrumental view of rationalization only makes sense if we find evidence that it was widely implemented (successfully or not) at the point of production, where it would have had a material impact on relations between workers and employers. Failing that, the narrow conception of rationalization as a thin disguise for intensified domination yields meager rewards for the historian's labors.

New developments in the historical profession, which can be succinctly described as "the linguistic turn," suggested a different and, I would argue, more rewarding approach. Rather than treating the industrialists' discourse as merely a "mask" for labor-control strategies in the material sphere, I began to consider the discourse itself as productive and as a source of power. Although the industrialist proponents of rational organization did aspire to remake the workplace and the workforce, their concern in the first instance was to remake *themselves*, or at least their class image. By identifying with new currents in rational organization and scientific management, these industrialists, engineers, and educators claimed for themselves the professional authority and technical expertise necessary to modernize Brazilian society.[5] In contrast to the "arbitrary" authority of the old-style planter or mill owner, these new industrial owner-managers defined a wide variety of problems affecting the organization of production in the workplace, and even life beyond the factory walls, as technical, not social, questions to be resolved on a systematic, scientific basis. Such an approach, they claimed, would not only increase productivity but also promote social peace.[6]

This effort by certain industrialists and their allies to capture the discourse of technical competence had formidable implications for labor relations and the work process, but workers were not the industrialists' sole concern. The industrialists also sought to change the perception of industry among politicians, professionals, and middle-class reformers who harbored doubts about industry's contribution to economic progress and social peace. By asserting the centrality of technical expertise as well as their privileged access to it, industrialists attempted to protect and expand their authority within the factory and claim an authoritative role in the making of public policies and programs.

This is not to imply that we can divorce the discursive realm from the material world. The advocates of rationalization actively promoted new forms of workplace organization and worker socialization that they genuinely expected to transform employer practices. After all, success in this realm would give further credibility to their claims of technical expertise and advance their own vision of modernity.[7] But such efforts hardly produced a linear progression to a rationally organized industrial society. Changes occurred fitfully and unevenly, with the very notion of what was rational or scientific being redefined or contested from one year to the next. In this regard, SENAI and SESI represented unusual attempts to institutionalize rational approaches to worker training and social services, but they, too, repeatedly had to revise their practices to conform to new managerial strategies, changing economic conditions, or pressures from labor unions.

Having jettisoned my earlier assumptions about wide-ranging transformations on the factory floor, I also had to rethink the position of workers and organized labor. If new work processes were not being systematically introduced until a later period, there was no reason to expect pitched battles between skilled workers and scientific managers. The few instances of such struggles that historians have unearthed have been eagerly presented as prize examples of workers' "agency."[8] But even these acts of resistance seem so sporadic and hapless that they reinforce an image of labor as a marginal participant in the entire process of industrialization, subject to repeated and inevitable defeats by a relentlessly modernizing bourgeoisie.

This view of Capital as representing the forces of modernity and of Labor as romantically resisting those forces breaks down even if we confine ourselves to the shopfloor, where workers sometimes pressed for "rational" innovations that their employers were reluctant to adopt. The picture changes even more substantially if we shift our focus to the discursive positions of those who presumed to speak for industrial workers. Some scholars have expressed their disappointment at early Brazilian labor leaders' failure to develop a more thoroughgoing critique of new technology and work processes, but it is difficult to imagine a viable standpoint from which to express such a critique in early twentieth-century Brazil. Labor activists could have little recourse to the past and tradition in a predominantly agrarian and hierarchical society that had only recently abolished slave labor. It is not surprising, then, that even militant labor leaders would seek to make Brazil more modern and link the prospect of a better life to economic progress.

Far from fighting a rearguard action against the forces of modernization, many labor leaders and activists cited workers' skills and expertise as crucial to any transformation of Brazilian industry. Furthermore, they used their own claims to technical expertise to criticize the "worst" employers— those who clung to antiquated machinery and shoddy methods and thus retarded economic growth. What was generally in dispute was not rationalization itself but how authority should be distributed within the rationalized enterprise. In contrast to the scenario of modernizing employers clashing with quixotic workers, this approach gives us a more complex picture of industrialist spokesmen and labor leaders operating in much the same discursive field, with both declaring themselves the champions of modernity and progress.

Since a central theme of this study is the industrialists' use of scientific management both to reorganize production and to reconfigure public debate about industrialization, it would be appropriate to discuss and clarify these concepts and define such terms as "Taylorism" and "Fordism." The term "rationalization" is used here to encompass a variety of strategies for reorganization of work and even everyday life along lines that its advocates regarded as "scientific." Common to all of these strategies was a rejection of empirical methods based on practice and tradition in favor of methods developed from "scientific principles" determined by experts. Whether applied to factory work, administration, transportation, or urban planning, these methods were expected to result in greater efficiency and productivity, which would redound to the benefit of employers, workers, and consumers.

The most famous, or perhaps most notorious, of these strategies is Taylorism. The North American industrial engineer Frederick Winslow Taylor in his *Principles of Scientific Management* (1911) elaborated a system designed to increase productivity without significant investment in new equipment. The key elements of Taylor's system were the simplification of tasks and the individualization of the labor force. The division and parcelization of tasks meant that they could be mastered quickly and that a small number of managers could monopolize the knowledge necessary for the operation of the firm. This led, in turn, to a more hierarchical organization of the factory and a reduction in the number of skilled workers, who tended to be more expensive and demanding than the unskilled. Those workers who remained in the reorganized factory would be expected to maintain a high level of productivity and would be paid according to individual output above a stipulated norm. This not only would be an incentive to increased productivity but would undermine collective movements for higher wages and reduce the appeal of unions. And to insure that there was no waste of movement or energy, Taylor and his colleagues in scientific management, "efficiency experts" Frank and Lillian Gilbreth, developed time-and-motion studies to determine the most efficient ways to perform individual tasks.[9]

The blatantly oppressive features of Taylorism, as well as its mechanical view of human physical and psychological characteristics, meant that, even in the United States, it was rarely implemented in its purest form. But several of the elements associated with it—division and simplification of tasks, concentration of technical knowledge in the upper levels of management, and linking of wages to productivity—had a significant impact on industrial organization in the United States, Europe (especially after World War I), and, eventually, Latin America.[10]

As ambitious as Taylorism was in pursuing its goal of reorganizing factory life, it did restrict itself, as a set of principles, mainly to the workplace setting. Taylor simply assumed that proper instruction and remuneration would be sufficient to mold a new, "Taylorized" industrial labor force.[11] He and his acolytes also focused their attentions almost exclusively on factory production as the center of industrial life and regarded scientific management as the responsibility and prerogative of the private sector.

The innovations and principles commonly referred to as Americanism or Fordism incorporated many aspects of Taylorism while broadening scientific management's purview and implications. The Fordist factory, with its assembly-line system, introduced Taylorist notions about parcelization of tasks and intensified work pace into the production process, relying on technical innovations to control work flow and rhythm. Advocates of Fordism, while still regarding the factory as the key location for change, believed that the transformation of the workplace required attention to aspects of industrial life beyond the production process. Whereas Taylor saw the threat of dismissal and the promise of reward as sufficient to discipline the new workforce, Henry Ford and his imitators viewed the problem as more complex: workers had to have the proper moral and social values and an internalized sense of discipline to perform well in the new industrial environment. The famous Department of Sociology that Ford installed in his factory precisely reflected the Fordist concern with and interference in the lives of factory workers beyond the assembly line. The Fordist "ethic," therefore, implied broader industrialist involvement in developing social services, instruction, and recreational activities for workers. All of these areas would be rationally organized to promote proper values and discipline that would be manifested by workers in all areas of everyday life, not just in the workplace.[12]

Perhaps the broadest and most fundamental ramification of Fordism was Henry Ford's notion that mass production, made possible by Taylorist and assembly-line methods, required a mass market. Therefore, while he demanded a high level of productivity from his workers, the standard wage he offered was correspondingly high—high enough, he calculated, for the workers to regard themselves not just as producers of industrial goods but also as consumers. This, he believed, would be the most effective means to resolve class conflict since the worker-consumer would have a direct stake in the development of more efficient forms of production that could provide inexpensive goods to a rapidly growing market.

The loose set of principles known as Fordism aspired to transform much more than the work process; its target was all of society, with the factory as the fulcrum for social reorganization and economic change. Like Taylor, however, Ford and his followers saw this great transformation as the responsibility and dominion of the industrialists, who would carry out the task without interference or compulsion from the state. Yet the very ambitiousness of the Fordist "philosophy," with its implications for social services, education, recreation, and standards of living, meant that industrialists' aspirations would eventually include state power itself.[13] As we will see, this would especially prove to be the case in predominantly agrarian countries like Brazil where a philosophy that placed the factory at the center of all social and economic life could have little impact without state support.

Another source of ideas that helped form the rationalization movement was the field of industrial or applied psychology, for many years known as *psicotécnica* in Brazil. Psychologists, educators, and other professionals in Europe and the United States began advocating various "scientific" methods of testing for job selection and orientation in the early twentieth century, but public response was limited until World War I. The massive, and now notorious, testing of recruits by the U.S. military during the war greatly increased the visibility and credibility of psychological testing and orientation and spurred their more widespread use in industrial settings after the war.

Proponents of applied psychology argued that it offered a uniquely rational and scientific means to determine the basic qualifications and proclivities of job candidates, whether for factory or office work. This would, in turn, reduce the incidence of maladjustment in the workplace and increase worker productivity and satisfaction. Industrial psychologists such as Henri Pieron and Elton Mayo also criticized Taylor and his followers for treating human beings merely as extensions of machines. While supporting many aspects of scientific management, advocates of psychological testing, selection, and guidance promoted what they viewed as a more rational method of job placement than simple financial punishment and reward. Moreover, they claimed that, in the interests of efficiency, the work environment should be adjusted somewhat to account for the necessities of human psychology and physiology rather than human beings adapting themselves to the needs of machines. Better "human relations" in the workplace were necessary to fulfill the rationalizers' goal of producing the most goods in the least time and with the least effort.[14]

These three elements—Taylorism, Fordism, and applied psychology—combined and modified formed the intellectual basis of the international movement for rational organization of work that gained momentum in the aftermath of World War I. Although we associate the enthusiasm for rationalization with postwar Europe or the new Soviet workers' state, industrialists and engineers in São Paulo were embracing the gospel of rationalization at precisely the same moment as their European and Soviet counterparts.[15] Indeed, its Brazilian proponents typically came from abroad or studied overseas at institutions where such ideas were all the rage. However, the concepts of rational organization and scientific management should not be regarded as "foreign" ideas, except in the most conventional sense of originating outside of Brazil's physical borders. Rather, these ideas would become so closely identified with modernity that they could easily migrate across the frontiers of any and all industrializing societies. At the same time, rational organization, broadly defined, was susceptible to modifications in particular national contexts. As we will see, the Brazilian advocates of philosophies such as Taylorism and Fordism regularly adapted aspects of the rationalizer's discourse to accommodate their own assumptions about Brazilian workers and Brazilian society.

In writing this study, I have had the advantage of building upon an extensive, revisionist literature on Brazilian industrialists and industrial relations that has grown steadily since the early 1980s. This scholarship has thoroughly dissolved earlier images of the Brazilian industrial bourgeoisie as politically weak, insufficiently modern, and incapable of developing its own economic or social projects for Brazilian society.[16] A major target of revisionist criticism has been the *estado de compromisso*. The notion of a "compromised state" emerged from the work of Francisco Weffort and other Brazilian social scientists who argued that the state, in the supposed absence of a hegemonic "national bourgeoisie," substituted for that class and created the conditions for Brazil to overcome its dependent position in the global economy. From this perspective, it is the state-centered elite, allegedly autonomous from any specific social group, that forges a viable project for industrialization and social control.[17]

The pioneering research of scholars such as Juárez Brandão Lopes, Leôncio Martins Rodrigues, and Fernando Henrique Cardoso in the 1950s and early 1960s provided the foundation for the construction of the *estado de compromisso* model.[18] By conducting extensive and often illuminating interviews with factory workers and industrialists, these Brazilian social scientists produced a portrait of both "industrial classes" as conglomerations of individuals with little consciousness or concern about collective issues or organizations and therefore incapable of effectively promoting a revolutionary or hegemonic class project. It was only "natural," then, for the state to step into the vacuum created by the incapacities of these social classes.

These ground-breaking studies, whose insights are still very useful for students of recent Brazilian history, suffer from the limitations of social science research of that era. These scholars brought to their research strong assumptions about the normative consciousness and behavior of industrial workers and employers—standard practice for social scientists in the postwar period. It is now nearly a matter of routine for social historians to criticize earlier research for its reliance on ideal types, which led to the predictable conclusion that Brazilian workers (and employers) were not sufficiently militant, progressive, or class-conscious.

These scholars' reliance on individual interviews and opinion surveys also created certain limitations, such as their assumption that a social class is equivalent to the sum of its parts. Since Cardoso, Brandão Lopes, and others defined class, in the first instance, as an objective economic relationship, the equation of the whole with the sum of its parts was tenable. But once we discard such a notion of class and approach it as a historical construct, we can no longer define it by summing up the views of "typical" workers or employers. Rather, we must consider the role of figures who are not themselves workers or employers in the formation of class identity, and we must take into account the relations and tensions between those who actively define and promote certain class objectives and those whose participation is intermittent or contingent. Throughout this study, I make a distinction between the ideas and discourses articulated by the industrial(ist) leadership and the often indeterminate ideas of the "rank and file." But I assume that a distinction between leaders and the groups they represent does not render the leadership "inauthentic" or unrepresentative; on the contrary, we should expect such distinctions given the particular compromises leadership entails. What is relevant is how successful the leadership is in recruiting support from or disciplining the members of the class it purports to represent.

The industrialists and industrial technocrats who will play central roles in this study bear little resemblance to the intellectually flawed and politically inept elites who figure in the *estado de compromisso* version of modern Brazilian history. Leading members of São Paulo's emerging industrial bourgeoisie and intellectuals closely associated with that class were trying to develop a more coherent approach to the problems of industrialization and social relations as early as the 1920s. Far from turning over their social and intellectual role to a corporatist state, the Brazilian industrialists and their technocratic allies aggressively sought to play a leading part in the reorganization of industrial relations and in the molding of a new urban-industrial society.[19]

The historian can approach the industrialists' role in this process from many angles, but I have chosen to focus on SENAI and SESI for a number of reasons. First, these massive agencies are interesting as original contributions by Brazilian industrialists to the realm of labor relations and modernization. More important, as agencies operated by employers' associations, they closely adhered to the industrialist leadership's ideological tendencies and objectives and were responsive to the industrialists as a class. Furthermore, I will argue that SENAI and SESI represented the culmination of long-standing aspirations by members of the industrial bourgeoisie to reorder work processes and industrial organization as well as labor relations. Neither agency ever fulfilled all of the goals laid out by its formulators, but they provide us with a particularly coherent outline of the industrial world the employers hoped to create. SESI's motto, "For Social Peace in Brazil," is especially evocative of industrialist aspirations.

Although SENAI and SESI are central to this study, it is both more and less than an institutional history of these two agencies. I will examine SENAI's and SESI's founding and operations in considerable detail, but I do not pretend to cover every aspect of their history. Rather, I am interested in exploring the ways in which their programs, services, and publications reflected and implemented the industrialists' strategies to "remake" the Brazilian worker and to insure social peace. Also, the unusual status of SENAI and SESI as public agencies functioning as private organizations effectively controlled by the employers further illuminates the relationship between the industrialist associations and the Brazilian state.

SENAI and SESI are national agencies with branches in every state of Brazil. However, I have chosen to focus on their history and operations in the city and state of São Paulo, by far the most industrialized region of Brazil and the one with the longest and most dramatic record of conflict between capital and labor.[20] Not only does over half of Brazil's industrial production take place in São Paulo, but it was the paulista bourgeoisie that was responsible for the conceptualization and creation of these two agencies. And the programs operated by the two agencies in the São Paulo area were by far the most elaborate and heavily funded. Finally, the paulista industrialists have played an exceptionally important political and ideological role in the history of twentieth-century Brazil, and their influence has extended well beyond the borders of their home state. Thus, their actions and objectives in the period under study had broad national implications even though they were played out in a local context.

The 1920s, a period of intellectual ferment, political conflict, and economic crises in Brazil, will serve as the starting point for this study.[21] During this decade, Brazilian industrialists, technocrats, and intellectuals began to discuss in earnest new forms of worker training and social services as part of a larger project for industrialization and even initiated some early experiments in these areas. In Chapter 1, I will explore these new trends among both industrialists and educators as well as the discourse of the emerging labor movement on technical progress and its consequences. Chapter 2 looks at the industrialists' role in the formation of new labor legislation and social policies during the 1920s and early 1930s and their changing attitudes toward the state and state intervention. I examine industrialist activity both in the formal political arena and in public/private ventures such as the Institute for the Rational Organization of Work (Instituto de Organização Racional do Trabalho, or IDORT).

Chapter 3 details the debates and proposals that led to the actual founding of SENAI and SESI. I look at the tensions between those intellectuals and technicians who favored a state-centered approach to worker training and social services and those who proposed a more "pragmatic" alternative that reflected what they perceived as the needs of the industrial sector. I also take into account historical contingencies, such as the wartime labor shortage and the postwar labor mobilization, that help explain the specific forms assumed by SENAI and SESI. Chapter 4 looks at the formative years of each agency and how they responded to the particular circumstances that produced them. It examines the practical problems involved in assembling a small army of instructors and professionals imbued with the appropriate attitudes about rationalizing Brazilian society and remaking the Brazilian worker. It also reflects upon the lasting impact of these formative years on SENAI and SESI and their relations with labor and the state.

In Chapter 5, I look at the responses of employers and workers to SENAI and SESI and to the projects they represented. Although both organizations were strongly identified with major industrialist associations, SENAI and SESI encountered a certain amount of resistance from the employer "rank and file," who evaded their obligatory contributions to the agencies and often proved less than enthusiastic about the services offered by SENAI and SESI. This chapter considers this mixed reaction and the means by which the industrial leadership disciplined its uncooperative colleagues. To gain some sense of how workers and the labor movement responded to SENAI and SESI, I look specifically at union newspapers and trace the changing attitudes toward these agencies from the time of their founding through the mid-1960s. I emphasize the receptivity of labor to certain programs sponsored by SENAI and SESI as well as the various discursive strategies used by labor to contest the industrialists' claims of being the champions of "social peace."

Chapters 6 and 7 examine more closely the programs sponsored by SENAI and SESI to "remake" the Brazilian worker and the working-class household from the late 1940s on. I look first at the tendency of both agencies to define the Brazilian worker as a "problem," which ran counter to the populist discourse of the period, with its celebration of workers' contributions and sacrifices for national development. In Chapter 6, I discuss the programs and courses developed specifically to promote more rational forms of amusement and a more hygienic family life, paying particular attention to the role assigned to working-class women in the formation of a new working-class *cum* middle-class culture. Chapter 7 explores the programs developed for the shopfloor, including intensive on-the-job training, courses for supervisors, instruction in human relations, and publications on occupational health and safety. In all of these programs, I argue, the tendency was to attribute the defects of Brazilian industry to worker ignorance or incompetence.

Chapter 8 analyzes the "politics of social peace." It looks at the industrial leadership's uneasy participation in the populist alliance that characterized Brazilian postwar politics and the roles SENAI and SESI played in this ambiguous relationship. Although the members of the Federation of Industries in the State of São Paulo (Federação das Indústrias do Estado de São Paulo, or FIESP) benefited from the developmentalist policies advocated by successive Brazilian presidents, industrialist spokesmen expressed growing alarm at state concessions to organized labor and the rise of Communist influence in the union movement. SENAI and SESI, as public agencies that were privately operated, provided the industrial leadership with a space to assert their technical and social authority in Brazilian society while distancing themselves from an increasingly dissonant political arena. And SESI specifically served as a vehicle for collaboration in the process that culminated in the 1964 military seizure of power. Finally, a brief epilogue examines the fates of SENAI and SESI after 1964, when the military dictatorship resorted to more conventional means of insuring social peace.

Rationalization
and Industry
in the 1920s

In December 1918, an enterprising young businessman named Roberto Simonsen addressed a crowd of friends and employees in the port city of Santos. The gathering was convened to honor those who had donated time or money to combat the tragic influenza epidemic that had marked the end of World War I. Expected to deliver the usual inflated and meaningless oratory, Simonsen surprised his audience by instead enunciating a strategy for postwar Brazilian prosperity, with an emphasis on new, more scientific and efficient methods of production that would raise both profits and living standards by lowering costs. Simonsen specifically assured the workers in attendance that the reduction in the costs of production would not come at the expense of their salaries but rather through the "maximum efficiency of labor," which would be obtained through "perfect organization, through intelligently adopted policies, that reduce the waste of time and effort to the minimum." Moreover, the "true principles of cordial cooperation between owners and workers would reign" as a result of such "perfect organization."[1]

Simonsen was speaking in earnest; he would spend much of his life promoting the policies that he advocated in this speech. Yet there is no better indicator of the yawning gulf between his vision of a "perfectly organized" industrial economy and the material practices of Brazilian industry than an account of production made some eight years later at a factory owned by Simonsen himself. Between 1923 and 1926, the Cerâmica São Caetano steadily lost money despite considerable investment in its productive capacity. Before resolving to sell the ceramics factory, which produced mainly building materials, Simonsen decided to consult an industrial engineer, Egydio M. de Castro e Silva, who was also a personal friend.

The conditions that Castro e Silva discovered in a factory owned by Brazil's most prominent advocate of rationalization must have been sobering. If his account is accurate, the Cerâmica São Caetano was a textbook case of everything proponents of rationalization, whether Taylorism, Fordism, or the more general "scientific management," decried. Castro e Silva's first improvement was to install a scale at the entrance to the factory to insure greater uniformity of weights and measures and thereby rectify the utter lack of standardization in the materials used. He then reduced the cost of transporting clay to the factory by purchasing the raw material from only one producer, located closest to the factory, instead of two. He also noted that both suppliers of clay were firms in which the factory's *mestre geral* was a partner, suggesting that they had been chosen for the head foreman's financial gain and not necessarily because they offered the best quality clay. Similarly, he found that the firm continued to use wood rather than high-quality coal in its ovens at least in part because the wood supplier was the father of the Cerâmica's commercial director. And in an amusing variation on the usual recommendations, the industrial engineer suggested that animal traction be substituted for the freight train that transported clay to the factory, arguing that the train was uneconomical for such a short haul.

In the sphere of production, Castro e Silva cited several areas where a waste of labor occurred, observing that "the exaggerated employment of *serventes* was notorious in almost all sectors of work." To remedy this problem in the clay-drying process, he installed a mechanical shovel, operated by animal power, "that permitted the dispensing of almost all of the *serventes* in this service." In the next step, he found that laborers deposited the dried clay in piles and then brought it to four "disintegrator" machines by the shovelful "in a constant and slow back and forth." This Castro e Silva remedied by designing a series of funnels that distributed the dried clay directly to the four machines. Next, young boys transported the moist clay powder in kerosene cans on their heads to the hydraulic presses. For this process, Castro e Silva substituted a simple and increasingly common apparatus—a conveyor belt. Still in the realm of production, Castro e Silva noted that the *mestre geral* mixed the raw materials "a olho" (by eye). He acknowledged the mestre's long experience but warned that "without the indispensable precision . . . he could not obtain a uniformly satisfactory and comparable result."[2]

Castro e Silva's comments and tone indicate that he believed immediate responsibility for the alarming state of the factory lay with the *mestre geral* and the commercial director. Wed to traditional, "nonscientific" procedures and a network of business associates and relatives who received preferential treatment, these men were unlikely to bring about the rationalization of the Cerâmica São Caetano. As for the workers, a dialogue between Castro e Silva and the furnace stokers that he reproduces in his report indicates that he saw them as inadequately trained and operating on erroneous assumptions. But he explicitly places the blame for this on management, which provided the workers with inappropriate raw materials and poor direction. Simonsen, the firm's president-director, shared responsibility for these problems, but as part owner of a construction company, a meat-packing plant, a banking house, and several other factories, he could hardly be expected to keep tabs on the day-to-day operations of the Cerâmica.

What were the "human" implications of the recommendations made by Castro e Silva? He never tells us, except for mentioning that the commercial director soon resigned his post and was replaced by none other than Castro e Silva. What became of the dispensable *serventes* we do not know. Nor do we know whether the workers operating the disintegrators or the hydraulic presses experienced any intensification in their work routines as a result of the more rapid and regular delivery of raw material, though it seems highly likely. It is interesting to note that the positions eliminated as a result of Castro e Silva's make-over of the factory were the most menial and unskilled jobs. At the same time, the employee who probably saw the most drastic reduction in his leeway and authority was the *mestre geral*, who was a supervisor and "technician," not a worker. Still, the overall impact of Castro e Silva's plan was what one would expect from an advocate of rationalization: greater discipline, increased mechanization, and the predominance of scientific calculation over practical experience.

The travails of this industrial engineer in the Cerâmica São Caetano illustrate how irregular, haphazard, and uneven the transformations in Brazilian industry were during this period. Despite considerable intellectual enthusiasm for "scientific organization of work" and "rationalization" of industrial life, few factories implemented such methods. This is not to say that the issue of rationalization during the 1920s should not be taken seriously. Too many important figures in the industrial community saw it as a solution to a wide range of problems—social conflict, high production costs, inadequately prepared workers—to dismiss it as a mere intellectual fad. Instead, we need to examine the nature of its appeal as well as the impediments to its broader material realization.

Brazil during the 1920s hardly offered the economic conditions usually associated with the dissemination of principles of scientific management or rational organization. Even its most rapidly expanding manufacturing center—São Paulo—had an industrial economy that consisted mainly of large textile factories and many small workshops. At the regional level, São Paulo's coffee-growing sector continued to surpass industry in terms of output and employment. Increased productivity, meanwhile, was not an extremely pressing matter considering that overproduction was a major problem, especially for the textile industry, during the 1920s. As for the supply of workers, the labor market seems to have posed few problems for potential employers since they had access to a swelling population of immigrants. A U.S. consul stationed in São Paulo reported in 1922 that "it is doubtful that there exists anywhere an industrial sector that offers better labor conditions from the employer's point of view. The workers in diverse industries and crafts are abundant . . . and earn only low salaries."[3] As for labor unrest, it had been reduced considerably by the combined forces of government repression and employer-sponsored antiunion activities.[4] And although political factions had made some attempt to impose legislation limiting child labor and mandating paid vacations, industrialists generally ignored these new laws with impunity.[5]

The majority of industrialists, like their counterparts elsewhere, paid little heed to the new wave of rationalization, and we have only a handful of concrete examples of industrialists or educators who consciously applied scientific principles to the workplace or to worker training. Yet it is difficult to dismiss the escalating interest in such ideas among influential industrialists, engineers, and educators during the 1920s. Far from being an intellectual fad that faded in subsequent decades, interest in rationalization intensified in the 1930s and 1940s, taking on increasingly institutionalized forms for its dissemination and implementation. How, then, do we explain the apparent precocity of the rationalization movement in the Brazilian context? To answer this question, it would be useful to take a closer look at the early careers of two men who will figure prominently in this story—Roberto Simonsen and Roberto Mange. These two Robertos, one an engineer turned industrialist, the other an engineer turned educator, represent in different but related ways the aspirations of those who advocated rationalization as the solution to a host of social and economic problems.

The Engineer as Industrialist

Roberto Simonsen was born in 1889, the last year of the Brazilian monarchy and the first year in which Brazilian property owners had to rely solely on free workers for their labor supply. Simonsen's father, Sydney Martin Simonsen, was an English citizen of Danish-Jewish descent who came to Rio de Janeiro in the 1870s to head an English banking house. In 1883 he married Robertina da Gama Cochrane, daughter of a prominent engineer and politician. Soon after the birth of Roberto, the family moved to the port city of Santos, where Simonsen spent his early years.

Since Roberto eventually distinguished himself by adopting ideas of mostly foreign origin, one might expect that his father was a key influence in his intellectual formation. However, Roberto, himself, and his subsequent biographers claimed that the formative influence in his youth was his maternal grandfather, Inácio Wallace da Gama Cochrane.[6] The latter had served as an engineer in the construction of several major railroad lines and was the founder of the Companhia City of Santos, dedicated to improvements in that city's public utilities. In addition, he had been a deputy in the São Paulo legislative assembly from 1870 to 1879 and owned a share of his family's coffee plantations in the Paraíba Valley. Thus, young Roberto had the benefit of a grandfather with both traditional political and social connections and a professional career that placed him in the vanguard of technical expertise in Brazil.[7]

Roberto's contact with his grandfather intensified as he moved to his grandparents' home in the city of São Paulo to attend the Colégio Anglo-Brasileiro. He remained in the state capital throughout his subsequent education in engineering at the Escola Politécnica, from which he graduated a few months before his twenty-first birthday. From there, Roberto followed in his grandfather's footsteps, working first for the Southern Brazil Railway (1909–10) and then moving to Santos, where he spent two years as chief engineer of the Santos Municipal Improvements Commission. In 1912 he left his job with the commission and founded the Companhia Construtora de Santos.

This private construction company, which Simonsen directed for the next eighteen years, would provide a testing ground for pioneering attempts at scientific organization and management. The annual reports that Simonsen prepared, especially from 1916 on, reflect a self-conscious and systematic attempt to apply rational methods of organization to the entire enterprise and to develop new approaches to labor relations, such as forming commissions of workers and managers to negotiate disputes. Several recent works suggest that these efforts were a response to the relatively long history of labor militancy in Santos and the apparent success of skilled construction workers in controlling the labor market. As one student of rationalization has argued, since the construction trades did not lend themselves to mechanization, the only means of increasing management control over the labor process was the simplification of tasks and the de-skilling of the workforce, which would allow rapid substitution of highly paid and militant skilled workers with unskilled laborers.[8]

There can be little doubt that social control was a high priority for Simonsen. This is particularly apparent after the 1917 general strike, which had substantial repercussions in Santos and halted work at the Companhia Construtora.[9] In the 1918 company report, Simonsen alerted his readers to the dilemma facing all employers: "The greatest problem currently facing engineers and administrators is, incontestably, the economical utilization of labor. . . . Today's industrialists must abandon the old patterns, recognize the worker's discontent, and firmly offer him fair remuneration; if not, they will witness the obstruction of production in the mistaken effort to decide this question by political means, when it can certainly be resolved by economic means."[10] The renewed strike activity and mass demonstrations of 1919, just months after the publication of this report, could only have reinforced Simonsen's concerns about impending "class warfare" in Brazil.[11]

Even so, we should not simply boil his interest in scientific management down to his need for better labor control. The broader concerns expressed by Simonsen in his two public addresses in December 1918, and even in the preamble of the company report for that year, indicate that he already held a view of the role of Taylorism and rationalization that went well beyond his specific firm and its particular labor relations problems. Several features of the passage cited above are worthy of further comment in this vein. Perhaps most striking is Simonsen's reference to engineers and administrators (obviously including himself) rather than *empresários* or employers. He apparently preferred to highlight the facet of his identity that implied technical expertise rather than his authority as owner of the enterprise. His reference to the "economical utilization of labor" raises an issue that will become a central theme in subsequent writings: that increased productivity is the surest means to raise wages and enhance workers' well-being. He then urges "today's industrialists" to "abandon the old patterns," a rather remarkable recommendation given that industry in São Paulo, on a significant scale, was barely a decade old. Finally, his plea to resolve this matter by "economic means" in order to avoid political solutions lays out a basic assumption of the technocratic discourse: that so-called "social questions" should be resolved through the systematic application of technical knowledge rather than through less "rational" political remedies. Labor control was a central concern, but not the sole element, in the vision Simonsen was developing.

Two experiences during the 1910s and 1920s contributed to Simonsen's awareness of the futility of applying scientific management to a single enterprise in the context of a broader and very unscientific economy. One involved a branch firm of the Companhia Construtora, the Companhia Santista da Habitação Econômica, whose specific mission was to construct affordable housing for working-class inhabitants of Santos. Although Simonsen's methods allowed the firm to build houses more cheaply than usual, he nevertheless discovered that the purchasing power of the proletarian population was so low that the price of even these very modest homes was beyond the average worker's reach.[12]

Simonsen's 1921 contract with the federal government to construct military barracks and hospitals throughout central and southern Brazil yielded much more positive results for his firm. In all, the Companhia Construtora, under Roberto Simonsen's close supervision, built forty-nine barracks, military hospitals, and other structures for the Ministry of War. An endeavor of this scale provided Simonsen with an unprecedented opportunity to apply his "industrial" methods to construction, with particular emphasis on standardization and workforce organization. Such methods, Simonsen claimed, allowed the company to spend less time and money than projected in the original plans.[13]

The problems encountered in such a massive and transregional undertaking were also highly instructive for the young engineer and businessman.[14] The project gave Simonsen a greater appreciation of the uneven nature of development in Brazil since much of the construction took place in areas with only the most elemental transportation facilities and since often even the simplest raw materials had to be shipped from São Paulo to the construction site. Along with the raw materials, the company usually had to send technicians and "specialized" workers since such skilled laborers were not available in sufficient numbers outside of São Paulo and Rio. Thus, although Simonsen touted the venture as a triumph of scientific methods, he also recognized the limits of rationalization in such an unevenly developed economy and labor market.[15]

These limits by no means discouraged Simonsen from formulating a genuinely national view of industrialization; indeed, this experience may have reinforced his sense that a reorganization and expansion of paulista industry alone was infeasible and undesirable. He made this position clear in his 1928 address to celebrate the founding of the Center of Industry in the State of São Paulo (Centro das Indústrias do Estado de São Paulo, or CIESP), of which he was the first vice president. The fact that the directors of the new organization chose Simonsen to give the main address on this occasion indicates his importance as a spokesman for the industrialists. Count Francisco Matarazzo, São Paulo's most successful businessman and CIESP's first president, contented himself with a brief speech and an introduction of Simonsen. Matarazzo referred several times in the speech to the state of São Paulo and CIESP's future role in realizing the legitimate aspirations of his class. Moreover, "these aspirations, far from conflicting with those of other classes, are in harmony with their aspirations for the fulfillment of a common objective: the ever-greater prosperity of the state of São Paulo."[16]

Simonsen certainly shared Matarazzo's belief that increased industrial prosperity would benefit all social classes, but he went considerably further than the count, repeatedly speaking of the "Brazilian industrial park" and the interests of Brazil as a whole, not just the state of São Paulo. Far from simply serving the narrow interests of a handful of factory owners, industry, in Simonsen's discourse, was essential for a nation to prosper and become truly independent. He began his celebration of industry by affirming that "everywhere industry is considered the path to advancement for a nation's people." Emphasizing industry's role in stimulating new ideas and forming new elites, he then extolled the role of the machine in society: "The machine, by increasing productivity, reduces manual and dehumanizing labor, sharpens the intelligence, permits the raising of wage standards, the reduction of work hours, favors educational opportunities for the proletariat, and generally improves the fate of humanity!"

Moving from the people to the nation, Simonsen articulated the broadest possible view of industry's role in Brazilian society: "In the current stage of civilization, the economic independence of a great nation, its prestige, and its political activity . . . can only be granted due consideration if that country possesses an efficient Industrial Sector, which matches its agricultural development."[17] And just in case anyone had missed the broader implications of industrialization for national life, he referred to the case of the United States, "where there is an intense campaign to improve methods in industry and business, which are regarded as a sort of public function, including social responsibilities and duties toward the community. In those nations that are in the vanguard of civilization, production in all of its aspects is considered a national, not individual, enterprise."[18]

The tenor of Simonsen's speech did not simply reflect his own ideological predilections. Much of what he said on that day was a response to widespread criticism of the paulista industrialists, especially among sectors of the elite and middle classes that at other times had been allies. The very founding of CIESP formalized the paulista industrialists' break with the Commercial Association of São Paulo, which had previously served as their main organ of representation. The decision to leave the Commercial Association and create an alternative body specifically designed to promote the interests of industry was a consequence of the debate over protective tariffs. Following President Washington Luis's implementation of an exchange rate stabilization program in 1926, merchants took advantage of the renewed purchasing power of the milreis to import large quantities of textiles into the Brazilian market, leading paulista textile manufacturers to argue that the existing tariff rates were insufficient to protect local industry. Although the industrialists succeeded in convincing the federal government to raise the tariff rates, they did so without the support of the Commercial Association; the latter's decision to side with importing interests in this matter precipitated the split and led to the founding of CIESP.[19]

Those who opposed higher tariffs and, by extension, the industrialists' policies did not simply argue in terms of conflicting sectoral claims. Critics routinely portrayed Brazilian industry as "artificial"—that is, economically viable only because of government protection.[20] They blamed the tariffs protecting industry for the steadily rising cost of living in Brazil's urban centers. Middle-class intellectuals also denounced industry for spreading the contagion of class warfare to Brazil and portrayed Brazilian industrialists as exacerbating the situation by refusing to make the most minimal concessions to their workers. Even the writer Monteiro Lobato, who published Simonsen's *O Trabalho Moderno*, noted in his 1927 translation of Henry Ford's *My Philosophy of Industry* that industrialization in Brazil had created "magnates in return for the perpetuation or aggravation of human misery." Therefore, he argued, "no country needs more than ours to understand and practice Fordism." In other words, attacks on the Brazilian industrialists, and especially the cohort derisively known as the "Italian Counts," came not from diehard antimodernists but from a more challenging position that questioned the industrialists' capacity to play a leading role in the process of modernization.[21]

The views Simonsen expressed at CIESP's inauguration reflected the industrialists' need to develop an alternative view of industrialization, and of their role in it, that would neutralize the arguments of their opponents. Many of the ideas Simonsen had already been airing in public a decade earlier served this purpose very well. It was not tariff protection that was driving up the cost of living but rather unscientific and irrational methods of production in all economic sectors that only industrial development could counter. Moreover, industrialization would expand purchasing power, thereby canceling out any tendency to make life more costly.[22] As for fears of class struggle, Simonsen had answered these years before by pointing out the advantages of cheap industrial production for all social classes. His speech in 1928, however, broadened his discourse by stressing the need for the business community to develop a sense of public service.[23]

Perhaps the material conditions of paulista industry in the 1910s and 1920s were not ripe for the large-scale introduction of rational or scientific methods, but the ideological and social context gave Taylorism, Fordism, and its correlates considerable appeal. The relative weakness of the labor movement, especially in factory production, made it unlikely that Brazilian manufacturers viewed these methods as providing them in an immediate sense with the "tools" to undermine the power and authority of skilled workers. Rather, the appeal seems to have lain precisely in the promise of increasing productivity and lowering production costs without lowering salaries or ostensibly increasing exploitation. Moreover, the Fordist philosophy offered the factory as a model for all of society and identified the industrial bourgeoisie, allied with a corps of technically trained managers, as the social class best suited to perform the civic duties of a modern elite because of its technical expertise and strategic position in the sphere of production. For an industrialist-engineer like Simonsen, energetically attempting to jettison the old image of the potbellied plutocrat, rationally organized industry and scientific management were the perfect panaceas for Brazil's economic and social ills.[24]

Due to his highly public and articulate presentation of industrialist views, Roberto Simonsen has emerged in recent scholarly works as the bellwether of his class. Far from being a peculiar or isolated figure, Simonsen seems to have been the guiding light for a group of young industrialists and industrial managers. Mariano Ferraz, Aldo Mário de Azevedo, Armando de Arruda Pereira, Antônio de Souza Noschese, Horácio Lafer, and Morvan Dias de Figueiredo all shared Simonsen's enthusiasm for scientific management as a way of increasing productivity and resolving social conflict. The first four had studied engineering, like Simonsen, and had gone abroad to learn the relatively new and more specialized subfield of industrial engineering. Several of them were ardent admirers of North American industrial organization and labor management, and all were active in local Rotary Clubs, Arruda Pereira eventually becoming the first Brazilian president of Rotary International.[25] Through the latter organization, these individuals had direct contact with intellectual trends that called for rational methods, service by businessmen to the broader community, and class cooperation as a means to defeat "extremism" (at least of the left). To be sure, during the 1920s, most of these men were relatively unknown figures in the paulista industrial milieu, a community still dominated by the "Italian Counts," but all would play leading roles in industrialist organizations during subsequent decades.[26]

Even among the intellectually inclined, significant variations existed in the industrialists' discourse. Octávio Pupo Nogueira, a minor textile manufacturer who served for many years as the secretary of the Center for the Textile Industry in the State of São Paulo (Centro dos Industriaes de Fiação e Tecelagem do Estado de São Paulo, or CIFTSP) and then of CIESP, produced a steady stream of reports and opinion papers on industrial issues. In contrast to Simonsen, his writings present a purely defensive view of social relations within industry.[27] Far more pessimistic in his attitude toward modern labor and technology, Pupo Nogueira claimed that mechanization had robbed work of its "poetic" aspect, so that "the modern worker, in his automatism, does not participate in the processes of production."[28] He also was more likely to treat the employer's authority within the factory as a natural function of property ownership combined with intimate knowledge of the specific workplace rather than as a consequence of technical expertise. Finally, Pupo Nogueira's writings leave the strong impression that he regarded physical force as the only guarantor of social peace.

Despite these differences, Pupo Nogueira's position was by no means diametrically opposed to that of Simonsen and his acolytes. None of the industrialists under discussion eschewed the use of force, whether in theory or in practice, as a tool for restraining the working class. While preaching social peace, Simonsen and others recognized that such "peace" might, at times, be purchased only by means of police intervention. What really separated the engineers *cum* industrialists from their more "conservative" colleagues is their persistently optimistic view of the social implications of modern work processes and their emphasis on technical competence as a source of authority.[29]

Another influential industrialist figure of the period who offered a somewhat different, if overlapping, set of ideas from those articulated by Simonsen is Jorge Street. This medical doctor turned textile manufacturer is one of the most interesting and controversial members of the early industrial bourgeoisie. The historiography frequently portrays Street as the epitome of the good *patrão*. His celebrated Fábrica Maria Zélia in São Paulo boasted a *vila operária* (worker village) that provided, aside from decent housing, a nursery and primary school for workers' children, a pharmacy, a grocery, recreational facilities, and a church.[30]

All post hoc categories are somewhat arbitrary, but Street's methods seem to embody the traditional paternalistic approach to authority, according to which the owner is the father figure who directly controls every aspect of his workers' lives. Easily confused with the Fordist strategy, it nevertheless envisioned a very different role for both employers and workers than the project Simonsen was advocating and portrayed the factory as a community closed off from the rest of the world rather than the world as a factory, writ large.[31] Although Street manifested touches of egalitarianism—his daughters would serve refreshments to workers in his home and dance with employees at company celebrations—he saw his workers as dependents who should submit to his authority, not because of his greater scientific knowledge but because he was the patriarch.[32]

Pupo Nogueira and Street, in their very different ways, demonstrate that Simonsen's discourse was by no means the sole expression of industrialist opinion during the 1910s and 1920s. If we move from discourse to practice, the limits of Simonsen's influence, or the influence of the ideas he promoted, become more obvious. Even Simonsen, in his own factory, did not necessarily practice what he preached. And the existing documentation reveals only a handful of cases in which industrialists or industrial engineers applied Taylorist methods to production during the 1920s.[33] CIESP and other employer associations paid considerable attention to the rationalizers' ideas. In 1929 the center, along with the governor of São Paulo, sponsored a series of lectures by Professor Leon Walther, a Swiss efficiency expert, whose themes included Taylorism, worker selection, workforce training, adaptation of instruments to the worker, and professional fatigue.[34] But the emphasis was on talk, not practice.

The experiment carried out by Paulo Nogueira Filho from 1922 to 1924 in the Santa Branca silk textile plant provides us with one of the few explicit accounts of Taylorism in the factory during this period. Nogueira Filho, a self-styled "progressive bourgeois" and eventual leader of the Partido Democrático in São Paulo, seized the opportunity presented by his new job as manager of this medium-sized factory to apply rational and scientific methods. Apparently, the firm's owners shared his interest in these methods: the president of the company, a relative, presented Nogueira Filho with a book by Taylorite Henry Gantt that became his guide in reorganizing the factory.[35] According to Nogueira Filho's retrospective account, he was able to gain the cooperation of the firm's employees by promising them participation in the increased profits and by guaranteeing a minimum wage to all who fulfilled the production quotas. With support from above and below, Nogueira Filho found it possible to apply "some Taylorist norms." These included instituting "a progressive salary scale, rationaliz[ing] the distribution of raw materials, specify[ing] the activities of foremen, and tak[ing] measures to suppress waste, to elevate the quality of work, and to facilitate the execution of tasks." Once in place, he claimed, the innovations had an immediate impact on the factory workforce. In a marvel of Taylorist self-selection, "the unproductive and lazy workers departed, and in their place came capable and energetic ones, attracted by the possibility of earning high wages through the new system."[36]

In Nogueira Filho's own words, he personally went to "radical extremes" in his enthusiasm for Taylorist principles. At the same time, he indicates that "certain efficient innovations" had been broadly implemented in paulista industries by the 1920s. Indeed, if we change the focus from conscious, systematic Taylorist practices to a looser definition of rationalization, the overall picture in São Paulo might prove more heartening to proponents of scientific management. Virtually all studies of industrialization in the 1920s describe a process of concentration and increased mechanization, especially in textile production but also in heavier sectors such as the metallurgical industry.[37] Since parcelization of tasks was most effective in large-scale industry, the trend toward industrial concentration provided more favorable conditions for rationalization. Increased mechanization, though not essential for all forms of rational organization, also facilitated the implementation of new methods and new forms of labor discipline in the factory.[38]

As for the Fordist injunction to provide a wide range of services for workers so as to improve their moral character and strengthen their identification with the goals of industry, here, too, we can see considerable progress in the 1920s, especially in larger enterprises. John French, in his study of São Paulo's industrial suburbs, notes that three very different companies—Simonsen's Cerâmica São Caetano, the French-owned Rhódia rayon-chemical plant, and the Italian-owned Pirelli metalworking factory—initiated similar "welfare-capitalist" policies during the 1920s.[39] These included systematic methods of hiring new workers and of rewarding productive and loyal employees with extra wages and bonuses. More generally, company housing became a regular form of recognition for "deserving" employees, and almost all large firms offered some sort of medical care for their workers and, less often, their families. Factory cafeterias and food cooperatives also became more commonplace, and many firms sponsored athletic clubs and other recreational facilities.

These innovations had many of the same features as the services offered to workers in Jorge Street's famous Vila Maria Zélia. The Pirelli and Rhódia plants also shared many of the objectives of the earlier *vilas operárias* created by textile manufacturers.[40] Factory-sponsored activities, in both cases, were usually designed to emphasize discipline and regimentation. And every employer assumed that workers who would face the loss of their homes as well as their jobs if they went on strike or complained about conditions would be more cautious about confronting their bosses. Still, it is important to delineate some of the ideological and practical distinctions between the older, paternalistic factories and the newer Fordist enterprises.[41]

First of all, whereas the older textile firms portrayed social services as products of the owner's benevolence and charity and identified such benefits with the figure of the *patrão*, the newer firms presented such facilities as emblematic of the advantages of employment in a modern and progressive industrial corporation. Typically, newer firms assigned responsibility for such services to personnel departments, which would administer them rationally and impersonally.[42] Advocates of Fordist innovations also stressed the direct connection between such services and increased productivity, particularly with regard to reducing accidents and illness. And systems of bonuses and extra wages were to operate on a scientific basis, not in the arbitrary and paternalistic manner exemplified by the Indústrias Reunidas Francisco Matarazzo, where bonuses were distributed on the patriarch's birthday and "special donations were passed out to those who married or who had children on the lucky day."[43] Finally, whereas the newer firms aspired to reinforce workers' ties to the company by providing housing, schools, and recreational activities, the rapid urban-industrial expansion of the 1920s and the constant labor turnover made Street's effort to create a self-contained factory community increasingly archaic and "unscientific."[44]

To be sure, Fordist innovations and welfare services were by no means universally available, even in the larger factories; physical conditions in many plants remained dangerous and unsanitary despite increased attention to safety and sanitation, and many workers had no access at all to the most rudimentary forms of hygiene or health care. In true Fordist fashion, even those industrialists who were most enthusiastic about such innovations did not argue that they should be compulsory or subject in any way to inspection by the state. The predictable result was a patchwork of improvements that did little to resolve the most basic problems of living and working conditions.[45]

A survey of the industrial scene in the 1920s must have been both encouraging and sobering for Simonsen and his followers. Here and there one could find evidence of the use of "scientific methods" or at least partial transformations in industrial organization. Mechanization and increased concentration of industry meant more opportunities for the implementation of their strategies. And a growing number of firms could boast that they offered at least some of the services associated with the modern, progressive, "hygienic" factory.[46] But on the other side of the ledger were thousands of workshops and small factories operating on an artisanal basis as well as many large plants that functioned as virtual agglomerations of workshops. Many owners and *mestres*, as well as workers, resisted or simply ignored methods associated with Taylorism and rationalization. At the same time, countless firms had not made a single serious improvement in the working conditions or services available to their workers. If Simonsen and his acolytes could take heart from some developments that occurred during this period, they could also conclude that there was still a great deal of work to be done.

The Engineer as Educator

Fortunately for this cohort of ambitious, young industrialists, they were not alone in their struggle. Several of them, such as Simonsen, Mariano Ferraz, and Aldo Mário de Azevedo, had frequent contact with a growing group of educators, journalists, engineers, and medical doctors based in São Paulo for whom rationalization was also an ideological touchstone. Many of the key members of this group had no direct involvement in the industrial economy, but they all had links, whether of parentage, patronage, or friendship, to important industrial figures. In Brazil, as elsewhere, intellectuals and professionals who often had little acquaintance with the inside of a factory played a crucial role in the development of discourses and policies to advance the industrialists' cause.[47]

For the members of this group, which would eventually coalesce in IDORT, scientific methods were a means to reorganize not just industry but all of Brazilian society. Such prominent educators as M. B. Lourenço Filho and Fernando de Azevedo saw scientific methods as the key to revamping Brazil's archaic and inadequate system of public instruction.[48] Hygienists such as Geraldo de Paula Souza and Moacyr Alvaro (the resident doctor at the Santa Branca silk factory) saw rational methods of sanitation and scientific organization of everyday life as the solution to a slew of health and medical problems.[49] And engineers such as Gaspar Ricardo Júnior and Roberto Mange considered the application of rational methods to worker training and apprenticeship the key to the formation of a more disciplined and appropriately skilled workforce.[50]

For the purposes of this study, Roberto Mange is the most significant figure in the group of intellectuals and professionals under discussion. Born in Switzerland in 1886, Mange completed his primary education in Portugal, where his diplomat father was briefly stationed. He trained as an engineer at the Ecole Polytechnique in Zurich; following his graduation in 1910, he went on to do an internship in the German railway system. It was in Germany that he gained exposure to new forms of organization and, particularly, to new methods of worker training. In 1913 he went to São Paulo to assume the chair in applied machine mechanics at the Escola Politécnica. A year later, he married into a traditional paulista family, and from that time until his death in 1955, he called Brazil his home.

Roberto Mange cut something of an odd figure when he first arrived in São Paulo. Described by his son as "a bit Teutonic," rigid, and as having "Calvinist principles," he presented a persona that must have been rather unusual even in the rapidly industrializing urban milieu.[51] But through his association with the Escola Politécnica and progressive educational circles, he quickly established a network of contacts with Brazilian intellectuals who shared his interest in scientific methods. Within a decade of his arrival in São Paulo, Mange had initiated his energetic campaign to transform the nature of vocational training and apprenticeship in Brazil.

As was the case for Simonsen and industry, the terrain of vocational education contained, for Mange, elements that were encouraging but also a great deal that was sobering. Organized and formal "professional education" in São Paulo had its roots in institutions founded by various religious orders. Such schools trained orphans and children of impoverished families for trades such as carpentry, shoemaking, and masonry but did little to elevate the prestige of vocational education or manual labor in paulista society.[52] Reflecting a then common view of manual training, the governor of São Paulo, in his 1909 message to the legislature, called for the creation of "industrial institutes," which he regarded primarily as a means to suppress criminality, "to bring together youths under twenty-one years of age who are not yet criminal, or even licentious, and to mold them into a moral life through work, study, and discipline."[53]

Not all politicians shared such a low and narrow view of vocational education. In 1911 a federal law mandated the creation of a national network of "professional schools" to be modeled on similar institutions in the United States and Europe that had a certain prestige in those societies. According to the director of São Paulo's Escola Profissional, writing in 1920, this 1911 law "mark[ed] the beginning of a new era, or perhaps even the advent of our society's emancipation from the rigid prejudice that we harbored against manual labor."[54] Similarly, by the early twentieth century, São Paulo's Liceu de Artes e Ofícios, a privately sponsored school previously devoted to "artistic" instruction, expanded into the area of industrial education.[55]

Despite these concrete developments in the area of vocational training, the vast majority of skilled workers and artisans in São Paulo during the early decades of the twentieth century learned their trade in the traditional manner. The aspiring (usually male) apprentice entered the workplace as an adolescent, performing menial tasks assigned to *serventes*. If fortunate, the young worker would become an *ajudante*, or helper, to a skilled worker or a group of skilled workers. Gradually, through observation, the apprentice learned the various aspects of the craft and after reaching a certain age and level of competence became a full-fledged practitioner.[56]

Predictably, Roberto Mange and other proponents of scientific training methods found this traditional system of apprenticeship thoroughly objectionable. From the very first moment the apprentice entered the workplace, it violated scientific principles by arbitrarily assigning certain functions to young workers rather than testing and selecting the tasks that matched their aptitudes. The learning process itself was haphazard and empirical, the latter representing the worst insult in the rationalizer's arsenal. The apprentice simply learned to mimic the actions of the skilled craftsmen rather than gaining any sense of the principles behind the techniques. And even worse, such a system impeded the adoption of newer, better methods since the apprentice learned to perform a task in the same way as his predecessors. Finally, by learning the craft strictly within the work environment, the apprentice was likely to absorb a variety of "bad habits" that would make him permanently resistant to new techniques.[57]

The first step in transforming this system, then, was to transfer at least part of the training or apprenticeship process from the workers' domain to schools or courses administered by experts in "professional" education. Next, to make that process both more rapid and more scientific, new methods of instruction would be needed.[58] In addition, training had to include some form of instruction that would mold good moral character and give the worker a sense of identification with industrial progress. In a 1926 interview, Mange stressed that "the worker of today has to be an enlightened citizen, conscious of his obligations."[59]

The preceding statement raises a central issue in the historical literature on vocational education. Although we might regard it as eminently "natural" that a burgeoning industrial economy would require a more formal and institutionalized training system, we need to examine the objectives of the various proposals being made in the area of "professional" education and determine whether there was, indeed, a growing demand for skilled work requiring formal training. In particular, we need to reconcile the frequent references by educators, public officials, and industrialists to the need for more vocational schools with the arguments developed by recent scholarship to the effect that the 1920s saw a general de-skilling of São Paulo's industrial workforce.[60]

Whether we address this question in terms of objective measures or subjective perceptions, it is difficult to formulate a definitive picture of the skilled worker's position in paulista society circa 1925. Not until the mid-1940s would industrialist organizations begin to gather statistics on the level and types of skills required in different industries. The closest we have to an earlier statistical estimate is Mange's claim that the state of São Paulo in 1926 had some 10,000 *mecânicos* whose jobs required apprenticeship-type training, leading him to conclude that 500 new skilled mechanics had to be "produced" each year to meet the expanding demand.[61] Not only is this rather sketchy, but as a recent study has pointed out, the very notion of "skill" is unstable and socially constructed rather than simply being a precise measure of the requirements of a particular craft. Tasks traditionally performed by women, for example, are more likely to be classified as semiskilled or unskilled than those performed by adult men, regardless of the amount of knowledge or experience they require.[62] The existence of a prior ideological construction must be kept in mind as we consider the various discourses about "professional" education in the context of actual and intended transformations in the urban-industrial sector.

Certainly a major portion of the new jobs created by São Paulo's industrial expansion involved little more than machine tending, with the typical factory worker becoming a "live appendage to a lifeless mechanism," to use Boris Fausto's grim phrase.[63] This was especially true in textile production, the most rapidly growing manufacturing sector, although even here we must exercise some caution. As two recent studies of the paulista textile industry observe, many "semiskilled" workers were highly valued by their employers due to their ability to work with raw materials of uneven quality and to tinker with old and fragile machinery.[64] Mange, by contrast, regarded such "improvised" knowledge with disdain.

There can be little doubt that the proposals made by Taylorist educators for scientific vocational training represented an attempt to diminish the worker's authority in the workplace and shift the locus of industrial knowledge away from skilled workers to middle-class technicians and engineers. Whether their motive was a desire for increased control over the labor force or a profound belief that modern industrial processes were beyond the grasp of Brazil's poorly educated workers, Mange and his confederates envisioned an industrial hierarchy in which the skilled worker had a limited and subordinate role. Even the position of *mestre* or *contramestre* (foreman)—traditionally a figure of great authority, not only over workers but over the production process itself—was increasingly envisioned as that of a supervisor who would merely transmit and enforce decisions made by upper management.

Despite the lack of statistics, it seems safe to say that the proportion of skilled workers in the urban workforce was declining and that the power and prestige of the skilled worker within the factory were also declining. Similarly, sufficient evidence exists to indicate an intensification of work rhythms with the increased mechanization of textile factories. But can we then conclude, in line with recent studies, that a massive "expulsion of skilled workers" from the urban labor force occurred?[65] And as a corollary, should we then conclude that concern for new forms of vocational training merely reflected educators' and employers' aspirations to produce a more disciplined and malleable workforce? In other words, was "professional education" nothing more than an instrument of social control?

The continuing employment of relatively privileged foreign craftsmen in paulista firms indicates that real deficits of skilled workers existed, at least in certain industries. Many accounts of early industrial life in São Paulo identify the most highly skilled workers in the factories as foreigners brought over at considerable expense from Britain, France, or Spain to fill jobs for which there were no qualified local candidates.[66] It was from this perspective that the state of São Paulo's education yearbook described vocational schools as "a secure vehicle for nationalization" and as a means to achieve "our emancipation from foreign labor."[67]

Neither impressionistic accounts nor scattered wage data indicate a massive devaluation of skilled labor during the 1910s and 1920s.[68] Thus, one author's claim that changes in these decades resulted in "the brutal and total elimination, both physical and social, of a significant segment of the paulista workforce" seems grossly exaggerated.[69] It is more reasonable to assume that the 1920s witnessed a restructuring of the urban labor force that reduced the importance of some skills but created a market for new ones. As one would expect with increased mechanization, the demand for highly skilled mechanics soared, along with the demand for workers in various metalworking trades.[70] At the same time, the ongoing proliferation of workshops and small factories, particularly in such areas as furniture-making, meant that artisanal work processes persisted in many sectors. In the same vein, construction was a major employer in a booming urban center, and even supposedly "Taylorized" construction sites depended on a wide array of skilled workers.[71]

Certainly the implications of rationalization included the reduction of the technical and social role of the skilled worker on the shopfloor. But in many areas the "forces of rationalization," whether due to worker resistance or employer indifference, had made only slight progress, and even in the most "modernized" sectors of industry, it proved impossible to eliminate the skilled worker. The task for Mange and his confederates, then, was to create a new kind of (male) skilled worker, steeped in a different "work culture" and prepared to take his (assigned) place in the new industrial hierarchy.[72]

The institution that gave the Swiss engineer his first opportunity to implement his project for vocational training was the Liceu de Artes e Ofícios, the most prestigious of São Paulo's "professional" schools. Founded in 1883, the Liceu was funded by private donations supplemented by a regular state subsidy.[73] Branching out from its initial artistic orientation, in 1902 the school launched a program of "industrial instruction" with fifty-three apprentices studying cabinet-making and woodworking.[74] Over the next three decades, industrial training expanded to include the metalworking trades, and the Liceu became increasingly responsive to the labor demands of the construction sector. Its workshops also began accepting orders for specific projects from private firms, which earned money for the institution and its apprentices but meant that the Liceu gradually came to resemble a branch of industry rather than a school for the arts. The school regulations even stipulated that the workshops duplicate the standard industrial hierarchy.[75] From the early 1900s on, industrial education in the Liceu reflected the growing interest of its directors in rational methods of organization.[76]

Roberto Mange found a particularly sympathetic reception for his new training methods at the Liceu, where he installed in 1923 the Escola Profissional Mecânica, the first institution in the state of São Paulo wholly devoted to the mechanical trades. Armed with a financial subsidy from the state government, Mange set about creating courses that utilized the "methodical series" apprenticeship system. According to this training technique, the apprentice progressed from the simplest to the most complicated task in orderly fashion, learning the "theoretical principles" behind each task while involved in its manual execution. Mange claimed that such training was more rapid than traditional techniques and that simultaneous instruction in theoretical principles and manual skills was the solution to "deadly empiricism."[77]

Another widely publicized innovation of Mange's school for mechanics was the Gabinete de Psicotécnica, created with the technical assistance of the Instituto de Higiene. In the early 1920s, Mange had made a brief trip to Europe, where he met with pioneers of applied psychology, and had returned an advocate of "psychotechnic" testing to determine whether an aspiring apprentice had the physiological and mental disposition for a specific craft. Mange and hygienists like Geraldo de Paula Souza claimed that such testing allowed schools to "guide" students into the courses most appropriate for their abilities, based on "scientific" data rather than on the arbitrary preferences of the neophyte worker. Indeed, for many educators, the Gabinete de Psicotécnica was the school's most significant innovation.[78]

Despite the considerable prestige and publicity that Mange's school and the Liceu enjoyed, they were by no means the only examples of new forms of vocational training in early industrial São Paulo. Perhaps most important, in numerical terms, were special courses created by or within industry. In 1928 CIFT noted the opening of a private school to train weavers already employed in the textile industry. It hailed the school as a solution to employers' frequent complaints about the lack of "trained" labor and called for the use of "theoretical" rather than "empirical" methods of instruction (indicating the diffusion of the principles advocated by Mange). In addition, it predicted that the school's graduates would form a "a veritable pool of good foremen."[79]

Certain firms, such as São Paulo Light & Power Company, commonly known as "Light," and the Italian-owned Pirelli metalworking factory, installed separate classrooms and workshops so that apprentices did not simply train by unsystematic observation of skilled workers. Light seems to have devoted particular attention to its apprentices; in a 1910 memo to department heads, the general manager outlined the company's plans for apprentices who had just completed their formal course of instruction: "Now, instead of going to classes the first thing in the morning, they should report directly to their proper department. It is desirous, however, that recreation and physical exercises *continue as heretofore*. . . . It is [also] intended that occasionally popular lectures be arranged for these boys in the evenings."[80]

In the public sphere, by far the most important institutions in the 1910s and 1920s were the Escola Profissional Masculina and the Escola Profissional Feminina, founded by the state government in response to the 1911 federal law requiring states to offer vocational education.[81] Both schools originally operated at the intermediate level, but the Escola Profissional Masculina reduced its entrance requirements from four to two years of primary schooling in 1924 to maintain its level of full-time enrollment. The three-year courses offered by the boys' school included mechanics (the most popular field), decorative painting, metalworking, electrical trades, and carpentry, as well as academic subjects.[82]

The schools seem to have been fairly successful in attracting students. The number of students enrolled in the Escola Profissional Masculina grew from 259 in its inaugural year to 799 in 1914, with an annual average of 882 from 1916 through 1920. The total number of students registered, including those in night courses, during its first decade of existence came to a sizable 9,079. Most illuminating, however, is the number of students who completed the course of study: of the 4,879 students who registered for vocational courses between 1911 and 1922, only 326 actually received their diplomas.[83]

There are several possible explanations for this massive dropout rate and the failure, or perhaps decision, of the vast majority of students not to finish the course. As the director repeatedly reported, many students from poor families had to terminate their training because their parents simply could not afford to keep them off the job market for so long. With what was probably unconscious poignancy, the director noted in his 1914 report that the free lunch program instituted that year had been a great success and that not a single case of a student fainting in class (previously a frequent event) had occurred since its inauguration. However, not all students seem to have dropped out from necessity; the director also repeatedly lamented the tendency of "apprentices" to be lured away by the ample job opportunities and relatively high wages offered to even incompletely trained craftsmen. Another possibility, never mentioned by the director, is that because of their limited education upon entering the school, students could complete their vocational training but lacked either the background or the motivation to fulfill the academic requirements.[84] Whatever the explanation, the statistics indicate that a serious gap existed between the conceptualization of vocational training and the actual circumstances of workers in early twentieth-century São Paulo.

The situation of the Escola Profissional Feminina, on the other hand, is highly illuminating with regard to the gender assumptions that informed the discussions of vocational education. In contrast to its masculine counterpart, the Escola Profissional Feminina seems to have had little trouble attracting and keeping students, turning away some 400 applicants in 1915.[85] And this was the case despite its rickety, claustrophobic, and unsanitary facilities, which one governor blamed for an outbreak of tuberculosis among its faculty and students.[86] One likely explanation for the school's greater success in attracting and retaining students was the absence of alternatives for women seeking marketable skills. There are also indications that a significant number of students who attended the school were from families clinging to the lower rungs of the middle class. To be sure, the young women enrolled in the regular courses were from very modest households, but perhaps they were less poor than the young men attending the Escola Profissional Masculina and had more years of primary schooling.

The Escola Profissional Feminina also differed from its masculine counterpart in that it taught skills relevant for employment in small workshops and ateliers rather than factories. The original course of study included (along with "domestic economics") dressmaking, needlework, lace-making and embroidery, flower arranging, and millinery, all traditional *artisanal* crafts for women.[87] A great deal of emphasis was also placed on the respectability of the institution, a concern that precluded, in the minds of its administrators, training women for *industrial* occupations. The advocates of industrial education apparently conceptualized such training, and, by extension, skilled factory labor, as a masculine domain. Working-class women who had no choice but to seek employment in industry simply would continue to perform those jobs defined as the least skilled and the lowest paid.[88]

Whatever the defects or limitations of the Escola Profissional Masculina, it did provide some systematic training to thousands of young workers during the 1910s and 1920s, especially in the areas of mechanics and carpentry. The school also had many features in common with Mange's program at the Liceu. Aprígio de Almeida Gonzaga, the educator who directed both the Escola Profissional Masculina and the Escola Profissional Feminina for the first two decades of their existence, emphasized the importance of vocational training in creating proper "work habits" and a sense of "moral discipline."[89] Like Mange, he stressed the need to provide complementary services, such as medical and dental care, and extracurricular activities, such as scouting or open-air exercises, in order to create physically and mentally sound workers. And Gonzaga was every bit as vehement as Mange in denouncing the "empiricism" of traditional apprenticeship, through which workers learned to execute tasks "just as their fathers and grandfathers had done" thirty years before and thus "unconsciously became impediments to the progress and technical evolution of our industries."[90]

Yet the contrast between the positions of these two advocates of vocational training points up Mange's deep commitment to advancing the interests of large-scale industry rather than serving the needs of the aspiring worker (or perhaps, to be more accurate, his belief that the latter should be wholly subsumed in the former). Whereas Mange enthusiastically embraced all forms of rationalization, regardless of their eventual impact on workers, Gonzaga viewed any innovation that undermined the position of the skilled worker with a critical eye. His reports frequently condemned worker "specialization," arguing that full knowledge of a craft was the worker's only "safe guarantee against the mechanization of the manual crafts."[91] The Escola Profissional Masculina's workshops also operated under conditions contrary to the Taylorist spirit. Answering unnamed critics, Gonzaga acknowledged that "in order to earn more money, we should adopt a plan of absolutely separate parts: one student will make the legs of a table; another, the drawers; another, the handles; another will do the sanding and staining. In this way, by the end of the year the school will have made an enormous profit, but this will have been accomplished by exploiting child labor and by doing just what the industrialists do."[92]

Despite insisting that professional schools needed to maintain close and friendly relations with industry, Gonzaga peppered his reports with attacks on the social and technical practices of Brazilian industrialists. He decried the widespread employment of women and children in industry, which he blamed for the low level of men's wages. He also endorsed the principle of unionization, arguing that individual struggle usually meant failure for a worker. Thus he called for "an intelligent union of workers" through which they could "participate in the resolution of the state's political and economic problems" and develop "democratic ideals for the resolution of the social question."[93] But he reserved his most caustic remarks for unskilled laborers in modern industry, whom he described as "morally dead, physically inadequate, mere human machines in the service of capital."[94] Such comments reveal a decidedly negative assessment of industry's social impact. Despite comments about the skilled worker's contribution to social and economic progress, Gonzaga appears to have regarded vocational training, first and foremost, as a means of protection for the industrial worker, who, otherwise, would become the helpless victim of an exploitative employer.

Mange, in contrast, maintained an unwavering pro-industry perspective.[95] He believed that the technical processes that characterized modern industry were well beyond the reach of the typical worker, even one who had intensive vocational training. And since he approached apprenticeship strictly within the context of scientific management, it was completely irrational, in his view, to resist the impact of mechanization or rationalization on a particular craft. Vocational training, Mange argued, should be finely tuned to the needs of industry and should continually evolve to meet those changing needs, as determined by highly trained engineers and technicians. For Mange, a skill did not endow a worker with a permanent identity that gave him a fixed position and a degree of authority within industry; rather, a worker's identity was constantly subject to processes of innovation and rationalization beyond his comprehension or control. For all of his attention to vocational training, Mange conceived only a limited and subordinate position for the skilled worker in production.

Nothing is more revealing than Mange's reply to a question posed by noted educator Fernando de Azevedo during his 1926 inquiry into the condition of public education in the state of São Paulo. In the final portion of this interview, Azevedo asked Mange what he thought of the idea of organizing "popular centers" to offer "(a) rapid basic technical education; (b) practical instruction in small domestic industries; (c) general culture through film, practical demonstrations, and lectures; (d) and to promote the 'cooperative spirit' among students, by means of producers' associations, for the application of crafts learned in school." Mange replied, "We agree with regard to letters 'a' and 'c.'"[96] He did not elaborate about his opposition to "b" and "d," but it is somewhat predictable. Mange viewed vocational training as serving the interests of modern, rational, and large-scale industry. Thus he had little interest in any scheme oriented toward smaller enterprises and would hardly endorse worker cooperatives, with their inattention to hierarchy and lack of "expert" knowledge.

As in the discussion of Simonsen and Pupo Nogueira above, it would be a distortion to portray Mange and Gonzaga as polar opposites. They shared many opinions about the role and character of industrial apprenticeship. What separated them, however, was the object of their efforts. For Gonzaga, it was the student, the future skilled worker, whose needs had to be considered even if they conflicted with those of industry. For Mange, it was large-scale industry, the modern factory, whose technical and social needs dictated the nature of industrial training. Although he was widely identified as an educator, Mange was first, last, and always an industrial technocrat.

As we will see, it was Mange's perspective on vocational education that emerged as the dominant strain in Brazil. Even in the 1920s, Gonzaga occupied an increasingly isolated position, whereas Mange's unabashedly pro-industry stance allowed him to forge important links with employers such as Gaspar Ricardo Júnior, the director of the Sorocabana Railway. And Mange's association with the Liceu de Artes e Ofícios linked him to a network of well-connected professionals and entrepreneurs who shared Mange's enthusiasm for rationalization and market-oriented training. It also meant that his efforts received generous publicity in the capital's leading daily newspaper, *O Estado de São Paulo*, whose contributors included several people involved in the Liceu.[97] It is therefore not surprising that Fernando de Azevedo interviewed Mange rather than Gonzaga (who was, after all, the director of São Paulo's leading *public* vocational school) for his educational survey. It was Mange's enthusiastic campaign for rational organization that appealed to Brazil's most innovative educators, who sought to provide their country with an unimpeachably modern educational system.

Worker Responses to Rationalization

Recent studies have given close attention to the opinions of industrialists and educators with regard to Taylorism, Fordism, professional education, and other related topics, but most of the existing literature has treated the worker's position on such matters as a given.[98] Since labor historians generally regard Taylorism and its correlates as mechanisms of social control, they portray the workers as naturally struggling against these mechanisms, using either dramatic forms of resistance such as strikes or less dramatic weapons such as slowdowns or frequent job changes.[99] It is assumed that workers would struggle against the reduction in skill and authority dictated by new production techniques or militate in favor of traditional craft prerogatives, and as we will see, this is often the case.[100] At the same time, however, substantial evidence exists to challenge the stereotypical image of the heroic worker fighting tirelessly, if somewhat quixotically, against the "dehumanizing" forces of modern industry.

I should declare at the outset that I am not seeking to recover the "authentic voices" of workers on these questions. Since much of the available documentation was produced by industrialist organizations, the historian often has to extrapolate the workers' position(s) from employer accounts. The labor press is a widely used source of working-class viewpoints, but it is most likely to reveal the perspectives of anarchist leaders or union officials rather than those of the "rank and file." And the enterprise is further complicated by the potential differences in position between, for example, artisanal workers protecting traditional prerogatives and unskilled workers whose only hope for sustained employment lay in the destruction of such prerogatives. The following analysis, then, does not presume to offer definitive conclusions about Brazilian workers' attitudes toward technical or organizational innovations. Rather, it seeks to illuminate the different positions workers adopted on such matters and to show that unremitting resistance is not a satisfactory description of working-class responses to the prospect of new work processes, apprenticeship methods, or factory conditions.

Studies of the early labor movement in Brazil reveal that workers frequently organized strikes or stoppages to protest work conditions other than wages and hours. If we examine the list of strikes in São Paulo and Rio between 1917 and 1920 compiled by Boris Fausto, we find that in over a quarter of the actions whose objectives are known, the complaints included denunciations of piece rates, fines, tyrannical foremen, and poor raw materials.[101] Although this provides us with clear evidence of workers' resistance to various forms of control, it cannot be interpreted as an indication of workers' opposition to rationalization per se. Simonsen himself wrote in 1919 of the "great conflicts between the two classes" caused by piece or task work, declaring that the latter "no longer serves to increase productivity."[102] Protests against foremen might seem to reflect objections to the increasingly hierarchical organization of factories dictated by rationalization, but it is more likely that they reflect opposition to traditional forms of industrial organization in which the foreman had a great deal of personal and arbitrary power and made many of the crucial decisions regarding work processes. In the "rationally organized" factory, the supervisory personnel would actually wield diminished authority, serving mainly as conduits for policies and work norms set by management.[103] As for the denunciations of employers who provided inferior raw materials (which caused hardship for workers and reduced the income of those paid by the piece), they could easily be echoed by any proponent of rationalization, who would certainly consider the use of such materials incompatible with the principles of scientific management.

More explicit examples of opposition to new work processes occurred in the 1920s. Perhaps the most conclusive evidence of worker resistance to the intensification of work routines as a result of increased mechanization is the 1928 strike at the Mariangela textile mill, owned by the Matarazzos. According to a letter circulated by the Matarazzos to other mill owners, the firm had attempted to increase the number of automated looms for which each woman worker in a particular section was responsible from eight to sixteen. The result was an immediate walkout, not only by the women in this section but by the entire factory workforce. The Matarazzo spokesman repeatedly insisted that the measure was merely an experiment and expressed astonishment that the workers had responded in this fashion since they were to be paid proportionally higher salaries if the experiment proved to be a success.[104] Such offers apparently had little appeal for the workers, and the Matarazzos' brief attempt at a Fordist policy of intensification of the work process in exchange for the promise of higher wages suffered a dramatic defeat.

Other evidence indicates that workers did not unilaterally and consistently reject new machinery or technical processes. The uneven nature of industrial development, in Brazil as elsewhere, meant that workers often had to weigh the advantages and disadvantages of various innovations. New techniques or machinery might reduce the value of their skills, but they also might reduce the physical fatigue or danger associated with a specific task. For example, the glassblowers of the Vidraria Santa Marina in the 1910s went on strike in favor of substituting compressed air for human effort—the very transformation that French glassblowers had bitterly resisted in the 1890s.[105] Similarly, in 1913 a meeting of textile workers resulted in a denunciation of the outmoded flying shuttles and a call for the implementation of new mechanical processes already being utilized in Europe.[106] Considering the relatively weak artisanal traditions in São Paulo compared to those in the United States, England, or France and the poor wages earned even by workers who had considerable control over the labor process, paulista workers may well have been more receptive to new production techniques than their American or European counterparts. Indeed, Paulo Nogueira Filho discovered, to his surprise, that the highly skilled *mestres* of a silk factory in Milan "considered labor that was specialized, planned, and controlled . . . a new form of slavery." Thus, in the mid-1920s, Milanese craftsmen stubbornly resisted "certain efficient innovations already in evidence in São Paulo's new industrial milieu."[107]

No one occupational group can illuminate all aspects of workers' responses to questions of rationalization, welfare capitalism, or apprenticeship. However, *O Trabalhador Gráfico*, the publication of the paulista printers' union, offers us considerable insight into workers' opinions on these issues. As members of a craft with strong artisanal traditions that was increasingly subject to mechanization and industrial organization but retained a level of skill requiring apprenticeship, printers routinely faced questions related to work processes and vocational training. They were also, on the whole, highly literate, and many contributed to their union's newspaper without being union officials themselves. Thus, *O Trabalhador Gráfico* expressed a relatively wide range of opinions, at least within the printing craft. In addition, it was the only union newspaper that appeared with any regularity during the period under consideration.[108]

Even the earliest issues of *O Trabalhador Gráfico*, published in 1905, reveal interest among the printers in the rationalization of their craft. In an article entitled "Wage Standards and Work Organization," the paper discussed the printers' attempt to formulate uniform wage rates and work processes through "technical commissions" for each area of specialization. *O Trabalhador Gráfico* wholeheartedly supported the effort and outlined the scheme's advantages in rather interesting terms: "The determination of a uniform wage and work process is felt to be necessary not only by the workers but also by serious and conscientious industrialists, who under the current disorganized conditions must contend with competition from shifty and abusive industrialists who only employ children or craftsmen stupefied by alcoholism."[109]

A year later, *O Trabalhador Gráfico* reiterated its conviction that a minimum and maximum wage standard for different types of work would greatly benefit both workers and owners. "It indirectly contributes to the prosperity of the printing and publishing firms that, paying the uniform wages, will not have to struggle with as many hardships as they currently face due to the abundance of makeshift workshops that, by paying miserable salaries to their workers, can compete with the large print shops equipped with all sorts of technical improvements and up-to-date machinery and where production is truly artistic." Indeed, attempts to regulate wages had failed, *O Trabalhador Gráfico* claimed, mainly because of resistance from "owners of a motley heap of machines . . . where the workforce consists of children who are despicably exploited . . . [and a] few craftsmen who . . . go unpaid; [these owners] will witness the impending doom of their workshops if the union succeeds in its effort."[110]

These statements indicate that employers were not alone in attempting to argue that all classes would benefit from rational organization, although it is important to emphasize that fairer wages, not higher profits, formed the starting point for the printers' rationalization scheme. It is also significant that the printers believed that they should set the terms for wages and work processes, based on their own technical expertise. But perhaps the most interesting aspect of these arguments is the fact that mechanization is associated with progressive employers, while shoddy machinery and little organization are associated with employers who hire underaged workers and alcoholics at disgracefully low wages.[111]

These statements were all the more remarkable since they were being made at the very moment that the printing arts were undergoing a technical revolution caused by the introduction of the typesetting or linotype machine. This innovation, already in use overseas by the 1880s, greatly reduced the role of the typesetter in the printing process. Yet in 1905 *O Trabalhador Gráfico* announced the impending arrival of linotype machines for the press shops of *Fanfulla*, São Paulo's most progressive daily paper, with great equanimity: "The arrival of these machines should evoke surprise from many of our colleagues who do not easily believe in the force of progress. For others it will serve, perhaps, as a cause for dismay; however, do not be alarmed—the machines are the workers' best helpers and will effectively aid us in the conquest of our emancipation."[112] Such an attitude may reflect, in part, the peculiar history of the printing craft, which traditionally associated itself with liberal, progressive ideals. Yet it also seems reasonable to argue that the "backward" methods and conditions maintained by the most openly exploitative employers made it easier to regard mechanization in a positive light.

Not all printers regarded the arrival of the linotype machines with such good cheer, as the *Trabalhador Gráfico* article acknowledged. Although the official position of the union was to welcome technical progress, printers who believed their jobs or wage levels were threatened by such progress were unlikely to share that position, a point perceived by Júlio de Mesquita, the patrician publisher of *O Estado de São Paulo*. In a 1906 meeting with striking printers, Mesquita described himself as a "protector" of the workers since he would be "the last to mount the linotype machines, which threaten to ruin the printer class."[113] Interestingly, the anarchist printer and writer Mota Assumpção made nearly the opposite argument three years later in an article written to discourage graphic workers from smashing the new machines. Presenting mechanization as inevitable and positive, despite some immediate negative effects, he contended that it was the "wickedness of certain owners and bosses" that was at the root of the printers' troubles. Returning to the equation of fairness with progress, he noted that one of the worst employers, Edmundo Bittencourt of *Corrêio da Manhã*, was also one of the last to install the machines.[114]

The system of apprenticeship and the abusive employment of apprentices were other workplace matters that received frequent attention in the printers' newspaper. Striking printers regularly demanded that new apprentices not be admitted into the shop or accused management of intending to "replace veteran workers with unconscious apprentices." One strike, by the printers of the Casa Duprat, began when the firm fired six workers who it claimed were producing less than some of the apprentices.[115] In these cases, the apprentice appears as a menace to the integrity of the craft.

Other articles referred poignantly to the hiring of "children" to work in print shops that were little better than dungeons, portraying the apprentice as a victim rather than a menace.[116] Contributors to *O Trabalhador Gráfico* lamented the lack of systematic instruction for apprentices and praised the Soviet Union, where minors worked a four-hour day and received "mandatory technical instruction."[117] The most severe commentary on the apprentices' plight came from a "young worker" who complained that "they deny us the most elementary education; and if they teach us anything it is to prepare us to serve the rich docilely and to tolerate without resistance a doubly brutal form of exploitation." Aside from a six-hour workday for minors, this youthful printer demanded "healthier work conditions, better salaries, [and] instruction paid for by employers."[118] Similarly, a column entitled "Our Labor" called for the creation of libraries, practical courses, and lectures to instill among apprentices "devotion to our association and to make them able workers, conscious laborers."

The double meaning printers invested in the word "conscious" is worthy of comment. At times, it meant being aware of one's class position and interests; at other times, it meant being knowledgeable, hardworking, and conscientious. This "confusion" of meanings was not a matter of sloppiness; rather, it reflected the printers' view that the worker who was socially conscious would also have considerable expertise and pride in his craft. To become an "able" worker, an apprentice had to be well trained in the technical aspects of the craft as well as conscious of the printer's obligations to his colleagues and employer.[119]

The printers were not the only workers concerned with technical education. Striking textile operatives in Rio included abuse of minors among their complaints and instruction for apprentices among their demands.[120] And one of the points reportedly discussed in the Third Brazilian Workers' Congress was the need for "schools for workers and the means to maintain and develop them within a rationalist orientation."[121] Although they were not major themes in the Brazilian labor movement, interest in formal vocational training for apprentices and criticisms of traditional forms of apprenticeship seem to have been fairly widespread among workers.

It is important to consider why workers themselves would propose dismantling the old worker-controlled system of training in which the apprentice observed and assisted another worker until he acquired the abilities necessary to join the craft. Earlier I argued that transferring the locus of training away from the shopfloor to specialized courses or schools would appeal to Mange and his colleagues precisely because it diminished workers' participation and discretion in the process. Yet the printer who condemned apprenticeship in his trade as occurring "without method and without obeying any fixed criteria" might have been quoting Mange.[122] It seems that the changing nature of manufacturing in São Paulo in the 1920s and its impact on craft-based production may have led workers as well to support professional education, if for a somewhat different reason.

Assuming increased mechanization and regimentation of industrial work—which was certainly the case in the printing trade—we can more easily understand the appeal of vocational courses to the workers. Under old systems of artisanal and craft production, established workers actually had real discretion over the work routines and instruction of apprentices. However, the changing conditions in manufacturing meant that "apprentices" were increasingly at the disposition of management and were likely to be minors employed in large numbers at very low salaries who performed only the most menial tasks and received little training in return.[123] Or they received only enough training to replace better-paid adult workers. In this context, professional education offered a form of protection for both the apprentice and the adult worker since it provided the former with real instruction in a skill and maintained the integrity of the latter's craft. Indeed, both workers and middle-class educators observed that a major obstacle to expanding vocational education was the employers' refusal to acknowledge that their workers performed tasks that required extensive training.[124] Under these circumstances, even the more specialized and accelerated training offered by Mange and his followers must have been attractive to many workers.

Unlike Mange, however, the printers whose views appeared in *O Trabalhador Gráfico* clearly expected the workers' organizations to play a direct and central role in vocational training, even if on a new footing. A very interesting example of this viewpoint can be found in a long article published during the 1923 printers' strike, a hard-fought campaign by the trade to force employers to recognize its union. Advising the "bosses" that recognition of the union was not "such a horrible thing," the article went on to assure owners that the union had no desire to "interfere in the discipline of each shop," but rather its intention was "to tutor our class in the technical and moral spheres, to the extent that they concern the general improvement of our art, because we wish to lift it out of the lethargy in which it has fallen, since there presently exist many workshops so badly organized and in such disorder as to make it impossible to work in them conscientiously."[125]

Again, we see the graphic workers adopting positions resembling those of Simonsen or Mange but from a rather different perspective. Their call for the moral and technical improvement of their craft and their explicit promise that all parties would benefit from the union's activities in this vein seem remarkably similar in some ways to the projects of the two Robertos. Yet implicit in the printers' remarks is the assumption that craft integrity is the key to creating more productive workplaces and that the workers themselves are best positioned to determine the terms of that integrity, not a group of outside experts operating according to reputedly scientific principles.

Several of the above quotes from *O Trabalhador Gráfico* demonstrate that the printers frequently presented their objectives in a quasi-Fordist manner, highlighting their potential contribution to the overall efficiency and organization of the printing sector, with benefits for both capital and labor. Similarly, they denounced unhygienic and dangerous conditions in the workplace—with the most extreme cases usually occurring in small shops—as harmful to both the interests of employers and the well-being of their workers.[126] But some aspects of the Fordist program met with little sympathy among the graphic workers. A 1929 article called for the creation of an athletics department in the printers' and other unions. The author argued that union-sponsored sports competitions would provide workers, and especially young ones, with an alternative to joining factory teams that were a form of propaganda for the *patrão*. This and several other remarks by contributors illustrate real concern among the printers for maintaining cultural and recreational activities separate from those organized by the employers.[127]

Again, the ecumenical character of the printers' journal makes it difficult to generalize about these workers' views of the relationship between capital and labor, both existing and potential. In the same month, *O Trabalhador Gráfico* might print an article discussing whether conditions were ripe in Brazil for a revolutionary union movement and an essay arguing that lazy, incompetent workers were the chief cause of the imposition of harsher work rules. There is also the matter of change over time. As the 1920s progressed, the growing presence of Marxists and supporters of the Bolshevik Revolution in the printers' ranks injected an anticapitalist theme into many of *O Trabalhador Gráfico*'s articles and illustrations.

The leaders of the printers' union consistently attacked organizations that gave priority to class conciliation over class struggle.[128] Still, they opened the newspaper's columns to dissenting opinions, and the leaders themselves frequently emphasized areas in which employers' and workers' interests overlapped. In the heat of the 1923 strike, Ambrogio Chiodi, a major figure in the union, wrote a remarkably calm article about the refusal of most owners to recognize the workers' association. He reminded the employers that unions were a fact of life in more developed societies and that although workers and owners in such societies did not coexist in an "eternal idyll," they also did not "spend the whole year fighting. Much to the contrary, the organization and identification of interests operates in the sense of eliminating, preferably in an amicable fashion, any misunderstanding that may emerge between owners and workers."[129] Nearly three years later, another article admonishing employers for their resistance to the union similarly argued that the owners simply did not understand that the union "will cooperate with them for the normalization, order, and discipline of their establishments, avoiding clashes and irregularities."[130]

Such language needs to be placed in the context of the union's struggle to survive during the repressive 1920s. In a later article, Chiodi reminded his readers that "for all the good will that might exist between owners and workers, their interests are opposed, they do not converge." This is in contrast to the view expressed by one anonymous contributor who rejected any notion of conflicting interests: "Capital and Labor are life. To destroy the former would be to kill the latter. And thus to kill life itself. Hence, us workers, instead of organizing Associations for Combat against Capital, should organize them to harmonize, from all points of view, these two things that cannot live without one another: Capital and Labor."[131] This quote, though hardly representative of the leadership's position, apparently had enough credibility to be published in *O Trabalhador Gráfico* and even to appear in the paper's May Day issue.

The most intriguing discussion of the need for class cooperation can be found in a series of articles, authored by "An Old Printer," published in 1926. In his initial essay, "Rights and Responsibilities," the author described himself as a longtime participant in the workers' movement but admitted that he was often chided for his "conciliatory spirit." He exhorted all printers to join the union, but the main theme of his essays was that printers should be good workers and thereby earn better treatment at the hands of their employers. Indeed, this writer reserved his most critical language for printers who arrived late or relaxed on the job, arguing that it was due to poor work habits that "the owners established the work bulletin, and conscientious workers suffer the annoyance of having to note the time used for the execution of tasks as if they were merely *idlers*."[132] In another article, he repeats his belief that "unconscious [unconscientious]" workers provide foremen and owners with justification for "rigorous measures that are perfectly dispensable." Summarizing his position in the final installment, the author acknowledged that employers had obligations: to respect their workers, to provide sanitary work conditions, and to pay a living wage. But the workers, too, had the obligation to respect both the bosses and other workers and "to produce the maximum amount permitted by one's abilities, always avoiding useless waste of material." If both parties fulfilled their duties, he concluded, they could avoid discord and disputes.[133]

It may be tempting to dismiss the elderly printer as himself "unconscious" in the political sense and outside the ideological mainstream of the labor movement. But, again, the editors considered his ruminations legitimate enough to provide him with ample space in at least three different issues of *O Trabalhador Gráfico*. Moreover, a careful reading of his remarks reveals a more complex position than a simple call for worker-employer cooperation. At two different points in his writings, he notes the increasing regimentation of work in the printing shops, which he perceives as an offense to the dignity of his craft. To remedy this situation, he calls upon his fellow workers to perform their appointed tasks assiduously in order to eliminate the need for closer supervision and control. He was particularly irked by printers who worked below their physical capacity to protest low wages, arguing that poor performance would only provoke harsher discipline and even lower wages. Thus his articles are more profitably read as a call to restore the integrity of the printers' craft at a time when labor relations were taking on an increasingly "industrial" cast rather than as an unconditional paean to "social peace."

As *O Trabalhador Gráfico* moved into the final years of the decade, its pages exhibited a more radical and partisan tone. Critical attitudes toward reformist socialists informed a long article published in mid-1927 entitled "Perspectives on Rationalization." Denouncing rationalization or Americanization as the "war cry of the bourgeoisie," the article discussed the impact of this movement in France, Britain, and Germany, where it had also gained support among Social Democrats and union bureaucrats. According to the author, the destruction caused by war had facilitated reconstruction with new technology and had launched ideologies of national development that emphasized cheap production to allow competition with foreign manufacturers—"and thus the intensification of labor, the overtime, the assembly line, Taylorism, the conveyor belts, etc."[134]

The article attacked rationalization on many fronts. First, it implicitly contradicted Simonsen's arguments by claiming that rationalization had been accompanied not merely by intensification of work processes but also by lower wages and longer work hours. In effect, the drive to reduce the costs of production had induced industrialists to employ both conventional and innovative methods to increase worker exploitation. At the same time, "technical progress" had equipped the employers with the means to "obtain the same level of output with a smaller number of skilled workers." The text also ridiculed the rationalizer's intellectual claims, referring to "so-called 'scientific' chronometry used to determine exaggerated norms." Finally, the article concluded that the two faces of rationalization—"one, technical progress 'useful' to the working class; the other, 'bad', abusive and exploitative rationalization"—were inseparable. "The diverse aspects of rationalization of the worker for the machine and the intensification of human labor, all these elements are indissolubly joined together in the capitalist system."[135]

This viewpoint probably had little resonance among *O Trabalhador Gráfico*'s readers. Judging from the majority of articles in the printers' newspaper, few graphic workers viewed capitalist development per se as antithetical to the interests of labor. In the same issue that ran this condemnation of rationalization, another article discussed the expansion of scientific knowledge about the physiology of work and encouraged workers to use such expertise to substantiate their demands for weekly rest and paid vacations.[136] In other words, it called upon workers to use scientific methods to their own advantage. Still, the antirationalization article is notable for introducing a many-sided critique of the transformations in industry and their underlying ideological justifications and for challenging the linkage between technical progress and progressive politics. Few workers would accept all of its conclusions, but many could identify with elements of this sophisticated diatribe. Indeed, echoes of this essay can be heard in a March 1929 article that explained to readers why the printers had decided, once again, to go on strike. The protest was not only for higher wages and paid vacations, the article explained, but also "to unmask the hypocritical humanitarianism of the Rotarians and eugenicists, employers without conscience or heart."[137]

It would be an exaggeration to speak of the "triumph of rationalization" in the 1920s. Many of São Paulo's factories had not yet embraced so-called scientific methods, whether in the realm of production, training, or social services. This was often due as much to lack of interest on the part of employers as to resistance on the part of workers. Generally speaking, neither economic nor social conditions made progress in this area a pressing matter for paulista industry.

At the same time, the views expressed by increasingly influential figures in São Paulo's industrial milieu demonstrate the strong ideological appeal of rationalization during these years. Rationalization provided Simonsen and his followers with a discourse that emphasized national progress through industrial development and social peace through greater productivity and efficiency, the latter a particularly serious concern after the 1917 and 1919 general strikes. And it placed the industrialists at the center of an elaborate project for reordering labor relations, both inside and outside the factory. Scientific methods also formed the basis for Roberto Mange's vision of a vocational education tailored to the needs of industry in terms of skill levels as well as worker attitudes. A whole generation of paulista intellectuals and technocrats found in rational organization a guide to the construction of a sanitized, orderly urban society in which they would provide the crucial technical expertise.

Moreover, rationalization did not operate strictly in the discursive realm. Material conditions within industry already reflected some aspects of rationalization by the 1920s, with increased mechanization and regimentation of labor accompanying the concentration of industrial production. In a haphazard and often uneven way, this signified a gradual restructuring of the labor force that reduced the number and authority of certain traditional craft workers while creating the demand for new types of skilled and semiskilled labor.

The role played by labor in the spread of Fordist and other such strategies is far more ambiguous than has been recognized in previous studies. Workers have usually been portrayed as both a goad and an obstacle to rationalization through their resistance to employer authority. Yet if we compare Brazilian industry with its counterparts in Britain, France, or the United States, we find weaker artisanal and craft traditions, with highly skilled positions often occupied by privileged "foreigners"—that is, non-Brazilians who were not typical of those who arrived in massive immigrant waves from Italy, Spain, and Portugal. Thus it is difficult to imagine that rationalization appealed to Brazilian industrialists and technocrats simply as a means to exert greater control over labor in the workplace rather than as a means to increase productivity or extol the advantages of industry. And it is equally difficult to imagine that workers in most occupations were able (or willing) to mount sustained resistance to new technologies and work processes. Again, this is not to say that the employer had a free hand; the experience of the powerful Matarazzo enterprise in the Mariangela textile mill demonstrates the contrary. But resistance was more likely to be spontaneous and isolated rather than sponsored by a well-structured and powerful craft organization.[138]

Even more important, scholars have mistakenly portrayed workers in this period as consistently and vigorously opposed to all forms of rationalization. Evidence from the printers' newspaper demonstrates that aspects of the rationalizer's discourse had some appeal to workers, at least in that craft. Contributors to the paper often reserved their harshest criticisms not for highly mechanized plants but for makeshift workshops utilizing inferior machinery and, by extension, poorly trained workers. Faced with the industrialization of their craft, printers increasingly turned to the union, which staged two major walkouts during the 1920s, to maintain their wage levels and improve working conditions. But the union repeatedly presented itself not as an enemy of technical innovation or workplace discipline but as the proper vehicle to promote better training, greater efficiency, and overall productivity. In their own ill-fated appeals for social peace, the union leaders borrowed a leaf from Simonsen's book, arguing that both labor and capital would benefit from recognition of the printers' union.

In light of the subsequent course of industrial relations in Brazil, it is interesting to note the almost total absence of the state in the various discourses emerging from industrialists, technocrats, and workers. For much of the period under discussion, the principal role of the state was to exercise repression on behalf of the employers and to provide some tariff protection for industry. Spokesmen for industry explicitly rejected state "interference" in relations between employers and workers, while unions rarely turned to the state for assistance. Even Mange's initial educational experiments occurred within a private institution.[139] But, as Edgar de Decca has noted, the Fordist strategy implicitly required some state intervention in the process of national development.[140] And political factions interested in creating new social legislation to modify working conditions increasingly forced employers to debate labor issues in the public arena as the 1920s drew to a close.

Rational Organization and Social Reform

During the period that stretched from the mid-1920s to the mid-1930s, enthusiasm for rationalization and scientific management continued unabated among leading Brazilian industrialists and their intellectual allies. Although the ideas first articulated by Roberto Simonsen and Roberto Mange in the previous decade underwent some modification, interest in basic Taylorist and Fordist principles intensified and took on new institutional forms. More important, these years saw a subtle but significant shift in the attitudes of the industrialist leadership regarding rationalization and state intervention. Increasingly, Simonsen and others explicitly assigned the state responsibility for facilitating harmonious relations between capital and labor and even viewed the state as a potentially useful mechanism for disciplining the members of their own social class. And this shift is all the more remarkable given the often turbulent political relationship between the paulista elites and the centralizing regime that came to power in 1930 under the leadership of Getúlio Vargas.

During Brazil's First Republic (1889–1930), a series of regional oligarchies monopolized political power, manipulating elections and minimizing popular participation.[1] From the outset, labor supply and labor control were questions of pressing importance for the republican leadership, but the initial emphasis was on the agrarian, not the urban, sector. Republican politicians throughout Brazil, acting primarily at the state level, addressed the labor problems created by the abolition of slavery in 1888. In São Paulo, the state used abundant revenues from export taxes on coffee to subsidize massive European immigration, successfully replacing the slaves who had previously tended the coffee estates with Italian, Spanish, and Portuguese families. In other regions, local political bosses used their formal and informal powers to prevent "vagrancy" and maintain peaceful relations with rural workers.[2]

It is hardly surprising, given the embryonic nature of industrial development in the 1890s and the liberal assumptions of most politicians about the role of the state, that the early republican leaders made no attempt to regulate the relations between capital and labor in the urban sector. But politicians did not have the luxury of ignoring what became known as the "social question" for long. The early years of the twentieth century brought the first major strikes in Rio and São Paulo. In 1906 São Paulo was the scene of a prolonged railroad workers' strike, and the next year witnessed the first attempt at a general strike. Demanding an eight-hour day, metalworkers walked off the job, followed by construction workers, stonecutters, shoemakers, and textile workers. In both cases, the state government became intimately involved, not in order to mediate or redress grievances but to mobilize the Força Pública, whose members kept the trains running, broke up demonstrations, and attacked the headquarters of working-class organizations and newspapers.[3]

Only a few important strikes occurred over the next ten years, and none took on a generalized character. This relative tranquillity, combined with the exclusion of workers from the formal political sphere, meant that occasional proposals for labor legislation or strike arbitration could go largely unheeded.[4] This was the case at least until the general strike of 1917, a movement of unprecedented scale and militance that united artisans and factory workers, men and women, in an effort to secure higher wages and better working conditions. Although middle- and upper-class observers recoiled at the sight of massive demonstrations and clashes between workers and police, there was considerable public sympathy for the strikers' demands. The European war and the consequent decline in imports had provided the paulista industrialists with a golden opportunity to increase their share of the local market. This led industrialists to extend working hours in an attempt to operate their factories at full capacity. Wages, meanwhile, generally rose during this period, but they failed to keep pace with the rising cost of living caused by war-related shortages. The demands of the workers, therefore, seemed eminently reasonable to many urban residents and especially to struggling members of the middle class who were themselves suffering the effects of inflation.

The general strike of 1917, closely followed by another strike movement in 1919, had a wide range of repercussions in the public and private spheres. The most concrete and immediate was an intensification of repression against anarchists and other labor activists. In the private sphere, the paulista textile manufacturers launched their own association in 1919 to defend their interests and soon inaugurated a blacklist of "undesirable" workers. In the public sphere, the state police began to address more systematically problems of public order peculiar to the urban milieu, establishing the Department for Political and Social Order (Departamento de Ordem Política e Social, or DOPS) in 1924.[5]

These were not, however, the only legacies of the 1917 and 1919 strikes. In the aftermath of the 1917 movement, São Paulo's State Department of Labor began an investigation into the feasibility of using federal labor legislation to regulate conflicts between capital and labor and to resolve certain worker grievances. It immediately consulted with the Centro de Comércio e Indústria de São Paulo, which held a well-attended meeting to discuss the issue and reported to the government that the center "always saw the necessity of adopting a labor code, to regulate relations between capital and the worker and to mediate contracts between the latter and employers."[6] The claim that the center "always" held this view should incite some skepticism, but it is clear from this and other documents that the terms of the debate had shifted so that it was no longer a question of preventing the state from intervening in labor relations. Now the objective was to modify and circumscribe that intervention.

It should also be noted that the employers' response to the State Labor Department called for the inclusion in the labor code of certain "guarantees" sought by the industrialists, meaning tariff barriers to protect their products from expected postwar competition. This indicates that the needs of manufacturers faced with competition from powerful foreign producers made opposition to all forms of state intervention untenable.[7] As we will see, the industrialists protested vigorously against every piece of labor legislation passed in the 1920s, but they could not completely reject the principle of state intervention.

Industrialists and Early Labor Legislation

Recent studies have examined either the growing elite consensus in favor of state regulation of labor relations or the growing enthusiasm among intellectuals and industrialists for rational organization, but little consideration has been given to the relationship between these two strains of thought, though both were concerned with restructuring the industrial milieu.[8] As a result, they appear as parallel ideological developments that at no point intersected or communicated. By the early 1930s, however, we can detect a convergence in these lines of debate, with labor legislation and state regulation of the labor movement becoming part and parcel of the rationalizer's vision.

This convergence was neither a natural nor an unproblematic process given the divergent discursive tendencies of social law and scientific management. For the advocate of Taylorism and Fordism, the point of departure was the scientific determination of conditions that allowed the factory to produce the most goods in the least time with the least effort. Worker welfare was simply subsumed by this increased productivity. Industrial psychology did pose some limits to the Taylorist program, but it did so on an allegedly scientific basis. Nowhere was there an explicit consideration or legitimation of workers' rights or needs, which were the usual point of departure for social legislation. Refracted through the rationalizer's lens, the "social question" became a technical question.

For example, at a 1931 meeting of textile manufacturers who gathered to discuss a projected eight-hour-day law, employers and engineers invariably justified their positions with "scientific" arguments. Those who supported the legislation argued that after eight hours productivity declined.[9] The leading spokesman for a nine-hour day (the majority position) claimed that a workday of this length would not be a burden to textile workers. "Since the machines work with electric motors, the [operative's] physical effort is minimal: the worker's function is to oversee the mechanical process." Still another employer proposed a longer day for some workers: "Ten hours would not tire a weaver, who has nothing more to do than keep track of the machine's actions in the propitious environment provided by large modern firms. His work level cannot be compared with that of stonecutters, ironworkers, etc., etc., who do need to work only eight hours."[10]

The different positions often rested on apparently contradictory arguments. On the one hand, the relative inefficiency of Brazilian textile factories made a longer workday necessary; on the other hand, increased mechanization and task simplification made a shorter workday *un*necessary. But whether logical or not, these arguments reveal the manufacturers' assumption that the length of the workday should be "scientifically" calculated according to the economic, physical, and mental demands of different industrial jobs, not according to the workers' cultural or political notion of a reasonable workday or the right to leisure.[11]

In its purest form, the rationalizer's discourse provided no space for labor legislation based on workers' definitions of their rights and identities. Indeed, the central thrust was to remove the debate over working conditions from the political arena and address such questions in a scientific, depoliticized context. To be sure, by privileging productivity and profitability, Taylorists and Fordists were expressing a preference with obvious political connotations, but they were always careful to cloak it in the language of science and its contribution to social welfare.

It was the pursuit of this last objective—the promotion of general well-being through greater productivity and efficiency—that made the rationalizer's discourse permeable to reformist sentiment. The Fordist project aspired to the reorganization of society as a whole, not just the factory, which required standard medical and educational services, some leisure time for consumption and healthy recreation, and a solid family structure. Furthermore, given the worldwide trend toward labor reforms, including the well-publicized recommendations in the Treaty of Versailles, rigid opposition to such reforms could only result in social disruption and disorder. This was no small consideration for the industrialist-rationalizers since they regarded social peace as a prerequisite for, as well as a consequence of, the implementation of their project. The need for class harmony might make certain concessions, even of an "unscientific" nature, unavoidable.[12]

The debate over social reforms also threatened intra-elite harmony as prominent members of paulista society, including individuals associated with *O Estado de São Paulo* and the Partido Democrático, embraced such ameliorative measures. Since several of these individuals also supported tariff reductions and had ties to agrarian and commercial elites, scholars have tended to view them as "anti-industry."[13] Yet many of these figures had ties to firms that were at least partially "industrial"; for example, Armando de Salles Oliveira, editor of *O Estado* and leader of the Partido Democrático, had a major interest in an electric utility, and *O Estado* itself employed hundreds of printers in a large, mechanized shop. And such figures as Salles and A. C. Pacheco e Silva were among the most enthusiastic advocates of rational methods of work organization and training.[14] What they objected to was not industry per se but the large textile industrialists, the so-called "Italian Counts," whom they portrayed as interested only in the pursuit of profits.[15] From the "reformists'" perspective, the textile magnates not only demanded high tariffs at the expense of urban consumers but also repudiated social reforms even at the expense of social peace. Thus, for "progressive" industrialist spokesmen such as Simonsen and Jorge Street, the challenge was to affirm the need for social reform in principle while presenting their objections to specific labor laws on a "rational" basis and to identify the fate of industry with the welfare of the nation.[16]

By the 1920s, few prominent industrialists denied the need for limited social reforms and better social services. But such a concession was not the same as accepting the active role of the state in such matters. Francisco Matarazzo, in the aftermath of the 1919 strike, may have been willing to grant an eight-hour day to his textile workers, but he surely would have opposed any legal measure compelling employers to shorten the workday.[17] At this point, most leading industrialists agreed that some legislation regulating work by women and minors and accident compensation was necessary. But reforms had to be limited and conform as much as possible to the interests of industry. In the words of Jorge Street, "It is absolutely necessary to avoid exaggerations and harmful excesses."[18]

Industrialists in both Rio and São Paulo regarded the 1925 law requiring paid vacations (Lei das Férias) and the 1926 restrictions on child labor as textbook examples of the danger of entrusting the formulation of labor legislation to politicians with no experience in the operation of industrial enterprises.[19] Industrialist organizations immediately protested both laws as economically ruinous and contended that the laws, by giving adult workers free time and enforcing "idleness" among the young, would provoke rampant vice and criminality. CIESP openly instructed its membership to ignore the laws and branded those who disobeyed CIESP's instructions as traitors to their class.

The passage of these laws and the resulting campaigns for their repeal or revision reveal the complicated political position occupied by Brazilian industrialists in the latter years of the First Republic. Within the space of a year, the federal Chamber of Deputies had passed two pieces of social legislation that were anathema to virtually every industrialist. However dubious the moral content of their arguments might be, the industrialists could effectively argue that legislative policies reflected neither the interests of industry (or to put it more broadly, industrialization) nor the level of class conflict in the industrial milieu. During these years, the federal deputies, most of whom represented regions with only marginal manufacturing economies, did not operate under the Fordist presumption that national and industrial interests were one and the same. Or if they did, they may have wondered, as did *O Estado de São Paulo*, whether the interests of the industrialists were identical to those of industry.[20]

Edgar de Decca cites 1928 as the key moment when a project formulated by the paulista industrialists and their allies crystallized and emerged as the dominant bourgeois discourse.[21] In many respects, 1928 was a year of triumphs for São Paulo's manufacturing class. The founding of CIESP signified a new degree of organizational unity and provided a forum to represent industrialization as crucial to the stability and welfare of the Brazilian people. The growing power of industrial interests in the Paulista Republican Party led to that party's successful intercession on behalf of higher tariffs on imported textiles. And industrialists did manage to stall the enforcement of two major pieces of labor legislation passed by the Chamber of Deputies.

Yet the industrialist leadership did not necessarily see itself as triumphant. Its efforts to repeal or drastically modify the labor laws had come to naught, confining CIESP and the Centro Industrial Brasileiro in Rio, champions of stability and order, to the ideologically and politically awkward strategy of noncompliance. And in the brief period when electoral contests began to take on some meaning, the industrialists fretted about their limited electoral clout or savvy. One of CIESP's first major projects was a voter registration drive at its members' factories, presumably including only persons of confidence and intended to induce industrialists to "abandon the indifference in which, until now, they have lived."[22]

Documents from CIESP's first full year as a functioning organization indicate that the center's own position on social reform was in a state of flux. In January 1929, the directorate circulated a ten-page opinion paper prepared by one of CIESP's legal consultants, João Arruda, in response to a series of questions about the Lei das Férias. His discussions of specific provisions of the law favored the employer's position, but his extended response to a question about constitutionality is of particular interest. He quoted a leading progressive law professor at the University of Chicago to the effect that "economic oppression generally proceeds with the apparent approval of the oppressed, whose weakness leads them to accept onerous terms, and such oppression can only be combated by restricting freedom of contract." Furthermore, he noted that Brazil, as a signatory of the Versailles Treaty, should voluntarily implement the treaty's social provisions.[23]

This paper was not a mere anomaly; CIESP's two major legal consultants, Plínio Barreto and Antônio Mendonça, also urged the application of the labor provisions in the Versailles Treaty, although they noted that the provisions did not explicitly address the issue of paid vacations.[24] Both consultants supported the modification of the traditional liberal "laissez-faire" position on labor relations in the interest of resolving certain persistent labor grievances in a peaceful and orderly fashion. The social reforms of the so-called Revolution of 1930 did not find the industrialists utterly unprepared.[25]

Paulista Industry and the Revolution of 1930

The initial response of industrialists to the 1930 seizure of power by a civilian-military coalition led by Getúlio Vargas was ambivalent at best. Since it came close on the heels of the worldwide economic depression and the virtual collapse of the coffee market, the fall of the First Republic was just one of several pressing issues facing the "conservative classes" in Brazil. In the national elections that preceded the Revolution of 1930, CIESP heartily endorsed the presidential candidacy of the paulista governor, Júlio Prestes, claiming that his state administration had been friendly to industry.[26] Moreover, industrialists in São Paulo, despite holding an increasingly national view of their economic interests, shared the paulista elites' assumption that their home state was the most progressive and productive in Brazil—or to use the metaphorical phrase, it was the nation's "locomotive." Given CIESP's position on the 1930 elections and its identification with a politically dominant São Paulo, the seizure of power by a politician from Rio Grande do Sul must have caused the leading industrialists some discomfort. Indeed, in the case of Roberto Simonsen, the discomfort was not slight. Suspicions of malfeasance by his banking house in the contracting of loans for government coffee purchases led to his imprisonment for two weeks during November 1930.[27]

Far more unnerving for the industrial bourgeoisie was the wave of popular violence, including the sacking and destruction of the notorious Cambucí Prison.[28] Throughout the month of October, CIESP nervously advised the industrialists to maintain business as usual; just a few days after the attack on the prison, CIESP assured members that the provisional government had "means to pacify disorders in the factories."[29] Under these circumstances, it is not surprising that CIESP quickly sought to develop a working relationship with the new federal interventor, the *tenente* João Alberto Lins de Barros. Three days into the new year, CIESP representatives met with João Alberto and convinced him to suspend temporarily the paid vacation law until a new labor code had been promulgated.[30]

Despite the turbulence associated with the regime transition and the proto-populist discourse articulated by Vargas, industrialists soon acknowledged the government's commitment to maintenance of order and protection of property.[31] In mid-1931 a massive strike broke out among paulista workers. Reacting to the hardships caused by the depression and to the renewed promise of social reform, as many as 70,000 operatives from the textile industry and other trades joined what CIESP tried to dismiss as mere "agitations." Both federal troops and the state Força Pública collaborated to protect strikebreakers' "freedom to work," and within days João Alberto issued a statement ordering workers to return to their jobs.[32]

Other aspects of the new government's policies gained easy acceptance from CIESP. In response to a government decree stipulating the creation of a hierarchical system of *sindicatos* and federations for both workers and employers, CIESP immediately petitioned the Ministry of Labor, Industry, and Commerce for recognition as the Federação das Indústrias do Estado de São Paulo, representing all industrial employer *sindicatos* in the state. CIESP officially became CIESP/FIESP in May 1931, and a visit from Vargas's minister of labor, Lindolfo Collor, marked the occasion.[33] With markets for manufactured goods contracting and factories operating at a mere 30 to 40 percent of capacity, industrialists also warmly welcomed the ministry's 1931 decree prohibiting the importation of textile and other machinery over the next three years (a measure undoubtedly prompted by a technical report from CIESP).[34] Furthermore, the decree expanded the power and purview of the industrialist associations since any request for exemption from the prohibition had to be channeled through the appropriate employers' *sindicato* and state federation.

Such matters, however, did not constitute the main subject of discussion and debate between industrialists and the state during the early 1930s. Rather, the spotlight was on the new social legislation. With uncustomary dispatch, Vargas kept his promises to popular groups by issuing a series of decrees during his first year in power that regulated working hours, vacations, child and female labor, and unionization as well as providing for collective bargaining, arbitration boards, and limits on the employment of foreign workers. Thus the industrialist leadership spent much of its energies during this period analyzing and criticizing drafts of the proposed labor laws.

Since the 1970s, historians have disputed the industrialists' role in the crafting of labor legislation from two sharply contrasting perspectives. Industrial spokesmen have been portrayed, on the one hand, as staunchly opposed to the entire enterprise (even if, after the fact, they might have benefited from the "disciplinary" effects of the new laws). On the other hand, some recent studies have portrayed Vargas and his advisers as virtual instruments of the employer class, who tailored the laws to suit the needs of industry. Both positions tend to caricature the relationship between Vargas and the industrialists and obscure the historical contingencies that affected the "legislative" process.

There is no dispute over industrialist participation in the process. The Ministry of Labor, Industry, and Commerce sent the texts of projected labor laws to FIESP and to other employer federations for comments and suggestions, some of which were inserted into the final versions. (No such courtesy was shown to the labor unions, whose "input" was restricted to questionable representatives in the National Department of Labor). The correspondence between FIESP and the ministry, though varying in tone, certainly does not support the claim that industrialists opposed the whole enterprise. Whatever specific protests FIESP lodged against Vargas's decrees, the federation did not challenge the state's right to formulate such regulations or deny the need for some sort of labor code.[35] It was more than a rhetorical flourish to end a letter to Lindolfo Collor regarding alterations in the labor code by assuring him that the members of FIESP "are unanimous in warmly applauding the great effort that Your Excellency is making to provide our country with a social legislation whose high, noble, and patriotic objective is to give aid and protection to the worker."[36] Though openly opposed to certain provisions and notoriously lax about implementing even those provisions they supported, members of the industrial leadership still wished to be identified with the government's project for social reform. Indeed, in a later and unusually indignant letter to a special delegate of the Ministry of Labor, FIESP claimed that "we [industrialists] sensed the need for social laws for many years, well before the nation's leaders contemplated them."[37] Here, too, the boundaries of the debate had been set.

Despite FIESP's generally mild response to the projected social laws, employers proved particularly unwilling to compromise on certain questions. The first "ante-projeto" (preliminary draft) sent to FIESP was for the "nationalization of labor," a law that would require two-thirds of the workers in a factory be "Brazilian" according to the decree's definition. FIESP reacted favorably, although it noted the need to allow for foreign workers whose services were "rigorously technical."[38] The one major controversy between the Ministry of Labor and FIESP over the Two-Thirds Law erupted two years later when a federal decree empowered labor unions to designate a member who would verify compliance at the factory level. Alerting its members to the decree, FIESP assured them that it would do everything possible to combat "the worst evil that could befall us, that is, the weakening of employer authority."

In a written communication to then minister of labor Joaquim Pedro Salgado Filho, FIESP cited the text of Decree no. 19,770, which delineated "legitimate" areas of union activity, prohibiting "any interference in the web of factory labor, whether in its technical, economic, or even social aspects." In nearly hysterical language, the letter claimed that the designated worker would become "strong with those powers bestowed on him by the law" and would "treat the owner with the superiority granted by legal powers." Noting previous attempts by unions to interfere in internal factory matters, the writer claimed that employers had repulsed all such efforts, "understanding, thanks to long experience with factory life, that the organization of work does not allow breaks in the hierarchy that must be in force among the various factors [of production] or the intrusion of elements from the working mass into the terrain of those who are in charge of the upper levels of management." Going even further, FIESP predicted that the decree would disrupt cooperation between capital and labor and inaugurate "a new era of discord." In his response to FIESP's vehement criticism, the minister of labor assured the industrialists that the union member would only have the power to denounce a suspected infraction, as any citizen can denounce a crime, and would not be empowered to demand information or compliance from a factory owner.[39]

FIESP accepted the new law on "syndicalization" of employers and workers with few reservations—hardly a surprise given the strict limits that the decree set on union activity. Joel Wolfe observes that as early as July 1931 São Paulo's federal interventor used the decree to suppress the textile workers' strike, which was led by organizations not formally recognized by the Ministry of Labor.[40] As for the provisions relating to employers, the paulista industrialists eagerly embraced the new guidelines by forming FIESP. At the same time, they campaigned, with eventual success, to exempt employer associations from many of the controls imposed upon workers' organizations. The result was the creation of a system of labor unions subjected to strict regulations and tight control and a network of employer *sindicatos* and federations that retained considerable autonomy.[41]

The very limited role that FIESP envisioned for trade unions in the new labor relations system can be detected in its response to proposed legislation for collective bargaining and in later comments about arbitration commissions. Collective bargaining, FIESP claimed, "would create the dictatorship of labor unions," and then it went on to argue that a proposed minimum wage law would dispense with the need for collective contracts or strikes.[42] In contrast, the projected laws for regulation of work by women and children met with the enthusiastic approval of industrialists. The provisions on child labor actually *lengthened* the maximum workday for minors from six to eight hours, a welcome change (for employers) from the 1926 code. As for the proposal restricting work by women, FIESP declared it "as nearly perfect as possible" and claimed that most of its provisions were already standard operating procedure in paulista industry.[43]

The two decrees that generated the strongest protests from industrialists were the eight-hour-day and paid vacation laws, even though the texts of both laws gave employers considerable room to maneuver.[44] What made these laws so troubling was not their actual provisions but rather the Vargas government's declared intention in 1932 of immediately enforcing them. The timing of the dispute over these laws is also crucial since it took place amid widespread strike activity among textile, glass, shoe, and other workers in São Paulo.[45] Although the Vargas administration and its representatives at the state level continued to provide police protection for property owners, the government also moved to appease the strikers by implementing the much ballyhooed labor legislation. The minister of labor ordered industrialists who had not granted workers vacation time during the previous year to indemnify their employees, and in March 1932, the state interventor announced his intention to decree unilaterally an eight-hour workday for São Paulo.[46]

Thus Vargas's representatives were moving to enforce provisions that would cost employers money at a time when industry had not yet recovered from the effects of the depression and would put the state of São Paulo at a disadvantage vis à vis other regions of Brazil. Furthermore, this transpired in the context of a serious challenge by labor to employer authority and at a time when key posts in the state government were occupied by military officials whose loyalties were ambiguous. Even the suppression of the Brazilian Communist Party (Partido Comunista do Brasil, or PCB) by the new interventor, Pedro de Toledo, in May 1932 did little to quell elite fears.[47]

If we take the confluence of all of these factors into account, it becomes easier to understand why the paulista industrialists who supported or tolerated Vargas's policies throughout his first year in power had moved by mid-1932 firmly into the opposition camp. To be sure, regional loyalty had something to do with the decision. Vargas's imposition of nonpaulista interventors and his inattention to the needs of the state's agrarian interests could only be construed as a usurpation of São Paulo's powers and prerogatives. In the same vein, officials appointed by Vargas were often regarded as unknown quantities by the industrialist leadership. This contrasts with their intimate knowledge of and frequently close ties with state officials appointed locally. For example, a 1931 FIESP letter to its membership assured factory owners that they need not feel intimidated by visits from state health inspectors since "the eminent director of inspection for workplace health and safety has a highly enlightened scientific spirit and in no instance would be given to excesses against the factories, having profound acquaintance with our industrial life."[48] The only federal appointee who merited similar confidence was Jorge Street, who Collor named to head the National Department of Industry and Commerce.

With the benefit of hindsight, one could argue that the long-term interests of the paulista industrialists lay with the "national" vision of economic development formulated by the Vargas regime. But in mid-1932 the industrialists perceived their immediate interests, whether in terms of financial solvency or social control, as being intertwined with the political future of the state of São Paulo. It was in this spirit that FIESP joined the "constitutionalist" revolt against Vargas, mobilizing the industrial sector's considerable resources to support the paulista troops throughout the three-month uprising.[49]

In the days following the outbreak of hostilities between federal forces loyal to Vargas and constitutionalist troops, FIESP called upon manufacturers of shoes and foodstuffs to donate their products to the rebel army. The federation also urged even overstocked factories to continue operations: "At this moment, a working factory is a demonstration of patriotism."[50] By early August, FIESP announced that the great majority of manufacturers had guaranteed the jobs and salaries of workers who joined the rebel effort and called on all employers to adopt this policy. Throughout the short-lived conflict, FIESP oversaw and orchestrated the "mobilization" of paulista industry to sustain the constitutionalist effort.[51]

Several experiences during the brief regional revolt had a lasting influence on the FIESP leadership; the industrial mobilization was one of them. The Industrial Registration and Mobilization Service, headed by FIESP president Roberto Simonsen, undertook the first detailed survey of industrial resources in São Paulo and directed programs to rationalize and reorganize industry on a war footing.[52] Roberto Mange, due to his background in mechanical engineering, personally oversaw the revamping of metallurgical factories for the production of armaments and successfully improvised ways to manufacture bullets and cartridges.[53] These experiences were extremely brief since the entire revolt lasted less than three months, but the hothouse atmosphere of the constitutionalist campaign gave Simonsen, Mange, and others an unprecedented opportunity to observe the workings of paulista factories and to experiment with various forms of technical and managerial innovation. According to one participant in the effort, Mange's methods led first to a doubling and then to a tripling of production in the participating factories.[54]

Another experience whose influence outlasted the campaign was the collection of funds to finance clinics offering free medical, dental, and pharmaceutical services for paulista workers. Alarmed by the lack of enthusiasm for the revolt among urban workers, FIESP openly admitted that these medical services were designed to enlist worker support for the rebel cause and assured members that they represented a short-term and temporary solution to a pressing situation.[55] However, soon after the revolt ended, the directorate reported that "many factories with an advanced vision of the current labor conditions requested that we continue this service on a permanent basis." Claiming that larger factories already offering medical assistance could economize through the centralization of such services, the notice solicited contributions to sustain the clinics, adding that, in the case of a weak response, FIESP would dismantle them "with great reluctance." A month later, FIESP informed its membership that only a small segment of industry had manifested support for permanent medical clinics, obliging the federation "to put an end to such an interesting and useful initiative."[56]

Traces of this brief experiment in collective "welfare capitalism" can be found in subsequent policies developed by the industrialist leadership. Most obviously, the popularity of the medical clinics highlighted the political utility of providing concrete services to workers. It also demonstrated the inadequacy of a social service network based solely on factory-level assistance. Although most large factories had doctors in residence and offered certain forms of medical care, such services were often deficient and were seldom extended to the nonworking members of an employee's family. Medium-sized and small factories, meanwhile, rarely provided even the most basic health care for their workers. But perhaps most important, the medical clinic scheme demonstrated the inefficacy of any plan that relied on voluntary contributions. If FIESP wanted industrialists to fund such services, it would have to find some means other than moral suasion to compel them to do so.

The defeat of the constitutionalist cause, which failed to attract active support from other regional elites, also demonstrated the infeasibility of political or economic strategies based solely on protecting the interests of the state of São Paulo. This is not to imply that FIESP immediately switched to unqualified support for the Vargas administration. The federation's president, Roberto Simonsen, had been forced into exile following the 1932 revolt, and FIESP now had to contend with a military governor, Waldomiro Castilho de Lima, who was Vargas's uncle by marriage. Still, within a month of the rebels' surrender, FIESP representatives met with Castilho de Lima to propose an alternative to the paid vacation law. Reporting on the meeting, the FIESP directors claimed that the governor had revealed "vast sociological knowledge" and had manifested his support for the "German system," whereby the state, employers, and workers all contributed to a social assistance fund.[57] Emboldened by this positive reception, FIESP followed up the meeting with a long letter to Castilho de Lima in which the industrialist Alexandre Siciliano Júnior outlined an elaborate plan for social services. It would include the construction of worker housing, the building of nurseries, kindergartens, and schools, the setting up of food and medical cooperatives, and the creation of a retirement fund. The most innovative feature of this proposal was its call for German-style, tripartite financing.[58]

Predictably, nothing became of Siciliano's proposal to replace the paid vacation law with a worker welfare fund. His scheme is interesting mainly to the extent that it foreshadows future social assistance projects and for what it reveals about the evolving attitudes of the industrialist leadership. Indeed, it is likely that FIESP viewed the proposal as a last-ditch and half-hearted effort to stop the implementation of the Lei das Férias. Less than a week later, the federation circulated a notice to its members describing the specific conditions for compensating workers who did not receive paid vacations between April 1931 and October 1932 and expressing its confidence that paulista employers would obey the law.[59] Even so, FIESP's conciliatory attitude did have limits. When the special delegate of the Ministry of Labor, charged with overseeing enforcement of labor legislation in São Paulo, proved too intrusive for the industrialists' tastes, the federation initiated a successful campaign to have him replaced.[60] And by December 1933, the government of São Paulo had struck an extraordinary agreement with the Ministry of Labor that delegated most ministerial functions to the State Department of Labor.[61]

Vargas's own conciliatory response to the paulista revolt indicates his shrewd perception of the prominent place São Paulo and its economy would occupy in any strategy for political centralization or economic development. Within months of the constitutionalists' surrender, Vargas granted the former rebels one of their major demands by calling elections for a constituent assembly. Roberto Simonsen immediately returned from his brief voluntary exile in Buenos Aires to run for the *constituinte* as an industrialist deputy, along with fellow FIESP members Horácio Lafer, Alexandre Siciliano Júnior, and A. C. Pacheco e Silva. It was through his speeches in the *constituinte*, several of which were published and widely circulated, that Simonsen emerged as a major national commentator on Brazilian economic and social policy.

Considering that the paulista industrialists had recently participated in the leadership of a failed revolt against the central government, their political prominence in the constituent assembly is nothing short of remarkable. Combining forces with the paulista Chapa Única (Single Slate) bench and other disgruntled regional factions when convenient, the industrialists became major figures in the assembly and important contributors to the draft of the 1934 constitution, fending off attacks by critics of tariff protection for industry. At the state level, Armando de Salles Oliveira—constitutionalist, engineer, industrialist, editor of *O Estado de São Paulo*, founding member of IDORT, and general enthusiast for scientific management—succeeded Castilho de Lima in 1933 as interventor. One of his first acts was to appoint the aging Jorge Street as head of the State Department of Labor. At the federal level, in 1934 Vargas created an interministerial commission to address the problem of vocational education; among its nine members were several educators closely associated with paulista industry and IDORT, including M. B. Lourenço Filho, Horácio da Silveira, and Roberto Mange.

This odd configuration of political participation and opposition by industrialists and their allies reflects the complicated historical conjuncture of the mid-1930s. For a brief period, traditional regional loyalties and liberal political assumptions would bind together the fragile paulista coalition and sustain industrialist ambivalence toward the Vargas regime, even as Vargas conceded to some of the industrialists' most significant demands.[62] It would be a few more years before the leading spokesmen for paulista industry would move solidly into the *getulista* camp.

Public Policy in the Private Sphere

The interaction of industrialists and rationalizers with the state during the period from the late 1920s to the mid-1930s reveals only one side of the process of formulating a project for rationalization and social peace. Many significant developments in the area of industrial social policy originated outside the public sphere, through organizations and institutes created by businessmen, engineers, and educators imbued with the spirit of rationalization. Despite the increasing prominence of the state in the realm of social policy as well as the growing participation of industrial elites in the public sector, advocates of scientific management continued to follow a semi-Fordist agenda that emphasized the role of industrialists and their technocratic allies in civil society.

The founding of IDORT in 1931 was only one of several signs of growing enthusiasm for rationalization among industrialist leaders. Once again, Roberto Simonsen attempted to set the agenda for industry, outlining his strategy in a speech delivered in 1931 at Mackenzie College, São Paulo's second oldest engineering school.[63] Simonsen used the occasion to analyze the problems that had hampered Brazilian industrial development during the previous decade. The solution he proposed for these problems, true to form, was the rational organization of production.

The text of the speech indicates, however, that Simonsen's view of rationalization had evolved over the course of the decade. Early in his talk, he compared Taylorism unfavorably with Fordist approaches to scientific management, criticizing Taylor's bonus system for crudely exciting the worker's appetite for material gain while commending Ford's emphasis on cooperation and service as well as higher levels of consumption.[64] Throughout the speech, Simonsen emphasized the need for a "full-scale rationalization of production," which would incorporate sociological and psychological insights as well as purely technical innovations.

Simonsen then shifted to a consideration of industrial development in other societies, citing the experience of postwar Germany as an appropriate model for Brazil. He noted that Germany, in the aftermath of the war, suffered from economic disorganization and capital scarcity, two impediments to industrial expansion in Brazil. Simonsen then described the progress of rationalization in Germany, emphasizing industrial concentration, standardization, and the use of assembly lines. In the social sphere, German industry had "adopted a system of high wages and efficient labor methods but also introduced applied psychology as the fundamental element for dealing with the human factor."[65] The direct references to industrial concentration, assembly-line production, high wages, and industrial psychology indicate that Simonsen had taken his commitment to rationalization several steps beyond his earlier Taylorist persuasion.

If some of Simonsen's previous writings implicitly allowed a role for the state in industrial development, this speech described state intervention in explicit and positive terms: "Affecting all of German social life, rationalization ceases to be a mere private economic issue and begins to have a profound impact on the public economy, and hence the justification for state intervention. The state, in the legislative and administrative domains, has taken important measures with respect to plant shutdowns, the application of labor legislation, arbitration of class conflicts, help for the unemployed, legislation on mergers, heavy subsidies for technical studies to advance rationalization, etc."[66] This interpenetration of public and private sectors, oriented by "impartial technical commissions," was now not only desirable but necessary for the progress of scientific management in Brazil. Simonsen had not simply conceded the legitimacy of state action in the arena of industrial policy but had recognized the auspicious opportunities for collaboration between public and private interests imbued with the rationalizing spirit.

As in his earlier work, Simonsen forecast an era of social harmony resulting from the scientific reorganization of society. After inspiring an advanced labor policy, rationalization would evolve into a "political system" based on "reason and technical knowledge." Simonsen next expanded upon this notion of a "true equilibrium among the elements that constitute the living forces of production. Rationalization has profound social effects and clearly counteracts the fundamental ideas of Marxism. . . . The continual development of technical and professional culture, for which the labor unions, themselves, clamor, the acceptance of worker control in the solution of economic problems, all naturally work together to cool off the class struggle forecast by Karl Marx."[67] Simonsen cited the opinion of sociologists who believed that a "veritable social doctrine," capable of absorbing all divergent schools of thought, would result from the "rigorously scientific" study of society then taking place in Germany—a belief that would take on a tragic irony just a few years later.[68]

Simonsen had also shifted, however slightly, his view of labor unions over the previous decade. In his 1931 speech, he portrayed workers as playing an active, if naturally circumscribed, role in the rationalization process and referred to labor unions in a matter-of-fact manner not characteristic of his earlier speeches. It is also interesting that he cited as common ground between unions and rationalizers support for "the continual development of technical and professional culture"—a rare instance in which an industrialist's claim to share the views of labor was probably accurate.

Just two months after Simonsen delivered this speech, a like-minded group of paulista businessmen and intellectuals held the founding meeting of IDORT. Since the late 1920s, Aldo Mário de Azevedo, Simonsen's cousin, had led the effort to create an institute devoted to scientific management modeled on the famous center in Geneva, from which IDORT took its name.[69] Briefly diverted from his goal by the onset of the Great Depression, Azevedo finally had the honor of delivering the inaugural address at the founding meeting of IDORT in June 1931. Praising Simonsen's recent speech for its "true vision of the potential of rationalization in Brazil," Azevedo went on to argue that the ongoing economic crisis made IDORT's mission even more pressing than before: "The crisis that exploded at the end of 1929 violently demonstrated the need for us to organize ourselves economically and financially, improving the quality of our production, lowering its cost, facilitating its circulation and distribution, and providing better remuneration for our workers, whose standard of living is blatantly inferior." He then outlined the objectives of IDORT as including research and the exchange of ideas, the application of scientific methods, and the transformation of class enemies into collaborators for "the common welfare."[70]

The composition of IDORT's organizing committee demonstrates its broad appeal to economic and technocratic elites. Aside from Azevedo, a textile manufacturer, its members included Gaspar Ricardo Júnior, director of the Sorocabana Railway; Geraldo de Paula Souza, the leading state official for workplace health and safety; Luis Alves Pereira, president of FIESP; M. B. Lourenço Filho, one of Brazil's best-known educators; Armando de Salles Oliveira, editor of *O Estado de São Paulo*; Henrique Villares, a member of São Paulo's leading construction machinery firm; and Roberto Mange, prominent expert on industrial training and *psicotécnica*. Other well-known paulista industrialists or bankers who were either founding or early members of IDORT were Simonsen, Gastão Vidigal, A. C. Pacheco e Silva, and Alexandre Siciliano Júnior. Distinguished members of the technocratic group included the prominent engineer Francisco Salles de Oliveira (related to Simonsen by marriage), the noted educator Damasco Pena, and the physician/hygienist Moacyr E. Alvaro.

Reflecting IDORT's aspiration to rationalize production from the top down and from the bottom up, its directors apportioned the institute's activities to two separate divisions. The first division, entrusted to Francisco Salles de Oliveira, dealt with the administrative organization of work, including specialization of functions, simplification and standardization of production, systems of administration and remuneration, and control of production inputs, stocks, and accounts. The second division, directed by Roberto Mange, dealt with the technical organization of work, including such matters as vocational training, occupational orientation and selection, industrial psychology, and workplace health and safety.[71]

IDORT set as its goal the rational organization of every corner of Brazilian society. Within this totalizing ideology, there was no activity, economic or social, that could not be subordinated to IDORT's creed of greater efficiency through scientific methods. The result, its members predicted, would be a productive, smoothly functioning society in which authority would be exercised by technical experts and increased wealth would allow all Brazilians to enjoy a higher standard of living. To be sure, broadly applied rationalization could have some negative repercussions, such as temporary waves of unemployment or intensification of work rhythms. But here, too, scientific methods could resolve whatever problems arose through reallocation of resources or applied psychology. As Mange observed in a meeting of IDORT's board of directors, "In fact there were certain technical or administrative deficiencies in industry that provoked discontent among the workers; the removal of that discontent has been one of the purposes of rational organization."[72] Appropriately, IDORT's regulations prohibited any affiliations of a religious or political nature; indeed, these were hardly necessary since an omniscient and beneficent science was IDORT's religion and its politics.[73]

In her pioneering study of IDORT, M. A. Antonacci describes Azevedo's inaugural address as defining the battlefield in terms of "rationalization versus skilled labor." His call to arms against inertia and routine was intended, according to Antonacci, "to complete the expropriation of skilled workers and to restructure the factory space to contain working-class organizing."[74] Reading IDORT's ideology from the perspective of a militant, skilled worker, Antonacci reduces the rationalizer's creed to a mechanism for labor control.[75] Certainly, the ideologues of IDORT wanted to subject workers to greater control by scientific experts and eliminate many skills through simplification of the work process. In his course on *psicotécnica*, Mange blandly noted that, with simplified tasks, "it becomes easy to recruit and replace personnel."[76] But such goals, however unsavory they might be, were articulated as means to an end—the formation of a prosperous, harmonious industrial society—not as the ends themselves. To read the modern romance of industrial and technological progress as merely a campaign against the "power" of skilled workers is to obfuscate its remarkably broad and enduring appeal to all social classes.

Constituted as a private institution, IDORT nonetheless embraced cooperation with the state. An introductory editorial in the debut issue of IDORT's monthly magazine explained: "In the highest sense, [rationalization] can be applied to an entire political economy, conceived and executed by the state or by a large industrial or financial group, usually in accord with the state." A few years later, another article affirmed that "the state, by its very nature, would always be the most efficient means to disseminate the mechanisms or regulations to achieve a more rapid generalization of rational methods."[77] However, IDORT's actual relationship with the state was rather complicated during the first decade of its existence. The conflict between the federal and state governments had inevitable repercussions for the "apolitical" IDORT. The second division under Mange directly participated in the reorganization of paulista industry during the 1932 uprising, and IDORT's most important patron was the persistently anti-Vargas *Estado de São Paulo*.[78]

IDORT's collaboration with the state government reached a high point in 1934 when the institute's former president, Armando de Salles Oliveira, occupied the office of interventor. Through Salles's patronage, the state government contracted with IDORT to reorganize and rationalize the state bureaucracy, and IDORT's successful innovations in this area eventually led to contracts with other state governments as well as with federal agencies.[79] At the federal level, several leading figures in IDORT, such as Mange and Lourenço Filho, began participating in "technical commissions" set up by the Vargas administration. The official documentation of IDORT rarely acknowledges political difficulties during this period, but it is likely that the close association of IDORT with the constitutionalist opposition and *O Estado de São Paulo* limited but did not eliminate its influence in the federal government during the early years of IDORT's operations.

The founders of IDORT saw rationalization as a solution to inefficiency and disorganization in all spheres of society, but their primary target was the industrial sector. Yet even though several prominent industrialists served in its leadership and the institute's activities in the industrial milieu were repeatedly publicized, IDORT awoke little enthusiasm in the "rank and file" of the paulista bourgeoisie. Soon after IDORT's founding, a São Paulo pottery factory contracted with Mange's second division to standardize ceramic plate production in its plant. But the director of this factory was a founding member of IDORT, and remarkably few other requests in this vein were made throughout the 1930s.[80]

Some broad-based studies of industrial conditions received cooperation from individual employers. In 1933 IDORT, in collaboration with the International Association for the Prevention of Blindness, undertook a survey of industrial lighting problems. FIESP announced this initiative with considerable enthusiasm, urging its members to cooperate with the IDORT representatives. Given the relatively innocuous subject of this study, it is interesting to note that FIESP felt obliged to assure its members that implementation of any recommendations would be purely voluntary and that only global results, not data from individual factories, would be published. Reinforcing its call for collaboration, the circular assured FIESP members that "the question of appropriate lighting in the workplace is of interest not only to those who work but, principally, to the employer because adequate lighting leads to greater and better output."[81]

Several articles in the *Revista IDORT* during the early 1930s pondered the reasons for the organization's limited membership and the dearth of requests for its services. Most of these essays focused on critiques of rationalization, especially common during the depression years, which blamed scientific management for unemployment as well as its "twin sister," overproduction.[82] But broad theoretical critiques of scientific management probably had little to do with the apparent lack of interest among industrialists. Unemployment, however, may have had some connection to employer "apathy" in the sense that low wages and an abundant labor supply, combined with a stagnant or shrinking internal market, hardly served to make rationalization a pressing concern for the average manufacturer.[83]

Another possible explanation is the factory owner's fear of intrusion in his operations, even by such an apparently owner-friendly organization as IDORT. "We are far from aspiring to compulsory intervention in production," Francisco Salles de Oliveira assured his readers in a 1932 report on the activities of the first division.[84] The fact that he perceived a need to make such a statement indicates suspicions on the part of employers, as does the language of the FIESP notice about the industrial lighting study. A brief article in an early bulletin of the Ministry of Labor, Industry, and Commerce places the industrialists' apprehension in a broader context. According to its author, a recent inspection of a rubber products factory revealed that the firm (in which Simonsen had an interest) was unnecessarily importing artificial rubber duty-free. The results of the inquiry, he claimed, revealed the need for special technical commissions to undertake such inspections and to inspire in the "sometimes egocentric and suspicious spirit of the industrialist interest in cooperating with the public powers."[85] Yet such "cooperation," even framed in terms of rationalization, was likely to be viewed by employers as representing a loss of their traditional prerogatives. At a time when firms perceived public agencies and myriad regulations as encroaching on the owners' domain, it is not surprising that virtually all requests for IDORT's industrial services came from firms whose owners or managers were active members of IDORT.

The institute did have some influence in other sectors of Brazilian society during the 1930s. Aside from its famed reorganization of the São Paulo state bureaucracy, IDORT staged highly publicized campaigns against waste and for the prevention of accidents. It worked with various public utilities, such as São Paulo Tramways, whose superintendent served as vice president of IDORT in the mid-1930s. Certain pet proposals of IDORT, including the use of psychotechnic testing for the selection of employees, became standard practice in many large firms and public institutions by the late 1930s. In addition, members such as Geraldo de Paula Souza, Roberto Mange, M. B. Lourenço Filho, Horácio da Silveira, and Moacyr Alvaro actively contributed to the formulation of federal health, educational, and labor policies. The second issue of the Labor Ministry bulletin included an unusually long article by the president of the National Institute for Social Welfare entitled "Combating Routine" that condemned "empiricism and obsolete practices" and called for rationalization in the same vein as in the United States and Germany. As for critics who blamed scientific management for unemployment and overproduction, the author replied, using language probably lifted from the *Revista IDORT*, that the solution was increased rationalization in all areas of society—"complete rationalization"—and not just in industrial production.[86]

The institute's success in these other areas, however, only partially compensated for its limited impact on the industrial sector, which it still considered the appropriate starting point for the rationalization process. IDORT's failure to elicit voluntary cooperation from private firms may have moved some of its more dedicated members to question the feasibility of a project for rationalization that lacked any form of compulsion. This disillusionment with private initiatives for social ends was displayed in an unusually explicit fashion by Aldo Mário de Azevedo in a 1936 session of the São Paulo state assembly. Representing industrial employers as a "class deputy," Azevedo proposed a .5 percent tax on insurance premiums to fund an educational campaign for the prevention of accidents. Similar campaigns, he noted, had been voluntarily funded by insurance companies in the United States and England, but his experience as a director of IDORT had convinced him that this was not possible in Brazil: "All efforts expended on the insurance companies . . . to obtain their necessary cooperation were useless due to the lack of interest among those who should be the greatest supporters of such an undertaking."[87] Such disappointments must have further eroded faith in the possibility of social and economic transformation within the context of a "liberal" society.

The early 1930s also saw the founding of the Escola Livre de Sociologia e Política, an institution with intimate ties to IDORT. Simonsen's 1931 speech at Mackenzie College had made evident his belief that the social sciences were essential for the resolution of problems associated with industrial development. Yet the law, engineering, and medical schools that dominated Brazilian higher education until the 1930s were hardly adequate for the preparation of social scientists equipped to handle the thorny problems presented by the urban-industrial milieu. According to Simonsen, in a speech at the school's inauguration in 1933, the Escola Livre "will serve to fill this obvious vacuum."[88]

Several studies of innovations in secondary education during this period, which included the creation of the University of São Paulo, cite a direct relationship between the paulista defeat in the 1932 revolt and the widely perceived need to create new institutions for the formation of "elites" and the discussion of social issues.[89] In the words of the Escola Livre's founding manifesto, the school would form "a numerous and organized elite, instructed in scientific methods . . . capable of comprehending the social milieu."[90] Inspired by positivist sociology, the school's founders considered "apolitical" and scientific inquiry by trained experts the appropriate means for resolving social conflicts as well as a way of removing such contested issues as wages, work conditions, and living standards from the arena of politics and class struggle. Such objectives were wholly consistent with the rationalizer's perspective.

Although the founders outlined the goals of the Escola Livre with admirable clarity, they encountered more difficulty attracting faculty and funding. Inaugurated a few months before the University of São Paulo, the Escola Livre had few local sources of social science expertise to draw upon. The immediate solution was to import two North American social scientists to serve on the faculty.[91] Simonsen himself was named to the chair in Brazilian economic history, and his frustrated search for adequate reading materials led to the publication of his *História Econômica do Brasil.* The school also enlisted Roberto Mange to teach Brazil's first course in *psicotécnica.* As for financing, aside from student tuition, the Escola Livre relied on the generosity of Simonsen and a few other industrialists, making its financial situation rather precarious.[92] Nevertheless, during the 1930s, the school's students and faculty undertook pioneering research on urban living standards, health and housing needs, and other issues from a scientific perspective.[93]

A very different sector of São Paulo's educational system, vocational education, experienced a series of important innovations in the early 1930s that owed their inspiration to the circle of educators and engineers associated with IDORT. Intermittent reforms in the structure of professional schools culminated in 1933 in an elaborate new educational code and the subsequent creation of a separate Superintendency for Professional and Domestic Education headed by Horácio da Silveira, a well-known educator and active member of IDORT.

Since its founding in 1911, the state's professional school system had expanded in size and capacity, with some 9,000 students enrolled by the mid-1930s. Qualitative changes were also afoot as the state educational bureaucracy created an explicitly two-track schooling system in the early 1930s. The new educational code called for the creation of "primary professional schools" and "prevocational courses" that would prepare working-class students for the existing professional schools, now elevated to the status of secondary institutions. Silveira, in a 1935 publication, attributed this new status to the increased industrial demand for highly skilled workers but also acknowledged its social value: "And if we wish to enter a different order of consideration, we should focus on the sociological problem of elevating the cultural value of the industrial trades, the manual and mechanical foundation so important for the democratic ideal."[94]

The new code also rigidified gender segregation within vocational education. Although several of the new schools were "coeducational," regulations explicitly excluded women from courses of an industrial nature, including those preparing workers for the textile sector.[95] At the same time, new rules compelled women at all professional schools to study "domestic education," which included classes in nutrition, infant care, cooking, housekeeping, and household economy.[96] Thus, even though the professional school system undertook the education and training of thousands of young women, it clearly defined the modern skilled worker as male and perceived the aspiring woman worker as, first and foremost, a future wife and mother.[97]

Other innovations in the state's vocational education system included formal training for school directors, and not surprisingly, the "theoretical" portion of this course highlighted "rational organization of work."[98] The educational code also established a Gabinete de Psicotécnica to develop and apply various tests for selecting and orienting students. Indeed, several accounts of the educational reform portray the psychotechnic movement as crucial to the pedagogical innovations of the 1930s. Silveira admitted that "empiricism" had dominated early vocational instruction but hailed the "new scientific spirit" at work in the professional schools, specifically citing the psychotechnic services installed by Roberto Mange.[99] The entire New School movement in Brazil owed much to the ideas and individuals associated with IDORT, but their influence was particularly conspicuous in the sphere of vocational education.

Although the changes occurring in the state vocational education system were significant, the most publicized innovation in worker training during this period originated in the private sector. From the time he founded his course for mechanics at the Liceu de Artes e Ofícios, Mange had maintained close contact with various railroad companies in São Paulo, major employers of skilled mechanics for operations and maintenance. Gaspar Ricardo Júnior, director of the Sorocabana Railway and an enthusiastic promoter of rationalization, subsequently invited Mange to collaborate more actively with his firm. In 1929 Mange traveled to Germany to review the latest developments in the training of apprentices for railroad work and returned in 1930 to found the Professional Education and Selection Service (Serviço de Ensino e Seleção Profissional, or SESP) of the Sorocabana Railway. The four-year course—two years of theoretical and general instruction and two years of practical application of knowledge—used both the classroom facilities of the Escola Profissional de

Sorocaba and the workshops of the railroad itself. Even more than the courses at the Liceu, SESP became a showplace for Mange's pet projects: the methodical series for apprenticeship training and the use of psychotechnic testing for apprentice selection and guidance.[100]

In strictly numerical terms, SESP had a limited impact even on the Sorocabana workforce. Each incoming class consisted of a mere thirty apprentices, and many of these failed to survive the first round of examination. But it served splendidly as a showcase for Mange's pedagogical innovations and for his denunciations of "common apprenticeship." Writing as director of SESP, Mange portrayed traditional artisanal instruction as dating from medieval times and as ludicrous in the context of modern industry. The twentieth-century craftsman, Mange argued, had neither the range of knowledge nor the leisure to instruct an apprentice within the workplace.[101] In contrast, the methods advocated by Mange allowed for quick, systematic, and effective training of apprentices. And there was an additional advantage to "rational instruction" for the apprentice: "Through the method learned at work, through discipline, through the regular verification of progress achieved, through the confidence in himself and his pleasure in his work, [rational methods] induce a true ethical and moral transformation of the individual."[102]

Seeking to demonstrate definitively the superiority of his methods, Mange staged an elaborate "experiment" in 1931 comparing the performance of SESP apprentices with railway apprentices who only had the benefit of "common instruction" and those in training at the Liceu. Each participant performed a series of standardized tasks; Mange and an instructor then judged their work according to "precision, perfection, and speed." The results revealed that, of the three groups, the apprentices who did not have the benefit of "rational instruction" demonstrated the greatest variation in performance, especially with regard to the time required for each task. The Liceu students did the best according to Mange's criteria, with the SESP students demonstrating a satisfactory consistency in their performance. These results, Mange triumphantly announced, were all the more spectacular because the "common" apprentices had, on average, three and a half years of training and an average age of eighteen. The SESP and Liceu students, in contrast, had an average of six and nine months of training, respectively, and were considerably younger than those in the third group.[103]

The results of Mange's famous experiment can be challenged from many angles, such as the tasks chosen and the emphasis on speed and uniformity. However, the accuracy of the experiment is historically less important than its reception by the paulista educational community. Reprinted in the *Revista IDORT* and widely publicized, the results of this experiment provided advocates of rational vocational training with the ammunition they needed to advance their proposals. The same applied to Mange's use of *psicotécnica* in SESP, which challenged the skilled workers' traditional (but irrational) prerogative of having their sons trained in their fathers' craft. Each applicant for the apprenticeship course underwent a battery of tests to determine physical capacity; general intelligence; memory; perception of forms; technical sense; visual, tactile, and muscular acuity; manual ability; and coordination of movements. The test results would then dictate whether an applicant was acceptable and what particular area of specialization was appropriate. Mange claimed that the apprentices' actual performances in subsequent practical exams showed a high positive correlation with their initial psychotechnic evaluation. To be sure, even Mange admitted that the expectation of a close fit between evaluation and performance was "utopian" and that psychotechnic testing could not illuminate certain areas, such as the applicant's medical condition and social tendencies.[104] Yet his efforts in this vein were considered successful enough to warrant the dissemination of his report to all professional schools in the state of São Paulo.[105]

In his official report for 1933, state interventor Waldomiro Castilho de Lima singled out SESP for special praise and offered an interesting explanation for the growing interest in Mange's program: "In all of the large foreign transport firms, the personnel expenses over the last few years have risen much more than expenses for materials, reaching a coefficient of 60 to 66 percent of total expenditures. Not being able to reduce salaries, it has become necessary to make personnel outlays as economic and productive as possible, a result that can be obtained by improving the quality of individual production, that is, through improvement in the *output of each worker*."[106] Mange's innovations in worker training apparently took place within a broader context of rationalization in the railroad sector. The relative strength of the transport workers' union and the consequently high proportion of wages compared to other expenses formed the immediate impetus for companies' adoption of scientific management.

Thus it is not surprising that within the next few years several other paulista railway lines sought to participate in Mange's apprenticeship program, leading to the formation in 1934 of the Railway Center for Professional Education and Selection (Centro Ferroviário de Ensino e Seleção Profissional, or CFESP). Within a decade, Mange's operations had expanded from a small course at the Liceu de Artes e Ofícios to a training center for all railroad lines throughout the state. In the same year, the new interventor of São Paulo, Salles Oliveira, placed CFESP under the official auspices of the state. According to Horácio da Silveira, this joint public-private initiative, drawing funding from both sectors, was a model for future expansion of professional education since the state government alone could not possibly provide vocational training for all who needed it.[107]

For the time being, public-private ventures involving the participation of paulista industrialists or technocrats would be largely confined to the boundaries of their home state. A persistent tendency to privilege region over nation as well as intermittently contentious relations with the federal government meant that the rationalizers' initiatives during the early 1930s were rarely national in scope. The latter years of the decade, however, would inaugurate a period of close cooperation between leaders of the industrial bourgeoisie and the Vargas regime and broaden the arena for the rationalizers' innovations and proposals in the areas of education and social policy.

3

Industrialists in the Nation's Service

In January 1934, Roberto Simonsen, serving as a class deputy, delivered a speech to the national constituent assembly. His initial purpose was to speak in support of a revision proposed by the paulista bench to an amendment in the constitution's section on the social and economic order. Intended to soften what the paulistas regarded as the overly statist tone of the original, the revised amendment read: "The economic order should be organized according to the principles of justice and the necessities of national life, with the aim of establishing, throughout the country, a standard of living compatible with human dignity. Within these limits, economic liberty is guaranteed."[1] In these brief lines, the paulista bench and its industrialist representatives manifested both their acceptance of the pressing need for a higher and more uniform standard of living in Brazil, which would require certain forms of government oversight or intervention, and their fear that such oversight would infringe on economic "freedom."

Simonsen, as was his custom, seized the moment to elaborate on his views concerning both state interventionism and the standard of living. With regard to the former, he argued that the Brazilian state was still "semicolonial" in many respects and that its failure, thus far, to resolve such fundamental problems as the education and elevation of the Brazilian people made it unwise for the state to expand into new fields of action. Simonsen conceded that the state could "stimulate and defend production, protect labor, [and] determine a sound course for these factors to proceed in an atmosphere of harmony." But he warned against undue intrusions in the sphere of production, which could dampen the "creative stimulus of progress." Furthermore, any state actions tending to limit or discourage production were particularly misplaced in Brazil, where, according to Simonsen, the key problem was not the distribution but the creation of wealth. As for living standards, Simonsen viewed their elevation as necessary for social peace and sustained economic progress. He cited knowledge and material wealth as "civilization's" two main causes of inequality and claimed that the diminution of these inequalities, through instruction and through the creation and extension of material goods, was the key to human dignity and social harmony.[2]

In the closing portion of his speech, Simonsen lamented Brazil's poor supply of what future economists would call human capital, citing deficient education and ignorance of hygiene as major causes of this "poverty." Adopting an urgent tone, he proposed the immediate formation of "practical schools for adults that will improve, within the shortest period of time, the degree of efficiency of the great mass of Brazilians." He also specifically deplored the lack of vocational training among Brazilian workers, citing his own experience in this regard: "In my work as an engineer, I have regretfully verified . . . that the most productive and best-paid positions, that is, those for skilled workers, are mainly occupied by foreign laborers, with national workers relegated to performing the heaviest and most thankless tasks due to their ignorance of specialized trades."[3]

Continuing with this account of his experiences as an employer, Simonsen described a project he directed in the late 1920s that required a medical exam for all potential workers. The results of these exams showed an improbably high rate of venereal disease of 45.5 percent among Brazilian workers, while foreigners who had been in Brazil over a year exhibited an infection rate of 22.1 percent, and those who had recently arrived, a rate of less than 5 percent. Moreover, if this was the case in the environs of the paulista capital, which he considered to have the most advanced health services in the country, how much worse must the situation be in other regions of Brazil? Arguing that an unhealthy population was unlikely to form an efficient workforce, Simonsen called for the creation of "social service and hygiene clinics" throughout Brazil alongside primary schools for adults.[4]

Thus, in early 1934, Simonsen was already promoting adult education, social services, and vocational training as central to the elevation of Brazil's population and therefore to the overall process of economic development. To be sure, the 1934 constituent assembly provided a perfect forum for politicians to expatiate on all sorts of ambitious solutions to Brazil's social and economic ills.[5] But Simonsen's words deserve particular attention since he represented an increasingly influential social class and would soon play a central role in the formation of national agencies to provide vocational training and social services to workers in the name of social peace.

The exaltation of social peace as the sine qua non of economic development frequently appears in the pronouncements of industrialist spokesmen in this period. In a 1934 speech to São Paulo's Rotary Club, Aldo Mário de Azevedo, textile manufacturer and IDORT founder, decried the traditional division of industry into "capital" and "labor." Capital, according to Azevedo, should be viewed as an element of production, the same as a tool, while labor should not be regarded as the exclusive domain of the worker. Indeed, Azevedo urged his audience to view the modern manager of a rationalized factory as a "different type of worker," to replace the old image of the capitalist, "that fat individual with heavy gold chains and diamond rings, cigar in mouth, and dressed in top hat and tails."[6]

Notices circulated by FIESP in this period called upon industrialists to support initiatives that the directorate regarded as advancing the cause of social peace. In 1933 FIESP announced to its members, with obvious pleasure, the founding of a Center for Social Action in São Paulo, which sought "to implant sound principles in the bosom of the laboring classes." The notice encouraged members to make financial contributions to this center of Catholic social work, claiming that the triumph of its principles would mean the "reconciliation of capital and labor."[7] Indeed, several major spokesmen for industry, including Roberto Simonsen and Morvan Dias de Figueiredo, increasingly incorporated language and concepts associated with Catholic Social Action to elaborate their positions on social services for workers and the role of industry in providing such assistance. Pope Leo XIII's 1891 encyclical on the condition of the working class, *Rerum Novarum*, became the key text for advancing a vision of social assistance as a means to maintain social order, nicely complementing the more technical but unemotional appeal of scientific management. Over the next decade, these two strains of thought—conservative Catholic activism and rationalization—become increasingly intertwined in industrialist discourse.[8]

FIESP enthusiastically endorsed other private ventures of a similar sort. A 1934 notice to all employers provided a glowing description of a network of health clinics for industrial and commercial workers founded by Arnaldo Lopes, a pharmacist and small industrialist. Lopes, who had briefly directed the clinics set up during the 1932 revolt, portrayed this latest initiative as a continuation of his earlier efforts.[9] FIESP similarly praised a 1933 proposal by the Associação Cívica Feminina to install night schools in large factories. Yet all of this noise about social services and health care for workers yielded few enduring results; during the mid-1930s, FIESP and its allies rarely succeeded in creating concrete services to match their rhetoric about class conciliation.

Furthermore, FIESP could not easily represent itself as the standard-bearer of social peace. Although the federation might shrug off "antisocial" actions by individual members as deviations from the norm, it could hardly deny its role in promoting and defending the interests of industrialists. The 1935 statutes of FIESP listed among their objectives "to facilitate for the members, and industrialists in general, the application of labor laws, seeking whenever possible to resolve by conciliatory means disputes between workers and owners."[10] In practice, FIESP consistently and predictably sought to apply the labor laws in such a way as to limit the costs to employers and diminish the benefits for workers. As late as 1935, the directorate of FIESP was searching for loopholes in the Lei das Férias to deprive large portions of the industrial workforce of paid vacation time. And the late 1930s saw a concerted effort by FIESP to limit the minimum wage and justify wage reductions for women, children, and apprentices.[11] In the January 1936 meeting of FIESP, the federation's president, Conde Sílvio Alvares Penteado, urged more concern for work conditions and workers' well-being.[12] But the very nature of the organization and its need to be responsive to the short-term interests of employers militated against such concerns.

New Industrialists for a New State

Although FIESP's leadership continued to register occasional complaints about state intrusion into the industrial sector, the mid- to late 1930s witnessed increasing collaboration between the industrialists and the state in several different spheres.[13] Simonsen, in particular, developed a close working relationship with Euvaldo Lodi, Vargas's main ally in the industrialist camp, and distanced himself from the liberal-constitutionalist position of São Paulo's Chapa Única.[14] By November 1937, when Vargas canceled the upcoming elections and declared himself dictator of an "Estado Novo" (New State), Simonsen had already broken with the traditional paulista leadership and emerged as a major participant in the formulation of government economic policy.

Simonsen's move into the Vargas camp was not an isolated development. Several prominent figures in São Paulo's industrial community who were closely associated with Simonsen shifted allegiances in this period, among them Morvan Dias de Figueiredo and his brother Nadir, the leading spokesmen for medium-sized and small manufacturers.[15] It is especially significant that the FIESP membership elected Simonsen president—a position he would hold throughout the Estado Novo—in 1937, precisely the time of his break with the paulista liberals. Although Simonsen's growing association with Vargas caused some rumblings within FIESP, Simonsen managed not only to get himself elected but also to double the federation's membership over the next two years.[16]

It is understandable that the Vargas regime of this period would be more appealing to Simonsen and his followers than the Vargas regime of the early 1930s.[17] Initial fears among industrialists about Vargas's populist "demagoguery" were quieted by his policies toward labor and the left from the mid-1930s on. Following a failed left-wing/nationalist uprising in 1935, the Vargas government brutally suppressed the PCB and extirpated Communists and leftist sympathizers from the labor union leadership. Police repression and surveillance reduced some previously vital unions to skeletal structures that barely existed except on paper, while other labor organizations survived because their leadership tacitly, or even enthusiastically, embraced the restrictions imposed by the Vargas regime.[18] Under such circumstances, industrial employers had little reason to worry about significant new concessions by Vargas to the working class or even the consistent enforcement of existing labor legislation.

In the context of this government-imposed social peace, the paulista industrialist leadership had little incentive to initiate ambitious new social programs. FIESP's preference for short-term solutions to pressing problems can be seen most clearly in its initial proposals for resolving the declared shortage of skilled workers. In his 1934 speech, Simonsen portrayed the low skill level among Brazilian workers as contributing both to their poor standard of living and to economic backwardness and called for the creation of institutes to train workers.[19] Leading industrialists admired Roberto Mange's successes in CFESP and praised Governor Armando de Salles Oliveira for promoting the expansion of vocational schools throughout the state of São Paulo. And a 1936 FIESP report to the Vargas government termed the number of professional schools manifestly insufficient. What did the authors of the report—Simonsen, Morvan, and Armando de Arruda Pereira—specifically suggest as a remedy? Rather than proposing ambitious plans to expand training, the FIESP directors argued that

Brazilian industry urgently needed access to foreign workers. Indeed, just a few months earlier, Simonsen and the president of FIESP had formally proposed the repeal of the Two-Thirds Law in the Federal Chamber of Deputies for that very reason.[20]

This had become a more urgent matter for industrialists in 1936 since the law's five-year exception clause—allowing employers to classify workers who had been in Brazil for ten years or more as Brazilian—was about to expire. FIESP assured its affected members that firms unable to meet the two-thirds requirement could apply to the State Labor Department for a certificate declaring a shortage of Brazilian workers with the qualifications to fill positions occupied by foreigners. Such certification, the FIESP notice insisted, would be virtually automatic "in view of the obvious fact that there does not exist a sufficient number of specialized national workers capable of replacing foreigners in industry."[21]

The considerable activity by FIESP in the mid-1930s aimed at the repeal or modification of the Two-Thirds Law casts doubt on assumptions historians have formed about the de-skilling process in industry from the 1920s on. As noted earlier, such a process likely occurred in some segments of certain industries, but new manufacturing activities, such as those in the growing metallurgical sector, created new demands for laborers defined as skilled that more than compensated for losses in other sectors. In addition, the ban on importation of new machinery must have increased the demand for maintenance personnel in the textile industry. For skilled workers in particular occupations—for example, shoemakers—who found themselves replaced or demoted by machines, the multiplication of jobs for workers with very different skills was of little consolation. Still, from the employer's point of view, the shortage of skilled workers seems to have been a genuine concern, not an imaginary or politically motivated complaint.

State Initiatives and Industrialist Responses

For the paulista industrialists and their organizational representatives, a key objective was to secure a sufficient number of skilled workers—sufficient not only to fill the increasing demand for workers in certain trades but also to limit the wage levels and bargaining power of skilled workers. Some of their spokesmen emphasized the role of education and training in promoting efficiency, rational organization, and moral character among the workers, but these were secondary themes. In contrast, the many educational reformers who filled the ranks of Vargas's bureaucracy viewed the shortage of skilled laborers and the promise of vocational education in the broadest possible terms.

Vargas himself was later characterized by one such official as a "fan" of vocational education. The platform of the Liberal Alliance, Vargas's political coalition in the ill-fated election of 1930, recognized the need for expanded vocational training. And in a 1933 speech, Vargas declared that "the education which we need to develop to the extreme limits of our possibilities is the vocational and technical kind. Without it, organized work is impossible, especially in an age characterized by the predominance of the machine."[22] But government interest in industrial training did not gain momentum until 1934, when the Ministries of Labor and Education created a commission to formulate a "Plan for Vocational Instruction." This commission included such prominent experts in the field as Roberto Mange, M. B. Lourenço Filho, Joaquim Faria Góes Filho, Horácio da Silveira, and Rodolpho Fuchs, inspector of industrial education. However, little seems to have been accomplished during this early period aside from the issuing of preliminary studies.[23]

The documentation of the Ministry of Education on industrial training from these years indicates the wide range of concerns and aspirations that these educational reformers attached to the question of vocational education. One of the earliest documents on industrial training, written by a trio of technicians, was an extended treatise on the "scientific organization of work." The authors discussed the origins and advantages of Taylorism and the role of the European war in eroding resistance to its implementation. It was not until the very end that they addressed the issue of vocational education, and then merely to insist that all schools be organized along the lines dictated by scientific management.[24] The authors plainly viewed vocational training as valuable only to the extent that it advanced the principles of Frederick W. Taylor, Henri Fayol, and Henry Ford.

Rodolpho Fuchs, who authored a 1935 report on the need for "rational and methodical training," shared this vision of Brazilian society as desperately in need of scientific organization. Fuchs, however, granted vocational education a much more central role in the transformation of Brazilian society, claiming that the only difference between North American employees of the Ford Motor Company and Brazilian workers was "rational training." Professional schools, he claimed, would provide the means to turn Brazilians into a rich and productive people. For Fuchs, unlike the previous authors, the promise of manual instruction lay in its social and political implications as much as in its economic ramifications.[25]

The process of reorganizing Brazil's "system" of industrial training really took off after 1937, during the highly authoritarian period of Vargas's rule known as the Estado Novo. Article 129 of the 1937 constitution declared that industrial firms were obligated to create "schools of apprenticeship" for their employees' children. At the same time, it affirmed, somewhat contradictorily, that professional education was to be "primarily the duty of the state."[26] Vargas and his dynamic minister of education, Gustavo Capanema, were sending a message to the members of FIESP and other industrial associations that reliance on foreigners was not an acceptable solution to the ongoing shortage of skilled workers in Brazil.

Vargas's minister of labor, Waldemar Falcão, moved relatively quickly to issue a decree that set the initial contours of apprenticeship training in Brazilian industry.[27] Decree-law no. 1,238 of May 2, 1939, actually consisted of two sections, the first requiring firms with over 500 employees to provide indoor dining space for all workers. The second section required the same firms to offer "courses for professional improvement for minors and adults." The specific structure and details of these courses would be defined by an interministerial commission appointed by the Ministries of Labor and Education.

The strange career of Decree-law no. 1,238 provides a revealing glimpse of the "legislative" process during the Estado Novo. One could hardly explain this decree as a response to pressure from labor unions since the late 1930s was the nadir of union militancy.[28] Yet Vargas's repressive actions toward the labor movement did not preclude a desire to maintain his populist image and appeal. Rather, Vargas's campaign against "subversives" made it all the more important to demonstrate his devotion to the "patriotic" Brazilian worker. To this end, Decree-law no. 1,238, which was issued immediately following a May Day pledge, could be portrayed by Vargas and his ministers as the state forcing capital to meet its obligations to the workforce.[29] Moreover, the provision of training opportunities for workers and their children so that Brazil would no longer need to rely on foreign craftsmen complemented the broader nationalist/populist vision of higher living standards and autonomous national development. A subsequent article in the São Paulo metallurgical workers' newspaper heartily praised Vargas for his attention to vocational training: "Today, principally due to the protection of our Nation's Leader, everywhere you look there are competent mechanics who learned their craft in Brazil and who are in no way inferior to the best mechanics of other countries."[30]

Despite the fact that Decree-law no. 1,238 addressed a major problem of Brazilian industry, its particulars were not at all to the liking of leading industrialists. Although FIESP encouraged members who represented large firms to meet the deadline for installing dining facilities, it assured them that the article requiring training courses would soon be modified and could be safely ignored.[31] Nevertheless, the issuing of the decree-law served as a challenge to the industrialists' inertia on the question of vocational training and forced consideration of alternative solutions.

The group that formulated this initial legislation on vocational training was not directly linked with either workers or employers. Instead, technicians in the Ministries of Education and Labor were responsible for the formulation of Decree-Law no. 1,238. Rodolpho Fuchs, a close colleague of Minister Capanema, was a guiding intellectual light in the discussions of vocational education within the Vargas government, especially prior to the formation of the interministerial commission. More specifically, Fuchs emerged as the most ardent advocate of linking industrial training with place of employment and of making such training obligatory for all young workers (or, more accurately, young *male* workers) entering the industrial labor force.

A 1938 report by Fuchs entitled "The Defects of Brazilian Vocational Instruction" argued that, at the current cost per student in the federally sponsored vocational schools, the government would have to spend an absurdly large sum to train the 70,000-plus "apprentices" who entered industry each year. Fuchs also criticized the vocational schools' extensive attention to academic subjects. This, he claimed, negated the central concern of all who worked in professional education, which was "to make apprenticeship as similar as possible to the industrial process on the shopfloor, so as to facilitate the concluding student's adaptation to the new environment." Going even further, he claimed that the skills of apprentices graduating from these schools were inferior to those of youths trained on the job. "It is precisely this distance between industry and the vocational school that is to blame for this situation." And to make matters worse, the faculty of the professional schools, in Fuchs's view, were not up to the task since most instructors either had no contact with industry or, worst of all, were women who could not even handle the young men's "problems of moral development, of civic and family education."

What was to be done? Fuchs strongly recommended that Brazil follow the example of France and Germany and make vocational instruction mandatory for all adolescents employed in industry. According to Fuchs's plan, boys between the ages of fourteen and eighteen would enter the factory as apprentices and would be granted eight hours per week, with pay, to attend a vocational school. This weekly classroom time would be dedicated to theoretical studies and a "good civic-moral and physical preparation," while the practical training would take place in the factory. Under this regime, the existing schools could accommodate six times as many pupils as were currently enrolled. And the limited schooling was perfectly compatible with Fuchs's restricted view of academic preparation as well as his injunction to avoid "too much training." Fuchs also predicted that this system would establish a "professional hierarchy for the worker" that allowed self-advancement through "professional ability" rather than through union politics.[32]

Fuchs's reference to the German system is not surprising since the Vargas government had recently provided funding for him to attend the International Congress on Vocational Education in Germany in July 1938. Upon his return, he presented a report entitled "Vocational Instruction in Germany" that was an unabashed endorsement of the German training process, instituted under Nazi rule. The German system, with its mandatory training for all males not going on to secondary school and its six to eight hours of weekly classroom time, directly inspired Fuchs's recommendations. Fuchs openly admired the way the Germans used the vocational schools to instill discipline, comparing them favorably to the German Army and the Hitler Youth as vehicles for socialization. And he praised the vocational guidance system whereby employment counselors steered young men into occupations that reflected the needs of the labor market.[33]

Not completely insensitive to the political connotations of this paean to German industrial training, Fuchs hastened to add that the same system had been instituted in democratic France, demonstrating the universal need for factory-based vocational education. Returning to the relationship between industrial training and social peace, Fuchs urgently called for Brazil to follow the German example: "We should not harbor the slightest illusion in this regard: either Brazil resolves to provide a straight and sure path to vocational training, or soon we will witness these demands becoming an arm of combat for the tireless Communist agitators." Although Fuchs viewed Brazilian workers as currently loyal to the government due to the new labor legislation, he feared that workers might over the next ten years mount new demands unless something was done to change their mentality. In his opinion, professional education was the best means of accomplishing such a change since it not only disseminated technical knowledge but also facilitated an understanding of "national politicosocial realities through the civic and moral education of the future worker."[34]

The interministerial commission first convened in May 1939, immediately following the publication of Decree-law no. 1,238. The original six-member committee included Fuchs, Joaquim Faria Góes Filho, and Lycério Schreiner, all nominated by Education Minister Capanema, and Saúl de Gusmão, Gilberto Crockett de Sá, and Edison Pitombo Cavalcanti, designated by Labor Minister Falcão. Although the committee included no industrialists (or workers, for that matter), one of its first actions was to seek industrialists' opinion on the decree through questionnaires distributed to the appropriate federations. The commission also invited several prominent industrialists to attend its weekly meetings and air their views on the subject and devoted an entire session to a report prepared by IDORT on the problem of industrial training.[35]

Four potentially controversial and closely related issues were before the commission: Who should oversee and administer vocational training? Should training courses be confined to factories with over 500 workers? What portion of the workforce would require extended and systematic training? And who should fund such courses? With regard to the first question, the members were apparently unanimous in their support of Fuchs's recommendation that training be linked to place of employment, with the state overseeing the educational aspects of the program. A preliminary report submitted in November 1939 deemed unacceptable the creation of a vast industrial education system autonomous from government control and spoke of industrialist participation in collaboration with the state.[36]

With regard to the second question, the commission rapidly concluded that there was little sense in restricting such courses to factories with over 500 employees. This stipulation had prompted immediate criticism from FIESP and the National Confederation of Industry (Confederação Nacional da Indústria, or CNI), headed by Euvaldo Lodi, as well as from state labor federations, whose representatives noted that the 500-plus requirement would deny the vast majority of Brazilian workers access to vocational training. The industrialists argued, moreover, that all but a few of the factories of that size were textile mills, which needed only a relatively small proportion of skilled workers.[37] To bolster its arguments, FIESP invited the commission to meet with the federation and to visit a sample of large factories in São Paulo.

The committee report on the meeting with FIESP noted with obvious pleasure that many prominent figures were in attendance. Aside from Simonsen, president of FIESP, these included Morvan Dias de Figueiredo (vice president), Antônio de Souza Noschese (secretary), Octávio Pupo Nogueira (president of the textile manufacturers' *sindicato*), Mariano Ferraz, Arnaldo Lopes, and the presidents of several employer *sindicatos*. Also present were Roberto Mange, representing both IDORT and CFESP, and Horácio da Silveira, superintendent of the state vocational education system. Judging from the turnout, paulista industrialists and vocational educators were taking the work of the interministerial commission very seriously.

The commission members spent the next eight days touring large factories in the state of São Paulo, including firms that produced cigarettes, machinery, pottery, beer, vehicles (General Motors), textiles, and metal goods. The members also made side trips to IDORT and to CFESP installations of the Paulista Railway. The first impression they gathered from this direct inspection was of "mechanization and assembly-line production in the majority, if not all, of the establishments visited." The two pottery factories, one of them Simonsen's Cerâmica São Caetano, were partial exceptions; in these two firms, the low level of mechanization meant that a significant number of workers performed heavy manual labor. However, the most important exception was the Indústrias Irmãos Cavallari, which manufactured and repaired large machines. According to the report, this firm of 200 workers, the only factory visited with a workforce under 500, was also the only one that employed large numbers of highly skilled workers. This confirmed criticism of Decree-law no. 1,238 as assigning industrial training to large factories without a rational basis for such a prescription.[38]

Inevitably, the debate over whether training should be provided in only large factories raised the question of how many workers, and in which specialties, needed prolonged vocational training. At the meeting at FIESP headquarters, Roberto Mange presented the preliminary findings of an IDORT study that classified only 15 percent of the industrial workforce as needing such training. Faria Góes enthusiastically concurred with Mange's statement and a few months later submitted a report echoing the IDORT findings. In this report, Faria Góes repeatedly emphasized the expanding role of the "semiskilled" worker in industry; this "attentive hand," to use Mange's phrase, generally needed only a few weeks' training to become competent at a repetitive task, in contrast to the skilled worker (or "thinking hand"). He pointed out that "the machine brings greater complexity, but it also assures, paradoxically, greater simplification." To support his argument, Faria Góes noted that in the Ford factories 70 percent of the workers acquired the needed "skill" in thirty days or less. In most industries, then, the vast majority of workers needed only a good general education "that enriches . . . the personality, gives them basic knowledge, awakens qualities of initiative, of cooperation, of loyalty; that creates habits that promote health, hygiene, thrift, hard work, discipline; that develops their capacity to reason, to observe, and to understand; and that makes them conscious of their duties as worker, head of a family, and citizen of a country of which they form an integral part."[39]

Throughout the debate over what type of education different workers needed and which positions should be designated as skilled, the main participants assumed that such questions could and should be resolved in a "scientific" manner. One could determine precisely the attributes and knowledge necessary for a particular task and the number of people industry needed to perform such a task and then design an instructional system accordingly. These premises made the opinions and interests of the workers themselves irrelevant. Not that workers usually played an active role in the formulation of educational policy, but traditionally members of particular crafts had wielded some influence over the definition of skill in the workplace through informal and organized forms of negotiation and resistance. Workers in a specific section of a factory might strike, for example, to force the owner to acknowledge their function as more highly skilled and therefore deserving of better remuneration. Or they might demand the hiring of "helpers" who, in effect, became apprentices in that trade. Although certain occupations could be more easily represented as a skilled craft than others, workers and employers based their notions of "skill" on a variety of elements that included the state of the labor market, craft-based protest, and gender roles, as well as a sense of how difficult it was to learn a particular trade. In contrast, the vocational program being developed by the interministerial commission relegated the power to designate occupations as skilled or unskilled to educational "experts" whose decisions would be based on narrow definitions of apprenticeship and industrial demand.

The subservient character of most labor unions in the late 1930s meant that these organizations were unlikely to contest the definitions of skill or appropriate instruction being formulated by Vargas's industrial education experts. Many unions already found themselves incapable of resisting employers' attempts to reduce the standing of their craft. Under such circumstances, official recognition of certain occupations as skilled could represent a victory for the labor movement. Yet a few examples from this period demonstrate that some practitioners of a particular craft did struggle to reconstruct or retain their identity as skilled workers. According to an article that appeared in *O Trabalhador Têxtil*, the official organ of the São Paulo textile workers' union, textile factories were suffering from a shortage of "specialized workers," particularly weavers, due to the low salaries they generally received. Although the article was entitled "Salary: A Social Question," its author argued not in terms of social justice but rather in terms of the significance of the weaver's expertise. Claiming that machines in many factories were idle because very few weavers "deserved the name," the author felt compelled to insist that weaving was, indeed, a skilled occupation: "Look, a weaver, that is to say, a worker who acquires a certain technical knowledge, through a period of apprenticeship, another of practice that varies according to the branch of textiles and the article being produced. . . . A weaver is not a worker that can be made from one day to the next. [The weaver] is a worker that, little by little, goes about absorbing the secrets of the profession and gathers an accumulation of small daily observations perhaps at great sacrifice."[40] Such sentiments, however, found little resonance among textile manufacturers and Vargas's educational experts. Quite the opposite: it was precisely this type of improvised and empirical approach to skill acquisition that the rationalizers scorned. Frequent comments about the limited number of skilled workers in textile factories indicate that these "technical experts" did not consider weaving to be a task requiring extended apprenticeship. Thus, by this definition, it was not a skilled craft.[41]

The increasing tendency to mold education for sons and daughters of the working class according to the demands of the urban/industrial labor market also evoked some criticism from labor organizations. During the 1930s, São Paulo printers founded the first union-sponsored Escola Proletária. A graduate of this institution deemed the school of great importance for young workers due to the limited nature of public education: "With the advent of industry and the rapid evolution of new production processes, that is, the rationalization of work, governments do recognize the need to administer elementary education to the proletariat; however, [this instruction] is strictly limited to the knowledge deemed indispensable for the exercise of the respective trades."[42] Expanded access to vocational training must have been a welcome innovation to many Brazilian workers, but others perceived the limitations of the instruction being offered.

The industrialists' representatives, meanwhile, were much more vociferous and systematic in their criticisms of the self-proclaimed educational experts in Vargas's government who were responsible for Decree-law no. 1,238. Simonsen presented the official position of FIESP in a memorandum sent to the interministerial commission two months after its 1939 visit to São Paulo. Annoyed at the government's promulgation of such an important decree without prior consultation with FIESP, Simonsen used the occasion to ventilate industrialist irritation at the cascade of labor legislation imposed by the Vargas regime. While hastening to note that the industrialists were not opposed to "good labor legislation," he denounced the law school graduates who allegedly dominated the government bureaucracy for their susceptibility to foreign precedents and their ignorance of domestic conditions. One consequence, Simonsen claimed, was "the sudden appearance [of laws] requiring *immediate* execution!" Switching to a more courteous tone, Simonsen acknowledged that the appointment of the "brilliant" interministerial commission and its careful attention to industrialist opinion offered some consolation. Nevertheless, he declared that it was not simply necessary to properly implement Decree-law no. 1,238; the offending law had to be repealed.

What, then, did the president of FIESP propose as an alternative? Assuring the commission that "all industrialists recognize the necessity for and the advantages of expanding vocational instruction," Simonsen called for the founding of additional manual training schools in already industrialized areas. The facilities would be extremely simple, and the skills taught would be only those in greatest demand. Furthermore, Simonsen suggested a modest beginning, with the schools concentrating on the training of *mestres* and the upgrading of experienced workers. As for funding, Simonsen insisted that the state, industrialists, and workers share the burden.[43]

The interministerial commission proved highly responsive to the criticisms offered by Simonsen on behalf of FIESP. The "conclusions and suggestions" they presented to Ministers Capanema and Falcão in late 1939 adopted almost all of Simonsen's premises and recommendations. The commission summarily dismissed the distinction between large and small industries as lacking a rational basis. It called for tripartite funding by employers, workers, and government. The report also endorsed Mange's view, echoed by Simonsen, that only 10 to 15 percent of the industrial workforce performed tasks that required an extended period of apprenticeship. Most industrial workers, it noted, were "manipulators," unskilled or semiskilled operatives who performed repetitive and easily mastered tasks.[44]

Although this distinction between skilled and semiskilled workers served to define more clearly the parameters of apprenticeship, it raised the troubling question of what to do about the 85 percent of the workforce that would not receive systematic vocational instruction. Indeed, as the work of the commission progressed, one can perceive an emerging tension between its emphasis on socialization and its attention to rational organization. And this tension characterized not just the commission members' discussions but also industrialist discourse. A Brazilian engineer who served as a consultant to General Electric's local operations claimed that "100 percent of Brazilian workers exhibit an insufficient general preparation."[45] And Simonsen himself vigorously argued that expanded vocational education would be useless unless incoming workers had better basic skills and attitudes. The commission thus found itself faced with the somewhat paradoxical task of creating a vocational education plan for an increasingly sophisticated and mechanized industrial sector in a society where the average urban worker still had less than two years of schooling in contrast to an average of eight or nine years in the United States and Germany.

In their 1939 report, the commission members asked rhetorically what previous schooling would be necessary to make good unskilled and semiskilled workers: "It is evident that one cannot expect more than primary schooling, and from that the creation, at the proper age, of habits of hygiene, of work, of discipline, of cooperation, of thrift." As something of an afterthought, the report further suggested that reading, writing, and elementary arithmetic would be "useful instruments" to such workers. Adult workers interested in self-improvement should be given access to courses in literacy, rational hygiene and nutrition, civic and moral values, and general technical knowledge. As for who would provide this instruction, the commission agreed with Simonsen that primary responsibility should lie with the government. Employers would be expected to provide the minimal manual instruction necessary for the performance of semiskilled tasks, preferably using "psychotechnic processes" to accelerate the procedure. Beyond that, at most, employers should be encouraged to offer literacy courses or retraining programs on a voluntary basis.

Moving to the fortunate 15 percent of workers who would enter the ranks of the skilled, the commission recommended two broad alternatives. One was for apprentices to study at existing "professional schools" and complete their education with a six-month internship in an industrial enterprise. The other alternative involved rational selection of primary school graduates who would enter factories as apprentices. Where concentrations of factories requiring similar skills existed, a common apprenticeship center would be set up to serve firms in the area. Finally, the commission cited the need to establish regional councils that would oversee both the internships and the apprenticeship courses and would include representatives from government, industry, and the labor unions.[46]

The emerging consensus on the shape vocational education should take, which was endorsed by the Ministry of Labor, the interministerial commission, and industrial representatives, did not enjoy the support of the influential minister of education. In July 1940, Capanema wrote to Vargas complaining of the new guidelines for industrial apprenticeship that were being prepared. He found it difficult to accept a vocational education program in which his ministry would play only a peripheral role and which would treat worker education as a function of industrial demand. In a subsequent letter to Vargas, he condemned any program dedicated to "an education that is merely the transmission of technical and unsuitable processes" and called for direct federal control over the new apprenticeship system.[47]

Vargas himself seems to have been most concerned with increasing the supply of skilled workers by the quickest means possible. The intensified pace of Brazilian industrialization that accompanied the outbreak of the war in Europe and the consequent inaccessibility of foreign craftsmen made the issue of vocational training far more pressing than it had been a decade earlier. Vargas was also highly receptive to Labor Minister Falcão's argument that Capanema's recommendations would prove very costly for the central government. Impatient for some tangible progress in this area, Vargas formed another commission whose task was to design a system of industrial training. This new three-member commission, convened in mid-1941, included Roberto Simonsen, president of FIESP; Euvaldo Lodi, president of the CNI; and Valentim Bouças, secretary of the Technical Council on Economy and Finances. In addition, the commission consulted with a formally constituted trio of experts in the area of vocational education: João Luderitz, Mange, and Faria Góes.

The direct intervention of the industrialists in the "legislative" process had come at Simonsen's behest. In July 1940, the president of FIESP had written to Capanema expressing his general support for the most recent proposal concerning vocational education but suggesting certain modifications that would improve the interaction between industry and the training centers. The thrust of Simonsen's suggestions was to expand the industrialists' administrative control, reduce the role of federal officials, and eliminate the participation of workers' representatives. Furthermore, he proposed that employers assume full responsibility for funding the new training program, even though this would constitute an "onerous burden" for the industrialist class.[48] As noted above, Capanema was hardly susceptible to such suggestions, but Labor Minister Falcão and Vargas himself apparently regarded Simonsen's proposal more favorably.

Simonsen's suggestions may seem surprising in light of his previous response to Decree-law no. 1,238, in which he supported the principle of government responsibility for professional education and sought to minimize the financial burden for employers. It is likely that Simonsen overstated his position in the 1939 memorandum; his vigorous opposition to the particulars of the decree-law and the ongoing wrangle over the minimum wage may have prompted him to utilize opportune arguments that did not necessarily reflect his broader views. At the same time, Simonsen recognized that some sort of legislation to expand industrial training was desirable and inevitable, given the international situation and Vargas's own commitment to the issue. In this context, it was preferable for industrialists to accept responsibility for training a portion of the skilled labor force and to seek to maximize their control over the process. This would also allow them to head off counterproposals such as those under consideration in the Ministry of Education that called for direct government supervision, obligatory apprenticeship for a large portion of the juvenile workforce, and even government interference in the labor market through compulsory hiring of trained workers. Moreover, the industrialists would be able to take full credit for an economically and socially valuable program. As a political scientist later remarked, "Simonsen had ingeniously turned the impending obligation into a political asset."[49]

The new "commission of employers" delivered its preliminary report, apparently authored by Simonsen, to Minister Capanema in September 1941. Simonsen immediately situated the commission's mission within the objectives of the Estado Novo, calling for accelerated industrial development in Brazil and claiming that "the rapid improvement of the national economy and the strengthening of our security can only be obtained through greater national industrialization."[50] This industrialization process would require not only the upgrading of the existing workforce but also the training of new technicians, craftsmen, and skilled workers. Still speaking in the language of the Estado Novo, Simonsen then argued that the employer *sindicatos* and regional federations recognized by the Vargas regime were the ideal organizations for funding and administering a new program for industrial training.

The report discussed in detail the number of incoming workers who would need apprenticeship. Simonsen estimated that of approximately 1,200,000 industrial workers in Brazil, 90,000 were technicians or supervisors, 200,000 were skilled workers, and 670,000 were semiskilled operatives. To meet the expanding needs of industry and improve the quality of the workforce, he calculated that the number of new workers who would require training each year would be approximately 15 percent of the number of workers in each of these three categories. Noting that Brazilian industry was "still insufficiently mechanized" and that increased mechanization and worker specialization would reduce the relative proportion of skilled workers in the industrial population, he nevertheless warned that due to the rapid growth of manufacturing, the deficit of trained workers would continue for some time to come. It would be industry's responsibility to train a third of these new workers as well as to upgrade an unspecified portion of the existing workforce.

For this purpose, the commission proposed the creation of the National Service for the Selection, Improvement, and Training of Industrial Workers

(Serviço Nacional de Seleção, Aperfeiçoamento e Formação de Industriários, or SENAFI). SENAFI's mission would be to train workers for relatively specialized and delimited functions within industry. The report cited
CFESP as its model of a training program that was rapid, systematic, and
responsive to the specific needs of employers. Simonsen used the example of
a mechanic (*ajustador mecânico*) to explain the difference between SENAFI
training and that offered by public vocational schools: whereas a typical all-
purpose mechanic required four years of instruction, a mechanic trained by
SENAFI would be taught a more specialized set of skills requiring only
two years of apprenticeship.

Funds for SENAFI would come from monthly contributions by industrialists in proportion to the number of employees in their firms. Regional
councils, formed by the industrial federations, would oversee state-level
operations, with the CNI coordinating SENAFI at the federal level. The
precise courses to be offered and the number of apprentices to be trained
annually would be determined through discussion with the relevant employer *sindicatos* in each region. Although the commission viewed SENAFI
as largely autonomous from government control, it did concede a small
role to the state. Representatives of the federal ministries would participate
in the national and regional councils, and the government would certify
SENAFI graduates and instructors.[51]

Nearly all of the conclusions in this report found their way into the
projected decree-law presented by the commission in December 1941.
Capanema once again expressed numerous objections to the commission's
proposals. He denounced the "regionalist spirit" of the project, which stipulated that funds should be applied in the region where they were collected.
He also recommended that the project be coordinated with proposals regarding primary and normal school reforms and urged that the training
program be overseen by the National Commission of Professional Education, which was staffed by educators, not industrialists. Capanema even
expressed his aversion to the organization's name, with its emphasis on
"improvement" rather than education, and suggested that the program be
called the National Service for the Professional Education of Industrial
Workers.[52]

Capanema's criticisms were to no avail, except with regard to nomen-
clature, and even there his victory was only partial: in the final text of the
decree-law, the new organization bore the name National Service for the
Training of Industrial Workers. Vargas clearly did not share his education
minister's reservations about the new program since he signed the project
into law with unusual dispatch. On January 22, 1942, Vargas and his ministers of education and labor issued Decree-law no. 4,048 establishing

SENAI. Eight days later, Vargas also signed Decree-law no. 4,073, the Organic Law of Industrial Education, which specified the various roles of the state in vocational education and reflected Capanema's desire to highlight continuing government involvement in that sphere. But the Organic Law amounted to little more than "a grand declaration of intentions," whereas the SENAI decree was a call to action.[53]

The "legislative process" that produced Decree-law no. 4,048 was unusually protracted and convoluted; even the issuing and implementation of the intensely debated minimum wage law proceeded in a more expeditious fashion. But even though it was not a typical case, the founding of SENAI reveals the way in which industrialists, under the Estado Novo, could intervene in the formulation of social legislation. Not only did Simonsen and Lodi immediately and effectively register their dissatisfaction with the 1938 decree-law, but they also actively influenced the workings of the interministerial commission. They countered Minister Capanema's proposals with their own recommendations, warmly supported by Labor Minister Falcão, and eventually took over the final phase of the "legislative" process.

Crucial to the industrial leaders' success in controlling the decision-making process was their use of "rational" and "scientific" arguments to bolster their positions. The factory visits arranged by FIESP for the interministerial commission provided vivid evidence of the federal technicians' ignorance of real industrial conditions in contrast to industrialists' intimate knowledge of their firms' operations. And FIESP presented such knowledge not as idiosyncratic or unsystematic but as reflecting a rational approach to industrial organization, verified by the scientific data produced by Mange and other industrial technocrats. Articulating their position within a discourse of technical competence, the industrialist spokesmen treated as self-evident the view that a rational system of vocational training should prepare only the number of workers required by industry, especially in a society with limited financial resources. Proposals for universal apprenticeship, then, could be discarded as irrational and wasteful. Throughout the process, the discourse of technical competence operated in such a way as to render the issue of vocational training a matter of industrial demand and not of educational goals or workers' rights.

In subsequent years, leaders of FIESP would unfailingly celebrate SENAI as the brainchild of the paulista industrialist leadership with Roberto Simonsen in the lead, assisted by such friendly technocrats as Roberto Mange. But Gustavo Capanema, in a speech marking SENAI's first full year of activity, predictably chose to emphasize his ministry's role, claiming that the 1938 report by Rodolpho Fuchs had planted the "seed" for the creation of SENAI.[54] To be sure, the final proposal submitted by the employers' commission cobbled together recommendations from several different sources. Fuchs's observations of training in Nazi Germany and his call for close cooperation between training organs and industry undoubtedly influenced subsequent policy.

Yet Fuchs himself hardly regarded the inauguration of SENAI (now definitively known as the National Service for Industrial Training) as a personal triumph. On the contrary, Fuchs wrote Capanema just prior to the solemnities to lament that the new program treated apprenticeship as a function of "the needs of the national economy" rather than the needs of Brazilian youth. Fuchs believed that restricting the number of apprentices would lead to arbitrary discrimination; indeed, it was a far cry from the German model, with its obligatory apprenticeship for all incoming male workers. "The training of industrial workers . . . has not become the great protective armor of the Brazilian adolescent who works but only an institution for the technical improvement of the manual labor required by industry."[55] For Fuchs, who envisioned industrial training as a vehicle for promoting discipline, social control, and worker integration into a state project for national development, SENAI was a profound disappointment.[56]

For Simonsen and Lodi, in contrast, the founding of SENAI was a clear-cut victory. It created a training program specifically geared to the needs and interests of industry and virtually free of state intervention. According to Faria Góes, the first director of SENAI in the state of Rio, control of the service by industrialist federations resulted in "a liberation from the well-known bureaucratic obstacles and a healthy continuity in its administrators and technicians."[57] The scheme for distributing revenue insured that the most industrialized areas would be the major beneficiaries of the new program. The structure of SENAI also eliminated any formal participation by labor unions in the training process, while allowing the industrialists to take credit for an initiative widely regarded as serving the nation's and the workers' interests. Even Capanema, in his speech at SENAI's inauguration, felt compelled to describe the new program as "an extraordinary badge of glory for the employers and industries of Brazil."[58]

This glory did not come without a price for the industrialists, who were now solely responsible for SENAI's financial survival. However, Lodi and Simonsen had succeeded in distributing this burden almost evenly among all enterprises. According to the decree-law, every manufacturing firm was required to make a monthly contribution of two cruzeiros per worker, later changed to 1 percent of the monthly payroll to insulate SENAI from the effects of inflation. Firms with over 500 workers did have to pay a 20 percent surcharge on their monthly payments, but this additional contribution went toward research and overseas internships that would be most beneficial to larger firms.

The ultimate configuration of SENAI also gave industrialist leaders like Simonsen and Lodi the leverage they needed among the "rank and file" of the industrial bourgeoisie.[59] Past experience had taught both men that the average industrialist was not likely to contribute on a voluntary basis to an ambitious project that offered little promise of immediate benefits for his specific firm. SENAI, however, did not have to depend upon the largesse of the average industrialist. Since SENAI had been established by a federal decree, contributions were compulsory, as would be the hiring of a specified number of apprentices in each industrial firm who would automatically receive release time for their studies. In this sense, SENAI had been organized to combine the best elements of both worlds: the state's capacity for coercion and the private sector's preference for autonomy.

Social Services for Social Peace in Brazil

Under the leadership of Simonsen and Lodi, the industrialist organizations simultaneously supported the labor policies of the Estado Novo and actively sought to shape new laws, whenever possible, to conform to employers' interests. Thus FIESP and the CNI could represent themselves both as champions of social peace and as dedicated defenders of their members' welfare. Of course, the debilitated state of the labor movement facilitated the industrialists' self-presentation as promoters of social peace since the labor unions themselves publicly proclaimed the need for class cooperation and harmony.

Despite occasional differences of opinion, industrialists during these years generally basked in the warmth of a cozy relationship with the state and with the upper levels of organized labor.[60] In 1942 Alexandre Marcondes Filho, a paulista and Simonsen confidant, replaced Waldemar Falcão as minister of labor, inaugurating a period of unusually close collaboration between FIESP and the central government. This collaboration took many forms over the next four years. A FIESP notice, circulated in April 1943, urged all members to support the labor minister's unionization campaign and to encourage their workers to join unions since "these organs, instead of being instruments of class struggle, are sources of equilibrium between owners and workers." Moreover, by "giving prestige to the unions . . . we industrialists collaborate in the execution of the broad and intelligent government policy of bringing together employers and employees." A later notice went so far as to suggest that preference be shown to unionized workers in hiring decisions.[61] Even the *sindicato* of the textile manufacturers, not previously noted for its pro-union policies, urged its members to cooperate with the campaign and praised the textile unions' leaders as men of "goodwill," teaching other workers their "rights and duties."[62]

The year 1943 may well have been the high point of this festival of class collaboration. In January the "working classes of the state of São Paulo," with the participation of sixty-three unions, staged a "Banquet of Fraternization," at which Morvan Dias de Figueiredo and Roberto Simonsen were the guests of honor "in recognition of our admiration for their efforts on behalf of harmonious cooperation between Labor and Capital." A few months later, Morvan was again a featured speaker at a gathering of some 100,000 workers in the Pacaembú Stadium to commemorate May Day. The graphic workers' newspaper, reporting on the festivities, noted that "without capital, labor cannot have stability, progress, and security in its future. . . . Without the worker, capital is an inert mass, useless to the collectivity and to those who possess it."[63] And when José Segadas Viana, director of the Labor Ministry's Division of Union Orientation, met with labor union leaders in São Paulo, he held the meeting in the headquarters of FIESP. According to one newspaper account, Segadas Viana "justified this meeting in the offices of the federation by saying that, today, the house [of industry], by virtue of the enlightened laws that orient the Brazilian labor code, is also the house of Brazilian workers."[64]

These celebrations of social peace can be understood only if placed against the backdrop of a world at war. By the early 1940s, the industrialists were enjoying a boom in production and consumption. Older industries, such as textile manufacturing, took advantage of new foreign markets, while newer industries, such as machine-tool and metals production, benefited from the reduction of imports.[65] These market conditions created windfall profits for many manufacturing firms. The initial impact of the war-related economic climate may have been beneficial to industrial workers as well since it rapidly expanded employment opportunities and drove up wages in some sectors. The combined effects of high profits, tightly controlled unions, and plentiful jobs briefly masked potential tensions and gave a certain credibility to a discourse of class harmony.[66]

Brazil's entry into the war in 1942 on the side of the "United Nations" created the perfect context for promoting an ideology of class collaboration. Vargas and his labor minister, Marcondes Filho, repeatedly called upon workers, "the producers of Brazil's wealth," to contribute to the collective effort and perform their duty to the nation, whether in the military or on the factory floor. In one of his widely disseminated radio broadcasts, Marcondes Filho enumerated the traits that make a nation great: "respect for authority, the spirit of sacrifice, the sense of order, constant labor, the intense desire to serve." Indeed, many Brazilians must have been stirred by these calls for national unity and by Brazil's new international status as a valued ally of the "United Nations."[67]

Some aspects of the war years, however, were considerably less appealing to poor Brazilians and gradually threatened to erode the fragile "social peace." First of all, Vargas used the pretext of the war mobilization to suspend or ignore many labor laws. The government regarded strikes and other forms of protest as "antisocial" activities and prohibited workers in "strategic" industrial sectors, such as metallurgy and even textiles, from changing jobs without employer permission. This meant that, despite the intensified demand for skilled and semiskilled labor, workers were not in a position to force increases in wages. The Vargas government did raise the minimum wage in 1943, but the increase was slight and was particularly favorable to the paulista industrialists, since it served to narrow the differential between the minimum in their region and that in less-industrialized states. Even the British ambassador to Brazil observed that "for a belligerent as little affected by the war as Brazil the regimentation of textile operatives introduced by this decree-law is fairly severe."[68]

To make matters much worse for the average worker, the cost of living rose acutely throughout the war years, with the sharpest increases occurring in 1943 to 1945. The possible repercussions of this spectacle of growing hardship for workers at a time of windfall profits for employers were not lost on the government or industrialist spokesmen. In 1942 Vargas ordered manufacturers to reinvest "excess" profits in order to increase industrial capacity and modernize plants. Simonsen, who in an earlier era surely would have denounced such government interference in the private sector, praised the measure as constructive and progressive and urged his fellow industrialists to observe it. Also in 1942 FIESP and the Labor Ministry joined in an effort to convince employers to grant workers voluntarily a wage increase of 10 percent or more to meet the rising cost of living. A FIESP survey that year indicated that nearly 90 percent of its members agreed in principle that wages should be higher, and the federation even circulated a sort of "honor roll" listing the names of firms that had made the wage concession.[69]

Small adjustments in the minimum wage and voluntary raises from some employers did little to help the working-class household keep pace with the skyrocketing cost of living. Commenting on the new minimum wage, *O Trabalhador Gráfico* noted its disappointment at the amount of the increase and claimed that workers would be better off if the government lowered rents and the cost of basic goods rather than adjusting wages. This echoed the argument of one FIESP member who wondered how workers could feed themselves on their current salaries but thought a wage increase would do little to improve their lot since it would only force up the prices of already scarce commodities.[70] Whatever its merits, this view of the situation clearly influenced government and employer social policy throughout the war years. Both public and private agencies intensified their efforts to extend social services and philanthropic assistance to the working-class community to stave off "pauperism" as well as an eventual popular explosion.

Vargas's government initiated its program to reduce the cost of living for workers in 1940 with the founding of the Social Welfare Nutrition Service (Serviço de Alimentação da Previdência Social, or SAPS).[71] Although SAPS was originally conceived as a multifaceted agency to provide classes in nutrition and hygiene, recreational activities, and dining facilities, after the onset of the war, it concentrated its efforts almost entirely on the creation of "popular restaurants" and "subsistence posts" that allowed workers to purchase food at below-market prices.[72] The state also encouraged labor unions and employer *sindicatos* to form consumer cooperatives. Such cooperatives became a major focus of union activity during the war years since they provided a safe haven for labor politics.[73] As for the employers, the textile manufacturers' *sindicato* enthusiastically recommended that food cooperatives be formed to ease the hardship of wartime for workers.[74]

The multiplication of agencies and programs to alleviate the growing poverty of São Paulo's working-class population accomplished little. Dependent upon very limited government funding or the highly variable "goodwill" of employers, these programs were overwhelmed by such problems as skyrocketing prices, the spreading urban squalor, and the deteriorating work conditions within factories operating around the clock, often with antiquated equipment. Moreover, by 1944, it was becoming clear to the industrialist leadership that the government-enforced social peace would not last forever. Several reports from U.S. consuls in São Paulo during that year noted a relaxation of controls on the press, speech, and association. Workers were beginning to ignore restrictions on strike activity, though few of their stoppages yielded tangible results. Labor leaders previously banned from union participation were reappearing at meetings or in print. And both the labor press and the mainstream press were becoming more openly critical of industrial interests in São Paulo, explicitly blaming manufacturers for the galloping inflation.[75] Faced with an increasingly explosive situation in the urban centers and threatened with the loss of his already diminished popular base, Getúlio Vargas began to remove the restraints he had earlier imposed on the labor movement.[76]

The triumphal tone that had characterized public statements by the industrialist leadership in the early 1940s rapidly gave way to an anxious consideration of the social and economic challenges posed by the impending resolution of the European conflict. Eager to develop coherent policies for the postwar period, leaders of the CNI and FIESP convened the first Brazilian Industrial Congress in December 1944. The chief concern of the conference was to discuss means to prevent the loss of new foreign markets and expand internal consumption once Brazilian goods were forced to compete again with European and North American products. Within this context, two highly pertinent issues were productivity and labor peace. To address these concerns, the congress recommended the "rationalization of work" and "the application . . . of modern industrial psychology to improve relations between employers and employees."[77] As for the labor force itself, the congress proposed that workers be given incentives for vocational education and encouraged the "creation and provision of an atmosphere more favorable to industrial workers, offering them better hygienic conditions and greater material and spiritual comfort," and the "promotion, through the creation of consumer cooperatives and other means, of greater assistance to workers' families."[78]

In addition to its apprehension about popular protest due to the rising cost of living, long working hours, and frequent workplace accidents, the industrialist leadership feared the growing opposition of urban middle-class groups to industry and its privileged relationship with the central government.[79] Since even higher protective tariffs and more extensive government support would be required to sustain fledgling firms during the postwar period, industrial interests could be seriously threatened if powerful urban political groups rejected the notion that industrial growth was crucial to national prosperity and security.[80] Much to FIESP's dismay, the influential economist Valentim Bouças, who had collaborated with Simonsen and Lodi on the creation of SENAI, immediately and publicly attacked the congress's recommendation of higher tariffs. According to Bouças, who aside from holding several important federal posts was a board member of "various and powerful North American firms in Brazil," the recommendations of the industrial congress were "contrary to the needs of the poor." Reverting to the language that had been used to criticize the industrialists in the 1920s, Bouças insisted that he was not against "honest, conscientious" industry—by which he meant firms that could survive without government protection or favors. Yet the proceedings of the congress revealed the participants' assumption that continued industrialization precisely depended upon increased government support and planning.[81]

Since the 1920s, paulista industrial leaders had been carefully constructing an image of their social class as forming the vanguard of technical expertise in Brazil.[82] More recently, they had also portrayed their class as increasingly aware of its social obligations. In a 1942 speech marking the publication of A. F. Cesarino Júnior's *Tratado de Direito Social Brasileiro* (Treatise on Brazilian social law), Simonsen assured his audience that "the concerns of factory owners today are divided between the solution of economic problems and social problems." Moreover, "in the house of industry [FIESP]," enlightened industrialists were "orienting more backward employers to recognize the need to harmonize their visions of profits with loftier aspirations."[83] By late 1944, this carefully cultivated image was under concerted attack by the press and even by government officials like Bouças, who portrayed the industrialists as creating, not resolving, social and economic problems.

FIESP memoranda and letters to the editor by industrialist spokesmen indicate that employers were not unaware of the political implications of the press's "unjust campaign" against industry. An article such as "Miserable Rice and Beans Is the Worker's Food," which appeared in a late 1944 issue of the São Paulo paper, *A Noite*, must have caused them some discomfort. Based on a lunchtime interview with workers at one of the capital's largest factories, the article not only highlighted the limited diet of rice and beans consumed by the workers but also caustically noted that the operatives had to sit on the sidewalk to eat their tasteless, cold lunch and were not allowed to enjoy even a quick cup of coffee.[84] And this was nearly seven years after a federal decree required all large factories to provide dining facilities.

The growing threat of labor turbulence and the popular view that hard living conditions were attributable to industrial policy quickened the resolve of industrial spokesmen to implement new social programs. In late January 1945, both FIESP and the Textile Industry Employers' Syndicate (Sindicato da Indústria de Fiação e Tecelagem, or SIFT) enthusiastically publicized Decree-law no. 7,249, which authorized factories with over 300 workers (or a combination of smaller firms) to establish *postos de abastecimento* (discount provision posts) for their employees. According to Simonsen, the decree-law was the result of a joint initiative between FIESP and Labor Minister Marcondes Filho, and the federation strongly urged its members to install the discount food posts in their factories.[85]

FIESP also expended considerable effort in early 1945 to improve its public image. Claiming that the press was unjustly and inaccurately disparaging industrialists for the "absence of social initiatives in the factories," the federation announced that it would create a Social Assistance Department, whose mission would be to gather information on and publicize such initiatives. To that end, FIESP distributed a questionnaire inquiring about the services offered "either spontaneously or *in accordance with the law*" by member firms.[86] Not surprisingly, the first few questions concerned dining facilities in the factory, followed by questions about medical assistance, child care, subsidized housing, subsistence posts, and recreational facilities.

During this same period, industrialist organizations exhorted their members to employ graduates of São Paulo's new schools for social work. As early as 1941, Social Action had sponsored "an intense campaign among the paulista industrialists to convince each and every one to hire a social worker for his factory."[87] In 1942 Aldo Mário de Azevedo wrote of this "new means of overseeing the well-being of one's workers" and the need to convince the directors of large firms that an in-house social service could significantly improve "human relations" in the workplace. But little notice was taken of the subject until 1945.

In January of that year, FIESP circulated a glowing report on Social Action's School of Social Service, which was "dedicated to the training of young women visitors, who establish contacts with the workers' milieu to verify deficiencies within the group and to provide solutions wherever possible." FIESP urged its members to enroll deserving employees in the school, which required only one year of full-time course work, adding that "it is indisputable that such courses serve the interests of industry since . . . firms can have at their disposal reliable elements that enable them to learn valuable details about their workers' lives."[88] By October 1945, the perceived need for such services had become so acute that SIFT devised an unprecedented arrangement with the two major schools of social work that allowed textile manufacturers to designate candidates, male or female, to enroll in special rapid courses for "social assistants." SIFT's newly formed Committee for Social Guidance had made this arrangement "with the goal of facilitating the organization of broader services for social assistance, in view of the current agitated situation."[89]

The description of the situation as "agitated" was not, for once, an overstatement. The relaxing of state controls that had been barely discernible in 1944 had turned into a full-scale *abertura* by early 1945.[90] Operating with relative freedom from government scrutiny for the first time since the inception of the Estado Novo, workers began forming factory commissions and electing union leaders committed to greater militancy. Communist activists who had suffered years of repression also reemerged, finding new recruits among young workers who sought alternatives to the hamstrung union movement.[91] Eager to shore up his flagging political power with expanded popular support, Vargas altered the composition of the labor courts to allow more favorable decisions for workers and formed an alliance of convenience with PCB secretary Luís Carlos Prestes, who had spent many years in government prisons.[92] The result was a crescendo of popular "agitations," including numerous strikes, political mobilizations, and spontaneous protests.

At first, industrialist *sindicatos* responded to the new worker mobilization by offering wage concessions.[93] But most employer discussions of working-class conditions continued to highlight the need for better social services and urban facilities to reduce the cost of living. In July SIFT initiated a "Campaign for Worker Assistance" to promote services for workers both inside and outside the factory. The *sindicato* requested that all members contribute ten cruzeiros per worker employed to the campaign's Fund for Social Assistance. At the same time, a member of the *sindicato*'s Committee for Social Orientation, Severino Pereira da Silva, who was described as "very knowledgeable on matters relating to worker assistance," formulated a highly ambitious Plan of Action. The seven objectives of this welfare plan for workers included comfortable, low-cost housing; an abundant and nutritious diet; complete medical coverage; recreational and cultural activities; religious, moral, and civic assistance; and the provision of child care "to relieve mothers of many of the worries that distract them from their labors throughout the day." Although little ultimately came of this proposal, the attention lavished on it by the *sindicato*'s leaders indicates that they considered it an appropriate response to working-class agitation.[94]

During the final months of 1945, the paulista industrialists faced a series of new challenges on several fronts. At the national level, the Brazilian armed forces ended Getúlio Vargas's fifteen-year rule with a preemptive coup. Vargas's fall from power is often traced to Brazil's entrance into the war since the authoritarian Estado Novo, with its fascist overtones, became more and more of an embarrassment for a military deeply involved in the fight against fascism. Vargas did move toward a democratic transition in 1945, scheduling a presidential election for the end of that year, but his previous disregard for such commitments made it expedient for his opponents to remove him from power before the election date. And, ironically, it may have been precisely the democratic opening and Vargas's switch to an explicitly populist strategy that sealed his fate. Concessions to workers, massive rallies of *queremistas* (from "nós queremos Vargas" [we want Vargas]), and a tacit alliance with the PCB raised suspicions that Vargas planned to extend his stay in office, and this time with a political base far less acceptable to Brazil's elites and military.

Many industrialists, alienated by Vargas's apparently prolabor stance during his last months in office, cheered the dictator's fall from power. But we should not assume that industrialists as a class welcomed Vargas's ouster. The representatives of FIESP and the CNI realized from experience that the labor leaders appointed by Vargas who managed to remain in office—presidents of unions and labor federations—were consistently the most "reasonable" and moderate. Moreover, Vargas had proved himself a dedicated supporter of industrialization and had incorporated industrial development as the central theme of his nationalist rhetoric.[95] In addition, the two most prominent spokesmen for the industrialists during these years—Simonsen and Lodi—were closely identified with the policies of the Estado Novo.[96]

Simonsen's political position during this period was rather ambiguous. Rumors circulated that he was negotiating with the now pro-Vargas Communist leader, Prestes, and was even subsidizing the PCB paper, *Tribuna Popular*. Yet a few months earlier, Simonsen and Horácio Lafer had attended the meeting of the newly formed Social Democratic Party (Partido Social Democrático, or PSD) that nominated Vargas's conservative minister of war, General Eurico Dutra, as a candidate for the presidency.[97] It is possible that Simonsen sought to prolong Vargas's rule until sufficient support could be amassed for the PSD candidate. As for Dutra, FIESP had found him to be a friend of industry in the past, and his conservative views made it unlikely that he would indulge in the type of populist rhetoric that had characterized Vargas's last year in power. Dutra, moreover, was greatly preferable to his main opponent, Brigadier Eduardo Gomes, the candidate of the National Democratic Union (União Democrática Nacional, or UDN) and a harsh critic of state-supported industrialization. Dutra's easy victory over Gomes in the December 1945 elections must have been welcome news for the paulista industrial leadership.[98]

In contrast, the news from the world of labor was hardly comforting. Despite the bonuses secured by many workers during the strike movements of mid-1945, the intensifying problem of *carestia*, a term indicating both dearth and costliness, created a widening gap between wages and cost of living. In some sectors, such as textile manufacture, the renewed influx of imported goods combined with export prohibitions caused cutbacks in production and a consequent loss of desperately needed overtime pay. Continuing deprivation during an unusually open and dynamic political conjuncture resulted in an unprecedented period of labor militancy. By early 1946, production in hundreds of textile factories had ground to a halt as workers walked off their jobs in protest. Widespread stoppages also occurred in other manufacturing sectors. Several important unions moved to increase their autonomy from state control, while insurgent members campaigned to eject *pelegos* (government-appointed officials) from their leadership.[99]

The initial reaction of FIESP could be characterized as an attempt to preserve the status quo of the Estado Novo. Far from disavowing the authoritarian constitution of 1937, industrialist spokesmen clung to the "principle" that strikes were illegal and turned to the police for assistance. In a revealing communiqué to its members, the federation asked that they report any "disturbances" in their factories to FIESP, assuring them that they could take such action "without prejudice to the customary and indispensable communications to the police." A week later, SIFT sent out a notice announcing that "strikes are an antisocial recourse condemned by the constitutional provisions in effect."[100]

The industrialists' response to the "crisis" was not purely recalcitrant. FIESP called a general assembly in mid-February to allow officials of the major employer *sindicatos* to meet with the directors of the principal labor federations to discuss "readjustment of wages and the lowering of the cost of living." The industrialists considered these labor leaders the voice of "moderation" in the labor movement and apparently hoped to work out some sort of compromise with them that stopped short of recognizing the legitimacy of the strike actions. In the same vein, when an "insurgent" group within the metallurgical workers' union pushed out the old leadership, FIESP sought Dutra's aid in restoring the *pelego* officials to their positions.[101]

Publicly, FIESP maintained a stance of vigorous condemnation, announcing that it would return to the subject of wage increases only after all disturbances had ended. Privately, FIESP informed its members that the participants in the recent assembly opposed a "general increase" in wages as "antieconomic" (that is, inflationary) and proposed instead that raises be granted on an individual basis "in view of the productivity, efficiency, and assiduity" of each worker. Such a strategy opened the door for negotiations with workers while rejecting collective labor militancy as the premise for such negotiations.[102]

In practice, individual employers began to break ranks and make concessions to their workers, compelling FIESP and the *sindicatos* to formulate a more coherent and flexible response to the workers' demands.[103] In April SIFT announced an agreement with the textile workers' federation to increase the "bonuses" granted in May of the previous year. The text of the accord acknowledged the "inflationary" character of the increases but noted that the textile industry alone could not be responsible for turning the tide of inflation. It described the agreement as fulfilling "the noble and patriotic objective of preserving social peace, the sole guarantor of Brazil's transformation into an industrialized nation and, hence, a creator of wealth." While the labor movement could claim a victory over industrialist intransigence, employers could portray themselves as insuring social peace and economic development. The industrialists could also take some consolation from having negotiated with the upper levels of the official labor bureaucracy rather than with grass-roots militants and from having conceded bonuses rather than increases in base pay. Moreover, most of the collective agreements did include an "attendance reward" that granted workers an additional 5 percent bonus if they maintained a perfect record. This preserved the principle of linking pay raises to performance and created a new instrument for combating absenteeism. Indeed, the textile industry accord described "respect for discipline and devotion to productivity" as the "essential corollary" for the recognition of workers' rights.[104]

Wage concessions bought the industrialists, at best, a fragile and temporary social peace. Leading figures within FIESP, such as Simonsen, Morvan, Antônio Devisate, Egon Felix Gottschalk, and Humberto Reis Costa, anxiously sought to mitigate the inflationary situation, establish new channels for influencing worker attitudes, and improve the industrial sector's public image, especially in light of the upcoming congressional elections. In February 1946, the federation asked its members to make a "pledge of honor" not to raise prices and to make donations to the federation's newly formed Committee for Public Relations. FIESP leaders also collaborated with government commissions implementing measures to reduce inflation.[105]

A key point of reference for FIESP officials during this period was the "Carta da Paz Social" (charter of social peace), issued in January 1946 by national leaders of industry who acknowledged the need for new social programs to bolster postwar Brazilian democracy and development. Designed to complement the "Carta Econômica de Teresópolis," which had called for economic planning and government incentives for industrialization, it promised employer attention to employee welfare and social justice in exchange for worker attention to productivity through rationalization and technical improvements. It recommended the formation of a Social Fund, with contributions from employers in every sector, to offer general social assistance "not only to continually improve employees' standard of living but also to provide means for their cultural and professional enrichment."[106]

FIESP undoubtedly took many of the proposals included in the charter seriously. The determination of the paulista industrial bourgeoisie to formulate an ambitious response to the new social and political climate is most evident from a FIESP notice circulated in March 1946. It announced the creation of a Mixed Committee of Employers and Employees to discuss salary increases and to seek government assistance in fixing factory prices for foodstuffs, medicines, and clothing. The notice also called for the founding of Committees for Efficiency and Social Welfare, whose objective would be to "attend to the needs . . . of workers and their families and to adjust the maladjusted and provide them and their families better housing, diet, treatment, and recreation." The same notice also announced plans to create a large nonprofit organization, with branches in working-class neighborhoods, to sell foodstuffs and other basic goods directly to the consumer at cost. Morvan called for each employer to make an initial contribution of twenty cruzeiros per employee.[107]

The FIESP leadership soon decided that it would be more convenient to combine these various "welfare" ventures in a single, centralized agency and in April announced the creation of the Fundação de Assistência ao Trabalhador (Foundation for Assistance to the Worker). Formed in collaboration with the labor federations, the foundation would function "to improve the lives of workers and for better understanding between the propertied and working classes" as well as "to combat subversive activities," although FIESP muted the latter objective in its public pronouncements. Within weeks, Morvan, then acting president of FIESP, cheerfully announced that "innumerable firms" had already pledged their "moral and financial support" for the new agency.[108]

No doubt firms closely associated with the FIESP leadership hastily enrolled in the foundation, but even a long-standing FIESP stalwart like the Companhia Antârtica Paulista did not join for several months and only did so after a visit by a federation representative. Smaller firms were even less responsive to FIESP's entreaties for funding; moreover, initially enthusiastic supporters could lose interest once the current social crisis had passed. Such considerations prompted Roberto Simonsen to seek government collaboration and to redesign the foundation along the same lines as SENAI.[109]

The result was a presidential decree-law issued by Dutra on June 25, 1946, forming SESI. The decree established a national council to oversee SESI's operations, with the president of the CNI presiding and with representatives from state-level industrialist federations and the Ministry of Labor, Industry, and Commerce. Regional councils would have a similar composition: in São Paulo, for example, the council included the FIESP president and a representative of the State Department of Labor. To fund SESI, all industrial firms would be required to make monthly contributions amounting to 2 percent of each firm's payroll. As for the service's objectives, Decree-law no. 9,403 specified "the defense of the worker's real wages (improvement in housing, nutrition, and hygiene), assistance for domestic problems resulting from difficult living conditions, socioeconomic research, and educational and cultural activities designed to enrich the individual and stimulate productive activity."[110]

A month later, at the installation ceremonies for SESI–São Paulo, Simonsen portrayed the new agency in a more explicitly political light. Noting that poor living conditions, contrasts between regions and classes, and the low educational level made Brazil's working class susceptible to "infiltration" by "extremist elements," Simonsen offered SESI, with its slogan "For Social Peace in Brazil," as a counterweight to such influences. In São Paulo, alone, SESI would directly affect some 600,000 Brazilian workers, and if their families were included, over a third of the state population would be served by the new organization. Part of SESI's mission would be to protect these workers from the impact of inflation, but Simonsen's emphasis was on SESI's role as an "instrument . . . for the popularization of cultural values in the proletarian milieu." By propagating "Christian" and "democratic" values, "SESI . . . will allow the Brazilian working masses to cross the Red Sea of oppressive and inhuman totalitarianism without wetting their feet."[111]

Simonsen hoped that employers would readily offer support for SESI, but as with SENAI, the industrialist leadership left little to chance or goodwill. SESI, like SENAI, was an "autarchy"—an officially recognized entity with the legal prerogatives of a private enterprise. Decree-law no. 9,403 guaranteed substantial funding for the new organization by making contributions compulsory at the same time that it placed SESI's operations entirely at the discretion of the industrialist associations and allowed for extensive regional autonomy. Although it was Eurico Dutra, not Getúlio Vargas, who issued the decree creating SESI, the new agency fit comfortably within the conceptual framework of the Estado Novo.[112]

Widely regarded as the brainchild of Roberto Simonsen and, to a lesser extent, Morvan Dias de Figueiredo, SESI actually represented the realization of a long-standing industrialist project.[113] The most relevant precedent was the proposal offered on behalf of FIESP by Alexandre Siciliano Júnior in November 1932 as an alternative to the Lei das Férias and partially inspired by the medical/dental clinics set up during the paulista uprising.[114] The objectives outlined for SESI also bore close resemblance to the plan proposed to SIFT by Severino Pereira da Silva a year earlier. Indeed, SESI was able to begin its operations in the interior city of Sorocaba before its mandated funding became available due to a generous loan from Pereira da Silva.[115] Simonsen, though, probably deserves the credit for the decision to structure SESI in SENAI's image.

Many features of SESI differentiated it from earlier projects, however, and reflected the particular historical conjuncture in which the organization emerged. Since the most pressing concern in the urban milieu was the problem of *carestia*, the largest share of the new organization's funding and efforts went to material forms of assistance, especially the discount food posts. However, for the industrialist leadership, the most threatening problem was renewed labor militancy and the revitalization of the PCB, whose candidate received a surprising 10 percent of the vote in the presidential election. Thus SESI sought to establish class cooperation and social peace and to serve as a bulwark of anticommunism. Finally, the challenge to Brazilian industry posed by the end of the war and the emergence of a significant political faction opposed to extensive government protection of industry meant that SESI consistently linked its material and ideological initiatives to the problems of labor discipline and productivity. To be sure, neither the fight against communism nor increased productivity were new concerns for the industrial bourgeoisie, but the specific historical context of SESI's founding made them particularly crucial and urgent issues for the new organization.

The years of the Vargas regime, especially the Estado Novo dictatorship, allowed the industrial bourgeoisie to refine its own "class discipline." Industrialist leaders further elaborated a project for state-supported industrialization and social peace and used their access to state power to impose that project on reluctant members of their own class. Indeed, the early 1940s, a period of high profits, friendly government officials, and hobbled labor unions—a period in which prominent "labor leaders" sponsored banquets for the likes of Roberto Simonsen and Morvan Dias de Figueiredo— must have loomed in the industrialists' memory as a "golden age" of class collaboration. Faced with the dramatic social and economic challenges of the postwar period, the industrialist leadership invested considerable financial and ideological resources in the two services created to address "labor problems" in the broadest sense. SESI and SENAI together would serve as the industrialists' moral and technical shields as they ventured into a new era of union mobilization, democratization, and populist politics.

Inventing SENAI and SESI

The founding of SENAI and SESI presented the industrialist leadership with an unparalleled opportunity to establish programs and activities aimed at rationalizing the industrial milieu both within and beyond the factory. The decree-laws that created SENAI and SESI and the subsequent legislation regulating these new agencies did little more than outline their skeletal structures. The government decrees, though very explicit about the composition of the administrative organs and the means for funding the agencies, described the respective missions of SENAI and SESI in perhaps purposely vague terms. In both cases, the government's role was to establish an entity that was little more than an empty vessel; it deliberately fell to the industrialists and their technocratic allies to fill these new structures with the appropriate programs and doctrines.

The ultimate forms that SENAI and SESI assumed proved flexible enough to accommodate changing political, economic, and ideological climates, but the historical contexts that spawned these two agencies account for enduring institutional features. In São Paulo, both agencies exhibited considerable continuity in certain key bureaucratic positions, allowing a handful of industrialists, technocrats, and professionals to exercise extensive influence over the operations of SENAI and SESI. The very structures of SENAI and SESI, which excluded labor organizations from direct participation and restricted the role of government personnel, meant that industrialists and their helpmates had an unusually free hand in setting the direction of these agencies and in maintaining their basic features, even across rapidly changing historical contexts.

The founding of both SENAI and SESI took place under "emergency" conditions. In the case of SENAI, the emergency was the intensifying shortage of skilled labor caused by the expanded industrial production and reduced immigration of the war years. In the case of SESI, the emergency was the postwar labor mobilization, caused in part by the problem of *carestia*. The first order of business, then, for both organizations was to address these problems, which meant delaying the implementation of programs that more fully expressed the ideological and programmatic orientations of their founders. Yet emergency conditions did not preclude consideration of long-term objectives.

SENAI and the Wartime Emergency

Wartime pressures moved SENAI to order its priorities during its first few years of operation to maximize its immediate impact on the labor market.[1] That meant virtually setting aside its main mission—to train juvenile "apprentices" for skilled industrial employment—and focusing instead on the rapid retraining or upgrading of adult workers for "skilled" positions, especially in the metallurgical sector. It also meant assembling a staff, both administrative and pedagogical, and arranging classroom facilities with great haste.

The three men appointed to the highest posts in SENAI were all well-known figures in the field of vocational training as well as long-standing allies of the industrialists. The first national director of SENAI, João Luderitz, had been involved in "professional education" since 1906, when he founded the Instituto Parobé in Rio Grande do Sul. In the 1920s, he directed a federal inspection of public vocational programs and oversaw subsequent reforms, and in the 1930s, he served as a consultant to the Ministry of Education on vocational matters. Equally important, he was one of the three technicians who advised the "employers' commission" that was responsible for the final SENAI project. Also among those technicians was Joaquim Faria Góes Filho, who as a member of the original interministerial commission had produced reports that consistently reflected the industrialist perspective. Perhaps as a reward for this service, he was appointed director of SENAI in the state of Rio, the second most important center for industrial training; when Luderitz resigned as national director in 1948, Faria Góes took his place and held the position for the next thirteen years.[2]

The obvious choice to head the SENAI department in Brazil's most industrialized state was Roberto Mange. Not only was he the director of the widely praised Centro Ferroviário, which in 1942 became a subdepartment of SENAI–São Paulo, but he was also regarded by those involved in the founding of SENAI as being personally responsible, together with Roberto Simonsen, for the "conceptualization" of the organization. Mange brought to SENAI his extensive contact with industrialists and railroad managers, his experience as a director of IDORT and as professor of mechanical engineering at the Escola Politécnica, and his considerable intellectual baggage packed with assumptions about proper methods for the instruction and socialization of industrial apprentices. In addition, Mange had surrounded himself with eager young engineers and fledgling industrial psychologists, such as Ítalo Bologna (who took over direction of CFESP) and Oswaldo de Barros Santos, who could quickly move into supporting positions in the SENAI bureaucracy.

During the first six months of 1942, the newly formed SENAI administration in São Paulo scoured the capital city and the interior for instructors, classroom facilities, and potential students. Offering salaries that were 20 percent above those paid to employees in the state school system, SENAI had little trouble attracting a teaching staff for conventional subjects such as mathematics and Portuguese. The recruitment of manual instructors, who were supposed to pass a qualifying exam and have at least five years of experience in the appropriate industry, proved more difficult. Desperate for personnel, SENAI found it necessary to hire instructors who failed the exam and had less experience than it deemed desirable. As for facilities, SENAI offered most of its initial courses, especially the night classes for adults, at state vocational schools. Additional courses found a home in the headquarters of the cabinetmakers' and woodworkers' union, the church-affiliated Instituto Dom Bosco, and the SENAI pavilion at the Fourth National Fair of Industry.[3]

To attract applicants, SENAI–São Paulo sent out over 25,000 notices during its first year of operations to manufacturing firms, employer *sindicatos*, labor unions, and working-class community organizations. Despite a lukewarm response from employers (discussed in greater detail in Chapter 5) and limited public knowledge about SENAI's mission, 3,291 workers and aspiring workers registered for the initial series of entrance exams. Of these, 2,245 were adults registering for either the Rapid Training Course or the Rapid Improvement Course. The remaining 1,046 candidates were divided almost evenly between the Courses for Craft Apprentices (Cursos de Aprendizes de Ofício, or CAOs) and the Courses for Working Minors (Cursos de Trabalhadores Menores, or CTMs). The former group—the true target of SENAI's efforts, at least from Mange's point of view—consisted of potential skilled workers under eighteen years old who were simultaneously enrolled in SENAI and employed in industry, while the latter consisted of minors destined for semiskilled positions.[4]

To select students for the "rapid courses," SENAI used a battery of tests developed at CFESP. Both adult and juvenile applicants were tested for basic educational skills and manual dexterity and underwent a physical examination. Only 962 of the original applicants for the "rapid courses" were actually admitted—less than half the number that registered to take the exams. Reflecting Mange's ongoing enthusiasm for *psicotécnica*, the new organization took a great deal of care with the selection process, even producing a film about the testing of applicants.

Due to the rudimentary nature of statistics on Brazilian industry at this time, much of SENAI's energies initially went into "mapping" São Paulo's industrial economy. The staff of SENAI's Department of Industrial Registry visited as many as a thousand manufacturing establishments each month to determine the physical location of industries, geographic concentrations of particular sectors (for example, textile or metallurgical firms), the percentage of skilled workers and apprentices, and other factors relevant in making decisions about the placement of schools and the number of apprentices firms would be expected to send to SENAI. Working closely with FIESP, by late 1943 SENAI had surveyed 8,122 industries in the capital and had begun to canvass firms in the industrial suburbs and the interior. The Control Department, meanwhile, "policed" the system to make sure that industrialists were paying the appropriate amount, through the Retirement and Pension Institute for Industrial Employees (Instituto de Aposentadorias e Pensões dos Industriários, or IAPI), into the SENAI coffers.[5]

The earliest SENAI courses were hardly elaborate affairs. The industrialists serving on the first regional council readily agreed that intensive training of adult workers for war-related production should be the agency's highest priority. The initial courses taught such skills as lathe operating, die casting, machine fitting, welding, and reading of technical design; they left little time for theoretical instruction or ancillary activities. Still, SENAI managed to find time for lectures in hygiene, preventive medicine, and nutrition. One graduate of SENAI's wartime "extraordinary course" for woodworkers and joiners also remembered a great deal of emphasis on patriotism, liberty, and the fight against fascism—concepts that stayed with him for many years after the war, if not precisely in the way SENAI's officials would have wished since he became an active member of the PCB.[6]

Less than a year after SENAI's inauguration, the textile manufacturers' *sindicato* informed its members that this "very important organization" could furnish "competent and honest lathe operators." By 1944, the "extraordinary courses" had certified 1,470 workers with "monotechnic" skills. The number in itself may not seem very impressive, especially placed against an industrial workforce of 550,000 in the state, with 290,000 in the capital alone. However, its significance is magnified if we keep in mind that SENAI considered its mission to be the training of a small portion of new workers with specific skills necessary for the wartime economy. SENAI had also made substantial progress in its efforts to publicize its operations. One of the most effective vehicles for public relations proved to be the school for textile operatives set up in the SENAI pavilion at the Fourth National Fair of Industry. In November and December 1943, 113,899 people, including President Vargas, visited the SENAI exhibit. The following year, nearly 11,000 people applied for SENAI courses in the capital and the interior.

SENAI's "emergency program"—the rapid instruction of adult workers—continued throughout the war, but Mange and his followers became increasingly anxious to shift the organization's focus to the training of apprentices. This sentiment is evident in Mange's opening paragraph for the 1944 annual report on SENAI's activities: "Although this emergency program should be maintained for several years in response to the current serious deficit of skilled labor, it cannot replace or retard the systematic technical instruction of young workers, which is the original objective of SENAI."[7] Of the twelve instructional units under direct SENAI supervision in 1944, six (three in the capital and three in the interior) already included apprenticeship programs. In addition, six schools operated under "the exemption system," whereby a firm installed its own instructional program according to rigorous criteria designed by SENAI. Once SENAI approved the program, the firm was exempt from the monthly contribution except for a 20 percent surcharge for firms with over 500 workers. All six of these schools offered apprenticeship programs.

As noted above, SENAI instruction for young workers during these years fell into two main categories. Students in CAOs worked half-time in industry and studied half-time in SENAI. The apprenticeship, open to students from fourteen to eighteen years old with at least a fourth-grade education, generally lasted three years and prepared a student for a position SENAI regarded as skilled. The recruitment process began with SENAI's Department of Industrial Registry determining the number of skilled workers in a particular firm; that employer would then be required to enroll a number of apprentices in SENAI equal to 5 percent of the firm's skilled labor force. Thus, São Paulo Light & Power, the state's largest industrial employer, had an initial SENAI quota of ninety-four apprentices. The short-lived CTMs, in contrast, were not intended to produce skilled operatives but only offered "general technical and cultural" instruction. SENAI regulations required industrial firms to hire a number of minors, who would participate in the CTMs, equal to at least 3 percent of their unskilled labor force.

Students entering the apprenticeship programs were almost exclusively male. Given the initial emphasis on metalworking, woodworking, and electrical skills—all masculine preserves—one would expect to find only young men in the programs. However, even some of the early textile apprenticeship courses, judging from the photographs, were not open to young women. Considering the prominent role women played in textile production, one can only assume that their absence from the apprenticeship courses indicated their systematic exclusion. Moreover, young women did participate in the courses for juvenile workers and were especially well represented in the many programs for *adestramento têxtil* (rapid textile training) set up during the war.[8]

SENAI's apprenticeship courses initially focused on metal, wood, and electrical work because of their "universal character," which made them useful to a wide variety of firms. By 1944, Mange declared SENAI's intention to expand its apprenticeship training to textiles, ceramics, shoemaking, and printing. The organization also rapidly extended its network of schools operating in the paulista interior; by the end of the war, Campinas, Jundiaí, and Taubaté all had SENAI programs, and the decision had been made to create an *internato* (boarding school) to serve students from areas of the interior where the density of the industrial population was too low to merit a separate school.

Aside from discussing which skills to teach, and in what locations, the early documentation of SENAI reveals an intense concern, especially on Mange's part, for the proper socialization of SENAI apprentices. Mange did not regard SENAI as a vehicle for *mass* socialization, having argued for a training program restricted to the small portion of the workforce that he classified as skilled. At the same time, the organization's officials understood that skilled workers tended to have stronger bargaining power and to assume more prominent roles in labor protests than semiskilled or unskilled laborers. And they were perceived as playing crucial roles in any campaign for greater productivity and efficiency in the workplace.[9] Thus, from the very beginning, Mange and his cohort conceived of SENAI as providing its students with something more than manual skills. The 1943 notice informing industrialists that SENAI could recommend competent

The spinning workshop in the textiles section of the SENAI school in Ipiranga, 1948. This course was unusual in that it included both boys and girls. Courtesy of the Núcleo de Memória, SENAI–São Paulo.

and *honest* lathe operators indicates that, even in the rapid courses for adults, SENAI claimed to instill moral as well as manual virtues in its graduates. (It also implies that lathe operators trained elsewhere might be dishonest.) One of Mange's "lieutenants" during this period recalled that SENAI aspired to form "a man, a citizen. . . . It doesn't do any good to have a well-trained professional whose aspirations are antisocial."[10]

Mange's commitment to providing social services for the apprentices also stemmed from pedagogical concerns. The early SENAI reports are full of pessimistic evaluations of the raw material that the staff had to transform into competent workers, implying that considerable social and medical intervention would be necessary to accomplish this task. According to Mange, "The observations made throughout these first two years . . . lead this regional department to the absolute conviction that, without a social service especially designed for the student-apprentices, and which provides them with medical and dental care, proper nutrition, and social assistance, the efficiency of the professional courses of instruction will be minimal."[11]

Reported deficiencies of SENAI candidates ran the gamut from easily correctable physical problems to perceived "defects" that reflected the ideological disposition of the staff. Nearly two-thirds of the adults who failed the medical exam for entrance into the *cursos extraordinários* did so because of defective vision; among the applicants for apprenticeship, over one-half had inadequate eyesight. Presumably, in most cases, the appropriate eyeglasses would have eliminated the problem. Regular physical and dental checkups also revealed that 80 percent of apprentices had intestinal worms and that apprentices averaged over thirteen cavities each.[12] SENAI began offering free lunches and regular snacks to supplement the students' poor diet, though nutritional deficiencies were seen by some staff members as resulting from ignorance as much as from poverty.

Besides evaluating these "objective" indicators of students' physical problems, Mange discussed the need for better personal and mental hygiene. Apparently, the staff felt that SENAI students did not bathe often enough and lacked the mental discipline to avoid disruptions in the classroom. The broad category of "bad habits," such as drinking, smoking, and the lack of appropriate recreation, offered a further challenge. According to Mange, "The current amusements, rather than being means for distraction and relaxation, merely aggravate the fatigue resulting from daily labors."[13] It would be SENAI's responsibility to provide healthy recreation for these working-class youths. To use Mange's favorite phrase, SENAI would give these apprentices a *formação integral*, a complete education in all aspects of work and life.[14]

Another reflection of this holistic approach to vocational education was the SENAI trinity, "School-Factory-Home." Not only did SENAI intend to bridge the gap between schoolroom and workplace, but it attempted to involve the student's family in his (and occasionally her) apprenticeship, so that parents understood the value of acquiring a skill and completing the SENAI training. Implicit in this objective was Mange's belief that the working-class household itself was defective and required socialization into the SENAI perspective: "In the social and familial atmosphere inhabited by the SENAI student, he finds little encouragement to improve his general culture and to elevate his civic and moral concepts. . . . [Thus the student's] preparation will be incomplete unless placed within a context of order and discipline, of morality and happiness in work, that would seek to create in these youths, who are the workers of tomorrow, a sense of

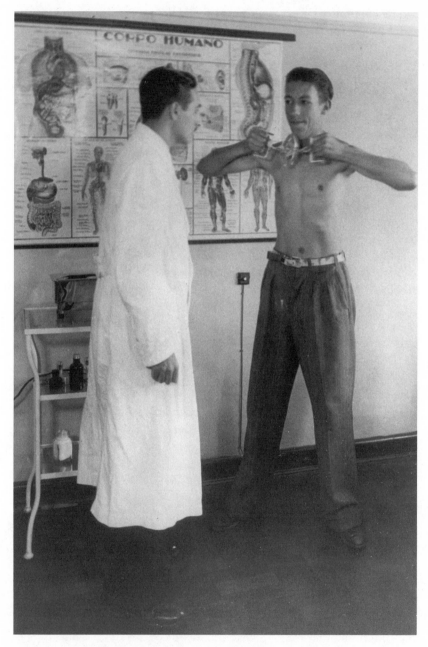

Medical examination for an applicant to a SENAI course, "test of strength,"
1943. Courtesy of the Núcleo de Memória, SENAI–São Paulo.

responsibility and an elevated interest in the progress of technology and the national labor force."[15] As one staff psychologist put it, SENAI would do for the student "what [his] family was too ignorant or incapacitated to do."[16]

The discussions of social services reveal a great deal about the underlying image of Brazilian workers that informed the policies of the director and division chiefs of SENAI–São Paulo.[17] The SENAI staff not only assumed, quite reasonably, that their students had limited formal education and poor standards of living but also concluded that they had poor moral standards, bad work habits, and little "culture." Summarizing an early study to construct a profile of the "average" SENAI apprentice, the psychologist Antônio d'Avila concluded that the SENAI student could not be considered "a typical adolescent. Rather, he is the point of convergence for various deforming personality influences: lack of familial assistance, uninteresting work, poor housing and nutrition, inadequate environments, prolonged contact with uneducated adults, premature responsibilities, etc."[18]

Thus, not only did the apprentices need to be trained, but they needed to be made over to approximate SENAI's image of the good worker. So daunting was the prospect of producing an adequate supply of skilled labor from these meager domestic resources that one industrialist representative on SENAI's regional council, Cyro Berlinck, became convinced that the only solution was to resort, once again, to massive Italian immigration. The textile manufacturer, in a rare (explicit) display of racial bias, confidently predicted that "the foreign industrial workers will dislodge the incompetent national workers toward rural labor."[19] Mange was less pessimistic. Although he was not especially sanguine about the "natural" gifts of Brazilian workers, he nonetheless believed that the appropriate programs could yield a serviceable skilled labor force.[20]

The effort to produce a "good worker" began with the battery of tests each applicant was required to take before being admitted to SENAI. The Division of Vocational Selection and Orientation used these tests not only to determine if the candidate possessed the required physical and scholastic abilities but also to discover whether the apprentice's "real" aptitudes suited him for a craft other than the one he had chosen to learn. If so, the division then attempted to guide the apprentice into the proper course of study, apparently with mixed success since SENAI officials frequently commented on the students' tendency to flock to courses for lathe operators even when other skills offered better employment opportunities.[21]

Once admitted into the program, the apprentice's socialization continued in the workshops and classrooms of the SENAI schools. SENAI always presented its manual instruction as purely technical and its entire training program as ideologically neutral, but Mange had long advocated the methodical series training method as a means to instill discipline and efficiency in the fledgling worker. When Rodolpho Fuchs wrote about the apprenticeship system in German industry, he admiringly noted the Nazis' concern to provide an "integral education" while eschewing "cheap lessons in moral and civic virtue." It was the training process itself that disciplined the will of students.[22]

SENAI, unlike Fuchs's Nazis, did believe in moral and civic instruction but also treated the workshop as a locus of socialization, with an emphasis on order, self-control, and hierarchy. The very conceptualization of SENAI reflected Mange's notion of an industrial hierarchy rigidly composed, in ascending order, of unskilled labor (anatomical hand), semiskilled labor (attentive hand), skilled labor (thinking hand), and supervisory labor (thinking and directing hand). In the words of Euvaldo Lodi, spoken at the inauguration of SENAI's Escola Roberto Simonsen: "The perfect order, the exact punctuality, the irreproachable cleanliness, the constant obedience, the sense of hierarchy in the industrial schools of SENAI constitute living lessons that all of our young students can imbibe."[23]

Mange and the head of the Division of Instruction, Atahualpa Guimarães, sought to make the training experience as uniform as possible through the distribution of detailed instructional packets that organized the apprenticeship program according to the logic of the methodical series approach. Guimarães also established an orientation program to explain SENAI's mission to all new instructors. At the same time, SENAI officials were aware that the instructors in the workshops were not SENAI products themselves and in many cases did not fit the desired profile. Few had any pedagogical experience beyond haphazard training of apprentices on the factory floor—precisely the model that SENAI intended to replace.

"We went to bed mechanics and got up the next day instructors" is the way Sebastião da Luz, who signed on as a SENAI instructor in the mid-1940s, described the process. With respect to technical knowledge, Luz was an excellent candidate. The son of a railroad worker, he had studied mechanics and industrial design at the Escola Industrial de Rio Claro and had participated in the production of the first Brazilian-made lathes, excavators, and escalators. At the time of his enlistment in SENAI, Luz was working as a machine designer for the Villares elevator factory. Ironically, his boss, Alfredo Dumont Villares, who was then a member of SENAI's regional council, tried to discourage Luz from applying, apparently to avoid losing a highly prized technician.

Despite his impressive resumé, Sebastião da Luz had no teaching experience whatsoever, and his own performance as an apprentice was poor preparation for SENAI. He claimed that he was always a perfectionist and would produce two or three machine parts for every ten made by the next trainee. Even more important, his very motive for seeking employment with the organization ran counter to the SENAI spirit. According to Luz's recollections, he ignored Villares's entreaties and overlooked the cut in pay because "working in industry . . . one is just a little screw, one more cog in the gears of the production process, and this cog itself disappears. . . . To work with people is different from working with machines." In other words, Sebastião da Luz used SENAI to escape from the routinized, mechanized industrial world that the organization portrayed as its ideal.[24]

In 1948 SENAI initiated a six-month training course for new instructors, which may have served to limit their pedagogical independence. Indeed, it is impossible to determine how representative Sebastião da Luz was of SENAI instructors in general, but his particular case demonstrates how an individual, while boasting excellent technical credentials, could "subvert" the intentions of SENAI's founders and directors. A SENAI employee who became director of the Escola Roberto Simonsen at the end of the war claimed that, despite Mange's intentions, SENAI in those days "functioned exactly like apprenticeship functioned in the Middle Ages," with the *mestre* imparting his personal knowledge to his students. This may well be something of an exaggeration, but it indicates that Sebastião da Luz was not so atypical.[25]

The other side of the training equation was the apprentice's experience within industry and the limitations this imposed on socialization. Many of the CAO students came from factories that lacked the rational organization espoused by SENAI or performed functions, such as that of messenger, in those firms that had nothing to do with their SENAI training or with the habits of routinization and discipline SENAI attempted to instill. Almost immediately, SENAI staff members voiced criticism of the system whereby apprentices alternated, on a daily basis, between school and workplace, claiming that such rapid changes in environment encouraged disruptive behavior and impeded the teaching of complicated techniques. Students working on a specific part often lost their place when they had to remove it, unfinished, from the machine and spent part of each lesson reviewing what had been done two days before.[26] By 1945, SENAI had switched to a semester system whereby apprentices spent seven months in the factory and five months in the school.

The personnel recruited to teach the general culture courses in math, science, and Portuguese to apprentices and CTM students were another potential source of socialization. Relatively well paid during these early years and often products of normal schools that advocated rational organization of the classroom, these largely middle-class teachers appear to have responded more enthusiastically to the SENAI message than the manual instructors. Still, their social distance from the students may have limited their influence. One math teacher recruited in the mid-1940s noted that SENAI encouraged its teaching staff to insert examples and images from industry whenever possible into their lessons. But having never set eyes on a lathe or any other common factory instruments, he found himself at a loss to know how to integrate such objects into his lesson plans. Mange, aware of this problem, required the general culture teachers to frequent night courses in vocational subjects to make them more sympathetic to their students and more familiar with the factory routine.[27] Some especially eager employees used their vacation time to undergo manual training, a sign of commitment that often yielded a promotion to subdirector or director of schools. Other teachers chafed at being treated like "an industrial worker" and at having to use their scarce free time to study subjects unrelated to their discipline or to publicize SENAI in São Paulo's factories.[28]

Mange and his acolytes certainly expected the classroom to serve as a locus of socialization, but they also believed that complementary services would be crucial to the formation of the SENAI worker. In his report for 1945, Mange declared that it would be an error to think of SENAI simply as an agency for industrial training. "Instead, a constant preoccupation for all collaborators of SENAI should be to maintain activities directed toward the moral, civic, and social formation of the apprentices."[29] By 1944, a plan was under way to install a social worker in every SENAI school in São Paulo. Once in place, the social worker organized students into teams of ten apprentices; the members of each group then collaborated in activities such as physical education, recreation, and discussions of moral and civic issues as well as the value of completing the SENAI training. The latter was of particular importance. The social worker had many functions—investigating physical problems or psychological maladjustment, organizing recreational activities and special celebrations, working out misunderstandings with employers—but none was more important than preventing students from dropping out of the SENAI program.

The dropout rate was alarmingly high during the first few years of SENAI's existence. Only 15 percent of the students who entered apprenticeship programs in 1943 were still enrolled in 1945, a year short of graduation.[30] The reasons for this distressing trend were hardly mysterious. Given the strong demand for skilled labor and the rising cost of living, it

Physical education classes for boys and girls at the SENAI school in Brás, 1946.
Courtesy of the Núcleo de Memória, SENAI–São Paulo.

was a constant temptation for apprentices to abandon their training and barter their limited skills for higher wages. Commenting on this tendency, Mange speculated that, paradoxically, SENAI was contributing to the "instability of the juvenile workforce" by improving the bargaining power of those who frequented its courses, however briefly.[31] Under such conditions, the school social worker had the rather thankless task of convincing SENAI students and their families that the students would be better off if they stayed in school. In 1945 alone, social workers visited nearly 600 families of SENAI students, usually with the objective of persuading the parents that the student should remain in the program. At the same time, SENAI officials expected the social workers to "take upon themselves the human and social development of these youths, which will protect them from the distorting influences of extremist propaganda and from miscomprehension of the worker-employer relationship, the work-salary problem, social classes, etc."[32]

Mange and other SENAI officials also sought to insure that the few training programs directed at young women conformed to what they perceived as the special needs of SENAI's female clientele. Women workers posed certain problems for SENAI since its ideal working-class home consisted of a skilled worker father and a homemaker mother; at most, SENAI expected working-class daughters to work a few years in semiskilled occupations until marriage placed them in the appropriate domestic setting. Yet women, young and old, made up over 40 percent of São Paulo's industrial workforce during World War II and formed the bulk of the textile labor force.[33] Industrialists often preferred women for semiskilled positions since they customarily received lower wages. And employers typically regarded women as "naturally" competent at tasks requiring manual dexterity. One prominent FIESP official, who was also a founding member of IDORT, went even further: warning that overtraining would produce discontented male workers unsuited to the industrial milieu, he suggested that women be recruited for the most monotonous and fatiguing tasks since they were more resistant to tedium on the job. As proof, he cited women's ability to knit for hours without becoming bored.[34]

Again, most young women enrolled in SENAI attended the CTMs, although some gradually entered the less sought-after apprenticeship courses in textile production and papermaking. The SENAI school in the interior city of Campinas reduced the number of hours its female students spent in Portuguese and math courses and sent them instead to the local Escola Profissional Feminina for lessons in cooking and home economics. The school proudly noted that these young women often prepared the meals for the rest of the student body.[35] And women were explicitly excluded from

SENAI's courses to train supervisors for the textile industry, even though female textile workers often complained bitterly about sexual and verbal harassment by male supervisors.[36] SENAI did occasionally boast of the technical progress made by its female students, noting that several young women in its textile school in the working-class neighborhood of Tatuapê were "teaching many things" to their *mestre* and that one had even been promoted to "supervisor's assistant."[37] But such comments were rare; in theory and in practice, SENAI regarded the "woman worker" as a separate subcategory of the working class.[38] Whether because women were expected to be employed only until marriage or to perform only semiskilled labor or to work a "double day" as adults, SENAI always insisted upon some instruction in the domestic arts for its women students.

Another area of special interest for SENAI was the education of children between the ages of twelve and fourteen in the "vocational courses." Ever since the debate over the child labor law in the 1920s, industrialists and social engineers of various stripes had been vigorously denouncing the "harmful hiatus" (*hiato nocivo*)—that is, the two years between the age of twelve, when children usually completed elementary education (if they were fortunate enough to go to school at all), and the age of fourteen, when they became legally eligible for employment. Although employers knew that many of these children filled the "hiatus" with illegal employment or jobs in the informal sector, educators worried that two years of unsupervised or unroutinized activity would encourage mischievous and even criminal behavior and make it more difficult for these future workers to conform to the factory routine. According to Mange, "It is precisely during this stage that the young boy acquires vices and suffers, due to the absence of schooling, a marked intellectual and moral regression." He lamented the "hundreds and hundreds of children [who] languish in dangerous idleness on the streets."[39]

The solution was to offer separate "vocational courses" for children below the minimum age for SENAI apprentices. SENAI began offering such courses at several locations in 1945, enrolling 145 students during this first year. The curriculum developed for these minors had two basic objectives: improving their "general culture" and introducing them to a variety of manual occupations. SENAI did not attempt to "train" these students for a particular skill but rather to expose them to the manual arts so that they, together with their instructors, might discover their particular "vocation" or calling, always presumed to lie, as a consequence of their social origin, in the sphere of industrial employment. Officials of SENAI's Division of Vocational Selection and Orientation promoted these courses with special zeal as a means to guide students in a more scientific manner toward the occupation that best corresponded to their aptitudes and inclinations. Oswaldo de Barros Santos, future head of the division, saw the vocational courses as counteracting the noxious tendency of young workers simply to emulate their fathers in the selection of occupation.[40]

Within a few years of the war's end, the Regional Department of SENAI in São Paulo had made considerable progress toward the development of a training system that reflected the ambitions of SENAI's "conceptualizers." Once the emergency climate of wartime had passed, SENAI switched its emphasis from rapid courses for adults to extended apprenticeship programs for minors. The SENAI administration in São Paulo particularly welcomed Decree no. 9,576, issued by President Dutra in August 1946, which facilitated the agency's stated objectives. This decree discontinued the CTMs, regarded by most of the SENAI staff as a deviation from the organization's true mission. It also explicitly required all industrial firms to send a number of apprentices equivalent to 5 percent of their skilled workers to SENAI schools each year. SENAI viewed the decree as rationalizing its recruitment process and praised it as indispensable for the "preservation of our industrial park."[41]

From 1943 to 1947, SENAI–São Paulo certified a total of 6,453 workers, of which 3,873 were adults and 2,580 were minors. Although such totals seem modest, they only partially reflect the scope of SENAI's impact since thousands of apprentices and adult workers underwent SENAI training for substantial periods of time but quit before certification. SENAI reports persistently complained that the number of apprentices enrolled was less than half of the targeted amount. Still, the nearly 8,000 workers registered for SENAI courses in 1947, three-quarters of whom were minors, represented a significant advance over the early years.

SENAI had also expanded its physical presence in the state of São Paulo with remarkable speed. By 1947, twenty-two SENAI units existed, not including those programs located within firms. SENAI schools sprung up in the industrial districts of the capital—Bras, Barra Funda, Belénzinho, Luz, Moóca, Ipiranga—and in such industrial suburbs as São Caetano and Santo André. Major interior cities, including Campinas, Jundiaí, Mogi das Cruzes, São Carlos, Ribeirão Prêto, Baurú, and Taubaté, had SENAI day and boarding schools by 1947. This burst of activity might seem to indicate confidence in the service's future, but early staff members claimed that the motivation for the hectic pace of construction was just the opposite. Fearing that, with the fall of Vargas and the writing of a new constitution, SENAI might be shut down altogether, its directors moved to make concrete progress that would impede any political move to consign SENAI to institutional oblivion.[42] In fact, a short-lived congressional

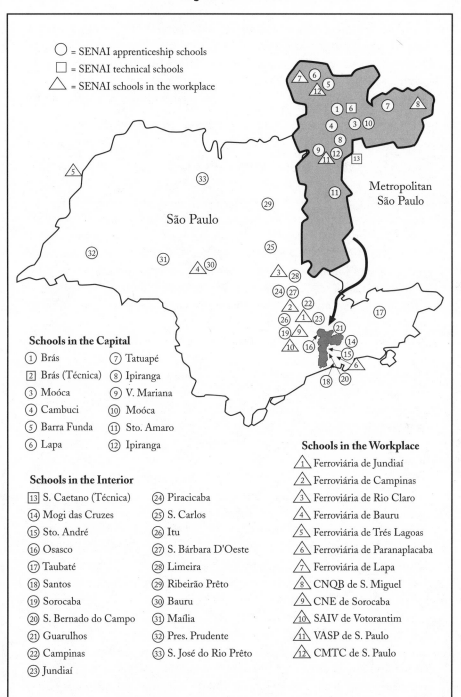

○ = SENAI apprenticeship schools
□ = SENAI technical schools
△ = SENAI schools in the workplace

Metropolitan
São Paulo

São Paulo

Schools in the Capital

① Brás	⑦ Tatuapé
② Brás (Técnica)	⑧ Ipiranga
③ Moóca	⑨ V. Mariana
④ Cambuci	⑩ Moóca
⑤ Barra Funda	⑪ Sto. Amaro
⑥ Lapa	⑫ Ipiranga

Schools in the Interior

⑬ S. Caetano (Técnica)	㉔ Piracicaba
⑭ Mogi das Cruzes	㉕ S. Carlos
⑮ Sto. André	㉖ Itu
⑯ Osasco	㉗ S. Bárbara D'Oeste
⑰ Taubaté	㉘ Limeira
⑱ Santos	㉙ Ribeirão Prêto
⑲ Sorocaba	㉚ Bauru
⑳ S. Bernado do Campo	㉛ Maília
㉑ Guarulhos	㉜ Pres. Prudente
㉒ Campinas	㉝ S. José do Rio Prêto
㉓ Jundiaí	

Schools in the Workplace

△1 Ferroviária de Jundiaí
△2 Ferroviária de Campinas
△3 Ferroviária de Rio Claro
△4 Ferroviária de Bauru
△5 Ferroviária de Trés Lagoas
△6 Ferroviária de Paranaplacaba
△7 Ferroviária de Lapa
△8 CNQB de S. Miguel
△9 CNE de Sorocaba
△10 SAIV de Votorantim
△11 VASP de S. Paulo
△12 CMTC de S. Paulo

SENAI Schools in São Paulo State, 1968

offensive did attempt to outlaw the various "autarchies" created under the Estado Novo, but it was easily defeated.[43] Meanwhile, the building campaign was so successful that subsequently SENAI had to focus much of its energy on convincing employers to send the legally mandated number of apprentices to the schools so that the organization would not be saddled with empty structures.

SENAI and the Gospel of Rationalization

If SENAI in São Paulo saw its mission vis à vis its students as being much broader than simple manual training, it also saw its mission vis à vis industry as consisting of more than the provision of adequately trained workers. The staff of SENAI viewed the agency as forming the advance guard of a campaign for industrial renovation and rationalization. Steeped in the programmatic ideologies associated with IDORT and the Escola Livre, SENAI officials considered every aspect of industrial production to relate in some way to SENAI's mission. After all, what purpose would well-trained apprentices or adult workers serve if the overall organization of the factory was weak or the chain of command deficient? To some extent, SENAI expected its graduates to be shopfloor ambassadors of the organization's rational methods.[44] Still, this was a slow and unreliable way to influence industrial organization and spread the rationalizer's gospel. To speed up the process, SENAI developed a range of complementary programs and courses that were only tangentially linked to the central mission of worker training.

The "courses in industrial psychology" were a prime example of such efforts. First offered by SENAI in 1945, these courses prepared men and women to "visit" industries and instruct supervisors in the selection of personnel, the rational distribution of tasks, and the psychology of command. The curriculum involved 46 hours of class work in the guidance, selection, and training of personnel, 44 hours in "human relations in the workplace" and the psychology of command, 32 hours in industrial organization, and 14 hours in social legislation.

The content of the courses closely reflected the philosophy embodied by IDORT in the early 1930s, which is hardly surprising if we consider that much of SENAI's personnel in these areas came from the Centro Ferroviário and that Mange required his staff at CFESP to join IDORT and read its publications religiously. The first segment of the course came straight out of Mange's lessons on *psicotécnica* at the Escola Livre. The second segment, on human relations, continued the effort first initiated in

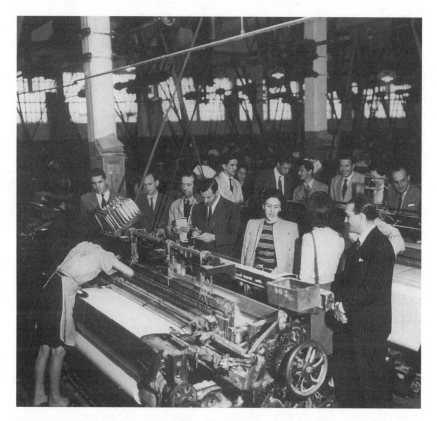

The middle class goes to the factory: Students in the SENAI course for industrial psychologists visit a textile factory, 1945. Courtesy of the Núcleo de Memória, SENAI–São Paulo.

Brazil by M. B. Lourenço Filho in the 1920s to modify scientific management so as to make it more compatible with "human psychology."[45] The segment on industrial organization focused on the theories and accomplishments of the same figures lionized by IDORT in the 1930s: Taylor, Gilbreth, Ford, and Fayol. The final segment, on social legislation, instructed the "visitors" in the "extent and limits" of legal protections for workers.[46]

SENAI prided itself on its pioneering role in the application of *psicotécnica*, with its elaborate, if questionable, array of tests for selection and orientation. SENAI's Division of Vocational Selection and Orientation developed a battery of exams, not only for aspiring students but also for internal job applicants. Important industrial firms based their own personnel selection process on techniques promoted by SENAI, and other educational institutions borrowed ideas from the agency. The high point of these efforts came in 1948 when SENAI, together with IDORT, sponsored the Seminário de Psicotécnica in the coastal resort city of Guarujá. SENAI's central role at this international conference, whose participants included North American and European industrial psychologists, established the organization as a stronghold of applied psychology.

Ironically, even as SENAI was proclaiming its devotion to the principles of *psicotécnica*, the type of testing it advocated was coming under attack in Europe and the United States. Whereas World War I had launched applied psychology as a "science" of selection and orientation, World War II, with its famous Royal Air Force study showing no correspondence between pilot performance and test results, damaged the field's reputation among professionals. Similarly, widespread acceptance of psychological theories emphasizing "irrational" aspects of human consciousness and behavior undermined the legitimacy of psychological testing techniques tied to mechanistic notions of human psychology. Experiments SENAI staged to evaluate the effectiveness of its testing techniques yielded results that were often disappointing or ambiguous.[47]

How, then, do we account for SENAI's ongoing enthusiasm for applied psychology? Part of the explanation lies with Mange, who continued to teach his *psicotécnica* course at the Escola Livre into the 1940s and who had trained several CFESP officials, who later joined SENAI, in "psychological techniques." SENAI, with its regionally decentralized administrative structure, provided these men with the perfect setting to apply and promote their expertise in this field. It is also important to emphasize that none of these individuals had formal psychological training; indeed, no such training was available in Brazil during the 1930s. This lack of contact with professional psychologists may well have insulated them from some of the criticisms being lodged against applied psychology. On the rare occasions when SENAI officials acknowledged debates about psychotechnic testing abroad, they defended its use in Brazil by noting that Brazilian workers had less uniform educational, physical, and cultural attributes than workers in more "advanced" nations. Consequently, psychotechnic testing was necessary in Brazil to detect those applicants who had inadequate preparation for vocational training. Furthermore, it should be noted that many industrial establishments in the United States and Europe continued to use psychotechnic testing during these years and similarly ignored such criticisms.[48]

The appeal of *psicotécnica* for Mange and his lieutenants also needs to be placed in a broader context of commitment to rationalization and belief that virtually all decisions related to education or production could be resolved with the application of appropriate and efficient techniques. Psychological testing offered SENAI officials a modern and "scientific" alternative to the presumably irrational and inefficient process that permeated Brazilian society whereby individuals gained access to schools or jobs through personal connections or influence. One of SENAI's psychotechnic experts recalled that Mange studiously ignored a job candidate's social or political connections and threw letters of introduction, a standard tool for job hunting in Brazil, into the garbage.[49] Indeed, SENAI officials frequently alluded to the "democratic" character of the institution; not only were its courses offered to workers free of charge, but the hiring of employees depended solely upon personal merit.[50]

Aside from its promotion of *psicotécnica* and internal programs such as courses for industrial physicians, SENAI involved itself in other areas only tangentially related to the training of industrial workers. SENAI officials apparently worried that their efforts to produce skilled workers would have relatively little impact on industrial efficiency if Brazil continued to suffer from a severe shortage of industrial engineers and "middle-level technicians." Back in 1939, Simonsen had delivered a speech at São Paulo's Institute of Engineering decrying the lack of engagement between his profession and the industrial sector. Citing recent statistics, he noted that of 1,680 registered engineers in the state, only 53 designated themselves as industrial engineers, and 37 of those were foreigners.[51] Moreover, the courses offered by the Escola Politécnica in subjects relating to industrial processes, including Mange's own course in mechanical technology, were among the most antiquated.[52] Of course, SENAI never presumed to get involved in the actual education of industrial engineers, but it did provide opportunities for engineering school graduates to do "internships" in industrial enterprises and even granted scholarships to fund internships in overseas industrial firms. Gentil Palmiro, who worked with Mange first in CFESP and then in SENAI, claimed that his boss managed to "germinate the very managers of industry within SENAI."[53]

Soon after Simonsen publicly lamented the shortage of industrial engineers, Mange gave an interview to the São Paulo daily, *Folha da Manhã*, in which he called attention to the related shortage of industrial *técnicos*, "technician[s] whose education is far more elevated than that of a skilled worker or craftsman."[54] But despite his deep interest in this matter, which became something of a personal crusade, the original conceptualization of SENAI *excluded* the training of technicians, a responsibility delegated to public technical schools. These institutions, however, due to limited funding, poorly prepared faculty, and inadequate facilities, produced few graduates who were of real utility to industry.[55] In response, SENAI actively

The middle class goes to the factory: Engineering students in the course for lathe operators at SENAI's Escola Roberto Simonsen, 1950. Courtesy of the Núcleo de Memória, SENAI–São Paulo.

publicized the need for more *técnicos* in Brazilian industry, publishing several articles in its monthly bulletin highlighting the deficit of middle-level technicians.[56] The organization also collaborated with North American agencies, such as the International Training Administration, to send aspiring technicians to study in the United States at such institutions as the Lowell Textile Institute.[57]

Meanwhile, SENAI operated in broader venues, collaborating during these early years with a variety of agencies and institutions concerned with the progress of rationalization and standardization in Brazilian industry. Aside from IDORT, with its many direct and intimate ties to SENAI, the agency also acted in concert with the recently founded Brazilian Association for Technical Norms (Associação Brasileira de Normas Técnicas, or ABNT), the Institute for Technological Research, the paulista State Department of Industrial Production (inaugurated in 1945), and, in the postwar period, SESI. SENAI was especially well placed to address the vexing problem of standardization. By providing virtually identical training of workers and supervisors in a variety of establishments, it contributed, in principle, to greater uniformity in work processes and design. Its corps of "industrial visitors" also formed a network for the dissemination of information on new technical norms. SENAI's role in this regard was most pronounced in the burgeoning metallurgical industry, where interchangeable parts, tools, and machinery constituted a matter of growing concern.

Organized attempts to promote scientific management and standardization in Brazilian industry dated back to the 1930s, but these goals took on particular significance in the 1940s, first due to the pressures of wartime production and then as a response to the "distorting inflationary wave" and the threat of foreign competition during the postwar years. The industrialist leadership knew that inadequate industrial production, whether translated into shoddy quality or inflationary prices, would strengthen the hand of those, at home and abroad, who clamored for fewer trade barriers and freer circulation of manufactured goods. Whereas in the past low wages and overproduction had minimized the impact of the rationalizer's message, the political and economic context of the postwar years served to infuse this message with renewed urgency.[58] It is not surprising, then, to find SENAI and SESI cosponsoring a "Campaign to Increase Production" in mid-1948 and participating in other activities geared toward reducing the costs and increasing the rate of industrial output.

The impact of such "campaigns" is always difficult to assess. Independent of any organized efforts by SENAI, SESI, IDORT, and company, many industrialists were using their accumulated profits from the war years to buy up new machinery as it became available from the United States and Europe.[59] The year 1945 saw a record level of capital goods imports as textile plants and other industries reequipped themselves to meet the demands of the postwar economic climate. To be sure, the importation of new machinery did not generate a miraculous overnight transformation of Brazil's industrial sector. A 1946 article in SENAI's national bulletin reiterated complaints about Brazilian industrialists that IDORT members had made fifteen years earlier: "Generally, impelled by the low cost of labor, industrialists reject the principles of assembly-line production, even when it can be demonstrated to have positive economic results. And very rare are the industries that assign the study of production control to specialized technicians, with the object of avoiding any waste in the executed task."[60]

Yet many industrialists recognized the danger of losing the footholds gained in foreign markets during the war or, even worse, having to share the internal market with more efficient competitors. As a leading SENAI official candidly observed, "With the disappearance of the German and Japanese textile industries from the competition, Brazil stood alone as the possessor of an industrial park with conditions for expansion, in the class of competitors with cheap labor, in view of the low national standard of living. This will guarantee us a privileged situation as long as we have equal conditions with our competitors in the other elements of production, to wit: technique and equipment."[61] SENAI, he argued, was the proper conduit for the dissemination of new manufacturing techniques and labor processes.

The need to rationalize and expand production became particularly acute during the first eighteen months of Dutra's rule. Lodi had warned Simonsen in early 1945 that Vargas's fall would unleash a liberal economic backlash against the state interventionism of the Estado Novo. Dutra's first year and a half in office seemed to confirm Lodi's worst fears.[62] The new president's decision to remove restrictions on foreign exchange and thereby open up the Brazilian market to imported goods reflected less an ideological proclivity for laissez-faire economics than the specific historical context in which he assumed the presidency. Faced with the rising social costs of *carestia* on the one hand and record levels of foreign exchange reserves on the other, Dutra had reason to assume that liberalization would rectify the distortions created by the wartime economy. Such considerations might have been enough to "determine" Dutra's economic policy; add to them input from liberal critics of the Vargas regime and pressures from a United States eager to expand markets for its burgeoning industry, and a situation emerges in which the industrialists' arguments carried relatively little weight, despite their friendly relationship with the president.[63]

The sudden influx of imported goods had precisely the effect on domestic manufacturing that industrialists had predicted. Many small and medium-sized firms went under, and larger firms had to resort to layoffs. Urban areas saw rising rates of industrial unemployment for the first time since the onset of the war. Even more distressing from Dutra's point of view was the virtual hemorrhage of foreign exchange, with reserves plummeting to $92 million by March 1947—about an eighth of the level in 1945. Faced with financial insolvency, an alarming proposition for a conservative military man, Dutra reversed his liberalization policy and restored controls on foreign exchange. This switch almost immediately revived domestic industrial production and initiated a period of "spontaneous," steady industrial growth.[64]

The political and economic currents of the postwar period converged to make industry more receptive to the rationalizer's gospel, and SENAI provided a network to facilitate its diffusion. As former director of the Centro Ferroviário, Mange brought to SENAI his many connections with railroad engineers and managers and with the growing metallurgical industry. In

Graduation ceremony for SENAI–São Paulo students, 1947. Roberto Simonsen, president of FIESP, hands a craft certificate (*carta de ofício*) to a young worker. To Simonsen's right is Roberto Mange; to his left is Antônio Devisate. Courtesy of the Núcleo de Memória, SENAI–São Paulo.

addition to its formal connection to FIESP, SENAI benefited from the enthusiastic patronage of such prominent industrialists and managers as Roberto Simonsen, Alfredo Dumont Villares, Armando de Arruda Pereira, and Antônio de Souza Noschese. Under these conditions, SENAI was able not only to train a substantial number of apprentices to staff the renovated factories but also, together with SESI, to instruct and advise many of their supervisors and even influence future engineers and technicians.

Evidence of the subsequent diffusion of the rationalizer's gospel can be discerned in many different contexts, including publications by private firms. Early issues of the magazine *Síntese*, published by the Indústrias Reunidas Francisco Matarazzo beginning in 1948, contained language that repeated, word for word, arguments found in the reports and journals of IDORT and SENAI. An article on Taylorism and standardization sang the praises of scientific management and assured readers that simplification and standardization were not incompatible with creativity and inventiveness; on the contrary, they fostered new and better methods of production. Another piece, entitled "Industrial Mentality and Education," discussed the role of "moral" instruction in encouraging workers to value their labors and feel contentment in the workplace. It particularly recommended such instruction for children who intended to seek industrial employment but were at risk of being corrupted by the "inactive" years (that is, the *hiato nocivo*). The article concluded that such children should be sent "as soon as they complete their primary education to a vocational school where they will be taught to love work and to work with perfection."[65] After only five years of operation, SENAI has made its mark on paulista industry.

SESI and the Postwar Challenge

Whereas SENAI, upon its founding, had to operate under the pressures of wartime, SESI had to confront a peacetime that posed far more serious challenges to the industrialists' interests. Inaugurated just two months before the promulgation of the new constitution, SESI faced immediate controversy over its legality. Even among its industrialist supporters, the demand for a 2 percent monthly contribution—twice the amount paid to SENAI—at a time when Dutra's trade policies were wreaking havoc on industrial profits was hardly welcome.[66] But to the founding fathers of SESI, by far the most serious challenge was the one presented by the labor movement and rising worker militancy. The strike wave, the resurgence of the Communist Party, open manifestations of class conflict, and the industrial elite's perceptions of these developments as profound threats to social peace are fundamental considerations for anyone seeking to understand both the creation of SESI and its activities during its first years of existence.

Unlike SENAI, which maintained a "neutral" technical image, SESI was, from the outset, an avowedly ideological organization. Although SESI did not openly endorse specific candidates or political parties, its founders designed it to advance a certain vision of the postwar Brazilian order and to disseminate their own social doctrine. Such goals were openly expressed in SESI's educational activities, but even its social welfare programs were infused, to the extent possible, with the proper ideological orientation. Simonsen, in his address at the inauguration of SESI–São Paulo, explicitly positioned the new organization among existing "educational" institutions for workers: "SESI . . . will also perform a pedagogical and educational mission imbued with clear ethical and social values. The technical-vocational instruction of our workers, whether administered by the state . . . or by SENAI, demands a complementary education that will permit the full civic development of the Working Man, integrated into his professional and social group. SESI will undoubtedly fulfill this objective. It will be an instrument par excellence for the diffusion of culture, for the popularization of cultural values in the proletarian milieu."[67] Simonsen imagined SESI as a means to fashion a truly "national" culture to counteract a supposed moral and cultural vacuum within the working-class community that would be filled with subversive "foreign" ideas in the absence of any coordinated effort on the part of capital.

We are more accustomed to discussing the utopian visions of the oppressed rather than the millenarian longings of the powerful, but it is useful in analyzing SESI's discourse and policies to consider the industrialists' vision of an ideal society. In the "Carta da Paz Social," issued in early 1946, the industrialist leadership acknowledged "the eminently social function of capital" and announced its commitment to the improvement of the workers' standard of living as the means to "social peace." What the industrialists proposed was not a welfare state of the sort being constructed in more developed capitalist nations but rather a form of welfare capitalism: the direct involvement of capital in the provision of cheaper goods and social services to fight "pauperism" as well as its indirect contribution to the improvement of social conditions through more and more efficient industrial production. They apparently hoped, or imagined, that such a commitment would mitigate the impact of *carestia*, strengthen the position of "responsible" elements within the union movement, and create a pact between labor and capital that would restore the "social peace" of the early war years, but in a new, democratic context.[68]

Among the many obstacles to the realization of this utopian vision was the workers' radically different view of the war years and the opportunities offered by the global wave of postwar democratization.[69] Forced to postpone their demands for higher wages and better working conditions and to accept only union leaders approved by the state while being repeatedly called upon to make sacrifices for the fight against fascism, industrial workers saw the easing of restrictions in 1944–45 and the subsequent return to elected government as finally offering them a chance to secure their long-promised rights as full Brazilian citizens. And the harsh impact of inflation on workers' standard of living—a poor reward for their constant labors—gave their demands particular urgency. For many industrial workers, the transition to democracy did not mean simply the restoration or expansion of popular suffrage. It also meant reclaiming the right to strike, to form factory committees, to elect union leaders, to join interunion confederations, to support anti-oligarchic political parties, and to seek government guarantees for such rights.[70] A promise from industrialists of cheaper food, better health care, and more recreational facilities, though appealing, paled against such aspirations.

The industrialists' evolving vision of the new order, moreover, excluded the very rights that the workers were demanding since the leaders of FIESP and the CNI increasingly regarded such prerogatives as incompatible with the quest for social peace, especially in light of recent successes by the newly legalized Communist Party. The surprising 1945 election results, the renewed strike agitation, and the highly visible role played by Communist militants in labor organizing may explain the hardening of employer rhetoric during the early months of 1946. The "Carta da Paz Social," authored in late 1945, recommended that unions be guaranteed "broad autonomy, whether in the selection and replacement of their officers or with regard to the administration of their social funds."[71] Such a statement indicates an unprecedented willingness on the part of employers, or at least influential industrialist spokesmen, to accept a labor movement operating nearly free of government restraints. In addition, the document explicitly associates democracy with social justice while omitting any mention of the need to combat communism or any other form of "extremism."

By contrast, less than a year later, in their statements marking the founding of SESI, Simonsen, Morvan Dias de Figueiredo, and others anticipated the rhetoric of the imminent cold war by defining democracy, first and foremost, as the antithesis of communism and as a safeguard of individual rights. In a September 1946 meeting of its advisory council, SESI–São Paulo adopted a list of "moral principles," which included a "man's right and duty to work, . . . to choose the form of government, . . . to constitute a legitimate family, . . . to improve his intellectual level, and to worship God. . . . Consequently," the document continued, "no government, organization, party, entity, firm, corporation, or individual can impede or restrict, by whatever means, economic freedom, political freedom, and spiritual freedom." According to these principles, a Communist Party or even such collective actions as industrial strikes had no place in a "true Christian Democracy."[72]

This appeal to Brazil's "Christian traditions" characterized virtually all of the statements made by the FIESP leadership in regard to the new social service organization. Simonsen's speech at the installation of the advisory council in São Paulo scolded members of the elite who immersed themselves in factional politics or the pursuit of easy riches, "unaware of the attempt at infiltration that is taking place among the working masses by extremist elements that . . . seek to destroy the foundations of our social order, creating a favorable environment for the involvement of our country in dangerous, alien political regimes, incompatible with our aspirations, with our traditions, and with the essential postulates of Christian civilization."[73] Simonsen viewed the Communist menace as particularly acute in Brazil due to the workers' poor standard of living and low cultural level, both of which made them susceptible to the charms of extremist ideologies. Thus he called for an anti-Communist crusade among workers that would combine material benefits with social education. Industrialists, through SESI, would form the front lines of this campaign, but Simonsen made no reference to a partnership with the labor unions, as had been suggested in the "Carta da Paz Social." Instead, he cited as SESI's comrades-in-arms the Dutra government, the armed forces, and the Catholic Church.[74]

Indeed, the shift in the industrialists' ideological emphasis may have been due not only to the intensified labor agitation but also to the opportunities offered by the newly inaugurated Dutra regime. Had Vargas been succeeded by a politician more sympathetic to a populist vision of Brazilian politics, the CNI and FIESP leadership might have leaned toward a more conciliatory course with labor, at least in the short run. But under a president like Dutra, already well disposed toward anticommunism and repression, the paulista industrialists had strong incentives to support and encourage a harder line against labor. Dutra's willingness to cooperate in this vein was almost immediately apparent. His first minister of labor, Octacílio Negrão de Lima, orchestrated a takeover of the São Paulo metalworkers' union by ministerialist (or, less politely, *pelego*) elements in early 1946.[75] Federal Law 9,070, issued in March 1946, made strikes virtually illegal by prohibiting them altogether within broadly defined "strategic" sectors and limiting them elsewhere to cases in which employers did not comply with the labor tribunals' decisions.[76] Dutra also prohibited any independent labor demonstrations or rallies on May Day during his first year in office. So impressive was the police presence in Rio and São Paulo on May Day that *O Estado de São Paulo* referred to "an unofficial state of siege," an image dramatically reinforced later that month when police in Rio opened fire on a Communist Party rally, wounding several workers.[77]

This is not to imply that the industrialists were the passive beneficiaries of Dutra's anti-Communist policies. Their representatives pressured politicians at both the state and federal levels to adopt measures favorable to industrial peace. For example, in March 1946 FIESP officials urged the federal government to declare a state of emergency if negotiations failed to contain the most recent strike wave.[78] In São Paulo, the industrialists warmly welcomed and undoubtedly influenced the decision to appoint Eduardo Gabriel Saad, a former DOPS official and a friend of FIESP, as head of the State Department of Labor. Moreover, the industrialists' role in the formulation of Dutra's social policies expanded over time. In the 1947 elections, Roberto Simonsen, running on the PSD ticket, won a seat in the federal senate despite his poor showing in São Paulo's industrial districts. As the leading industrialist spokesman in congress, Simonsen tirelessly campaigned for economic planning and industrial protection and against a legalized Communist Party.[79] In the formal political sphere, perhaps the most triumphant moment for FIESP came in December 1946 when Morvan Dias de Figueiredo, acting president of the federation, replaced Negrão de Lima as head of the Ministry of Labor, Industry, and Commerce.

The appointment of Morvan as minister of labor points up a significant difference between Dutra and his predecessor. Vargas imposed many controls on the labor movement and used repression when workers' demands overflowed the prescribed boundaries, but it is almost inconceivable that he would have appointed as minister of labor someone as intimately identified with the industrial bourgeoisie as Morvan Dias de Figueiredo. Even Alexandre Marcondes Filho, who was a personal friend of Roberto Simonsen and a political backer of the paulista industrialists, maintained some distance from his employer allies, most vividly illustrated by his prominent role in Vargas's Brazilian Labor Party (Partido Trabalhista Brasileiro, or PTB).[80] Dutra, in contrast, found Morvan—a longtime FIESP official and a founder of SESI—to be a comfortable choice to head the Ministry of Labor and to oversee social policy.

The paulista industrialists immediately anointed Morvan the "minister of social peace." Brief biographies of the new labor minister published by FIESP and SESI highlighted his modest origins, noting that the Pernambuco-born Morvan worked for several years as a sales clerk, first in Belo Horizonte and then in Santos. In the latter city, the biographical accounts claimed, Morvan had helped organize sales clerks to establish their first food cooperatives and sports associations, making him an authentic "union leader." This experience allegedly continued to influence him decades later, after he founded, with his brother Nadir, an industrial enterprise that by the 1940s had 3,000 employees, instilling in him a profound commitment to social peace.[81]

Independent labor leaders regarded Morvan's calls for social peace and class collaboration as ironic at best. Left-wing newspapers portrayed Morvan as "responsible for the *carestia*" and labeled him the "profiteer-minister" due to his membership in the industrial bourgeoisie.[82] More important, such epithets did not simply amount to guilt by association; in the unions' eyes, the actual measures implemented by the Ministry of Labor during Morvan's tenure made a mockery of his supposed devotion to social peace. Among his more memorable acts was his role in shutting down the General Confederation of Brazilian Workers (Confederação Geral dos Trabalhadores do Brasil, or CGTB), an intersindical organization that had promoted autonomous union activity and cooperation among unions in different industries. In accordance with a May 1947 presidential decree, the ministry first outlawed the CGTB and then, "to eliminate extremist elements," intervened in the directorates of 143 unions that had adhered to the confederation.[83] Throughout Morvan's twenty months as minister of labor, the ministry systematically replaced elected union leaders with appointed officials, continually postponed union elections, and once again made non-Communist credentials a prerequisite for union officeholding. The federal government not only condemned the briefly legalized Communist Party to clandestinity but also banished its members and sympathizers from leadership roles in the labor movement. It was Morvan who oversaw this aspect of the anti-Communist crusade.[84]

This campaign directly affected only a small number of Brazilian workers, and it is perfectly plausible that Morvan's actions against the CGTB and the PCB would have excited little lasting hostility if they had been combined with significant concessions to the labor movement.[85] But the minister of labor apparently regarded the services offered by SESI to be a sufficient demonstration of employer goodwill and made no attempt to broaden state assistance or protection. On the contrary, not a single increase in the minimum wage was enacted during Dutra's presidency, and labor unions explicitly blamed Morvan for postponing such scheduled reforms as paid weekly rest and a mandatory Christmas bonus.[86] During Dutra's final year in office, the printers' newspaper lamented the state of the Brazilian labor movement, noting that "a large majority of the labor organizations [are] chained to the whipping post of the Labor Ministry," and declared as labor's first priority "to reconquer the union autonomy that was torn away from us by the claws of the ex–minister of labor, the profiteer Morvan Dias de Figueiredo."[87] So egregious were Morvan's antilabor policies that even *pelego* union leaders must have breathed a sigh of relief in October 1948 when he announced that, due to ill health, he was resigning his post.[88]

Implementing the SESI Agenda

If we define "social peace" in the narrowest sense, the industrialist leadership could score itself a victory during the Dutra years. The Communist Party had been forced underground, the strike wave had diminished dramatically, and "ministerialist" elements had seized control over the major labor unions.[89] At the same time, the unabashedly antilabor policies of the Dutra era and the industrialists' close identification with those policies meant that those union leaders who rose to (or regained) positions of power during Morvan's tenure had little legitimacy in the eyes of the broader labor movement. And by the same token, SESI, whose early activities coincided and collaborated with the government onslaught on labor, initiated its institutional life with a blatantly politicized image and with very little credibility among union activists.

Often apparently "neutral" activities such as establishing the discount food posts reflected ideological ends and generated tensions with other organizations. Since SESI placed a very high priority on combating the problem of *carestia*, the agency invested much of its initial resources and efforts in opening these posts. The immediate results in São Paulo were impressive: by May 1947, a total of 77 SESI posts were in operation, 37 of them in the capital and 40 in the interior.[90] Even critics of SESI admitted that the posts had been set up with unusual efficiency and that they offered economical prices to their working-class clientele.[91]

The campaign against *carestia* was not the only consideration involved in the founding of food posts and especially the selection of locations for the posts. In a July 1947 meeting of SESI's regional council, Armando de Arruda Pereira proudly announced that "with the installation of our food posts in certain zones of the city, we have managed to close eight Communist posts." At the same meeting, a textile manufacturer from Sorocaba urged that more attention be given to the interior, and principally his hometown, "where there is a large number of Communist elements."[92] The SESI posts also undermined union cooperatives, even in cases where no "Communists" were involved. In the metalworkers' newspaper, a leading activist complained bitterly when the president of the metallurgical workers' federation, José Sanches Duran, refused to support a "class cooperative" and endorsed the SESI posts instead. Sanches Duran curtly replied that the organization of the SESI network had prompted all unions to abandon "class cooperatives" as no longer necessary.[93]

The posts were the main sources of material assistance offered to industrial workers by SESI during its early years, but other services were available as well. SESI's Division of Health, Nutrition, and Housing benefited from the energetic direction of Geraldo de Paula Souza, an eminent authority on public health issues, a major figure in IDORT, and a founder of São Paulo's Instituto de Higiene. By 1947, the division had inaugurated its first medical clinics, located in the working-class neighborhoods of Tatuapê and Belénzinho. Under Paula Souza's guidance, each clinic included, along with the usual medical personnel, social workers and hygienists who could be consulted in the clinic and were also available for home visits. This reflected SESI's concern to inculcate better health and sanitary habits in its working-class patients. The clinics also, as a matter of policy, charged modest fees for their services. SESI had decided against completely free health care since its clients were not "indigent" and it wished to avoid the appearance of offering charity.[94]

SESI's preoccupation with combining assistance and education could even be detected in its scheme for district kitchens. These central cooking installations provided "hot" meals, delivered by special trucks to participating factories, at low prices. It was an innovative response to the ongoing complaints by industrial workers about the lack of decent dining facilities, especially in smaller firms or in industrial districts far removed from the workers' residences. Since the midday meal was, by tradition, the largest and most elaborate, Brazilian factory workers deeply resented having to eat uncooked food or cold fare, making the SESI service a desirable alternative, despite its shortcomings. Indeed, SESI regarded the kitchens, like the food posts, as a means to appease "disorderly" workers: in 1948 SESI decided to install District Kitchen no. 4 in Santos due to "labor problems among the port workers."[95]

By 1950, six district kitchens had been opened in the state of São Paulo, together serving well over 3,000,000 meals a year. SESI devoted considerable publicity to the kitchens, holding banquets for visiting dignitaries in these facilities and always stressing that the distinguished visitors consumed the same food as SESI's worker-clients. But almost all of the organization's comments about the program emphasized its role in teaching Brazilian workers the rudiments of good nutrition. A retrospective account of the district kitchens claimed that during the early years workers refused even to allow green vegetables to be put on their plates, forcing SESI nutritionists to disguise the vegetables in various ways until their working-class customers became more amenable to such foods. At the same time, SESI claimed that its rational nutritional standards were "contributing to greater productivity in the workplace."[96] The organization must have been enormously pleased when an industrial firm using SESI's district kitchen reported that after two months of its meals, the company could boast increased production and reduced illness as well as an average weight gain of one kilo among its workers.[97]

SESI also liked to portray its welfare services as indirectly increasing workers' salaries by expanding their purchasing power. Indeed, in the context of ongoing inflation, SESI could claim that its benefits represented "real" improvements in the workers' standard of living rather than the supposedly ephemeral benefits offered by higher wages. Furthermore, as employers noted among themselves, SESI's services insured that the workers' expanded purchasing power went toward what employers considered genuinely useful ends. An official of São Paulo Light & Power, in an appraisal of SESI, made just such a point: "A simple raise in salary doesn't always contribute strongly to this improvement [in the standard of living] since, due to a lack of guidance for the beneficiaries, part of the raise is, generally, wasted on unnecessary or unjustified expenditures."[98] Thus, SESI would serve to introduce workers to proper habits of hygiene and nutrition while fueling them for greater productivity and guiding their behavior as consumers.

Soldiers of Social Peace

As much as SESI trumpeted the material benefits it was offering workers, the organization's founders regarded many of the early programs, such as the discount food posts, as temporary emergency measures that regrettably drained resources and personnel from SESI's more fundamental mission of worker education.[99] Such education did not simply consist of literacy classes but entailed a broader and more elaborate approach to worker orientation and cultural elevation. Moreover, SESI intended to address the "problems" of the entire working-class population rather than just the worker on the job or the head of household. Within a few months of its founding, SESI in São Paulo had contracted hundreds of young, middle-class paulistas to join its growing corps of social workers and "social educators." Indeed, in 1947 nearly 60 percent of the budget of SESI–São Paulo went toward paying salaries, and the president of its regional council assured the board of directors that this was understandable since SESI essentially consisted of "personnel."[100]

The hundreds of social workers hired by SESI in the late 1940s were almost all products of the Escola de Serviço Social and the Instituto de Serviço Social, run by Social Action. Since their curriculums shared SESI's emphasis on Christian social doctrine, anticommunism, and the adaptation of individuals to the existing social structure, their graduates could easily immerse themselves in SESI's programs and objectives.[101] Operating out of social service posts at the medical clinics and other SESI units, social workers made initial contacts with working-class families at these facilities to discern whether they were in need of orientation or counseling. If the social worker perceived a problem, she would follow up this first contact with a home visit, presumably with the worker's prior consent. This extended interview could yield suggestions for medical treatment, job training, legal assistance, or, in more complicated cases, ongoing therapy. Statistics from 1948 and 1949 reveal 69,000 contacts between SESI social workers and SESI clients, indicating a very active corps of social assistants.[102] Considering the embryonic state of the social work profession in Brazil during the 1940s, SESI's programs must have initiated a whole new phase of respectability and influence for these professionals, most of whom were middle-class women.

Typically, these women social workers concerned themselves with working-class problems of a personal and domestic nature rather than explicitly political or work-related questions. To deal with the latter, SESI "invented" a whole new category of professional, the "social educator." Working within the department that became the Division for Social Orientation (Divisão de Orientação Social, or DOS), these functionaries were to serve as the frontline troops in SESI's war on communism and campaign for social peace. Even before SESI's official inauguration in São Paulo, A. F. Cesarino Júnior, president of the Institute for Social Law, presented a plan for an intensive, six-month course to prepare social educators, indicating that from the outset they were expected to play a central role in the agency's activities. SESI recruited students for the course among young, middle-class paulistas majoring in such disciplines as law, sociology, philosophy, and social work. The original curriculum included "social doctrines, social economics, social politics, social psychology, [and] techniques of social education," with moral and civic education being added the following year.[103] Required readings ranged from the "Carta Econômica de Teresópolis" to works by Pope Pius XI and Bishop Fulton Sheen.[104]

As for the mission of these social educators, the "Regulations for the Function of Social Educator" stated it in the broadest possible terms. In regard to the "collectivity," the social educator had the obligation to "cooperate in all initiatives of a clearly democratic character" and "to develop a spirit of solidarity and an atmosphere of collaboration between employers and employees for the improvement and expansion of national production and social welfare." In regard to industrial workers, the social educator had the responsibility to "develop their moral and civic education," "to educate them for democracy," and "to explain the true meaning of social legislation." The social educator also was directed to demonstrate to the workers "the possibility of complete improvement in their economic, social, moral, and intellectual conditions and their elevation on the social scale, without requiring the subversion of our institutions or the rupture with the traditions of our Christian civilization." Finally, with regard to employers, social educators were to "explain to them the social function of private property" and "to make them appreciate the benefits of conscious, spontaneous, and faithful observance of social legislation."[105]

This was a rather tall order for the 114 men and women who formed SESI's first battalion of social educators and the hundreds of others who joined them over the next few years. By the end of 1947, DOS had grown to include 766 functionaries. Moreover, their task was made even more daunting by the absence of specific guideposts for their activities vis à vis industry and the industrial workforce. The result was a period of experimentation as the division developed a variety of means by which social educators could make contact with workers and employers and disseminate the SESI message.

The most frequent activity of the novice social educator was the factory visit. The pretext for the visit was usually to provide information to both employers and workers on SESI programs ranging from the food posts to boy scout troops. But the social educator had to be alert to all opportunities to deliver SESI's message or to discuss aspects of SESI's social doctrine, especially with workers. The folklore of these early years includes many stories of SESI functionaries being refused admittance to factories or even having the dogs set on them by suspicious employers.[106] Undoubtedly, there were cases in which the factory owner regarded any outsider as an intruder or resisted allowing a social educator to interrupt the work routine on the shopfloor. However, SESI's internal documentation seldom mentions the barring of social educators from factories. At one regional council meeting in early 1948, a SESI official claimed that out of 4,000 visits to 1,259 firms, only 4 resulted in the social educator being sent away.[107] This suggests that such stories serve mainly to highlight these SESI pioneers' struggles against adversity—in the form of less enlightened members of the bourgeoisie—during the early years of the battle for social peace. As for the workers' response to these early initiatives, they were generally described as cordial, especially if the chat or lecture provided an excuse to stop work.

Many other potential points of contact existed outside the factory. A report on the first few months of activity by the social educators in São Paulo and its industrial suburbs listed 107 factory visits but also 54 visits to worker clubs, 24 to discount food posts, 21 to schools, 21 to Catholic Workers' Circles (Círculos Operários, or COs), 14 to benevolent associations, 12 to churches, and 11 to union meetings. Such activities intensified considerably in subsequent months since DOS reported nearly 20,000 "visits" by social educators during 1948 alone. The contacts also became more extended and elaborate over time, graduating from brief lectures to ongoing discussions and formal courses. SESI promoted certain activities in part to facilitate such contacts.[108] For example, within a year of its founding, SESI was offering dozens of sewing courses to working-class girls and women, and this service seems to have been eagerly sought by labor organizations. As the number of such courses multiplied, a member of SESI's regional council asked whether they were invading SENAI's territory. Arruda Pereira, then regional director of SESI, allayed his fears by assuring him that the sewing courses were of a purely domestic character and that they constituted "not an end in themselves but a means of greater contact between workers and social educators."[109]

Throughout the late 1940s, with the inauguration of its first Worker Club (Clube do Trabalhador) and its network of "social centers," SESI expanded the opportunities for social educators to perform their mission. Workers visited the club in Bras or the social centers in Lapa, Ipiranga, and other working-class districts to take advantage of SESI's adult literacy courses or inexpensive legal services, but they might stay to hear a lecture by a social educator or even enroll in a course on such subjects as labor legislation, human relations in the workplace, and social doctrines. Recreational programs such as athletic events, picnics, and other types of excursions also offered an opportunity for closer contact between workers and social educators.[110] Regardless of the context, SESI apparently assumed that most Brazilian workers presented a tabula rasa on which the well-trained social educator could inscribe the appropriate beliefs. As Antônio Rodrigues de Azevedo, SESI's chief administrator, wrote to Octávio Pupo Nogueira a year after SESI's founding, "The human aspect that we always respect in our direct contacts, our goal of educational orientation, and the Christian basis of our social action will surely result in our complete recuperation of those men who are marginalized by bitterness, by neglect, and by miscomprehension."[111]

DOS also used its functionaries in a variety of capacities that reflected the particular demands of the period in which SESI was founded. For example, SESI's directors expected social educators to mediate factory disputes before they escalated into strikes and to assist in the process of reconciliation once a strike had begun. The report of early activities cited above also noted five visits to the Ramenzoni hat factory for "prevention of a strike" and sixteen visits to factories on strike, such as Atlas Elevators and Rhodiaceta, to facilitate a settlement.[112]

One of the most prolonged and dramatic strikes to occur in the state of São Paulo during the turbulent years following World War II was the stoppage by the workers of the São Paulo–Goiás railroad line. The dispute, which began in July 1946, continued for almost a year, nearly paralyzing service on a line that ran through one of the richest agrarian districts of São Paulo. It also attracted considerable attention from government officials, both state and federal, as well as from labor unions and commercial organizations that sympathized with the railroad workers.[113] It is not surprising, then, that SESI dispatched two of its new social educators to

Bebedouro, a small town near the capital that served as the center of the railroad workers' community, to study the situation and investigate the possibility of installing a discount food post.

The report dispatched to SESI by Roberto Azevedo and Irineu Senise in March 1947 reveals the difficulties experienced by the social educators in adopting a position that accurately reflected SESI's assumptions about the labor movement while attempting to create a positive relationship with local workers, especially in the context of a serious labor dispute. The report began, in proper SESI fashion, by noting that the striking workers had no idea of the importance of the railway line to the larger collectivity or the fact that the slightest lapse in service "places the welfare of the community in serious imbalance." Witnessing the impact of the strike, "we saw and felt from up close the disastrous effects of the use of a right [to strike] when exercised in a precipitous fashion."[114]

At the same time, it was difficult to deny, from up close, the validity of the workers' claims. The São Paulo–Goiás line, due to serious financial reverses, had been angling to sell off its holdings since early 1946 and had been refusing all requests for higher wages despite the obvious impact of inflation on its workers. Wages for adult workers on the line had fallen below the average for juvenile workers in the capital. The social educators acknowledged this situation, claiming that a food post was badly needed due to the workers' "minuscule salaries." Delays in the regional labor courts' response to the workers' demands prompted the original strike declaration, but an intervention by the state government had temporarily settled matters, with the state pledging to reach a permanent solution by December. When no further progress occurred, the railroad workers revived the strike, prompting the company to begin firing 280 workers for "serious infractions." The social educators made no attempt to hide their aversion to the company's decision, noting that "dozens and dozens of workers, prematurely aged by their daily labors for the railway, were fired and find themselves at the moment in serious financial straits." Moreover, they described the sympathetic reaction of the surrounding community to the strike as perfectly understandable since the workers were only demanding their rights.

One of SESI's motives for sending the social educators was to investigate rumors that the strike was not only led by Communists but was being funded, and therefore prolonged, by the PCB.[115] Azevedo and Senise reported that two of the leaders of the strike commission were followers of the "red creed" and lamented that "such a legitimate manifestation suffers from the demagogic influences of the Communist Party's pernicious orientation." However, they discovered that the PCB had been able to contribute only a trifling amount to the strike fund and that most strikers had sought temporary employment to survive. Invited to speak at the union's headquarters, the SESI functionaries had a chance to evaluate the workers' political and social tendencies, which they described as "guided by the preachings of agitators." However, they assured their SESI supervisors that most of the workers could be easily reoriented "through real monetary assistance and effective social education." Clearly, they had concluded that it would be useless to provide the latter without the former.

The social educators' remarks about the local Catholic COs are particularly interesting in light of SESI's close alliance with the *circulistas* during its early years and its correspondingly awkward relationship with most labor unions. According to Azevedo and Senise, the local circle, run by the parish priest, had 300 members, only 32 of whom were railroad workers. Over half of the latter stopped participating once the strike began, "having realized that the circle was not capable of truly defending their rights nor of solving their problems."

The report ended with a series of recommendations, including the installation of a SESI post, a measure the social educators described as supported by everyone from a well-known capitalist to a former Communist Party candidate for the state legislature. They also endorsed the proposed takeover of the São Paulo–Goiás line by the Companhia Paulista, a possible solution that they claimed was widely supported by the strikers due to the company's reputation for good treatment of its workers. Finally, they urged SESI to create a "mobile team" of social educators who would travel throughout the interior, working with the COs and other associations, and to escalate its publicity to counteract the ignorance or, worse, misinformation about SESI's mission. They noted with particular regret that a local priest attributed to SESI "political concerns of a factional nature."[116]

Although SESI was an eminently political organization, it did generally refrain from overt involvement in party politics. One significant exception during this period was its deployment of social educators to participate in the campaigns on the PSD ticket of Roberto Simonsen and Armando de Arruda Pereira for the federal senate and the state Chamber of Deputies, respectively. Aside from the fact that Simonsen and Arruda Pereira were two of the most influential figures in SESI and FIESP, the 1947 municipal, state, and federal elections were of particular concern for the paulista industrialists in light of the surprisingly strong showing of the PCB in the 1945 elections. As a result, DOS regularly assigned social educators to attend Communist rallies "to follow the development of the Brazilian Communist Party."[117] Even as the first class of social educators was graduating from the Institute for Social Law, DOS sent two of its new functionaries to monitor the progress of the industrialists' campaigns in the highly industrialized "ABC" suburbs of São Paulo.

The municipalities of Santo André, São Bernardo, and São Caetano were important targets for SESI since they had emerged as political strongholds of the Communist Party, and São Caetano was the home of Simonsen's ceramics factory, which Arruda Pereira managed for twenty years. It is probably no coincidence that two SESI food posts appeared in São Caetano in the months before the election. Meanwhile, the FIESP duo sought proletarian support by placing advertisements in a local newspaper declaring, "Worker, your vote belongs to Roberto Simonsen and Armando de Arruda Pereira."[118] To discover how the workers of these districts were responding to the industrialists' campaign, SESI dispatched social educators to attend rallies for Simonsen in Santo André and to strike up conversations about his candidacy with workers.

The content of their reports could not have been very encouraging. Reporting on an indoor rally, José Eduardo de Toledo Abreu noted that only sixty people were in attendance, and that number included several SESI functionaries. The audience "politely applauded" after the speeches but generally remained "impassive." In her report on an outdoor rally, Ana Rosa de Camargo Moura estimated the number of "listeners" at eighty, including employees of Simonsen's factory and customers at nearby bars. She and other SESI functionaries then initiated a discussion with several workers in a bar, one of whom she described as "really black" and another whom she noted wore mended clothing and "smelled from *pinga* [cane liquor]." The workers immediately started complaining about high prices and long lines at polling places, but according to Camargo Moura, "we purposely moved the conversation to an ideological terrain," asking the workers if they planned to "vote for communism." The man with the mended clothing, an employee of São Paulo Light & Power, claimed ignorance on the issue, prompting a lecture by a SESI employee on the situation of workers in Russia. Next, the social educators conversed with a young man who worked at the Fábrica São Caetano and claimed to have "no complaints" against his boss. However, when asked how the 2,500 employees of the plant intended to vote, the young man replied that "almost all are going to vote for Dr. Adhemar," referring to Adhemar de Barros, the populist, Communist-backed candidate for governor. The social educator ended her report by concluding that these workers in the bars had not listened to the speeches delivered at the rally.[119]

These instances of "fieldwork" by social educators, though very different in nature, illustrate the obstacles and contradictions these middle-class men and women faced in promoting the SESI agenda. Among the self-selected sample of workers associated with the COs, they could find subjects who were readily amenable to SESI's concept of social peace, but among the general working-class population, reactions to industrialists ranged from indifference to hostility. Furthermore, the initial SESI strategy meant deploying social educators to "trouble spots" where workers tended to have the greatest rancor against their employers, creating a virtually impossible situation for the SESI functionaries, who were, after all, ambassadors of the industrial bourgeoisie. And although some social educators may have been deeply conservative and may have thoroughly identified with SESI doctrine, others sought a career in this area for more altruistic reasons and found themselves functioning in a capacity that led them to become highly critical of employers' behavior. Yet SESI, and especially DOS, existed to improve the industrialists' image among the larger population, and the organization could hardly expect employers to continue to contribute monthly payments if it became a vehicle for negative representations of the "conservative classes." Somehow, social educators had to be supportive of workers and solicitous of their needs while also being responsible for burnishing the image of the industrialists who often bore direct responsibility for the workers' problems. It is no wonder that DOS administrators worried about the social educators' "doctrinal confidence."[120]

Aside from the efforts of its social educators, DOS conducted other operations to strengthen support from friendly union leaders and to influence the course of the labor movement in São Paulo. The key figure in such operations, some of which were shrouded in secrecy, was Eduardo Gabriel Saad, the former DOPS official who briefly served as head of the State Department of Labor and then joined SESI as the director of DOS in 1947. The hiring of Saad for this post is an indication of the industrialists' commitment to a conservative policy toward unions since the new director was openly identified with the most repressive period of state-labor relations.

Saad's previous political posts meant that he had established a network of personal connections to union bureaucrats throughout the state, with particularly strong contacts in the interior and at the upper levels of the labor union structure (the federations), where ministerialist elements wielded the greatest influence, especially after the interventions carried out by the Ministry of Labor in 1947.[121] Upon assuming the direction of DOS, Saad began receiving requests for SESI assistance from "sympathetic" union officials. Often couched in sycophantic language, the requests were for everything from a SESI-sponsored sewing course to funds for a union picnic to technical help in renovating union headquarters. DOS also received several appeals from unions to intervene in disputes with management and thereby prevent open conflicts with employers.[122]

Whether or not SESI granted a union's request depended on a variety of factors, such as cost, purpose, and employer opinion (which, as Saad informed one labor leader, SESI consulted "before doing anything else").[123] However, the internal correspondence discussing these matters indicates that a common deciding factor was the political behavior of the union and the extent to which its officials adhered to SESI's philosophy. To be sure, the very act of requesting assistance from SESI or, for example, thanking the agency for a free subscription to the conservative newspaper, *O Diario de São Paulo*, indicated that a union was not among the more militant labor organizations in São Paulo. But even among the more cooperative unions, SESI held some in particularly high esteem for their services in the pursuit of social peace. For example, Saad was usually solicitous of the needs of the construction workers' union, whose president, Luiz Menossi, he described as "one of the most efficient union leaders and a great friend of SESI."[124] Similarly, Saad supported a request for assistance from the textile foremen's union, describing its president, Fernando Garcez, as "a good and dedicated friend of SESI."[125] Favors and funds sought by the metallurgical workers' union in Santa Barbara D'Oeste also met with positive responses. In aiding this union, Saad commented, "we are dealing with a class organ directed by individuals with a sound orientation, who observe the same principles that guide our own activities."[126] Occasionally, a particular industrialist might intercede on behalf of a highly valued union. Humberto Reis Costa, a textile manufacturer and member of SESI's regional council, seconded a request for recreational funds from São Paulo's textile workers' union, which he claimed was "one of the few unions that is always at our disposition with all goodwill and always seeking to UNITE."[127]

SESI might also grant a favor if it perceived a "friendly" union directorate as threatened by insurgent workers less concerned with social peace. For example, Saad wrote to Mariano Ferraz, then regional president of SESI, supporting a request for funds from his "friends" in the meatpackers' union in Barretos in the following terms: "Considering that, in the near future, they will be holding elections in the union under discussion, and that we need to do whatever we can to prevent a victory by the agitators, it is evident that projects of the kind that they currently want to carry out in the union can only advance our 'plan of defense.'"[128] Similarly, Saad recommended that SESI grant 3,000 cruzeiros to the directorate of the construction workers' union to defray expenses associated with a recent union election, "since we are dealing with a contest in which the elected directorate had to make extraordinary efforts to keep the union from falling into the hands of leftists."[129]

Union leaders also quickly learned to play upon SESI's fears of "extremist elements," framing even the mildest proposals as contributing to the fight against subversion and the campaign for social peace. A union based in Campinas asked SESI to fund a picnic at the shore for its members, arguing that the occasion would strengthen loyalty to the union and therefore protect its members from "dangerous influences." And João Cabral, president of the hydroelectrical workers' union, made an unusually impassioned plea for SESI's help in expanding his union's headquarters. The plans included space for a lecture room that could be used for "social education." Cabral contended that this was especially urgent because many union members "had been 'worked over' by disruptive ideas, as we have perceived on the occasion of our assemblies, many of them attended by SESI visitors; when you enable us to install [the lecture room], we will hold discussions with workers who have been the most frequent targets of creeds harmful to order and social peace."[130]

Only a few recorded instances exist in which SESI openly rejected a union request on political or ideological grounds. In a couple of cases, local SESI delegates advised against helping unions that were not sufficiently sympathetic toward the industrialists' organization or were too influenced by subversive ideas.[131] In one case, Saad chewed out the SESI delegate in Campinas for agreeing to speak at and fund the railroad workers' May Day celebrations without consulting him. Saad apparently felt that the festivities the year before had been too "political."[132] In a different vein, SESI denied a subsidy for an amateur theater production by a union in the town of Jaú, complaining that the play, "A Case of Love," criticized legal and moral codes and was therefore "pernicious." But DOS hastened to offer support if the union chose instead one of the many plays "already approved by its censors" that SESI could provide.[133]

Close collaboration with SESI could become a tricky matter for a union, and for SESI itself, since even the most cooperative union leaders might face demands from the rank and file that could create tensions with SESI. The potential for both friendship and discord is nicely illustrated by SESI's relationship with Heraldo Marques, the ambitious president of the hydroelectrical workers' union in Campinas. The official correspondence between Marques and SESI began in December 1947 with a letter from Marques to Saad in which the union president described the "brilliant success" of a "party of confraternization" jointly organized by SESI and the union to celebrate a wage agreement between the Companhia Paulista de

Força e Luz and its employees. Marques's description of the festivities must have been intensely gratifying to the director of DOS: "It is a special pleasure to report on the atmosphere of discipline and respect in which these particular festivities occurred, and which had the virtue of eloquently displaying a valuable lesson, at this tumultuous time when social peace is being threatened by criminal proposals and practices that proclaim force and brutality, extremist and antisocial recourses, as the only remedies capable of providing solutions to the problems of equilibrium between the two major powerful forces of our nationality: capital and labor." The union president, a politically astute man, also wrote to Simonsen and Morvan, then minister of labor, rhapsodizing about the gala and attributing the success of the wage negotiations to SESI, "whose actions are recognized as being in harmony with the unions' objectives."[134]

A few months later, Marques invited SESI to set up sewing courses at his union's headquarters, a request that seems to have been favorably received.[135] However, the relationship became more complicated in August 1948 when Marques sent SESI a copy of a letter he received from union members asking him to negotiate another salary increase. The electric company workers argued that inflation had wiped out gains from the previous negotiations; moreover, a recent increase in utility rates would provide funds for higher wages. The letter immediately elicited a negative response from José Vicente, DOS's representative in Campinas, who asserted that the workers' demands were unjustified.[136]

Marques obviously sent a copy of this letter to SESI in order to demonstrate that he was under pressure from the rank and file to adopt a position he might otherwise have chosen to avoid. In any case, relations between Marques and SESI worsened after an October 1948 union assembly attended by José Vicente. According to the latter's report, Marques informed the members that he had tried to reach a friendly agreement with the company on the wage demands but claimed that management had not even favored him with a response. Consequently, the workers voted to file a "collective grievance" (dissídio coletivo) with the labor court. Vicente reiterated his opposition to the workers' demands in light of their "recent" salary increase and, more importantly, accused Marques of fabricating the story about management's refusal to respond; according to the DOS official, the manager had responded in person rather than in written form. "We lament," wrote Vicente, "that with this attitude the president of the union serves to harden attitudes against the employer, creating a hostility that, being unjustified, seems odious." Vicente then tried to delay the filing of the grievance, even recruiting assistance from João Cabral, Marques's counterpart in the capital.[137]

DOS's efforts in this vein seem to have been unsuccessful. Moreover, tensions between Marques and SESI escalated a few days after the assembly when the Division for Food Supply refused his many requests to allow his union's members to buy on credit at the SESI food post. Marques angrily replied that Saad had told him purchases on credit were possible; the union president also claimed that he knew Matarazzo workers had reached an agreement with SESI to purchase food on credit. With what was probably calculated anger, Marques denounced this demonstration of "unjust preference" and concluded by saying that he had no alternative but to distribute the SESI notice rejecting his request to the union membership. Forced to choose between currying favor with SESI and maintaining the support of his union's rank and file, Marques at least temporarily opted for the latter.[138]

Apparently, SESI managed to work out some sort of accord with Marques because, by year's end, the union president was again writing to SESI to thank the organization for its material assistance and to praise José Vicente for his role in recent negotiations. And in April 1949, Marques sent SESI a copy of a notice distributed to his union membership announcing a compromise wage settlement that granted workers, depending on their wage levels, between one-half and two-thirds of the amounts originally demanded. That same month, DOS agreed to fund a picnic at the seashore for the hydroelectrical workers of Campinas, with Saad describing Marques as "a good union leader." The record is incomplete, but it seems likely that SESI adopted an intermediate position that was acceptable to the electrical company and allowed Marques to save face with his membership.[139]

For many union officials, a working relationship with SESI meant that they could offer the rank and file concrete services such as dental care, recreational activities, or sewing courses. Such benefits would have particular significance for new unions in small urban centers that had few resources of their own, and it was precisely those unions that had little experience with strikes or other labor disputes that might erode their friendship with SESI. But even in these relatively cooperative unions, officials might feel compelled to correct certain abuses or be pressured by the rank and file to make demands beyond what management would willingly concede. It was at those moments that a working relationship with SESI, whose first loyalties were always to employers, could become awkward or even untenable.[140]

No such awkwardness was likely between SESI and the Workers' Circles, which collaborated extensively with the organization during the late 1940s. Within weeks of SESI's inauguration, the organization began receiving requests for material assistance from COs throughout São Paulo, especially those located in the interior.[141] The activities of the *circulistas* were, by and large, quite compatible with SESI's programs—hardly a surprise since SESI used the prior experiences of Social Action in developing its own operations. Many of the COs sought SESI assistance in establishing sewing schools, adult education, or courses on labor legislation. Even more common were pleas for SESI to set up discount food posts in isolated and impoverished areas or to help COs offer inexpensive medical and dental care—important drawing cards in small urban centers where unions were far too poor to offer such services.

Occasionally, COs would seek sizable sums of money for new headquarters or low-income housing. Letters making such requests almost always invoked the pressing need to combat the rising tide of subversion. The circle in Botucatú, a railroad workers' community, accompanied its request for a medical clinic with the following description of the local situation: "For a long time, there has existed in the bosom of the local railway worker family a group of aggressive and very adept leftists who frequently disturb the climate of social peace, unleashing serious clashes and conflicts." A few months later, the CIESP delegate in Botucatú wrote urging SESI to grant the circle another 100,000 cruzeiros, claiming that the organization had almost 1,000 members and was very active. "So much so that, during the most recent strikes on the Sorocabana line, it was the *circulistas* who resisted the movements of rebellion." Going into more detail, the CIESP representative noted that the circle had organized thirty-five "cells" in various workplaces "with the aim of gathering and attracting working-class elements who were moving toward the Communist columns." SESI granted the Botucatú CO half the amount requested, still a hefty sum.[142]

The Rational Organization of Repression

This description of anti-Communist activity by *circulistas* did not come as news to SESI or its Division for Social Orientation. Within months of the installation of the regional governing body, SESI's council members had already approved an agreement for joint action with the Social Action Department of the São Paulo archdiocese, to be lubricated by an initial donation from SESI of 80,000 cruzeiros. This money financed a variety of activities, but the major objective of the collaboration was to influence the ideological orientation of Brazilian workers and, more specifically, to affect the outcome of impending union elections.

Through regional council members Morvan, Arruda Pereira, and Theophilo Olyntho de Arruda (Arruda Pereira's friend and relative), SESI developed connections to Catholic activist organizations dedicated to the fight against communism, regarded as being at the root of all worker militancy.[143] Particularly interesting is the transcript of a regional council meeting held in December 1947, attended by Padre Joaquim Horta, representative of the Federation of Workers' Circles. The discussion focused on ways in which SESI could collaborate with the Movement for Professional/Craft Organization (Movimento de Organização Profissional, or MOP), organized by *circulistas* as an alternative to the Communist-led Workers' Unifying Movement (Movimento Unificador dos Trabalhadores, or MUT). Predictably, Padre Horta claimed that MOP was having a wide-ranging impact among the "proletarian masses" and was advancing "the spirit of unionization," so crucial to any project for reorientation of the working class. Indeed, both SESI and the COs believed that only a small, though highly dedicated, minority of Brazilian workers had extremist leanings; therefore, an expanded union membership would dilute the strength of these radical elements. And the dilution would be even more effective if new members had the benefit of moral and spiritual guidance from MOP and other such organizations.

Following Padre Horta's glowing introduction of his movement's activities, the council members got down to brass tacks. Antônio Devisate, a shoe manufacturer and leading figure in both FIESP and the PSD, asked the priest "how the penetration of the unions would be carried out." Padre Horta "explained that the movement possessed cells in the unions, and these [cells] received orders from traveling agents." In the spirit of fighting fire with fire, the leaders of MOP had apparently co-opted what they presumed to be the tactics of their "enemy." Impressed by this description, Devisate then informed his colleagues of "the need to speed up the preparation of workers for the [union] elections that have been scheduled for the near future," reminding them that Morvan was "giving [them] a period of six months," referring to the Labor Ministry's recent postponement of union elections.[144]

Not all of the regional council members viewed SESI's commitments of this sort with unadulterated enthusiasm. Manoel da Costa Santos, a manufacturer from Sorocaba, repeatedly criticized the organization for its neglect of the interior and its general disregard for providing material assistance.[145] He dramatized the latter in a 1948 meeting by noting that the 400,000 cruzeiros per month that SENAI spent on such auxiliary services as health care and school lunches was more than SESI spent monthly on all of its district kitchens and medical clinics. He also questioned the large amount of money being donated to Catholic activist organizations and the large share of SESI's budget—nearly one-quarter—allotted to DOS in 1947.[146] Costa Santos doggedly pleaded for a rechanneling of funds into divisions providing "concrete" benefits as well as a survey of industrialist opinion on this matter. His remarks indicate that he assumed *his* views were more representative of mainstream employer opinion than those of the powerful but highly ideological coterie that controlled SESI and FIESP. However, within the regional council, his was the minority view. Even the Ministry of Labor representative, a Morvan appointee, argued that "the struggle that is emerging globally has been defined as Catholicism versus communism" and that communism in Brazil could not be combated "with our usual ingenuous policies." At the very meeting in which Costa Santos raised his most serious objections, the council voted "unanimously" to donate an additional 30,000 cruzeiros a month to the Federation of Workers' Circles.[147]

SESI officials frequently attempted to demonstrate that the accord with MOP was yielding tangible results. At one meeting, SESI's chief administrator informed the council members that 2,800 workers had joined unions at MOP's urging since the unionization campaign had begun. And a few weeks after the council approved the additional 30,000-cruzeiro monthly donation, Padre Horta reappeared to ask for more funds. Devisate seconded this new request, though for the first time he did stipulate that future support be based upon the outcome of union elections. But Morvan and his paulista successor as minister of labor, Honório Monteiro, continually postponed the elections, making it extremely difficult to judge the results of the *circulistas'* efforts. Despite growing doubts about the efficacy of their organizing tactics, SESI regularly renewed its funding commitment to the Catholic organizations.[148] Still, Costa Santos persisted in his criticisms of DOS and its financing of activities by the COs, even demanding that Saad be invited to give an account of his expenditures to the regional council.[149]

Saad did describe DOS's operations to the council at its next two meetings, but the content of the discussion went unrecorded in the minutes, indicating the highly sensitive nature of the matters being discussed. Information and remarks in subsequent meetings, however, suggest that Saad and his minions in DOS worked closely not only with the COs but also with DOPS and other police groups to "remove" subversive elements from the unions and to suppress strike movements. Such collaborative activities intensified in 1949 and early 1950 with the revival of labor agitation.[150]

The minutes of the meetings offer few precise details on DOS's relationship with DOPS, but one council member spent a considerable amount of time in mid-1950 praising the "assistance lent to the public authorities by personnel from DOS on the occasion of extremist agitations and threats of a strike wave."[151] A year later, in a different context, the council touched on the relationship between DOS and DOPS in a debate over whether to provide free health care to DOPS employees (who did not officially qualify for SESI services). The industrialist José de Paula e Silva argued for such assistance, describing DOPS as "an official entity . . . that effectively provides São Paulo industry and the industrialists of Brazil a service of great significance." Small donations from SESI and Morvan's family had already allowed DOPS to create the "'Morvan Dias de Figueiredo' Medical Service," but Paula e Silva termed its facilities inadequate. Concluding his remarks on behalf of DOPS, Paula e Silva referred to the department's most recent contributions to social peace: "The members of this council know of the services that the functionaries of that department have provided and surely know that the strikes by bank workers, by workers on the Santos-Jundiaí and Paulista Railroads, by the workers of the metallurgical industry, were delayed by more than sixty days, thanks to the efficient operations of that department, in collaboration with one of SESI's divisions." Apparently, despite the elaborate array of services and programs developed by the paulista industrialists, on some occasions the social question was still a matter for the police. Indeed, in a later meeting, Paula e Silva, referring to DOPS, bluntly affirmed that "this police division is the most solicited by paulista industry during worker mobilizations."[152]

Saad's personal role in these matters is particularly shadowy, but it seems that not all SESI officials and council members approved of his modus operandi. In August 1950, Rodolpho Ortenblad, an industrial manager and director of SESI, suddenly rearranged the agency's organizational structure, demoting DOS to a subdivision of the Division of Social Assistance. Predictably, this downgrading of DOS provoked the resignation of its arrogant and freewheeling director, causing considerable consternation among his supporters on the regional council. The details are cloudy, but it seems that some SESI officials considered Saad guilty of financial irregularities. This prompted his supporter, Paula e Silva, to reveal that the former DOS director had had at his disposal a "secret fund" that had been endorsed by the FIESP leadership and whose uses were made known only to Simonsen, Morvan, and Arruda Pereira. The revelation of this fund may have been due, in part, to the recent deaths of Simonsen and Morvan, which deprived Saad of his most influential patrons.[153]

Saad, however, still had many friends on the regional council, and they immediately clamored for the restoration of DOS and its erstwhile director. Diniz Gonçalves Moreira, an industrialist who would soon head São Paulo's Department of Industrial Production, claimed that Ortenblad had no authority to restructure SESI without consulting the regional council and vociferously objected to the downgrading of DOS. According to the minutes, "In his view, services of this kind, which require special knowledge and contacts with strikers, agitators, etc., cannot remain subordinated to a division with such a markedly technical character as Social Assistance." Paula e Silva, in the same session, praised Saad and his efforts on behalf of the recently deceased Morvan and industrialists in general. Within months, these efforts began to pay off: DOS merged with SESI's Education Division to form the Division of Social Education and Orientation, a definite improvement in status. And in 1952, largely as the result of an unrelenting campaign by Gonçalves Moreira, the council voted to resurrect DOS as a separate division with Saad back at its helm.[154]

These tales of union infiltration, covert collaboration, and secret funds would be of merely prurient interest if they were not manifestations of a political and ideological agenda that had considerable impact on industrial relations during this period and often brutal implications for urban workers. A consular report on labor conditions in São Paulo during 1950 quoted a state official's description of the situation: "The police intervene, down comes the club, and then the strike's over."[155] As the operations of DOS make plain, SESI, far from offering an alternative to such a violent and uncompromising policy, actively colluded in the repression of labor militancy under Dutra.[156] And it was precisely those industrialist leaders who fancied themselves progressive and enlightened—Roberto Simonsen, Morvan Dias de Figueiredo, Armando de Arruda Pereira, and Antônio Devisate—who bore the greatest responsibility for this repressive orientation.

Although it is tempting to ascribe the direction of SESI policy to the rigid conservatism and chronic anticommunism of the industrialists and dismiss their declarations of social concern as superficial nonsense, it makes more sense to focus on the specific historical moment that spawned SESI. The revival of labor activism, the conservatism of the Dutra regime, and the increasingly chilly cold war climate all reinforced the conceptualization of SESI as, first and foremost, an instrument of social and ideological control. In a 1951 regional council meeting, Paula e Silva bluntly described SESI's purpose as "to combat left-wing extremism, the greatest menace to social peace," and no one disagreed.[157]

In contrast, the Fundação de Assistência ao Trabalhador, SESI's short-lived forerunner, had emphasized currying favor with workers by providing badly needed social services and discount food posts that would mitigate the effects of *carestia* and promote an alliance of employers and workers. Its goals, too, were political and ideological, but its methods, if widely employed, would have had considerable appeal to an economically strapped proletariat. After all, even the most skeptical labor militant could not easily condemn an organization providing inexpensive medical care and cheap food. But only the worst *pelegos* could heartily endorse an employer-run organization that included officials like Saad and actively collaborated with DOPS to break up strikes and arrest agitators.

Both SENAI and SESI operated to advance the interests of the industrialists who funded and administered them, all the while describing themselves as initiatives taken on behalf of the workers. But as we will see in the next chapter, there was a discernible difference between the two agencies with regard to their images and reception among the working class. SENAI, despite a similar ideological orientation to SESI and a commitment to a rationalization process that often negatively affected working conditions, offered workers, at least male workers, something they genuinely sought—marketable skills. SESI also offered workers some tangible benefits, but they were paltry compared to the needs of the urban working class and were provided by an organization widely identified with the most repressive social policies. In such a context, SESI's motto, "For Social Peace in Brazil," could only have seemed ironic to many paulista workers.

Employers and Workers Respond

The process by which the industrialist leadership formulated its social policies and the institutions to implement them was by no means consensual, even within the narrow confines of the industrial bourgeoisie. A coterie of Brazilian industrialists and managers, which one North American observer characterized as "the more wide-awake element among the employers," assumed the role of "vanguard." Working closely with the federal and state governments, such leading figures from the CNI and FIESP as Roberto Simonsen, Euvaldo Lodi, Morvan Dias de Figueiredo, Armando de Arruda Pereira, Mariano Ferraz, and Antônio Devisate were able to realize their highly ambitious plans to promote new forms of industrial organization and social control.[1] Moreover, the founding of SESI and SENAI and the legislation that made employer contributions compulsory expanded the power and purview of FIESP and its regional counterparts throughout Brazil.[2]

Simonsen and his colleagues could argue that they legitimately represented the interests of the industrial bourgeoisie since they had been repeatedly elected by their peers to official positions within FIESP over the past two decades. But for the most part, the "vanguard" acted independently of the industrialist "rank and file," which did not participate substantially in the processes that led to the founding and subsequent operations of SENAI and SESI.[3] This distance between the leadership and mainstream employers meant that one of the primary objectives of the two

Inauguration of the Escola Roberto Simonsen, SENAI–São Paulo, 1949.
From left to right: Euvaldo Lodi, Roberto Mange, Morvan Dias de Figueiredo,
Armando de Arruda Pereira, Mariano Ferraz (at microphone), and Raphael
Noschese, all members of the "Simonsen circle." Courtesy of the Núcleo de
Memória, SENAI–São Paulo.

agencies during their early years—and even well into the 1950s—was to
convince industrialists that they should make their compulsory financial
contributions and avail themselves of the organizations' services.

The industrial workers who were the targeted clientele of the new training and social service agencies had even less of a say in the matter. To be
sure, SENAI and especially SESI emerged partly in response to pressures
from workers that elicited new strategies for "social peace" from the industrial leadership.[4] But at no point did the industrialists invite labor leaders, even those known to be highly cooperative with employers, to play a
significant role in the creation or operation of these new services. Yet the
extent to which SENAI and SESI could be deemed successful would depend upon their reception both among the "rank and file" of employers and
among the workers that they were intended to serve.

The question of employer and worker responses to SENAI and SESI
during the period under consideration is one that cannot be answered in a
definitive or precise fashion. Even data from surveys of worker or employer opinion are of limited usefulness since, aside from a host of other

problems, they reflect a momentary judgment that might evaporate with changing political and economic circumstances. My objective, then, is not to measure reactions to SENAI and SESI by employers and workers in any exact or quantifiable sense but to examine their respective responses to different aspects of these institutions or to specific programs and to discern changes in these responses over time. I will also explore the ways in which SESI and SENAI responded to criticism or indifference from the industrial community.

In 1956 Robert Alexander, the noted North American scholar of Latin American labor movements, visited São Paulo to survey the state of labor-management relations in Latin America's leading industrial center. His itinerary included stops at SESI and SENAI facilities as well as discussions with various industrialists about these services. Though favorably impressed by these organizations, Alexander admitted that "the employers tend to regard [them] as one more thing for which they have to pay money, but not exactly something which they, the individual employers, have much control over."[5] Alexander associated employer apathy or intransigence toward SENAI and SESI with the smaller industrial firms, whose owners he regarded as less politically aware and more hostile to financial burdens that might narrow their often slim profit margins.[6] But the records of the organizations themselves indicate that many of São Paulo's largest firms, and even those owned by businessmen regarded as "enlightened" by their peers, withheld cooperation from SENAI and/or SESI, especially during the services' early years. Similarly, one cannot easily generalize about domestic- versus foreign-owned companies: the Italian-owned Pirelli factory, managed by FIESP stalwart Rodolpho Ortenblad, generally cooperated with the organizations, while several traditional Brazilian firms relented only under duress.[7]

FIESP, in its campaign to recruit employer cooperation and support for SENAI and SESI, could resort to the leverage provided by the government decree-laws that made contributions and even certain forms of participation mandatory. The industrialist leadership, however, was loathe to compel its colleagues to cooperate. Having frequently criticized the government for undue interference in the factory routine, FIESP officials apparently felt uncomfortable invoking the power of the state to bring fellow industrialists into line. Their general preference was to cajole and compromise, leaving coercion as a last resort.[8]

Industrialist discourse consistently lumped together SENAI and SESI as complementary institutions dedicated to increased productivity and social peace, and it is likely that for some employers the two services were indistinguishable. But in practice, SENAI and SESI were hardly identical, and the two organizations elicited different sets of objections from the industrialists they were designed to serve. Indeed, employer resistance rarely stemmed from a broad-based critique of these agencies or ideological opposition to their activities. Rather, employers objected to the financial burdens imposed by these agencies and to specific features of SENAI or SESI programs. Therefore, it is appropriate to consider employer responses to SENAI and SESI separately.

Employer Reception of SENAI

Upon its founding in 1942, SENAI had the formidable task of convincing employers both to meet their monthly financial obligations to the organization and to allow a certain number of workers, adults and minors, to enroll in SENAI courses. Many employers acknowledged the shortage of skilled workers and were immediately responsive to SENAI's appeals, but others proved resistant to SENAI's attractions on a number of counts. Although SENAI devoted much of its attention at the outset to compiling statistics on the structure of the labor force, it was a challenge to coordinate the offerings of its schools with the needs of industry. SENAI believed it could identify such needs in a rational and scientific manner, but it had to contend with contrary judgments by employers, who often regarded "skilled" positions as requiring considerably less preparation. An early SENAI official admitted that many employers belittled the tasks performed by their workers and had to be convinced that even a small portion of their labor force required extended training. A survey of SENAI "dropouts" conducted in the early 1950s revealed that employer pressure was a major factor in the decision to leave the program. And a technician in the State Department of Labor in 1948 attributed the precarious situation of young industrial workers to "the almost complete disdain that employers have for their instruction."[9]

It was also difficult for SENAI to balance the increasing demand from certain sectors, such as the metallurgical industry, for relatively specialized workers with the needs of other sectors for workers with a wider range of abilities and skills. And SENAI's growing emphasis, especially after the war, on apprenticeship training was problematic since the industries that required the largest number of skilled workers generally hired the fewest minors, whereas the textile industry, with few jobs classified as skilled, employed large numbers of workers between the ages of fourteen and eighteen.

Perhaps most vexing of all to the founders and champions of SENAI was the complaint frequently aired by industrialists that apprentices sent to the organization had no obligation to remain with their original employers. In response, SENAI officials strenuously argued that their goal was not to prepare workers for a specific employer but to expand and improve the national pool of skilled craftspeople from which all industrialists would draw. According to Raphael Noschese, a member of SENAI's regional council during the 1940s, "SENAI prepared men for every factory, not just for João's or Pedro's or Paulo's. . . . Our objective was not to produce a worker just for you, but for São Paulo, for Brazil." But such arguments offered little comfort to smaller firms that could ill afford to squander resources on training an apprentice who would wind up working for someone else.[10] Indeed, the objections raised by employers in this regard sharply illustrate the tension between individual industrialists, with their understandable attention to the bottom line, and the ideologues of SENAI who advanced a broader vision of industrial progress.

Larger firms often sought to avoid making payments to SENAI by claiming that they already offered adequate internal training programs and could dispense with SENAI services. The response of SENAI was to set very rigorous standards that a program had to meet in order to qualify as a SENAI school operating under a "regime of exemption." Such standards appear to have been rigorously enforced; after all, Roberto Mange and João Luderitz did not want firms to use such claims as a ruse to dodge paying the SENAI contribution, nor did they want to wink at the preservation of traditional, empirical methods of job training. Thus the programs had to use pedagogical materials supplied by SENAI, offer general culture courses as well as manual instruction, and be located in structures separate from the rest of the factory. In zones where no other SENAI facilities existed, the firm had to open its school to a certain number of nonemployees. Given these stiff requirements, it is not surprising that only three large industrial enterprises in São Paulo qualified to operate under the regime of exemption.[11]

The reminiscences of those involved with SENAI during these early years regularly refer to industrialists' initial indifference or hostility to the organization. According to a SENAI official involved in the area of *psicotécnica*, the industrialists viewed SENAI as "one more government institution that was out to get money from them." Several accounts claimed that, at first, industries sent their least promising apprentices, the "worst students," to SENAI since they regarded the program as a waste of time. Predictably, these same accounts asserted that employers soon "began to perceive that SENAI students, and those trained by SENAI, were the best."[12] Even an educator who claimed that industrialists were always very supportive of SENAI recalled the early years in this fashion: "The first stu-

SENAI course for glassmakers in the Nadir Figueiredo glass factory, 1951.
Despite SENAI's modern, technically sophisticated image, the physical setting
and equipment for this course were quite rudimentary. Courtesy of the Núcleo
de Memória, SENAI–São Paulo.

dents sent to SENAI were selected from among the worst apprentices in
the workshop; [the employers] wanted to be rid of them and sent them to
the SENAI schools just to get rid of them. To meet their legal obligations.
But [the apprentices] returned [to the workplace] with an outstanding attitude, and those same students brought to industry, to their superiors, a
completely different image, a completely retouched portrait of their character. From then on, the supervisors chose the best apprentices to be sent
to SENAI."[13] It is difficult to know how literally we should take such
memories. It does seem that SENAI, innovative in its structure and in its
public/private character, encountered considerable skepticism among industrial employers. At the same time, the image of SENAI as Pygmalion,
transforming the least capable or least cooperative youths into competent,
honest, and dedicated workers and thereby winning the confidence of industrialists, has to be taken with a grain of salt.[14]

Again, some smaller firms—those with much fewer than 500 workers—
proved especially reluctant to cooperate with SENAI and often objected
to the idea of paying even half the minimum wage during the months an

apprentice spent in the classroom rather than in the factory. A SENAI official who took over the direction of the new school in Ribeirão Prêto in 1951 recalled that the larger local firms—the Matarazzo textile factory, the Antarctica beer factory, the leading construction firm, and the nearby electric power plant—faithfully sent apprentices to SENAI. But a smaller dental equipment factory, owned by a "rather irascible German," adamantly refused to enroll students in SENAI. When the school director visited the factory to inquire about the firm's refusal, the owner simply replied that he saw no reason to send an apprentice, whom he would have to pay, to SENAI when he could recruit a skilled worker, trained for free, from the local vocational school.[15]

The ideal vision of SENAI, developed by Mange and shared by his coworkers, was of a training organization oriented toward the working minor who would alternate between instruction and practical experience in his place of employment. But the frequent lack of cooperation from industrialists meant that many SENAI schools had to resort to *aspirantes a indústria*—unemployed minors—to fill their quota. Yet it was widely acknowledged that these students had less motivation, and thus a higher turnover rate, than those already employed in industry. In fact, many of these "aspirants to industry" chose to drop out once they found the industrial employment they aspired to. SENAI social workers made regular attempts to place the unemployed youths with companies that failed to meet their apprentice quota, but such efforts yielded limited success. In short, SENAI had to modify the ideal vision of its mission due to the choices made by young workers and to the withholding of cooperation by many industrial firms.[16]

The records of São Paulo Light & Power provide an unusually detailed glimpse of the interaction between an urban employer and the new training service. A Canadian/North American firm operating in Brazil since the beginning of the century, Light was the largest urban employer in São Paulo at the time of SENAI's inauguration. Of course, Light was not a manufacturing firm in the usual sense; it was a utility that provided electrical power (and urban transport until the late 1940s) throughout the state of São Paulo. Thus its workers operated in a variety of settings: power plants, construction sites, repair shops, and transport systems. Due to the structure of its operations, Light employed a higher proportion of workers classified as skilled—electricians, mechanics, machine operators—than other large-scale "industrial" firms. Indeed, for internal purposes, Light classified nearly half of its labor force as skilled, that proportion being reduced to approximately one-quarter of the workforce once the firm applied SENAI's criteria.[17] In this sense, Light may have been atypical, but its labor needs were not dramatically different from those of other industries in the metallurgical and electrical equipment sectors.

Light's interest in apprenticeship training dated back to 1910, when it began providing both manual instruction and cultural fare to young workers. Although the São Paulo firm had allowed its formal training courses for minors to lapse by the 1930s, Light continued to acknowledge the need for more and better skilled workers.[18] After the federal government issued the 1939 decree-law requiring firms with over 500 workers to offer vocational education, the head of personnel strongly recommended that Light comply by creating its own courses not only because it was a "legal exigency" but also because "we have noted the need for this, in view of the scarcity of technical professionals, clerks, and workers." The superintendent of Light in São Paulo, Odilon de Souza, confirmed this sentiment in his answers to the 1939 questionnaire distributed by the interministerial commission. In response to the question, "What are the principal faults observed in the workers regularly employed in your firm?," de Souza, an active member of IDORT, wrote: "Since Brazil is not an industrial nation, and always suffers from a scarcity of specialized technical workers, it becomes difficult to find, in the labor market, Brazilians to meet the percentage required by [the Two-Thirds] law. . . . In these conditions, the national element available to us represents, generally, a level of efficiency below that demanded by positions of responsibility."[19]

Under these circumstances, Light was highly enthusiastic about any sort of program that would provide systematic training for *adults*. That, however, was the fly in the ointment: the main objective of the interministerial commission and the organs that succeeded it was to develop means to train *minors* through some form of apprenticeship, whereas Light only hired minors as messengers. Here, again, its practices may have been atypical of large industry in São Paulo; most metallurgical factories employed larger numbers of workers under the age of eighteen than did Light. But even in those cases, the minors most likely worked as *serventes* and had very little contact with the actual production process. Thus the eventual creation of SENAI meant not only a new financial obligation but also a partial revision in hiring practices.

Despite Light's repeated lip service to the cause of vocational training, the company made a brief attempt to excuse itself from participation in SENAI, claiming that its status as a utility and transport enterprise exempted it from contributions to an "industrial" service. However, SENAI promptly informed Light that its classification as a member of FIESP and the CNI meant that the firm had to make a monthly contribution to SENAI.[20] By January 1943, Light had entered into direct negotiations with

Roberto Mange, who had collaborated in various Light projects in the past, to determine the amount of back payment Light owed the training organization and to set the quota for apprentices.[21]

The most taxing aspect of compliance was not the financial contributions but the recruitment of apprentices. According to SENAI's guidelines, Light had to hire and enroll in SENAI approximately ninety apprentices—a number equal to 5 percent of its total skilled workforce. SENAI policy on recruitment had two potentially contradictory features: it required the enterprise to pretest candidates for admission to SENAI and to give preference to the children, orphans, and siblings of the firm's employees. With regard to testing, Light responded in a way that SENAI would have considered ideal: the head of personnel not only embraced this practice but also seized the opportunity to expand testing to all potential employees, examining them for educational level, manual ability, and "moral character."[22]

As for the policy of favoring (qualified) relatives for entrance into SENAI courses, Light initially depended almost entirely on recruitment among the sons and brothers of existing workers to fill its quota. Despite having thousands of workers to draw on, the company found it difficult to locate employees who had relatives of the proper age (fourteen to fifteen years), with the required level of schooling, who wanted to study in SENAI. Finding candidates proved particularly difficult in the interior, where the workforce was smaller and the educational level lower. For example, in 1944 the Light plant in Jundiaí had only three minors in its employ, one of whom was about to turn eighteen. The other two, meanwhile, were uninterested in SENAI since they were already enrolled in a local commercial school. Only one employee had a son of the correct age; as for local youths unrelated to Light employees, management claimed that "the majority are already taking courses in the said SENAI school." Although this last assertion seems questionable, it is clear that the local personnel department was having a hard time finding potential apprentices, especially once the kinship networks failed to yield a sufficient number of appropriate candidates.[23]

Even in the capital, after several years of participation in SENAI, Light struggled to meet its quota. The head of personnel claimed that Light had tested 149 minors for apprenticeship positions in 1945, but only 106 passed the initial examination. Meanwhile, 34 of those who passed the test decided not to enroll in SENAI, and another 24 quit their jobs with Light soon after being admitted. As a result, Light, despite its good intentions, enrolled only 48 new apprentices in the SENAI program that year. Furthermore, the personnel department found that its ability to determine the craft selected by its apprentices was limited. By 1945, Light had apprentices enrolled in four areas: mechanics, electrical work, carpentry, and adjustment. But the number of apprentices enrolled in each area was by no means an accurate reflection of Light's internal job distribution. By 1948, Light had 218 youths studying to be lathe operators, but it employed only 221 adult workers with this skill. Sixty-two Light employees were apprentice electricians, as compared to 494 adult electricians. And only 15 minors had enrolled in courses to learn carpentry or adjustment, despite the fact that the number of adults practicing these skills at Light totaled 740.

Indeed, SENAI simply could not meet the demand for the lathe operator courses; at one point, the local SENAI school informed Light that it only had openings for students in its carpentry courses. When the firm responded that none of its apprentices had any interest in acquiring that trade, Mange reluctantly reduced Light's quota until SENAI could accommodate the existing demand. Subsequently, the director of the SENAI school and the Light personnel office attempted to rationalize the distribution of apprentices, setting target numbers for each skill, but such efforts met with continual frustration as a result of strong student preferences.[24]

Early on in Light's experience with SENAI, the issue arose of who would be responsible for justifying an apprentice's absence from class. In most school settings, it would be the parents' role to do so, but a Light official argued that the spirit of the law creating SENAI gave the employer-apprentice relationship a "paternal character"; therefore, the Light personnel department, not the apprentice's family, should oversee his progress and monitor his performance. This created a sort of "double jeopardy" for the SENAI apprentice since incompetent classroom performance or inappropriate behavior could cost him not only scholastic advancement but also his job. Whereas parents rarely sever their relationship with their offspring if they do poorly in school, Light—as current and perhaps future employer—was quite prepared to do so.[25]

Light did exhibit a certain "parental" pride when its apprentices placed first in the SENAI exams or boasted a 100 percent promotion rate to the next year of training. The personnel department, in particular, cited such early successes as proof of the efficacy of its testing and selection methods. But Light could be a stern guardian when apprentices—who were, after all, adolescent boys—violated the norms of "proper" behavior. The most common infraction was excessive absences from class or work. Light quickly established a policy of issuing warnings, followed by dismissals, if the apprentice did not improve. More serious acts of indiscipline also occurred, many of them at work. For example, Light briefly suspended nine apprentices for turning on an expensive machine, breaking a spare part, and playing with fire hydrants. Another apprentice, who manifested "lack of discipline and disrespect to the foremen," suffered a two-day suspension without pay. And in the most extreme case, the police detained a Light apprentice for stabbing a fellow SENAI student.[26]

Poor performance or indiscipline among SENAI apprentices could be particularly trying when the son of a long-term and trusted employee was involved. One SENAI student suspended for ten days "for an attempted act of aggression against his instructor" turned out to be the son of a Light employee. The case of the Zinneck brothers, whose father was head foreman at a power plant (Usina Isabel) in the interior, serves as another example. Delighted to find an employee with several sons of the right age to enroll in SENAI, the personnel department convinced the foreman to send the older boys, Alfredo and Rodolfo, to the SENAI boarding school in Taubaté. The school director, however, soon expelled Alfredo for indiscipline—which, in turn, meant that Light had to fire him from his apprenticeship post. Alfredo's place was taken by his brother Darwin, who initially appeared to be a considerable improvement over his older sibling, placing first among forty-one students in his year. But within a year, Light began receiving reports that both Darwin and Rodolfo were cutting afternoon classes. Moreover, the personnel supervisor for the interior claimed that the SENAI apprentices doing office work in Jundiaí, Mogi das Cruzes, and especially Taubaté "do not have a disposition to work" and created a disruptive presence. Out of consideration for the Zinneck brothers' father, Light held off dismissing them and informed the father of their bad behavior and "ill will." But Rodolfo persisted in his absences, leading to his dismissal despite the fact that, in terms of course work, he had placed first in his class at the beginning of the fourth year. The only one of the three brothers who may have completed the SENAI course was Darwin, and even he had hardly compiled a stellar record with regard to "moral character."[27]

Although the Zinneck brothers may have proven especially problematic, theirs was not an isolated experience. After only a few years of participation in SENAI programs, the Light personnel office acknowledged that the firm's apprentices exhibited a general decline in both classroom performance and discipline, especially during the last two years of instruction. Upon inquiry, a school director suggested that this decline could be attributed to the fact that Light apprentices did not perform tasks in their place of work that had any relationship to the skills they were learning at SENAI. High-level Light officials accepted this explanation and immediately contacted the managers of various plants, urging them to employ the apprentices "in the functions of this agency that pertain to the training that they are doing." At least one manager replied that the apprentices could not be usefully employed in his workshop and would have to continue performing office work. Indeed, it is understandable that a supervisor of a shop with expensive machinery and much potential for accidents would be reluctant to take on apprentices who had earned a reputation for indiscipline.[28]

This brief period of disappointment over the apprentices' performance moved Light to create a more elaborate system for monitoring student progress, with accompanying rewards and penalties. By the end of 1948, Light had begun classifying its apprentices at the close of each semester as either excellent, good, average, or poor. The company began automatically firing any apprentices who failed to be promoted to the next year of studies while granting small wage increases to those apprentices who achieved high rankings. Perhaps most effective, with the certification of Light's first class of SENAI students, the firm established a policy of rehiring only those graduates who had demonstrated good classroom performance and conduct and rejecting those who had proved unsatisfactory. Moreover, their wages at entry would reflect how they performed as apprentices. In the words of one divisional superintendent, "We believe that the promotion of the good elements and the dismissal of those not up to standards will help to stimulate the effort of these future craftsmen."[29] And the head of Light's legal department approved the classification/wage-increase policy "because it will serve as an incentive to the apprentice, who will begin to work with more interest and will develop a greater sense of responsibility since his efforts are being compensated."[30]

This system of reward and punishment seems to have achieved its purpose since subsequent classes of Light apprentices showed higher rates of promotion and lower rates of indiscipline. Light began "rehiring" larger numbers of its SENAI graduates, usually rejecting only those whose grades were among the lowest in their class. Outstanding class work, however, did not compensate for a bad attitude. According to a Light memorandum, one SENAI graduate, though "one of the best of our apprentices throughout the entire course, will not be hired due to his behavior, which has left much to be desired."[31] The implementation of the new policy also hit a few rough spots. Upon learning of his dismissal for failing to be advanced to the second year of training, one apprentice complained to the hydroelectric workers' union. He and other apprentices, with the support of their fathers, caused enough of a fuss that Light eventually had to modify its policy and allow for extenuating circumstances. And one SENAI graduate who had not been rehired by the company immediately filed a grievance with the local labor tribunal.[32]

Such actions and the assorted tales of indiscipline among Light's apprentices demonstrate that the socialization involved in the SENAI experience yielded mixed results. There were, to be sure, model apprentices like young Claudio Mallada, who, having received a letter of congratulations from the superintendent of Light for placing third in his class, wrote back that "words of praise from your excellency for a modest apprentice-worker like myself have an immense value since they will serve as a great incentive for me."[33] And management must have been pleased when its apprentices published a piece in the union paper entitled "Exaltation of Work." The closing paragraph, presumably composed by the apprentices, was particularly illustrative of SENAI's ideological efforts: "Always keep in mind: it is your effort that will make you triumph. However, it is only from harmonious relations between employees and employers that we can have true social peace, the indispensable precondition for the order and progress of our nation."[34]

SENAI could not boast of a perfect track record in instilling a sense of "duty" and employer loyalty in its students, but it did offer Light and other employers a means to winnow out undesirable or incompetent workers and to identify promising candidates for positions requiring some skill and responsibility. Judging from the jobs in which Light generally placed SENAI graduates, the firm valued SENAI training as much for its socializing and "winnowing" function as for the actual technical skills the apprentices acquired. Despite SENAI officials' claims that their organization produced "ready-made" workers, no Light apprentice, upon certification, ever assumed a position as a full-fledged practitioner of his craft. Light openly described SENAI's electrician courses as "elementary instruction"; graduation from the program merely made the apprentice eligible for Light's internal course for electricians. Graduates from the other courses were consistently rehired as *ajudantes* (helpers) to craftsmen. Only by observing and assisting a skilled worker and absorbing his practical knowledge could the SENAI graduate become eligible for promotion to fully skilled status. In other words, at least in Light's case, SENAI had not managed to eliminate the face-to-face, empirical training Mange deplored. It merely added another layer and at best compressed the process of shopfloor training by improving the apprentices' educational level and technical background.[35]

Light's practices cannot be generalized to all of paulista industry. Smaller firms (that is, all other urban employers in São Paulo), with fewer skilled workers, more precarious finances, and less demanding managers, may have hired SENAI graduates, fresh out of the classroom, as craftsmen. But even SENAI officials acknowledged that older, more experienced workers objected to an eighteen-year-old "kid" assuming a position of status and responsibility on the factory floor and often insisted that the SENAI graduate gain experience as an *ajudante* prior to promotion. Moreover, the employer had reason to sympathize with workers' sentiments in this regard since he could pay the *ajudante* lower wages while expecting similar output.[36] In this respect, SENAI's ideal scenario for its graduates, once again, had to undergo modification in response to employer interests and shopfloor conventions.

Despite Light's initial token resistance to participation in SENAI, occasional criticisms, and difficulties in filling its quota of apprentices, the firm regarded SENAI as a useful and practical initiative. Light regularly enrolled hundreds of apprentices—the equivalent of the workforce of a substantial, medium-sized factory—in SENAI courses and faithfully made its monthly contributions. Indeed, in 1944, when SENAI changed its levy from a fixed amount per worker to 1 percent of the monthly payroll, Light made no objection even though the new system tripled its monthly obligation from 21,863.60 cruzeiros in November 1943 to 63,143.20 cruzeiros in January 1944. Similarly, when SENAI increased the ratio it used for determining the expected number of Light apprentices (and those in all metallurgical industries) from 5 to 10 percent, the firm accepted the new quota without protest.[37]

How typical such responses were is hard to say since SENAI did not keep careful records of the percentage of firms making their contributions and sending apprentices to SENAI (or if it did, it never made them public). One source for gauging employer responsiveness to SENAI is a 1951 study carried out by the national office to explain the high dropout rate among SENAI apprentices. The data from São Paulo revealed that nearly 10 percent of the ex-students cited "difficulties stemming from the work environment"—that is, pressure from their employer or supervisor—as their motive for dropping out. Usually, the employer wanted the apprentice to work full-time and threatened dismissal if the student did not terminate his studies. One ex-student who lived with his family in company housing poignantly explained that his foreman "insisted on my dropping out of school, under penalty of dismissal, which would have meant that I and my entire family would have had to move out of the house where I live." In other cases, employers offered wage increases on the condition that apprentices withdraw from SENAI. In one instance, confirmed by the researchers, an employer actually tripled an ex-student's salary for dropping out.[38]

The investigators had no choice but to conclude that a significant number of employers and supervisors saw little or no value in SENAI training. Moreover, their additional research on employer attitudes offered small comfort in this regard. Of the 558 firms surveyed in São Paulo, only 134 (24 percent) indicated that they employed SENAI apprentices. One hundred seventy-nine firms (32 percent) responded negatively, and another 245 (44 percent) claimed not to know whether the firm employed apprentices studying in SENAI. The report did what it could to present these statistics in a more favorable light, noting the more cheering results obtained if one disaggregated the data by industry. Whereas the statistics for employment of SENAI apprentices in São Paulo's construction and food-processing industries were low, half of the firms surveyed in the metallurgical, textile, and printing industries—precisely the sectors targeted by SENAI–São Paulo—responded affirmatively to the question about employing SENAI students.[39] Furthermore, the researchers could cite with pride the high level of satisfaction expressed by the 134 paulista firms that reported employing SENAI students. One hundred seven firms (80 percent) claimed to have a "good impression" of the apprentices' job performance, while 24 (18 percent) described their performance as "satisfactory," and only 3 firms registered a "bad impression."[40]

Nonetheless, the researchers admitted that "the majority of employers . . . continue to be uninformed about professional training, not even being conscious of the apprenticeship arrangements in their own industrial establishments and lacking awareness of this issue. . . . This lack of awareness is congruent with the nation's economic formation and with the Brazilian national identity and, thus, with the conditions of our industry shaped, in large part, around the employment of unskilled, low-quality labor."[41] Rather than consider the possibility that SENAI-type training had little utility for many of the industries in question, either due to a lack of appropriate courses or the sector's limited skill requirements, the SENAI officials issued a lament reminiscent of statements made by IDORT directors in the 1930s. Despite the efforts of an "enlightened" industrialist vanguard and its technical advisers in SENAI and SESI, the researchers regretfully acknowledged, many employers remained oblivious to the issue of vocational training and uninterested in programs that served to advance industrial productivity.

Employer Reception of SESI

SESI's reception among paulista industrialists was bound to be more complicated than that of SENAI given SESI's openly ideological character, broader preoccupations, and more varied programs, not to mention a monthly contribution that was twice as large as the one due SENAI.

Funeral procession for Morvan Dias de Figueiredo, 1950, in front of SENAI's
Escola Roberto Simonsen. Courtesy of the Núcleo de Memória, SENAI–
São Paulo.

Moreover, whereas SENAI could point to concrete accomplishments—a
tangible increase in the supply of skilled workers—as evidence of its value
for the industrial economy, SESI's successes and accomplishments were
likely to be much more intangible and thus debatable. In its defense, the
founders of SESI could argue that there was a widespread perception
among industrialists in the immediate postwar years that more vigorous
and coordinated efforts were required to combat "extremism" among the
workers and to increase productivity. But employers had reached little consensus about the shape such efforts should take. As we have seen, some serious dissent had been voiced within SESI's own regional council about the
direction of the new organization.[42]

SESI gained considerable prestige and credibility among employers
from its close identification with the two most prominent industrial
spokesmen in São Paulo—Roberto Simonsen and Morvan Dias de Figueiredo. But Simonsen would only live long enough to witness the first two
years of SESI's operations; he died of a heart attack while delivering an

address to the Brazilian Academy of Letters in May 1948. And Morvan, who resigned in 1948 from the Ministry of Labor because of ill health, died less than two years later. Thus, in quick succession, SESI lost its two most important patrons.

With few exceptions, SESI's councillors and top officials regarded themselves as champions of Roberto Simonsen's approach to "social peace." In its biographies of such figures as Mariano Ferraz, Rodolpho Ortenblad, and Antônio Rodrigues de Azevedo (SESI's first superintendent and Simonsen's cousin), *SESI-Jornal* described these men as members of the "team assembled" by Simonsen since his days with the Companhia Construtora de Santos. They considered themselves, due to their experience, education, and "progressive" views, to be uniquely situated to shepherd Brazilian industry through the thickets of social tension and class conflict clogging the path to rapid industrial growth. They could not, however, ignore industrialist opinion on the workings of SESI since they depended upon employer goodwill for the punctual contributions that made its operations possible. They could turn, as a last resort, to state coercion, but it had been Simonsen's wish that industrialists "willingly" support SESI, both ideologically and financially.[43]

Thus industrialist opinion was a frequent agenda item at the meetings of SESI's regional council. Significantly, the councillor who most often raised the matter was Manoel da Costa Santos, an "outsider" from Sorocaba who frequently criticized SESI policy, especially its relative neglect of the interior. Costa Santos was particularly insistent upon the need for careful surveys of industrialist attitudes and suggestions regarding SESI and proposed the organization of roundtable discussions in which employers could air their views and grievances.[44] As early as October 1947, SESI's Division for Social Orientation presented statistics gathered by its social educators showing that 85 percent of the firms visited affirmed their "complete support" for SESI, while only 6 percent were skeptical, and 1.5 percent were negative. Moreover, SESI director Rodrigues de Azevedo claimed that sixty-five firms initially hostile to SESI had become enthusiastic as a result of factory visits.[45] Such figures may have cheered the council members, but even SESI's supporters regarded the survey as unscientific, yielding highly questionable results.[46]

SESI tried again in 1950, surveying 5,915 industrial employers in the capital and its industrial suburbs. The published results showed that nearly 40 percent of employers supported SESI "with enthusiasm," while 31 percent simply supported it, and another 12 percent were hostile or indifferent.[47] For public relations purposes, SESI and FIESP could highlight the finding that some two-fifths of industrial employers were enthusiastic about the social service agency. But in private they had to acknowledge that a clear majority of industrialists, if they contributed to SESI at all, probably did so because they had to.

Indeed, during the first decade of SESI's existence, a major concern of its regional council was the failure of firms to make any contributions whatsoever to the new organization. And it must have been particularly distressing for the council members to learn that many of the intransigent firms were among the oldest and most prestigious industrial enterprises in São Paulo. SESI's champions could take some consolation in the knowledge that few firms framed their refusal to contribute in ideological terms. Several firms explicitly endorsed SESI's mission even though they withheld their stipulated contributions. How, then, do we explain their lack of cooperation? Their objections mainly stemmed from two concerns. Most common was the argument by a firm that it already offered sufficient services to its workers, making SESI's facilities and programs superfluous and the contribution an unwarranted burden. In addition, employers in the interior frequently claimed that the concentration of SESI activities in the capital and its suburbs meant that their workers had little access to its facilities.[48]

The firm that most doggedly insisted that it had no need for SESI was the Companhia Nitro-Química, a chemical company with thousands of workers located in the industrial suburb of São Miguel. Part of the huge complex eventually known as the Indústrias Votorantim and overseen by the self-styled progressive industrialist, José Ermírio de Moraes, Nitro-Química originally met its financial obligations to SESI. However, it argued that its facilities—which included a *vila operária*, free medical assistance and inexpensive dental care for workers and their families, a resident social worker, a recreational club, literacy courses, and a SENAI school—allowed it to dispense with SESI services. The first social educator to visit Nitro-Química did conclude that the firm was "carrying out all of the immense program that the Serviço Social da Indústria has proposed" and recommended that SESI either take over the operation of the company's services or grant it an almost total subvention.[49]

A higher-ranking SESI official revised the social educator's conclusions, noting that Nitro-Química fulfilled "*almost* all of SESI's objectives. . . . SESI also carries out a social policy and a program of social orientation that transcend the private activities of a particular firm, and thus that firm cannot implement the entire mission attributed to SESI."[50] The latter comment gets at the heart of the dispute between SESI and Nitro-Química (and many other firms that withheld payment). SESI early on realized that it would have to make some concessions to firms that already offered many of the services it was providing; indeed, the organization could use the possibility of a partial subvention as an inducement for a firm to improve internal conditions.[51] But SESI assumed that no subvention should amount to more than 50 percent of the monthly payment since SESI organized a broad range of social and cultural activities directed at the entire working-class community that could not be replicated in the services offered by a single company.

Nitro-Química's objections did not amount to an explicit ideological rejection of SESI, but they do reveal a different perspective on the proper means to maintain social peace. José Ermírio, along with the owners of such traditional industrial enterprises as São Paulo Alpargatas, the Cotonifício Rodolfo Crespi, and the Vidraria Santa Marina, apparently felt that services and assistance offered by management directly to the workers, in the conventional welfare capitalist mode, were more effective in promoting social peace than the programs developed by SESI. Such a view also indicates that the recalcitrant factory owners believed they were better off concentrating on improving relations with their own workers rather than cultivating good relations with the larger working-class community.[52]

By contrast, SESI officials and the industrialists most closely associated with SESI's operations positioned their organization as a healthy alternative to paternalistic welfare schemes, which it portrayed as antiquated, nonscientific, and even demeaning to workers. One official, upon returning from a SESI-sponsored visit to the United States, announced that paternalism had become a dirty word to organized labor in that country. The North American workers saw paternalism as "protection originating directly and personally from the employer," a definition that absolved SESI and its services of the taint of paternalism, at least in theory.[53] Another SESI official described the two main threats to the organization as paternalism, on the one hand, and "statization" on the other—leaving SESI a rather narrow discursive space to occupy.[54]

SESI took the challenge from Nitro-Química seriously enough to send its most prominent functionary, Geraldo de Paula Souza, to conduct personally the evaluation of the firm's services. It even formed a special advisory committee, whose members included Roberto Mange and A. F. Cesarino Júnior, to decide the matter.[55] Ultimately, the committee upheld the notion that firms should be granted only partial subventions, and then only if they accepted SESI's orientation in the implementation of services and made services available to people other than their own workforce. In the specific case of Nitro-Química, SESI offered the maximum subvention of 50 percent, but the firm regarded this amount as inadequate and flatly refused to make any further contributions. To SESI's embarrassment, Nitro-

Química then began criticizing the quality of SESI services, citing delays and ill treatment of its workers at the medical clinic in Ipiranga and accusing SESI of causing the death of an employee whose ulcer perforated while he was awaiting hospitalization.[56]

Whereas few firms directly challenged the legitimacy or efficacy of the SESI project, several employers had excellent reasons to doubt whether a new array of social and educational services would advance the cause of social peace. The report of the social educator who visited Sorocaba's Companhia Nacional de Estamparia in 1948 reveals the confusion SESI personnel experienced in evaluating a firm that provided excellent services but was plagued by worker unrest. After detailing the firm's many medical, residential, and educational facilities for workers, the SESI functionary turned to the subject of relations between labor and management: "As is common knowledge, Sorocaba is a center of Communist expansion, where innumerable general demonstrations of discontent have taken place." In a massive enterprise with over 8,000 employees, it was "easily admissible" that some workers would suffer from such influences. But the social educator immediately minimized their importance: "We perfectly understand, therefore, that even though there have been strikes in the 'Companhia Nacional de Estamparia' this does not signify aggression against the management, which seems to enjoy the esteem of its workers." In a blatant act of wishful thinking, the social educator concluded that the workers could not fail to recognize all that the firm had done for them.[57] Apparently, the management was not so optimistic.

The case of the Companhia Taubaté Industrial, a textile firm in the Paraíba Valley, must have been even more perplexing to SESI officials. Fellow industrialists remembered the recently deceased founder of the firm, Felix Guisard, as a pioneer in the introduction of services for workers; according to one biography, his innovations in this area "anticipated" subsequent labor legislation.[58] Yet a social educator who visited the plant in 1949 admitted that, despite the "romantic spirit" of its management, the workforce "is positively not sympathetic." The SESI functionary also recalled an attempt by CIESP a few years earlier to honor the firm for its social services, an idea that met with an odd reception from the founder's son and heir. Felix Guisard Filho declined the honor, noting that, despite all of his firm's efforts, the workers continued to be hostile to management: "In spite of the affection with which this company has treated this matter, it is with sincere regret, if not with extreme disappointment, that we are forced to inform you gentlemen that Taubaté's Communist cell is installed in our factory and among the workforce of this company, and its head is one of our employees."[59] It is hardly surprising, then, that the firm initially refused to make its contributions to SESI and even went so far as to offer funding instead to the local labor union—a move that especially enraged SESI's regional council.[60]

To be sure, a major consideration of firms that withheld payments was the amount of money involved. Guisard Filho noted that his company already spent a million cruzeiros a year on assistance to its workers. The additional SESI contribution, amounting to 300,000 cruzeiros annually, would undoubtedly raise the cost of production—the very opposite of SESI's intentions. Concern with costs was even more explicit in the case of São Paulo Light & Power. Light proved far more stubborn in its refusal to contribute to SESI than it had been in its objections to SENAI. Estimating its obligation to the new organization at nearly 11 million cruzeiros during the first year alone, Light resolved to avoid the payments by any means possible.

Light was very careful not to criticize or challenge SESI on ideological grounds. On the contrary, in its correspondence on the matter with the minister of labor, Octacílio Negrão de Lima, Light freely praised the SESI project: "At the outset, we wish to add our applause to an idea that translates into a real increase in salary, allowing a better standard of living for our working classes. . . . The creation of a fund that seeks to contribute, in a direct manner, to the resolution of problems such as nutrition, housing, health, and education is sure to be received with goodwill and the desire for cooperation on the part of the employers, conscious of their obligations in this delicate phase of our national life."[61] Undaunted by the latter declaration, the Light representative went on to argue that utility and transport enterprises should not be included in SESI's domain due to their distinctive character. And, of course, he mentioned that such enterprises generally provided their own services that they would be forced to close down if SESI insisted upon payment.

The Light management apparently hoped it would find some legal loophole that would allow it to avoid paying SESI. It watched anxiously as members of congress challenged the legality of the government-created autarchies, only to see the campaign go down in defeat. Light continually pressed the issue of the exemption of utilities from the SESI contribution. When SESI and the government countered such arguments, the firm retreated to the traditional position of employers opposed to costly legislation: it simply refused to meet its obligations.[62]

Light realized that such a position was morally questionable, especially for a foreign-owned and highly visible firm. Not surprisingly, its director of public relations was the official who argued most strongly in favor of a settlement with SESI. His internal memorandum on the matter noted that

SESI "has been undergoing tremendous growth in São Paulo since its management is in the hands of persons who direct it with efficiency and in an apolitical manner. Its development is already substantial, with nearly 100 discount food posts, as well as medical clinics, community kitchens, and schools for social workers." And its formal communication to the government presenting its rationale for nonpayment actually ended by declaring that Light "also cannot fail to give its entire support and collaboration to the task that SESI proposes to undertake."[63] But the money Light saved by adopting this tactic of refusal apparently outweighed any public relations concerns.

Finally, in a few cases, firms withheld payment due to resentment over SESI's intervention in relations between labor and management, despite the organization's tendency to err in favor of the employer. The Cotonifício Guilherme Giorgi twice wrote to Eduardo Gabriel Saad complaining about SESI functionaries who appeared to be siding with workers against management or providing retroactive medical justifications for absences from work.[64] And it would be interesting to know the responses of the companies involved in certain cases that were mediated by SESI's legal service and proudly described by the organization's internal newspaper. A firm referred to only as "CML" (possibly Companhia Minerva Lanifício, a long-time holdout) could not have been too pleased with SESI when a worker it attempted to fire proved with the help of a SESI lawyer that he had a right to job tenure.[65] Still, few employers criticized SESI for overzealousness on the workers' behalf; apparently, most SESI functionaries were careful not to overstep the bounds imposed by the organization's mandate.[66]

SESI employed a variety of methods to improve its relations with industrialists and to solicit contributions from those employers who were persistently delinquent in their payments. Aside from factory visits by social educators, prominent FIESP officials and members of SESI's regional council penned personal notes to industrialists seeking their cooperation. Even after the deaths of Simonsen and Morvan, SESI benefited from the "activism" of such eminent figures in political and industrial circles as Antônio Devisate and Armando de Arruda Pereira, the latter of whom would soon be appointed mayor of São Paulo. SESI also concentrated on familiarizing industrialists with its operations and involving them in its programs. Between 1947 and 1951, social educators arranged visits to SESI facilities for 332 employers located in the capital and invited them to participate in innumerable SESI functions.[67] Leading industrialists—including those who refused to make their stipulated payments—found themselves bombarded by a steady stream of invitations to such events as banquets for foreign dignitaries at the district kitchens, inaugurations of social centers, New Year's Eve galas, and May Day athletic competitions. In its efforts to germinate enthusiasm among employers, SESI also took a leaf from SENAI's book: from the outset, the training organization had invited representatives from the relevant industries to preside over graduation ceremonies, thus giving employers a more intimate connection with SENAI's graduates. Since SESI offered hundreds of courses, ranging from literacy classes to sewing instruction, it could also organize a multitude of graduation ceremonies and invite local employers to officiate. This served the double purpose of reinforcing the employer's personal identification with SESI and strengthening the worker's identification of SESI benefits with the industrialists.[68]

Although SESI's regional council greatly preferred persuasion to other tactics in securing employers' support, it reluctantly recognized that measures beyond personal appeals and public relations might be necessary, especially considering what was at stake financially. During the first year of SESI's existence, Light calculated the amount it theoretically owed the organization to be nearly 11 million cruzeiros—at a time when the entire operating budget of SESI–São Paulo was a mere 15 million cruzeiros.[69] The members of the council seem to have found it particularly annoying when large, foreign-owned companies refused to cooperate, as was the case with Johnson & Johnson, which opened its first pharmaceuticals plant in São Paulo in 1937. The North American firm replied to the initial request for payment from IAPI by claiming that it was "exempt due to being a private entity."[70] SESI immediately sent a social educator to explain the situation; at this meeting, Johnson & Johnson pleaded ignorance, claiming that the management did not know the SESI payment was obligatory and giving the SESI representative the impression that the firm would henceforth pay its SESI contributions promptly. But a year later, Johnson & Johnson had yet to make any payments to SESI, inciting the wrath of several regional councillors. Devisate, in a rare display of anger, argued that "SESI's attitude of tolerance toward industries delinquent in the collection of their contributions cannot continue." Costa Santos echoed his remarks, insisting that "in no way can we justify SESI's tolerance, especially toward powerful industries, when it is certain that very small firms, most of them struggling with enormous difficulties, are fulfilling their obligations."[71]

Once other means to secure payment had been exhausted, SESI turned to the government agencies to initiate judicial proceedings against the delinquent employers. Even this step, however, did not automatically resolve matters, especially in the case of a large company whose legal staff could delay a court injunction indefinitely. For example, Light managed to defer its contributions to SESI until the mid-1950s. But in most instances, the combination of personal pleas from SESI, peer pressure from other employers, and intermittent judicial harassment eventually softened the delinquent firm's resistance. In addition, SESI developed a standard policy of granting subventions and forgiving a major portion of a company's past debt if the firm would commit to making future payments. By December 1959, SESI had formulated 423 such agreements with delinquent companies, often at considerable cost to the organization. For example, SESI forgave half of the 19 million–cruzeiro debt owed by São Paulo Alpargatas and also conceded a 50 percent subvention to the firm, even though the services it offered by no means justified exempting such a large percentage of the payment. SESI officials apparently regarded half a debt as better than none and recognized the publicity value of receiving contributions from companies long identified as holdouts.[72]

As with SENAI, the prompt payment of the monthly contributions was not all that SESI expected from employers. The organization also wanted employers to solicit its services: to buy meals from SESI's district kitchens, to welcome lectures by its social educators, and to offer facilities for the various SESI courses at their factories. In addition, SESI urged firms to participate in its May Day festivities and other annual social events. Generally, employers proved responsive to SESI's offers of services and courses, in part because they cost the firms little in the way of time and effort and had the potential to earn them considerable goodwill among a portion of their workforce. Especially well received by employers were the literacy courses; by 1949, these *cursos populares* were being offered in over 100 factories throughout São Paulo, with an enrollment of 4,249 students.[73]

It is interesting to note that nonpayment of the SESI contribution was no obstacle to using SESI services and participating in the organization's activities. The most striking example of this involved the Cotonifício Guilherme Giorgi, which had built up a debt of over 2 million cruzeiros to SESI by the late 1950s. Yet in 1958 the textile firm boasted that it housed literacy and sewing courses organized and staffed by SESI personnel, had monthly screenings of films provided by SESI, and offered dental care to its workers and their families through a SESI accord. Most of the firm's 3,000 employees had enrolled in a nearby SESI discount food post, and its foremen received training in a SESI Course for Supervision of Personnel in Industry (Curso de Supervisão do Pessoal na Indústria, or CSPI). Moreover, the Cotonifício Guilherme Giorgi was a faithful participant in SESI's annual May Day parades. Similarly, the Companhia Taubaté Industrial, one of the fiercest holdouts, nonetheless turned its consumer co-op into a SESI food post and housed a SESI literacy course with ninety-three students.

Far from denying its services to enterprises that withheld contributions, SESI actively offered them as a means to convince recalcitrant firms that it was worth their while to make the payments. Light found itself in an awkward situation as hundreds of its workers enrolled in SESI food posts and sought company certification of their status as *industriários*. Athletic teams from various Light subsidiaries also began participating in the May Day Workers' Olympics. In 1950 the soccer team from the Cubatão power plant emerged as the champion in the Santos region, making it virtually obligatory for upper-level management to attend FIESP's award ceremonies. And Light's director of personnel certainly had to attend the "First Marathon on Labor Legislation" in 1954 since three of the firm's employees, designated by the hydroelectrical workers' union, were participating. A year later, Light finally settled its accounts with the social service organization.[74]

The number of firms that utilized SESI services directly is impossible to determine since the organization only recorded aggregate data with respect to the number of students in its courses or patients assisted in its clinics. Given that a firm merely had to provide physical space to accommodate a SESI course, it seems likely that a significant number of medium-sized and large factories sponsored literacy or sewing instruction or one of the more ideological courses organized by DOS. Even Light, which employed virtually no women among its production workers, requested a SESI sewing course for the wives and daughters of its workers in the Itupararanga power plant. The Light personnel chief expected the course not only to provide a useful domestic skill but also to encourage "the strengthening of social relations among the functionaries' families."[75]

At the same time, few industrialists seem to have embraced SESI with the enthusiasm and commitment that characterized its founders. Despite SESI's direct appeals and constant positive publicity from FIESP and the State Department of Labor, many employers remained indifferent to the new organization and unresponsive to pressure from the industrialist leadership for participation and contributions. It seems significant that FIESP, in its many articles extolling the achievements of SESI, constantly invoked the name and spirit of Roberto Simonsen, even many years after his death. Although this can be interpreted as testimony to his enduring influence, it also indicates that no one had emerged from the industrialists' ranks with the same degree of prestige and authority as SESI's patron saint.

Perhaps due in part to the fact that relatively ineffectual figures replaced Simonsen, SESI proved largely unsuccessful in "disciplining" the industrialist class. Implicit in SESI's project was its intention to persuade factory owners to adhere to existing labor legislation and to offer welfare services at their firms above and beyond what was stipulated by law. However, in practice, the SESI leadership emitted mixed signals on the matter of labor legislation since employers quickly discovered, during Morvan's tenure as minister of labor, that they could commit violations with virtual impunity. And many factory owners came to regard their participation in SESI programs as a substitute for providing the type of services certain larger firms routinely offered their workers during the 1920s and 1930s. In these matters, as well, the FIESP/SESI leadership provided something less than consistent inspiration to its fellow industrialists. For example, Teobaldo de Nigris, owner of a medium-sized printing firm and a prominent figure in FIESP and SESI during the 1960s, came under repeated attack by the printers' union for his failure to provide a lunchroom for his employees. In his own defense, Nigris claimed that the law required such facilities only in firms with over 300 workers, whereas his workforce fluctuated between 260 and 270, an explanation that prompted the union to accuse him of deliberately firing employees in order to remain below the limit.[76] Whether or not there was any truth to this last allegation, other employers could reasonably conclude from this incident that even members of SESI's own regional council were making merely halfhearted efforts to insure social peace.

SENAI and SESI: The View from Organized Labor

In the closing pages of his *História das Lutas Sociais no Brasil*, published in 1962, former printer and longtime socialist Everardo Dias tossed a bouquet to the Brazilian industrialists:

> We cannot fail to recognize that a new consciousness has formed in our nation. National industry, its principal leaders, today think in a way that is diametrically opposed to the thinking of captains of industry, commerce, and finance in 1905/6, in 1910/12, in 1917, in 1924, in 1927, and even in 1930. . . . This can be observed not only in the treatment of the workforce . . . but also in the provision of means for [workers'] subsistence.
>
> There exists a form of social comprehension that has come to be known as "human" or "public relations" and that is undeniably one of the collateral conquests of socialism. . . . No, today it is understood that the worker must be technically trained, adept, capable, encouraged, and inspired to be a good producer, a competent operative. Thus, there are specialized, theoretical, and practical courses—

technical schools such as those of SENAC [the National Service for Commercial Training (Serviço Nacional de Aprendizagem Comercial)] and SENAI—that are truly massive enterprises that would be fitting for the state to oversee but that were organized, paradoxically, by the leaders of industry and commerce. This should have been the culminating idea, concept, endeavor of the labor government of Getúlio Vargas, and instead it became the idea and project of an enlightened, advanced, progressive, understanding, and very truly nationalist bourgeoisie.[77]

Such flattery from a prominent participant in Brazil's early labor struggles must have given the industrialist leadership considerable pleasure and affirmed its belief that employer-funded training and social programs would add luster to the industrialists' image. But by the time Dias wrote these lines, he had long ceased to have any active connection to the Brazilian labor movement or to the larger proletarian community. His views of the industrialists and their organizations could hardly be categorized as representative of working-class opinion.

Where, then, should we look to find more "authentic" working-class views of the industrialists' efforts to construct social peace? One much-used source is the labor or union press, but these newspapers present their own problems. Especially during the 1940s and 1950s, the tone and ideology of a union paper shifted drastically according to changes in that organization's leadership. During a period of *pelego* control, a union paper was likely to express conservative and class-collaborative views, whereas under a more autonomous directorate, it was likely to offer a more critical perspective. At the same time, the union newspapers were not party organs and published articles with wildly contrasting opinions. And we have limited means to determine which position in such debates found more resonance among the "rank and file." Indeed, it is always difficult to know whether the positions adopted by relatively politicized union leaders or activists have any relevance to the attitudes of the "average" worker.[78]

With these cautions in mind, it still seems most fruitful to discuss the reception of SENAI and SESI among paulista workers in the context of the labor unions. After all, the industrialists created SENAI and SESI specifically to increase productivity and promote social peace, and the unions would play crucial roles in advancing or obstructing both items on the industrialists' agenda. It also seems reasonable to assume that union leaders freely elected by the membership are somewhat more likely to reflect the views of the rank and file than union officials who are simply ministerial appointees. Of course, even more independent union leaders cannot be assumed to be speaking for the mass of the working class since the very position of leadership moves them to formulate criticisms of industrialist discourse and policy that may have only an oblique relevance to the day-to-day experiences of industrial workers. Consequently, we should not be at all surprised to find a labor leader denouncing SESI or SENAI even as hundreds of thousands of workers eagerly seek these organizations' services. This does not necessarily imply that union leaders were "out of touch" with their constituencies; rather, it indicates the predictably loose connection between political discourse and material practice. As one militant metalworker put it, he saw "no reason not to patronize" the SESI food posts if the prices were, indeed, lower than in other stores.[79] Few Brazilian workers could afford to refuse cheaper food or medical assistance, but that hardly signifies that they enthusiastically embraced SESI's ideological messages.

In exploring the responses of the labor movement to SENAI and SESI, it makes sense to cast our net as widely as possible and consider commentary not just on these specific institutions but also on the broader aspirations they professed. We need to examine labor's responses not only to the courses offered by SENAI but also to the goals of rationalization and increased productivity so intimately tied to SENAI's project. And in the case of SESI, it is particularly important to analyze labor's responses to the industrialists' calls for class collaboration and social peace, objectives explicitly identified as the organization's raison d'être.

The industrial labor force that these unions represented was rapidly expanding and changing during the 1940s and 1950s. With just over a half-million industrial workers by the end of the war, the state of São Paulo was both the biggest industrial producer in Brazil and the fastest-growing manufacturing center in all of Latin America. By 1951, SENAI–São Paulo recorded over 700,000 workers employed in the manufacturing and transport sectors, and by 1960, the industrial labor force in the state of São Paulo had topped the one million mark. At the same time, growth was by no means even across the industrial spectrum. Whereas the textile labor force virtually stagnated, growing by only 4,500 workers during the 1950s, the number of workers employed in the metallurgical sector doubled to approximately a quarter million, making it the single largest employer of industrial workers by the end of the decade.

The composition of the workforce—by skill level, gender, and age—also changed. By 1960, the percentage of textile operatives *classified* as skilled had dropped precipitously from 38 percent in 1950 to under 8 percent. In the metallurgical industry, the percentage of skilled workers also decreased, but only from 34 percent to 29 percent. The growing percentage of workers employed in that sector overall meant that the absolute number of skilled workers in industry continued to climb. Meanwhile, the percentage of women in the São Paulo workforce steadily declined as textile production lost ground to the metallurgical and related industries. Whereas women accounted for over 40 percent of industrial workers in São Paulo during World War II, by 1955, less than a quarter of the workforce was female. Among workers under eighteen, however, females continued to predominate; only in the late 1960s did the number of male minors in the workforce surpass the number of female minors. The proportion of minors in the workforce also declined, but only slightly, from 11 percent in 1953 to 10 percent in 1963.[80] This continued presence of minors in substantial numbers represents the main idiosyncrasy in the evolution of São Paulo's industrial workforce. Otherwise, the decline in the percentage of women workers and the growth of sectors with a higher proportion of skilled male workers replicated a familiar pattern of industrial development.

The 1950s and early 1960s also saw dramatic increases in the number of workers joining unions and participating in strike actions. During the early 1940s, only a minuscule portion of workers joined the unions in their category; even the relatively well-heeled São Paulo metallurgical workers' union could count a mere 5 percent of workers in that industry as formal members.[81] The relaxation of government controls on unions in the early 1950s, the return to open elections, and calls from President Vargas for workers to organize increased unions' membership rolls.[82] Successful strike actions such as the 1953 Strike of the 300,000 in São Paulo gave unions new meaning and greater credibility among the growing industrial labor force, composed mainly of recent migrants from the northeast or from the interior of São Paulo. Most workers still did not formally join the union representing their sector, but they were much more likely to be aware of union activities and to respond when unions called for walkouts or demonstrations. Although it would be misleading to claim that the union leadership embodied the views of the rank and file, the positions adopted by unions and expressed in the labor press became more widely disseminated and more sensitive to (and constitutive of) rank and file opinion by the latter half of the 1950s.

SENAI, Organized Labor, and National Development

The initial reception of SENAI by the labor unions, then operating under the tight controls of the Estado Novo, was a predictably warm one. Given the close collaboration of the government-sanctioned unions with the war effort, it is not surprising that several emergency courses organized by SENAI between 1942 and 1945 were offered in union headquarters. After the war, union officials played only a peripheral role in the new training organization, but several labor leaders did visit SENAI facilities and serve as observers when SENAI administered final exams to its students. In his 1947 report, Roberto Mange claimed that SENAI's relationship with industry was improving, and not just with regard to employers. "There has also been progress . . . in the way SENAI is considered within the core of industrial workers, with outstanding support coming from the labor unions, which thus contribute to broadening the interest of apprentices in the SENAI schools."[83] Mange noted that there was particular enthusiasm among union leaders for the "craft certification" (*carta de ofício*) earned by those SENAI students who passed the final battery of exams.

In its official monthly newspaper, the Union for Workers in the Metallurgical, Mechanical, and Electrical Material Industries of São Paulo (Sindicato dos Trabalhadores nas Indústrias Metalúrgicas, Mecânicas e de Material Elétrico de São Paulo, or STIMMMESP), controlled by "ministerialist" elements throughout the Dutra presidency, waxed euphoric over SENAI's programs. After a tour of SENAI facilities by some twenty-five directors and members of STIMMMESP, *O Metalúrgico* cheerfully noted that "the visitors, favorably impressed by what there was to see, did not mince words in expressing their admiration for this grandiose project that is being undertaken with regard to vocational instruction in our nation." The union officials placed particular emphasis on the "nationalist" aspects of SENAI's programs, contending that Brazilian workers in the past could only acquire skills in the metalworking industry at great personal sacrifice, leading employers, and even the government, to prefer foreign technicians and mechanics. In his speech at a SENAI graduation ceremony in 1948, STIMMMESP president Mário Sobral went so far as to claim that the creation of SENAI was a direct result of pressure exerted on the federal government by the labor unions themselves. And the union's secretary rhapsodically described SENAI as giving workers "the sweet hope of better days, the hope of [Brazil] becoming a genuine industrial power."[84]

Again, the heavy hand of state intervention and the relatively conservative union leadership in the late 1940s have to be kept in mind when evaluating such comments.[85] Yet the more independent and militant faction that took control of STIMMMESP following union elections in 1951 continued to hold SENAI in very high regard. The new secretary, Aldo Lombardi, wrote to the director of the SENAI school in Taubaté thanking him for the opportunity to observe the final exams for craft certification. According to Lombardi, SENAI "stimulates the student to be a worker, uniting and producing for the progress of Brazil."[86] The metallurgical

Members of the metallurgical workers' union visiting a metalworking section of SENAI's Escola Roberto Simonsen, 1951. Courtesy of the Núcleo de Memória, SENAI–São Paulo.

workers were hardly alone in their praise of SENAI. The textile workers' paper declared SENAI "an undertaking of truly great social and patriotic proportions" and described SENAI training as occurring in an "atmosphere of discipline, but healthy and cheerful."[87] Even *O Trabalhador Gráfico*, published by the relatively militant printers' union, foreshadowed Everardo Dias's remarks, praising "the services provided to the collectivity by this magnificent institution, the source of well-deserved pride for national industry."[88]

In the case of the metalworkers, support for SENAI and the depiction of SENAI as a nationalist enterprise were quite logical given the situation of the metallurgical industry. An official policy favoring national development with an emphasis on greater self-sufficiency promised to expand the metallurgical sector and increase employment opportunities for STIMMMESP's "category." Although SENAI could not meet all of the needs of the rapidly expanding sector, the training agency served as an example of Brazil's ability to provide appropriately skilled workers, adjust to new labor demands, and eschew its traditional dependence upon foreign

craftsmen and mechanics. And the many SENAI courses for the metallurgical industry reinforced its image as a highly skilled category.[89]

In an earlier period or in a different economic context, SENAI's active
promotion of standardization and parcelization of tasks in the metallurgical industry might have provoked furious objections among metalworkers.[90] Few Brazilian workers in this category, however, drew on the traditions of craft production that had characterized the metalworking trades in
Britain or the United States in the late nineteenth century. Even those
metalworkers who had specific skills experienced difficulty gaining recognition as craftsmen, and with the rapid expansion of the postwar years, the
metallurgical sector witnessed a massive influx of inexperienced workers
eager for any training that would allow them to rise above the minimum
wage.[91] To be sure, episodes of worker resistance to standardization on the
shopfloor occurred, but union leaders, juggling relations with the state,
employers, and a diverse category of workers, often welcomed changes in
the work process as guaranteeing more jobs and greater competitiveness.

To the textile workers' union, the appeal of SENAI was somewhat different. The union had long defended the integrity of the textile workers'
craft and the productivity of their category against manufacturers' attempts
to treat textile workers as, at best, semiskilled laborers easily replaced by
new recruits, most of them poorly paid women and minors. Thus, the existence of a variety of SENAI courses for training textile workers aided the
union leadership in its efforts to upgrade (and masculinize) the image of
the textile workforce and create a hierarchy of textile "professions" with
corresponding increases in salary. Also to the textile workers' advantage
was the provision of the law on training of minors that restricted payment
of half the minimum wage to those apprentices enrolled in SENAI or
SENAI-approved programs. Many textile manufacturers abused the half-
wage provision, but the union could cite the law to bolster its campaign
against the substitution of underpaid minors for experienced workers.[92] As
for SENAI's promotion of mechanization and rationalization—trends
that threatened to reduce the rate of employment in the textile industry—
the union did not yet perceive these processes as major threats in the early
1950s. On the contrary, O Trabalhador Têxtil occasionally took factory
owners to task for their inefficient production strategies and failure to replace outmoded equipment.[93]

The printers presented a third variation. Having a strong craft tradition,
they were more like the metalworkers than the textile workers, but unlike
the former, the printers no longer viewed rapid industrial development and
the attendant mechanization as strengthening their position as skilled
workers. Although the source of the menace had shifted from the linotype

Members of the textile workers' and textile supervisors' unions visiting a textile workshop in the SENAI school in Ipiranga, 1950. Courtesy of the Núcleo de Memória, SENAI–São Paulo.

machine to the computer, many printers regarded their trade as threatened by rationalization and technological innovation. It is not surprising, then, that the only sour notes with regard to SENAI and its mission were sounded by *O Trabalhador Gráfico*. The printers' paper criticized articles written by a SENAI instructor about their craft, and in response to SENAI's call for emergency courses to end the shortage of printers, the editors claimed that the scarcity of printers was not due to lack of training but rather to low salaries.[94]

Anxiety about the status of the printing profession, with its implicit criticism of new training methods, became even more apparent in the 1950s. In an article commemorating the thirtieth anniversary of the 1924 printers' strike, *O Trabalhador Gráfico* offered a balance sheet of the gains and losses of the Brazilian working class during the previous three decades, including an evaluation of the social impact of changes in the work process: "The great industrial boom, surging in the course of World War I and then taking on even greater proportions during World War II, with the accelerated introduction of machines and resultant assembly-line production, is rapidly making the specialized worker dispensable, easily replaced by new strata of workers, submitted to rapid training and therefore having no need for the extended apprenticeship that in the past served to help them identify with the traditions of their class. All these factors tend to subvert the professional and human structure of the working class."[95]

Although this particular article did not make a direct attack on SENAI, a subsequent piece on "professional classification" was much more explicit in its criticisms. It discussed the union's efforts to define desirable wage levels for different degrees of skill, a project that was especially important in light of employers' tendency to "constantly lower the level [of our craft], in both the technical-professional and the economic sense." The piece then offered more precise details:

> We can verify this with the concrete case of the linotype sector, undoubtedly the most advanced in terms of both consciousness and economic status within our category. Because of this, it is the sector that has received the greatest attention from the employer class, acting both individually and collectively, as with the ongoing "manufacture" of linotypists by SENAI on the collective plane of employer policy, or individually with the "little schools" that have proliferated in [print shops of] various newspapers with the sole aim of constantly reducing the level of this professional category, whether it be in terms of wages or its technical-professional capacity.[96]

Though without success, the printers' union did make some attempt to regulate the apprenticeship process for its craft.

The printers did not remain alone in their denunciations of mechanization and rationalization. By the late 1950s, *O Trabalhador Têxtil* also began publishing articles critical of "automation," including one that baldly stated that "the plan for rationalization of the work process has not yielded benefits to anyone."[97] But the printers' union maintained the most energetic campaign on this issue, led by a printer-turned-politician, José da Rocha Mendes Filho, who had been elected to the São Paulo state assembly in the late 1950s. Mendes Filho authored a series of articles that linked "automation" to unemployment, especially among skilled workers, whom he claimed were the first to be displaced by new machinery. Consequently, Mendes Filho argued, automation and rationalization depressed wages while promoting illnesses and accidents related to the intensification of the work regime. The former printer admitted that automation was still in an embryonic stage in Brazil but claimed that it was already having a significant impact on the graphic, textile, construction, and metallurgical industries.[98]

Given Mendes Filho's constant attention to the issue of mechanization, he must have been disappointed by the silence that greeted most of his pronouncements on this matter, even within the labor movement itself. His arguments, it turned out, were poor competition for the much stronger theme of national development that had been taken up by virtually every major union in the 1950s. Organized labor had not just responded to the nationalist appeals of populist politicians; union leaders were often in the vanguard of the movement for rapid industrial expansion. Acutely aware of Brazil's difficulties in competing with technically advanced foreign industries, and often critical of domestic employers for their failure to adopt the most up-to-date technology, labor leaders were unlikely to join a major campaign against automation per se.[99] In light of this, Mendes Filho had to circumscribe his critique, assuring his readers that "the worker is not opposed to progress or to science. On the contrary, without [the workers], science would have no resources and human progress would not be possible."[100]

Conceding the need for technological innovation, Mendes Filho retreated from his initial attack and argued for measures to mitigate the impact of rapid mechanization, including unemployment insurance, retraining facilities, a shorter workday, and job stability. This last measure—formally guaranteed by the Brazilian labor code to workers employed for ten years in the same firm—had been widely ignored or evaded by Brazilian factory owners. As a result, the enforcement of job tenure provisions became a major demand of the labor movement, whose leaders denied that "stable" workers were less productive or an impediment to industrial progress. In other words, organized labor's strong support for national development did not move it to accept uncritically the industrialist's view of what was necessary for economic progress.[101] Even STIMMMESP, by the late 1950s, adopted a more selective posture on technical progress, proposing that "the syndical and labor organizations approach the question of technical advances introduced into the production process, among them automation, in terms of their consequences for the standard of living, the physical state, and the social conditions of work for the laboring masses."[102] At the same time, the unions' strong commitment to the project of national development often muted such considerations or led them to cede authority for the resolution of such questions to technical experts.

As noted earlier, the very conceptualization of SENAI transferred responsibility for the definition of skill levels to educators and professionals. Yet SENAI's identification of certain jobs as skilled also aided unions (intentionally or not) in developing a salary scale based on professional categories to counteract the employer tendency to "flatten" the wage scale and undervalue workers' skills. As leaders of the paulista federation of textile workers noted in a 1959 congress, "The victorious struggle to raise the minimum wage throughout the nation has created a certain equalization of salaries between skilled hands and unspecialized workers. Thus we have partially liquidated the wage hierarchy. This leveling of salaries has caused profound discontent among specialized workers . . . since employers have remained intransigent, refusing to attend to the wage demands of the various professional categories."[103] As this statement indicates, unions pursued a two-pronged strategy, seeking to raise the minimum wage for unskilled workers while maintaining wage differentials for more skilled (and usually male) workers. SENAI classifications could be used to support claims for these differentials. Thus the proposal for setting "professional salaries" at the 1960 congress of paulista unions indicated that the unions sought to create steps in the professional hierarchy that closely matched those defined by SENAI.[104]

SENAI, however, was a dubious ally for such efforts. The boundaries drawn by SENAI between skilled and unskilled occupations changed over time and usually not in a direction favorable to labor. SENAI guidelines might, at one point, serve to support workers' claims that they performed skilled labor and therefore deserved higher wages and, at the next, provide evidence that a task was, at best, semiskilled.[105] SENAI presumably based its reclassifications—almost always from skilled to semiskilled—on purely "technical" criteria such as "objective" changes in the work process, but it was also susceptible to various forms of pressure from industrialists on such issues. Labor unions, meanwhile, had virtually no say in the matter and generally seem to have accepted the question of skill definition as beyond their control.[106]

The industrialists and educators who founded SENAI were hardly sympathetic to workers' demands for job stability or "professional classification," but SENAI never became closely associated with employer resistance to such measures. Rather, labor unions continued to view SENAI as a major advantage for workers, and especially minors, who would otherwise have little access to formal training and instruction given that most working-class families relied upon additional income from their adolescent sons and daughters. Indeed, the main thrust of union policy with regard to SENAI was to push for an expansion of its network of schools. At the 1959 congress of metalworkers, and again in 1961, participating unions called for the installation of SENAI courses in all industrial municipalities of São Paulo. Construction workers and printers made similar motions at their conventions. At these meetings, the proposals for improving the situation of juvenile workers usually included scrupulous observance of SENAI regulations with regard to the definition of apprenticeship and expanded training opportunities.[107]

The positive aspects of the training opportunities offered by SENAI apparently overshadowed aspects of its operations that organized labor might have found less appealing.[108] From time to time, labor congresses called for more state participation in worker training or direct involvement by unions in apprenticeship programs, but labor leaders eschewed explicit attacks on SENAI except to cite its existing facilities as insufficient. Once again, only the São Paulo printers' union offered genuinely critical commentary on SENAI's operations. In a subdued tone undoubtedly related to the recently imposed military dictatorship, a 1965 article in *O Trabalhador Gráfico* evaluated the union's relationship to SENAI. Politely acknowledging the agency's contribution to the training of Brazilian youth, the author went on to call for an expansion of technical education, "including the participation of the labor unions, and excluding the cheap demagoguery of course-installation ceremonies." Furthermore, "it is not enough just to train a technician; it is also necessary to give the young worker a sense of social solidarity, something only the union can offer." But this was a rare case of a union taking SENAI to task on ideological grounds, and it came from a long-established craft devastated by ongoing technological innovations.[109] Considering the exceptional nature of the printers' plight and the broader political context, it is hardly surprising that such criticism produced few echoes from other labor unions.

Organized Labor, SESI, and the Pursuit of Social Peace

The moment of SENAI's birth cast the new agency in a distinctly positive light. As noted earlier, a longtime Communist labor militant fondly remembered the SENAI carpentry course he took during the war not only for the skills he acquired but also for the instructors' comments about Brazil's participation in the fight against fascism and for democracy. The founding of SESI, in contrast, took place at a moment of unusually intense class conflict, and thus the appearance of the new agency immediately created widespread suspicion of its objectives among labor activists and even "ordinary" workers. Quickly identified with the *pelego* leadership, including officials who assumed control of major unions during Morvan's tenure as minister of labor, SESI never enjoyed any sort of honeymoon with the more militant or autonomous segments of the labor movement. And whereas SENAI's technical image shielded it from attacks by other social groups, SESI's more openly ideological intent made it a prime target for criticism from competing or hostile political factions and organizations. From the outset, the industrialist leadership was forced to devote a good deal of energy to defending SESI, branding its critics as unpatriotic and opposed to national development.[110]

Even SESI's most solicited services—its "popular courses" and discount food posts—encountered some initial hostility and resistance from workers and labor leaders. The literacy instructors openly recounted early instances of worker reticence or criticism. One SESI functionary admitted in a 1949 issue of the *Diário de São Paulo* that "at the outset the popular courses were received with certain reservations on the part of the employers and the employees themselves. [The workers] were suspicious after so many years of exploitation."[111] Another SESI literacy teacher recalled his experiences in Vila Zelina, a very poor neighborhood on the outskirts of São Paulo mainly inhabited by Eastern European immigrants. He claimed that the original eighteen students enrolled in the course suffered harassment from the local residents, forcing some to drop out. Locals also pelted the school with stones and garbage and made threats against the SESI staff, who had to seek police protection.

The author offered no explanation for the residents' aversion to the presence of the SESI instructors, implying simple ignorance, but an additional anecdote from his account indicates that there was considerable political awareness among Vila Zelina's inhabitants. According to the author, two young men who were not regular students in the course asked to sit in on a session, framing their request with compliments about SESI's efforts on behalf of workers. However, as the session drew to a close, the author claims the young men (in chorus?) declared the following: "Sir, you stated that we should seek instruction so as not to be led astray by false indoctrinators. I know that for SESI every Communist is a false indoctrinator. But SESI itself is in the service of the Americans who give it money."[112] Although the accusation that SESI received "American" funding was probably inaccurate, these visitors were quite aware of SESI's anti-Communist objectives and its sympathy for the cold war ideology being energetically disseminated by the United States. The instructor, of course, responded that SESI was apolitical, seeking only to "disseminate the truth, by means of the truth."

SESI's version of the "truth," however, often rang false to workers' ears. The instructor for the "reading orientation course" in the Jafet textile factory noted that several of her students used the class as an occasion to air grievances about wages and work conditions. Her response was to advise self-improvement through "good discipline," reading aloud a rags-to-riches story called "The Millionaire Worker" from SESI's official collection. The students immediately protested that the story's upwardly mobile hero, depicted as deeply concerned with his workers' welfare, bore no resemblance to their own employer. Undaunted, the instructor reminded them of the benefits they derived from their reading classes, offered in space "donated" by Jafet and made possible by the staff and materials provided by SESI.[113]

As in virtually all of these accounts, the upshot was positive. The instructor noted that her students, unruly at first, became more polite and disciplined. The professor who suffered such trials and tribulations at Vila Zelina triumphantly reported that, after eighteen months, enrollment increased fivefold. Indeed, the literacy courses were eagerly sought after by workers, especially recent migrants from the northeast, and were soon offered in hundreds of factories, social centers, and union headquarters. SESI even set up a literacy course in the São Paulo Electoral Tribunal to allow illiterate workers to gain the credentials necessary to qualify for the vote. How workers received the political messages embedded in these "popular courses" is another matter entirely. Upon the first anniversary of Roberto Simonsen's death, all of SESI's literacy classes dedicated a week to the study of his life and work. During that week, the distinguished jurist Cesarino Júnior gave a speech inaugurating the reading orientation course in the Armour meat-packing plant. Alluding to the figure of Simonsen, he urged the workers' to keep in mind "the example of a man who, born into prosperity . . . looked to the legions of his less-privileged compatriots and immersed himself in the herculean task of educating, instructing, and improving the standard of living of the Brazilian worker."[114] As the above anecdotes suggest, workers did not necessarily accept such hagiographic portraits of the industrialist leadership or, if they did, often compared them to their own employers and found the latter wanting.

The popular response to the SESI food posts was also very positive, with inflation-pressed workers eagerly taking advantage of the lower prices charged for basic goods. But opposition factions within certain unions, such as STIMMMESP, openly objected to the replacement of union-sponsored cooperatives with SESI food posts. In unusually vivid language, Aldo Lombardi denounced the collaboration between SESI and the president of the metallurgical workers' federation, José Sanches Duran, claiming that by "giving support to SESI's food posts . . . [Sanches Duran] has helped further enslave the worker to the owners . . . naturally allowing [the owners] control over the workers' lives and, in their expensive propaganda, to portray themselves as tribunes who will show [the workers] the way to paradise."[115] The criticism lodged against SESI by the Lombardi faction reflected, first of all, concern that cooperatives formed to foster worker solidarity and interunion collaboration would be transformed into publicity vehicles for the industrialists.[116] At the same time, the growing conflict between autonomous union activists and *pelegos* within the union hierarchy fueled and magnified the dispute over SESI.[117]

As minister of labor from 1947 to 1948, Morvan was in a particularly advantageous position to rally ministerialist union officials—many of whom owed their jobs to his "intervention"—in support of SESI's programs and activities. With Saad overseeing local relations, SESI established a network of supportive union officials who could be counted on to make public endorsements of SESI initiatives or to appear at important SESI functions to demonstrate organized labor's enthusiasm for the industrialists' good works. Similarly, these union leaders invited SESI or FIESP officials to attend labor functions such as inaugurations of new directorates or Christmas parties.

During the early years of its existence, SESI frequently called upon these union officials to speak publicly on behalf of SESI initiatives. Sebastião de Paiva, the highly cooperative president of the paulista railroad workers' union whose tenure ended with open union elections in 1951, obliged SESI by speaking at the inauguration of the first district kitchen and cafeteria. Paiva described the cafeteria, founded specifically to serve maintenance workers of the Santos-Jundiaí line, as representing "an important conquest in the economic and eugenic life of the railroad worker, and it is the most obvious proof that all social questions can be resolved perfectly well within a climate of harmony, understanding, and cooperation."[118] Another frequent participant in SESI festivities was Luiz Menossi, president of the construction workers' federation. At a SESI-sponsored celebration of Brazilian independence, Menossi figuratively "kiss[ed] the hands" of SESI's *professoras*, whom he praised for "organizing the grand army of social peace."[119]

Other statements by cooperative union leaders indicate that their support for SESI was not necessarily shared by all segments of organized labor. At the 1948 installation of literacy courses in the industrial center of Perús, an event attended mainly by workers, a labor federation official gave the following address:

> We constantly hear declarations, some of them malicious, by men who pretend to be enlightened, claiming that the union does nothing; other such [declarations] are pronounced by people of goodwill who merely repeat what they hear, according to whom unionism in Brazil is dead.
>
> They go so far as to say, my friends, and I am not afraid to say it here, they have the utter nerve to say that it is SESI that killed the

UNION! They forget that we, the unions and the federations, are working side by side with SESI for our mutual ideals.

We welcome everyone who, in good faith, undertakes something practical and effective in favor of the worker. If SESI harmed the worker, if it were an instrument of oppression against the less privileged classes, then we would combat it with all the strength of our souls and we would not declare a truce until it had disappeared.[120]

The highly emotional and defensive tone of this statement reveals that conservative union officials were aware of the potential drawbacks of a close alliance with SESI. Nonetheless, the influence of government and industrial officials, combined with the material benefits offered by SESI, outweighed any reservations—strategic, not ideological—these union leaders may have harbored about the organization.[121]

As one would expect, union newspapers published during the late 1940s usually reported positively on activities sponsored by SESI or offered only muted criticisms of the organization. Still, tolerance of opposition opinion meant that occasional denunciations of SESI appeared even in the publications of *pelego*-controlled unions, such as STIMMMESP. And the newspaper of the relatively independent printers' union took every opportunity to attack Morvan, the "profiteer-minister," and even dismissed a "recommendation" to industrialists by Roberto Simonsen to grant workers pay for Sundays and holidays, noting that Simonsen sought to persuade industrialists to grant on a voluntary basis what should be recognized as a worker's right.[122] Published criticism of this sort was exceptional during the final years of the Dutra presidency, but the treatment accorded SESI changed, in some cases drastically, with the election of more independent union leaders and the intensification of class conflict during the subsequent decade. Most revealing of this shift in attitudes was the changing union response to the SESI-sponsored May Day festivities. Whereas literacy or sewing courses offered members and their families tangible benefits that many unions welcomed even after their relations with SESI had soured, the blatantly ideological May Day events organized by SESI had no redeeming material features to blunt criticism from organized labor.

Beginning in 1947, SESI sought to reproduce and expand the May Day ceremonies of the Vargas dictatorship with the explicit purpose of transforming a traditional commemoration of worker militancy and sacrifice into a celebration of social peace.[123] The centerpiece of the May Day activities was the inauguration of the Workers' Olympics, a multisport athletic competition in which factories and other worker organizations fielded teams that competed for several weeks until one emerged as champion.

Oath being administered to "worker-athletes" at the opening of the fifth Workers' Olympics, May Day, 1951. Courtesy of the Núcleo de Memória, SENAI–São Paulo.

SESI always marked the opening of the games with a gathering of employers and workers in Pacaembú Stadium, where the proceedings included speeches by high-ranking political and military officials, prominent industrialists, and carefully chosen union leaders. But unlike the festivities of the Estado Novo years, the spotlight was on industry, not the state, with an emphasis on the similarity of interests between capital and labor. This theme became even clearer in 1951 when SESI initiated an annual May Day parade to precede the opening ceremonies of the Workers' Olympics. Groups representing factories, SENAI schools, and SESI courses marched with elaborate costumes, floats, and banners proclaiming workers' commitment to social peace.

O Metalúrgico described SESI's first May Day festivities in adulatory terms, noting the participation of 150 athletic clubs with a total of 2,500 worker-members and the presence of Senator Roberto Simonsen, Armando de Arruda Pereira, and Governor Adhemar de Barros, "who addressed the workers with a brilliant speech."[124] In contrast, O Trabalhador Gráfico regularly questioned attempts by SESI and the government to turn

May Day into a festive occasion rather than a demonstration of labor militancy and solidarity, although it had to moderate its normally acerbic remarks in recognition of the popularity of the SESI games, especially among younger workers. In an editorial entitled "The First of May, Not a Festive Date," the editors excused the enthusiasm of their younger colleagues by noting that "for the last twenty years, the First of May has been monopolized, managed, and exploited by the bourgeois class."[125]

Participation in the SESI-sponsored May Day Olympics grew slowly during the late 1940s, with SESI officials blaming apathy among employers and transport problems for the relatively small increases in the number of teams participating each year.[126] However, a major public relations campaign in the early 1950s paid off, with the number of those partaking in the festivities statewide jumping from 11,249 in 1950 to slightly over 40,000 in 1952.[127] Flushed with success, SESI president Antônio Devisate sent the following communication to employers in early 1953: "Conducted with the spirit that seeks to commemorate Labor Day in an atmosphere of social peace, suitable to the Christian character of Brazil's working class, thus the OLYMPIC GAMES have become, year after year, the high point of the May Day festivities in São Paulo, and the athletic tournaments . . . have succeeded in monopolizing the interest of the entire working population of the city and its surrounding areas."[128]

Devisate's inflated claim about SESI's success in "monopolizing" worker interest soon proved unfounded. In March 1953, workers in the capital initiated the largest general strike in Brazil's history, the so-called Strike of the 300,000.[129] By May Day of that year, the strikers had returned to work, but the movement had at least temporarily dampened workers' enthusiasm for the SESI festivities, causing participation to drop to 21,138 people statewide. Following the 1953 strike, many unions that had previously cooperated with SESI in promoting the annual Workers' Olympics began adopting more critical stances, and those that had already expressed misgivings sharpened their rebukes. Articles on May Day in the metallurgical and construction workers' newspapers stressed its historical significance as the "starting point of labor's struggles" and urged union members to participate only in those commemorative activities endorsed by organized labor.[130] Similarly, *O Trabalhador Têxtil* called for a May Day celebration "independent of organizations such as SESI, SESC [the Commercial Social Service (Serviço Social do Comércio)], and others that only entertain workers to deceive them."[131]

As was often the case, the printers published one of the earliest and broadest-ranging critiques of SESI's May Day festivities: "Friends, we have arrived at May Day of 1954, a year of hunger, of energy shortages, of high prices and low wages, of bourgeois demagoguery and general scarcity. The job of softening us up . . . has been prepared, as usual, by the employers' DIPS: SESIs, SESCs, etc. The schedule of Labor Day festivities has already been programmed: parades in Anhangabaú, worker gatherings, sports contests and other 'spontaneous' demonstrations of gaiety."[132] The editors closed with a reminder to their readers that May Day should be an occasion for protests "against those who, forgetting that class struggle is inseparable from the capitalist system, try to extinguish it by decree."[133]

Few unions in the mid-1950s went as far as the printers in their denunciations of SESI's Workers' Olympics, and the first year of the presidency of Juscelino Kubitschek even saw a move by several paulista unions to collaborate with SESI on May Day.[134] But as labor militancy intensified, so did the criticisms of the May Day festivities. By the early 1960s, even an organization like the bakery workers' union, which had long been regarded as moderate and cooperative, urged its members to avoid commemorating May Day "with festivities of a recreational or athletic character, which is the way some pseudo-organizations for worker protection commemorate it every year, disparaging the true meaning of its historical content."[135] The railroad workers' union went even further, describing May Day as the first step toward the eventual triumph of the workers and socialism and declaring that "the distortions practiced by SESC and SESI with their fanfare and festivals will be to no avail in obstructing the glorious day of the working class throughout the world."[136]

As one would expect, SESI's May Day festivities persisted in spite of union criticism. The games seem to have been genuinely appealing to worker-athletes, whose numbers rebounded after the decline in 1953.[137] Recognizing this appeal, militant unions began organizing their own sports competitions for May Day, thereby providing a "classist" alternative to the SESI Workers' Olympics but nevertheless acquiescing to a schedule of events on May Day that was more festive and less political. The SESI parade, on the other hand, had increasing difficulty attracting union participation.[138] This is obvious from an account of the parade written by Light's personnel director for distribution to the upper echelons of management, who were debating future participation. According to the Light functionary, "We are not talking about a workers' parade, *strictu sensu*, since it actually has more of an athlete-student character, and when we say student, we are referring to SESI students." Going into further detail, the account noted "a very small number of worker delegations, almost always in connection with a display of agricultural machinery, privately owned fire engines, etc. There were a few union representatives and, unless I am mistaken, none from public utilities . . . with the exception of the Municipal Collective Transport Company."[139]

SESI parades may have succeeded in drawing large crowds, but they curried little favor among union leaders.[140] The parades' failure in this regard, leading to their ultimate demise, illustrates what types of strategies and practices yielded positive results for the employer-run organization. SESI services that were perceived as being of a practical nature tended to draw support from workers and labor leaders regardless of the educational objectives SESI might attach to such activities. But events of a more "festive" sort, whose ideological implications were difficult to mask, were especially vulnerable to criticism from union leaders, and all the more so in the case of May Day, an occasion packed with symbolic significance for the labor movement.

Thus many unions, even while balking at participation in the SESI May Day celebrations, continued soliciting SESI courses for their members. But not all SESI courses were equally desirable or acceptable. Literacy or sewing classes had almost universal appeal, but other SESI courses—such as those on labor legislation, oratory, and unionism—met a chillier reception among the more militant unions. Unions representing paper, clothing, construction, and hydroelectric workers, all of which were friendly to SESI throughout the 1950s, eagerly sought such courses for their members. But the metallurgical workers' union, for example, rebuffed SESI attempts to create such courses for its category during this period. And representatives of the printers' union openly rejected the idea of an employer-run organization offering courses of this nature. "This employer-controlled entity seeks to lure into its orbit those workers who stand out among their colleagues, enrolling them in the courses it sponsors, such as the seminar in labor legislation, the course for orators, the course for union leaders, etc., then worming a heap of fanciful ideas into their heads with the goal of having them serve as their agents (though they do not call them this) among the workers." To learn about their rights, the author concluded, workers simply needed to frequent union meetings, not attend a SESI seminar.[141]

Material services offered by SESI, though initially more attractive to labor unions than the ideologically oriented programs, were by no means exempt from criticism. Indeed, the very fact that certain services came from an employer-run agency seems to have made them a lodestone for complaints by increasingly militant labor unions. The most common examples of a SESI service that incited as much resentment as gratitude from workers were the district kitchens. Given SESI's almost exclusive emphasis on meeting carefully calculated nutritional standards, it is not surprising that workers often found the food lacking in taste and volume—after all, a "rational" meal is not necessarily a satisfying one. Furthermore, SESI's "thermal" delivery trucks often proved inadequate for keeping hundreds of prepared meals warm for an extended trip through sclerotic city traffic, thereby defeating the purpose of providing hot, nutritional lunches to urban workers.

As early as 1950, the printers' union used the occasion of a speech by the president of the employers' *sindicato* on conditions in a North American printing plant to wax ironic about SESI's food services. Citing the employer's highly favorable description of the U.S. company's cafeteria, *O Trabalhador Gráfico* remarked that its readers need not be envious since "here we have the 'plentiful' and 'tasty' gruel served by SESI."[142] This was merely the opening salvo in a barrage of criticism directed at SESI's district kitchens and cafeterias. The carpenters' union ran an article in 1955 entitled "Rotten Meat Served by SESI," quoting workers at a furniture factory who complained that SESI food tended to be of poor quality and cold by the time it was delivered.[143] But it was the railroad workers and busdrivers—the two groups most dependent on SESI for their lunches—who mounted the fiercest campaign against the district kitchens. Describing SESI meals as arriving spoiled, bug-infested, and with only half the nutrition required, *O Condutor* declared that Antônio Devisate would not feed SESI food to his dog.[144] Meanwhile, the president of the busdrivers' union, recently elected to São Paulo's municipal council, broadened the polemic. In a speech to his fellow *vereadores*, Timoteo Spinola claimed that the small portions served by SESI caused "physical weakness" and made workers vulnerable to illness. Thus he declared SESI policy during the recent influenza epidemic as nothing short of "criminal."[145]

Although some of these complaints smack of exaggeration (as do SESI's earlier claims that its meals increased worker productivity), they surely reflected some real dissatisfaction on the workers' part. One longtime union militant remembered that his fellow metallurgical workers eventually shunned SESI food services as "too plebeian," indicating that the workers themselves had a rather different estimation of their needs than the "rational" nutritionists responsible for elaborating SESI's menus.[146] Moreover, SESI's own statistics show a drastic decline in demand for its food services from the mid-1950s on. In 1956 alone, forty-one firms that had previously purchased over 2 million meals per year from SESI opened their own restaurants, establishing a trend that continued throughout the decade.[147]

Thus we cannot dismiss the complaints about SESI food services as mere pretexts for political attacks, but the inadequacy of the district kitchens certainly provided an excellent opportunity to deride SESI's over-all project to promote social peace. The article in the busdrivers' paper de-voted as much space to criticizing SESI's ideological goals as it did to com-plaints about its food. The author did not mince words in denouncing SESI and its larger objectives: "By developing a program of apparent 'so-cial assistance,' SESI—an employer agency—seeks to convince the work-ers that it is Santa Claus. But its only intention is to instill in workers' heads its own way of thinking, which is exactly the opposite of ours since the interests of employers and employees are irreconcilable."[148] Further-more, the article warned that SESI "sticks its nose into everything related to workers, and if we don't keep our eyes open, even into the union." Judging from the language of this denunciation, the author's hostility to SESI had little to do with the poor quality of its food services, but his criti-cisms surely had greater meaning for the rank and file when expressed in the context of an exposé of the district kitchens.

The article in *O Condutor* was unusually vituperative in its condemna-tion of a specific SESI service, but it echoed the rhetoric of many other union newspapers when it attacked SESI's cherished concept of social peace: "The much-proclaimed social peace is nothing more than a slogan of the employers that, translated, means: 'We can live in peace as long as you think like us and do what we want.'" Indeed, it is interesting to see how thoroughly the phrase "social peace" had penetrated the realm of in-dustrial labor relations in São Paulo, but it was increasingly used by orga-nized labor as a vehicle for sarcasm and criticism lodged against the indus-trial bourgeoisie.[149]

Although the phrase "social peace" was an old one, it gained greater currency at the end of World War II with the issuing of the "Carta da Paz Social" by the industrialists and with the emergence of a "Christian demo-cratic" discourse that stressed class collaboration and opposition to com-munism. It was in this spirit that SESI chose "For Social Peace in Brazil" as its motto, and FIESP leaders dubbed Morvan Dias de Figueiredo "the minister of social peace." Several features of the phrase appealed to SESI's founders, such as its apparent neutrality in comparison to, say, "for social justice," which uncomfortably implies the existence of injustice. It also conveyed the need for stability and calm—so essential, from the industri-alists' point of view, for national development—while avoiding the stento-rian and un-Christian tone of the Republican/positivist motto, "Order and Progress." And it positioned SESI as promoting an indisputably desirable state of affairs. After all, who could oppose a project for social peace except those professional (i.e., Communist) agitators who, alone, would benefit from the instability and disorder generated by strikes and other forms of open class conflict?

Workers from the outset paid little heed to the industrialists' definitions of social peace. The hundreds of thousands of industrial workers who went on strike in 1945 and 1946 did not hesitate for fear of disrupting the social order. But as we have seen, the Dutra government quickly replaced the more independent labor leaders who led or endorsed the strikes with ministerialist officials who eagerly took up the cause of social peace. These new union leaders, whether committed anti-Communists or simple opportunists, affirmed the importance of social peace for national prosperity in public and in print. According to a December 1948 article entitled "Peace and Work" in *O Metalúrgico*, "São Paulo is prospering . . . due to constant collaboration between the working class and employers." And its article describing May Day that year declared, "The First of May—The workers of São Paulo know how to maintain a climate of order and high output."[150]

Deposed labor leaders and union militants may have been deeply unimpressed by this ubiquitous exaltation of social peace, but they could not completely ignore the implication that those who supported strike actions or argued for the inevitability of class conflict were promoting social disorder and undermining national development.[151] Rather than merely ignoring the industrialists' rhetoric, representatives of organized labor began to use the concept of social peace to question the goodwill of the industrialists and to indict the employers' intransigent attitudes and exploitative policies as the "true" causes of social instability. After all, industrialist associations openly admitted that "social peace" could only thrive if both owners and workers recognized their duties as well as their rights, leaving employers open to charges that they were not fulfilling their part of the bargain.[152]

Even under Dutra, we can already detect examples of labor spokesmen using the phrase "social peace" in ways that must have caused the industrialist leadership some discomfort. In effect, the unions subtly shifted the burden of insuring social peace from themselves onto the industrialists. A 1947 article in *O Metalúrgico* praised a firm that met with STIMMMESP's legal department in order to reach a voluntary accord regarding a worker's complaint, citing the company as an example to be followed "by all industrialists who truly want social peace." Similarly, *O Trabalhador Gráfico* congratulated employers who granted their workers Sunday pay or a Christmas bonus, describing their policies as a reproach to greedy industrialists who "merely proclaim the marvels of social peace" while doing nothing to promote it. Another article in the printers' newspaper acknowledged the

Members of the construction workers' union listening to a lecture about SENAI courses in the union headquarters, 1950. Construction work was both dangerous and poorly paid compared to other trades; a large number of the members of this "category" were recent migrants from the northeast. Courtesy of the Núcleo de Memória, SENAI–São Paulo.

potential benefits of social harmony for both workers and owners but predicated harmonious relations on whether the employers paid decent salaries and learned the workers' language.[153]

Even organizations that collaborated most closely with SESI during this period, such as the construction workers' union, occasionally interpreted the preconditions for social peace in a way that challenged the industrialist perspective. Despite its moderate position, the construction workers' union participated in the 1952 campaign against the "assiduity clause" that made certain labor benefits contingent upon rates of worker attendance (a principle cherished by the FIESP leadership). Assuming that increased production required perfect cooperation between capital and labor, the union official argued that "such cooperation can only exist in a climate of freedom, mutual respect, and confidence." Calling the clause an instrument of oppression, the author concluded by urging the "employing classes" to give up this "absurd demand for perfect attendance [*assiduidade integral*], in the name of social peace."[154]

With the intensification of strike activity and the election of more militant union directorates in the 1950s, these gentle invocations of social peace gave way to increasingly acerbic and sarcastic references to the industrialists' stated goal of class harmony. When one of the largest publishing firms in Brazil instituted a new work regulation that the union deemed illegal, *O Trabalhador Gráfico* declared that "instead of social peace [the company] prefers the law of the jungle." After other graphics firms followed suit, the union paper complained that the bosses no longer found existing labor legislation sufficient to "maintain discipline and order" and therefore "intend to impose 'social peace' with arrogance and abuses."[155]

As one would expect, elaborate critiques of the notion of social peace were particularly common in the aftermath of bitter industrial conflicts. In early 1958, an alliance of São Paulo unions (the Interunion Unity Pact [Pacto de Unidade Intersindical, or PUI]) staged a three-day general strike to protest the failure of various employers to make the salary adjustments agreed upon in a recent labor settlement. According to a union account, FIESP responded by inducing the police to harass, beat, and arrest workers, despite the legality of the strike. As a result of this action, *O Metalúrgico* declared that "the 'social peace' of the bosses and SESI is dead and buried. . . . The workers who, for so many years, had instilled in their brains the idea that the social peace propaganda eagerly promoted by the employers through their machines of deception (among them SESI) was sincere were deeply disappointed and finally had to open their eyes."[156] Although the author of the article, for rhetorical purposes, may have overstated workers' credulity with regard to employer discourse, he clearly believed that "social peace" no longer had any credibility as a shared goal for workers and employers.

Interestingly, an article published during the same month in *O Trabalhador Gráfico* adopted a critical but more conciliatory tone. The author of "For Social Peace" began by faulting the industrialists' behavior: "In spite of the slogan 'For Social Peace in Brazil,' so often used and abused by SESI, its founders have still not tried to do anything to secure the much-praised social peace." Instead, inhumane treatment had created a constant state of hostility between workers and owners in Brazil. But far from regarding social peace as dead and buried, the printer reminded the industrialists that each class must contribute to its maintenance, "the employer conceding rights and the employee fulfilling obligations." He reaffirmed that "we all desire the much discussed social peace; however, we want a social peace founded on justice, on understanding, and on a spirit of humanity." Once workers had decent homes and the means to clothe, feed, and educate their children, "you can be sure that 'social peace' will be an established fact."[157]

These two articles, though both found fault with SESI and the "imperative" of social peace, represent two rather different strategies of criticism that characterized union discourse about FIESP and SESI.[158] In some cases, unions used the employers' stated desire for social peace to advance labor's campaigns for expanded rights or higher salaries (or rather, salaries that kept pace with inflation). Such a strategy was not confined to the more moderate or less militant unions.[159] The president of the metallurgical workers' union in the ABC region of São Paulo, Marcos Andreotti, was a long-standing member of the PCB and a dedicated labor leader. In 1961, as part of a campaign to secure a thirteenth-month salary for his category, Andreotti sent a letter to all firms in his district appealing for cooperation. Although he admitted that the additional salary would not, by itself, resolve the grave situation of the working masses in Brazil, he claimed it would "undoubtedly contribute to the strengthening of relations between capital and labor, a decisive step toward the much desired and proclaimed SOCIAL PEACE, and it will make [capital] more humane and [labor] more productive, with real benefits for the entire collectivity."[160]

The other strategy, which became increasingly common as the strike activity of the late 1950s gave way to the massive labor mobilization of the early 1960s, was simply to reject the very idea of social peace or treat it as a farcical concept in light of Brazil's vast social problems, much of the blame for which organized labor assigned to the industrialists. Union newspapers regularly referred to "social peace" in an ironic sense when revealing what they considered to be illegal or unethical practices by employers. When *O Trabalhador Têxtil* published an article exposing the routine harassment of older workers with job tenure to force their early retirement, the headline read, "Social Peace Applied to Elderly Employees." And when Antônio Devisate, president of FIESP and SESI, wrote to President Jânio Quadros advising against minimum wage increases, *O Metalúrgico* commented, "Here you see how the bosses regard 'social peace' and hold it in such high esteem."[161]

Union newspapers also took advantage of the growing militancy among the employees of SESI and SENAI (and their commercial counterparts, SESC and SENAC) to expose the intransigence of the employers. *O Trabalhador Gráfico*, after briefly detailing the history of these services and the recent attempts by their employees to unionize and press for higher wages, drew the following conclusion: "See how the 'producing classes' [employers] even after sixteen years have not managed to attain their objective, that is, to implant the much-discussed SOCIAL PEACE, since even in their own redoubts (SESI—SESC—SENAC—SENAI), the struggle for better salaries is more intense today than ever."[162]

Other union newspapers took the gloves off altogether, ridiculing "social peace" as a preposterous goal and denouncing the phrase as a simple bit of trickery. An editorial in the railroad workers' journal cataloged Brazil's many social ills and then claimed that "those responsible for this calamitous state—in order to be able to continue exploiting the people—preach the necessity of maintaining this 'SOCIAL PEACE.'" Exhibiting a similar tone, an article in the bakery workers' paper carried the blunt title, "Social Peace: An Unscrupulous Lie," and asked, "How can there be social peace in a society where the social disparities are unprecedented?"[163]

Such statements do not necessarily represent the sentiments of the rank and file or even of the entire union leadership. Moreover, these attacks on SESI's ideological project did not mean that the union publishing such articles rejected any sort of relationship with SESI. For example, one union newspaper ran a strongly worded denunciation of a FIESP representative who had condemned job stability and the right to strike as "the worst social cancers in Brazil" and a threat to social peace. But the very same issue included two pages of SESI advice on how to improve one's home life and a long, SESI-authored article, "The Ten Commandments of Worker Safety."[164] Many unions continued to take advantage of SESI materials and services, but with a marked preference for those elements of the SESI program that were less explicitly ideological. And many individual members found SESI's medical and legal assistance preferable to the often underfunded services offered by unions.[165]

SESI officials took comfort in the ongoing popularity of certain programs, assuring themselves that the "typical" Brazilian worker continued to appreciate SESI's services and sympathize with its notion of social peace. Criticism of SESI could then be attributed to the militant minority who, due to their oratorical skills and ideological zeal, had captured control of the labor movement. Rather than perceiving this new leadership, voted into power through open union elections, as more legitimate or representative, SESI construed it as increasingly alien to the interests and attitudes of the "authentic" Brazilian worker.[166]

Whether or not the rank and file shared the view of labor militants that socioeconomic conditions in Brazil made the "imperative of social peace" impossible, or even farcical, the running critique of the industrialists' use of this phrase had gradually emptied it of its original meaning and transformed it into an instrument for exposing employer hypocrisy. Thus labor spokesmen successfully transformed language meant to express the industrialist leadership's utopian vision of Brazilian society into a serious political liability for the employers and for SESI, an organization officially dedicated to the struggle for social peace. Whereas, in the view of organized labor, SENAI had only a tangential connection to rationalization processes that negatively affected only some workers and could be defended as necessary features of industrial development, SESI was clearly and emphatically identified with increasingly objectionable ideological precepts and with the most compromised sectors of the labor movement. Indeed, it can be argued that, by the early 1960s, an organization and a discourse developed to advance industrialist hegemony were serving to erode the political and ideological position of the industrial bourgeoisie.

Remaking the Worker at Home and at Play

The transition in 1951 from Dutra's repressive regime to the populist politics of the now democratically elected Getúlio Vargas inaugurated a period in which the Brazilian worker occupied an ever more prominent place in public discourse. Populist politicians from Vargas to the paulista opportunist, Adhemar de Barros, heartily praised the contribution of Brazilian workers to national development and sympathetically portrayed their struggles to maintain a decent standard of living despite adverse circumstances. The urban working "masses" emerged in electioneering rhetoric as the backbone of the new democratic, industrializing Brazil.[1]

At first glance, this rhetoric seems perfectly compatible with the programmatic thrust of SESI and SENAI, which were committed to elevating the cultural and material level of the Brazilian worker. Yet there were sharp differences in the assumptions that informed the industrialist-sponsored agencies and the rhetorical positions adopted by populist politicians. Far from portraying the (male) worker as a hero who toiled selflessly and tirelessly for his family and country, SENAI and SESI defined the worker, first and foremost, as a "problem." All public discourse acknowledged the difficulties experienced by workers because of their low pay, limited access to education, and poor living conditions, but the populist solution lay in better wages, more schools, and better public services—benefits defined as workers' "rights." To SENAI and SESI, however, such measures would provide at best partial solutions given the typical Brazilian worker's lack of proper culture, hygiene, and motivation and the disorganized state of the average working-class household.

The other major theme in politics and policy during the 1950s—developmentalism—fit more comfortably with the outlook of these industrialist-funded organizations. Inspired in part by the writings of Roberto Simonsen and policies long advocated by the paulista industrial leadership, developmentalism in Brazil favored joint public/private efforts to promote economic development and especially industrialization. Echoing Simonsen's earlier arguments, developmentalists saw new, more efficient industries as the key to national independence and higher standards of living. As for the hardships of the working class, developmentalists attributed these primarily to objective or structural factors rather than to any political failure to grant workers their rightful share of the national wealth.[2]

Although SENAI and SESI acknowledged the relevance of structural factors (especially when such factors relieved employers of responsibility for their workers' shortcomings), both organizations continued to place particular emphasis on the cultural and educational deficits of Brazilian workers. In their construction of the worker as an obstacle to modernization that could not be removed by higher wages alone, SENAI and SESI could draw upon a long discursive tradition that portrayed the "popular classes" as ignorant, unhealthy, and dangerous and denigrated manual labor and those who practiced it.[3] To be sure, a major theme in the SENAI and SESI literature was the value and dignity of manual labor, but recognition of its value could only come in the context of a modernizing, industrializing economy in which industrialists, through SENAI and SESI, would oversee the creation of responsible worker-citizens.

The Working-Class Household and the Problem Worker

In effect, this position could be described as "antipopulist" in its unflattering depiction of the "people." Of course, few leading industrialists were as fatalistic (or openly racist) as Cyro Berlinck, who came to the conclusion that São Paulo could only obtain a competent labor force through another massive wave of European immigration. And even fewer were as crude and obtuse as Eduardo Jafet, who at the 1944 Industrial Congress argued that Brazilian consumption levels were low not as a result of poverty but due to Brazilian workers' apathy toward material acquisition.[4] But references to the workforce as "immature," easily misled, and poorly prepared for the demands of modern industry and urban life appear in many public statements by major industrialist leaders. Far from exalting workers and working-class culture, FIESP spokesmen and their technocratic allies adopted programs that aspired to construct an alternative, nonproletarian culture within and beyond the factory.[5]

These "antipopulist" premises constantly emerged in the policies and programs of SENAI and SESI and generated a series of studies and strategies for "improving" working-class culture outside the workplace. As noted in an earlier chapter, SENAI officials repeatedly stated that the low moral and cultural background of their students presented a serious obstacle to successful apprenticeship training. Moreover, they attributed the poor physical and educational levels of incoming students as much to worker ignorance and apathy as to the absence of adequate social welfare facilities or wage levels in Brazilian society. Such assumptions about Brazilian workers persisted into the 1950s, even as SENAI boasted of increasing enrollments and higher standards for the selection of prospective students.

Despite the overall improvement in the qualifications of the apprentices, the continually high dropout and failure rates caused considerable concern among SENAI officials. In São Paulo, for example, of 74,005 students enrolled from 1942 to 1952, fewer than 15,000 earned their final certification.[6] The national directors of SENAI were so distressed by the high number of apprentices who failed to finish their training that they launched an extensive inquiry into the causes of the phenomenon. The study, initiated in 1951, analyzed thousands of SENAI dropouts in the cities of São Paulo, Rio, Porto Alegre, and Recife, comparing them with a "control group" of students who had successfully completed their training. The investigators, who included SENAI and SESI technicians as well as staff from various schools of social work, surveyed the dropouts to ascertain their reasons for leaving SENAI. In addition, they canvassed employers' attitudes toward SENAI students and compiled detailed information on the family backgrounds and living conditions of SENAI dropouts.[7]

The researchers reported with obvious relief that only a small minority of students cited factors internal to SENAI as causing their decision to withdraw. To be sure, the study defined such factors narrowly, so that former students who expressed a general lack of interest in continuing their education were not classified as critical of SENAI per se. Similarly, the researchers emphasized that many of the students who withdrew from textile or carpentry courses claimed that they would eagerly return to SENAI should openings become available in the metallurgical or mechanical trades. Other motives mentioned by the ex-students included frustration at being unable to find a job that allowed them to practice what they were learning in class, the need to work full-time, and poor educational preparation, which made it difficult for them to keep up with the general culture courses. Such explanations might suggest the need for better selection methods, placement programs, and social assistance but did not necessarily call into question the basic structure or mission of SENAI.[8]

As noted in the previous chapter, a substantial number of students attributed their withdrawal from SENAI to "difficulties stemming from the work environment"—that is, pressure from their employers or supervisors to drop out of SENAI.[9] Furthermore, a survey of industrialist opinion conducted in conjunction with the dropout study largely confirmed such testimony. Although many students dropped out for purely personal reasons unrelated to employer behavior, the results of the survey offered cogent evidence for viewing the high dropout rate as directly related to employer practices and the apprentices' perception that completing the SENAI program would not necessarily improve their employment situation and might even cost them their jobs.[10] Such an argument, however, had little appeal for the authors of the report since it questioned the very viability of the SENAI enterprise and placed the burden of the dropout problem on employers rather than on workers. Thus the researchers downplayed the job-related issues and highlighted instead the socioeconomic characteristics of the "dropout population," seeking to uncover weaknesses in the family backgrounds of the ex-students that could explain their failure when compared with the control group of SENAI graduates.

If we compare the main characteristics of the two São Paulo groups— 344 SENAI dropouts (and their families) and 20 households of SENAI graduates—the most obvious feature is their startling similarity. Consequently, the data collected for the study allow us to compose a portrait of the "typical" SENAI student in the early 1950s. The apprentice was very likely to be male since the student body was overwhelmingly male and "white" since only 12 percent of the households surveyed for the study were described as predominantly black or *pardo*.[11] He was a native of São Paulo state and, in over 80 percent of the cases, came from a household whose head could read and write.

The data classified 60 percent of the apprentices as contributing financially to the maintenance of the household. The report gave this finding considerable emphasis, noting that the head of the typical "SENAI household" in São Paulo contributed only 43 percent (37 percent in the control group) of the total family income. This was well below the 65 percent and 71 percent registered in two previous surveys of working-class households in São Paulo.[12] Most of the difference could probably be explained by the fact that a SENAI student had to be at least fourteen years of age, making it likely that the household had a larger number of working-age children than the average family. Indeed, the researchers reported that the typical household head earned a salary that was higher than the industrial average. Nevertheless, they surmised that most families had only recently emerged from straitened financial circumstances and depended upon their children's earnings to maintain a standard of living somewhat above the "level of misery." As the report bluntly put it, "The heads of households from which SENAI students come . . . do not have the resources they need to live. . . . The budget of these families thus depends, fundamentally, on the contribution of its dependents. Without this contribution, and with the same composition, the family would register a budget deficit characteristic of misery."[13] In light of this, one can easily imagine the pressure on unemployed SENAI students to find steady work or on working apprentices to keep their jobs, even if this meant leaving SENAI.

In addition to determining the income levels of SENAI households, the study examined the pattern of household expenditures. The "principal revelation" was the large share of household income classified as "autonomous expenditures"—that is, at the "free" disposal of the individual members. Among the "dropout households," 23 percent of income fell into this category, and the proportion was even higher—26 percent—within the control group. Given the presence in the average household of several employed dependents, this partial retention of income by its earners seems reasonable and not especially ominous. The researchers, however, interpreted this finding as revealing a "structural weakness" in the SENAI household. Arguing that the average percentage of income spent for food consumed within the household—35 percent in São Paulo—was *lower* than expected, the SENAI officials concluded that the members of the household spent most of the day away from the family, with the home becoming merely a place to sleep or gather on weekends and holidays. This tendency toward "separatism" among the members, reflected in the "autonomous expenditures," was interpreted by the researchers to indicate a "low level of domestic group cohesion."[14]

Going even further, the study concluded that in households where dependents had such a high level of autonomy as consumers, one would also expect to find "individual moral and social autonomy, generally characterized by the diminution of the authority of the family heads over the dependents who have their own income."[15] To be sure, the study could not argue that this domestic situation was a distinguishing characteristic of SENAI dropouts since such patterns of expenditure were even more pronounced within the control group. Rather, the researchers intimated that the reduction in parental authority and the low level of domestic cohesion were general problems that limited the working-class family's ability to

Families of SENAI apprentices visiting a workshop for mechanics at the Escola
Roberto Simonsen, 1950. Courtesy of the Núcleo de Memória, SENAI–
São Paulo.

instill discipline and encourage apprentices to continue their SENAI
training.

The study also examined, in depth, the housing and sanitary facilities of
the SENAI students. It found that the great majority of SENAI students'
households were located in outlying and "interstitial" areas and that the
homes were typically "shacks, shanties, huts, and other types of rudimentary structures." In São Paulo, only 35 percent had indoor toilets, and the
average household had nearly three persons per bedroom—well above the
number the researchers accepted as "normal" for a typical-sized room.
Taken altogether, such data indicated the "precarious living conditions" of
the average SENAI student.[16]

Revealing what the researchers considered to be a singularly important
discovery, the report went on to note "significant differences" in the living
conditions of the control group versus those of the dropouts. The families
of SENAI graduates in every city except Porto Alegre were more likely to
have indoor bathrooms, running water, and electricity. They were also

more likely to own radios and sewing machines and to have fewer persons per bedroom. And this was true in São Paulo even though the average income of the dropout household was similar to that of the control group household.

How, then, did the study explain the "superior living conditions" of the latter group? The researchers argued that it was a question of mentality: "Such families have a more positive social motivation than those of the boys who drop out. The families of those boys that complete their courses overcome the negative aspects of [the student's] educational background with a psychological propensity to progress in the satisfaction of social needs that surpasses the imperative of mere subsistence. This propensity constitutes an intangible factor in the student's educational progress. When [this propensity] does not exist, or is weak, in the student's domestic context, he is easily involved in the dropout process."[17] In effect, the researchers were arguing that the success or failure of the SENAI student largely depended upon the social aspirations of the student's family. If the household strived for a better lifestyle, as indicated by domestic conditions and patterns of consumption, then it would encourage the student to complete the SENAI course as a path to social mobility. Implicit in this argument was the conclusion that the high failure and dropout rate of SENAI students reflected the limited aspirations and motivations of the working-class household, placing the burden of the problem on the workers themselves.[18]

It is worth examining the São Paulo data on which the researchers based this momentous conclusion. First of all, given the small size of the control group—20 households—one would immediately expect greater uniformity in living conditions than the diversity exhibited by the main cohort of 344 households. Once we consider the two groups by income category, we see that no household in the control group fell into the lowest four categories, whereas 53 "dropout households" (15 percent) were so classified—hardly surprising since a number of ex-students indicated very difficult financial circumstances as the motive for their withdrawal from SENAI. The average income of the two groups, again, was very similar, but this was due to the relatively large number of dropout households that could be found in the highest income category, thereby compensating for the poorest families. But once the study turned to such issues as radio ownership or persons per bedroom, the presence of 53 very low income families among the dropout households yielded results that were not "counterbalanced" by the higher income households. Indeed, even with these poorer households included, the differences in the living conditions of the two groups were, in most respects, quite small, and if we control for income category, the differences disappear. In short, the researchers could have easily concluded that the better living conditions of the control group households were a function of higher income rather than a matter of social disposition or psychological motivation.

Although one might assume that the researchers' conclusions simply resulted from a sloppy interpretation of the data, such an explanation seems inadequate. From the outset, SENAI officials had regarded the SENAI student as "problematic" and the student's family as unwholesome. No less an authority than Roberto Mange had declared just a few years earlier that "in the social and familial atmosphere inhabited by the SENAI student, he finds little encouragement to improve his general culture and to elevate his civic and moral concepts."[19] In light of such assumptions, it seems reasonable to surmise that the SENAI officials involved in this research project actively sought an explanation for the high dropout rate in the supposedly flawed character of the working-class family.

Strikingly absent from the study is any serious attempt to evaluate and criticize SENAI itself or the premises on which SENAI operated. At no point, for example, did the researchers consider whether a young worker actually derived significant benefits from the completion of the SENAI course as opposed to one or two years of study. No questions were asked about whether the apprentice could reasonably expect to earn more or gain greater job security with SENAI certification.[20] As for the study of industrialist opinion, the researchers automatically assumed that SENAI-type apprenticeship would be beneficial to all firms in all sectors, despite the fact that SENAI's own emphasis on rationalization and simplification of tasks should have moved the investigators to consider whether certain industries actually required the type of worker SENAI trained. This omission is especially startling in light of the massive reorientation of SENAI just a few years later toward greater emphasis on rapid training within industry.[21]

The particular questions asked by the researchers as well as the questions they omitted indicate a presumption that the main obstacle to SENAI's full success was the "low moral and cultural level" of Brazil's industrial workers (and some of its industrial employers). Through a selective reading of the data collected, the researchers concluded that only a very small portion of that working class—represented by the control group—exhibited the values and aspirations that insured social mobility. Manifested in superior consumption patterns and living conditions, the values of these families approximated the SENAI officials' notion of "middle-class" standards.[22]

Thus, even SENAI, with its more technical and less explicitly ideological orientation, fashioned an image of the "typical" Brazilian worker as an

impediment rather than a contributor to national development and regarded Brazilian working-class culture as decidedly inferior or defective, if
not an outright oxymoron.[23] Wherever possible—in its celebrations of national holidays, ceremonies honoring leading industrialists, extracurricular
activities, and alumni associations—SENAI impressed upon its apprentices
the organization's goal of transforming them into responsible citizens aware
of their obligations and capable of contributing to industrial development.[24]
By implication, SENAI's message classified those workers who did not have
the benefit of SENAI instruction—the vast majority of the laboring population—as ill-prepared for citizenship and socially irresponsible.

As we have seen, SENAI's ideological predisposition did not irrevo-
cably dim its image among workers or union leaders, who viewed it in
practical terms as often the only means for young operatives or unskilled
adults to acquire a trade. But SENAI's orientation—its simultaneous emphasis on the low moral and cultural level of the Brazilian worker and on
the progressive character of the industrial bourgeoisie, combined with the
exclusion of labor representatives from its administration and the lack of
attention to workers' rights and concerns—limited its political impact.
Even those unions that valued SENAI highly for its practical advantages
ultimately regarded it as an organization that trained workers but served
the interests of industry (as opposed to SENAI's slogan, "An industrial organization at the service of the Brazilian worker"). And SENAI's promise
of training and individual social mobility for only a small segment of the
industrial workforce was hardly the stuff of populist dreams.

This image of the Brazilian worker permeated even the "technical"
aspects of SENAI's operations, with their emphasis on the need for discipline, order, cleanliness, and hierarchy. But it is likely that within the
workshop the SENAI apprentice was little affected by the sociological
assumptions of the organization's directors.[25] In the case of SESI, however,
the images constructed of the Brazilian worker were central to every phase
of its operations. Such images guided the activities of SESI's diverse
staff—social workers, social educators, home economics teachers, nutritionists, industrial safety experts—and therefore deserve a particularly
careful consideration.

Constructing the Brazilian Worker

The SESI staff constructed its image of the Brazilian worker from a number of different ideological sources—reformist Catholic doctrine, Fordism,
liberal sociology, and corporatist "social law"—all informed by a historical

narrative that emphasized the moral degradation of Brazilian workers and the denigration of manual labor (at least prior to the founding of SENAI and SESI). In addition, SESI personnel were constructing a portrait of the "Brazilian working man" at a moment when the composition of São Paulo's industrial workforce was visibly shifting from a population of predominantly European-immigrant origin to a more diverse group that included large numbers of recent rural migrants, many of whom were people of color. These "national" workers, assumed by SESI staffers to be especially inexperienced and "ignorant" of the demands of modern-industrial life, reinforced the tendency to view the urban labor force as maladjusted and in dire need of moral and cultural uplift.[26]

A certain amount of ideological variation always existed among individual staff members, but the efforts of divisional directors to produce a uniform SESI "doctrine" allow us to discern the most prevalent images of the Brazilian worker in the SESI literature. A very useful publication in this regard is the monthly magazine *Educador Social*, first issued by DOS in 1952. DOS mailed thousands of copies of the magazine, free of charge, to factory managers and supervisors, union headquarters, SESI's own social centers, and other appropriate locations. Although it is impossible to determine how much of a regular readership *Educador Social* attracted, the magazine is a convenient source for uncovering the messages that SESI wished to disseminate among industrial workers and the social constructions that informed those messages.

Educador Social published brief articles written either by SESI staff members or by outside authors whose views were compatible with SESI doctrine. The contents of its debut issue offer an excellent sample of the magazine's style and orientation. One article, entitled "Democratic Equality," set the antipopulist tone of the publication. Using a historical anecdote involving French politicians, it ridiculed "excessive declarations" of equality and proclaimed the impossibility of "total equality." Immediately following this brief essay was a longer article by a Jesuit detailing the "worker's rights and duties." According to Father Soder, the worker's duties included "*respect and obedience* to the just demands of the owners" and the obligation to "remain immune to *subversive doctrines and insinuations* that tend to destroy the friendly and fraternal relations between employees and employers."[27] The worker's rights included access to the "fruits of his labor," defined as a wage sufficient for a "decent existence." But some rights were accompanied by prescriptions for proper behavior: the good father viewed "Sunday rest" as necessary since it "allows the worker to fulfill his religious obligations and to spend one day a week in the happy conviviality of his family." Other articles touched on subjects such as the need to honor the Brazilian flag and to support scouting.

In subsequent months, *Educador Social* diversified its contents to include advice about various types of labor legislation and accounts of SESI activities. But certain themes appeared with remarkable regularity, prominent among them being calls for increased productivity and paeans to hard work and self-discipline. These articles occasionally highlighted the career of a particular worker, such as the employee of a clothing factory who in ten years had not missed a day of work or arrived a minute late.[28] Others consisted of advice to workers. "How to Increase the Pleasure You Get from Work" urged workers to improve themselves, suggesting that each "put himself in the owner's place. Then do your job as he would like it to be done. Don't limit yourself to merely 'fulfilling your obligation.'"[29] Similarly, "Self-Control" claimed that "discipline is essential to a man's development." And a series of articles simply entitled "Work" assured its readers that society no longer regarded work as degrading but rather as a source of pride.[30] A piece commemorating SESI's seventh anniversary repeated the standard line about the organization's apolitical character, affirming that "SESI's only intention is to make the Brazilian worker . . . a good family head, conscious of his duties and responsibilities, and to increase his technical and productive capacity."[31]

As in the case of SENAI, the worker emerges in the pages of *Educador Social* as a problem; with rare exceptions, he is portrayed as unaware of his obligations and incapable, without assistance, of contributing fully to industrial production. All manner of problems are attributed to the workers' alleged lack of discipline: operatives chatting on the job are blamed for the high incidence of industrial accidents, and unnecessary motions are cited as a leading cause of fatigue and industrial waste. Moreover, the worker's alleged flaws, far from being the product of circumstances beyond his control, are described as a matter of attitude. Hence, with the correct motivation and discipline, provided by SESI programs, an individual worker could overcome his cultural and educational deficits and, by implication, achieve a certain degree of social mobility and security.[32]

The magazine not only placed the burden of industrial problems on the workers' shoulders but also implicitly exonerated Brazilian industrialists of any blame for low levels of industrial productivity or poor standards of living. The only other figure on the industrial scene that *Educador Social* consistently criticized was the supervisor who lacked the appropriate psychological and technical training and thus often exacerbated misunderstandings and maladjustments among workers. But the editors of *Educador*

Social viewed this as no surprise since the vast majority of industrial foremen were themselves simply workers who had obtained their positions through seniority and experience rather than scientific selection and training.[33]

One could expect the technicians involved in the production of *Educador Social*—industrial psychologists, social workers, social educators—to emphasize the "problem worker" given their training in professions dedicated to social adjustment and assistance. But the SESI staff went further, regarding Brazilian workers on the whole as problematic, with only exceptional workers displaying the moral, cultural, and technical qualities regarded as necessary for rapid industrial development. As one SESI publication bluntly put it, São Paulo's industrial workforce, "needless to say, finds itself maladjusted."[34]

Significantly, not all "experts" on labor and economic development expressed such views. It is interesting to contrast SESI's assumptions about the Brazilian worker with those expressed in studies of Brazilian manufacturing during this period. Reports by the United Nations Economic Commission on Latin America and the Joint Brazil–United States Economic Development Commission, published in 1951 and 1954, respectively, cited many obstacles to full-scale industrialization in Brazil, including transport problems, expensive raw materials, capital scarcity, and energy shortages. Both studies did acknowledge that the shortage of highly skilled workers was a problem, and the latter report also noted a deficit of technicians and engineers. But neither study described the workforce, overall, as unproductive or defective. Similarly, a survey of paulista firms in the late 1950s found that employers consistently ranked intensification of worker productivity as the least important factor in expanding industrial output.[35] Then again, such reports treated workers almost exclusively as economic actors; SESI, meanwhile, may have stressed economic performance but was at least equally concerned with the worker's political and social behavior.

Thus far, references to the Brazilian worker have repeatedly made use of the masculine pronoun, and deliberately so: the typical worker constructed by SESI was, unfailingly, a male worker. The organization did not completely neglect the working-class woman, but its conceptualization of her role and the "problems" she presented were quite different from that of the working-class man. This was even reflected in the structure of the institution: programs and courses directed at men were offered by the Division of Social Orientation, while activities organized specifically for women were the province of the Division of Family Assistance.[36]

Home economics class (not a vocational course) in sewing for female apprentices at the SENAI school in Campinas, 1946. Courtesy of the Núcleo de Memória, SENAI–São Paulo.

SENAI also perceived the roles of men and women in the labor force very differently. Even though SENAI's own statistics showed that girls composed well over half of the industrial labor force under eighteen, the organization operated on the assumption that most of these working girls would, and should, withdraw from the industrial labor force once they reached marriageable age.[37] SESI, meanwhile, virtually ignored the woman worker, treating the working-class woman as, first and foremost, a housewife and mother. SESI's mission with regard to the working-class woman who was already a wife and mother was to teach her to perform her domestic functions in a more rational and cost-effective fashion. As for the tens of thousands of girls employed in factories, SESI's objective was to prepare them for the day when they traded in their work card for a marriage license. SESI's staff members knew that many women remained in the factories well beyond the age of majority; the textile, clothing, and soap industries continued to rely very heavily on women operatives. And many women workers found their withdrawal from the industrial labor force to be only temporary as straitened economic circumstances pushed them back into factory work. The SESI course for *māezinhas* (little mothers), which trained adolescent girls to care for the household in their mothers' absence, acknowledged this possibility. But SESI regarded a return to factory work, however unavoidable, as an unfortunate deviation from the normal routine of family life anchored by a full-time wife and mother.[38]

Reconstructing the Brazilian Worker

Having constructed the working-class population as problematic, the social workers and educators of SESI and SENAI undertook to resolve these problems by rational and scientific means. SESI and SENAI strived to instill not just the value of self-discipline and hard work—the sine qua non of social advancement—but also the need for careful budgeting, rational consumption habits, good nutrition, improved hygiene, and healthy recreation.[39] But such rationalization of life beyond the factory had to be accompanied by certain moral and civic guidelines so that the workers could be integrated into a national culture based on patriotism and Christian ethics. This culture, though superficially Brazilian in its celebration of national holidays and historical events, could be defined more accurately as "transnational" since it reflected the social workers' notions of modern, middle-class life in more industrialized societies.

Beginning in the 1950s, SENAI intensified its efforts to assure the social and moral "adjustment" of its apprentices, going beyond its previous emphasis on extracurricular activities and instituting "systematic social education," offered in regular weekly classes, in addition to courses in family education for the parents of SENAI students. SESI, meanwhile, viewed all of its operations as including a social educational component; even the discount food posts supposedly taught workers habits of thrift and economy. But certain programs lent themselves more readily to the inculcation of appropriate cultural and moral values. A 1955 report by SESI's Division of Education and Culture made this explicit in describing the achievements of its literacy teachers:

They do not limit themselves merely to teaching the ABCs, arithmetic, and basic notions for various facets of human activity. Oriented toward the social aspects of their work, they equally undertake to develop in the student habits and attitudes favorable to his integration into society; they stimulate the acceptance of values such as coopera-

tion, solidarity, and respect for human dignity; they examine the problem of human relations, indicating to the worker how he can participate, harmoniously and effectively, in his work group, his family, and
in other social circles.[40]

The report also proudly noted that the division had turned its *cursos populares* into "a veritable school of *brasilidade*." This effort entailed not only
lectures on Brazilian history and discussions of the constitution and democratic government but also elaborate observance of every national holiday,
such as Independence Day, Proclamation of the Republic Day, Flag Day,
Day of the Soldier, and Abolition of Slavery Day. The report mentioned
with particular pleasure a recent rally staged by some 5,000 SESI students
in the capital (with smaller gatherings throughout the interior) to commemorate Brazilian independence.

It is striking how much attention SESI and SENAI paid to these national holidays, including those like Flag Day that had no particular tradition or popular appeal. For example, the debut issue of *Educador Social*
contained detailed instructions on how to honor and handle the Brazilian
flag.[41] SENAI students religiously observed all such commemorative occasions and participated in rallies and parades organized by SESI. At the
same time, SESI and SENAI carefully distinguished their patriotism from
the rising nationalism of populist and left-wing groups.[42] The industrial
organizations celebrated the *Pátria* as the source of a common culture and
traditional institutions—the Church, the Family, the Armed Forces—to
be respected and strengthened. But such love for one's country did not en-
tail the exaltation of the "State" or the exclusion of foreign investment and
influence—except when incompatible with national interests and traditions, as would be the case with the "totalitarian" Communist nations.

SESI's instructional staff made little effort at subtlety in conveying the
appropriate messages. A text issued in the early 1950s for SESI's advanced
literacy courses, *The Worker's Second Reader*, took every opportunity to instill the correct moral and civic values in its audience. Using simple language and ample illustrations, the primer gave lessons in proper living as
well as basic literacy skills. It opens with an illustration of a domestic scene
in what is obviously SESI's ideal working-class (*cum* middle-class) household. A father in shirt and tie is photographing a young child seated in a
high chair while an attractively attired wife (complete with apron, lest anyone remain ignorant of her domestic function) looks on approvingly. This
simple tableau includes several lessons for the worker-student: emphasizing the trappings of middle-class respectability, such as proper attire, it
portrays the worker as a devoted family man enjoying the company of his

wife and child, rather than his workmates, and shows him wielding a camera, an object of consumption, like a radio or sewing machine, that workers could aspire to own.

In subsequent pages, the text instructs workers to bathe regularly, to make a constant effort to avoid accidents, to drink milk instead of alcohol, and to fulfill their obligation as citizens to vote. The final lesson for the reader is illustrated by a drawing of a manager with his arm around the shoulders of a worker, with the text stating, "Cooperation, the link between workers and management, mutual interaction, in short, teamwork, are the most effective means for improving each person's welfare and overall production."[43]

An interesting aspect of this final illustration is the fact that the worker is not only white—as were all of the other figures in the reader—but blond as well. Of course, São Paulo's working-class population still included many European immigrants whose appearance may have approximated that of the illustrated figure, but they could hardly be regarded as typical. Meanwhile, the substantial portion of the working class that was black or *pardo* went completely unrepresented in the SESI reader and in most of the organization's other publications. Not that SESI adopted an overtly racist posture. It offered literacy and sewing courses at the headquarters of the Associação José do Patrocínio, one of São Paulo's few organizations for people of color.[44] And an article in *Educador Social* expressed the classic liberal view that "there is no such thing as superior or inferior races; all men have the same mental potential."[45] But it seems that, having declared all men equal, SESI relieved itself of any obligation to address issues of racial prejudice or discrimination. Rather, it eagerly embraced the "myth of racial democracy," frequently endorsing the idea that no racial problems existed in Brazil.[46]

SESI's literacy courses provided an excellent medium for the dissemination of lessons in moral and civic virtue. In 1955 alone, 431 such courses were operating in the capital and the interior, with over 20,000 students enrolled. The SESI official who oversaw literacy instruction during these years claimed that the organization received more requests for the courses than it could handle.[47] SESI also tended to the civic education of more literate workers. In its social centers and in factories, SESI offered courses in "orientation for reading" to develop better reading habits among already literate workers. Such classes placed less emphasis on basic skills and more emphasis on the content of reading materials and the themes introduced by SESI in its literacy courses.

SESI also encouraged workers to read by providing circulating libraries and bookmobiles that would drop off portable bookcases, containing hundreds of volumes, at interested factories or union headquarters. SESI took care to make sure that the readings offered to workers were ideologically and morally suitable; a committee of SESI officials and outside advisers met every year to review the books being added to the collection. One book excluded from the bookmobiles during the Vargas administration was a polemic on the Brazilian petroleum industry that SESI regarded as too nationalistic and critical of the United States. A worker interested in reading a prohibited book could borrow it from SESI's central library, but he or she would first have to chat with a librarian, who would determine whether the worker was really "capable of understanding" the text in question.[48]

The orientation of reading courses became increasingly popular over time. In 1954 SESI recorded 121,165 worker "appearances" in these courses, five times the number recorded four years earlier. In that same year, over 65,000 books were consulted or borrowed from SESI's library facilities in São Paulo.[49] But this still represented a very small portion of SESI's potential clientele, and courses in "civic instruction" and "social doctrines" offered by DOS at SESI's social centers only attracted a few hundred students per year. To reach a wider audience, SESI turned to a medium that had thoroughly penetrated São Paulo's working-class communities: the radio.

SESI personnel recognized the educational potential of the radio but also feared its capacity to disseminate undesirable messages since "many programs . . . do not obey moral norms and principles."[50] Beginning in 1953, every Monday evening SESI broadcast a half-hour program on Rádio Tupi that discussed work-related questions such as accident prevention, social legislation, domestic problems, and community issues. The program solicited questions from São Paulo's industrial workers that would then be addressed on the air and enlivened its offerings with classical and popular music.

Rational Recreation

Courses for popular instruction accounted for only a portion of the activities of the Division of Education and Culture. SESI concerned itself with every facet of working-class life, a concern that included the organization of appropriate recreational activities for workers' leisure time.[51] In this respect, too, the Brazilian worker was problematic, failing to fill his or her free time with wholesome entertainment or relaxation. A SESI publication lamented that Brazilian workers "do not know how to entertain themselves." Thus it was up to SESI to "teach the worker to enjoy himself and,

Apprentices at the SENAI school in Brás during a period of recreation, 1947.
Courtesy of the Núcleo de Memória, SENAI–São Paulo.

enjoying himself, to contribute to the formation of a social spirit in our land." Moreover, such assistance was urgently needed since "the lack of appropriate and accessible recreation causes the workers to seek meeting places that are not always recommendable and that induce the formation of harmful habits." Or as SESI's house publication bluntly put it, "In general, the working-class population seeks to amuse itself in the 'corner bar,' and it's hardly necessary to mention the consequences of this 'sojourn.'"[52] Once again, SESI regarded the worker either as lacking in culture or developing a culture that was undesirable by SESI's standards.

SESI's efforts to reorganize workers' recreational activities began modestly. Aside from the May Day Workers' Olympics, which absorbed much of the energy of the sports subdivision, SESI created a handful of "workers' clubs." Located in the capital and the interior, these clubs provided space for such wholesome pastimes as dominoes, chess, and checkers as well as facilities for social gatherings and in the case of the São Caetano club, an art gallery.[53] SESI's sports service also sought to bring "discipline" to amateur soccer in urban centers, organizing and "legalizing" *futebol* clubs associated with factories or working-class neighborhoods. In distributing financial and technical assistance, SESI gave priority to those clubs with over 500 members, preferably associated with a single firm, and made sure that the club's leaders were willing to "disseminate among its members and those of other clubs SESI's policy of cooperation between employees and employers." SESI's first major grant of this type was awarded to the soccer club associated with the Santa Marina glass factory. According to SESI's regional council, this club was "among those with the strongest Christian democratic orientation."[54]

The service's technicians not only provided financial aid and athletic instruction but also made every effort to affiliate teams with amateur sports federations, thereby subjecting their competitions to rational record-keeping and officiating. Such disciplined play by factory teams, according to the director of SESI's sports subdivision, created among the workers "a feeling of participation and pride so necessary for maintaining, within and outside the workplace, a climate of collegiality and friendship and good relations with the management of the firm." At the same time, care was taken to avoid "excessive enthusiasm," which the SESI officials considered an unfortunate aspect of amateur athletics.[55]

By the 1950s, SESI had expanded its technical and organizational services in the recreational sphere to include boxing, handball, Ping-Pong, basketball, bicycling, swimming, track, volleyball, and chess. In 1955, not counting the Workers' Olympics, SESI organized 2,331 sports competitions with 21,072 athletes participating. As one would expect, SESI's sports technicians directed most of their efforts at working-class men and boys. However, some of the activities were open to women, with women's teams holding competitions in track, volleyball, and chess during the May Day festivities, although women were specifically excluded from participation in soccer.[56]

SESI also offered various forms of wholesome entertainment to fill the working-class family's leisure hours. Among the most popular programs were screenings of recent films at union halls, workers' clubs, and other gathering places. From 1948 to 1954, SESI recorded 7.5 million paulistas in attendance at these showings, which attracted particularly large crowds in interior cities where there were few commercial options for such entertainment. As with its literary offerings, SESI carefully monitored the contents of these films to make sure that they met its cultural standards. SESI's amateur theatrical productions also attracted substantial audiences, with attendance from 1950 to 1954 approaching 300,000.

Annual festivities such as the Party for Worker Confraternization (Festa de Confraternização Operária) on New Year's Eve formed another important facet of SESI's recreational activities. The gala that inaugurated the year 1954 had some 8,000 paulistas in attendance, and the number rose

SENAI salutes SESI: The delegation of SENAI apprentices in the parade for the fifth Workers' Olympics, May Day, 1951. Courtesy of the Núcleo de Memória, SENAI–São Paulo.

to approximately 12,000 the following year. Among the participants in 1954 were high government officials, prominent industrialists, and union leaders such as José Sanches Duran of the metallurgical workers' federation, Luiz Fiuza Cárdia of the clothing workers' federation, and construction worker federation head Luiz Menossi. The high points of the event were the annual message to paulista workers from the president of FIESP and the crowning of a young working-class woman as "Queen of the Workers."[57] Pleased with the success of this event, SESI began sponsoring an annual Spring Ball, which the organization portrayed as providing an opportunity for working-class *brotinhos* (teenagers) to imitate the "coming out" parties of upper-class debutantes.

SESI also began organizing ever more elaborate ceremonies to mark workers' "graduation" from its various courses. When a factory cosponsored a literacy course, for example, the teacher urged the owner not only to attend the closing ceremonies but also to award small gifts to those who achieved certification and provide refreshments for a celebration. Even more of a fuss was made at the close of courses in the interior. It was by no means unusual for several dignitaries of a small urban center to attend the certification ceremonies for graduates of SESI's sewing or literacy courses. The mayor of Santo André, one of the capital's oldest and largest industrial suburbs, served as *paraninfo* (patron) at the graduation ceremonies for a SESI sewing course. And gracing the inauguration of home economics courses in São Carlos were both the president of the municipal council and the local bishop.[58] Thus such festive occasions served to reinforce SESI's links with various influential sectors of urban communities while giving the courses' graduates a sense of accomplishment and importance.

SESI encouraged students who took its courses or workers who frequented its facilities to celebrate virtually all traditional religious and folkloric events with the glaring exception of *carnaval*. Despite the central role that the pre-Lenten festivities played in the social and cultural life of Brazilian cities, SESI (at least in São Paulo) registered only disapproval of the annual revelries. This policy reflected, in part, the profound influence of the Catholic Church on many of SESI's social workers and educators since the church had long decried the hedonistic and irreligious aspects of Brazilian *carnaval*. But even if the church had not been critical of *carnaval*, it is difficult to imagine SESI officials lauding the celebration, with its apparently anarchic character, lewd overtones, "deafening samba music," and unhygienic practices such as overcrowding and excessive drinking. SESI personnel also regarded *carnaval* as incompatible with São Paulo's sober image as Brazil's center of rational organization and hard work. In many ways, *carnaval* represented the most extreme aspects of the popular culture that SESI was trying to rationalize and/or replace. Apparently regarding the pre-Lenten celebration as beyond rationalization, SESI officials simply encouraged its nonobservance, counseling "intelligent" paulistas to avoid participation in the revelry.[59]

The Hygienic Housewife

Whereas such messages were aimed at both men and women, SESI officials regarded cultural respectability and good health practices to be the domain of the working-class wife and mother. From the outset, SESI had focused some of its attention on women, the sewing courses being among its first and most popular instructional programs. SESI's social workers also took every opportunity to visit workers' homes, survey conditions, and make suggestions for improving the domestic sphere. Typically, when a worker sought SESI's medical services but could not make the modest payments, a social worker paid a home visit to determine if the financial problems were a matter of poor household management. As Antônio Devisate revealingly put it, the social worker would investigate "to see why the workers' wives were not able to make their husbands' wages go as far as they should."[60] Often, after this initial contact or an encounter at a SESI social center, the social worker tried to organize a group of women in the neighborhood to meet and discuss their personal and economic problems, with the SESI representative gently guiding the conversation and suggesting solutions to domestic dilemmas. One SESI social worker described such gatherings as an incentive for the working-class woman to clean and decorate her home, "since this is not the typical condition of their residences."[61] SESI's subdivision for family assistance, meanwhile, set up various courses in child care, home economics, and cooking, the latter being held at its district kitchens.

By the early 1950s, SESI had decided to concentrate these courses for working-class women in the Centers for Domestic Instruction (Centros de Aprendizado Doméstico, or CADs). By 1954, the organization had inaugurated twenty-five such centers throughout the state. The centers offered three different cooking courses as well as classes in child care, household management, domestic hygiene, and preparation for marriage. Sewing courses, previously held in factories or union headquarters, were now also available at many of the centers. And to complement the centers' activities, SESI began publishing two monthly magazines, *Dona de Casa* and *SESI-Higiene*.[62]

The centers offered instruction for women of all age groups, with the courses for *mãezinhas* aimed at nine- to fourteen-year-olds, the preparation for marriage courses aimed at young women, and all other courses open to anyone sixteen and older.[63] The centers also reached out to the families of their students; for example, many parents with daughters in the *mãezinha* program attended monthly meetings with the center's staff to be informed of their child's progress and to discuss domestic matters.[64] Students, especially in the cooking courses, frequently organized parties and contests that involved friends and families, and every certification ceremony was an occasion for celebration. The women associated with the centers also participated prominently in other SESI activities, such as the May Day parade and the Spring Ball. After completing the courses, an ex-student could maintain social contact through the center's alumnae association.

Again, all of these courses operated on the assumption that working-class women were, first and foremost, wives and mothers or future wives and mothers. Women might work before marriage or work outside the home intermittently after marriage to alleviate financial distress, but their

The SENAI "jeep" in the SESI-sponsored parade to inaugurate the fourth Workers' Olympics, May Day, 1950. Courtesy of the Núcleo de Memória, SENAI–São Paulo.

major contribution to the household would come in the form of a rationally organized budget, a healthful atmosphere, and well-raised children. As the premier issue of *Dona de Casa* put it, referring to the magazine's title, which means "Housewife," "Here you have, in just three words, the golden dream of almost every young woman."[65] Moreover, *Dona de Casa*'s editors apparently regarded the role of housewife as biologically determined. In a later article, the magazine answered the question, "Is the masculine sex superior to the feminine?," by claiming that it was not a matter of superiority or inferiority but of difference, grounded in different hormonal activity. "As a result, women have the ability to note the small details, while men see only the broader picture." Continuing this emphasis on separate abilities and spheres, the magazine concluded that "although the man has his triumphs in the workplace . . . the woman has the reward of raising strong children."[66]

   With varying degrees of subtlety, the home economics courses taught their students that housewives, though not wage earners, were largely responsible for the standard of living and quality of life in their homes.[67]

Thus *Dona de Casa* roused its readers with its call to initiate, "by any means possible, a campaign against malnutrition and the neglect of Brazilian homes." Similarly, an account of a cooking contest between students from the CADs in Santo André and São Caetano assured readers of the *SESI-Jornal* that "if all future housewives acquired the knowledge of the culinary arts, nutrition, and diet that are provided in the CADs, soon there would no longer be any problems resulting from nutritional deficiencies." Speaking at this same contest, FIESP president Antônio Devisate informed his audience that "ignorance" about domestic tasks on the part of working-class women was a major cause of marital disputes. He claimed some 90 percent of the separation cases brought to the attention of SESI's legal service had such domestic incompetence at their root. Thus the competent housewife could not only provide a comfortable home and balanced diet for her family but also save her marriage.[68]

Much of the cooking and housekeeping advice dispensed by the SESI courses amounted to routine information that could be extracted from the home economics manuals used by São Paulo's vocational schools for women since the early twentieth century.[69] But SESI infused its courses with its own preoccupations, emphasizing the rationalization of housework and adherence to a code of proper conduct. An early issue of *Dona de Casa* asked its readers, "Did you know that our organism is similar to a machine?"[70] In contrast to the home economics literature of wealthier societies, the SESI publications did not emphasize the acquisition of modern, labor-saving household appliances, most of which were beyond the financial reach of SESI's audience. But precisely because of this, the Brazilian working-class household had to be very carefully organized and managed.[71]

SESI courses and publications also advised young women to be "modest, simple, and sweet," claiming that men might go out with boisterous, flirtatious, and heavily made-up women but chose more demur types to be their wives. "Dona Nicota," the fictional advice columnist for *Dona de Casa*, warned young women to avoid any form of premarital sexual activity and urged them to think less about love and marriage and more about domestic tasks. Women were also counseled to remain demur even after marriage. *Dona de Casa* faulted a wife who became angry with her husband when he went out for a drink with his friends and arrived home late for dinner. The real solution to the problem, it contended, was to make their home more pleasant so that the husband would *want* to arrive on time.[72]

The question of proper morality emerged even more conspicuously in the discussion of health matters, both in *Dona de Casa* and *SESI-Higiene*. The latter publication, issued by SESI's Industrial Hygiene and Safety Service, was clearly targeted at women since the vast majority of its articles dealt with marital, domestic, and child-rearing matters. Only rarely did the magazine raise the subject of industrial accidents, and it usually did so in relation to some domestic practice that indirectly contributed to their incidence. Like much of the SESI literature, *SESI-Higiene* treated good health as a function of knowledge about hygiene and proper morality, regarded as two sides of the same valuable coin.

The close association of hygiene and morality is best illustrated by the extensive attention SESI paid to the problem of syphilis. Since its founding, the organization had devoted a sizable portion of its resources to test hundreds of thousands of factory workers for the disease. This campaign may have been inspired by Simonsen's claim, based on a supposedly scientific survey he sponsored in the 1920s, that 45 percent of Brazilian-born workers were infected with syphilis.[73] The actual results of massive testing in the late 1940s and early 1950s revealed a much lower rate of infection—3.5 percent—among industrial workers, a rate that was lower, in fact, than that found in many advanced industrial nations.[74] Despite this heartening discovery, SESI continued to treat syphilis as a major health risk for the Brazilian working class and a major concern for working-class women. Publications aimed at workers (that is, men), such as *Educador Social* and *CIPA-Jornal*, rarely made any mention of syphilis or other contagious diseases, whereas the woman-oriented magazines constantly discussed the menace of venereal infection. The debut issue of *SESI-Higiene*, for example, included two separate articles on the subject, one of which warned its readers that you could contract syphilis from a mere kiss.[75]

Given SESI's identification of venereal disease as a major social problem for women, it is not surprising that a large portion of the material in the preparation for marriage course dealt with syphilis testing and prevention. Instructors advised prospective brides to choose their husbands carefully and to give special attention to their future mate's physical condition. A premarital examination was a must, as was constant vigilance for signs of the disease. Much emphasis was also given to the impact on future offspring. SESI literature warned students of the large number of infants who died from the effects of syphilis, claiming that these tiny victims had been "murdered" by their parents.[76] To illustrate this point, *SESI-Higiene* devoted an entire issue to the hypothetical tale of Lili and Maricota. The former agrees to marry the first man she meets, fails to insist on prenuptial exams, contracts syphilis, has only one child who dies in infancy, and ends up ill, abandoned, and childless. The latter, in contrast, patiently seeks the proper mate, insists on prenuptial exams, and becomes the perfect wife and mother, a happy ending verified by the accompanying illustration showing Maricota holding an infant in her arms and surrounded by six other children.[77] It seems that nobody at SESI found any irony in the idyllic portrayal of a working-class housewife with seven young children, a situation that would almost certainly have spelled poverty for her household.

Syphilis was not the only contagious illness that received attention in the "domestic arts" courses. Tuberculosis— a real scourge of the paulista working class that was spread by poor living conditions—was a matter of similar concern. During its first decade, SESI tested over a million factory workers and their families for tuberculosis and provided treatment centers and a sanatorium. Yet the SESI literature paid less attention to this disease than it did to syphilis, perhaps because the contraction of tuberculosis could not be so easily attributed to a moral failing. SESI's obsessive preoccupation with syphilis had less to do with the incidence or severity of the disease than with the means of transmission.

Another major preoccupation of the SESI domestic arts instructors and the related publications was to steer women away from midwives and home births and toward doctors and hospitals. *SESI-Higiene* and *Dona de Casa* portrayed the midwife as "Dona Ignorancia's inseparable friend" and regarded the advice of doctors as unimpeachable.[78] In its discussions of high infant mortality rates, *SESI-Higiene* mentioned widely recognized factors such as lack of medical attention during pregnancy and infancy but, in typical fashion, assigned primary culpability for the problem to the parents: "It is necessary that the parents understand that they themselves are the most responsible for this high rate of mortality."[79]

Although much of the literature produced by SESI on domestic arts reflected strong North American influences—bolstered by frequent internships by SESI "technicians" in the United States—SESI displayed more traditional Brazilian attitudes with regard to the ideal family size. Unlike North American social workers, who increasingly considered large families to be a major factor in household impoverishment, SESI's personnel and publications portrayed the ideal family as consisting of numerous children—seven in the case of the fortunate Maricota. This tendency can be attributed at least in part to SESI's strong ties to Catholic organizations, which precluded any overt reference to family planning. The only published allusion to this subject during the early 1950s can be found in an article entitled "Crime and Punishment" that stridently denounced the reputed increase in abortions. Claiming that the high cost of living was driving women to commit "veritable murders," *SESI-Higiene* accused lay abortionists, midwives, and "even some unscrupulous doctors who dishonor their noble title" of "tremendous barbarities." The article reminded its readers that the "cost" of abortion, aside from the sin of "killing a human being," included serious physical risks for the woman. Not only did a perforated uterus "invariably lead to death," but also "sterility and uterine cancer usually have their origins in these hideous acts, which are, unfortunately, so common among us."[80]

Another "vice" that SESI's courses and publications routinely condemned was alcohol consumption, including even recreational drinking. According to *SESI-Higiene*, "Alcohol destroys domestic happiness, causes the degeneration of the race, and disturbs the social tranquillity." Even though SESI regarded excessive drinking as a predominantly male activity, it delegated the woman the responsibility for discerning signs of such vices in a prospective mate and for creating a domestic environment conducive to clean living. In its only (oblique) reference to domestic violence, *SESI-Higiene* noted the constant headlines in daily papers about murders and suicides, which it blamed on the victims, who "are ignorant of the great responsibilities that marriage entails."[81] In short, it was the woman's role to stretch the family budget, give birth to healthy children, create a wholesome home environment, defeat the spread of syphilis, respect the advice of experts, and avoid circumstances conducive to vice and violence. No wonder that SESI scolded women who sought to marry as a way to stop working by reminding them that "their labors [after marriage] will be greater and their responsibilities greatly increased."[82]

One might expect such daunting prescriptions for competence as a wife and mother to discourage working-class women from enrolling in the SESI courses, but the CADs proved to be among the most popular of SESI's programs. From 1948, when the domestic arts courses first started functioning, to 1959, the centers granted nearly 200,000 certificates of completion to paulista women and another 14,000 certificates to women who completed courses by correspondence. Some women took multiple courses, reducing the total number of individuals represented in these figures. However, the statistics probably underestimate the centers' impact since they exclude women who attended several classes but failed to complete a course, relatives who participated in the centers' activities, and the 51,000 graduates of the sewing courses.

We can only speculate about the appeal of these courses since the occasional remark quoted by SESI hardly amounts to a random sample of student opinion. In the case of the sewing courses, which SESI portrayed as vehicles for social education and for reducing household expenses, it is evident that many women enrolled for other reasons. Virtually every comment about these courses by former students mentions the value of learning a skill that allowed them to earn extra income and supplement their husbands' salary. SESI may have denied that these were "professionalizing courses," but the women who enrolled in them insistently disagreed.[83] The same explanation could not apply to most of the other courses, however. Except for the most advanced phase, the cooking classes were too rudimentary to provide a means to earn additional income, and the other courses were only relevant for unpaid work in the domestic sphere.

Why, then, did thousands of women flock to these courses on cooking, child care, and other domestic arts? Perhaps the center attracted them because it was a place for women only, where they could congregate with other working-class women and discuss problems that were genuinely relevant to their everyday lives. After all, what institution offered urban, working-class women a similar meeting place or forum? Certainly not the male-oriented union headquarters, the priest-centered church, or the typically masculine neighborhood bar. Although SESI's approach to the problems of working-class women appears, in retrospect, overly moralistic and often unrealistic, it did treat matters central to most women's lives—cleaning, shopping, cooking, child rearing—as serious responsibilities that deserved thoughtful consideration. In a society that barely took notice of women's unpaid labor, SESI's careful attention to these activities, whatever the ideological underpinnings, provided a refreshing contrast.[84]

It is also likely that SESI accurately assumed that most working-class women aspired to the role of housewife and mother. In a society that had long conceptualized the female industrial worker as an unskilled operative with little opportunity for vocational education, professional advancement, or active participation in her union, few women could regard lifelong factory employment as a desirable alternative.[85] Although girls continued to constitute a majority of factory workers under the age of eighteen, they almost always found themselves assigned to highly monotonous, semiskilled positions with little promise of promotion. In this context, the daily routine of the skilled "household manager" must have seemed quite attractive.[86]

Again, SESI made every effort to give its women students a sense of accomplishment and importance when it granted the certificates of completion (as well as a sense of gratitude to the organization's sponsors). The prominent role of FIESP "First Lady" Anita Devisate at such ceremonies and the presence of political and church officials may smack of noblesse oblige, but their participation undoubtedly heightened the solemnity of the occasion. This was surely an unusual experience for working-class girls and women accustomed to seeing their considerable domestic efforts go unacknowledged. Similarly, the various festive events promoted by SESI offered rare opportunities for these women to wear formal dresses—often sewn in SESI courses—and emulate a lifestyle normally inaccessible to them. Whereas working-class men had access to an industrial work culture that created attainable images of masculinity—emphasizing strength, skill, and wage earning—working-class women were constantly bombarded with images of femininity and sexuality that were normally beyond the reach of the financially constrained and overworked housewife.

SESI, in its particular fashion, celebrated women's current or future roles as wives and mothers while downplaying or denigrating their status as members of the working class. In the domestic sphere, too, working-class Brazilians were treated as lacking in skills, culture, and hygiene. The reconstructed working-class housewife would be expected to eliminate these deficiencies. Her goals were to cultivate an elegant appearance, stretch the budget, decorate the home, and organize the domestic sphere so that it approximated, as much as possible, the ideal middle-class household—goals that surely led to frustration for many of the centers' graduates. An article instructing housewives to wax their floors on a weekly basis must have seemed, at best, ironic to the many working-class women who lived in makeshift housing with "natural" floors.[87] But the SESI staff took considerable pleasure in the perceived transformation wrought by the CADs. As one female social educator, surveying a graduation ceremony, remarked: "Look at how these young ladies, with very rare exceptions, are now free of embarrassment and proudly lift their heads. *They don't even seem like women workers.*"[88]

Remaking Working-Class Youth

For rather different reasons, SESI also concerned itself with the proper socialization of working-class youth, especially boys, who would eventually become the backbone of the industrial workforce. Although SENAI existed to train and socialize these future workers, its students had to be fourteen or older, and the training organization served only a fraction of the total working-class population. SENAI was not unaware of these limitations; a major subject of discussion among its staff members was the old problem of the *hiato nocivo*—the two or three years between the completion of formal schooling and the initiation of factory employment. More specifically, this was seen as a problem only for working-class boys since girls could be occupied more easily with domestic tasks until they reached the legal work age and boys of higher class status would be expected to continue their education.[89]

As noted in Chapter 4, the *hiato nocivo* may well have been a "social problem" that was all construction and no substance. Many working-class boys, though not legally registered, began steady wage-work well before the age of fourteen, and some who worked with family members received legal permission to work by age twelve. Nonetheless, the specter of working-class adolescent males walking the streets, undisciplined and unsupervised and exposed to unwholesome influences, continued to haunt the psychologists, educators, and social workers employed by SENAI and SESI. Isaac Mielnik, SESI's leading child psychologist, published an article on "abandoned children," using that phrase to refer not to homeless children but to those who spent all their time on the vice-ridden streets for lack of alternatives, an experience that would forever distort their moral, professional, and civic development. Mielnik recommended that parents provide these youths with a more stimulating home environment or send them to "supervised parks" sponsored by SESI and other organizations.[90] Another DOS staff member, Fajardo da Silveira, authored an even more alarmist and lurid account of this danger in "O Problema do Menor de 14 Anos." According to Silveira, less than a quarter of the students who graduated from primary school had the means to continue their schooling; the remaining youngsters, "having left school but not being able to enter the workplace, remain on the streets, disposed toward crime, seeking out vices, and causing serious disturbances, especially in their own families."[91]

The ideal measures to "protect the minor from the dangers of the street" were SENAI's "vocational courses," open to boys and girls between the ages of twelve and fourteen. Surrounded by manual instructors, social workers, guidance counselors, and industrial psychologists, the students in these courses could be shielded from pernicious influences and guided into the "appropriate" career paths.[92] The only drawbacks of these courses were the high cost and the limited number of spaces: although enrollment grew from 280 in 1947 to 1,136 in 1953, the latter figure represented only a small fraction of the potential student population. Inhibiting further expansion was SENAI's precarious financial state, which made programs like the vocational courses something of a luxury. As a result, in the mid-1950s, SENAI, despite its enthusiastic endorsement of the endeavor, suspended these courses, which were then resurrected by SESI, working in collaboration with SENAI.

SESI and SENAI's preoccupation with youths in this age group also reflects their social workers' view of the big city as corrosive of family authority. The literature emanating from the United States on "juvenile delinquency" during the 1950s undoubtedly reinforced such concerns. Programs for this age group, then, tended to emphasize self-discipline as well as obedience to authority. One activity heavily promoted by SENAI and especially SESI was scouting. During its first year of existence, *Educador Social* published articles on scouting in nearly every issue, including an essay on "Boy Scout law" and its ten commandments. To commemorate the "Day of the Boy Scout" in 1953, the labor-oriented magazine even placed a portrait of the organization's founder on its cover.[93]

SESI scored occasional successes in its efforts to organize scouting troops, as indicated by a letter received in 1960 requesting subsidies for the purchase of Boy Scout uniforms. Signed by 500 residents of a low-income housing project in the industrial suburb of Santo André, the letter extolled the impact of the SESI scouting initiative. The petitioners introduced their request by noting that in the past it was not unusual to see groups of kids "who lived without the least control . . . smashing windows and trees . . . learning bad habits that harmed their health and morality, speaking a lingo loaded with slang and obscenities, always being disrespectful to their parents and their elders." Then, with SESI's help, the residents organized a scout troop, immediately enrolling 150 boys, "all workers' children." The results, the petitioners claimed, amounted to a radical transformation: "Applying an educational approach based on SESI's teachings, and scouting and military discipline, we elaborated an intensive program of instruction."[94] Now those same boys obeyed their parents and helped keep the community clean. But this was an unusual case; for the most part, SESI failed to disseminate its enthusiasm for scouting among the working-class youth of São Paulo. Requests for technical assistance were few and far between, and by 1954, SESI had inaugurated only two troops with a total of seventy members.[95] At a loss to explain this lack of interest, SESI blamed the shortage of qualified troop leaders, ignoring other possible factors such as the expense of scouting and the culturally unfamiliar rituals that accompanied it.

SESI also sponsored supervised parks where working-class children could play, staffed some factory schools for workers' offspring, and issued the monthly magazine *Sesinho*, one of Brazil's first regular publications exclusively for children. But such efforts were modest compared to programs for adult workers and working-class housewives. The only SESI initiatives that genuinely appealed to large numbers of young working-class males were the athletic programs and sports competitions. Pointing to SESI's success in this area, a militant printer admitted that "sometimes our enemies teach us good lessons" and urged his union to sponsor its own sports events to lure juvenile workers away from the activities organized by employer-run entities.[96]

This same union militant also complained that the cultural programs sponsored by SESI on the radio and television were full of images or material "imported" from the United States, thus causing Brazilian youths to despise their own culture. Although such criticism certainly overstates the extent of SESI's influence, it should not be completely dismissed. An idealized version of North American middle-class culture—a culture it purveyed as accessible even to workers if they applied themselves—informed SESI's recreational, educational, and cultural activities. Even its patriotic commemorations were virtually identical to those for corresponding holidays in the United States. Perhaps the major discernible difference was the influence of the Catholic Church within SESI, but this influence manifested itself clearly only in SESI's policies on birth control and family planning and its emphasis on Brazil's "Christian traditions." SESI literature also included some criticisms of "rampant individualism," with sporadic references to the need to place collective welfare above the desires of individuals, in the Christian democratic mode.[97] But in practical terms, SESI's programs and messages emphasized individual self-improvement and mobility, not collective forms of advancement. To be sure, it is an exaggeration to imagine that SESI's efforts caused widespread rejection of Brazilian popular culture, but the organization certainly played an important part in disseminating commercial and cultural images from the United States. At the same time, SESI probably reduced its impact and appeal within the working-class population by failing to utilize or explicitly rejecting the familiar idioms and images of Brazil's vibrant popular culture.[98]

The social education programs developed by SENAI and SESI addressed issues related to the domestic and recreational spheres as part of a larger campaign to promote worker productivity and workplace harmony. The worker who lived in an orderly home, practiced wholesome leisuretime activities, and had the proper "civic and moral formation" would be, by logical extension, a more cooperative and dedicated employee. He or she would also be a more reliable and responsible citizen, celebrating occasions important to all Brazilians and embracing values (discipline, social mobility, self-improvement) that presumably transcended class boundaries. At least superficially, SESI and SENAI encouraged members of the working class to take pride in their class identity, but both agencies labored to redefine the content of that identity so that "working-class culture" would resemble, as much as material limits permitted, middle-class culture. In a society where the celebration of the worker had only recently begun and where the industrial worker was increasingly identified as male, the SESI message undoubtedly had considerable appeal to segments of the working-class community.

Remaking the Worker at Work

All activities sponsored by SENAI and SESI, whether cooking courses or soccer tournaments, shared a discourse of scientific management and rational organization that its enthusiasts had first applied to the industrial firm. Yet it was painfully apparent to the agencies' directors and staffs that few Brazilian factories in the postwar era approximated this industrial ideal. And to complicate matters, innovations in industrial technology and psychology were rapidly redefining the parameters of rationalization. In response, SESI and especially SENAI developed a range of programs during the 1950s intended to revise and reorganize social and productive relations within the workplace—the ultimate concern of both agencies.

SENAI and the Modernization of Brazilian Industry

The policies pursued by SENAI during the 1950s reflect a number of crucial factors, including the rapid expansion of the metallurgical industry in São Paulo and the massive influx of multinational corporations during the administration of Juscelino Kubitschek (1956–60). But SENAI also experienced a series of institutional crises during these years that help explain new directions in the organization's operations throughout the 1950s. Both SENAI and SESI passed through repeated periods of insecurity during the Vargas presidency as they were challenged by two groups with utterly opposite motives. The more statist and nationalist *getulistas* lamented the employer-funded organizations' independence from government control and attempted to subordinate them to the federal bureaucracy. Meanwhile, Vargas's implacable foes in the UDN regarded SENAI and SESI as legacies of the Estado Novo and part of *getulista* "corruption" and agitated for reforms in their organizational structures or their outright abolition.[1]

With strong support from the leadership of the CNI and FIESP, the two organizations survived these efforts at "deprivatization" and even temporarily evaded demands that they submit their financial records to the federal fiscal tribunal. But SESI was briefly mired in the "Sea of Mud" scandals arising from revelations of corruption in the Vargas administration just prior to the president's August 1954 suicide. UDN leader Carlos Lacerda accused officials of the CNI of using SESI funds to help found the pro-Vargas daily newspaper, *Última Hora*.[2] Euvaldo Lodi, still Vargas's most unrestrained supporter in the CNI, was so dispirited by these attacks that he "confessed his apprehensions" about the survival of SENAI and SESI at a July 1954 meeting of SENAI's national council.[3]

Although SENAI escaped any direct accusations of corruption, it suffered continuously from the financial malfeasance of the federal bureaucracy during the Vargas presidency. IAPI, the federal social security institute that received and disbursed the lion's share of employer contributions to SENAI, repeatedly held up the disbursement of funds or skimmed off portions of SENAI funding for other purposes. Somewhat tense relations between Roberto Mange, still director in São Paulo, and various figures in the national headquarters of SENAI served to exacerbate this situation. The cause of this tension, aside from Mange's generally arrogant and rigid personality, was Mange's ongoing commitment to a vision of SENAI that was much broader and more ambitious (and more expensive) than that of its administrators on the national level or in other regions.[4]

During the 1940s, under Mange's supervision, SENAI–São Paulo had rushed headlong into the construction of a network of schools that encompassed most of the state. By the early 1950s, São Paulo's twenty-eight schools accounted for over a quarter of the SENAI schools in operation throughout Brazil. Moreover, Mange insisted that each institution include a full complement of social, medical, dental, and recreational services, which he considered essential to the proper development of apprentices. Consequently, Mange was hostile to any movement toward vocational training within industry that lacked the complementary services and instruction provided by the SENAI schools.[5]

SENAI's financial resources did not keep up with Mange's expansive vision, however, or with inflation, for that matter. SENAI–São Paulo inaugurated only one new school in the early 1950s despite offers of free land from various municipalities. Instead, almost all funds went toward the maintenance of existing facilities, and even that expense steadily outran SENAI's resources. SENAI could boast that the quality of the students entering its courses was gradually improving due to greater competition for openings, but this was small consolation in light of the rapid expansion of the industrial labor force. And this expansion was especially pronounced in the metallurgical industry, with its relatively high proportion of skilled workers.

Mange's annual report for 1952 acknowledged the challenges posed by rapid industrial growth in those sectors most in need of skilled workers, declaring that SENAI still regarded itself as operating under a "state of emergency." Considering that an estimated 50,000 new workers were entering São Paulo's factories each year, Mange admitted that SENAI, with some 9,000 students enrolled in its courses during 1952, was far from keeping pace with demand. But rather than propose a streamlined solution to the skilled labor deficit, Mange argued that the massive influx of new workers meant SENAI had an even greater obligation to "be concerned with the formation of a healthy mentality, firm and conscientious, within the new labor generation."[6] In short, he rejected any proposal to cut corners in the preparation of apprentices.

Mange maintained this position despite being well aware of the shifting role played by "skilled" workers in the industrial labor force. As will be discussed below, an ongoing process of mechanization and rationalization was reducing the proportion of skilled workers required in certain sectors. Throughout the 1950s, the textile labor force barely grew, while the industry's output increased sharply, indicating rising productivity.[7] Responding to both new technology and new definitions of skill within the textile sector, by the mid-1950s SENAI was classifying only 7 percent of textile occupations as requiring prolonged training. And Mange foresaw the same process occurring in the metallurgical sector. In one of his last public lectures, the SENAI director reported on machinery displayed at recent European expositions, concluding that "the tendency in mechanics is toward automation, thus eliminating almost all interference by the human factor."[8]

The massive increase in the size of São Paulo's metallurgical, mechanical, and electrical industries, however, meant that the absolute demand for skilled workers in these sectors continued to grow rapidly despite technical innovations. From 1946 to 1956, the number of workers employed in these industries grew 113 percent, and in some subsectors, SENAI classified as many as a third of the workers as skilled. New types of production also

created the need for new skills, so that de-skilling in some phases of manufacturing was offset by the lively demand for, say, tool-and-die makers.
Thus, despite increased training of lathe operators, mechanics, adjusters,
and electricians, the vocational training agency simply could not keep up
with expanding demand, whether from workers seeking to take advantage
of new employment opportunities or employers eager to staff their new
factories.[9]

SENAI's inability to meet the demand for skilled workers facilitated
employers' efforts to revise the legal definition and status of apprentices.
Initially, the federal decrees on apprenticeship training specified that only
juveniles enrolled in SENAI or a program approved by SENAI could be
paid half the minimum wage. By all accounts, most minors received the reduced wage regardless of their training status, but such practices sparked
concerted criticism from organized labor. Thus industrialists began to press
the government to reconsider and redefine the conditions for apprenticeship. The result was an October 1952 executive decree reaffirming that only
apprentices could be paid the reduced wage but including in the definition
of apprentices those being trained within industry. Employers now had less
of an incentive to pay a SENAI apprentice for the five months he or she
spent each year in the classroom.[10]

Important figures in the national organization did not share Mange's
distaste for the trend toward training within industry. Paulo Novaes, subdirector and then national director in the early 1960s, enthusiastically supported the new orientation as more appropriate to the ample needs but
limited resources of Brazilian society. At one point in his tenure as national
director, Novaes even went so far as to propose the selling off of all SENAI
structures to the various state governments so that the agency could focus
exclusively on training within industry—a proposal defeated by the horri-
fied paulistas and their allies in FIESP.[11]

Further impetus for training on the factory floor came from the various
North American and international agencies addressing the issue of vocational education in Brazil. Immediately following the end of World War II,
the U.S. government, in cooperation with Brazilian authorities, set up the
Rio office of the Brazilian-American Commission for Industrial Education
(Comissão Brasileira-Americana de Educação Industrial, or CBAI).[12] Its
original mission was to enhance the preparation of vocational teachers
throughout Brazil and improve the pedagogical material in use, particularly in the public schools. But by the early 1950s, CBAI was actively promoting training within industry (TWI) as the most effective solution for
Brazil's "manpower" needs. In a similar vein, an official report of the Joint
Brazil–United States Economic Development Commission issued in 1954

also endorsed this approach. The author of the section on "manpower problems" in the metallurgical industry wrote approvingly of SENAI and proposed that it be given "every support." But the subsequent passage indicates that the author had his own idea of the form SENAI training should take: "I am informed that the training program works better when conducted in industrial plants and that this should be recommended. I am very much in agreement with this, for experience in other countries supports it. On-the-job training is a most important activity in the United States—and elsewhere, particularly in England—and should be supported."[13] Not surprisingly, as direct investment in Brazil by U.S. corporations grew, agencies like CBAI stepped up their promotion of the TWI format and energetically promoted internships in North American industries for vocational instructors.

Mange's growing isolation in the 1950s as an advocate of *formação integral* helps us appreciate the specificities and ironies of his particular worldview. Mange's conception of vocational training as part of a vast rationalizing enterprise meant that he granted first priority to the needs of industry and not to the young workers who attended SENAI schools. His lifelong devotion to the principles of scientific management led him to promote avidly all forms of rationalization and mechanization that might increase productivity, even if such innovations downgraded or made superfluous the skilled workers who had been trained in Mange's own vocational centers. But his persistently Fordist vision of society as a factory writ large led him to reject an approach to worker training that was narrowly focused and purely functional.[14] Instead, the skilled worker, the figure he regarded as so crucial to industrial harmony and productivity, had to be socialized to act as a productive citizen in every sphere. Thus his adherence to rational organization had a certain "utopian" quality, and Mange advanced a vision sharply at odds with the pragmatism of North American and Brazilian advocates of TWI, who viewed worker training simply as a way to plug up holes in the labor market.

Mange's physical health and SENAI's fiscal health declined precipitously during the early 1950s. The financial crisis reached a peak in 1954 when delays in the disbursement of funds forced SENAI to stop all works in progress and reduce the number of functionaries.[15] Under such circumstances, SENAI–São Paulo proved more amenable to low-cost innovations, and toward the end of that year, the organization initiated, with the help of CBAI, its first five in-plant training programs for foremen and supervisors. The target enterprises—Elevadores Atlas, Máquinas Piratininga, Ford Motor Company, Metalúrgica Matarazzo, and Jafet Textiles—were among the largest and most important manufacturing firms in the state. The choice of these industries would give the new program maximum visibility.

Mange's death in May 1955 at the age of sixty-nine was a traumatic event for those in the upper echelons of the SENAI administration in São Paulo. Mange had imposed not just his philosophy but his personality on the organization, and even though his rigid punctuality and emphasis on rational principles had frequently intimidated members of his staff, he had also earned their sincere admiration. In their eyes, Mange was a "pioneer" who had transformed Brazilian vocational training with his centers for railway apprentices and who had worked hand in hand with Roberto Simonsen to found SENAI. In their recollections of this period, many longtime officials of SENAI–São Paulo cite Mange's death as bringing to a close an era of intellectual ferment and educational innovation.[16]

From a purely institutional perspective, however, Mange's death could hardly be considered untimely. As long as he was in command, SENAI–São Paulo would have remained at odds with the national headquarters and reluctant to participate in the new workplace programs. Such recalcitrance was inappropriate at a time of budget cuts and funding delays. Not that SENAI abandoned Mange's vision; after all, his successor as regional director was Ítalo Bologna, the engineer who had first worked with Mange in the railway apprenticeship centers and who had long been regarded as Mange's closest collaborator. But Bologna possessed neither the strong ideological commitment of his predecessor nor Mange's personal identification with specific policies. Indeed, the new director had briefly served as superintendent of CBAI from 1949 to 1950.[17] He was therefore willing to be more flexible about changing trends in vocational training.

Illustrative of the new, if still slightly reluctant, attitude of the SENAI administration under Bologna is the director's 1956 "Plan of Action." It begins with the significant admission that some 70 percent of skilled workers in the mechanical and metallurgical sectors were being trained within the factory and that SENAI had to respond accordingly. "It is necessary for us to face reality, accepting the fact that in the factories there are also conditions favorable to the training of certain types of skilled personnel; it is appropriate for SENAI, meanwhile, to help them improve this instruction, providing guidance and technical assistance through its specialized departments."[18] Not completely enthusiastic about this new reality, Bologna believed that the best course for SENAI was to position itself as central to this new form of training.[19]

The TWI approach by no means implied a return to earlier arrangements in which an apprentice informally and gradually learned a skill from an older, more experienced worker. Rather, TWI prepared supervisors to train workers systematically and "rationally" in the performance of specialized and routinized tasks. Operating on the assumption that foremen already had the requisite technical knowledge, the first stage of TWI, "correct instruction of a task," sought to teach the supervisor the most effective and rapid means of instructing his subordinates. Where there was sufficient interest, the TWI team offered two further stages: courses in "simplification of tasks" and in "human relations in the workplace."[20]

As should be apparent from the names of these courses, TWI shared many of the assumptions that informed SENAI's own training methods. But the intensive nature of the TWI courses meant that they prepared even more narrow and specialized "skilled" workers. Indeed, the diffusion of TWI coincided with and facilitated a blurring of the division between skilled and semiskilled in many industries, typically to the detriment of the skilled worker. Similarly, SENAI's growing involvement in workplace training stimulated a gradual differentiation of the institution: its schools increasingly focused on the training of juvenile apprentices for positions in industry that required a wide range of technical skills or theoretical knowledge—mechanics, carpenters, and electricians involved in repair and maintenance, for example.[21] Meanwhile, its courses in industry, whether for adults or minors, concentrated on the rapid preparation of workers performing relatively routine tasks, such as machine operators. As Bologna succinctly put it, "An initiative of this sort [TWI] shows that SENAI, rather than being simply a network of vocational schools, should be seen as a veritable system of preparation and improvement of the labor force, in whatever format is most adaptable to each case."[22]

SENAI had little trouble finding clients for its new services, which combined the TWI approach with instruction of a more technical character. By 1956, SENAI-trained instructors using SENAI material were instructing 825 adults and 1,300 minors in 75 paulista firms, and by the following year, the number of minors had grown to 3,413—well over a third of the number enrolled in SENAI's schools. By 1959, SENAI was collaborating with nearly 300 firms for in-house training. The organization's efforts in this regard undoubtedly received a boost from new federal guidelines on apprentices issued in 1956 that required all apprenticeship programs in the workplace to be inspected and approved (or "normalized") by SENAI.

The new direction of SENAI training also coincided with the rapid rise of the automobile industry in São Paulo. Although a Ford factory had been operating in the state since the 1920s, for decades the auto firms amounted to little more than assembly plants. By contrast, the mid-1950s saw the influx of several new foreign manufacturers with the specific intention of producing cars and car parts in Brazil. The development-minded government of Juscelino Kubitschek created a special program, the Executive Group for the Automobile Industry (Grupo Executivo da Indústria Automobilística, or GEIA), to induce foreign firms to initiate all phases of vehicle production in Brazil and to persuade Brazilian companies to engage in the manufacture of basic components.[23] SENAI meanwhile emerged as a crucial supplier of the skilled workers needed to convince firms to "Brazilianize" production and as an important collaborator in the development of local technology.

This collaboration began in the mid-1950s when Luiz Gonzaga Ferreira, then director of SENAI's flagship Escola Roberto Simonsen, convinced Mange to install a "metrology" laboratory in the school. The first of its kind in Brazil and equipped with the latest precision measuring instruments, this lab played a key role in preparing struggling auto parts firms for the rigorous demands of large-scale vehicle manufacturing. According to Gonzaga Ferreira, SENAI began by assisting COFAP, a leading parts manufacturer, in the creation of a quality-control system. In his personal recollections, the longtime SENAI official claimed that the rate of rejection for COFAP parts dropped from 81 percent to 12 percent after the company's technical staff consulted with SENAI.

Whatever the truth of such claims, the school director soon became the key figure in the collaboration between SENAI and the car manufacturers' *sindicato* to train supervisors and other skilled personnel for the auto industry. Gonzaga Ferreira recalled, probably with some exaggeration, that "80 to 90 percent of all foremen and supervisors of production in the automobile industry" during the 1950s were graduates of SENAI.[24] Rather than bypass the Brazilian training agency and create their own in-house programs, most of the corporations in this sector opted for a cooperative agreement that made SENAI responsible for workplace instruction. This arrangement received further encouragement from abroad in 1958 when the U.S. Import-Export Bank granted Brazil a $4.5 million loan for the specific purpose of expanding and updating SENAI's operations, with $2 million earmarked for São Paulo.[25]

The most innovative facet of SENAI's collaboration with the auto industry was its role in setting up the first systematic courses in Brazil for training tool-and-die makers, a prerequisite for a genuinely "national" auto industry—that is, an industry where all phases of production occurred in Brazil. To prepare himself for this enterprise, Gonzaga Ferreira did a four-month internship in France; meanwhile, SENAI recruited experienced tool-and-die makers from Spain and elsewhere to instruct the apprentices. Attended by much interest from both manufacturers and potential students, SENAI inaugurated its first *ferramenteiro* courses in the early 1960s.[26]

One notable aspect of Gonzaga Ferreira's and SENAI's collaboration with the auto producers' *sindicato* is their attempt to counteract market forces in the setting of wages for skilled workers in this sector. The sudden and massive expansion of the auto industry inevitably caused intense competition for the limited supply of skilled workers. Moreover, even SENAI's energetic efforts could not increase that supply quickly enough to reduce the bargaining power of craftsmen in the metallurgical trades. According to Gonzaga Ferreira, "There was at the time a veritable process of cannibalism among the firms. There were some very noteworthy cases: a tool-and-die maker who worked for Ford was hired by Willys, after that was hired by Mercedes, after that was hired by International; in other words, it sometimes happened that he left a firm, and six months later he returned to that same firm earning 5 or 6 times more than he earned six months before. Such was the demand for tool-and-die makers."[27] He also recalled personnel recruiters from the various auto companies donning overalls and riding bikes to rival factories, where they would surreptitiously locate skilled workers and offer them higher wages to change jobs.

Not only did the employers' *sindicato* predictably regard such a situation as problematic, but so did high-level SENAI officials. Accordingly, Gonzaga Ferreira worked with the *sindicato* to produce a catalog of occupations in the auto industry, including an assessment of "appropriate" wage levels for the different job classifications. The obvious purpose of this project was to create more uniform wage standards throughout the industry and thus sharply reduce the bargaining power of scarce skilled workers. To use Gonzaga Ferreira's telling phrase, the catalog was intended as an antidote to industrial "cannibalism." Apparently, neither the auto companies nor SENAI would permit the breakneck pace of Brazilian development to "distort" the income levels of skilled workers.[28] This project, however, was not intended for public consumption; when a disgruntled employee of Mercedes-Benz informed a journalist of the catalog's existence, the revelation caused considerable embarrassment to the foreign companies that dominated the auto industry.

The influx of foreign car manufacturers into São Paulo even prompted a modification of SENAI's long-standing approach to the instruction of apprentices—an innovation surely facilitated by Mange's death in 1955. Since the days of his mechanics courses at the Liceu de Artes e Ofícios, Mange had assiduously promoted the "methodical series" as the most rational form of worker training. Organized around a restricted number of progressively more difficult operations, the methodical series did not lend itself to the demands of the auto industry or to new trends in the machine-tool industry, where parts had to be fashioned according to written specifications. Thus, with the help of a technical adviser from the International Labor Organization, SENAI began to incorporate other methods into its instructional repertoire, including use of "operation sheets," "technical information sheets," and "directed study"—techniques designed to prepare apprentices for industries in which written instructions dictated the specific task to be performed.[29]

Under Bologna's leadership, SENAI diversified its activities in several new directions. In the late 1950s, SENAI–São Paulo became directly involved for the first time in the training of middle-level technicians, inaugurating the Escola Têxtil Francisco Matarazzo in 1957. The decision to focus on technicians for the textile industry probably reflected the declining demand for skilled workers in that increasingly mechanized sector. The technical school, in effect, prevented SENAI from becoming irrelevant to the still vast textile sector. This supposition is supported by the inauguration of technical courses a few years later in the Escola Cerâmica Armando de Arruda Pereira, since the ceramics industry also had little need for skilled workers as previously defined.[30]

By the close of the 1950s, SENAI had revived its financial fortunes, at least temporarily, and involved itself in a wide array of operations it deemed essential to the current phase of industrial development. It had created working relationships with many of the large multinational firms located in São Paulo, and its programs served to make the state a more attractive place for foreign investment.[31] SENAI also proudly and justifiably boasted of its role as a model for vocational training in other Latin American nations—agencies such as SENA in Colombia, SENATI in Peru, and CONET in Argentina had borrowed heavily from SENAI and benefited from close consultation with SENAI officials. Even a delegation from socialist Czechoslovakia visited SENAI to gather ideas for reforming that country's training system.[32]

Ironically, SENAI emerged as a model for other ventures in industrial education precisely at a time when the identity of the institution had become ambiguous and ill-defined. By the early 1960s, SENAI had moved even further away from its original conception as an organization devoted to the educational and professional needs of working-class youth. To be sure, SENAI had always oriented its activities according to the perceived needs of industrial employers, but under Mange's leadership, it had played a major part in defining those needs—emphasizing the formation of worker-citizens—rather than simply responding to shortages in the labor market. In that sense, the claim made by one longtime SENAI official that the organization stagnated after Mange's death amounts to more than nostalgia. SENAI survived and thrived in the post-Mange era, but it did so by downplaying its in-school apprenticeship programs and responding to the demands of large, often multinational, corporations. SENAI was still at the center of industrial training, but it no longer played a significant role in setting the agenda.[33]

Remaking the Worker/Foreman

Among the many implications of the new trends in industrial training and organization was the transformation of the foreman or supervisor. At first glance, it might seem that the foreman's role would be greatly enhanced by rationalized production and instruction, but in most respects, the foreman's personal power and discretion were declining in the new industrial order. In Brazil as elsewhere, early factories often consisted of a series of semi-independent "shops"; within those shops, the *mestre* functioned as manager, master artisan, and head foreman. His wide-ranging powers to hire, fire, promote, and set the pace of production made him a frequent target of complaints about unfair and abusive treatment (especially of women workers) and oppressive work rhythms. Rather than expand his authority, one of the objectives of the rational organization of production was to subordinate the foreman to a more efficient and scientifically oriented management and to reduce his discretionary powers.[34] In the modern factory, the foreman (*contramestre*) became, first and foremost, a transmitter and enforcer of work norms and production methods defined by management. Moreover, the assembly line, with its machine-defined production rhythms, further reduced the foreman's role as an enforcer of work pace or an evaluator of performance.[35] Foremen did not lose all ability to reward or punish individual workers, but such powers would be greatly diminished by the modern industrial firm.[36]

It may seem curious that at the very moment when the foreman's authority was declining, he should become the object of intense scrutiny and attention from SENAI and SESI. Yet it was precisely the foreman's subordinate position that made it possible for vocational instructors, social educators, industrial psychologists, and others to intrude on his routine and attempt to rationalize it. At the same time, the foreman's position as a transmitter of the orders and expectations of management made him a crucial actor for human relations within the factory. Indeed, as a former worker himself, with all the problems that such an identity implied to SESI, and usually lacking any specialized training in pedagogical or leadership skills, the foreman quickly emerged in the SESI literature as the weak link in the industrial hierarchy. After all, what was the use of installing the latest machinery and introducing scientific management principles at the upper levels if unschooled and ill-prepared foremen alienated or antagonized production workers on the shopfloor?

This preoccupation with the *mestre* and the *contramestre* and their role in maintaining social peace dates back to a speech delivered by Armando de Arruda Pereira to a Rotary Club meeting in 1933. Arruda Pereira evidently considered the speech worthy of repetition because he expanded it and delivered it as a series of lectures at the first Brazilian Industrial Congress in 1944 and at a union meeting of textile *mestres* and *contramestres*. SESI then issued the text as a pamphlet entitled *Roteiro do Mestre*, using it, along with a monograph published by the North American National Foremen's Institute, as the basis for its Course for Supervision of Personnel in Industry (CSPI), inaugurated in 1952.[37]

Emphasizing social peace, Arruda Pereira designated the *mestres* and *contramestres* as "the necessary and indispensable links for the realization of that ideal." The themes he discussed as crucial to the supervisor's performance included "how to avoid wasted time," "safety and accident prevention," "maintaining discipline," "how to place a worker in the correct job," "horseplay on the workfloor," and "the discontented worker." Significantly, under "responsibilities of the *mestre* toward the employer," Arruda Pereira listed, among other items, "to identify himself with the administration," "to be capable of cooperating with superiors," and "to know the limits of his responsibility and authority." Thus, by the 1930s, members of the industrialist "vanguard" were conceptualizing the *mestre* in his modern incarnation.

Arruda Pereira's references to proper psychology, fair treatment, and better understanding and his declaration that "the era of the 'tough guy' foreman is passing" indicate the early influence on Brazilian industrialist-intellectuals of the "human relations in the workplace" movement. During the 1930s, leading figures in IDORT, such as M. B. Lourenço Filho and Aldo Mário de Azevedo, had already begun to criticize Taylorism for its insensitivity to human psychology and to denounce employers who implemented time and motion controls in such a crude fashion as to fuel class conflict.[38] Such criticisms easily found an appreciative audience in SESI's corps of enthusiastic social workers and social educators, who initiated courses on "human relations in the workplace" for supervisors and production workers.

The emphasis on closer interaction between supervisors and workers in the human relations approach was not meant as a challenge to hierarchy in the workplace. On the contrary, the idea was to attenuate the impact of a hierarchy in which the worker had virtually no say over the basic conditions of his or her work life. This is evident in a wide range of SESI material, particularly in the manual accompanying SESI's human relations course for workers. In its discussion of the "problem of discipline," the manual described anything that disturbed the factory hierarchy as "indiscipline." Furthermore, "although the supervisor is responsible for good guidance and the maintenance of discipline, it is the subordinates' obligation *to accept the disciplinary norms*."[39] Even when workers discern a better way to perform a task, they should accept the orders of their superiors, limiting themselves to "presenting suggestions at opportune moments." Finally, "the worker must always keep in mind that it is the foreman's job to resolve the most difficult problems. . . . The foreman is responsible for this function; that is why he is the *supervisor*."[40] Indeed, SESI tended to portray even the "humanized" foreman as a figure of towering stature vis à vis the workers. An especially literal example of this is an illustration accompanying an article in *Educador Social* that shows a smock-wearing, authoritative-looking supervisor surrounded by what initially appear to be small children dressed in overalls and caps. A closer examination reveals that the "children" are, in fact, workers.[41]

Although SESI continued to offer human relations courses for workers throughout the late 1950s and 1960s, staffing problems led the organization to concentrate its limited resources on supervisors. In practical terms, this made good sense since courses for workers had few repercussions beyond their impact on the actual participants, whereas courses for supervisors theoretically affected not only the students but also all of their subordinates. SESI explicitly stated its aspiration to transform industrial supervisors into "true auxiliary agents of the social service." Thus the 500 supervisors who had graduated from the CSPI by mid-1953 represented a significant extension of SESI's activities within the workplace.[42]

Moreover, well-adjusted workers would simply be frustrated in their efforts to improve workplace relations if their supervisor proved insensitive or poorly prepared. Given the hierarchical structure that SESI considered a prerequisite for rational organization, the supervisor or foreman inevitably emerged as the linchpin of industrial relations. Accordingly, the SESI staff gradually shifted primary responsibility for social peace from the factory owner to the supervisor. In a speech delivered to the first Latin American Conference on Scientific Organization in 1953, a major figure in SESI's Division for Social Orientation attributed the growing number of work-related conflicts to the foreman's lack of training in human relations and to the fact that the typical supervisor "is merely a more senior worker."[43] Meanwhile, *Educador Social*—a publication that increasingly focused on issues of interest to supervisory personnel—repeatedly blamed foremen for such problems as worker discontent, the high accident rate, and low productivity. According to Hélvio Pinheiro Lima, who regularly wrote on these matters for the monthly magazine, "There is no need for a very profound analysis to understand that the discipline problem is, principally, a question of good direction since there are very few people who are incorrigibly undisciplined or who are incapable of benefiting from good guidance."[44] In other words, a well-prepared *contramestre* should have little trouble keeping workers disciplined and contented. Conversely, a single badly given order by an incompetent *contramestre* could disturb the "natural harmony" between workers and management.

SESI backed up its insistence on human relations training with the testimony of foreign experts. An issue of *Educador Social* summarized a series of articles by Louis James, director of the Institute for the Instruction of Scientific Administration in Rio, who argued that the supervisor played a central role in increasing productivity. Going even further, Professor James claimed that "moral and psychological factors, much more than technical factors, were hampering the productivity of the Braziliam employee."[45] The appeal of such an argument to an employer-funded and -directed organization is obvious; after all, it was far cheaper and easier to subject supervisors to human relations training than to renovate a factory's physical plant.

According to the SESI literature, supervisors had to convey management's demands for greater productivity in such a way that workers would understand the reasons for the intensification of work rhythms and accept it affably. Supervisory staff had to be sensitive to the psychological fragility of adolescent workers, remembering to compliment young employees on an individual basis. They also had to correct workers' misconceptions about Brazilian labor law and deflect resentment away from management. Only rarely did the SESI literature recognize the difficult and contradictory demands that employers were placing on the modern foreman. In contrast to other articles that posited a "natural" harmony of interests in the factory, a 1958 essay in *Educador Social* plainly stated that "the very nature of the supervisory function, by the fact of controlling productivity, makes it disagreeable to the workers."[46] In other words, the author accepted the notion that workers might have opinions or preferences that were not simply a matter of poor understanding or insensitive communication.

The SESI courses for supervisors, which often complemented the TWI courses offered by SENAI and the state, penetrated São Paulo's industrial milieu to a significant extent. The late 1950s saw a huge increase in the number of students enrolled in courses offered by DOS, indicating that thousands of supervisors, or aspiring supervisors, were taking the CSPI and other courses. By 1964, a summary of DOS activities reported a total of 991 such courses offered since the program's inception, with 58,869 graduates.[47] Many supervisors followed up the CSPI with additional courses offered by DOS on "notions of productivity," "rationalization of work processes," and "notions of oratory."

SESI representatives also made a serious effort to involve supervisors and their families in the activities of SESI's social centers, where, according to one DOS official, they could "imbibe sentiments of Christian solidarity and of respect and dignity for the human being." Wherever possible, the CSPI included social functions that encouraged family participation. SESI organized one group of foremen's wives and daughters to sew clothing for the indigent during the Christmas season. The goal, claimed a SESI author, was to teach the foremen to perform well out of a deep belief in human dignity and not just in order to increase output. Indeed, in this author's view, the supervisors formed the "true middle class" of industrial organization.[48]

In some firms, foremen may have enrolled in these courses as a result of pressure from a management that was enthusiastic about better human relations in the workplace. The labor relations director for the Matarazzo industries in the mid-1950s believed that the SESI course for foremen was the best means to improve the company's relations with workers.[49] But many supervisors eagerly sought an opportunity to discuss the problems they faced on the job as well as a relatively painless way to improve their credentials and chances for further promotion.[50] As with the courses for working-class housewives, SESI may have placed an unequal burden on the supervisor in terms of maintaining social peace and productivity, but at the same time, the SESI programs took the supervisor's role and responsibilities very seriously. In larger companies, the SESI and TWI courses allowed supervisors to create their own networks and internal bulletins. The *Boletim do Supervisor* of São Paulo Light & Power began publication in 1956, and its debut issue repeated, word for word, SESI doctrine: "Discipline . . . is merely a matter of good direction, while indiscipline is a result of poor supervision."[51] Of course, there was always the occasional dissenting view: a foreman from the industrial suburb of São Bernardo informed *Educador Social* that, in his opinion, "it doesn't help for the boss to be good since some workers have indiscipline in their blood." SESI, with its nearly infinite faith in the efficacy of proper technique, assured the writer that this was not the case and cheerfully encouraged him to get to know his workers better.[52]

Workplace Hazards as a Technical Problem

In their dealings with supervisors, both SESI and SENAI placed a great
deal of emphasis on the role of the foreman in reducing workplace hazards.
The concern of the two organizations with this matter is hardly surprising:
during the postwar decades, Brazil repeatedly earned the dubious distinction of being a world leader in industrial-accident rates. Moreover, such
key figures in SENAI and SESI as Roberto Mange and Geraldo de Paula
Souza had long cited improvements in occupational safety and health as
prerequisites for increased productivity. One of Mange's most famous
achievements as director of IDORT's Division for the Technical Organization of Work during the 1930s was his study of accidents on the docks
in Santos, which led to significant reorganization of the work process
among the stevedores. And Paula Souza's Instituto de Higiene joined
forces in 1942 with the Rockefeller Foundation to survey health and hygienic conditions in paulista factories "with the goal of improving and increasing production."[53]

The war years sharpened the interest of reformers and employer representatives (not to mention workers) in the issue of industrial safety as the
hectic production pace and run-down machinery created ever more precarious work environments.[54] FIESP invited the president of the newly
formed Brazilian Association for the Prevention of Accidents to address a
meeting of the federation's directorate; the association itself had been
formed by industrialists and industrial engineers. The federation also issued a steady stream of notices calling attention to the problem. To be
sure, FIESP always related the issue of industrial health and safety to the
goal of increasing productivity; economic, not moral, considerations should
prompt the industrial employer to eliminate workplace hazards.

Vargas's Estado Novo, meanwhile, was slow to take any significant action on the issue of occupational safety. The minimum wage law did allow
for an increment in salary for those workers employed in "insalubrious" activities or conditions, such as jobs that involved exposure to lead.[55] And the
Ministry of Labor issued minimal requirements and guidelines for factory
safety. But these were rarely enforced, and only toward the end of the war
did the government begin to consider measures to decrease the rate and se-
riousness of accidents. At Vargas's behest, A. F. Cesarino Júnior and a
group of paulista law students undertook a study of workplace accidents in
São Paulo's factories with an eye to proposing new legislation. FIESP, in a
notice to its members, enthusiastically endorsed the study; indeed, it is
possible that the FIESP leadership actively encouraged government action
on the matter since Cesarino Júnior, aside from being one of Vargas's lead-

ing advisers on social legislation, was a FIESP consultant and close friend of Roberto Simonsen.[56]

As with many other issues, the FIESP leadership placed itself in a delicate position by calling attention to the high industrial-accident rate. The rules of scientific management made such accidents strictly irrational, especially when severe enough to stop production. Moreover, a high accident rate, whatever the cause, could only serve to provoke worker resentment and undermine social peace. At the same time, the FIESP leadership, which had to answer to its industrialist constituency, could not endorse a slew of regulations and penalties that would have the immediate effect of increasing production costs and interfering with employer authority on the factory floor. The Vargas government, however, had no intention of "burdening" employers with harsh new regulations. The decree issued in June 1945, authored by labor official José Segadas Viana, addressed the problem of industrial accidents while remaining sensitive to employer authority.

The 1945 decree provided the guidelines for the creation of an Internal Commission for Accident Prevention (Comissão Interna para a Prevenção de Acidentes, or CIPA) in every factory with over 100 employees, already stipulated by the 1943 Consolidated Labor Laws (Consolidação das Leis do Trabalho, or CLT). In some respects, the CIPAs represented an innovation in Brazilian industrial relations—they were not only the first factory committees of any sort mandated by the government, but the guidelines also required that they include at least three workers designated by the appropriate labor union. At the same time, the official composition of the CIPA virtually guaranteed that management would be the dominant force in its proceedings. Each CIPA was to have a minimum of seven members, including a "president" intended to be the owner or manager of the firm, a secretary designated by the president, the company physician, and the factory's engineer. Thus, even if the union appointed three worker-members who were not intimidated or co-opted by management, they typically would have only a minority voice in the CIPA's proceedings.

The CIPA, mandated to meet at least once a month, had many functions, but most of them were of an educational or advisory nature. According to the decree, the CIPA had the obligation to promote the observance of federal health and safety legislation, to study the causes of and potential solutions for accidents in the workplace, to promote "professional selection" of workers, to sponsor competitions and awards for contributions to workplace safety, and to facilitate the activities of federal labor officials from the Division of Health and Safety. Only one of its functions involved any real enforcement power—its authority to set penalties for workers who refused to submit to safety standards. In theory, a CIPA could also denounce violations of workplace safety regulations by the employer, but the composition of the committee made such action unlikely.[57]

It is not surprising, then, that FIESP endorsed and embraced the CIPAs. For the federation's leadership, the CIPAs were technical commissions with token worker participation that could tackle the problem of workplace accidents and demonstrate industrialist concern over the matter without penalizing or stigmatizing the employer. But as was often the case, the industrialist "rank and file" did not share the leadership's enthusiasm. Given the loose government implementation of the regulation, relatively few employers rushed to form CIPAs in their factories. Thus SENAI and particularly SESI became vehicles for the stimulation of employer consciousness about workplace safety questions. SENAI set up a Service for Workplace Hygiene that consulted with firms whose apprentices trained in SENAI to propose measures for improving occupational safety. And the organization incorporated health and safety questions into its curriculum for apprentices and adults, even forming CIPAs in its workshops as examples for its trainees.

Far more ambitious were the activities developed by SESI to promote interest in workplace safety issues. In October 1948, FIESP announced the founding of SESI's Service for Industrial Hygiene and Safety, whose personnel could assist factory owners in the formation of CIPAs. Moreover, SESI infused virtually all of its activities with safety-consciousness; as previously noted, the basic readers for literacy courses included allusions to the need to avoid on-the-job accidents. Accident prevention was a central theme in the courses for supervisors and in the human relations seminars, and even the domestic arts courses warned against habits or behaviors that might cause accidents.

The first director of SESI's industrial hygiene service was Fernando de Barros Ferraz, whose career trajectory was typical of many high-level SESI and SENAI officials. Barros Ferraz graduated from the Escola Politécnica and went to work for the Sorocabana Railway, an enterprise that was a veritable breeding ground for industrial technocrats. He then pursued additional studies in sanitary engineering at the University of North Carolina. During his four-year tenure as director, Barros Ferraz concentrated his efforts on educational campaigns and the formation of CIPAs. He also initiated a bimonthly publication entitled *CIPA-Jornal*; the 12,000 copies of each edition were distributed to factories, labor unions, and other agencies.[58] But few industrialists immediately sought SESI's occupational safety services, and after three full years of operation, the division had helped set up only sixty CIPAs.

Barros Ferraz's sudden death in 1952 led to the appointment of Bernardo Bedrikow as director of the industrial hygiene service. Bedrikow was a well-known expert on industrial safety issues, and he brought new energy and a new orientation to the service. Like his predecessor, he drew heavily on technical material from the United States and studies conducted in North American industry. Among his accomplishments was overseeing an agreement in 1957 with the U.S. government's Technical Cooperation Program to install a laboratory on SESI premises for more precise study of industrial hazards, the first facility of its kind in Brazil. Under Bedrikow's leadership, SESI–São Paulo became the nation's most important center for the study of occupational health and safety.

Having only an advisory rather than a "coercive" function, SESI could not intervene in any dramatic way to improve workplace conditions, but it could exert considerable influence over the way accidents were perceived. Predictably, some of the early SESI literature and similar publications by individual firms placed the "blame" for industrial accidents on careless and ignorant workers or incompetent supervisors.[59] But not all of the articles authored by industrial technocrats adopted a crude "blame the victim" position that could be easily disputed by labor leaders. A long article in the national bulletin of SENAI argued against distinguishing the causes of workplace accidents as "subjective" or "objective" (that is, worker carelessness versus dangerous conditions). Such distinctions, the author argued, were not only fruitless but exacerbated conflict between workers and owners, with each party seeking to blame the other. Instead, the author proposed approaching workplace hazards in organizational terms: even when it seems that the worker is "at fault," the real problem may be poor training and selection, for which the worker is not responsible. Improving workplace safety, he suggested, was a matter of "worker education, that is, his preparation for the performance of the job through methods of selection and instruction that enable him to defend himself spontaneously from potential dangers."[60] Similarly, "objective" hazards could be reduced through the application of rational organization.

This approach still indirectly placed the burden of accident prevention on the worker but transformed the issue from a moral or political matter to a "technical" question by making workplace hazards a problem to be resolved through scientific management. Wider adherence to this approach is indicated by the composition of São Paulo's Council on Occupational Health and Safety, founded by Governor Lucas Nogueira Garcez in 1951. An engineering graduate of the Escola Politécnica, Nogueira Garcez appointed representatives of SENAI, SESI, SESC, the State Departments of Labor and Industrial Production, and IDORT to the council but did not include a single representative of organized labor.[61]

Social educators and other SESI staff who frequently visited industrial workplaces did not always share the view that advocating a more rationally organized work environment was all that was necessary to reduce Brazil's prodigious accident rate.[62] During a visit to a metallurgical firm that, in requesting a subvention, had invited SESI to inspect its facilities, which boasted a normally functioning CIPA, the SESI staffperson found "terrible" health and safety conditions on the factory floor. These included poor lighting, oil slicks and holes in the floor, a scarcity of fire extinguishers, and insufficient machine guards. Yet this same firm published an article in its internal newspaper, addressed to workers, that began, "Accidents happen . . . but they wouldn't happen if safety norms were obeyed." Similarly, a metallurgical firm in Sorocaba with a functioning CIPA had its subvention reduced in part because the SESI official found "very poor hygienic conditions in all sections" of the factory. In this case, the hazards included holes in the floor, lack of air circulation, missing fire extinguishers, and filthy walls. According to the report, in a ten-month period 194 accidents had occurred in this factory, 38 of them "serious."[63]

As head of SESI's Industrial Hygiene and Safety Service, Bedrikow diverged from a pure "worker education" approach to the issue. Throughout the 1950s, under his direction, the service's *CIPA-Jornal* primarily emphasized the need for better protective equipment and sanitary facilities in paulista factories, squarely placing the burden of reform on management rather than the workers. Arguing that Brazil's stage of industrialization resembled that of the United States at the onset of the twentieth century, *CIPA-Jornal* contended that Brazilian industrialists should follow the safety and hygiene measures adopted in U.S. industry during that earlier period and ignore much of the current literature. That meant attention to machine guards, tool maintenance, and other physical aspects of the workplace such as adequate lighting and ventilation. It also meant providing hygienic drinking fountains, changing rooms, bathrooms, and showers—facilities, according to *CIPA-Jornal*, that even some larger industries failed to furnish for their employees. Among its many suggestions, *CIPA-Jornal* flatly recommended that the government ban the importation of "unprotected" machinery.[64]

The editor of the bimonthly magazine, Haroldo Pataracchia, explicitly addressed the "worker negligence" issue in an article entitled "Personal Factors and Material Factors." Pataracchia remarked upon the tendency in CIPA meetings for committee members to blame workers (*fator pessoal*) for accidents, bolstered by their knowledge that international statistics show 80 percent of industrial accidents to be the worker's fault. However, the editor argued that such statistics came from factories in more advanced economies with much better safety conditions. In Brazil, on the other hand, a much larger percentage of serious accidents could be attributed to the lack of machine protectors and other safety equipment (*fator material*). To strengthen his point, Pataracchia noted that SESI found a high percentage of accidents caused by personal negligence only in well-equipped paulista factories with low overall accident rates.[65] *CIPA-Jornal* even had the temerity to quote Henry Ford's *My Philosophy of Industry*—a virtual bible to some members of the FIESP leadership—to support its position. According to Ford, the major causes of accidents included defects in construction and machinery, lack of machine guards, and insufficient space, light, cleanliness, and air. Only at the bottom of his list did Ford include personal negligence.

Under Bedrikow's leadership, SESI's industrial hygiene service rapidly expanded its activities; in 1954 the division racked up nearly 2,000 consultations or lectures in industry—a tenfold increase over the early years of its operation.[66] The next few years saw another decline in its activities, but in 1959 the number of consultations jumped dramatically to over 20,000. Although many of these "consultations" consisted of the distribution of safety posters and other printed matter, they did include fifty-two courses on the prevention of accidents. In the early 1960s, the regional council of SESI–São Paulo agreed to deemphasize traditional medical services and concentrate on industrial health and hygiene. SESI also elevated the industrial hygiene service in 1960 to the status of a subdivision.[67]

Intensifying interest in industrial safety meant that the subdivision received many more requests for its services than it could meet. Indeed, by the early 1960s, CIPAs were becoming commonplace in medium-sized and large factories, as were the numerous posters and placards designed by SESI to alert workers and supervisors to workplace hazards. But the subdivision's efforts had scant effect on the overall accident rate and fell far short of defusing the explosive issue of work-related injury and illness. During the late 1950s, labor unions began paying closer attention to issues of workplace safety, exposing dangerous conditions and denouncing ineffectual CIPAs.[68]

One particularly detailed account was given in an article in *O Metalúrgico* describing the working conditions in the foundry section of Indústria Semeraro, a Brazilian-owned metallurgical firm with over 400 workers. According to the union paper, there was no ventilation in the smoky, low-ceilinged foundry area, except perhaps for the air circulation provided by leaks in the ceiling. Since there was no dining area, workers often ate their lunches in this unhealthful environment, and the absence of toilets meant that workers had to use the bathroom of a neighboring factory. The firm did have a CIPA, but it was not run according to the rules. No elections were held for worker representatives, and when an employee tried to attend a meeting and discuss how the CIPA should function, the committee president, Francisco Semeraro, expelled the intruder. The article accused the foundry foreman of running a "slave regime" but did not confine its arguments to moral outrage. *O Metalúrgico* also accused the foreman of being "technically incompetent" and informed its readers that workers in this firm "will never have the conditions to produce at a high rate, working without safety and without even minimal social, moral, and hygienic assistance." In conclusion, the article claimed that workplace inspectors would be performing "a patriotic service" by forcing the firm to improve these conditions.[69]

As labor unions' denunciations of ineffectual CIPAs and dangerous workplace conditions intensified, SESI's industrial hygiene service began to back off from its sharply critical attitude toward lax employers and focused more and more on the collective and individual errors committed by workers. The new subdivision was especially opposed to the union campaign in favor of supplementary pay for those who worked in hazardous conditions, a campaign that yielded new federal regulations in 1962. According to a subdivision report, "It is well known that the legislation on this matter . . . is of a more punitive than preventive character. As has been said by many, numerous times, this situation opens the way for worker demands for additional payment due to insalubrity, seeking compensation in the form of money instead of improvements in working conditions or in a situation that places their health at risk. . . . This fact discourages many industrialists, who stop making improvements 'since they are making the additional payments.' The efforts of industrial hygienists are utterly futile in these conditions."[70] Not only did SESI's industrial safety experts roundly condemn the particular strategies adopted by organized labor, but SESI also shifted its position on the issue of "fault" in industrial accidents. In a 1964 article entitled "Supervisor and Safety," *CIPA-Jornal* overtly addressed this issue, claiming that until recently technical experts had regarded accident prevention as a question of installing machine guards and posting safety notices. Although such measures were important, "we now know that this alone is not sufficient to get good results. . . . Many accidents occur due to the personal errors of the workers."[71]

This is not to say that the subdivision's position had undergone a complete reversal. On the one hand, *CIPA-Jornal* continued to publish occasional articles revealing horrendous physical conditions in (unnamed) paulista factories.[72] On the other hand, the subdivision's past pronouncements had not exempted workers from all blame: a widely distributed pamphlet, "Why Workplace Accidents Occur," issued in 1958 gave considerable emphasis to worker indiscipline or carelessness and stressed the supervisor's obligation to prevent such behavior. However, the same pamphlet also cataloged aspects of the physical plant that were basic to worker safety and that were strictly the responsibility of management. In effect, the discourse of the subdivision, though not radically revised, underwent a significant shift in emphasis during the 1960s, with more and more attention paid to the need to train and discipline workers and less and less to industrialists' obligation to invest in safety equipment and hygienic facilities.

Given the continuity in the service's personnel from the 1950s to the 1960s, we have to look beyond individual conviction or orientation to explain this shift. Bedrikow and his lieutenants portrayed the new emphasis as a response to new research; therefore, it was a rationally formulated change in policy. There could be some substance to this argument. With the influx of large, highly capitalized firms and the increased dissemination of basic information about safety equipment and hygiene, there may well have been an increase in the number of factories that met minimum safety standards or that made protective goggles and gloves available to workers.[73] Since the incidence of accidents and work-related illnesses continued to be high, SESI officials could conclude that ignorant, inexperienced workers, not greedy or indifferent owners, were at fault.

The changing tenor of discussions of industrial accidents in union newspapers indicates that organized labor also recognized the spread of innovations that, in principle, should have served to improve safety conditions. Alongside articles such as the profile of Indústria Semeraro, which revealed clearly appalling conditions in "backward" firms, the union press began discussing the specific hazards posed by more modern firms, with their high degree of mechanization and demands for greater productivity. According to the labor press, many workers, pressured to tend increasing numbers of machines or to repeat the same task at ever greater speeds, had to forego safety precautions to maintain a production pace that would allow them to keep their jobs. Similarly, protective equipment such as masks and gloves often slowed workers down and made it all but impossible to meet production quotas. And then there were the firms that purchased safety equipment but did little to modify the shopfloor temperature or ventilation, leaving the worker with an agonizing choice between extreme personal discomfort or physical insecurity.[74] Thus, if workers failed to follow safety precautions or use protective equipment, it usually was not due to ignorance or carelessness but to the work conditions created by management.[75]

SESI, in contrast, aggressively promoted the view that the worker's behavior, even though it was the immediate cause of most accidents, could be modified with the rational application of employee selection and training. After all, simply attributing an accident to worker carelessness made the incident seem unavoidable. But according to *CIPA-Jornal*, "In order to be [judged] really careless, the worker must first have been taught to be careful, or rather, we should only say that the worker erred if he had been given the conditions to succeed."[76] Apparently, the new direction in the SESI subdivision's policies allowed it to join the trend toward training within industry and thereby dramatically expand the scope of its activities.

As organized labor intensified its polemic about hazardous working conditions, the SESI subdivision may have found it increasingly uncomfortable to highlight the failures and transgressions of employers. Within the institution, SESI staff members responsible for organizing CIPAs often became the targets of employer complaints if the organizer was too insistent about workers' prerogatives.[77] On a more global level, SESI's industrial safety experts probably welcomed occasional exposés of particularly recalcitrant firms; a report from the early 1960s lamented the subdivision's inability to enforce better safety standards.[78] But labor's criticism of rationalization and mechanization with respect to worker safety and its demands for higher wages for dangerous jobs went against the philosophy of the subdivision and of SESI in general. Again, SESI's response was not to deny the high rate of industrial accidents but to attribute it to the poor preparation and limited experience of the average industrial worker.[79]

As for the role of the government in regulating working conditions, the Labor Ministry's Division of Workplace Health and Safety seems to have lacked the funding, personnel, and prestige necessary to make a serious impact on safety in the workplace. In February 1960, a group of federal deputies attempted to remedy the government's ineffectiveness in this area by creating the Brazilian Institute of Occupational Health and Safety, to be funded by the imposition of a tax on accident insurance policies. Its proposed powers would have included the inspection of imported machinery for safety features and the certification of safety devices. FIESP's lawyers immediately attacked the initiative as redundant given the prior existence of a health and safety division within the Labor Ministry and denounced the inspection provisions as "highly prejudicial and inconvenient" for industry. Instead, they recommended "a collaborative effort among public organs and private entities concerned with this question." Ultimately, the measure went down in defeat, sparing employers the threatened inconvenience.[80]

SESI on the Shopfloor

Since its founding, SESI had tried various means to strengthen its links with the workplace, to influence relations between capital and labor, and to alter routines on the factory floor. In the late 1940s, social educators attempted to extend their contacts by creating Internal Councils of Social Orientation within industrial firms. These committees consisted of supervisors, the company's doctor or social worker, and worker-graduates of SESI courses. Their role was to disseminate information about SESI, encourage workers to use its services, promote SESI courses within the firm, alert SESI to potential industrial conflicts, and direct "maladjusted" workers to the appropriate SESI agency. This elaborate scheme had little success, however. Even where SESI managed to establish these committees, employee turnover frustrated its efforts. And in several firms, workers regarded the committee members as spies for management and resented the intrusion into their routines.[81]

To a small extent, the CSPIs were a substitute for this program. SESI hoped CSPI graduates would form a corps of informal social workers and rationalizers who would disseminate SESI doctrine throughout the industrial milieu.[82] But this form of influence was haphazard at best, and there were limits to what SESI could expect from individual foremen. Thus, in the mid-1950s, DOS initiated an experimental program to send social educators or social workers to a specific factory for an extended visit (*estágio*). Over a period of one or two weeks, the SESI staff member was to survey "human relations" within the factory, alert management to the most immediate problems, and cooperate with foremen in the implementation of further suggestions to improve output and maintain social peace.

Within a few years, the experiment proved successful enough to be institutionalized as a regular feature of DOS's operations, guided by the internal publication, *Manual do Estagiário* (1958). Indeed, SESI seems to have regarded the initiation of this program on a regular basis to be something of a triumph. Antônio Devisate, in his brief introduction to the manual, noted that "it took ten years of contacts and relations with paulista firms to allow the dedicated soldiers of social peace to initiate these extended visits."

Envisioning these visits as especially useful to small and medium-sized factories, Devisate expressed his hope that more and more firms would open their doors to these SESI functionaries, who were "entrusted with removing points of misunderstanding between capital and labor that by chance exist within the factories."[83]

The handbook for SESI's industrial visitors is, in itself, an interesting and revealing document. Authored by a major figure within DOS, Lucy Marx Gonçalves da Cunha, the manual offers a set of general precautions and suggestions for the fledgling industrial visitor. The text advises the *estagiário* to "place himself in an equidistant position of neutrality, impartiality, . . . taking all precautions to avoid becoming, inadvertently, the repository of unfair demands by badly advised workers or of unreasonable impositions on the part of unenlightened managers."

The tasks that lay before the *estagiário* encompassed nearly every aspect of the DOS agenda. The stated objectives of his or her visit to a factory included, in the social realm, the "development of good human relations within the firm," the clarification of the worker's role in the enterprise, the improvement of working conditions in the factory, and the prevention of accidents. In the technical realm, the SESI functionary was expected to contribute to increased productivity by facilitating better collaboration between employers and employees, by suggesting processes to reduce costs and raise output, and by generally collaborating to perfect "the scientific organization of work along with its humanization." Finally, the visitor was instructed to seek to integrate the firm into the larger community and strengthen its relationship with SESI in general and DOS in particular.

The handbook then went on to detail the types of suggestions the *estagiário* should make, where appropriate, to management. If no CIPA existed, the SESI representative was to recommend its formation, even if the size of the firm made it legally exempt. Firms were to be encouraged to publish an internal newspaper, to set up a suggestion box, and to use the latest psychotechnic testing methods for personnel selection. Of course, the SESI representative was only permitted to advise the firm, in the gentlest manner possible, in order to avoid alienating the management whose good offices had made the visit feasible in the first place.[84]

Needless to say, SESI did not bother to obtain the permission of the firm's workforce before it initiated an *estágio*. Thus, unless the social educator was a fairly sensitive and discreet individual, it is easy to imagine that the workers resented the intrusion. After all, one of the expressed functions of the SESI representative, who worked for an employer-controlled agency, was to identify maladjusted workers. And although the handbook prescribed sending such workers to the nearest SESI social center, the workers may well have suspected that their evaluation as problematic would lead to their dismissal. The *estagiário* was also instructed to seek out existing and potential union leaders among the factory's employees, a process that may have aroused some workers' suspicions.

Indeed, the objectives of the visiting SESI representative went beyond work relations on the shopfloor. According to the handbook, "if there were no objections on management's part," the *estagiário* was to carry out a unionization campaign within the factory. This meant encouraging workers to join their union and explaining its "legitimate" functions, "the objective being to give the worker greater professional consciousness and to connect him with the union in his category, where he can act in a positive manner and make sure that his class interests are being well and correctly defended."[85]

This objective must have placed the visitor from SESI in an extremely delicate position. It is likely that many employers, especially owners of smaller firms who relied on personal forms of negotiation, rejected outright any attempt to encourage unionization, even if placed within the context of DOS's struggle against "extremist" elements. The workers, meanwhile, would not necessarily welcome SESI's attempts to cultivate "promising" labor leaders—that is, those who conformed to its appropriate ideological profile—or its efforts to involve the firm, as much as possible, in union elections.

It appears that relatively few employers were eager for an extended visit by a SESI functionary. Although DOS never published statistics on the number of *estágios* carried out by its staff, the sparse references to this service in the SESI literature and correspondence indicate that demand was limited. In at least one case detailed in the SESI archive, a large papermaking and printing firm appealed for a subvention, but a visit by a social educator revealed few social services, poor health conditions, and an absence of rational organization. The company then admitted an *estagiária* from DOS into the factory, and SESI soon granted the firm an unusually generous subvention of 35 percent.[86] It is unclear whether SESI systematically used the possibility of a higher subvention to convince firms to open their doors to *estagiários*, but even if it did, the success rate was still low. DOS's social educators continued to visit thousands of firms every year to deliver lectures, advertise SESI services, and resolve conflicts. But factory owners were less enthusiastic about admitting SESI representatives who installed themselves for a week or two and requested carte blanche to investigate conditions in the firm. Even a SESI functionary—who could only advise and suggest, not coerce, and who represented an employer-friendly organization—seems to have been regarded as an undesirable presence by many industrialists.

Other forms of "intervention" in the workplace proved much more successful. SESI, SENAI, and similar programs such as the state-sponsored TWI courses all had considerable impact on the work routines and organization of São Paulo's factories during the 1950s. Although SENAI did not eagerly embrace all new trends in vocational instruction, it played a key role in the redefinition of skilled and semiskilled occupations and was central to the creation of new skills in the burgeoning automobile industry. SESI, meanwhile, spread the gospel of human relations in industry and strongly contributed to a revision in the role of the supervisor. It also trained hundreds of personnel directors, disseminated a doctrine of worker selection through psychotechnic testing, and convinced many firms to make social workers a fixture in large factories.

The constant efforts of the industrialist organizations to promote rational organization and scientific management also yielded considerable success in the 1950s. To be sure, much of the mechanization and reorganization of production that occurred in paulista industry during this period reflected foreign managerial trends and the influx of highly capitalized multinational firms—factors with no direct connection to campaigns mounted by SENAI, SESI, or IDORT. Yet the industrialist leadership could reasonably conclude that its organizational offspring had contributed to a pervasive consciousness throughout industry about the need for rationalization, mechanization, and *psicotécnica* in the workplace.[87] It could also claim to have created the programs and ambience necessary to attract so many large foreign firms to São Paulo, thereby facilitating a whole new phase of Brazilian industrialization. As Mariano Ferraz claimed at a 1952 FIESP meeting, "Through mere contact with SENAI, these [North American] industrialists will be able to appreciate the magnitude of São Paulo's industrial park."[88]

Although smaller firms lagged behind, large industrial firms, foreign and domestic, adopted many of the methods and services associated with rational organization and "human relations in the workplace." An exuberant SESI social educator, in a 1956 report on labor relations in a multinational firm, breathlessly remarked that "from the director to the doorman, everyone works in a spirit of hierarchical solidarity."[89] This latter phrase, however odd it may seem and however unlikely in practice, succinctly expresses the ideal of factory organization purveyed by SENAI and SESI. It was the formula that seemed to guarantee both greater productivity and social peace.

Yet the efforts of SESI and SENAI to remake the worker and the work-place yielded mixed results. Their proposed technical solutions to work-place problems had limited success in both the discursive and material realms. This is particularly evident in the case of occupational hazards, a problem that may have been most glaring in "backward" domestic firms but stubbornly persisted even in the presumably modern multinational enterprises. Moreover, SESI could not easily represent itself as an objective and purely technical actor in this realm given its institutional connection to employer associations and its need to avoid fueling worker criticism of industrial employers. To varying degrees, the same problem emerged in virtually all of SENAI's and SESI's workplace programs, as technical experts or supervisors supposedly occupying a middle ground "between labor and capital" found that space to be exceedingly narrow and usually tilted toward the employers who founded and funded their agencies in the first place.

The Politics
of Social Peace

The political conjuncture of the early 1950s presented the first in a series of excellent opportunities for the industrial leadership to advance its project for social peace and increased productivity. Although some industrialists regarded the newly elected president of Brazil, Getúlio Vargas, with misgiving, others had contributed funds to his campaign for the presidency and welcomed his election. As FIESP informed the readers of its weekly bulletin, Vargas was a politician who "had always sought to establish cooperation among the different social classes and never sought to incite class conflict."[1] Vargas, with his populist rhetoric and working-class base, might not be as quick to repress unruly workers as his predecessor, but he had a long track record of advancing the cause of industrialization while currying workers' favor—a talent whose value was increasingly obvious in the new democratic context. FIESP particularly praised Vargas's inaugural address to congress for its emphasis on national development, an issue that the industrialists identified as appealing to all social classes.[2]

Industrialist discourse during the initial years of the Vargas presidency exhibited a discernible shift away from appeals to Christian values and anticommunism and toward an emphasis on the mutual benefits for workers and capitalists of expanded industrial production and increased productivity. To strengthen relations between organized labor and employers, SESI began in 1951 to sponsor luncheons that brought together representatives from each group. At one such gathering, Mariano Ferraz urged union leaders not to regard SESI's services simply as manifestations of employer generosity. "Do not think that the Brazilian employer is giving you something as a gift; on the contrary, he is returning to you a small part of what is rightfully yours, due to the increase in production."[3] Ferraz even went so far as to ask the workers present to forgive industrialists for past errors.

The two most important figures in the FIESP leadership during these years were Ferraz and Antônio Devisate, and the former seems to have been unusually energetic in attempting to redefine the basis for interclass cooperation and harmony. An innovative engineer who had worked for the Sorocabana Railway early in his career, owned a medium-sized firm that manufactured transport equipment, and was a founding member of IDORT, Ferraz had long emphasized the need for more standardized and rational production methods in Brazilian industry. Moreover, like Simonsen, he regarded greater productivity and the worker's access to a share of the additional income generated by that productivity as the sine qua non of social peace.[4] Ferraz proudly pointed to the fact that, in over twenty years of operation, workers at his company had never gone on strike, and he readily attributed his firm's "clean slate" to its advanced production methods and its complicated formula for redistribution of profits among employees. Of all the leading figures within FIESP, Ferraz articulated most forcefully the classic Fordist vision of industrial relations. Speaking at a SENAI graduation ceremony, Ferraz exalted the value of manual labor and promised the graduates a better future: "Brazilian industrialists support the policy of high wages for our workers, low prices for consumers, and reasonable profits for those who invest their capital. We are for the constant reduction of poverty and for the raising of the living standards of our people, which are directly linked to the level of efficiency in 'production.'"[5]

Ferraz once again aired his views on these matters at SESI's Party of Worker Confraternization, the organization's annual New Year's Eve celebration. According to a report on the festivities in *O Estado de São Paulo*, significantly headlined "Paulista Industry and the 'New Deal,'" Ferraz appealed to workers and employers to unite in a common effort for the "successful implementation of a new way of life, with more ample and equitable distribution of wealth and a more dignified existence for the proletariat." *O Estado* regarded these remarks as signaling a new, more progressive attitude among industrialists. The newspaper also described prospects for the nearly 800,000 industrial workers in the state of São Paulo as increasingly favorable due to a relative shortage of labor and to "the conduct of certain enlightened industrial leaders." For that matter, *O Estado* claimed that

Ferraz had made these statements not only to encourage workers but also to "put on alert those backward industrialists who, in their relations with their workers, without knowing it, still live in the past."[6]

A few months later, *O Estado de São Paulo* published an article entitled "Industry and Social Problems." Praising the various programs sponsored by SESI, the newspaper explained such initiatives in the following terms: "Again and again, the leaders of paulista industry have demonstrated their unequivocal devotion to improving the workers' standard of living. Do not conclude, however, that they have assumed this attitude merely out of humanitarian sentiments, though these are much to be commended. . . . To reasons of the heart we must add arguments of an eminently practical order. . . . In truth, they know full well that national development largely depends upon the purchasing power of the working class and that, by increasing it, they are naturally expanding their own business opportunities."[7] The article went on to praise SESI programs, such as the discount food posts and medical clinics, that served to increase workers' real income and concluded that "far more than all the speeches and promises [by politicians], this organization's activities have contributed efficiently to the improvement of the workers' standard of living, to economic stability, and to the social harmony reigning throughout the nation."

A significant motive behind *O Estado*'s praise for SESI and for social initiatives from the private sector was the newspaper's historical antagonism to Vargas. Thus the editors described SESI's food posts as far more effective than government price controls in holding down prices and voiced a thinly veiled criticism of Vargas with its reference to "speeches and promises."[8] But whatever the motive, the newspaper's analysis of SESI's objectives and impact perfectly echoed Ferraz's representation of the organization. No longer identified, first and foremost, as a bulwark against communism, SESI—the social welfare arm of FIESP—was presented as the linchpin of industrial development by virtue of its ability to expand the internal market, increase productivity, and promote social peace.

FIESP's internal report on its activities for 1951 similarly indicated that the new decade had initiated a new attitude on the part of the industrialist leadership, who now saw social peace as a goal to be fulfilled through interclass cooperation, not police repression. In the section on wages, the report acknowledged "partial disturbances" in the labor market toward the end of the year but avoided the alarmist language of previous documents, noting only that the workers, "claiming an increase in the cost of living, peacefully demanded better wages." The report mentioned that employers in the textile and metallurgical sectors had conceded cost-of-living raises, and then it closed on a self-congratulatory note: "The movement to demand better wages, though spreading to other branches of industry, did not assume disturbing proportions due to the prevailing understanding between employers and workers made possible by the federation and center [FIESP and CIESP]."[9]

Ambivalent Industrialists and the Populist Alliance

The political and economic conjuncture of Vargas's election briefly created the perfect "populist moment" during which industrialists, the state, and labor leaders could imagine a rough commonality of interests.[10] Their shared commitment to expanded industrial production, based on expectations of greater productivity and a broader internal market, offered ideal conditions for the articulation of an alliance incorporating the state, the industrial bourgeoisie, and the labor movement—an alliance long identified as the populist ideal. Under such circumstances, employers could accommodate workers' "reasonable" demands for higher wages and tolerate the tendency of government leaders to indulge in occasionally "excessive" populist rhetoric. The state and labor could, in turn, moderate legislation and agitation that would have a negative impact on industrial productivity. And such an alliance would allow Brazilian democracy to develop without posing a threat to the perceived economic interests of the industrial bourgeoisie.

This perfect populist moment, however short-lived, was not completely illusory. Aspects of the state-industry-labor alliance survived into the early years of the subsequent decade. But the "new deal" being offered by the industrialist leadership proved very limited in scope, and even the most progressive FIESP representatives demonstrated little flexibility in the face of fresh challenges posed by mass-based politics and the emergence of a more autonomous union movement. As in the immediate postwar period, industrialists underestimated the extent to which labor repression under Dutra had forced workers to mute grievances that would rise to the surface once unions could free themselves of state-imposed directorates. Thus Vargas's election, though welcomed by FIESP spokesmen, created certain conditions that industrial leaders would soon regard as inauspicious for social peace.

The paulista industrialists, despite their largely enthusiastic response to Vargas's electoral victory, also continued to exhibit considerable ambivalence about the role of the state in economic development and labor relations. An editorial published in the FIESP bulletin during Vargas's first year in office adhered to the Simonsen line, claiming that in an undertaking as vast as the industrialization of Brazil, "private initiative, alone, cannot prevail; the public sector, itself, must participate." The editorial hastened to add, however, that state intervention should not be regarded as a substitute for private activity; rather, "it is the state's role . . . to create indispensable opportunities to direct private initiative."[11] Vargas, committed to a policy of developmental nationalism, readily obliged the industrialists by implementing measures to encourage rapid industrial growth and government investment in less profitable spheres of production. But the increasingly populist president, who drew much of his support from urban workers, also used the powers of the state to control prices and soften the impact of inflation, policies that prompted the FIESP publication to denounce "state intervention in the economic domain."[12] Similarly, Vargas's intensifying nationalist rhetoric, which called for the exclusion of foreign capital from strategic sectors of the economy, found little resonance among industrial spokesmen who regarded foreign investment as crucial to rapid industrialization and the expansion of infrastructure.[13]

Persistent energy shortages during the early 1950s had both economic and social repercussions for industrialists. Rationing of electricity repeatedly forced factories to interrupt production; workers' testimony also indicates that many firms responded to the shortened work week by speeding up the production process.[14] Indeed, workers seem to have suffered doubly as a result of the energy problem, losing wages from reduced working hours and experiencing more intense work routines on the job. Moreover, due to Vargas's loosening of government control over the labor unions and the holding of open union elections, São Paulo's labor movement now had at its helm leaders who were more responsive to the interests of the rank and file. Thus, in March 1953, when the employer *sindicatos* rejected demands from several major unions for substantial wage increases, those unions—embracing hundreds of thousands of textile, metallurgical, furniture, and glass workers—initiated a massive work stoppage coordinated by the newly formed PUI. This Strike of the 300,000 was the largest such movement in São Paulo since the general strike of 1917.[15]

Despite Mariano Ferraz's earlier proclamation of a "new regime" in industrial relations, FIESP and the employer *sindicatos* responded to the massive strike in predictable fashion. FIESP members blamed "Communists" and "outside agitators" for the stoppage, and the federation's directorate, now headed by Antônio Devisate, urged employers to maintain a united front of resistance to union demands. The industrialists called upon the state security forces to discourage worker demonstrations and to guarantee the "right to work." And FIESP orchestrated a highly publicized accord with the paper workers, who had not joined the strike, for salary increases below those demanded by the striking workers but high enough, FIESP hoped, to tempt other unions to break ranks.

To the employers' chagrin, labor's united front held, with factories in the capital remaining paralyzed for nearly a month. Indeed, it was the *industrialists'* unity that cracked when metallurgical firms accepted the ruling of the regional labor tribunal that granted workers in their sector the stipulated salary increases. Even then, the metalworkers resisted returning to work unless employers in the other paralyzed sectors made similar offers to their employees. At that point, the employer *sindicatos* in the remaining three sectors caved in, settling the strike by conceding almost all of the strikers' demands.[16]

This rare defeat for paulista manufacturers provided an important lesson for the FIESP leadership about labor, the state, and industrial relations in the context of populist politics. Although the industrialists could hardly claim that they had been abandoned by the state and federal governments, in many respects this strike and its aftermath diverged from the pattern set by previous industrial disruptions. The actions of the union leadership demonstrated how different labor relations could be once the *pelegos* were removed from power and the directorates had to respond to the rank and file, not the Ministry of Labor. Moreover, no crackdown on labor activists followed this strike, as had occurred under Vargas in the mid-1930s or under Dutra in the mid-1940s. The government had also shown itself unusually susceptible to pressure from the labor movement in the rulings of the regional labor tribunal and in the limits set by Governor Nogueira Garcez on police violence against the strikers.[17] To be sure, those workers who were beaten or jailed during the course of the strike may not have been very impressed by these "limits"; the industrialists, on the other hand, may have felt that the illegality of the strike and the illicit PUI justified much more strenuous repression.[18]

In its public discourse, the FIESP leadership did not portray the 1953 strike as a catastrophic event. In a statement on strike negotiations, FIESP avowed its intent to "make a decisive contribution to social peace . . . maintain[ing] constant and direct contact with the authorities and, in the courts, with the labor leaders in a climate of goodwill and cooperation."[19] But the strike plainly demonstrated that the balance of forces had shifted and that industrial employers could no longer automatically count on the unqualified support of the state or the disunity of the labor movement to defeat labor's demands. It also illuminated the differences in the discourse and social policies of the Vargas government and those of the industrial bourgeoisie. Despite the state and the industrialists' apparent identity of interests in the project of developmental nationalism, political expediency moved the *getulistas* to place increasingly heavy emphasis on the workers' well-being, whereas the industrialists continued to place primary emphasis on profits and productivity.

The limits set on the industrialists' "new deal" by their concern for increased profits and productivity and their assumptions about what such goals entailed are nicely illustrated by two controversial features of industrial relations during this period: assiduity clauses and job tenure. Since the end of World War II, the industrialist leadership had demanded that salary increases and benefits such as Sunday pay be tied to *assiduidade integral*—that is, perfect attendance.[20] Otherwise, employers argued, there would be rampant absenteeism among their workers. FIESP reinforced its position by pointing to "scientific" studies showing a positive relationship between wage increases and absences from work.[21] Moreover, industrialists assumed this stance despite the opposition of virtually all unions—including those notoriously cooperative with employers—to such measures. Union opposition stemmed, in part, from employers' abuse of attendance requirements to fraudulently reduce workers' wages. But union leaders also opposed these clauses as an offense to workers' dignity. Even officials of the construction workers' union, a stronghold of conservative unionism in the early 1950s, rejected the idea, insisting that cooperation between capital and labor "can only exist in a climate of liberty, mutual respect, and trust." And it is significant that the paper workers, who "betrayed" the 1953 strikers by signing a separate accord with their employers, nonetheless insisted upon adding a clause in the contract stating that "the wage increase resulting from this agreement will not be conditional upon assiduity or any other such requirement."[22] Thus the controversy over assiduity clauses had a symbolic meaning for organized labor, and probably for workers in general, that went beyond material considerations.

The issue of job tenure brought into even sharper relief workers' demands for dignity and security and the ways in which these demands clashed with the employers' quest for greater productivity. According to the 1943 CLT, after ten years with the same firm, a worker automatically achieved "stability"—that is, the worker could not be fired unless he or she committed a "serious violation" (*falta grave*) recognized by the labor courts as such. In a society utterly lacking in unemployment benefits and where many firms routinely fired experienced, and even skilled, employees in order to hire younger workers who could be paid lower wages, it is hardly surprising that labor unions rallied around the stability issue.

At the same time, given the industrial leadership's preoccupation with rationalization and scientific management, it is equally unsurprising that employer spokesmen bitterly opposed a measure that threatened to saddle factory owners with relatively well paid workers who might become redundant upon the introduction of new machinery or production methods. Considering that certain Taylorist concepts were still accepted doctrine among industrialist spokesmen and their technocratic allies, it is easy to imagine their discomfort with regulations that blocked the firing of "unproductive" workers and removed what they perceived as the most powerful incentive for good job performance—the threat of dismissal.[23] Thus industrialists regularly attacked the law by arguing that a worker's productivity almost inevitably declined upon achieving tenure. And in practice, many employers circumvented the law by routinely dismissing workers who had completed nine years or less with their firm.[24] Once again, the employers' position, while consistent with strategies for rationalization, denigrated Brazilian workers and their contributions to industrial production. It therefore produced the opposite effect of classic populist rhetoric, which exalted workers' struggles and sacrifices.[25]

The challenge, then, for the industrialist leadership was to position itself amid the crosscurrents of developmentalism and rising urban populism while maintaining its emphasis on rational organization. In their public utterances, FIESP and CNI officials portrayed the industrial bourgeoisie as committed participants in the populist alliance. After all, industrialist spokesmen were early and vigorous proponents of industrialization as an antidote to underdevelopment and external dependence, and the industrial leadership continued to demonstrate its concern for the elevation of the Brazilian poor with the creation of SENAI and SESI. One needed only to compare the lifestyle and opportunities available to a rural laborer with those available to an urban worker to appreciate the progressive contribution of Brazilian, and especially paulista, industrialists to the general quality of life.[26]

Remaking Organized Labor

SESI's statements and publications portrayed the industrial sector as the bulwark of national development, of support for organized labor, and of democratic rights. Given the practices of industrial employers and their official organizations, it is tempting to see such representations as a smokescreen for the industrialists' "real" agenda. But a close examination of SESI's public discourse and programs reveals the extent to which these positions were always, and openly, subject to a series of contingencies. Developmental nationalism was a salutary doctrine as long as it avoided the "extremist" position that advocated exclusion or restriction of foreign investment.

Unions were positive participants in labor relations and the forging of social peace as long as they did not become vehicles for "extremist" agitation, including strikes, or obstacles to greater productivity. And democracy was the preferred basis for politics as long as the people knew how to exercise the precious right to vote and knew enough to resist "extremist" ideologies.

The social education programs discussed in the previous chapters were all meant to strengthen these contingent circumstances, but such programs were usually directed at the individual worker or a specific workplace. Their cumulative effects on labor relations were, even under the most auspicious circumstances, gradual and partial. Therefore, SESI—as the social arm of FIESP—continually sought direct means of guiding and influencing the Brazilian labor movement, a mission made both more pressing and more complicated by the decline of *peleguismo* in the larger unions.[27]

Beginning in 1952, DOS functioned as a seedbed for moderate union "leaders." To that end, the division formed the Union Squad (Equipe Sindical), "whose goal it was to contribute to the strengthening of the unions, led by enlightened men . . . attending to the particular interests of their class, without demagogic attacks, violence, or subtle deviations from their prescribed objectives." The purposes of the squad also included stimulating unionization and "collaborating with the public authorities in union elections."[28]

The initial emphasis was on preparation of union leaders imbued with "healthy principles." In a 1956 interview, Eduardo Gabriel Saad, director of DOS, described the division's seminars as constituting "a rounded course in union leadership training." Aware that its classes in "notions of oratory," "labor legislation," and "unionism," with their limited number of spaces and erratic appeal, could not function as vehicles for mass socialization of the working class, DOS hoped to magnify its influence by forming skillful, proficient union leaders who would extend SESI doctrine to the wider labor movement. More specifically, DOS sought to create an alternative pool of leaders to counteract the burgeoning influence of Communist union officials, who Saad regarded as the only well-trained elements in the Brazilian labor movement.[29]

SESI specified what it expected from a good union official in its 1953 publication, *O Guia dos Dirigentes Sindicais* (Guide for union leaders), and supplemented this pamphlet with frequent words of advice in *Educador Social*. The 1953 guide closely adhered to the letter of union regulations as elaborated during the Estado Novo while highlighting those points that SESI considered most relevant in the contemporary political context. For example, in the section entitled "Conditions for the Functioning of the Union," the guide quoted article 521 of the CLT, which prohibited propaganda in favor of "doctrines incompatible with the institutions and interests of the nation." As for the "objectives of the union," the guide again quoted the CLT, which described the unions as serving "the purposes of study, defense, and coordination of their economic and professional interests."[30] But this terse statement left considerable room for interpretation, moving the guide's author to seek additional guidance on the question from the works of a Chilean "syndicalist," Alberto Hurtado.

According to Hurtado, whose arguments betray strong Christian Democratic influences, the union existed to "elevate man." Moreover, the object of the union was "man," not a social class or the state. The union could also play a limited political role by educating its members for "legitimate democracy" inspired by Christian principles. A third objective of the union was to advance "social justice," but the fourth objective implicitly restricted the means to pursue such justice, stating that the union's goal was to "suppress the causes of class conflict, and not to encourage it." Unions were admonished not to make exorbitant demands that would harm the "just interests" of other parties. In addition, unions had to contribute to the "general welfare" and "national greatness."[31]

In its discussion of the union's "duties," the guide adopted the classic Estado Novo line, citing the union's obligation to "collaborate with public authorities for the development of social solidarity" and declaring the goals of union and state to be identical—namely, social justice and social peace. Finally, the union had a duty to offer social, legal, and educational services to its members and to sponsor consumer and credit cooperatives. Lest any doubt remain about the purpose of this guide, FIESP president Armando de Arruda Pereira included a cover letter to union officials noting that the enclosed pamphlet was meant not only to assist those who led the labor unions "but above all to contribute to making these class organs true instruments of social peace, guiding them to collaborate on behalf of greater understanding between employers and wage earners."[32]

Once an aspiring labor leader had completed the full complement of DOS courses—on labor legislation, social security, unionism, social doctrines, and oratory—SESI often recommended membership in a Catholic CO to supplement this training. After 1953, SESI could also endorse promising and sufficiently anti-Communist "leaders" for additional instruction in one of the many programs funded and directed by the U.S.-based American Federation of Labor or its hemispheric affiliate, the Regional Organization of Inter-American Workers.

Again, SESI's view of the union's rationale and purpose had a much wider acceptance among labor leaders during the Dutra regime, when *pelegos* dominated the most powerful unions and labor federations, than it did in the 1950s. But the composition of the labor leadership did not change overnight, and most federation officials and many union leaders, especially in interior cities, continued to espouse an ideological position similar to that advanced by SESI. For example, at a 1954 ceremony for graduates of SESI's labor law seminar in Piracicaba, Serafim dos Santos, the president of the foodworkers' local, described education as the only means to a better life: "We do not wish to learn just to intensify class conflicts or to make unjust demands but only to defend our legitimate rights in a climate of harmony and social peace. Having left behind the era when the interests of employers and employees were considered antagonistic, we understand that these two groups are intimately linked. We must, therefore, always struggle to maintain this atmosphere of harmony among the forces of production, the only situation conducive to national greatness and well-being."[33] It is very likely that dos Santos derived much of the language contained in his speech directly from a SESI text.

Dos Santos was not an isolated case. During the mid-1950s, graduates of SESI courses held offices in the construction workers' union, the hotel workers' union, and many union locals throughout the interior. SESI also developed close working relationships with several well-entrenched officials of São Paulo's union bureaucracy, most of whom would be regarded as thoroughgoing *pelegos* by the more militant labor leaders.[34] As previously noted, the confederation and federation presidents tended to be more intimately linked with the Ministry of Labor and less dependent on rank-and-file support for their survival, making them more amenable to cooperation with SESI. Regular participants at SESI luncheons and confraternization parties included José Sanches Duran, Olavo Previatti, Luiz Fiuza Cárdia, Francisco José de Oliveira, and Luiz Menossi, presidents of the metallurgical, paper, clothing, food, and construction workers' federations, respectively. Perhaps the most infamous *pelego* of all, Deocleciano de Holanda Cavalcanti, president of the National Confederation of Workers in Industry (Confederação Nacional de Trabalhadores na Indústria, or CNTI), frequently spoke at events organized by FIESP or SESI. The presence of these federation officials lent superficial credence to FIESP's claims of an alliance with labor, but most of these "leaders," in practice, had meager grass-roots support.

DOS's social educators also participated in surreptitious campaigns to influence the union rank and file. DOS personnel attended union meetings "disguised" as workers, where they would argue against more militant positions or make pronouncements in line with SESI doctrine. Social educators also regularly attended union assemblies for the election of new officials to check for irregularities in procedures and to gather information on prominent participants and new ideological orientations in the organizations.[35] Whenever appropriate, Saad generously shared the data gathered at these meetings with his former colleagues at DOPS. Indeed, Saad regarded SESI's educational programs as long-term strategies to combat the problem of Communist influence in the union movement. Until such strategies began to bear fruit, repressive measures would continue to be necessary as a stopgap strategy against the Communists; hence his frequent exchange of information with the political police.[36]

Despite its efforts, SESI's Division for Social Orientation garnered more frustrations than successes during this period, with the 1953 strike in São Paulo providing dramatic evidence of the increasing militancy of organized labor and the extensive support, even pressure, for strike actions from the rank and file. Attempting to adjust to the new tendencies within organized labor, Saad began to patronize more independent union leaders—those who were clearly not *pelegos* but who were not closely associated with Communist factions within their unions. One example is Remo Forli, a Catholic metallurgical worker who played a leading role in the 1953 strike and later joined the Brazilian Socialist Party. Saad claimed in a 1956 interview that he had advised the group led by Forli to "go slow" and consolidate grass-roots support, but Forli allegedly ignored his advice, which resulted, according to Saad, in a complete takeover of the union leadership by the Communist faction.[37]

Several somewhat contradictory assumptions informed DOS's union activities. The SESI staff initially treated the issue of union leadership as a matter of "technical skill"; thus the Communists were gaining dominance in several unions because they, alone, had the training necessary to speak authoritatively, to carry out a successful union election campaign, and to articulate labor demands. In SESI's view, authority and legitimacy within the labor movement were not related to experience in factory-level struggles, personal sacrifices, or grass-roots support but to oratorical and organizational skills and some knowledge of labor legislation.

Yet as Saad's account of Forli's experience with the metallurgical workers demonstrates, fledgling leaders had to build a following within the rank and file to maintain their positions. How did SESI, with its insistence on the "Christian" traditions of Brazilian society, explain the successful appeals of Communists to the rank and file in certain unions? In Saad's view, the Communists' successes were the result not only of their technical abilities but also of Brazilian workers' ignorance and their consequent susceptibility to demagogic appeals—an increasingly prominent theme in the literature of SESI and FIESP.[38] Saad complained that, unlike their North American counterparts, Brazilian workers had no idea why they should oppose communism and support democracy. But without any sense of contradiction, he also claimed that the Communists, recognizing the limited sympathy for Marxism within the Brazilian working class, often carefully concealed their political affiliation.

Not all observers of the labor movement during this period shared this view of the Brazilian worker as "ignorant." In the words of a U.S. labor attaché stationed in Brazil at the time of the 1953 strike and its aftermath, "It is said that every working man in São Paulo carries a copy of the labor laws in his pocket." The attaché assured his audience in the State Department that this was not literally true, "but what is meant is that practically every industrial worker is familiar with the wording of the labor laws and determines much of his activities by his interpretation of the laws."[39] This not only conflicts with SESI's image of the typical worker as unknowledgeable but also recognizes, unlike the SESI literature, that the laws lent themselves to multiple interpretations. The DOS courses, in contrast, claimed to instruct their students in the single, correct meaning of the laws, depicting alternative interpretations as errors resulting from ignorance or willful deception.

DOS's demonization of "communism" in the labor movement meant that its officials rarely examined the specific proposals and objectives championed by party members within the unions and generally dismissed Communist activism as sheer opportunism or subversion. One can discern, however, a gradual realization on SESI's part that the proposals of moderate union leaders had less appeal for union members than those of the "extremist" leaders. Moderate officials preaching restraint, interclass cooperation, and modest gains needed time and a more "educated" rank and file to attract a following, according to SESI logic. Even as FIESP rhetorically claimed that the average worker opposed the increasing frequency of strikes and other labor protests, SESI could not ignore the fact that radical leaders who advocated such actions were expanding their influence within the labor movement. No wonder Saad continued to profess the need for the police's "short-term" approach to the problem of communism.[40]

The mid-1950s even saw a weakening of SESI's relationship with its formerly stalwart supporters in the labor bureaucracy. SESI's "loss" of Melchiades dos Santos, the deeply anti-Communist president of the São Paulo textile workers' union and an active participant in the "Moral Rearmament" movement, was the result of natural causes. Mariano Ferraz personally wrote to the union leader's family to express SESI's grief over his death, FIESP held a memorial in his honor, and *SESI-Jornal* ran a brief obituary—a rare "honor" for a labor leader.[41] Other allies faded from the organized labor scene as the new militancy made it difficult for federation leaders of the old school to survive. Sanches Duran of the metallurgical workers' federation had actively supported SESI activities since the organization's founding. His anti-Communist reputation also earned him a 1956 training visit to the United States, where he became acquainted with prominent officials of the American Federation of Labor, including its president, George Meany. But with his support slipping even among unions in the interior, Sanches Duran sought to cut his ties with "imperialist" and employer-oriented organizations and curry favor with the labor left. Despite this opportunistic ploy, a left-wing activist defeated Sanches Duran in the 1957 elections for the federation presidency, bringing the erstwhile *pelego*'s career to a close.[42]

Perhaps most interesting is the strain on SESI's relations with Olavo Previatti, president of the paper workers' federation and one of the most durable anti-Communist labor leaders. Previatti was a fixture at SESI's public events throughout the early 1950s, and he regularly invited SESI personnel to his union's functions. A 1950 communication from a SESI official described the organization's relationship with Previatti and his union as "among the best."[43] Yet in a 1956 interview, Previatti criticized SESI for the inadequacy of its services, its excessive bureaucracy and red tape, and its "espionage" activities within unions in the name of fighting communism.[44]

At the time of this interview, Previatti was busy negotiating with both SESI and employers in his sector to create the Social Service for the Paper, Cardboard, and Cork Industry (Serviço Social da Indústria do Papel, Papelão e Cortiça, or SEPACO), designed to provide free medical and dental care and other forms of assistance for paper workers. According to Previatti's plan, SEPACO, which would begin functioning the following year, would receive the 2 percent payment firms previously contributed to SESI and would be run by a board of six employer representatives and five workers. Previatti's bitter remarks about SESI apparently indicate that the organization had put up some resistance to the proposal to channel the entire contribution from employers in his sector to SEPACO. However, Previatti soon reached an agreement with SESI, in part because the employers' *sindicato* strongly backed the federation president, who had built up their confidence by successfully excluding Communists from positions of authority within the federation and union locals.[45] Indeed, Previatti's motives for creating SEPACO are transparent: with SESI offering limited material benefits to his membership, particularly among his strong supporters in the interior, and alienating even moderate leaders by meddling in union affairs, Previatti needed an alternative means to bolster his position and to protect his left flank. Despite the ostensible ideological compatibility, SESI had become something of a liability for the paper workers' federation president by the mid-1950s. And by 1958, DOS had quietly dissolved its Union Squad.[46]

Circumventing the State

Even before the 1953 strike shattered any lingering illusions about Vargas's presidency inaugurating an era of social peace, the discourse of the industrialist leadership had shifted away from the relatively bold declarations made by Mariano Ferraz at the onset of the decade. Ferraz's successor as president of FIESP and SESI, Antônio Devisate, had a large enough following among his fellow industrialists to hold the office for the duration of the 1950s.[47] A shoe manufacturer and influential figure in the paulista directorate of the PSD, Devisate had long played a prominent role in the industrialists' federation and São Paulo politics. However, the new FIESP president did not have Ferraz's broad intellectual background and favored a more conventional and paternalistic discourse on relations between capital and labor. In contrast to Ferraz, who had used the previous New Year's Eve radio speech to call for a "new way of life, with more ample and equitable distribution of wealth," Devisate dwelled on the benefits provided by SENAI and SESI to the Brazilian worker, and especially the organizations' "efforts . . . on behalf of moral instruction."[48] Devisate underscored his point by referring to a recent congress of the International Labor Organization at which "the most electrifying issue . . . was the so-called Brazilian solution to the social question, by means of SESI and SENAI."[49]

This formulation of the "Brazilian solution" conspicuously omitted the state and insistently individualized workers rather than addressing them as a class, as Ferraz had tended to do. This tendency was even more pronounced in Devisate's 1954 speech for São Paulo's Day of Industry: "The workers of São Paulo understand that industry is the field of opportunity, par excellence, where anyone equipped with the qualities of intelligence and hard work can aspire to a more favorable situation in the economic sphere. The move up to more satisfactory standards of living and in many cases to prominent management posts in our industrial enterprises occurs, in our milieu, almost always as a function of each person's intelligence and capacity for work."[50] In Devisate's rhetoric, the antipopulist assumptions that already informed much of FIESP discourse and practice clearly rose to the surface. Devisate and his clique seem to have eschewed any serious attempt to reconfigure industrial relations, abandoning the bolder vision of Simonsen and his cohort for a more conventional discursive strategy.

The events of Vargas's final years in office served to reinforce this anti-populist drift in FIESP discourse and to discourage the use of more innovative approaches to labor relations on the industrialists' part. Aside from the 1953 general strike and the subsequent appointment of João Goulart as minister of labor, energy shortages persisted and the inflation rate continued to rise steadily. Partly because of inflation, organized labor pressured the Vargas government to decree a substantial raise in the minimum wage and Goulart called for a 100 percent increase in February 1954—a proposal that received a predictably chilly reception from industrial employers and other conservative political factions. Indeed, hostility toward the "radical" Goulart, especially within the military, moved Vargas first to disavow the labor minister's proposal and then to remove him from office.[51]

Vargas's brief attempt to allay the fears of the military and assuage his more moderate supporters proved futile as his opponents intensified their unrelenting campaign against his government. To fend off his attackers during what proved to be the final months of his administration, Vargas reversed his position on the minimum wage and infused his rhetoric with a more radical tone. Seeking to expand and mobilize his support among Brazilian workers, on May Day of 1954, Vargas announced a doubling of the minimum wage. He also urged workers to wield greater power and influence through the electoral process: "As a class, you can make your ballots the decisive numerical force. You constitute the majority. Today you are with the government. Tomorrow you will be the government."[52]

Industrialists decried the minimum wage increase as not only inflationary but also beyond the means of many firms. Some employers simply refused to pay the stipulated wages, thereby inducing unions throughout Brazil to organize strikes and protests.[53] At the same time, the major industrialist organizations never overtly sided with the opposition or called for Vargas's resignation. Again, many industrial employers had supported Vargas's election and had derived considerable benefit from his pro-industrialization policies, whereas his opponents included political figures who had shown little sympathy for the politics of industrial development.[54] Furthermore, Vargas's unquestionable popularity among Brazilian workers made it problematic for industrialist organizations to sever all ties with his government, which would mean disavowing any sort of alliance with organized labor.

Instead, FIESP sought to distance itself from Vargas's policies while portraying the paulista industrialists as stalwart supporters of the working class. In a June 1954 issue of its official bulletin, an editorial entitled "Social Peace" laid out the image that FIESP wished to convey to organized labor. Regional in emphasis, it opened with the claim that paulista industry, from the beginning, "recognized the rightful and indisputable value of labor, doing everything it could so that the natural differences between the latter and capital could be smoothed out as much as possible." The article claimed that the disputes between employers and employees in São Paulo were "minimal and perfectly resoluble" and that industrialists had long ago abandoned the "narrow and egotistical" mentality that had provoked such bloody social conflicts in the "Old World." SESI and SENAI, the editorial noted, provided tangible evidence of all that industry had done "in favor of the material and cultural improvement of the working class." In conclusion, the piece referred to recent negotiations between FIESP and unions to restructure wages and noted Devisate's opinion that "it is through this path of open cooperation and solidarity between employees and employers that we will arrive at the true social peace."[55]

The scenario outlined in the editorial indicates a move away from the government-supervised labor relations of the past. In its place, FIESP proposed direct negotiation between employers and workers' representatives, citing a recent amicable meeting between union leaders and industrialists as demonstrating the value of this new approach. Just a week after the editorial appeared, however, FIESP leaders experienced some of the potential drawbacks of this strategy in negotiations with metallurgical and textile workers. Despite a positive initial response from union leaders, including Remo Forli, to a proposal from the metallurgical employers' *sindicato*, the labor officials insisted that they had to present the tentative agreement to their general assemblies for rank-and-file approval. The employers openly manifested their annoyance with this insistence on democratic procedure by the union leaders—and not without reason, since more militant factions could block the progress of negotiations in the general assemblies.[56]

Initial negotiations between textile manufacturers and the textile workers' union president, Nelson Rusticci, yielded even fewer positive results. The employers' representative elaborately declared his category's willingness to consider the demands of the textile workers and emphasized the need for direct negotiation between the respective *sindicatos*. The Communist-backed Rusticci, whom textile employers regarded as a reasonable union leader, if not as agreeable as his *pelego* predecessor, nonetheless had to answer to an increasingly militant rank and file and presented demands that the employers' *sindicato* dismissed as "exaggerated." The meeting ended with the manufacturers' representative threatening to await a "legal" resolution of the wage question, which meant abandoning the very strategy FIESP had proposed of face-to-face bargaining without government interference.[57]

Vargas's suicide in August 1954 ushered in a period of uncertainty and caution in the industrial arena. The crisis of political transition during the caretaker government of former vice president João Café Filho froze many social arrangements, and labor unions proceeded with particular care, wary of the interim president, a conservative military officer and a lightning rod for anti-*getulista* sentiment. Thus the paulista textile workers accepted a proposal in early 1955 from the employers' *sindicato* for a modest 25 percent increase, citing the union's desire to "develop and consolidate good and friendly relations" with employers.[58] Only when a preemptive military coup guaranteed the presidential succession of the legally elected candidate, Juscelino Kubitschek, did the context become more propitious for reorganizing labor relations and constructing new strategies for industrial development and social peace.

Social Peace at Risk

The new president, affiliated with the PSD, began his career as the *getulista* mayor of Belo Horizonte, capital of his native state of Minas Gerais. In most respects, Kubitschek was the perfect president for the FIESP leadership—a moderate politician with strongly anti-Communist views but with a profound commitment to national development through industrialization. However, some aspects of his election cast something of a shadow on the new administration, at least from the industrialists' point of view. Aside from Kubitschek's narrow electoral plurality and the need for a military coup to insure his inauguration, there was the election of the radical *trabalhista*, João Goulart, as vice president. But, on balance, the immediate future looked highly promising for the industrial bourgeoisie.

Indicative of the expectations that Kubitschek's presidency incited among industrial employers is the "Carta de Princípios da Indústria," issued by the CNI in the months following Kubitschek's electoral victory. This statement of principles, formulated in the first plenary session of the CNI since the 1940s, reiterated most of the positions first adopted in the "Carta Econômica de Teresópolis" in 1945. It treated industrialization as central to Brazilian development, national security, and general welfare. The document called for state intervention in the economy, but never to the detriment of private initiative, and supported foreign investment, but never in preference to domestic capital.[59] It gave considerable attention to the need for greater productivity, which it described as having three components: "technical efficiency, organization, and human relations." In the area of worker training, it called for greater efforts by the public sector to complement the work of SENAI. And although it did not refer to SESI by name, the "Social Policy—Assistance" section proposed an "expansion of public assistance services, preferably in cooperation with private agencies." Virtually all proposals regarding social policy in the document made major improvements conditional upon increased productivity and national income.[60] Moreover, in language nearly identical to that articulated by Simonsen in the 1920s, the *carta* rejected "redistribution of national income" as offering only ephemeral advantages, arguing instead for improvements in the standard of living through overall growth.

The *carta* reveals both the great expectations excited by the Kubitschek presidency and ongoing reservations about the state's role in industry, especially in relations between capital and labor. Aside from hedging calls for state intervention with an emphasis on private initiative, the document carefully restricted the state's sphere of action in labor relations. With regard to wage policy, it said, the state should limit itself to setting the minimum wage. And in its section on "social order," the *carta* stated simply that "social order is the result of perfect understanding between employers and employees, based on the mutual observance of rights and obligations." Apparently, the state was to play no *overt* role in the maintenance of this social order. In a similar vein, during the 1955 plenary session, CNI president Augusto Viana Ribeiro dos Santos glowingly referred to SESI and SENAI as "two organizations that place our nation in the vanguard with respect to human relations in the workplace."[61] According to this speech, Brazil's reputation as a progressive industrializing nation lay not in its state-directed system of labor legislation and unions but in the social welfare agencies created by the industrialists themselves.

Despite the employers' trumpeting of their own achievements, the spotlight during the latter half of the 1950s remained fixed on the state as Kubitschek's government energetically promoted both unprecedented industrial expansion and a broadly popular ideology of national development.[62] FIESP embraced most aspects of Kubitschek's economic strategy, including a reform in the tariff schedule that increased protection for domestic industrial production. Indeed, paulista industrialists could reasonably argue that their ongoing campaigns to define Brazil as a potential industrial power and to highlight productivity and efficiency as the key to social well-being had created the preconditions for Kubitschek's developmental juggernaut.

FIESP devoted considerable energy during the Kubitschek years to promoting industrial productivity. The federation stepped up its activities in this vein both within its own organization and through its auxiliary agencies, SENAI, SESI, and IDORT.[63] In March 1956, FIESP inaugurated its Technical Council on Productivity, a committee of specialists in scientific management operating under the auspices of SESI's Division for Social Orientation. The committee's mission included publishing articles and pamphlets on means to increase productivity and consulting directly with industrial firms, especially smaller firms, widely regarded as bastions of inefficient organization.[64] Also in 1956, FIESP announced the founding of the Instituto de Tempos e Métodos in São Paulo. The FIESP bulletin described this entity, affiliated with IDORT and directed by managers from large industrial firms, as the first of its kind in all of Latin America. Its purpose was to disseminate information on methods designed to improve economy of movement and to "increase productivity with greater saving of manpower and material."[65]

Aside from its more technical initiatives, FIESP expanded its "intellectual" activities during this period with the resurrection of CIESP. The center had remained virtually dormant since the 1930s, when it was subsumed under the FIESP rubric; presidents of the federation also held the nominal title of CIESP head. But in the mid-1950s, CIESP, though still subordinated to FIESP, began functioning as a separate entity with its own president, industrial engineer Waldemar Clemente. The center, which included the newly founded Forum Roberto Simonsen, became a locus for debate and discussion of political, economic, and social problems, with invited speakers including prominent industrialists, military leaders, state officials, and even left-wing nationalist intellectuals.[66]

With the industrial economy booming and a moderate-developmentalist politician occupying the presidency, one might expect the discourse at the forum to assume a self-congratulatory tone. Yet much of the discussion in the recently resurrected CIESP focused on a growing or imminent "political crisis." Kubitschek's unstinting support for industrial development did relatively little to allay industrialist fears and criticism of a political system that seemed to be functioning in a dangerously "irrational" manner. To be sure, in a society where a popular president had been driven to suicide by fierce political opponents and where his elected successor took office courtesy of a preemptive military coup, a perception of crisis may not seem unreasonable. Yet this is a very different view of industrialists' attitudes from the standard portrayal of a warm and mutually beneficial relationship between Kubitschek and manufacturing interests during his government.

The reigning interpretation of the Kubitschek years highlights the government's skillful negotiation of agreements between employers and workers and its maintenance of curbs on union militancy.[67] Although this view admits that Kubitschek's Ministry of Labor "permitted a certain amount of liberty at the lowest levels" of the union structure and that the president was often "more generous" in his wage policy than recommended by economic advisers, the emphasis is on the co-optation and manipulation of labor. Scholars generally have construed Kubitschek's policies and his "ideology of national development" as having a negative impact on the labor movement, whereas employers are seen as benefiting from the state's mediation between capital and labor. This perspective assumes that industrialists did not find the pattern of increasingly frequent strikes and steady wage hikes disturbing but instead gratefully accepted the state's mediation of quick conclusions to industrial conflicts.[68]

Certainly, there were many aspects of the Kubitschek administration that industrialists could regard with approval, but if we look at the period from 1956 to 1960 through the eyes of the paulista manufacturers, we can also see much that they found disconcerting. Although Kubitschek's discourse emphasized harmony between capital and labor, once in office he made a series of concessions, formal and informal, to an increasingly militant labor movement to secure its support for his sweeping industrialization policies. Encouraged by his *trabalhista* vice president and pressured by radical-nationalist union leaders, Kubitschek further loosened government controls over the labor movement, allowing the stronger unions and their federations an unprecedented degree of political autonomy and financial independence. It was also under Kubitschek that the Brazilian congress removed most restrictions on the right to strike, and labor unions won increased representation on the governing boards of the social security institutes.[69]

This record of compromise with and concessions to the labor movement formed a sharp contrast with the Dutra presidency or the early years of the Estado Novo, when the state had energetically intervened in the labor unions to restrain militancy and insulate "leaders" from the demands of the rank and file. Instead of restraining labor, the state now provided the means for the unions to expand their influence and respond to rank-and-file demands. Paulista industrialists took particular offense in 1958 at the legal initiatives that dramatically expanded the right to strike for most private-sector employees. Although the constitution of 1946 guaranteed workers this right, Dutra's Decree-law no. 9,070 had effectively prohibited such actions. Under Kubitschek, congress both revoked Dutra's decree and created regulations to make the constitutional guarantee more meaningful.

Maintaining its earlier position that the elaborate network of labor tribunals established under Vargas made strikes unnecessary except in the most unusual circumstances, the FIESP leadership repeatedly denounced and criticized the campaign to expand the right to strike.[70] Editorial remarks in the FIESP bulletin characterized the legislative proposals as "absurd" and portrayed recent strike movements as the work of a handful of politically motivated activists. Egon Felix Gottschalk, a director of CIESP and a self-styled industrialist-intellectual, argued that a strike should be "the final resort for resolving a purely economic conflict, once all the means for conciliation have failed."[71] In effect, that meant strikes should remain illegal except in cases where the decisions handed down by the labor courts were not implemented by employers. Gottschalk justified FIESP's position by emphasizing the "disastrous" consequences of strikes: "The collective paralyzing of labor in any sector of the national economy would signify a serious disturbance and do undeniable harm to the potential for productivity." To reinforce this point, FIESP published detailed statistics demonstrating the losses incurred by paulista industry due to work stoppages in 1957.[72]

Even more than the economic effects, Gottschalk emphasized that "labor conflicts, inevitably, will begin to undermine the atmosphere of understanding and collaboration between the factors of production" and would put "social peace at risk." The latter phrase became a favorite of the FIESP leadership; it highlighted the employers' position that strikes represented a dangerous disruption of the economic and social order rather than a routine aspect of industrial relations. In this vein, the FIESP bulletin declared the proposals for an expanded right to strike "an incentive to anarchy" and "an act of insanity."[73]

The issue of the right to strike seems to have fed the industrialists' fears of impending crisis in Brazilian society, as demonstrated by a frankly alarmist public statement by FIESP official Jorge Luiz. Serving as the FIESP representative on the 1958 Minimum Wage Commission, Luiz deviated from the meeting's agenda to read a long document urging workers to cooperate in the maintenance of social peace. Speaking in the most lurid terms, he declared that "Brazil is no longer at the edge of the abyss, but rather is in the abyss, merely waiting to crash and explode; that the demagoguery of politicians leads the workers along the wrong path, thus hindering the construction of the much-desired peace; that job tenure and the right to strike are the worst social cancers in Brazil, particularly the right to strike."[74]

Within São Paulo itself, relations between labor unions and industrialist organizations had been relatively harmonious during the early months of the Kubitschek period. For example, after years of ignoring or denouncing SESI's May Day festivities, several major unions decided to participate in the SESI-sponsored parade and Workers' Olympics. According to Aldo Lombardi, general secretary of the São Paulo metallurgical workers' union, SESI's deeper pockets had routinely allowed the industrialist organization to stage more spectacular—and better-attended—festivities than those sponsored by the labor unions. Thus several of the unions belonging to the Interunion Commission decided to join SESI in 1956 and 1957 and take advantage of the heavy turnout at its May Day commemorations.[75]

The unions abruptly terminated this symbolic collaboration in the aftermath of the October 1957 strikes in São Paulo. This ten-day walkout, whose participants included metalworkers, printers, shoemakers, and textile workers, had been staged to pressure employers to accept a labor tribunal ruling granting workers in these categories an across-the-board 25 percent wage increase. In its account of the (apparently legal) strike, *O Metalúrgico* angrily reported that the industrialists called upon the police and the civil guard to arrest, beat, and harass strikers. Interestingly, the article claimed that the forces of law and order only responded after three days of pleading from the employers. And the attempted intimidation proved fruitless since the labor tribunal reconfirmed the workers' salary demands. There was one major consequence, however: in the words of *O Metalúrgico*, the strike "buried once and for all the 'social peace' proclaimed by the bosses and SESI."[76] And from the unions' perspective, it was the employers, not the strikers, who were responsible for its death.

The leaders of São Paulo's industrial organizations even encountered resistance and protest on their home turf. During the late 1950s and early 1960s, employees of SENAI and SESI took the first steps toward unionization as their salaries lagged behind inflation. The upper echelons of both agencies initially treated these efforts as a form of betrayal or mutiny, summarily dismissing employees who dared to go public with their criticisms. Especially revealing is the indignant response of SESI's regional council to a 1960 petition for higher wages from the newly formed employees' union, the Association of SESI Employees (Associação dos Servidores do SESI, or ASSESI). Council president Antônio Devisate denounced the petition as written "in highly disrespectful terms" and branded it a "veritable act of indiscipline." Another council member declared the petition a "serious manifestation of indiscipline and disregard for hierarchical superiors," and the council voted to cancel its recognition of ASSESI as well as to halt paycheck deductions for the union contribution. Most seriously, it called for the firing of the petition's signatories.[77]

Since the petition itself was not included in the SESI archive, it is impossible to uncover precisely what these industrialists found so offensive, but the terms in which they discussed the matter and their response to the petition demonstrate how anxious they were to preserve their authority and the existing organizational hierarchy. They also indicate how deeply disturbed the industrialists were by insubordination among the "soldiers of social peace." Eventually, both the regional representative of the Ministry of Labor and the president of the CNTI would intervene on behalf of the ASSESI directorate, but the council refused to alter its position unless the signatories provided a written apology and retraction. To save their jobs, the ASSESI directors acquiesced, composing a letter to Devisate requesting that he "consider nonexistent any terms or expressions that could be construed as indelicate or offensive" in the petition. In response, the regional council canceled the order to dismiss the employees, but the incident created considerable bitterness and set the pattern for a series of subsequent conflicts, including a threat to strike by SESI's 6,000 employees in São Paulo the following year. Moreover, leaders of various industrial unions seized upon SESI's internal labor conflicts as proof of the hypocrisy of the industrial bourgeoisie and its authoritarian approach to labor relations.[78]

Unnerved by the new era of union militancy, the rapid influx of foreign capital, and the accelerating rate of inflation, the industrialists did not hesitate to describe Brazilian society during the final years of the Kubitschek presidency as entering a state of crisis. The FIESP leadership regarded the political sphere as increasingly "irrational" as elected officials unfamiliar with the needs and complexities of the workplace made concessions to workers without recourse to any "scientific" consideration of the new regulations' impact. Retreating to a neo-Fordist position, industrialists pointedly contrasted the sphere of production—rational, harmonious, hierarchical—with this chaotic political arena, spinning out of control.

Pronouncements by the FIESP leadership focused, more and more, on the factory as the building block of society. The workplace was not only the point of production but also the key element in national security and the prime location of cross-class collaboration. The representations of the factory by spokesmen for FIESP, SESI, and SENAI revolved around the somewhat paradoxical concept of "hierarchical solidarity."[79] That is, the factory was a space in which a rational, and therefore (by the industrialists' logic) hierarchical, organization reigned. At the same time, industrialists emphasized the teamwork and cooperation that characterized the production process. Thus the factory was a virtually utopian space where authority and democracy could coexist without disturbance and where men and women, "whether in command of the most important positions or in the execution of the simplest tasks," struggled together to improve the standard of living for all Brazilians "through the strengthening of the national economy."[80]

An excellent example of this discursive tendency is a FIESP editorial commemorating the Day of Industry in 1956:

> Those who only perceive antagonisms and differences between capital and labor are utterly mistaken, for in the intimacy of the factory or workshop, more than anywhere else, one always feels a powerful force for closer cooperation among men—there is a community of interests and objectives that transforms every captain of industry into a worker with broad responsibilities and each worker into a party interested in the output of the firm, in which all participate as members of a collectivity whose vital necessities are satisfied through the complex mechanisms of production.[81]

FIESP even liked to emphasize the strategic importance of the factory in the event of a national emergency, arguing that under the conditions of modern warfare the industrialist at the head of his factory was at greater risk than the military commander at the head of his troops.[82]

The factory, then, served two functions in industrialist discourse. First, it was the source of the employer's authority in the social and political realm, given the financial, even physical, risks that such investments entailed and the privileged information and technical expertise gained by those intimately involved in overseeing the production process. Second, it provided a microcosm of "democratic" cross-class collaboration and social peace as all participants cooperated in the heroic enterprise of national development. In both respects, it presented a salutary contrast to the political sphere, where those who made decisions often lacked the knowledge/authority to do so and where class conflict was increasingly open and disruptive.

This portrait of the factory as a harmonious and rational space contradicts recent research in the history of Brazilian labor, which emphasizes ongoing worker resistance to new work processes, day-to-day attempts to subvert the chain of command, and other forms of struggle at the point of production.[83] But it is important to keep in mind that such resistance in Brazilian factories, at least prior to the 1970s, tended to occur on an individualized and episodic basis and that labor leaders even in the most highly unionized categories had little success in organizing workers on the shopfloor.[84] Factory commissions that emerged during strike movements often faded quickly, and attempts to create networks of union-elected shopfloor delegates repeatedly ended in failure. The dozens of interviews conducted by Robert Alexander with industrialists during the 1950s and early 1960s did not reveal a single firm with a shop-steward system, and most employers explicitly preferred direct negotiations with the union leadership.[85] According to a 1963 article in the North American journal *Business Topics*, there were "no shop stewards of the U.S. pattern in Brazilian industry." Furthermore, the author claimed that "organized labor is not a serious factor limiting managerial prerogatives" and that "unions are relatively weak, *except as a political force.*"[86]

The industrialists' view of the factory as the sphere of order and rationality was not, then, pure fiction. Placed in contrast to the increasingly conflict-ridden political sphere, the factory could be constructed as an orderly space where managerial prerogatives suffered few serious challenges. Especially in the larger factories, industrialists and their organizations controlled the vocational programs that trained workers for skilled jobs, offered the literacy courses for adult workers, introduced modern methods of organization and human relations to the supervisory personnel, and closely monitored the activities of committees formed to prevent workplace accidents. And when the state tried to intervene in the shopfloor routine or in the workings of the industrial labor market, employers usually could fend off such attempts with impunity.[87]

Several studies of the Brazilian labor movement have addressed the question of the unions' "weakness" at the factory level, directly or indirectly, typically assuming that the explanation lies in the corporatist system of labor relations. The result was, presumably, a union structure that became top-heavy in bureaucracy but sank only shallow roots into the workplace.[88] Union leaders, either to retain the benefits of their sinecures or in response to the vanguardist politics of the PCB, supposedly collaborated to maintain a structure that was only weakly rooted in the shopfloor. Not all historians of Brazilian labor accept this argument, and several studies have documented efforts by militant union leaders to set up a network of shopfloor delegates or factory commissions during the postwar period.[89] Yet these efforts were sporadic and isolated and usually met with frustration and failure.

If we shift the emphasis from state control of the union structure to industrialist power in the workplace, new elements appear to explain such failures.[90] In the first instance, it was management's ability to squelch workplace organizing that caused these efforts to fail. How, then, do we explain management's success? One possibility is to emphasize the weaker "class-consciousness" of Brazilian workers during this period as compared, say, to the mid-1970s, when São Paulo gave birth to the "new unionism." But another way to approach the matter is to consider, on the one hand, the extent to which industrialists managed to preserve the workplace as their nearly exclusive domain in exchange for their collaboration in Vargas's corporatist-populist project. From the outset, they effectively limited the intrusion of federal inspectors or other representatives of the state into the workplace and relegated to themselves functions that, in other settings, would be the concern of the state bureaucracy. And they most strenuously and effectively resisted any delegation of authority to union officials in the sphere of production. On the other hand, labor unions encountering the many obstacles erected by employers to organization at the factory level (whether those obstacles were frequent firings or positive inducements for workers) could be expected to turn to the more receptive political sphere to press for better wages and working conditions.[91]

This configuration of labor relations, then, served to reinforce the industrialists' view of the factory as an orderly, rational space where social peace reigned in contrast to the political arena, where conflict was not only intensifying but even threatening to "infect" the sphere of production. Similarly, within the factory, industrialists and managers could maintain the ideal hierarchy of knowledge and command, safe for the time being from the disruptive effects of political conflict. For all the talk of teamwork and democratic cooperation, life inside the factory walls reinforced employers' habits of command and their sense of privileged authority.

At the same time, industrialist leaders regarded Kubitschek as insufficiently respectful of their expertise and authority.[92] One political scientist has described the CNI as "strangely inactive" in the late 1950s, arguing that there was no need for industrialists to assert themselves publicly under an administration so clearly committed to industrial development.[93] But at least within FIESP, there seems to have been a growing sense of unease and little consensus about whether industrialists could rely on Kubitschek and other supposedly sympathetic politicians to act in their interests. True, the FIESP leadership put forth no serious alternative program or systematic critique of Kubitschek's policies; one FIESP director publicly lamented his colleagues' "lack of a political-economic doctrine" in the face of mounting crisis.[94] This lack of alternatives, however, does not signal contentment or even acquiescence.

SENAI and SESI in the 1960s

A scandal that erupted during the short-lived presidency of Kubitschek's successor, Jânio Quadros, demonstrated that industrialist leaders were hardly immune from the corrupting influences of the public sector. From 1956 to 1961, Lídio Lunardi served as president of the CNI. A prominent member of the PSD, as were many other industrialists throughout Brazil, Lunardi also had close ties to PTB leaders João Goulart and Hugo de Faria. At the very end of the Kubitschek period, Lunardi approved the deposit of SENAI and SESI funds totaling 180 million cruzeiros in a Rio de Janeiro bank owned by a businessman with personal ties to Lunardi, Goulart, and Faria. The bank was in a state of near insolvency, and the deposits apparently were made in the hopes of restoring its financial health. But Lunardi's machinations were to no avail, and the bank began returning checks written on its accounts by directors of SENAI and SESI. This prompted the anticorruption Quadros, whose campaign symbol was a broom, to intervene in the CNI and the National Departments of SENAI and SESI, appointing an emergency governing board to oversee all three entities.[95]

No FIESP leaders were implicated in the scandal, but the government's intervention in the CNI was certainly a source of embarrassment for industrialist spokesmen already concerned with their somewhat diminished stature on the national stage. And although the São Paulo departments of SESI and SENAI had previously operated with virtual autonomy from the national offices, the scandal seems to have affected their ability to collect sufficient funding, forcing them to adopt a series of austerity measures during the early 1960s.

Despite these hardships, both SENAI and SESI were able to maintain most of the activities developed during the 1950s and even expand into new areas. SENAI–São Paulo lavished particular attention on its courses to produce skilled workers for the massive automobile plants. The Escola Roberto Simonsen introduced its first full-scale course in tool-and-die making in 1962, and a year later, SENAI commemorated the 100th anniversary of the São Paulo suburb, São Bernardo, by opening a school in that *município* specifically designed to train metallurgical workers.[96] SENAI also maintained its programs to train technicians for the textile and ceramics industries and expanded its program for training within industry.

Perhaps in response to the discouraging financial outlook, SENAI–São Paulo actively sought to develop as many schools and programs as possible in collaboration with other entities. For example, in early 1961, SENAI signed an accord with the São Paulo state government in which the state agreed to build ten new schools in the capital and another twenty in the interior and SENAI agreed to administer and staff the new institutions. According to FIESP, the state had decided to establish the new professional schools in cooperation with SENAI "with the purpose of making their organization as objective and rational as possible and fitting them within the framework of the state's manufacturing sector."[97]

The annual governor's reports from the early 1960s reveal a persistent anxiety about the shortage of skilled workers, especially in the metallurgical trades. In 1960 Governor Carlos Alberto de Carvalho Pinto went so far as to attribute an industrial slowdown in part to the scarcity of skilled workers. Aware of the inadequacy of the state's own vocational schools, the governor proved eager to encourage SENAI's activities throughout the state. SENAI also set up a series of accords with French and North American agencies to expand access to new technical information and industrial training materials. These various strategies—training within industry and collaborative efforts with the state government and foreign agencies— allowed SENAI to maintain slow but steady growth during these years. Statistics from 1961 indicate this upward trend: between 1942 and 1960, SENAI–São Paulo awarded a total of 46,493 certificates to apprentices, whereas in 1961 alone, there were 23,000 minors being trained by SENAI in São Paulo. But it is important to note that over half of these apprentices were being trained within industry.[98]

Both financial and political pressures moved SESI to reorder its priorities during the early 1960s. The Kubitschek years had seen ever more lavish parades and ceremonies to commemorate May Day (including an elaborate torchlight procession through the industrial suburbs of São Paulo on May Day eve). SESI activities in the flush years of the late 1950s culminated in the inauguration of its first *conjunto assistencial*. This complex, located in the capital and named after Antônio Devisate, was designed to serve as a combined social, recreational, and educational center.[99] Its unveiling was attended by considerable fanfare, including a speech by Kubitschek himself, who treated the occasion as a confirmation of his social policies: "My government has sought to establish a solid and stable equilibrium between the two great organizations that oversee the expansion and progress of the nation. On one side, the men of initiative, the men of capital, who are engaged in an extraordinary effort to give Brazil these instruments of progress, and on the other side, the worker, who provides the intelligent labor and extremely efficient collaboration in this process of development."[100] Although Kubitschek's concern for social peace echoed SESI doctrine, few industrialists would have echoed his populist affirmation of the Brazilian workers' "extremely efficient collaboration" in the process of industrialization.

In the aftermath of the highly publicized inauguration of this first *conjunto*, municipal politicians throughout São Paulo besieged SESI with requests for similar centers, usually offering a free piece of land as inducement. SESI actually signed agreements with the *municípios* of Santo André and São Caetano do Sul to build *conjuntos* in those locations, but a shortage of funds and more pressing obligations caused SESI to postpone construction for several years. Similarly, by the early 1960s, SESI had decided to forego the expensive May Day parade, opting instead for a modest flag-raising ceremony at the opening of the Workers' Olympics.[101]

By 1962, the SESI regional council, with new FIESP president Raphael Noschese presiding, formally adopted a fresh list of priorities, shifting emphasis from social welfare to educational programs.[102] The new priorities reflected in part SESI's continuing conception of itself as a vehicle for socialization and not simply a dispenser of social services. SESI repeatedly affirmed that its mission was "not only to provide assistance to the worker and his family but to create a veritable school of culture and civic and social orientation."[103] At the same time, these decisions reflected new social and political trends. For example, the council argued that the "evolution" of the National Institute for Social Welfare (Instituto Nacional de Previdência Social, or INPS) would gradually make SESI's medical clinics redundant. Instead, the council members decided to stress "preventive medicine," especially in the area of occupational health and safety.[104] Similarly, the growing housing shortage in the urban areas—evidenced by mushrooming squatter settlements—made low-cost housing an urgent matter. Noschese also emphasized the ideological value of expanded home ownership for industrial workers, arguing that housing was "the fundamental issue for safeguarding the integrity of the worker's family and for simultaneously giving the family unit a sense of stability and participation within a free society."[105]

The most dramatic reorientation in SESI's activity was its sudden massive involvement in the area of primary education, dictated by a 1961 executive decree. Issued by Jânio Quadros during the first few months of his abortive presidency, the decree implemented article 68 of the 1946 constitution, which required all firms with over 100 employees to provide primary schooling for workers' children.[106] This decree illustrated, once again, the imprecise relationship between state initiative and industrialist inclination. Prior to the decree, industrialists had made only piecemeal, "voluntary" efforts to implement the constitutional provision. As of 1961, SESI sponsored a mere 65 elementary school classes in São Paulo, with a total enrollment of 1,600 students.[107]

The industrialist associations responded to the enactment of the decree with either mild or enthusiastic approval. FIESP officials, in a telegram to Quadros, expressed "the satisfaction of paulista industry to be able to surmount one more hurdle in the struggle against the prevailing elements of underdevelopment, in this case illiteracy."[108] Central to the easy acceptance, even embrace, of the decree by industrial enterprises was the role SESI was to play in its implementation. SESI assumed responsibility for the training of teachers, the preparation of pedagogical material, and other details involved in the organization of factory schools. Indeed, a document from SESI certifying that a firm had taken appropriate steps toward the inauguration of a school constituted formal proof and allowed the firm to "unfreeze" its funds in the Banco do Brasil. By 1963, SESI–São Paulo had organized 1,758 classes with a total enrollment of 71,242 students—a fortyfold increase since the promulgation of the decree.[109] Through SESI's good offices, industrialists could establish a primary school in their firm with a relatively small outlay of money or energy and rest assured that the instruction in the school reflected some of industry's particular concerns regarding education.[110]

Social Peace and National Security

In his "state of FIESP" speech delivered in early 1961, Antônio Devisate spoke about the labor conflicts of the previous year in measured tones, optimistically noting that the strikes had not spurred broader or deeper upheavals. And he greeted the election of paulista politician Jânio Quadros with enthusiasm, endorsing the new president's strategy to bring inflation under control. Except for a critical reference to increasing statism, the speech revealed little anxiety about the past or the future. But if we look at the editorials of FIESP's weekly bulletin during this period or the content of the talks sponsored by CIESP's Forum Roberto Simonsen, we see continuing evidence of industrialist anxiety about Communist influence in the labor unions, monetary instability, and general incompetence in the political sphere, even as the latter expanded its purview. And such anxiety was bound to intensify after Quadros's unexpected resignation from the presidency in August 1961. His replacement, Vice President João Goulart, drew his main political support from the radical wing of *trabalhismo* and was so objectionable to a faction of the military that he barely managed to take office after Quadros's resignation.[111]

Goulart's presidency, however, did not initiate a new line of discourse within FIESP so much as an amplification of existing themes. Under Kubitschek, the industrialists already spoke of the threat of subversion and displayed increasing eagerness to collaborate with segments of the armed forces in political and intellectual pursuits. Military officials became regu-

Lunch for officials of the Second Army Division at the SENAI restaurant in the Escola Roberto Simonsen, 1949. Roberto Mange is speaking; to his left is General Henrique Teixeira Lott. This was one of many such luncheons held for visiting dignitaries. Courtesy of the Núcleo de Memória, SENAI–São Paulo.

lar speakers at the Forum Roberto Simonsen, and leading industrialists gave lectures or even studied at the Superior War College, the intellectual center of the Brazilian armed forces.[112] A typical event was the visit of 150 "high officials" of the Brazilian military to FIESP headquarters, SENAI, SESI, and various paulista factories in late 1958. According to a FIESP publication, the military men were especially impressed by SENAI and SESI for producing "civically superior citizens." A week later, Antônio Devisate delivered a lecture to student-interns from the Superior War College in which he affirmed FIESP's concern for the "valorization of the Brazilian" and talked extensively about SENAI and SESI as evidence of this concern.[113]

The "intellectual" collaboration between FIESP and the military culminated during the early 1960s in a series of lectures at the Forum Roberto Simonsen on national security. The speakers in this series included the future dictator, General Humberto Castello Branco, and General Edmundo de Macedo Soares e Silva, "mastermind" of the Volta Redonda Steel Mill. The effusive introduction for the latter speaker was delivered by A. C. Pacheco e Silva, longtime member of IDORT and FIESP and graduate of the Superior War College.[114] He described Macedo Soares, an engineer, as a perfect example of the close collaboration between industry and the military. According to Pacheco e Silva, "The army and industry have affinities between them that become more accentuated with the advance of science and technology." In his lecture, entitled "Industry and National Security," Macedo Soares responded in kind, citing "social peace" as one of the main objectives of national security and ending with the declaration that "without industry there will be no progress." [115]

The affirmation of the industrialists' role in promoting the general welfare of the nation was a recurring theme in the dialogue between FIESP and the armed forces. Both industrialists and military men regularly drew upon conservative Christian doctrine to define their social positions. More concretely, SENAI and SESI repeatedly served as the chief evidence of the industrialists' compassion and the private sector's efficiency; rarely did an industrialist spokesman deliver a speech without making some reference to one or both of these organizations. [116] These services also provided the basis for praise of the industrialists from some unexpected sources, such as socialist and former printer Everardo Dias. As noted earlier, Dias closed his account of early labor struggles in Brazil by contrasting the retrograde bosses of the past with the "enlightened bourgeoisie" responsible for creating such agencies as SENAI and SESI. [117]

Few active union leaders would have echoed Dias's opinions. For much of the period from the late 1950s to the early 1960s, the industrialists adopted a defensive posture in response to a torrent of criticism from the labor movement and populist politicians. Even members of the military were not above questioning the industrialists' commitment to advancing social peace. In 1962 prominent FIESP official Mário di Pierro delivered a lecture entitled "Industry, the State, and the National Economy" to the Círculo Militar de São Paulo. Perhaps the most interesting feature of the event was the introductory speech made by General Oswaldo C. Dória. According to Dória, then head of the Círculo Militar's cultural department, there were two types of industrialists:

> ONE has the Lord, our God, in his body but has an empty heart and a hollow head; he ignores [workers' rights] and only under penalty of the Law and collective grievances does he yield to the workers' demands and sacred rights; in the current moment of social evolution, he lives, despite frustration and bitterness, off the remnants of feudalism and slavery. The OTHER has GOD in his conscience, a human heart, and an intelligent head; enlightened, he adapts himself to new social conditions; humane, he has no slaves but collaborators, whom he stimulates with promotions and bonuses; progressive, he often spontaneously

anticipates the claims that the other concedes only in the face of strikes. ONE is the boss, the OTHER is the captain of industry![118]

To be sure, this criticism of the "old-fashioned" factory owner left the way open for Pierro to construct the typical paulista industrialist as corresponding to the second, more "progressive" archetype. Indeed, Dória's "captain of industry," with his rational mind and compassionate heart, closely matched the image that FIESP always tried to convey of its membership.

Pierro's lecture, in contrast to the public utterances of Antônio Devisate, went beyond the usual praise for the industrialists and their contributions to the formation of Brazilian society. Influenced by the "strong state/ weak bourgeoisie" model elaborated in that era, his talk exemplified the industrialists' difficulties in defining their political and economic position during this period of crisis. In the tradition of Roberto Simonsen, Pierro admitted the need for significant state intervention in the economy but also warned against the tendency of the state to stifle private initiative. Then, echoing many progressive sociologists and political scientists of the period, Pierro described the state's "protective intervention" as "perhaps one of the causes of the difficulties we have in forming an authentic class of prominent national entrepreneurs and the resulting recourse to the state."[119]

Even though industrialists might be politically and culturally weak on the national level, their enterprises were still, according to Pierro, the basic building blocks of society. To bolster this argument, Pierro referred to the recent papal encyclical, *Mater et Magistra*, and its apparent reaffirmation of the centrality of personal and private initiative in the economic world. Going further back, he cited a statement issued by the Assembly of French Bishops in 1944 which insisted that "the unity of command and . . . the authority of the firm's director . . . should be fully recognized." Having established the industrialists' claim to being the central authoritative actors in the economic sphere, he then called for "the formation of a new and solid mentality within the industrialist class, with an awareness of its historical responsibilities toward the nation and capable of being a true ruling class."[120]

The other discursive tendency among FIESP leaders during this period was, more predictably, the denunciation of growing subversion and "insurrectional tendencies." Reviving the passionately anti-Communist rhetoric of the mid-1940s, FIESP spokesmen regularly attributed social conflicts to a cabal of subversives and increasingly identified democracy with anticommunism. Under Kubitschek, leading FIESP figures were already sounding the anti-Communist alarm. In December 1959, Pacheco e Silva delivered a lecture at the Forum Roberto Simonsen entitled "The Advancing War of Subversion." Pacheco e Silva warned his audience that "techniques designed to implant indiscipline and revolt among the masses, to sow conflict between the classes, discord within the armed forces, agitation in the student ranks, and disturbances in the heart of the population, are being skillfully implemented." Similarly, a panel of industrialists and military men who spoke at the Forum Roberto Simonsen at the very end of the Kubitschek administration concluded that "there exist throughout the nation symptoms of insurrection."[121] The main speaker, an army officer, specifically cited Pacheco e Silva's lecture thirteen months earlier and fully endorsed the FIESP director's arguments.

In contrast to this escalating rhetoric, the initial public reaction of the FIESP leadership to Goulart's ascendance to the presidency was measured and even mildly positive. To be sure, the preconditions of Goulart's succession—the imposition of a quasiparliamentary system that greatly reduced the power of the executive—made him seem less threatening. But it is also important to recall that several directors of FIESP, such as Devisate himself, were active members of the PSD, a party that regularly formed alliances of convenience with Goulart's PTB. Devisate and Nadir Figueiredo, Morvan's brother, traveled to Brasília to attend Goulart's formal inauguration, and the FIESP president took advantage of the trip to confer with the new chief executive. Reporting back to the membership, Devisate emphasized Goulart's "conciliatory attitude" and assured his fellow industrialists that the new president "will not undermine measures designed to attend to the necessities of national production." A week later, FIESP/CIESP took the unusual step of issuing an official statement "reaffirm[ing] its confidence in the nation's democratic institutions" and extolling the "enlightened and patriotic action" of President Goulart.[122]

Despite subsequent events and considerable diversity of opinion among prominent FIESP members, it seems safe to argue that Goulart's inauguration did not, in and of itself, transform the federation into a strident opponent of the existing regime. But Goulart's announced social programs, proposed amid an accelerating rate of inflation, did little to dispel industrialists' ongoing sense of a politically inspired crisis. Indeed, the postinauguration honeymoon was exceedingly brief, with FIESP adopting a much harder and more critical line by the close of 1961. The specific issue that altered the course of FIESP rhetoric was the congressional debate over a measure to require all firms to grant employees a thirteenth-month salary. Industrialists opposed this on the grounds that it was inflationary and unduly onerous at a time of credit scarcity, positions that were eminently predictable.[123] However, what provoked an outraged response from industrialists was not the proposal itself but an announcement by the most militant unions in São Paulo that they would call a strike to pressure congress into passing the bill.

After calling an emergency meeting of its general assembly, FIESP issued a statement, "Paulista Industry to the Nation," detailing its planned response to the proposed strike and some broader considerations on the current situation. Describing the strike as illegal, the manifesto claimed that it was being organized by those who wished to undermine Brazilian institutions by encouraging disorder and fueling runaway inflation. The "designs" of those engaged in such provocative activities, it noted, were "unconfessable." Moving to specifics, the industrialists called upon the state government and its police force to insure "the right to work" during the strike. In the event that the public powers did not provide such guarantees, the federation announced that it would recommend that all firms "lock their doors in order to guarantee the physical integrity of their workers and the preservation of their property."[124]

The industrialists' challenge to the mobilization for a thirteenth-month salary campaign was initially successful. The employer-friendly governor of São Paulo, Carlos Alberto de Carvalho Pinto, readily acceded to FIESP's demands to guarantee the "right to work" and thereby foiled the threatened general strike. The subsequent "Opinion" column of FIESP's weekly bulletin savored this triumph and claimed that the manifesto signaled a new "virile and firm" position on the industrialists' part. Perhaps more telling, the bulletin editor claimed that the "virus of demagogy" in Brazil increasingly "comes from up above, from the top," especially at the federal level. Meanwhile, "words of stability, of good sense, of the just measure of things, which everywhere is the discourse of responsible governments, are no longer being enunciated by those who hold the reins of the administration but by the men of private enterprise."[125] This perspective could only have been reinforced by the eventual passage of the thirteenth-month salary law.

From late 1961 on, FIESP and other industrialist federations published a steady stream of articles and declarations criticizing the federal government. Even apparently innocuous issues with few political ramifications provided opportunities for diatribes against demagogues and inefficient bureaucrats. Thus a FIESP article praising efforts by the employer *sindicato* in the plastics industry to train high-level technicians and establish research laboratories placed these activities into a political context. According to the account, the plastics producers' achievements demonstrated, once again, that the private sector had to take such matters into its own hands since the state sector was inefficient and subject to "spurious and demagogic" influences.[126]

The changing of the guard at the upper levels of the FIESP hierarchy also contributed to a more strident and unrelenting criticism of the federal government. In October 1962, Antônio Devisate, claiming illness, stepped down after ten years as president of the federation. His newly elected replacement was Raphael Noschese, scion of a paulista industrial dynasty allied with the opposition UDN and the first FIESP president from the postwar generation. Noschese wasted no time in adopting a more alarmist tone than his predecessor. Even before assuming office, the president-elect lectured the São Paulo Rotary Club about the threat to Brazil from "totalitarian forces." In his inaugural address, Noschese began by discussing the current economic conjuncture and the impending exhaustion of the import-substitution model of industrialization. But Noschese devoted most of his unusually lengthy speech to political matters, assuring his fellow industrialists that "we must not and will not be indifferent to the war declared against Brazil and its free institutions."[127]

Aside from its overtures to the armed forces and its rhetorical attacks on statism and communism, FIESP continued its efforts, mainly through SESI, to influence the course of the labor movement and worker consciousness despite intense hostility from union leaders. To promote better coordination of such efforts, Noschese appointed high-level members of the SESI and SENAI bureaucracies to positions within FIESP. Nelson Marcondes do Amaral, a longtime employee of SESI and recently retired as director of the National Department of Labor, became Noschese's assistant for public relations. And Eduardo Saad, head of DOS, was named FIESP's assistant for sociopolitical and union matters.[128] Official activities included a growing number of seminars in "civic formation." In 1962 SESI–São Paulo offered 140 such courses as well as a series of radio programs on the subject. In a similar vein, SESI's regional council made a special allocation of 2 million cruzeiros so that DOS could purchase and distribute the pamphlet *Você é a Democracia* (You are democracy) in massive quantities.[129]

SESI also continued its policy of supplying covert subsidies and support for certain organizations and movements.[130] One of the most fascinating episodes during the early 1960s was SESI's response to a prolonged strike at the Aymoré biscuit factory in the port city of Santos. The stoppage began in July 1960 as an expression of solidarity with striking workers at the nearby Moinho Paulista, who were protesting an unfavorable decision by the regional labor tribunal. But the Aymoré workers must have had grievances of their own since their stoppage continued even after the Moinho Paulista employees returned to work.

The situation at Aymoré quickly became a cause célèbre in the labor movement and a cause for alarm among employers. Devisate called a special news conference in which he emphasized that the solidarity strike, "a movement devoid of either economic or juridical content," was completely illegal. He also bitterly denounced the use of pickets at the Aymoré factory, claiming that their presence challenged property rights. He ended by reiterating FIESP's solidarity with the owners and their firm resistance to the strikers' demands. Despite this tough talk, the strike at Aymoré continued, and by November 1960, Devisate had shifted his position on the need for firm resistance by employers. Arguing to SESI's regional council that "the strike movement that has exploded in this firm is now becoming a focal point for disturbances of the social peace," Devisate called for a grant of 1,026,000 cruzeiros to be distributed by the owners to the striking workers "in such a way as to facilitate a more rapid settlement." The SESI council voted its approval.[131]

Aside from such episodic interventions, SESI also maintained its interest in courting and supporting allies within organized labor. As we saw earlier in this chapter, even during the 1950s SESI's efforts in this regard were being repeatedly frustrated as old-guard *pelegos* either lost their bases of power in the labor movement or avoided close association with the industrialist organization. By the early 1960s, the industrialists' opposition not just to known Communist labor leaders but to any union official adopting a militant posture left SESI with fewer and fewer options in the sphere of organized labor. The only significant faction that SESI, and more specifically DOS, could enthusiastically support and promote was the Democratic Union Movement (Movimento Sindical Democrático, or MSD). Representatives of DOS attended the first national meeting of the MSD and described the event in glowing terms to SESI's regional council, whose members readily voted the movement a 1-million-cruzeiro subsidy.[132]

Openly anti-Communist, the MSD was composed of "bitterly anti-Goulart *pelegos*," according to one student of Brazilian organized labor. Indeed, the MSD's leaders were quite different from those *pelegos* who had been SESI's allies in organized labor during the late 1940s and early 1950s. The latter group, which we might regard as "genuine" *pelegos*, had little grass-roots support, deriving their power and influence mainly from their connections to the federal Labor Ministry and the fledgling PTB. But the MSD leaders lacked both popular support and ties to the federal labor bureaucracy. Rather, they were what one labor official termed "*pelegos da FIESP*," or to use the traditional disparaging labor term, "yellow" trade unionists. Their rhetoric was one of conciliation and compromise with employers, and in contrast to both Communist and radical-nationalist labor leaders, they eschewed all discussion of basic reforms.[133]

Both the MSD's program and its sources of support outside the labor movement did little to enhance its appeal among the rank and file. Though claiming support from seven labor federations and seventy-four trade unions in São Paulo as of 1963, the MSD represented a small and declining segment of organized labor. Its only remaining stronghold at the federal level was the National Confederation of Commercial Workers, but even the confederation's powerful president, Antônio Pereira Magaldi—a leading figure in the MSD—was increasingly unpopular and being challenged by an insurgent slate backed by the Labor Ministry.[134]

Prominent industrialists attempted to portray the close relationship between the MSD and FIESP as proof of the ongoing potential for cooperation between capital and labor. A 1963 issue of the FIESP bulletin summarized a letter sent to the MSD leadership in São Paulo by Antônio Devisate expressing his thanks for a ceremony honoring himself and fellow industrialist Mário di Pierro. In the letter, Devisate described himself as having done everything he could, through FIESP, SESI, and SENAI, to create better relations between employers and employees. He declared that the words of homage from the MSD members led him to believe that his lifelong efforts in this vein were "beginning to bear fruit."[135]

The MSD homage to Devisate and Pierro is vaguely reminiscent of the banquet held by union officials in 1943 to honor Roberto Simonsen and Morvan Dias de Figueiredo.[136] But the latter event took place at the height of corporatist politics and *peleguismo* under the Estado Novo. In an authoritarian, repressive context in which organized labor was rigidly controlled by the state, such a celebration of harmony between capital and labor had a certain credibility specific to the period. But by 1963, such professions of class harmony were made amid intensifying political conflicts and even factory-level struggles that rendered the MSD's homage to Devisate and Pierro a mere caricature of the earlier event.

SESI officials also increasingly departed from their tacit acceptance of a single union for each industry, turning in some cases to a local CO as an alternative for labor organizing. Saad, for example, designed an especially elaborate program for the Santos area to combat the influence of the increasingly militant petrochemical workers' union. The scheme involved paying a monthly subsidy of 150,000 cruzeiros to COs in the industrial suburbs of Santos and providing extensive medical and dental facilities so that workers would not have to resort to using union installations. Nevertheless, the continuing prohibition against union pluralism limited how far SESI could go with such machinations.[137]

In their more sober moments, FIESP spokesmen acknowledged their estrangement from organized labor (though not the working class, broadly defined, since the "average worker" could still be portrayed as having little sympathy for union activists). An editorial entitled "Example of Cooperation between Capital and Labor" that appeared in a 1962 issue of the FIESP bulletin celebrated industrial relations not in Brazil but in the United States. More specifically, it described the transformation of United Mine Workers president John L. Lewis from an implacable foe of the bosses to a collaborator with the large mining enterprises in the campaign to increase productivity and thereby improve workers' standard of living. According to the author, the U.S. coal-mining industry had become the most productive and efficient in the world due to "a new spirit of cooperation on the part of the workers led by John L. Lewis." As part of this collaboration, Lewis accepted the closing of smaller, less efficient mines and the replacement of certain workers by machines. He understood that rationalization would mean greater efficiency and higher wages for those who survived the process. In short, the editor regarded Lewis as a perfect "role model" for Brazilian labor leaders: after all, he was a man with impeccable credentials as a labor militant who had embraced rationalization as the means to advance the workers' cause. But the editor closed by making it perfectly clear that Brazil still awaited its own John L. Lewis.[138]

As one might expect, the industrialist organizations modulated the tone of their pronouncements on the crisis of the early 1960s according to the author and the audience. In contrast to the *Boletim Informativo*, circulated mainly among FIESP members, SESI's *Educador Social*, which targeted an audience of union officials, factory supervisors, and even the rank and file, took more moderate positions on existing controversies. Whereas articles on labor law and union regulations continued to emphasize such features as limitations on the right to strike or activities that were illegal in the course of a strike, the general perspective could be described as "Christian democratic," with an emphasis on developmentalism, moderate social reform, and cooperativism. This may reflect the background of the magazine's collaborators, many of whom had studied in the Catholic School of Social Work founded by Social Action. There were frequent references to the papal encyclicals, *Mater et Magistra* and *Pacem in Terris*, and not just to the passages that affirmed private-property rights. Indeed, during the early

1960s, *Educador Social* regularly advocated agrarian reform and argued that such a reform involved an expansion, not a denial, of property rights. Several articles also invoked agrarian reform as part of the larger campaign to develop and rationalize Brazilian society.[139]

To be sure, among the proposals for basic reform, land distribution posed the smallest challenge to the industrialists' interests. The typical response to new forms of union militancy was to adhere to a rigid interpretation of corporatist labor regulations. Yet we should not simply dismiss the positions adopted by *Educador Social* as window dressing or a smokescreen for industry's alliance with more reactionary forces. Rather, for all of the contradictions and evasions, they represent an attempt by SESI officials and employees to situate themselves politically in such a way as to maintain some claim to a socially progressive agenda while gingerly avoiding any positions that could prove too threatening to industrialists. The publication's heterodox arguments may also indicate a tendency toward greater "doctrinal" independence among SESI staffers.

Within the halls of FIESP, by contrast, there was less and less concern with maintaining a progressive stance in the face of growing labor militancy. Rather, employers increasingly turned to more conventional means of preserving social peace. A 1963 visit to FIESP by General Adelvio Barbosa Lemos, the secretary of public safety for São Paulo, provoked a steady stream of pleas for "protection." Former FIESP president Humberto Reis Costa claimed that previous state administrations had left industry without such guarantees and only fortune had allowed them to avoid "depredations" and other grave developments. Much to the pleasure of those in attendance, General Barbosa Lemos assured his audience that he would "seek to guarantee, intransigently, the right to work" and would not allow pickets "since they are a form of coercion against the free will of the citizenry." Illegal strikes would be dispersed by any means at his disposal, and public tranquillity would be maintained, by force if necessary.[140] Such open appeals to security forces paralleled the constant references to the national crisis and to the actions of "demagogues serving interests alien to the Brazilian nation." In this context, it seems both ironic and fitting that SESI's May Day festivities in 1962 featured a "performance" by the German shepherds of the Police Canine Corps.[141]

Subsequent accounts of the coup against Goulart reveal that well before March 1964 prominent members of the industrialist elite had shifted from polemical attacks on the government and labor militants to covert activity with the objective of overthrowing the existing political regime.[142] With the benefit of hindsight, we can detect many signs of FIESP's collusion in the 1964 coup. In October 1963, the Forum Roberto Simonsen initiated a series of lectures entitled "Democratic Doctrine and the National Reality." The leadoff speaker, Júlio de Mesquita Filho, was the publisher of the strongly anti-Goulart *O Estado de São Paulo* and a leading agitator for military intervention. At FIESP's annual Christmas luncheon, Raphael Noschese expressed even more vigorously than usual his belief that the current economic crisis was mainly of political origin.[143]

The dramatic events of March 1964 finally produced an open identification of FIESP, as an organization, with the opposition forces.[144] Leading industrialists, including Raphael Noschese, participated in the massive March 19 demonstration organized by right-wing, middle-class paulistas to protest the reputed left-wing drift of the Goulart administration. The editorial in that week's FIESP bulletin described the "productive classes" as "a force in the service of democracy" and praised the "decision made by men of production in our state to come to the public square and confront demagoguery." Perhaps most important, it referred to the "abyss" that separated the two conflicting conceptions of Brazil's social and economic future.[145]

In his personal account of this period, recollected with obvious pride, Noschese claimed that preparations for the coup and FIESP's role in it began eighteen months before the actual overthrow of Goulart—in other words, from the time Noschese assumed the presidency of FIESP. He recalled weekly meetings with the presidents of the other employer associations and an officer representing the Second Army Division, based in São Paulo, to coordinate activities. FIESP's responsibilities included the purchase of twenty-five "blank" airline tickets to allow the command of the Second Army to meet undetected with commanders of other divisions. Furthermore, in a move reminiscent of the 1932 revolt against Vargas, FIESP and SESI created the Industrial Mobilization Service, which would provide meals, clothing, and transport for the armed forces once the maneuvers leading to the coup had begun. One FIESP official interviewed in 1966 claimed that the federation's leadership had collected 1.5 billion cruzeiros, equal to more than a million dollars, to aid the armed forces in the seizure of power.

Philippe Schmitter, a North American political scientist who was among the first to discuss the paulista industrialists' role in the coup, cautiously observed that "important as this activity might have been materially and spiritually, . . . it was not decisive. The coup of 1964 was primarily a military affair."[146] More recent research by Brazilian scholars has placed greater emphasis on and attributed greater significance to the covert activities of civilian elites in Goulart's overthrow.[147] To be sure, the contribution of the paulista industrialists was not decisive in strictly strategic terms. But the industrialists' ideological positions and narrow conception of what constituted social peace certainly contributed both to the growing sense of political crisis and to the labor movement's increasing recourse to the political sector for benefits and empowerment. In this sense, the industrialists helped to pave the way for the coup long before they became involved in the material preparations.[148]

In the aftermath of the successful coup, FIESP proved quite eager to accentuate its role in the events of April 1. The lead editorial in the federation bulletin published immediately after the coup described FIESP and CIESP as playing a "decisive" role in the mobilization. Explicitly using military language, it praised the industrialist organizations for "remain[ing] at their posts, uninterruptedly, day and night." And the editorial assured the membership that the industrialists would continue at their posts to pursue the "task of redemocratization" that lay before them.[149]

Although both SESI and SENAI maintained a "business as usual" tone in the months following the coup, SESI quickly involved itself in a range of new activities that reflected the new military order. Some predictable areas of SESI's involvement included its 500,000-cruzeiro donation and participation in the "Campaign for Civic Education."[150] But more unusual was the obligation SESI–São Paulo assumed to fund (up to the amount of 10 million cruzeiros) the installation of a regional office of the newly formed National Information Service (Serviço Nacional de Informações, or SNI), a government agency that would play a central and often brutal role in the suppression of dissent over the next two decades. The text of the resolution, issued by the executive directors of SESI–São Paulo in September 1964, seems an appropriate way to end this discussion of the industrialists and the politics of social peace in Brazil:

> Keeping in mind that Law no. 4,341 of June 13, 1964, which created the National Information Service, in its article 3 recognizes this service, an advisory organ to the president of the Republic, as especially responsible for establishing and securing the necessary connections and agreements with private entities in the orientation and coordination of information and counterinformation operations . . . and considering that the Industrial Social Service [SESI] has as its purpose, among others, to stimulate action in favor of the public welfare and social peace; considering moreover that the National Information Service also has as its purpose to supervise and coordinate activities related to national secu-

rity, which naturally includes the [maintenance of] public order and social peace. We authorize, in our capacity as executive directors of the Industrial Social Service . . . the acquisition and delivery, by means of FIESP, of the material necessary for the installation of the São Paulo Regional Agency of the National Information Service.[151]

This statement demonstrates how easy it had become for SESI to elide the concept of social peace with the doctrine of national security.

Epilogue and Conclusion

"We are living through a time of light and splendor after . . . a long and anguishing period of heavy darkness." Thus did the newly appointed president of SESI's national council, Colonel Alberto de Assumpção Cardoso, describe the moment of transition to military rule.[1] For the men who occupied prominent positions in FIESP and the São Paulo agencies of SENAI and SESI, the "revolution" of 1964 was a cause for rejoicing, a victory for Christian and democratic forces in Brazilian society.[2] The new military dictatorship (a term that the industrialist leadership studiously avoided) seemed to offer a new world of untrammeled opportunity for institutions dedicated to the advancement of social peace and productivity.

The paulista industrialists' intimate relationship with Brazil's new military rulers allowed FIESP, SENAI, and SESI to avoid government-dictated changes in personnel. At the national level, the military did immediately intervene in the CNI, appointing a board of administrators until December 1964, when new elections were held for confederation president.[3] The man chosen by the membership, General Edmundo de Macedo Soares e Silva, undoubtedly pleased the paulista industrialists. The general held directorships in several paulista industries and was an active, long-standing member of FIESP. One clear indication of Macedo Soares's allegiance to the industrialist leadership in São Paulo was his appointment of Roberto Mange's acolyte, Ítalo Bologna, as director of SENAI's National

Department, a position he would hold for the next ten years.[4] And in his Christmas message for 1964, the general was unstinting in his praise for the Brazilian industrialist, "worker at the pinnacle, upon whose hard work and dedication rest the index of productivity and golden ring of development that we all seek."[5]

Both the changes at the federal level and the demobilization of organized labor offered industrial employers and their technocratic allies ideal conditions for "social peace." In its personnel report for the year of the coup, São Paulo Light & Power noted, with nearly audible relief, that "the panorama of intranquillity that characterized the early months of 1964 has been replaced by a climate of greater serenity."[6] Underlying this rather mild statement were the hundreds of interventions suffered by labor unions in São Paulo at the hands of the new military regime, which allowed some of the most conservative, anti-Communist labor officials to move into positions of authority. The São Paulo textile workers' federation, in the July 1964 issue of its monthly newspaper, hailed the "victorious revolution of April 1" as well as the new era of unionism it inaugurated. The orientation of organized labor in this new era would be "compatible with the democratic and Christian traditions of our people." The article also noted that the government had intervened in 19 out of 33 unions affiliated with the federation; the other 14 escaped this fate thanks to their being "authentically democratic."[7]

The changes in Brazilian society celebrated by the Light personnel manager and the textile federation *pelegos* ushered in a new era for SESI and SENAI as well. Aside from bringing about the felicitous changes in personnel at the national level, the military regime provided them with a smoother playing field on which they could implement their programs and projects unencumbered by "irrational" political interests, inefficient bureaucrats, or recalcitrant union militants.[8] SESI, an institution founded for the purpose of immunizing Brazilian workers against the contagion of communism, could logically expect to play a central role in the process of "redemocratization" and could look forward to serving a more receptive working-class clientele, free from the influence of Communist activists. SENAI, meanwhile, maintained a more politically neutral demeanor, as befit its primarily technical orientation and image. Asked about SENAI's role in the events of 1964, Raphael Noschese simply remarked that the vocational training agency "remained immune to such things."[9] Yet SENAI, too, could expect to benefit from a new era in which programs for increased productivity could be implemented without meeting even mild resistance or criticism from labor unions. Under these new conditions, apprenticeship and retraining, not strikes and collective grievances, would hold the key to worker advancement, thereby increasing SENAI's value to the urban labor force.

The Militarization of Social Peace

SESI had to make few discursive or programmatic adjustments to accommodate the new order. The military representation of the coup as rescuing Brazilian democracy from the "suffocating web of international communism" was perfectly compatible with SESI's notion of democracy as, first and foremost, a defense of order, private property, and conservative Christian values.[10] During the months immediately following the coup, SESI's *Educador Social* published a rash of articles with such titles as "Cooperativism and Democracy," "Enterprise and Democracy," and "Democracy and Authority" without exhibiting the slightest intellectual discomfort. And the final issue of 1965 carried a rhapsodic account of the military's achievements during the first twenty months of the dictatorship.[11]

One of the few innovations that occurred in the aftermath of the military seizure of power actually involved the reactivation of an old program. In response to a proposal from FIESP's Commission on Social Policy, in 1964 DOS resurrected its Union Squad. This squad, armed with its "Union Education Plan," devoted itself to training union leaders and to encouraging the participation of "all" union members, thereby "avoiding a situation where the unions become fiefdoms of a small group acting in the service of political or private interests absolutely foreign to [the unions'] true objectives." To insure that unions remained in the hands of acceptable leaders, it offered a "course in union orientation" for interventors appointed by the Ministry of Labor as well as for those members of union directorates who had survived the government purges.[12] Classes were cosponsored by the Labor Ministry and were held in the ministry's regional headquarters; they were deemed successful enough for SESI to offer two more such courses in the city of São Paulo as well as three in the interior. Graduates of the "class of 1972" included thirty-two federation and union officials, many of them from the largest categories in São Paulo.[13]

Also new among SESI's activities after the coup was the Campanha Operário Padrão, a "model worker" competition that grew out of a collaboration between the Rio-based newspaper, *O Globo*, and the National Department of SESI. *O Globo* had conceived the idea for the contest ten years earlier in an attempt to create some popular appeal for the right-wing newspaper. The initial effort, based on advertising, roused little interest among either employers or workers, but by 1964, the political context had become considerably more favorable for such a venture. In addition, *O Globo* had enlisted the cooperation of SESI, which could draw upon its many contacts with employers, supervisors, and personnel departments to stir up support for the contest. From SESI's perspective, the Campanha Operário Padrão was a convenient vehicle for a discourse that emphasized individual effort and cooperation with one's employer as the key to social advancement for workers.[14]

The amount of effort required to select an *operário padrão* at the factory level and compile the appropriate dossier meant that only relatively large firms with well-organized personnel departments were likely to field candidates. Indeed, a mere fraction of even large firms consistently participated in the contest. But the combined public relations capacity of SESI and *O Globo* made the Campanha Operário Padrão a regular feature of mass culture during the early years of the military regime. The national winner could be seen in photographs in *O Globo* and on the covers of mass-circulation magazines, usually being congratulated by the president of Brazil. He also appeared on television and in newsreels regularly shown in movie theaters.[15]

What impact the Campanha Operário Padrão had on the Brazilian public is difficult to say, but the contest certainly allowed SESI to celebrate the "virtues" that it had been laboring to disseminate among Brazilian workers. A survey of the nominees' dossiers quickly reveals certain recurring patterns in the narratives of their career paths and experiences. Many of the early winners came from impoverished rural communities; their move to the city and entrance into the industrial labor force typically represented the first step toward a better way of life. Still, they often languished in unskilled and poorly paid jobs until they either found a large, "progressive" firm that provided them with opportunities for internal mobility or gained access to formal vocational training. Especially in the case of older candidates, the narratives usually made much of how difficult it was to learn a trade prior to the advent of SENAI. These dossiers would then list a half-dozen or more courses sponsored by SESI and SENAI by means of which the candidates had upgraded their professional and personal abilities.[16]

This combination of skill, self-improvement, and loyalty to a "progressive" firm was the key to the worker's ability to scale the factory hierarchy. Indeed, in the vast majority of cases, the nominees were no longer regular workers but supervisors: foremen who had risen beyond the ranks of the *horistas*, or workers paid by the hour. The *operário padrão* symbolized, above all, individual mobility and success within industry—a fitting symbol for a period during which workers had little opportunity to better their situations through collective action.[17]

SESI's social educators also became involved in publicizing and explaining post-1964 alterations in the CLT to workers throughout São Paulo. The most significant legal innovation prior to the promulgation of the 1967 constitution was the September 1966 law establishing a Severance Pay Fund (Fundo de Garantia por Tempo de Serviço, or FGTS) that a worker could opt for instead of the preexisting job tenure arrangement. As noted in Chapter 8, manufacturing firms had long opposed the job tenure provisions of the CLT. Indeed, a 1963 survey of industrialists revealed that 64 percent regarded *estabilidade* as having a negative effect on their enterprises.[18] It is not surprising, then, that SESI vigorously proselytized the virtues of the FGTS among its proletarian clientele.[19]

According to SESI, the new system "caused no harm to the employee," especially since, in theory, an employee could still choose the old *estabilidade* arrangement. But in practice, the FGTS meant the virtual extinction of job tenure since most employers refused to hire or retain employees who opted for *estabilidade*.[20] SESI's enthusiastic support for the FGTS also revealed its very superficial commitment to a Christian democratic position. Despite the occasional attacks on liberalism and the brutality of the unregulated market in the literature produced by its Division for Social Orientation, SESI showed itself quite eager to dispense with a regulation that had attempted to reduce workers' vulnerability to the laws of supply and demand. Emphasizing the attractive features of the new FGTS, SESI avidly endorsed the alternative that the industrial bourgeoisie regarded as the most "rational" and profitable for their firms.[21]

Yet the very law that created the FGTS also reduced the mandated employer contribution to SESI from 2 percent to 1.5 percent.[22] This reduction was primarily intended to ease the burden of the required deposits for the FGTS, but it also reflected the lower priority enjoyed by SESI in the context of the military's forced demobilization of the labor movement. The industrialist leadership had always faced some resistance from rank-and-file employers, many of whom viewed the SESI payment as a pointless expense. Now, with the labor movement apparently under control and industrialists considerably less concerned with their public image, the arguments in favor of SESI, whether moral or economic, lost some of their force. The military, after all, hardly seemed to need SESI to promote "social peace."

Not that the new military order had made SESI superfluous. Many of the organization's activities, such as its courses for supervisors, its adult literacy classes, its primary schools for workers' children, and its scholarships for managerial personnel, were highly compatible with the military's campaign for industrial development and increased productivity. Local governments continued to plead with SESI to construct *conjuntos assistenciais* in their municipalities, and impoverished labor unions increased their requests for SESI assistance, whether in the form of cash or facilities.[23] At the same time, SESI had to contend with a series of measures that reduced or delayed its funding as well as new regulations that decreased the demand for certain SESI services. In 1968 Minister of Labor Jarbas Passarinho issued a decree prohibiting loans or donations to unions unless approved by the ministry. Subsequently, SESI had to refuse all direct requests for assistance, even from the friendliest labor unions.[24] SESI, originally conceived by Roberto Simonsen as a major instrument for improving industrial relations and the cultural level of Brazilian workers, had become by the late 1960s a minor handmaiden of the military regime, with the diminished status that role implied.

SENAI under Military Rule

The final year of the Goulart presidency had been a difficult time for SENAI; financial exigencies forced the São Paulo department to close most of its night classes for adults, among other cutbacks. These troubles were not due to hostility from the populist president, who exhibited considerable interest in vocational education, especially rapid retraining of adults, and had created the Intensive Preparation for Industrial Labor program (Preparação Intensiva para Mão de Obra Industrial, or PIPMOI) to complement the prolonged instruction offered by SENAI and the state vocational schools. Rather, SENAI's predicament was due to more mundane factors such as galloping inflation and delays in the transfer of funds.[25]

Whatever Goulart's intentions, the financial chaos of his final months in office took its toll on SENAI's operations and undoubtedly moved many SENAI officials to welcome the military seizure of power out of institutional as well as ideological concerns. The new military regime, with its technocratic and modernizing orientation, certainly promised to improve conditions for SENAI and enhance the institution's prestige. In immediate and concrete terms, this meant more efficient collection and transfer of funds and the resurrection in São Paulo of SENAI's night courses for adults.[26]

In a broader context, SENAI also warmly welcomed the new regime's endorsement of "social improvement" (*promoção social*), a concept that meshed well with Mange's notion of "integral education" and the organization's overall emphasis on training as a prime source of social mobility and increased productivity. A 1966 SENAI publication traced the roots of the movement for workers' "social improvement" to postwar France and listed its "four essential characteristics: (1) human valorization through cultural and professional betterment; (2) access to posts of great responsibility through new skills and experiences; (3) training programs and methods oriented toward the acquisition of abilities and attitudes favorable to improving productivity; (4) humane and democratic sense of social access through work."[27] *Promoção social* emphasized individual effort and self-enhancement through precisely the kinds of programs sponsored by SENAI and SESI.

SENAI's resources and activities expanded markedly under the regime of Humberto Castello Branco (1963–67). Laws issued in 1965 and 1967 made contributions to SENAI and SESI part of the overall payments of employers to the social security institutes. This reduced the likelihood of employer evasion or delay of contributions to SENAI and SESI, which were previously made on a separate basis. The greater resources allowed SENAI to increase the number of places for apprentices in its schools, but the expansion in this realm paled in comparison to the massive growth in rapid training of semiskilled workers.

Under the military, PIPMOI (renamed PIPMO in 1972) emerged as a wide-ranging organization for preparing industrial workers, with SENAI assigned responsibility for compiling didactic materials and coaching instructors. The dramatic increase in SENAI enrollments during the late 1960s was mainly due to its involvement in the PIPMOI courses. To illustrate this trend, in the second semester of 1967, SENAI–São Paulo enrolled 7,330 minors in apprenticeship courses, 6,218 adults in night courses, and a mere 1,834 workers in rapid-training programs. By the second semester of 1970, SENAI had 12,125 apprentices and 12,612 adults enrolled in courses to produce skilled workers and a whopping 23,779 adults and minors enrolled in its rapid-training courses. All phases of SENAI's operations had expanded, and total enrollment had more than tripled, but apprentices—the original focus of SENAI activity—accounted for less than a quarter of its "student body."[28]

Ítalo Bologna, as SENAI's national director, continued to claim a privileged place for apprenticeship programs in the vocational-training system. Young workers, he wrote, were the most "susceptible" not only to new techniques and information but also to the "educative action" necessary for the formation of healthy personalities and for integration into private enterprises. Apprenticeship, he argued, was a "profound experience" designed to produce the most highly qualified workers and future supervisors, a veritable aristocracy of labor.[29]

Yet even those youths who managed to secure a place in a SENAI school could not confidently expect to join this reputed aristocracy. Rapid technological change, accelerated by the influx of multinational firms, often had a negative impact on the job outlook for SENAI graduates. In some fields, such as printing, SENAI machinery and techniques were too antiquated to prepare an apprentice for a secure position. At the same time, simplification and mechanization of certain work processes made some skills acquired in SENAI courses superfluous. Often graduates emerged from SENAI apprenticeship programs only to find themselves lumped together with the ever-increasing number of rapidly trained semiskilled workers.[30] Even the most progovernment labor publication to circulate in São Paulo during these years admitted that industrial employment was expanding at a rate well below the growth in the supply of workers and that this was especially true for positions paying up to three times the minimum wage "as a result of the rationalization measures that firms find themselves obliged to introduce."[31]

Various legal innovations made by the military regime also had an adverse effect on SENAI's apprenticeship programs. The constitution of 1967, "in an incredible setback for labor law" (to quote a union newspaper), had lowered the legal working age to twelve and endorsed a three-tier wage system based on age.[32] According to the new scheme, any worker under age sixteen could be paid half the minimum wage, regardless of whether that worker had the benefit of being enrolled in a training program, and those between sixteen and eighteen could be paid 75 percent of the minimum wage. As a result, a major material inducement for an employer to send a young employee to SENAI—the right to pay him or her half the minimum wage—immediately evaporated. Lecturing in Rio, the new director of SENAI–São Paulo, Paulo Ernesto Tolle, lamented the steadily declining number of apprentices being channeled into SENAI schools by industrial employers. He contended that, if the trend continued, SENAI's apprenticeship programs would be left with only "aspirants to industry."[33] Indeed, he was so alarmed by the decreasing enrollment of this particular type of student that he asked why there were so few female candidates—a question studiously avoided by his predecessors.

SENAI's collaboration with PIPMOI and increased attention to on-the-job training expanded its scope and activities but also reduced the significance of the programs for which it had been originally conceived. One serious consequence of this was SENAI's waning prestige with the military regime, which began to regard the SENAI schools as an unnecessary luxury and the monthly payment to SENAI (and SESI) as an undue burden on employers. This led to the imposition of a ceiling on such payments in 1974, fixed according to multiples of a "value of reference," a formula that provoked a sharp drop in SENAI's financial resources.[34]

This is not to imply that, after an initial period of euphoria and cooperation, SENAI suffered nothing but defeat and disillusion at the hands of the military regime. The 1969 reform of the educational code fulfilled a long-standing aspiration of SENAI officials by creating equivalencies between the regular educational system and SENAI courses.[35] Thus apprentices who successfully completed the SENAI course could enter nonvocational institutions at the level of intermediate education. This enhanced SENAI's appeal to young Brazilians who were undecided about their professional future or who needed to work for several years before continuing their education. But it also increased the likelihood that an apprentice would see his or her SENAI training as a pause, a temporary solution, on the way to a job as a technician, engineer, or white-collar employee.

Ultimately, even with this educational reform, the military regime proved something of a disappointment to SENAI officials, as it did to SESI. Despite their ideological and programmatic compatibility with the military project for national development, both organizations found themselves marginalized by the military's minimalist and no-nonsense approach to worker training and socialization.[36] And it was not just SENAI and SESI that suffered a loss of influence and prestige but also the industrialist associations that sponsored and supervised them.[37]

In Pursuit of Social Peace

In some respects, the Brazilian economic "miracle" of the early 1970s was the ultimate fulfillment of Roberto Simonsen's dream of a modern, rationalized, industrialized Brazilian economy. The industrialists' long-running campaign to create a "natural" link between national welfare and industrialization had proved successful beyond their wildest dreams as successive regimes, elected or imposed, emphasized industry, productivity, and efficiency as the means to a better way of life. But although the outlines of this picture seemed to conform to Simonsen's vision, many of the details ran counter to the imagined design.

This study has focused on SENAI and SESI as the leading institutional expressions of the paulista industrialists' vision of employer-worker relations. Despite their rather different spheres of action, both organizations worked to promote rational organization and industrial efficiency and to advance their particular notion of social peace. Designed primarily as the means to remake the emerging industrial working class, SENAI and SESI also aspired to change the mentality and public image of the industrialist "rank and file," introducing the less enlightened to scientific management, applied psychology, human relations, and welfare capitalism.

It is difficult to calculate the success or failure of SENAI and SESI with any precision. FIESP publications trumpeted these agencies' achievements with frequent tallies of the numbers of workers enrolling in their courses, attending particular performances, or shopping at the discount food posts. Such statistics are hardly meaningless; it is of some importance that by 1964 several hundred thousand paulista women had graduated from SESI home economics courses and several thousand factory foremen had enrolled in special courses sponsored by SENAI and SESI. But there is no "objective" or quantifiable way to judge the impact of such organizations on a society, especially if we give a privileged place to the discursive aspects of SENAI and SESI and their roles in constructing new identities for industrialists and workers.

It is precisely in this arena that I wish to consider the impact, limitations, and implications of SENAI and SESI. Here it is crucial to stress, again, the unusual status of SENAI and SESI as organizations created by the state but funded by industry and controlled by industrialist associations. Elsewhere, such educational and social welfare programs have operated under the aegis of the state, have emerged from a collaborative effort among government, industry, and labor, or have been the responsibility of individual firms. In Brazil, by contrast, a particular segment of the industrial bourgeoisie, a self-styled "vanguard" of that class, assumed control of programs they considered vital for industrial progress and social peace, minimizing the role of the state and utterly excluding organized labor. As we have seen, this arrangement had several advantages. The industrialist leadership had a free hand to determine the contents of these programs, in terms of both the concrete services and courses offered and their ideological dimensions. Except for occasional threats of "statization," SENAI and SESI did not have to be formally concerned with the demands of populist politicians or militant labor leaders, as was the case with the social security institutes.[38]

Industrialist spokesmen also used SENAI and SESI as evidence of employers' social conscience, constantly emphasizing that they alone were responsible for the services and instructional opportunities that SENAI and SESI provided for workers. This served, at least in some contexts, to enhance the image of the industrial bourgeoisie and to deflect demands for increased employer contributions to government social welfare programs. Similarly, FIESP officials liked to stress how efficient these organizations were in comparison to state-run agencies, an opinion echoed even by some of their severest critics and one that reinforced industrialist claims to technical competence.[39]

SENAI and SESI offered a host of employment opportunities to middle-class technocrats and professionals—engineers, educators, psychologists, social workers, home economists, industrial hygienists—who became valuable and articulate supporters of the industrialists' cause. Both SENAI and SESI actively contributed to the process whereby certain functions in Brazilian society and the expertise deemed necessary to perform them became the province of "professionals." Both organizations expanded the authority of technical personnel and members of the "helping professions" in industrial life within and beyond the factory. The discourses of authority promoted by these professionals ranged from a purely technical conception of industrial accidents to the medicalization of marriage and childbirth.[40]

Thanks in large part to Michel Foucault, few scholars these days regard the members of these professions, in any context, as completely benign. Rather, their professional expertise is widely seen as a source of power and their ministrations as a form of discipline. Yet the recognition of their expertise and authority has allowed such professionals, in other national contexts, to play a significant role in advancing programs and legislation sought by organized labor.[41] In the Brazilian case, however, leading members of these professions worked for employer-controlled organizations rather than the state or independent agencies. Not only were they likely to lose their jobs if they strayed too far from the industrialists' perspective, but they themselves were subjected to a process of socialization once they joined SENAI or SESI to insure that they shared these organizations' vision of social peace. Not that such socialization was entirely successful— a DOS official's anxiety about the "doctrinal confidence" of the social educators indicates its limitations.[42] Also, Paulo Freire's early experience as a director of SESI in Recife does not seem to have dampened the innovative spirit of this renowned radical educator. But most of the professionals employed by SENAI and SESI were less exceptional; they remained within the boundaries of acceptable activity and sometimes drew those boundaries even more narrowly than their industrialist employers.[43]

The industrialists and technocrats who "masterminded" SENAI and SESI also regarded these organizations as a means to remake and discipline their own social class. Throughout this study, I have emphasized that members of the industrialist leadership were not "typical" of industrial interests as a whole, nor should we expect them to be. Their intricate involvement in a series of political, social, and economic questions bred concerns among industrialist spokesmen that were of limited relevance to the "average" factory owner. At the same time, prominent industrial figures were able to expand their power through intellectual prestige, government connections, and control of official industrial associations, allowing them to impose a certain vision of industrial relations on the employer rank and file. Using the federal decree-laws as leverage, the leadership obliged its fellow employers to fund vocational schools and social welfare programs and gently pressured them to create CIPAs, consult industrial psychologists, and install literacy classes, among other things. Here, too, the socialization process was hardly a complete success; even large employers with long-standing links to FIESP often evaded the contributions, failed to designate apprentices, or showed little interest in SESI services. FIESP officials, in turn, displayed little inclination to coerce its members into compliance or to embarrass publicly those employers who were lax in these areas. Dependent upon at least tacit support from the employer rank and file and loath to fuel the fire of industry's critics, the industrialist leadership proved disinclined to police its own class.

On occasion, prominent industrialists did ventilate criticisms of their less "progressive" brethren, whose antiquated production methods or crude labor-control strategies impeded the pursuit of social peace and productivity. As *O Estado de São Paulo* commented in the early 1950s, the FIESP leadership was promoting a "new deal" not only to appeal to workers but also to "put on alert those backward industrialists who, in their relations with their workers, without knowing it still live in the past."[44] This was, of course, a convenient construction for the industrialist vanguard, which could attribute problems in industrial relations or productivity rates to this remnant of the old factory regime, whose weight in the industrial economy was bound to diminish over time.

Yet how "enlightened" was this industrialist vanguard? And what constituted progressive policies and attitudes within industrial circles? In this study, the concepts of rational organization and scientific management have been highlighted as central to the discourse of such "progressive" industrialists and technocrats as Roberto Simonsen, Euvaldo Lodi, Mariano Ferraz, Armando de Arruda Pereira, Morvan Dias de Figueiredo, Roberto Mange, and Aldo Mário de Azevedo. The members of this cohort shared with their colleagues in post–World War I Europe and the United States the widespread belief that scientific and rational principles could be applied to industrial society—within and outside the workplace—to create a more productive, efficient, and harmonious way of life.

This broad formula for industrial organization, however, had many variants; the version that was most widely diffused among Brazilian industrialists privileged hierarchy, technical authority, and close supervision in the workplace.[45] It was a version that allowed little or no space for worker participation; indeed, it assumed that workers, with their low cultural and educational levels and limited experience with modern economic life, constituted a major obstacle to rational organization in all spheres of society. The position adopted by FIESP in the early 1930s—that "the organization of the work process does not allow a break in hierarchy . . . or the intrusion of elements from the working masses into the sphere of those in charge of the firm's upper management"—proved remarkably enduring.[46] Occasionally a prominent figure at an opportune moment, such as Mariano Ferraz during the early 1950s, might shift to a somewhat more democratic language, with an emphasis on rights and redistribution. But this "new deal" language never emerged as the dominant discourse.

One could argue that all versions of scientific management, with their interest in subordinating workers and the work process to managerial experts, take a low and uncharitable view of workers' culture and capabilities. But this tendency seems to have been particularly pronounced among Brazilian advocates of rationalization, who insistently referred to the low moral and cultural level of the Brazilian worker. Despite their declared belief in the (eventual) dignity and value of manual labor, these industrialists and technocrats shared the view common among elite Brazilians that those who performed manual tasks were likely to exhibit cultural, physical, and moral deficits. Simonsen, after all, gave his speech on the promise of rational organization only three decades after the abolition of slavery and at a time when Brazilian society was still overwhelmingly agrarian.

Whether, or how, racism contributed to this image of a deficient working class is difficult to discern. A few industrialists did declare a preference for European immigrants as the tide of northeastern migrants to São Paulo swelled in the 1940s. Judging from Simonsen's account of his syphilis survey—in which immigrants who had lived in Brazil a year or more showed rates of infection approaching those of national workers—he at least blamed environmental factors for the degradation of Brazilian workers.[47] Meanwhile, most industrialist spokesmen eagerly adopted the view that Brazil was a "racial democracy" and would not have regarded their unflattering construction of the Brazilian worker as related in any way to racial prejudice. In a narrow sense, it probably was not. But their very notion of the working class as morally and culturally inferior incorporated contemporary elite attitudes about race and culture without ever resorting to explicit racial references. Then there was the tendency to split the labor movement into two distinct segments: one, a thin stratum of artful, competent, and highly ideological activists; the other, a mass of "average" workers who had no inclination toward radicalism but whose ignorance made them vulnerable to the activists' blandishments. The resemblance of this view to earlier stereotypes about immigrant versus "national" (that is, nonwhite) workers cannot be dismissed as coincidental.[48]

This negative construction of Brazilian workers as either subversive or maladjusted made it unlikely that the industrial leadership would see them as potential partners in the creation of educational or social programs. Industrialist control of SESI and SENAI, however, proved to be the proverbial double-edged sword. Programs represented as evidence of employers' social conscience could also become easy targets for criticism from union leaders during periods of industrial conflict. Unsatisfactory meals delivered by SESI's district kitchens, rude service at the discount food posts, antiquated machinery at the school for apprentice printers, or the absence of a SENAI program in a particular industrial suburb—all could provide further evidence of the industrialists' callousness and indifference to workers' welfare. Stated simply, employers had to take the criticism along with the credit, and credit might be in especially short supply during periods of industrial conflict.

The identification of SENAI and SESI with the industrial bourgeoisie rather than with the state profoundly affected the way in which organized labor received these programs and activities. Even SENAI, with its technical and apolitical image, suffered occasional attacks for its "manufacture" of apprentices or for the "cheap demagoguery of the course installation ceremonies."[49] In the case of SESI, its identification with the employer class, not the state, had more severe consequences. Throughout the period from the 1940s to the 1964 coup, populist politics and developmental nationalism elicited enthusiastic responses from sectors of the Brazilian working class. Central to this appeal was a state that could support the labor movement in certain strategic ways, make political and material concessions, and emphasize the role of labor in the national enterprise, thereby constructing a national identity that was meaningful to industrial workers.[50] By contrast, SESI's attempts to appeal to workers as members of an imagined industrial community through rituals such as the May Day parades and New Year's Eve confraternization parties were far more problematic since there was little basis on which it could construct a common identity between "capital and labor" that would be meaningful to workers. Instead, it was easy enough for labor militants to portray the Labor Day observations orchestrated by SESI as the May Day of the "bosses" or to subject SESI's calls for social peace to cutting sarcasm. And rank-and-file workers evinced little interest in the civic rituals and festivities that SESI and SENAI imported, with few modifications, from the United States.

Overtures to organized labor (as opposed to individual workers) were also likely to be frustrated by the industrialist attitudes toward unions. To be sure, by the 1940s Simonsen, Lodi, and other industrialist spokesmen had discarded their traditional hostility to labor unions per se. Endorsing the corporatist and hierarchical scheme for organized labor devised by Vargas and his advisers as a rational means to minimize class conflict, employer associations publicly urged members to encourage unionization, echoing Vargas's claim that "these organizations, instead of serving as instruments of class conflict, contribute to the equilibrium between owners and workers."[51] But this legitimization of organized labor was premised on an extremely narrow view of the functions and scope of activity acceptable for trade unions. Legitimate labor leaders, in this view, recognized that workers should only formulate "rational" demands that would not have a negative impact on productivity. Actions such as strikes and slowdowns were irrational and harmful to national development as well as unnecessary in a nation with an elaborate system of labor tribunals. And the structure of state-sanctioned unions presumably precluded any form of shopfloor organization, with its implicit threat to managerial authority.

Such a vision of organized labor did not materialize in a historical vacuum. As I have argued, the years of the Estado Novo, at least prior to 1945, formed a sort of golden age of labor relations in the industrialists' collective memory. With major unions in the hands of *pelegos* eager to collaborate with employers and the state and with the rank and file inhibited by police repression and wartime restrictions, it is little wonder that employer associations actively promoted unionization. In those days, Simonsen, Lodi, and Morvan could represent themselves as champions of the workers' welfare with little fear of dissenting opinion. Thus the industrialists may have expanded their view of labor relations to include a rationally organized union structure, but that did not imply any significant democratization of relations between capital and labor. And it certainly did not include any redistribution of authority or power in the workplace.

Brazilian industrialists throughout this period proved remarkably successful at discouraging any form of union representation on the factory floor, thus leaving the way open for SENAI and SESI to arrange various aspects of factory life unfettered by demands and pressures from organized labor. It was the industrialist-appointed technocrats of SENAI who determined what jobs should be considered skilled, how much training they involved, and how many practitioners of each trade should be produced.

Workers faced with rationalization and mechanization often welcomed the categories and classifications designed by SENAI, but they were still relegating such functions to an agency directly controlled by employers—and an organization dedicated in part to the extinction of skilled positions whenever its notion of rationalization required it.

Labor unions also had little means to challenge SENAI's view of vocational training as a form of instruction destined for only a minority of the industrial workforce. By allowing young workers to apprentice and study while employed, SENAI opened up training to a segment of the population that had been previously excluded from the state professional schools, which offered only full-time study. But the prerequisites for SENAI, formal and informal, meant that most successful applicants would be children of workers already employed in industry with sufficient resources to complete at least a few years of formal schooling. This left recent rural migrants at a distinct disadvantage, especially as entry to SENAI became more competitive.[52]

Those at the greatest disadvantage were women workers. With the exception of a few courses for women in the textile, paper, and clothing industries, SENAI provided virtually no training for women. Of course, there were strong and long-standing social biases against women working as lathe operators or mechanics, but SENAI formalized the sexual division of labor by making no attempt to recruit young women into new skills and by excluding them from courses designed to train supervisory personnel. Year after year, female operatives accounted for a majority of minors employed in paulista industry but a tiny minority of those training to become skilled workers. By the late 1960s, women constituted a mere 3 percent of the workforce classified as skilled. It is highly probable that more women performed tasks requiring substantial preparation and experience but that their jobs were not classified or remunerated as skilled work. Since they were excluded from access to better-paying and more secure industrial positions, it is little wonder that only a small segment of these young women workers remained in the industrial labor force as adults.[53]

SESI's impact on the factory floor was more diffuse and ambiguous. The organization had considerable weight in the realm of workplace health and safety, setting up and orienting CIPAs, organizing national conferences, publishing a steady stream of literature, training inspectors, and minimizing intervention by the state or labor unions. SESI's courses for supervisors and personnel directors also played a significant role in the reorganization of factory life. Through the techniques associated with "human relations," SESI sought to make as palatable as possible a hierarchical and tightly supervised system of production. Social educators, meanwhile, disseminated SESI's notions of rational organization and dispensed gentle suggestions for more efficient work processes.

Although most of the programs sponsored by SENAI and SESI were open to public scrutiny, both organizations, and SESI in particular, engaged in a certain amount of "covert activity." SENAI surreptitiously collaborated with automakers to control the wages of scarce skilled workers, while SESI engaged in a vast array of clandestine operations to maintain social peace. From the moment of its founding, SESI involved itself in secretive campaigns to influence union elections and made improper expenditures to curry favor with the political police. Such activities climaxed in 1964 with SESI's concession of support to the newly formed National Information Service following the military coup.

Two aspects of these "operations" deserve emphasis. One is their remarkable continuity from the mid-1940s through the early 1960s. Goulart's accession to the presidency undoubtedly intensified the industrial leadership's involvement in anti-Communist activity, but the history of SESI is fraught with precedents for such operations. The other is the leading role played by such figures as Simonsen, Morvan, Arruda Pereira, Ferraz, and Raphael Noschese in promoting these clandestine activities. Far from representing a remnant of an older, traditional manufacturing class, these men were precisely those who most energetically promoted rational organization and were avid advocates of agencies like SENAI and SESI. They were the industrial spokesmen who claimed to have their fingers on the pulse of modernity, who studied in engineering schools abroad, who served as presidents of Rotary Clubs, and who played active roles in technical organizations within and outside Brazil. Their support for covert activities was not a product of an insufficiently "modern" mentality; rather, it was perfectly compatible with their concern for social peace as an essential precondition for Brazil's modernization.[54]

In the broadest sense, SENAI and SESI formed part of a long-term campaign to premise all discussions of social welfare on rapid economic development and the attendant notions of heightened productivity, rational organization, and technological progress. It was a resoundingly successful campaign, producing a hegemonic discourse whose underpinnings went unchallenged even by the most critical and militant labor organizations of the early 1960s. Labor spokespeople might demand that workers receive a larger share of the benefits from increased productivity; or that measures be taken to cushion workers in affected industries from the impact of "automation" and rationalization; or that the state play a larger role in the process of industrialization and economic development. But the need to industrialize, to become more efficient, to adopt new methods and machinery as the key to a better way of life for the Brazilian people, went undisputed.[55]

At the same time, if we consider SENAI and SESI as forming part of the industrialists' strategy for social control—or to use their language, social peace—we can see obvious limits to their hegemonic ambitions. Such limits became especially clear in the 1970s with the revival and transformation of labor activism in the state of São Paulo. Many scholars have already traced the rise of the "new unionism" in Brazil, with specific attention to the workplace struggles initiated by metallurgical workers during the second decade of military rule.[56] There is no need to repeat the details here, especially since the story goes well beyond the scope of this study. But it is worth noting the leading role played by skilled workers, a surprising number of them SENAI graduates, in the insurgent labor movement. By the mid-1980s, the presidents of the four most militant metallurgical workers' unions in São Paulo were all tool-and-die makers trained by SENAI. And the two most prominent figures to emerge from the new union movement over the last fifteen years—Jair Meneghelli and, of course, Luiz Inácio Lula da Silva—were both SENAI graduates.

It is not just in retrospect that the salient role of skilled workers, and SENAI graduates in particular, has gained attention. Back in the mid-1970s, several years before the dramatic metallurgical strikes at the close of that decade, a study of "worker consciousness" in Brazil noted the tendency of skilled workers to be more activist than their unskilled colleagues. In the words of one metallurgical worker, "Normally, the workers who belong to a higher category are those who are most interested [in labor activism]. They're the ones who go to the union and make strikes. I believe that it's a matter of culture. The fellow who has a craft, perhaps a course in SENAI, has more experience and greater facility to speak."[57]

Those industrialists and educators who regarded SENAI, first and foremost, as a means of producing compliant skilled workers inoculated against the temptations of labor militancy would surely regard all of the above as evidence of the organization's "failure." The militancy of these SENAI graduates would also seem to demonstrate the folly of those members of the dominant classes who took the concept of "social control" too literally. And it gives the lie to assumptions, common within both SENAI and SESI, that "culturally elevated" workers would be more likely to seek compromise and cooperation with employers (on the employers' terms). Finally, it indicates that even systematically and rationally trained craftspeople derive a sense of pride and autonomy from their identity as skilled workers and therefore may find the close control and hierarchy of Brazilian factory life especially intolerable.[58]

In his 1931 speech in praise of rationalization, Roberto Simonsen declared that this "veritable social doctrine" would neutralize the "fundamental ideas of Marxism" and moderate class conflict. Rationalization, according to SENAI and SESI's future founder, would accomplish these ambitious goals by allowing "the continual development of technical and professional culture" and by accepting "worker control in the solution of economic problems."[59] By the 1970s, SENAI and SESI had contributed substantially to the first phase of Simonsen's formula. An account of the rise of the new unionism in metropolitan São Paulo notes the "enormous growth in technical and vocational schools, in night courses, and generally even in the educational level of the working classes."[60] A rapidly growing cohort of workers, especially in the metallurgical sector, was developing a sense of pride in its skills and an estimation of its importance in the production process. But the second phase of Simonsen's formula—the acceptance of "worker control" in some spheres or aspects of the economy— failed to materialize. Instead, a 1978 study of large metallurgical plants in São Paulo revealed the dominant mode of organization to be a Brazilianized Taylorism. Factories were organized in a markedly hierarchical fashion so that workers had little contact among themselves and almost no participation in decisions affecting production. Considerable emphasis was also placed on simplification of tasks, thereby allowing for easy substitution of workers, and in place of the monetary incentives and bonuses that characterized classic Taylorism, the factories substituted close supervision and the threat of dismissal.[61]

Metalworkers at all points of the production process chafed at these conditions, but they were particularly incompatible with the skilled workers' sense of pride and expertise. The anger and frustration of these lathe operators and tool-and-die makers proved strong enough to fuel the most important labor insurgency in Brazil's history. Yet, without minimizing the radical and dramatic departure that the new unionism represented, it would be inaccurate to view the attitudes and identities of the leadership as the *negation* of the SENAI/SESI discourse. Many of the insurgent leaders' concerns—access to training, innovations in the production process, "professional" salaries, more attention to occupational health and safety— adapt and reconfigure aspects of the rationalizers' discourse.[62]

Both the militant skilled worker and the *operário padrão* see themselves as "good workers." The father and son in Brazil's most famous fictional representation of working-class life, the film *They Don't Wear Black Tie*, express these shared attitudes. The father, a longtime labor militant, declares that, despite his activism, he has never had trouble finding employment because he is a "good worker"—a phrase that expresses both his expertise and his recognition of certain obligations to the employer. And the strikebreaking son, leaving his family home in disgrace, comforts himself with the knowledge that he has a "profession" and therefore can start a new life elsewhere. Despite their ideological differences, both men share an identity as skilled industrial workers and a stake in an industrializing and modernizing Brazil.

Appendix

TABLE A-1.

Comparison of Graduates of SENAI–São Paulo, Minors and Adults, 1943–1971

Year	Minors[a]	Adults[b]	Total	Minors/ Total (%)
1943–47	2,580	3,873	6,453	40.1
1948–52	6,683	4,999	11,682	57.2
1953–57	10,813	6,893	17,706	61.6
1958–62	11,959	15,171	27,130	44.1
1963–67	15,955	48,272	64,227	24.8
1968–71	19,428	175,398	194,826	9.9
Total	67,416	254,606	322,024	20.9

Source: PM, SENAI-SP, "Relatório do Departamento Regional de São Paulo pelo Ano 1971."
[a]Minors include all apprentices, ages 14–18.
[b]Adults include all trainees, ages 18 and over.

TABLE A-2.

Enrollments and Completions of Selected SENAI Courses, São Paulo State, 1953–1964

Year	CAO/CAI[a] Enroll.	Comp.	CR/CA[b] Enroll.	Comp.	TIA[c] Enroll.	Comp.	TIM[d] Enroll.
1953	6,635	1,092	1,138	564	—	—	—
1954	7,968	1,488	1,214	738	75	21	—
1955	7,416	1,808	1,137	698	482	237	—
1956	7,873	1,874	1,141	734	811	705	—
1957	8,006	1,667	1,119	692	650	544	—
1958	9,035	—	1,205	—	621	—	9,234
1959	9,551	2,195	1,668	1,090	1,006	—	8,444
1960	10,147	2,486	1,856	1,348	1,709	1,096	13,603
1961	10,914	2,421	3,813	1,810	936	—	18,225
1962	11,202	2,770	3,394	2,334	2,053	1,325	23,654
1963	11,469	—	5,112	—	1,965	—	25,619
1964	12,161	2,818	7,692	7,208	2,351	—	26,922

Sources: SENAI-SP, "Relatório" (1957–64); *Informativo SENAI*, 1961–62.

[a] *Cursos de Aprendizes de Ofício/Cursos de Aspirantes a Indústria* (apprenticeship courses for minors, both employed and unemployed). Statistics on completion include diplomas and craft certification.

[b] *Cursos Rápidos de Formação/Cursos de Aperfeiçoamento* (rapid courses and improvement courses for adults).

[c] *Treinamento na Indústria—Adultos* (training of adults in industry).

[d] *Treinamento na Indústria—Menores* (training of minors in industry). Statistics were not kept on minors completing this program.

TABLE A-3.

Selected SESI Services in São Paulo State, 1947–1964

Year	Meals Served[a]	Customers[b]	Med. Clinics[c]	Dent. Clinics[d]
1947	215,000	1,557,653	22,550	—
1948	1,154,606	2,237,963	80,626	31,478
1949	2,626,128	2,925,210	124,343	45,475
1950	3,312,139	2,320,158	116,664	63,585
1951	4,336,790	2,661,920	198,040	147,078
1952	6,316,160	3,722,908	252,658	248,331
1953	5,989,227	4,573,118	323,534	248,245
1954	6,008,422	4,768,285	375,187	228,810
1955	4,777,424	4,897,239	413,209	282,068
1956	5,459,584	5,744,333	430,893	344,198
1957	4,930,242	5,670,170	470,701	396,878
1958	4,734,994	5,806,913	458,510	488,853
1959	5,000,410	6,775,797	486,630	602,747
1960	4,892,328	6,841,321	416,865	588,802
1961	4,270,370	6,849,076	408,713	602,812
1962	4,469,412	7,514,729	403,595	610,538
1963	4,103,997	7,790,204	437,493	637,613
1964	3,838,292	7,997,313	388,935	649,101

Sources: SESI-SP, Divisão de Assistência Social, *SESI—18 Anos* (1965); SESI-SP, Divisão de Alimentação, *SESI—18 Anos* (1965).
[a]Total number of meals served annually in district kitchens.
[b]Total number of customers served annually in discount food posts.
[c]Total number of consultations and treatments in medical clinics.
[d]Total number of consultations and treatments in dental clinics.

TABLE A-4.
Selected SESI Educational Services in São Paulo State, 1948–1959

Year	CP[a]	COL[b]	CAD[c]	CCC[d]	DOS[e]
1948	1,049	—	365	87	—
1949	1,858	5,073	1,427	375	—
1950	2,383	24,676	7,119	1,140	—
1951	3,111	71,449	15,866	2,500	—
1952	3,856	111,516	14,559	3,271	412
1953	2,847	103,379	18,367	3,655	776
1954	3,909	121,165	20,220	5,542	944
1955	5,238	121,068	22,365	5,708	1,542
1956	5,883	134,735	25,389	7,174	7,417
1957	3,172	163,819	29,018	4,262	9,281
1958	5,715	193,236	33,630	7,257	14,453
1959	10,047	263,621	25,107	9,973	19,063

Source: SESI-SP, *SESI em Algarismos* (1960).

[a] Graduates, *Cursos Populares* (adult literacy courses).

[b] Attendance, *Cursos de Orientação de Leitura* (reading guidance courses).

[c] Graduates, domestic arts courses, Centros de Aprendizado Doméstico (after 1952, includes correspondence courses).

[d] Graduates, *Cursos de Corte e Costura* (sewing courses).

[e] Graduates, *Seminários e Cursos Especializados*, DOS (includes supervision of personnel in industry, human relations for the worker, notions of oratory, labor legislation).

Notes

Abbreviations

In addition to the abbreviations used in the text, the following abbreviations are used in the notes.

AA	Arquivo da Administração, São Paulo Light & Power
AC	Assessoria de Comunicações, Serviço Social da Indústria, São Paulo
AE	Arquivo do Estado, São Paulo
AG	Arquivo Geral, SESI-SP
AIDORT	Arquivo do Instituto de Organização Racional do Trabalho, São Paulo
AMF	Arquivo Alexandre Marcondes Filho
AP	Robert Alexander Papers, Rutgers University, New Brunswick, N.J.
ACIFTSP/ SIFTSP	Arquivo do Centro dos Industriaes/Sindicato da Indústria de Fiação e Tecelagem de São Paulo
BARS	Biblioteca e Arquivo Roberto Simonsen, São Paulo
BCNI	Biblioteca da Confederação Nacional da Indústria, Serviço Nacional de Aprendizagem Industrial and Serviço Social da Indústria, Rio de Janeiro
BI	*Boletim Informativo* (FIESP)
BIT	*Boletim Informativo do Trabalho*
BMIDET	*Boletim Mensal Informativo do Departamento do Trabalho*
BMTIC	*Boletim do Ministério do Trabalho, Indústria e Comércio*
CIESP Circular	CIESP Circular, Biblioteca e Arquivo Roberto Simonsen, São Paulo
CIFTSP Circular	CIFTSP Circular, Arquivo do Centro dos Industriaes/Sindicato da Indústria de Fiação e Tecelagem de São Paulo

EE	SENAI-DN, "Pesquisa sôbre Evasão Escolar: O Problema da Escola de Aprendizagem Industrial no Brasil," 6 vols. (Rio de Janeiro: SENAI-DN, 1952)
EPF	Escola Profissional Feminina
EPM	Escola Profissional Masculina
ES	*Educador Social*
ESP	*O Estado de São Paulo*
FGV, CPDOC	Fundação Getúlio Vargas, Centro de Pesquisa e Documentação, Rio de Janeiro
FIESP Circular	FIESP Circular, Biblioteca e Arquivo Roberto Simonsen, São Paulo
GC	Arquivo Gustavo Capanema
LF	Arquivo M. B. Lourenço Filho
MET	*O Metalúrgico*
NA	National Archives and Records Administration, Washington, D.C.
PH	Patrimônio Histórico, São Paulo Light & Power
PM	Projeto Memória, SENAI-SP
RG	Record Group
SENAI-DN	SENAI, Departamento Nacional
SENAI-SP	SENAI, Departamento Regional, São Paulo
SESI-DN	SESI, Departamento Nacional
SESI-SP	SESI, Departamento Regional, São Paulo
SHSI	Subdivisão de Higiene e Segurança Industrial
SIFTSP Circular	SIFTSP Circular, Arquivo do Centro dos Industriaes/ Sindicato da Indústria de Fiação e Tecelagem de São Paulo
SJ	*SESI-Jornal*
TG	*O Trabalhador Gráfico*
TT	*O Trabalhador Têxtil*
VCC	*A Voz da Construção Civil*
VF	Arquivo Valdemar Falcão

Introduction

1. Two structurally similar agencies, SENAC and SESC, were also founded in the 1940s to provide training and services for commercial and clerical employees.

2. Classic works on the expanding role of the state in the early twentieth century include Maier, *Recasting Bourgeois Europe*; James Weinstein, *Corporate Ideal*; Skocpol, *Protecting Soldiers*; Fraser and Gerstle, *Rise and Fall of the New Deal Order*; and Hamilton, *Limits of State Autonomy*.

3. See, for example, Rago, *Do Cabaré*; Wolfe, *Working Women*; Antonacci, "A Vitória da Razão"; and Moraes, "A Socialização da Força de Trabalho."

4. Aside from the obvious impact of Thompson's *Making of the English Working Class*, a more recent influence has been Montgomery, *Workers' Control* and *Fall of the House of Labor*.

5. For a broad discussion of this issue in the context of Brazilian society, see Chauí, *Cultura e Democracia*.

6. A study that predates the linguistic turn but adopts a similar view of ideology and social control is Bresciani, "Liberalismo, Ideologia e Contrôle Social."

7. I owe this phrase to Nolan, *Visions of Modernity*. Her study of debates about rationalization and Fordism in Germany has been very helpful in my own research.

8. Historical studies of "social control" in the 1980s eschewed an earlier view that treated control strategies as, by and large, effective. Following Stedman Jones ("Class Expression versus Social Control?"), they emphasized the ways in which workers resisted or modified elite attempts at social control, retaining a notion of elites and workers as operating within very different conceptual frameworks and struggling primarily over conflicting material interests.

9. Nelson, *Frederick W. Taylor*; Haber, *Efficiency and Uplift*; Montgomery, *Fall of the House of Labor*; Maier, "Between Taylorism and Technocracy." For an example of Taylorism in the Latin American context, see Winn, "Worker's Nightmare."

10. On resistance to scientific management, see Montgomery, *Workers' Control*, esp. pp. 40–44, 101–8; Edwards, *Contested Terrain*, pp. 102–4; and Haydu, *Between Class and Craft*, chap. 2. Montgomery cites the observations of Belgian sociologist Henri de Man, who visited industries in the United States during World War I. According to de Man, Taylorism in its classic form was "liquidated" by worker opposition and its own conceptual flaws, but "'scientific management' was not [eliminated] by any means" (Montgomery, *Fall of the House of Labor*, p. 249).

11. Taylor expected his methods to make unions superfluous. See Montgomery, *Fall of the House of Labor*, pp. 253–54.

12. Most of the literature on U.S. industry defines Fordism as a system of control based on the technological innovations—such as assembly lines and conveyor belts—characteristic of the Ford factory. See Edwards, *Contested Terrain*, pp. 115–22. Other works emphasize the standardized production, mass consumption, and high-wage aspects of Fordist industry. See Meyer, *Five Dollar Day*, and Gerstle, *Working-Class Americanism*, pp. 7–8. When consumed abroad, Fordism or Americanism became a broader set of practices that included technological change and standardized production as well as "human rationalization" as exemplified by Ford's Department of Sociology. Whereas in the United States "welfare capitalism" emerged somewhat independently from the rationalization ideas associated with Taylor and Ford, elsewhere welfarism was seen as part and parcel of rationalization. The most famous exponent of the latter view was Antonio Gramsci. See Gramsci, "Americanism and Fordism." Gerstle (*Working-Class Americanism*, p. 12 [n. 7]) contends that Gramsci mistakenly interpreted Ford's interference in workers' personal lives as part of the new bourgeois ideology rather than as a paternalistic, idiosyncratic throwback. But if we view his firm's sociological activities as part of the campaign for human rationalization, we can understand their appeal to Fordist enthusiasts abroad, especially in societies with weaker traditions of democracy and support for the individual rights of workers. For an excellent discussion of the Fordist mania in Germany, see Nolan, *Visions of Modernity*, pp. 30–57. On Fordism and liberalism in Brazil, see Vianna, *Liberalismo e Sindicato*, pp. 63–77.

13. The implications of the Fordist project for industrialists' relations with the state are discussed in Gomes, *Burguesia e Trabalho*, p. 195, and de Decca, *O Silêncio*, chap. 4.

14. For an account of a pioneering project to promote human relations in the workplace, see Roethlisberger and Dickson, *Management and the Worker*. For critical discussions by historians and social scientists, see Edwards, *Contested Terrain*, pp. 97–104; Montgomery, *Workers' Control*, pp. 37–38, 123; and Cohen, *Making a New Deal*, pp. 173–74. For a comparative analysis of these models of managerial authority, see Guillén, *Models of Management*.

15. On European interest in Taylorism and Fordism after World War I, see Nolan, *Visions of Modernity*, pp. 30–57, and Maier, "Between Taylorism and Technocracy." On Taylorism in the Soviet Union, see Linhart, *Lenin, os Camponeses, Taylor*, pp. 75–115; Van Atta, "Why Is There No Taylorism?," pp. 327–37; and Siegelbaum, *Stakhanovism*, chap. 1.

16. See De Decca, *O Silêncio*; Pinheiro and Hall, *A Classe Operária*; and Trevisan, *50 Anos em 5*.

17. In chronological terms, this *estado de compromisso* supposedly took shape during the dictatorship of Getúlio Vargas (1930–45). See Weffort, *O Populismo na Política Brasileira*, pp. 45–78, and Rowland, "Classe Operária e Estado de Compromisso." For a rather overheated critique of this concept, see Munakata, "Compromisso do Estado."

18. The most important works on industrial relations in this period are Fernando Henrique Cardoso, *Empresário Industrial*; Juárez Rubens Brandão Lopes, *Sociedade Industrial* and *Crise do Brasil Arcaico*; José Albertino Rodrigues, *Sindicato e Desenvolvimento*; and Leôncio Martins Rodrigues, *Conflito Industrial*. Only Cardoso's work focuses primarily on industrialists.

19. This argument is made most forcefully in de Decca, *O Silêncio*, pp. 135–82. Warren Dean, in his pathbreaking study *The Industrialization of São Paulo*, revealed early efforts by industrialists to organize their class and institutionalize forms of control. But Dean also saw industrial employers as politically rigid and lacking in vision, whereas this study will emphasize the capacity of the industrial leadership to adopt innovative strategies in both the political and productive spheres.

20. Two recent studies on industrial labor in São Paulo are French, *Brazilian Workers' ABC*, and Wolfe, *Working Women*.

21. On the "crises" of the 1920s and the new ideological currents they provoked, see Prado, *A Democracia Ilustrada*, and de Decca, *O Silêncio*.

Chapter One

1. Simonsen, *O Trabalho Moderno*, pp. 11–12. All translations are my own.

2. Egydio M. de Castro e Silva, *Agua, Cerâmica, Celulose e os Homens*, pp. 77–95. I am grateful to John French for providing me with this source.

3. Quoted in Pinheiro and Hall, *A Classe Operária*, p. 126.

4. Ibid. According to the U.S. consul in São Paulo, "Unions are practically unknown . . . and strikes are not encouraged, to say the least, in any sector of work." In 1927 the Italian consul in São Paulo wrote of the "absolute repression by the Brazilian authori-

ties of any attempt at trade union organization, even the most peaceful." See Hall and Garcia, "Urban Labor," p. 171.

5. On the industrialist response to early labor legislation, see Chapter 2.

6. Highly complimentary portraits of Simonsen can be found in Heitor Ferreira Lima, *Três Industrialistas*, pp. 149–85, and Fanganiello, *Roberto Simonsen*, chap. 1.

7. Under the same influence, another da Gama Cochrane grandson, Aldo Mário de Azevedo, became a noted engineer and industrialist as well as the founding director of IDORT. See Chapter 2.

8. This argument is made most forcefully in Antonacci, "A Vitória da Razão," pp. 17–18. Kazumi Munakata claims that, by 1909, construction workers in Santos had managed to take control of the labor market in their sector (*A Legislação Trabalhista*, p. 21).

9. Companhia Construtora workers were the last to go on strike of the workers at firms, in the capital or in the interior, listed in Simão, *Sindicato e Estado*, pp. 155–58.

10. Simonsen, *O Trabalho Moderno*, p. 37. This oft-cited monograph consists of three different texts by Simonsen—two speeches and a company report— entitled "Pelo Trabalho Organizado," "Pela Organização da Produção," and "Pela Administração Scientífica." The quote is from the latter text.

11. For an excellent discussion of Simonsen's writings during this period, see Vieira, "O Pensamento Industrialista de Roberto Simonsen," chap. 1.

12. Heitor Ferreira Lima, *História do Pensamento Econômico*, p. 160 (n. 1).

13. Howes, "Progressive Conservatism," pp. 91–92. My thanks to Rosa Maria Vieira for providing me with a copy of this very useful thesis in addition to her own excellent M.A. thesis, "O Pensamento Industrialista de Roberto Simonsen."

14. Heitor Ferreira Lima, *Três Industrialistas*, pp. 159–60.

15. Simonsen, *A Construção dos Quartéis para o Exército*.

16. The text of Matarazzo's brief speech can be found in Pinheiro and Hall, *A Classe Operária*, pp. 222–23.

17. Ibid., p. 224.

18. Ibid., p. 228.

19. On the split between commercial and industrial interests, see Luz, *A Luta pela Industrialização*, pp. 162–63, and Leopoldi, "Industrial Associations," pp. 88–93. Industrialists' triumph on the tariff question owed much to their alliance with the Paulista Republican Party, whose board Simonsen joined in 1928.

20. For a discussion of complaints lodged against industry by spokespeople for commerce, labor, and an ill-defined middle class, see Capelato and Prado, *O Bravo Matutino*, pp. 79–81, and Luz, *A Luta pela Industrialização*, pp. 140–63.

21. Dean, *Industrialization of São Paulo*, pp. 174–75. The phrase "Italian Counts" is cited in Leopoldi, "Industrial Associations," p. 369.

22. Pinheiro and Hall, *A Classe Operária*, pp. 227–28. Another leading paulista industrialist, Alexandre Siciliano Júnior made a very similar argument in his pro-tariff pamphlet, *Agricultura, Comércio e Indústria*.

23. Simonsen was by no means the first to link industrialization with nationalism. On early pro-industry thought in Brazil, see Luz, *A Luta pela Industrialização*, pp. 67–84.

24. On Simonsen's infatuation with Fordism, see his "As Finanças e a Indústria," pp. 229-31.

25. Lafer was president of the São Paulo Rotary Club in the late 1920s, and Arruda Pereira eventually founded thirteen other clubs throughout Brazil. Certain employers and technocrats were so closely identified with the Rotary Clubs that a union newspaper, referring to industrialist spokesmen, denounced the "hypocritical humanitarianism of the Rotarians" (*TG*, Mar. 20, 1929, p. 1).

26. Aside from Francisco Matarazzo, the "Italian Counts" would include textile manufacturers such as Nicolau Scarpa and Rodolfo Crespi. The Simonsen cohort, by contrast, tended to invest in newer sectors, including transport equipment (Ferraz), ceramics (Simonsen and Arruda Pereira), and even rudimentary steel plants (Souza Noschese).

27. Octávio Pupo Nogueira's *Indústria em Face das Leis* includes several opinion papers written for textile manufacturers in the late 1920s. On Pupo Nogueira's career as a front man for industry, see Dean, *Industrialization of São Paulo*, pp. 163-67.

28. Pupo Nogueira, *A Indústria em Face das Leis*, pp. 23, 27.

29. Pupo Nogueira claimed that because Brazilian workers bounced from one job to another without acquiring any specialization, "the methods for rationalization of industrial work are unknown here, or are difficult to apply" (ibid., p. 39).

30. On services for the workers in Street's factories, see Teixeira, *A Fábrica do Sonho*, pp. 85-94. For a more negative view of Street, see Dean, *Industrialization of São Paulo*, p. 156.

31. For an excellent discussion of Street's patriarchal language and his attempt to create a self-contained factory-village for his workers, see Rago, *Do Cabaré*, pp. 178-80.

32. Dean argues that "paternalism is, itself, a form of rational labor exploitation the moment it becomes self-conscious" (*Industrialization of São Paulo*, p. 156). I see paternalism as operating according to a different rationality than Fordism and scientific management, although all may be concerned with control.

33. Antonacci mentions Taylorist experiments in the 1920s but overstates their ideological or functional significance during this period ("A Vitória da Razão," p. 31).

34. CIESP Circular no. 66, Aug. 26, 1929.

35. Nogueira Filho, *Ideais e Lutas*, p. 122. The author refers to a book by A. Gant but apparently meant Henry Gantt's widely read *Work, Wages, and Profits*, which outlined a Taylorist "task-and-bonus" plan.

36. Nogueira Filho, *Ideais e Lutas*, p. 124.

37. On concentration and mechanization during the 1920s, see Ribeiro, "Condições de Trabalho," chap. 2; Suzigan, *Indústria Brasileira*, pp. 150-52, 165-66; Versiani, *A Década de 20*, chap. 3; and Wolfe, *Working Women*, pp. 42-43. Stanley Stein calculated that "nearly three times as much textile machinery by weight entered Brazil in the years 1922-27 as in the preceding seven years" (*Brazilian Cotton Manufacture*, p. 108).

38. Eileen Keremitsis, in her study of the early shoemaking industry in Rio, notes increased mechanization, replacement of adult shoemakers with apprentices, and the transformation of the master artisan into a less autonomous foreman ("Early Industrial Worker," pp. 145-46, 158).

39. French, *Brazilian Workers' ABC*, pp. 75-76. Also on São Paulo, see Wolfe, *Working Women*, pp. 45-46. One of Rio's oldest textile mills instituted "modern tech-

niques of personnel management" in the 1920s (Von der Weid and Bastos, *O Fio da Meada*, pp. 157–264). Such techniques were rare even in North American factories prior to the 1920s. See Brandes, *American Welfare Capitalism*, and Lizabeth Cohen's wonderful study, *Making a New Deal*, esp. chap. 4.

40. Rago, *Do Cabaré*, p. 181.

41. For a document describing the application of "rigorously scientific" organizational principles to a predominantly female workforce at the Companhia Telefônica do Rio de Janeiro, see Pinheiro and Hall, *A Classe Operária*, pp. 142–46.

42. On the creation of a central personnel office at the São Paulo Tramway, Light & Power Company, the capital's largest employer, see PH, Correspondência da Light, Subsérie 24 (General Orders), Nov. 26, 1925, June 6, 1928. After the latter date, foremen could hire only "common laborers" without going through the firm's employment bureau.

43. Dean, *Industrialization of São Paulo*, p. 174. On personalistic forms of control in a northeastern textile factory, see José Sérgio Leite Lopes, *A Tecelagem*, chap. 2. Lopes claims that among the workers he interviewed "the examination of hands and eyes done by the boss in flesh and blood was viewed with nostalgia when compared to the psychotechnic texts and physical exams of the 'modern' factories, generally affiliated with southern firms" (ibid., p. 60).

44. In 1922 Gaspar Ricardo Júnior claimed that worker housing benefited employers by making it possible for them "to have the worker near the workplace and much more subject to their influence and direction. Aside from housing, industrialists can favor their workers by providing meals . . . allowing the employers to inspect and restrict the use of alcoholic beverages, thus securing a workforce that is well nourished and therefore capable of better production" ("Qualidades Pessoais dos Trabalhadores—seu Melhoramento," *Revista da Associação Comercial de São Paulo*, Sept. 1922, cited in Antonacci, "A Vitória da Razão," p. 30).

45. Dean, *Industrialization of São Paulo*, pp. 151–55. Rago, *Do Cabaré*, and Wolfe, *Working Women*, focus on the discourse of rationalization and a few prominent cases of Fordist management policies but understate the uneven application of these policies even beyond the 1920s. Again, limited implementation does not neutralize the importance of such discourses, but it does raise problems once we move to the terrain of worker resistance.

46. On the hygienic factory, see Rago, *Do Cabaré*, pp. 37–47.

47. For a discussion of this emerging group of intellectuals and technocrats, see Antonacci, "A Vitória da Razão," pp. 31–44.

48. In a 1929 article entitled "Escola Nova," Lourenço Filho proposed a new system of pedagogy, testing, and guidance for Brazilian schools based on the principles of Taylorism. In 1926 Fernando de Azevedo carried out a survey of leading educators for *O Estado de São Paulo*. The responses were later collected and published, along with his commentary on how to create a more rational and modern system of instruction. See Fernando de Azevedo, *A Educação Pública*, esp. pp. 175–92.

49. On Paula Souza, Alvaro, and the Instituto de Higiene (which became an autonomous entity in 1925), see Rago, *Do Cabaré*, pp. 134–35, and Guzzo Decca, *A Vida fora das Fábricas*, pp. 73–88. I have translated "higiene" as "hygiene" rather than "health" since the thrust of this movement was to change habits and behavior.

50. For an early presentation of Roberto Mange's educational views, see the text of Fernando de Azevedo's 1926 interview with him in *A Educação Pública*, pp. 222–36.

51. By far the best study of Roberto Mange's career is PM, *De Homens e Máquinas*. Information on Mange can also be found in Bologna, *Roberto Mange*, pp. 13–18, and interviews with Ernest Mange, Apr. 11, June 19, 1990, and Roger Mange, June 3, 11, 1990, PM.

52. On early vocational education in São Paulo, see Ana M. C. Infantosi da Costa, "A Educação para Trabalhadores," pp. 3–10, and Moraes, "A Socialização da Força de Trabalho." The latter has been especially helpful in this study.

53. Albuquerque Lins, *Mensagem Enviado ao Congresso Legislativo*, pp. 412–13.

54. EPM, *Relatório* (1920), p. 1. See also favorable coverage of the schools' inauguration in *ESP*, June 11, 1912.

55. For an insider's view of the Liceu, see Severo, *O Liceu*. For a detailed analysis of the Liceu's evolution, see Moraes, "A Socialização da Força de Trabalho," chap. 2.

56. John French, in discussing the background of skilled electrician and labor leader Marcos Andreotti, describes this process of apprenticeship in "Social Origins of Resistance," p. 4.

57. For Mange's views in this vein, see CFESP, *Relatório* (1931), pp. 5–18, and CFESP, *Relatório* (1933), p. 3. In the latter report, Mange argued that the modern craftsman, "confined by the feverish activity [of the workshop]," no longer has the time to instruct an apprentice properly in a craft. "The apprentices are thrown into the workshop, learn whatever they want and whatever they can, and often copy defective work processes and acquire bad habits."

58. For a discussion of the *série metódica* proposed by Mange and its origins, see Moraes, "A Socialização da Força de Trabalho," pp. 205–7.

59. Mange interview, in Fernando de Azevedo, *A Educação Pública*, p. 226.

60. On the need for more vocational schools, see ibid., pp. 175–283. On the alleged de-skilling of paulista workers in the 1920s, see Rago, *Do Cabaré*; Segnini, *Ferrovia*; Antonacci, "A Vitória da Razão"; Moraes, "A Socialização da Força de Trabalho"; Ribeiro, "Condições de Trabalho"; and Wolfe, *Working Women*. These studies are at least partially inspired by the pioneering work of Braverman, *Labor and Monopoly Capital*.

61. Fernando de Azevedo, *A Educação Pública*, pp. 224–25.

62. Joan W. Scott, *Gender and the Politics of History*, p. 175. For a similar point, see Wolfe, *Working Women*, p. 201 (n. 15).

63. Fausto, *Trabalho Urbano*, p. 117.

64. Wolfe, *Working Women*, pp. 35–36; Veccia, "Women, Work, and Family Life."

65. Antonacci, "A Vitória da Razão," p. 22. Antonacci takes a particularly intemperate view of the transformation of the industrial workforce given the sketchiness of her evidence. Wolfe provides hard evidence of work pace intensification: in all of Brazil from 1921 to 1927, the number of looms increased 33 percent and spindles, 59 percent; the number of workers grew by only 17 percent (*Working Women*, p. 42). Even considering that plants often functioned far below capacity, this surely indicates accelerated work rhythms.

66. By the 1920s, many textile manufacturers had replaced the original European *mestres* with "Brazilian" workers. See Stein, *Brazilian Cotton Manufacture*, pp. 73–75,

and Ribeiro, "Condições de Trabalho," pp. 141–42. But highly paid European craftsmen continued to hold positions of authority in newer firms. Joan W. Scott mentions that several skilled glassworkers displaced by new equipment in the factories of Carmaux, France, were contracted to work for a Brazilian firm (*Glassworkers*, p. 170). See also Dean, *Industrialization of São Paulo*, pp. 176–77; Moraes, "A Socialização da Força de Trabalho," p. 174; and PH, Correspondência da Light, Subsérie 40, Jan. 27, 1908, Apr. 16, 1909.

67. *Anuário do Ensino do Estado de São Paulo* (1918), p. 533, and *Anuário do Ensino do Estado de São Paulo* (1920–21), p. 368, cited in Moraes, "A Socialização da Força de Trabalho," p. 174. This also reflects the disillusionment among middle-class paulistas with immigrant workers following the general strikes and the valorization of "national" workers. See Andrews, *Blacks and Whites*, pp. 85–89. Many immigrant workers also regarded imported craftsmen as privileged "foreigners."

68. This reliance on foreign skilled workers continued well into the 1930s. See FIESP Circular no. 762, Aug. 25, 1936.

69. Antonacci, "A Vitória da Razão," p. 25. A comparison of the wages of skilled and unskilled workers over time shows no evidence of a massive devaluation of skilled labor. Data from Light (PH, Correspondência da Light, Subsérie 40, Sept. 30, 1908) show skilled workers earning 60 to 100 percent more than unskilled. A table composed by the U.S. consul in 1922 reveals that skilled workers were earning 50 to 150 percent more than unskilled workers (Pinheiro and Hall, *A Classe Operária*, p. 126).

70. The director of the Escola Profissional Masculina claimed in 1920 that the demand for skilled mechanics was so strong and their wages so high that the school could not afford to hire them as instructors. See EPM, *Relatório* (1920), p. 18.

71. French notes the persistence of handwork in São Paulo's growing furniture industry (*Brazilian Workers' ABC*, p. 50).

72. In Mange's words, rationalized training would produce "healthy individuals, of disciplined character, conscious of their obligations" ("Escolas Profissionaes Mecânicas," p. 17).

73. Moraes, "A Socialização da Força de Trabalho," pp. 95–96.

74. Severo, *O Liceu*, p. 36.

75. Ibid., p. 84.

76. See Moraes, "A Socialização da Força de Trabalho," chap. 2, and Segnini, *Ferrovia*, p. 75. The Liceu had not completely joined the Taylorist camp; as of 1918, three times as many of its students were enrolled in design and fine arts as in vocational instruction. See Severo, *O Liceu*, p. 193.

77. CFESP, *Relatório* (1931), pp. 9–10.

78. Fernando de Azevedo, *A Educação Pública*, p. 233; Horácio da Silveira, *O Ensino Technico-Profissional*, pp. 13–15; Antonacci, "A Vitória da Razão," pp. 38–39.

79. CIFTSP Circular no. 779, May 10, 1928. The notice did not exclude women, but the reference to the preparation of foremen suggests that the sponsors had only male workers in mind.

80. PH, Correspondência da Light, Subsérie 24 (General Orders), July 8, 1910 (emphasis added); Subsérie 52, July 20, 1907, Jan. 20, 1920. The main instructor of these apprentices was Moysés Marx, a mechanical engineer who would later become Mange's collaborator in the school for mechanics.

81. Rodrigues Alves, *Mensagem Enviada ao Congresso Legislativo*, p. 567; Guimarães, *Mensagem Enviada ao Congresso Legislativo*; EPM, *Relatório* (1914). The state also established a third professional school in the interior town of Amparo.

82. EPM, *Relatório* (1924), p. 3. A textile course was offered for a short time but was discontinued due to weak and irregular demand.

83. Moraes, "A Socialização da Força de Trabalho," Anexo 15.

84. EPM, *Relatório* (1914), p. 12; EPM, *Relatório* (1920), p. 9; EPM, *Relatório* (1924), p. 3. In the latter report, the director noted that the students' need to begin working as soon as possible had prompted the school to cut back on its "theoretical" courses.

85. Rodrigues Alves, *Mensagem Enviada ao Congresso Legislativo* (1915), p. 659; EPF, *Relatório do Diretor*, p. 11.

86. Campos, *Mensagem Enviada ao Congresso Legislativo*, pp. 18–23.

87. EPF, *Relatório do Diretor*, p. 11.

88. Aprígio de Almeida Gonzaga directed both schools and defended the women's school against attempts to shift its emphasis to home economics. But his hostile comments on women workers in industry make it clear that he opposed employment of women in factory production. See EPM, *Relatório* (1920), p. 6. For more on vocational education for women, see Besse, *Restructuring Patriarchy*, chap. 3.

89. EPM, *Relatório* (1924), p. 5.

90. Ibid., p. 7; Moraes, "A Socialização da Força de Trabalho," p. 219.

91. EPM, *Relatório* (1920), p. 4. Moraes compares the positions adopted by Gonzaga and Mange in considerable detail in "A Socialização da Força de Trabalho," pp. 226–29.

92. EPM, *Relatório* (1920), p. 23.

93. EPM, *Relatório* (1923), p. 12.

94. EPM, *Relatório* (1920), p. 22.

95. Mange, "Escolas Profissionaes Mecânicas," pp. 17–21. In this essay, Mange described scientific methods as a "technical response" to the campaign for the eight-hour day. According to Mange, "the widely desired, but dangerous and pernicious 'reduction in the workday'" made it necessary "to seek, through perfect, accurate, and rapid labor, with all unnecessary movement eliminated, the means to produce more and better in a shorter space of time." For an account of Mange's career that puts more emphasis on his evolution away from a rigidly "rational" position, see PM, *De Homens e Máquinas*.

96. Fernando de Azevedo, *A Educação Pública*, pp. 234–35.

97. Severo, *O Liceu*, p. 46.

98. Two studies that examine workers' responses in a more complex fashion are Rago, *Do Cabaré*, and José Sérgio Leite Lopes, *A Tecelagem*.

99. The pioneering work of David Montgomery (*Workers' Control in America*), among others, stimulated a new line of inquiry for labor historians that focused on craft control and resistance to reorganization of the work process. But Montgomery's approach may be less useful in studying industrial economies in which "craft control" barely existed, if at all. Workers still resisted changes in the work process, but we cannot assume, a priori, that they would resist or that they would offer the same type of resistance.

100. The recent historiography of Brazilian labor has also been profoundly affected by the "new unionism" that emerged in the 1970s. The success of grass-roots organiz-

ing during a repressive dictatorship prompted historians to focus on forms of resistance outside the context of formal labor union struggles. See Paoli, Sader, and Telles, "Pensando a Classe Operária."

101. Fausto, *Trabalho Urbano*, pp. 253–73.

102. Simonsen, *O Trabalho Moderno*, p. 41.

103. Ibid., p. 35. Simonsen specifically criticized the "military" model of industrial organization according to which an expanding firm simply multiplied the initial "cells" of production under the control of foremen and subforemen.

104. Details of this "experiment" and the subsequent strike were circulated by the textile manufacturers' association. See CIFTSP Circular no. 758, Jan. 24, 1928. On this strike, see also Rago, *Do Cabaré*, pp. 57–58, and Wolfe, *Working Women*, p. 48. Rago and Wolfe assume that the strike was triggered by the introduction of automated, or semiautomated, looms. The circular's language is ambiguous, but it seems that automated looms were already in use, and Matarazzo was doubling the number assigned to each woman.

105. Fausto, *Trabalho Urbano*, p. 119. On the French glassworkers, see Joan W. Scott, *Glassworkers*, pp. 72–107.

106. Fausto, *Trabalho Urbano*, p. 119.

107. Nogueira Filho, *Ideais e Lutas*, pp. 128–29. Rago argues that even anarchist artisans in São Paulo, with their critical view of capitalism, did not form a thoroughgoing critique of the new technology (*Do Cabaré*, pp. 57–59).

108. For the pre-1930 period, I was able to find issues of *O Trabalhador Gráfico* from 1905 to 1906 and from 1920 to 1929, with frequent gaps even during these periods. On the role of the printers' union in early labor struggles, see Dias, *História das Lutas*, and Gomes, *A Invenção do Trabalhismo*, pp. 171–72.

109. *TG*, Feb. 16, 1905, p. 2.

110. *TG*, Jan. 1906, pp. 1–3.

111. Margareth Rago's manifest disappointment at the limits of the anarchist critique of new technology (*Do Cabaré*, pp. 57–59) reflects the dominant narrative in the recent historiography of early labor movements and industry. Historians have routinely seen technical innovations as de-skilling workers, creating ever more elaborate means for their control, and intensifying work processes. The articles in *O Trabalhador Gráfico*, by contrast, express a more complex and ambivalent view of modernity and make the opposite association between levels of skill and levels of technology.

112. *TG*, Apr. 1905, p. 4.

113. *TG*, Jan. 1906, pp. 1–3. On the position of this key newspaper with respect to the emerging labor movement, see Barbara Weinstein, "Impressões da Elite."

114. Rago, *Do Cabaré*, p. 59.

115. *TG*, Apr. 4, 1906. This was a special supplement devoted to the strike at Casa Duprat.

116. *TG*, Sept. 24, 1920, p. 4.

117. *TG*, Nov. 1922, p. 4.

118. *TG*, Mar. 7, 1926, p. 1.

119. *TG*, Apr. 1905, p. 4. In Portuguese, the term was "consciente." For a good discussion of workers' pride in craft as a form of "personal affirmation," see Rago, *Do Cabaré*, pp. 49–50.

120. Fausto, *Trabalho Urbano*, p. 271.

121. Pinheiro and Hall, *A Classe Operária*, p. 189.

122. *TG*, Aug. 1927, p. 2.

123. *TG*, Jan. 1906, pp. 1-3. One of the major objectives of the printers' attempt to standardize wage and job classifications was "to put an end to the exploitation of apprentices so widely practiced in this capital."

124. EPM, *Relatório* (1920), p. 15. Moraes quotes Mange to this effect in "A Socialização da Força de Trabalho," pp. 210-11.

125. *TG*, Feb. 21, 1923, p. 3.

126. *TG*, Oct. 15, 1926, p. 1.

127. *TG*, Jan. 10, 1929, p. 3. See also Pinheiro and Hall, *A Classe Operária*, p. 130.

128. The newspaper bitterly criticized the Grêmio Typographico Paulistano, an association that rejected strikes as well as all other confrontational tactics. See *TG*, Jan. 1906, p. 3.

129. *TG*, Feb. 27, 1923, p. 1.

130. *TG*, Dec. 13, 1925, p. 2.

131. *TG*, May 1, 1925, p. 1.

132. *TG*, Feb. 7, 1926, p. 2 (emphasis in original).

133. *TG*, Mar. 7, 1926, p. 1; July 21, 1926, p. 3.

134. *TG*, Aug. 1927, p. 7.

135. Ibid.

136. Ibid., p. 4. On "scientific" studies of human work capacity and fatigue, see Rabinbach, *Human Motor*.

137. *TG*, Mar. 30, 1929, p. 1. Considerable enthusiasm for eugenics existed among Brazilian educators, technocrats, and hygienists during these years, but their conception of eugenics had more to do with social than biological engineering. See Stepan, *"Hour of Eugenics."*

138. For a comparable case, see Lobato, *El "Taylorismo."*

139. Simonsen, in his early writings, urged employers to institute new forms of worker compensation so as to preempt efforts to resolve the social question through "political means" (*O Trabalho Moderno*, pp. 37-39). John French also notes Simonsen's concern about state intervention but overstates the case when he claims that Simonsen saw a political solution to the social question as "the main threat" (*Brazilian Workers' ABC*, p. 76).

140. De Decca discusses the big industrialists' formation of CIESP, their campaign for a revision of tariffs, and their involvement in the Paulista Republican Party. These developments indicate that the industrialists had come to believe that industrial development was dependent upon a privileged relationship with the state. See de Decca, *O Silêncio*, pp. 149-55. Luiz Werneck Vianna describes industrialists during the 1920s as advocating a purely "liberal" project that excluded state participation (*Liberalismo e Sindicato*, pp. 63-77).

Chapter Two

1. On the politics of the First Republic, see Love, *Rio Grande do Sul*, and Lewin, *Politics and Parentela*. The term "oligarchy" here refers to the monopolization of power

by a small group of families and their clients, especially during the early decades of the Republic. At the same time, legal and financial transformations indicated an emerging "bourgeois" ethic among the dominant state elites. See Saes, *A Formação do Estado Burguês*, and Topik, "Brazil's Bourgeois Revolution?"

2. On São Paulo's immigration program, see Hall, "Origins of Mass Immigration"; Kowarick, *Trabalho e Vadiagem*; and Andrews, *Blacks and Whites*, chap. 3. On post-emancipation labor control in the northeastern sugar zones, see Eisenberg, *Sugar Industry*, and Huggins, *From Slavery to Vagrancy*.

3. On these early strike movements, see Simão, *Sindicato e Estado*, chap. 3; Fausto, *Trabalho Urbano*, chap. 3; and Barbara Weinstein, "Impressões da Elite," pp. 141–58.

4. "Patrões e Operários," *ESP*, June 2, 1907, p. 1; "As Paredes Operárias," *ESP*, June 10, 1907, p. 2; "Os Operários nas Fábricas," *ESP*, June 27, 1907. Henrique Coelho, a dissident Republican, was an early advocate of social legislation. For a discussion of Coelho's writings, see Barbara Weinstein, "Impressões da Elite," pp. 157–58.

5. There are many accounts of the 1917 and 1919 general strikes. See, for example, Fausto, *Trabalho Urbano*, pp. 157–243; Khoury, *A Greve de 1917*; French, *Brazilian Workers' ABC*, pp. 30–34, 41–44; and Wolfe, *Working Women*, pp. 16–25.

6. José de Souza Martins, *Conde Matarazzo*, p. 95. See also Gomes, *Burguesia e Trabalho*, p. 160, and Emilia Viotti da Costa, "Brazilian Workers Rediscovered." For an interesting description of the government response to the general strike of 1919, see Moraes Filho, *O Problema do Sindicato Único*, pp. 204–5.

7. São Paulo's textile manufacturers (together with those in Rio and Minas Gerais) successfully lobbied against tariff reductions in 1919–20. See Leopoldi, "Industrial Associations," p. 88. The 1930 Manifesto of Vargas's Liberal Alliance turned their argument on its head, claiming that "if our protectionism favors the industrialists . . . it is our duty also to assist the proletariat" (cited in Gomes, *Burguesia e Trabalho*, p. 104).

8. Gomes, *Burguesia e Trabalho*, includes an insightful analysis of the potential conflict between the industrialists' "liberal" views on the social order and increasing calls for state intervention in the process of economic development. For a study that examines pre-1930 social legislation in light of Fordist tendencies among the industrial bourgeoisie, see Vianna, *Liberalismo e Sindicato*, chaps. 1–2.

9. CIFTSP Circular, Representação a Lindolpho Collor, Jan. 14, 1931, enclosure.

10. Ibid. The arguments about the appropriate length of the workday were followed by a two-page discussion of Taylorism and other strategies for rationalization of the textile industry.

11. On workers, leisure, and the struggle for the eight-hour workday in the United States, see Rosenzweig, *Eight Hours For What We Will*.

12. For a provocative discussion of the conflict between discourses of justice and reason, see Baker, "A Foucauldian French Revolution?," pp. 198–99.

13. Boris Fausto, disputing a simplistic view of the Partido Democrático as representing "new, supposedly dynamic sectors," portrayed the party as hostile to industry (*A Revolução de 1930*, pp. 32–38). Although some members of the party were anti-industry, many of its adherents viewed industrialization as the key to Brazil's future development. For an excellent discussion of the Partido Democrático's proposals to resolve the social question, see Prado, *A Democracia Ilustrada*, pp. 150–72.

14. On Salles's ties with *O Estado de São Paulo* (of which he became publisher in 1927),

with various electric utilities, and with the founders of IDORT, see Pacheco e Silva, *Armando de Salles Oliveira*, pp. 63–94.

15. Fausto, *A Revolução de 1930*, p. 38. According to Fausto, critics portrayed the industrialists as "a group of foreign exploiters, producers of shoddy goods, responsible for the rise in the cost of living."

16. Leopoldi argues that by 1931 the industrialist leadership was also arguing for "rationalization" of tariff policy ("Industrial Associations," p. 95 [n. 1]).

17. José de Souza Martins, *Conde Matarazzo*, p. 94.

18. Gomes, *Burguesia e Trabalho*, p. 159.

19. On the opposition of industrialists in Rio to the new labor legislation, see Carone, *O Centro Industrial*, pp. 103–8.

20. *ESP*, Nov. 29, 1928, cited in Capelato and Prado, *O Bravo Matutino*, p. 80.

21. De Decca, *O Silêncio*, chap. 4.

22. CIESP Circular no. 63, Aug. 12, 1929. The quote is from an article published in *A Folha da Manhã*, Aug. 11, 1929, which praised CIESP's registration campaign.

23. CIESP Circular no. 20, Jan. 21, 1929. Arruda's opinion paper was also circulated by CIFTSP. The quote is from Ernst Freund, *Police Power*, p. 501.

24. CIESP Circular no. 20, Jan. 21, 1929. The two opinion papers were circulated together.

25. In this respect, I disagree with Vianna (*Liberalismo e Sindicato*) and Gomes (*Burguesia e Trabalho*), who portray the industrialists as rigidly opposed to labor legislation at the time of Vargas's seizure of power. For a similar view to mine, see Leopoldi, "Industrial Associations," which describes Vargas as having "accentuated and accelerated a political trajectory which [industrialists] had already been following, rather than setting a different course" (pp. 338–39).

26. Leopoldi, "Industrial Associations," pp. 90–93, 350–55.

27. Vieira, "O Pensamento Industrialista de Roberto Simonsen," pp. 48–49. Simonsen's case proved atypical. Since he was more closely associated with the old regime than most employers, he was especially vulnerable to public scrutiny. Leopoldi claims this experience moved Simonsen to turn over all his business dealings to associates and confine himself to public service ("Industrial Associations," p. 367 [n. 1]).

28. Wolfe, *Working Women*, p. 50.

29. CIESP Circular no. 113, Oct. 28, 1930. Plínio Barreto, a staunch CIESP ally, was provisional governor until December.

30. CIESP Circular no. 117, Jan. 3, 1931. The *tenentes* (lieutenants) were young nationalist military officers who supported Vargas's seizure of power and generally favored significant social reforms. See Borges, *Tenentismo*.

31. Love, *São Paulo*, p. 185; Leopoldi, "Industrial Associations," p. 93.

32. CIESP Circular no. 161, July 18, 1931; no. 162, July 20, 1931; no. 163, July 21, 1931; no. 164, July 22, 1931; no. 166, July 30, 1931; Wolfe, *Working Women*, pp. 53–62.

33. Leopoldi notes that the paulista industrialists were the first group to reorganize themselves along the new syndicalist lines but oddly attributes this fact to the employers' "weakness" ("Industrial Associations," p. 49). A more likely explanation is that the industrialists expected that they, unlike the workers, would be able to manipulate the new system to their advantage.

34. Sáenz Leme, *A Ideologia dos Industriais*, p. 56.

35. It was probably not coincidence that Horácio Lafer replaced the unyielding Octávio Pupo Nogueira from 1931 to 1934 as secretary of CIESP. See Antonacci, "A Vitória da Razão," p. 78.

36. FIESP Circular no. 228, Dec. 17, 1931. Enclosed was a copy of the long letter (probably authored by Simonsen) to Collor containing FIESP's comments on the proposed labor laws.

37. FIESP Circular no. 375, Jan. 25, 1933; copy of letter to Adail Valente do Couto, special delegate of the Ministry of Labor, Jan. 18, 1933, enclosure.

38. FIESP Circular no. 123, Feb. 23, 1931; no. 167, Aug. 4, 1931; no. 174, Aug. 19, 1931; no. 430, July 19, 1933; no. 451, Oct. 10, 1933. FIESP was still named CIESP when it received the first draft of this decree.

39. FIESP Circular no. 430, July 19, 1933; no. 451, Oct. 10, 1933.

40. Wolfe, *Working Women*, pp. 55–56.

41. On the conflict between Oliveira Vianna and Simonsen over the extent of the state's corporatist powers, see Howes, "Progressive Conservatism," chap. 8. Among the concessions that the industrialists wrung from the Vargas regime were the retention of "parallel" organizations (for example, CIESP) not subject to government control and the right to reelect officials without restriction. See Leopoldi, "Industrial Associations," pp. 57–63.

42. FIESP Circular no. 228, Dec. 17, 1931 (letter to Collor enclosed); no. 346, Nov. 14, 1932.

43. FIESP Circular no. 206, Oct. 26, 1931; no. 212, Nov. 5, 1931.

44. FIESP Circular no. 173, Aug. 18, 1931.

45. FIESP Circular no. 266, May 9, 1932; no. 268, May 14, 1932. See also Wolfe, *Working Women*, pp. 58–62.

46. FIESP Circular no. 246, Feb. 17, 1932; no. 253, Mar. 7, 1932; no. 279, June 6, 1932.

47. Love, *São Paulo*, p. 120.

48. FIESP Circular no. 221, Nov. 20, 1931. I assume the director in question was Geraldo de Paula Souza.

49. For more detail on the circumstances leading to the paulista revolt, see Love, *São Paulo*, pp. 119–22; Hilton, *1932*; Borges, *Getúlio Vargas*; and Capelato, *O Movimento de 1932* and *Os Arautos do Liberalismo*, pp. 171–89.

50. FIESP Circular nos. 293–95, July 13, 1932; no. 297, July 18, 1932; no. 319, Aug. 3, 1932.

51. On the industrialists' role in the constitutionalist revolt, see Clovis de Oliveira, *A Indústria e o Movimento Constitucionalista*.

52. Heitor Ferreira Lima, *Três Industrialistas*, p. 184.

53. Costa Júnior, "Roberto Mange," pp. 399–410.

54. Ibid., p. 404.

55. FIESP Circular no. 327, Sept. 5, 1932; no. 328, Sept. 14, 1932; no. 330, Sept. 20, 1932. See also Sáenz Leme, *A Ideologia dos Industriais*, p. 144.

56. FIESP Circular no. 333, Oct. 7, 1932; no. 343, Nov. 3, 1932.

57. FIESP Circular no. 341, Oct. 28, 1932.

58. FIESP, Correspondence, letter to Gal. Waldomiro Castilho de Lima, Nov. 1, 1932, BARS.

59. FIESP Circular no. 344, Nov. 7, 1932.

60. FIESP Circular no. 456, Nov. 11, 1933.

61. FGV, CPDOC, VF/c 37.11.12-A, P17, 2, "Convênio Celebrado . . . entre o Gov. Federal e o Gov. do Estado de S. Paulo."

62. One setback for industry was Vargas's 1935 reciprocal trade agreement with the United States, which threatened gains from the 1934 tariff reform. Simonsen, anticipating developmental nationalism, claimed that such agreements led to the "progressive enserfment" of less-advanced nations. See Leopoldi, "Industrial Associations," p. 124.

63. Simonsen later published this lengthy speech with the title "As Finanças e a Indústria."

64. Ibid., pp. 230–32.

65. Ibid., pp. 234–35.

66. Ibid., p. 239.

67. Ibid., p. 243.

68. For a similar discussion of Simonsen's "industrialism," see Vieira, "O Pensamento Industrialista de Roberto Simonsen," pp. 88–91. Alcir Lenharo's insightful analysis of this speech is marred by his claim that Simonsen was referring in 1931 to an as yet nonexistent Nazi Germany, thereby exaggerating the explicitly totalitarian aspects of Simonsen's enthusiasm for rationalization (*A Sacralização da Política*, p. 149).

69. Aldo Mário de Azevedo, "Discurso do A. M. de Azevedo na Ocasião da 1ª Reunião do IDORT, June 23, 1931," p. 11.

70. Ibid., p. 10; AIDORT, Livro de Actas, Acta da Assemblêa de Constituição do Instituto de Organização Racional do Trabalho de São Paulo, June 23, 1931.

71. For an excellent discussion of IDORT's structure and objectives, see Antonacci, "A Vitória da Razão," chap. 2. See also Tenca, "Razão e Vontade Política."

72. AIDORT, Livro de Actas, Acta da 34ª Reunião da Diretoria, Apr. 25, 1938.

73. IDORT's international ties illuminate the cross-ideological appeal of rationalization. IDORT had close contacts with its counterparts in Nazi Germany and Fascist Italy. At a 1938 meeting, director Moacyr Alvaro reported on his visit to the Reichskuratorium für Wirtschaftlichkeit in Berlin. See AIDORT, Livro de Actas, Acta da 24ª Reunião, Jan. 31, 1938; Acta da 26ª Reunião, Feb. 14, 1938.

74. Antonacci, "A Vitória da Razão," pp. 96–97.

75. Ibid., p. 102.

76. Mange, *Lições de Psicotécnica*, p. 4.

77. "O Que Somos," *Revista IDORT*, no. 1 (Jan. 1932): 2, and Nelson Malta, "Deve o Estado Sugerir ou Impor a Racionalização?," *Revista IDORT*, no. 45 (Sept. 1935): 196, both cited in Antonacci, "A Vitória da Razão," pp. 97, 176.

78. Antonacci, "A Vitória da Razão," pp. 90–91. *O Estado de São Paulo* provided IDORT with office space, publicity, and financial subsidies; its editor, Armando de Salles Oliveira, served as the institute's first president.

79. Ibid., p. 172; Pacheco e Silva, *Armando de Salles Oliveira*, p. 83.

80. Antonacci, "A Vitória da Razão," pp. 136–40. Margareth Rago's claim (*Do Cabaré*, p. 39) that Taylorization of production was widely implemented during the 1930s seems overstated; implementation continued to be piecemeal and uneven.

81. FIESP Circular no. 393, Mar. 3, 1933.

82. Antonacci, "A Vitória da Razão," pp. 141–44.

83. On the failure to excite greater interest among textile producers, see AIDORT,

Livro de Actas, Acta da 10ª Reunião da Diretoria, Sept. 13, 1937; Acta da 27ª Reunião, Mar. 7, 1938; Acta da 34ª Reunião, Apr. 25, 1938.

84. "Introdução ao Relatório dos Estudos Feitos na Firma X pela 1ª Divisão," *Revista IDORT*, no. 19 (July 1933): 147, cited in Antonacci, "A Vitória da Razão," p. 134.

85. "Fiscalização Industrial," *BMTIC*, no. 2 (Oct. 1934): 160.

86. Aristides Casado, "O Combate a Rotina," *BMTIC*, no. 2 (Oct. 1934): 119–32; "O Phenômeno da 'Racionalização,'" *BMTIC*, no. 3 (Nov. 1934): 156–61. For an incisive discussion of IDORT as an intellectual influence during the Vargas regime, see Lenharo, *A Sacralização da Política*, pp. 147–50.

87. Aldo Mário de Azevedo, "Discurso Pronunciado pelo Eng° Aldo Mário de Azevedo na Sessão de 30/X/36 da Assembléa Legislativa."

88. Simonsen, *Rumo à Verdade*, p. 5, and *Evolução Industrial*, pp. 461–65.

89. Simonsen, in his address at the school's opening, referred to São Paulo as "morally wounded by the distasteful events of recent years" (*Rumo à Verdade*, p. 7). Donald Pierson, a U.S. sociologist who joined the faculty in 1939, stressed the 1932 defeat in his account of the school's founding (FGV, CPDOC, LF/c 43.06.22-A, "Escola Livre de Sociologia e Política"). See also Vieira, "O Pensamento Industrialista de Roberto Simonsen," p. 92, and O'Neil, "Educational Innovation," p. 57.

90. Cited in Vieira, "O Pensamento Industrialista de Roberto Simonsen," p. 92.

91. The choice of North American social scientists reflects the Escola Livre's preference for applied sociology. In contrast, the University of São Paulo drew upon European sociological traditions from the outset. See O'Neil, "Educational Innovation," p. 59, and Morse, *From Community to Metropolis*, p. 250.

92. According to O'Neil, many students deserted the Escola Livre once the University of São Paulo inaugurated its Faculdade de Filosofia largely because the tuition at the Escola Livre was five times higher than at the university ("Educational Innovation," p. 58 [n. 7]).

93. Pierson, "Escola Livre"; Guzzo Decca, *A Vida Fora das Fábricas*, pp. 15–95.

94. Horácio da Silveira, *O Ensino Technico-Profissional*, p. 23.

95. Ibid., p. 21. The women's courses, aside from those in domestic arts, were oriented toward such traditional crafts as embroidery.

96. Ibid., p. 43.

97. The 1936 governor's report notes the creation of "child care dispensaries" at vocational schools to teach female students child-rearing skills. See Oliveira, *Mensagem Apresentado pelo Governador a Assembléa Legislativa*, p. 42.

98. Horácio da Silveira, *O Ensino Technico-Profissional*, p. 12.

99. Ibid., pp. 13–15. The general assembly of IDORT praised Roberto Mange for his role in the 1933 reform of São Paulo's educational code. See AIDORT, Livro de Actas, Acta da Assembléa Geral, June 28, 1933. See also d'Avila, *O Código de Educação*.

100. On Mange's training of railroad mechanics, see Segnini, *Ferrovia*, chap. 4, and Medeiros, "Estradas de Ferro."

101. Mange, "Ensino Profissional Racional," p. 31.

102. Mange, *Lições de Psicotécnica*, p. 84.

103. Mange, "Ensino Profissional Racional," pp. 41–57. This report first appeared in a 1932 issue of *Revista IDORT* and was also published as a pamphlet by the Sorocabana Railway in 1936.

104. SESP, *Relatório pelo Anno de 1931*, pp. 22–27. To compensate for the limits of psychotechnic testing, Mange collected data on students' home and family lives.

105. Horácio da Silveira, *O Ensino Technico-Profissional*, pp. 13–15.

106. AE, "Mensagem do Gal. Waldomiro Castilho de Lima no Governo de São Paulo, como Interventor Federal no Estado" (1933), p. 281 (emphasis in original).

107. Horácio da Silveira, *O Ensino Technico-Profissional*, pp. 44–45.

Chapter Three

1. Simonsen, *Discurso na Assembléia*, p. 9. The original paragraph was modeled on a section of the Weimar Constitution.

2. Ibid., pp. 12–14.

3. Ibid., p. 27.

4. Ibid., p. 28. Simonsen's analysis of syphilis rates reflects the peculiarly Brazilian environmental eugenics that Stepan describes in *"Hour of Eugenics,"* pp. 46–54, 153–69.

5. On class representation in the *constituinte* and social reforms in the 1930s, see Conniff, *Urban Politics*, pp. 117–34.

6. Aldo Mário de Azevedo, "O Capital e o Trabalho." Azevedo noted that "labor no longer refers to the ragged, starving worker bent under the weight of eight huge sacks of coffee."

7. FIESP Circular no. 406, Apr. 8, 1933.

8. The best discussion of Catholic social discourse is Vianna, *Liberalismo e Sindicato*, pp. 155–72. While Catholic social doctrine penetrated industrialist discourse, the theme of rationalization also appears in conservative Catholic circles. According to a leading Catholic thinker of the period, Alceu Amoroso Lima, "The works of Ford have already familiarized us with the new position of the modern economy in the United States, and on this point we are in complete agreement. . . . The modern rationalized economy meets the greatest and most pressing demands of Christian economic ethics" (cited in ibid., p. 166).

9. FIESP Circular no. 514, May 3, 1934; no. 518, May 28, 1934.

10. FIESP Circular no. 675, Nov. 9, 1935.

11. FIESP, "Relatório do Exercício, 1938–39," pp. 97–100, reprinted in Carone, *O Pensamento Industrial*, pp. 497–501. For a discussion of the industrialists' response to the minimum wage, see Howes, "Progressive Conservatism," chap. 9.

12. FIESP Circular no. 709-A, Jan. 23, 1936.

13. On the changing relationship between the Vargas regime and industrialists, see Diniz and Boschi, *Empresariado Nacional*, chap. 2, and Leopoldi, "Industrial Associations," pp. 364–86.

14. Leopoldi, "Industrial Associations," pp. 133, 364–81; Carone, *O Centro Industrial*, p. 173. Simonsen's appointment in mid-1937 to the Federal Council for Foreign Trade marked his new status as a government insider.

15. On the alliance between Simonsen and Morvan, see Leopoldi, "Industrial Associations," p. 59 (n. 1).

16. Howes, "Progressive Conservatism," pp. 117, 218; Clovis de Oliveira, *Do CIESP à FIESP*.

17. In his influential *A Revolução de 1930*, Boris Fausto argued that "industrial development was not the objective of Vargas's political practice between 1930 and 1937" (p. 49). Vargas's industrialization policy did become more coherent after 1936, but I disagree with historians who see Vargas as initially anti-industry. This overstates the impact of the 1936 reciprocal trade agreement with the United States and understates the protective tendencies of the 1934 tariff reform.

18. On the aftermath of the leftist uprising, see French, *Brazilian Workers' ABC*, pp. 62–70.

19. As early as 1919, in an article cowritten for the London *Times*, Simonsen had noted the need for broader technical education in Brazil. See Simonsen and Britto, "Technicos para o Brasil."

20. FIESP Circular no. 756, July 27, 1936; no. 792, Dec. 28, 1936; Simonsen, *A Indústria em Face da Economia Nacional*, p. 36.

21. FIESP Circular no. 762, Aug. 25, 1936.

22. Vargas, *A Nova Política*, 1:25, 2:121–22.

23. For this documentation, see FGV, CPDOC, GC/g 34.11.28, "Organização Geral do Ensino Profissional."

24. FGV, CPDOC, GC/g 34.07.24, "Sôbre Instalação e Organização das Universidades Technica e do Trabalho."

25. FGV, CPDOC, GC/g 34.11.28 (1935).

26. Góes Filho, *O SENAI*, p. 3.

27. Howes ("Progressive Conservatism," p. 201) speculates that Falcão was eager to get a vocational education law on the books before he left for the 1939 International Labor Organization meeting in Geneva. This would help explain why the Ministry of Labor drew up the law without consulting FIESP.

28. On the limits imposed on worker activism during these years, see French, *Brazilian Workers' ABC*, pp. 85–92, and Wolfe, *Working Women*, pp. 89–93.

29. Gomes, *A Invenção do Trabalhismo*, p. 235.

30. *MET*, Mar. 1943, p. 4. See also *TG*, May 1940, p. 3.

31. FIESP Circular no. 94/40, Sept. 2, 1940; no. 96/40, Sept. 12, 1940.

32. FGV, CPDOC, GC/g 34.11.28 (1938), "Os Defeitos do Ensino Profissional Brasileiro."

33. On the Nazi vocational training system, see Gillingham, "'Deproletarianization' of German Society."

34. FGV, CPDOC, GC/g 35.12.00, Doc. I-10, "O Ensino Profissional na Alemanha (Berlin, 1938)."

35. The minutes of the meetings of the interministerial commission can be found in FGV, CPDOC, GC/g 38.04.30, P3.

36. FGV, CPDOC, GC/g 38.04.30, Doc. IIa-1. For other accounts of the founding of SENAI, see Leopoldi, "Industrial Associations," pp. 400–407; Alexim, "Origem e Concepção"; and Bryan, "SENAI, Estrutura e Funcionamento."

37. For a report by a commission member that followed the industrialists' line of argument very closely, see FGV, CPDOC, GC/g 38.04.30, Doc. IIa-1, Joaquim Faria Góes Filho, "A Aprendizagem nos Estabelecimentos Industriais."

38. FGV, CPDOC, GC/g 38.04.30, Doc. III-2, "A Viagem de Estudos e Observações ao Estado de São Paulo."

39. Góes Filho, "A Aprendizagem nos Estabelecimentos Industriais," pts. 4–6. Mange's views on the number of workers who required extended training were published in *A Formação dos Técnicos*.

40. *TT*, Nov.–Dec. 1939, p. 4.

41. Góes Filho cited a textile mill in Rio that employed 906 workers, of whom it classified only 50 as skilled ("A Aprendizagem nos Estabelecimentos Industriais").

42. *TG*, Feb. 7, 1936, p. 3. This article is remarkable because it postdates the union's subordination to state control.

43. Simonsen's 1939 memorandum to the interministerial commission has been reprinted in Carone, *O Pensamento Industrial*, pp. 273–84 (emphasis in original). Leopoldi contends that the ongoing dispute over the minimum wage fueled Simonsen's irritation at the new labor legislation ("Industrial Associations," pp. 400–407).

44. FGV, CPDOC, GC/g 38.04.30, Doc. IIa-1 (Nov. 7, 1939).

45. FGV, CPDOC, GC/g 38.04.30, P3, Ata da 11ª Sessão (July 7, 1939).

46. Góes Filho, "A Aprendizagem nos Estabelecimentos Industriais," pt. 6.

47. FGV, CPDOC, GC/g 38.04.30, Doc. IIb-1. For a discussion of this dispute, see Schwartzman, Bomeny, and Costa, *Tempos de Capanema*, p. 238.

48. FGV, CPDOC, GC/g 38.04.30, Doc. IIa-1, letter from Simonsen to Capanema, July 7, 1940.

49. Schmitter, *Interest Conflict*, p. 184.

50. FGV, CPDOC, GC/g 41.09.13, Doc. I-1 (Sept. 13, 1941).

51. Ibid. Since Lodi chaired the commission, the report appeared under his name, but it was clearly authored by Simonsen.

52. FGV, CPDOC, GC/g 41.09.13, Doc. I-2.

53. Schwartzman, Bomeny, and Costa, *Tempos de Capanema*, p. 239.

54. FGV, CPDOC, GC/g 41.09.13, Doc. I-15.

55. FGV, CPDOC, GC/g 41.09.13, Doc. I-6 (July 21, 1942).

56. On the conflict between the industrialists and Capanema and Fuchs, see Schwartzman, Bomeny, and Costa, *Tempos de Capanema*, pp. 239–41.

57. Góes Filho, *O SENAI*, p. 15.

58. FGV, CPDOC, GC/g 41.09.13, Doc. I-8 (Aug. 6, 1942).

59. Simonsen frequently referred to the need to "orient the more backward employers" ("O Direito Social," p. 258).

60. During these years, the upper echelons of the union hierarchy (the federations) were controlled by *pelegos*, or ministerial appointees with little support at the grassroots level. See French, *Brazilian Workers' ABC*, pp. 88–92.

61. FIESP Circular no. 59/43, Apr. 7, 1943; no. 120/43, July 20, 1943.

62. SIFTSP Circular no. 2,307, Sept. 11, 1943. John French claims that employers continued to oppose labor unions, but such opposition was undoubtedly less widespread and less vehement than in the past (*Brazilian Workers' ABC*, chap. 3).

63. *TG*, Feb. 1943, p. 4; May 1943, p. 1; Arquivo FIESP (São Paulo), Ata da 17ª Reunião Semanal, June 17, 1942, courtesy of Joel Wolfe. For Simonsen's speech at the banquet, see "Confraternização Social," pp. 270–74.

64. FGV, CPDOC, AMF/j 42.01.31 (Recortes de Jornais), *Correio Paulistano*, July 15, 1943.

65. Pereira, *Estrutura e Expansão*, pp. 27–30; Baer, *Industrialization*, pp. 26–34.

66. French, *Brazilian Workers' ABC*, p. 141; Gomes, *A Invenção do Trabalhismo*, pp. 242–68. For a grim portrait of labor conditions during the war, see Wolfe, *Working Women*, pp. 101–8.

67. Wolfe, *Working Women*, pp. 95–96; FGV, CPDOC, AMF 00.00.00/10, Alexandre Marcondes Filho, "Três Meses de Palestras com Operários do Brasil," palestra II (Jan. 29, 1942).

68. Howes, "Progressive Conservatism," p. 193.

69. FIESP Circular no. 160/42, Sept. 4, 1942; no. 201/42, Oct. 24, 1942. The latter includes a list of 170 paulista firms that "voluntarily" conceded wage increases. During this same period, *O Trabalhador Gráfico* printed an appeal to owners ("Higher wages and more production are the imperatives of the moment") to raise wages voluntarily. See *TG*, Mar. 1942, p. 1.

70. *TG*, Jan.–Feb. 1944, p. 3; Arquivo FIESP, "Relatório" (1942), 1:36, cited in Wolfe, *Working Women*, p. 105.

71. Sáenz Leme, *A Ideologia dos Industriais*, p. 154; Gomes, *A Invenção do Trabalhismo*, p. 264.

72. FGV, CPDOC, VF/c 37.11.12, P14, Docs. 5, 13, 14; AMF/j 42.01.31 (Recortes de Jornais); AMF 45.10.20, Doc. 1, "Postulados da Proteção Jurídico-social do Trabalhador no Brasil," pp. 66–67. Directing SAPS was Edison Pitombo Cavalcanti, who had served on the interministerial commission.

73. French, *Brazilian Workers' ABC*, p. 92; FGV, CPDOC, AMF/j 42.01.31, *Folha da Manhã*, July 14, 1943. FIESP received a request for financial support from the Cooperativa de Consumo dos Trabalhadores Sindicalizados do Município de São Paulo. See FIESP Circular no. 30/44, Mar. 7, 1944.

74. SIFTSP Circular no. 2,097, Mar. 25, 1942; no. 2,110, Apr. 22, 1942; PH, Correspondência da Light, Subsérie 24 (General Orders), Apr. 23, 1941; Arquivo FIESP, Ata da 11ª Reunião Semanal, Mar. 20, 1946, courtesy of Joel Wolfe.

75. Wolfe, *Working Women*, p. 120; FGV, CPDOC, AMF/j 43.12.24, *A Noite*, Nov. 27, 1944; FIESP Circular no. 39/45, Feb. 21, 1945.

76. On this "opening," see French, *Brazilian Workers' ABC*, pp. 93–99, and Gomes, *A Invenção do Trabalhismo*, pp. 201–2.

77. Carone, *O Pensamento Industrial*, p. 377.

78. Ibid., p. 369.

79. Dean, *Industrialization of São Paulo*, p. 235.

80. FIESP Circular no. 146/45, Aug. 7, 1945. This notice reprinted a lecture by Mariano Ferraz entitled "Equipping Industry for International Competition."

81. FIESP Circular no. 3/45, Jan. 3, 1945. Bouças's position was similar to that of Eugênio Gudin, the economist and businessman with whom Simonsen carried on a highly public debate over economic planning and state intervention. Simonsen's writings in favor of economic planning can be found in *Evolução Industrial*, pp. 281–342. On the Gudin-Simonsen debate, see Vieira, "O Pensamento Industrialista de Roberto Simonsen," pp. 125–55.

82. See, for example, Simonsen, "As Finanças e a Indústria," and Aldo Mário de Azevedo, "Na Era do Machinismo."

83. Simonsen, "O Direito Social," pp. 257–59.

84. FGV, CPDOC, AMF/j 43.12.24, *A Noite*, Nov. 27, 1944.

85. FIESP Circular no. 19/45, Jan. 19, 1945; SIFTSP Circular no. 2,516, Feb. 5, 1945.

86. FIESP Circular no. 39/45, Feb. 21, 1945 (emphasis added).

87. Antonacci, "A Vitória da Razão," p. 226; Yasbek, "A Escola de Serviço Social," p. 49.

88. Aldo Mário de Azevedo, "Uma Nova Forma de Zelar," p. 3; FIESP Circular no. 27/45, Jan. 31, 1945.

89. ACIFTSP/SIFTSP, SIFTSP letter to members, Oct. 25, 1945.

90. On the 1945 *abertura*, see Maranhão, *Sindicatos*; Vianna, *Liberalismo e Sindicato*, pp. 243–54; French, *Brazilian Workers' ABC*, pp. 103–51; and Wolfe, *Working Women*, pp. 127–42.

91. Wolfe, *Working Women*, pp. 135–36.

92. Ibid., p. 126; French, *Brazilian Workers' ABC*, pp. 118–22; Skidmore, *Politics in Brazil*, pp. 48–53.

93. Wolfe, *Working Women*, p. 138; FIESP Circular no. 55/45, Mar. 16, 1945; SIFTSP Circular no. 2,576, May 30, 1945; PH, Correspondência da Light, Subsérie 24 (General Orders), Jan. 10, 1945. SIFT hoped a wage increase would also reduce the shortage of skilled workers.

94. SIFTSP Circular no. 2,599, July 11, 1945; no. 2,611, July 25, 1945. It is unclear whether the reference to women's labor means domestic or paid labor, but it probably meant the latter given the large number of adult women employed in textile factories.

95. The two most prominent paulista industrialists to join the anti-Vargas (UDN) forces in 1945 were José Ermírio de Moraes and Antônio de Souza Noschese. Simonsen, Lafer, Morvan, and most other major figures joined the PSD. See Leopoldi, "Industrial Associations," pp. 381–86.

96. Howes, "Progressive Conservatism," p. 311 (n. 25); McCann, *Brazilian-American Alliance*, pp. 448, 464; Leopoldi, "Industrial Associations," p. 385. A letter that circulated in January 1945, supposedly from Lodi to Simonsen, urged that industrialists do everything possible to keep Vargas in power. This letter is now widely regarded as apocryphal, but there is no doubt that Lodi was a committed Vargas supporter.

97. Robert Howes interviewed Rômulo de Almeida, an economist who was closely acquainted with Simonsen and Lodi during these years and who denied their involvement with the *queremistas* ("Progressive Conservatism," p. 311 [n. 25]).

98. On the brigadier's presidential candidacy, see Skidmore, *Politics in Brazil*, pp. 49–60, and French, *Brazilian Workers' ABC*, pp. 113–30.

99. "Liberdade Sindical," *MET*, Jan. 1946, p. 1; Wolfe, *Working Women*, pp. 137–38.

100. FIESP Circular no. 42/46, Feb. 20, 1946; no. 45/46, Feb. 25, 1946.

101. FIESP Circular no. 39/46, Feb. 15, 1946. This "urgent" notice called for a general assembly to discuss the unions' proposals. It asked firms to send representatives with the power to implement any agreement reached. On the struggle over the metallurgical workers' union, see Maranhão, *Sindicatos*, pp. 47–49, and Wolfe, *Working Women*, p. 137.

102. FIESP Circular no. 45/46, Feb. 25, 1946. This announcement was published in several newspapers and quoted a labor federation official who supported FIESP's position.

103. Wolfe, *Working Women*, p. 138.

104. SIFTSP Circular no. 2,804, Apr. 22, 1946.

105. FIESP Circular no. 45/46, Feb. 25, 1946; no. 46/46, Mar. 8, 1946; no. 57/46, Mar. 23, 1946. These measures included a six-month prohibition on textile exports to increase supplies.

106. The text of the "Carta da Paz Social" has been reprinted in Carone, *A Quarta República*, pp. 399–403.

107. FIESP Circular no. 54/46, Mar. 13, 1946.

108. FIESP Circular no. 75/46, Apr. 23, 1946; no. 83/46, May 2, 1946; AG, Correspondência, P474, June 4, 1946.

109. For a similar account of SESI's founding, see Leopoldi, "Industrial Associations," pp. 407–14.

110. FIESP Circular no. 122/46, July 6, 1946.

111. The text of Simonsen's inaugural address has been reprinted as "O Problema Social no Brasil."

112. Anti-Vargas forces in congress regarded SENAI and SESI (and their commercial counterparts, SENAC and SESC) as spawn of the Estado Novo and repeatedly tried to have the state take them over. See interview with Luiz Gonzaga Ferreira, Aug. 10, 1989, PM.

113. Simonsen, "O Problema Social no Brasil," p. 452.

114. On Siciliano's plan, see Chapter 2.

115. SIFTSP Circular no. 2,611, July 25, 1945; FIESP Circular no. 162/46, Sept. 28, 1946.

Chapter Four

1. Morris L. Cooke, the Taylorite chief of the American Technical Mission to Brazil during World War II, left his impressions of the Brazilian "manpower" situation in *Brazil on the March*, pp. 53–86.

2. For an official history of SENAI's early years, see Stênio Lopes, *Uma Saga da Criatividade Brasileira*. The history of SENAI–São Paulo is chronicled in PM, *O Giz e a Graxa*.

3. Interviews with Ophir Corrêa de Toledo, May 10, 1990, and Sebastião da Luz, Apr. 5, 1990, PM; interview by author with Pedro Senna, July 3, 1986; Mange, *Missão*, p. 6.

4. PM, SENAI-SP, "Relatório do Departamento Regional de São Paulo, Sept. 1942–Dec. 1943" (1944), pp. 13–20.

5. Luderitz, in a 1944 meeting of SENAI's national council, mentioned that the organization paid a "gratuity" to employees of IAPI to speed the transmission of its funds (BCNI, Atas do Conselho Nacional do SENAI, Nov. 22, 1944).

6. Interview by author with Lázaro Maia, July 18, 1986.

7. SENAI-SP, "Relatório" (1944), p. 1.

8. Ibid., p. 24. Female employment in the metallurgical trades did increase during the war. Joel Wolfe notes that women even moved into jobs as machinists and other positions previously reserved for men (*Working Women*, p. 103).

9. Mange, *Planejamento*, pp. 14–16.

10. Interview with Oswaldo de Barros Santos, June 12, 1990, PM.

11. SENAI-SP, "Relatório" (1944), p. 3.

12. SENAI-SP, "Relatório" (1945), p. 91. For similar remarks on health and vision problems of Brazilian workers, see Cooke, *Brazil on the March*, p. 75.

13. SENAI-SP, "Relatório" (1944), pp. 54–55.

14. "Formação" is difficult to translate. It refers to education but also implies general development and socialization.

15. SENAI-SP, "Relatório" (1945), p. 75; Mange, *Planejamento*, p. 14.

16. SENAI-SP, *Curso de Aperfeiçoamento para Instrutores: Noções de Psicologia do Adolescente*. The probable author, Antônio d'Avila, was one of Mange's closest disciples.

17. This emphasis on socialization was strongest, by far, in São Paulo. At a 1945 meeting, the national council debated setting a ceiling on social assistance expenditures, with some members insisting that apprenticeship should be given first priority, indicating that not everyone involved in SENAI saw the two as intrinsically linked. See BCNI, Atas do Conselho Nacional do SENAI, May 16, 1945, pp. 2–3. A subsequent resolution affirmed that social assistance programs revealed the "humanitarian and patriotic sentiments" of the directors. At the same time, it stated that other departments need not imitate the example of SENAI–São Paulo. See BCNI, Atas, May 17, 1945, pp. 4–5.

18. "O Aluno SENAI," *Informativo SENAI*, no. 11 (Sept. 1946): 3. D'Avila's notion of "typical" (*comúm*) did not reflect numerical preponderance since working-class adolescents were far more numerous in Brazil than the members of the middle class used by the author as a point of reference. "Normative" more accurately describes what d'Avila meant by "typical."

19. AG, Correspondência, P109, Mar. 31, 1948. Berlinck, the manager of a textile factory in the interior, made these remarks in a confidential letter to SESI's director.

20. Euvaldo Lodi also called for increased immigration but was careful to note the virtues of Brazilian workers ("Precisamos de 20,000 Técnicos," *Boletim SENAI*, no. 10 [May 1946]: 36).

21. Interview by author with Pedro Senna, July 3, 1986.

22. FGV, CPDOC, GC/g 35.12.00, Doc. I-10, "O Ensino Profissional na Alemanha," pp. 13–14; SENAI-SP, *Curso de Aperfeiçoamento para Instrutores: Elaboração e Aplicação da SMO*. This notion of socialization through discipline resembles the "technologies of power" discussed by Foucault in *Discipline and Punish*.

23. Lodi, *Positivos os Indícios*, p. 5. See also "Disciplina e Conduta como Fatores de Progresso nas Escolas de Aprendizagem," *Revista SENAI*, nos. 30–31 (Jan.–Feb. 1948): 5–6. For a critical analysis of SENAI that emphasizes socialization through manual instruction, see Frigotto, "Fazendo pelas Mãos," pp. 38–45.

24. Interview with Sebastião da Luz, Apr. 5, 1990, PM.

25. Interview with Luiz Gonzaga Ferreira, Aug. 10, 1989, PM.

26. Interview with Ophir Corrêa de Toledo, May 10, 1990, PM.

27. Ibid.; interview by author with Pedro Senna, July 3, 1986; interview with Luiz Gonzaga Ferreira, Aug. 10, 1989, PM.

28. Interview with Sebastião da Luz, Apr. 5, 1990, PM.

29. SENAI-SP, "Relatório" (1945), p. 10.

30. Ibid., p. 11. The dropout rate was higher in the CTMs, but this was of little con-

cern to Mange, who regarded them as lying outside SENAI's real agenda.

31. Ibid.; "O Maior Entrave do SENAI," *Boletim SENAI*, no. 10 (May 1946): 8–9. On the high dropout rate, see Chapter 6.

32. "O Aluno SENAI," *Informativo SENAI*, no. 11 (Sept. 1946): 4; "A Mão de Obra Juvenil e o SENAI," *Boletim SENAI*, no. 10 (May 1946): 22–24; FIESP Circular no. 76/43, May 12, 1943. In the latter document, Pupo Nogueira informed his fellow industrialists that "thanks to SENAI we will have technical instruction molded on a foundation that encompasses the very soul of the worker."

33. Wolfe, *Working Women*, p. 103.

34. A. C. Pacheco e Silva, "A Fadiga Industrial," *Boletim SENAI*, no. 16 (Nov. 1946): 11–13.

35. SENAI-SP, "Relatório" (1945), p. 29.

36. *Informativo SENAI*, no. 60 (Jan. 1951): 2.

37. *Informativo SENAI*, no. 13 (Nov. 1946): 2–3. An article on a SENAI school in Rio noted that "there are trades that are indicated for young female apprentices. In the graphic arts course, the job of stapling [*grampeação*] is an example" (*Revista SENAI*, no. 41 [Dec. 1948]: 31). For the comments of an observer from the U.S. Women's Bureau on the limited opportunities offered by SENAI to women workers, see Wolfe, *Working Women*, pp. 103–4.

38. Joan W. Scott has written extensively on the historical construction of the "woman worker" category (*Gender and the Politics of History*, esp. pp. 93–177). See also Barbara Weinstein, "As Mulheres Trabalhadoras."

39. SENAI-SP, "Relatório" (1946), p. 35. See also "O Aluno SENAI," *Informativo SENAI*, no. 11 (Sept. 1946): 3, in which the vocational courses were applauded for protecting youths "from the dangers of the street."

40. Interview with Oswaldo de Barros Santos, July 12, 1990, PM; SENAI-SP, "Relatório" (1945), p. 14.

41. SENAI-SP, "Relatório" (1946), pp. 7–8.

42. Interview with Luiz Gonzaga Ferreira, Aug. 10, 1989, PM. According to Gonzaga Ferreira, SENAI rushed to build facilities before the promulgation of a new constitution in 1946.

43. AA, SESI, P1, Feb. 12, 1948.

44. "Formação de Pessoal para a Indústria Têxtil," *Revista SENAI*, no. 51 (Oct. 1949): 68–72.

45. "Cursos de Psicologia Industrial," *Boletim SENAI*, no. 5 (Oct.–Dec. 1945): 12–15; FGV, CPDOC, LF/pi 42.11.09, "Relações Humanas no Trabalho."

46. FIESP Circular no. 182/45, Sept. 25, 1945; no. 29/46, Jan. 26, 1946. FIESP notified its members of the availability of these "visiting industrial psychologists" and mentioned that SENAI had made sure to train psychologists of both sexes.

47. Interviews with Oswaldo de Barros Santos, June 12, July 12, 1990, PM. On broader trends in the field of psychology, see Burnham, *Paths into American Culture*, esp. pp. 69–112.

48. SENAI-SP, *Curso de Aperfeiçoamento para Instrutores: Noções de Psicologia do Adolescente*, pp. 27, 37–38. Antônio d'Avila, who worked for Mange at the Centro Ferroviário, developed the course material. Many SENAI officials interned in the

United States and reported on the use of industrial psychology by North American corporations. See PM, Oswaldo de Barros Santos, "Relatório Final de Viagem de Estudos aos Estados Unidos, 1956–57."

49. Interview with Oswaldo de Barros Santos, July 12, 1990, PM.

50. Stênio Lopes, *Uma Saga da Criatividade Brasileira*, pp. 187–88.

51. Simonsen, "Os Objetivos da Engenharia."

52. Interview with Ernest Mange, June 19, 1990, PM. Ernest, Roberto's son, described "Poli" during the 1940s as "archaic, obsolete."

53. Interview with Gentil Palmiro, Sept. 28, 1989, PM.

54. *Folha da Manhã*, Aug. 8, 1940, reprinted in Mange, *A Formação dos Técnicos*.

55. For a report on a leading technical school that details its many problems, see FGV, CPDOC, GC/g 36.10.07, Doc. IV-16, "Relatório da Escola Técnica de São Paulo" (1942). The report mentioned only six students who completed the course in that year.

56. João Luderitz, "Educação Técnica no Brasil," *Boletim SENAI*, no. 3 (Apr.–June 1945): 7–8; "Precisamos de 20,000 Técnicos," *Boletim SENAI*, no. 10 (May 1946): 36.

57. "Precisamos de 20,000 Técnicos," *Boletim SENAI*, no. 10 (May 1946): 36.

58. "Instalada a Confederação Nacional do Comércio," *Boletim SENAI*, no. 9 (Apr. 1946): 29–33.

59. "O Reequipamento da Indústria Têxtil," *Revista SENAI*, no. 51 (Oct. 1949): 3–16, 47, 89. A table included in this issue showed productivity per worker in the textile industry declining from 1924 to 1940 but increasing immediately after World War II.

60. M. Salles, "Organização: Industrialização," *Boletim SENAI*, no. 16 (Nov. 1946): 9–11.

61. "A Fabricação da Maquinaria Têxtil: Uma Imperiosa Necessidade," *Boletim SENAI*, no. 10 (May 1946): 14–15. This author was inverting Simonsen's logic: instead of arguing that industrial development guaranteed better wages and a higher standard of living, he claimed that low wages would guarantee industrial development.

62. McCann, *Brazilian-American Alliance*, p. 448.

63. On Dutra's postwar economic policies, see Skidmore, *Politics in Brazil*, pp. 69–73, and Baer, *Industrialization*, pp. 45–48. On U.S. influence in this period, see Haines, *Americanization of Brazil*.

64. Draibe, *Rumos e Metamorfoses*, pp. 138–76.

65. "A Organização Científica do Trabalho, o Taylorismo, a Estandardização," *Síntese*, no. 4 (July 1948): 17; "Mentalidade Industrial e Educação," *Síntese*, no. 5 (Sept. 1948): 8–11.

66. The initial response of industrialists to the founding of SESI is discussed in greater detail in Chapter 5.

67. Simonsen, "O Problema Social no Brasil," p. 449.

68. "Instalada a Confederação Nacional do Comércio," *Boletim SENAI*, no. 9 (Apr. 1946): 29–33; "Carta da Paz Social, 1946," in Carone, *A Quarta República*, pp. 399–403.

69. Virtually all authors who have studied the immediate postwar period agree about this. See, for example, Maranhão, *Sindicatos*, chap. 2; French, *Brazilian Workers' ABC*, chap. 5; and Wolfe, *Working Women*, pp. 123–24. For a broader perspective, see Bethell and Roxborough, "Latin America between the Second World War and the Cold War."

70. French, *Brazilian Workers' ABC*, pp. 146–49.

71. "Carta da Paz Social," in Carone, *A Quarta República*, p. 402.

72. Roberto Simonsen, "Os Princípios Morais de Orientação do SESI," *Boletim SENAI*, no. 17 (Dec. 1946): 13.

73. Simonsen, "O Problema Social no Brasil," p. 444.

74. Ibid.

75. Maranhão, *Sindicatos*, p. 48.

76. Ibid., p. 58; FIESP Circular no. 61/46, Mar. 27, 1946.

77. Maranhão, *Sindicatos*, p. 84; Carone, *A Quarta República*, p. 11. The latter event became known as the Massacre of the Largo do Carioca.

78. Maranhão, *Sindicatos*, p. 58. FIESP sought to assure its membership that it was working closely with the federal government and state police. See FIESP Circular no. 42/46, Feb. 20, 1946; no. 46/46, Mar. 8, 1946.

79. Simonsen, "As Classes Produtoras," pp. 455–58. On Simonsen's poor election returns in the industrial suburbs of São Paulo, see French, "Workers and the Rise of Adhemarista Populism."

80. Gomes, *A Invenção do Trabalhismo*, p. 290.

81. *SJ*, no. 1 (Mar. 31, 1948): 6; *BMIDET*, no. 1 (May 1948): 7; SENAI-SP, *Morvan Dias de Figueiredo*.

82. Maranhão, *Sindicatos*, p. 76; *TG*, Mar. 1947, p. 4. The latter lambasted Morvan's two predecessors, Marcondes Filho and Negrão de Lima, but reserved its harshest criticism for Morvan's "short but calamitous administration." The term "ministro-tubarão" (which I have translated as "profiteer-minister") implies that all manufacturers made windfall profits during the war. "Tubarão" literally means "shark."

83. Skidmore, *Politics in Brazil*, p. 67; Telles, *O Movimento Sindical*, p. 40. The latter study claims that Morvan ordered interventions in some 400 unions, but the lower figure is probably more accurate.

84. Officially, the PCB had a no-strike policy in 1945–46, but many militants ignored the party line and played prominent roles in the movement. See Wolfe, *Working Women*, p. 121.

85. French, *Brazilian Workers' ABC*, p. 234.

86. *TG*, Mar. 1947, p. 4.

87. *TG*, Feb. 7, 1950, p. 1.

88. Ill health is often a convenient excuse for political resignations, but it may have been a genuine motive in this case. Morvan's health deteriorated rapidly and he died less than two years after leaving the ministry. Apparently, Dutra offered the position of interim minister to Armando de Arruda Pereira, who declined it. See *SJ*, Nov. 30, 1948, p. 1.

89. On the changing trends in strike activity from 1945 to 1950, see Sandoval, *Social Change*, pp. 81–82.

90. Simonsen, *As Atividades do Serviço Social da Indústria no Estado de São Paulo*; FIESP Circular no. 165/46, Sept. 28, 1946; SESI-SP, Divisão de Abastecimento, *SESI—18 Anos*, pp. 9–30. About a third of these posts were originally run by COs, SAPS, and the labor unions and then taken over by SESI.

91. AA, SESI, P1, Aug. 12, 1947. Light's director of public relations described the SESI services as having been organized in an "efficient and apolitical manner." Another

Light official, based in Santos, noted that the nearby SESI food post sold goods at prices well below those in local markets. See AA, SESI, P1, July 18, 1947. But Light refused for many years to contribute to SESI (see Chapter 5).

92. AC, SESI-SP, Atas do Conselho Regional, July 10, 1947. See also Alexander, *Labor Relations*, p. 108.

93. *MET*, Jan. 1947, p. 6; Mar. 1947, p. 9. The author was Aldo Lombardi. Another article (*MET*, Feb. 1947, p. 2), signed by a "Nortista," complained that the walls of the union headquarters were "plastered with propaganda pamphlets" from SESI. A study of worker politics in the 1940s notes the sudden appearance of SESI posts in working-class districts when Simonsen and Arruda Pereira began campaigning for political office. See French, "Workers and the Rise of Adhemarista Populism," pp. 11–12.

94. AA, SESI, P1, Mar. 24, 1947 (letter from Arruda Pereira, acting president of SESI-SP, to "Senhores Industriais"); Reis, *O Serviço Social da Indústria*.

95. SESI-SP, Divisão de Alimentação, *SESI—18 Anos*, pp. 9–11.

96. Ibid. Despite SESI officials' claims that theirs was not a "paternalistic" organization, this account of trying to get workers to eat their vegetables certainly smacks of a parent-child relationship.

97. AC, SESI-SP, Atas do Conselho Regional, Oct. 24, 1947.

98. AA, SESI, P1, Aug. 2, 1946.

99. AC, SESI-SP, Atas do Conselho Regional, Mar. 8, 1949. In 1956 the SESI official responsible for overseeing food posts in São Paulo, Roberto Simonsen Sobrinho, argued that they should be dismantled once local merchants learned the value of selling goods cheaply. See interview with Roberto Simonsen Sobrinho, Apr. 12, 1956, AP.

100. AC, SESI-SP, Atas do Conselho Regional, Jan. 14, 1948. Council member Manoel da Costa Santos repeatedly urged the SESI administration to provide more funds for "concrete" benefits.

101. Yasbek, "A Escola de Serviço Social." Yasbek emphasizes the school's conservative bent, but at least one early graduate characterized the "priest-instructors" as "very progressive." See interview by author with Maria Antonieta Guerriero, June 10, 1986.

102. *SJ*, June 30, 1955; interview with Hugo Guimarães Malheiros, Apr. 13, 1956, AP.

103. AG, P3/114 (Instituto de Direito Social), July 20, 1946; SESI-SP, DOS, *SESI—18 Anos*, p. 65. Scholarship students had to submit a certificate of good character from the police and a letter of support from an industrialist in order to qualify for funding. They also had to be men, although exceptions were made if there were no male candidates. See AC, SESI-SP, Atas do Conselho Regional, Oct. 18, 1949.

104. Texts required for the second graduating class of social educators included J. A. de Assis Pacheco, *Prevenção de Dissídios Trabalhistas*; M. Vincent, *Questão Social*; Pio XI, *Sôbre o Comunismo Ateu* and *Sôbre a Restauração e Aperfeiçoamento da Ordem Social*; Leão XIII, *Sôbre a Condição dos Operários*; Bishop Fulton Sheen, *O Problema da Liberdade*; and Victor Kravechenko, *Escolhi a Liberadade*. See AG, P3, July 11, 1947.

105. AG, P3/114, n.d.

106. Interview by author with Hélvio Pinheiro Lima, July 14, 1986. Pinheiro Lima was among the first social educators employed by SESI.

107. AC, SESI-SP, Atas do Conselho Regional, Jan. 23, 1948; FIESP Circular no. 127/47, Sept. 3, 1947.

108. Hélvio Pinheiro Lima claimed that the factory visits "soon became mechanical"

and recalled contacts in clubs and other settings more favorably. See interview by author with Hélvio Pinheiro Lima, July 14, 1986.

109. AC, SESI-SP, Atas do Conselho Regional, Mar. 5, 1948. The students, however, did not necessarily share this view of the sewing courses. See Chapter 6.

110. Interviews by author with Maria Antonieta Guerriero, June 10, 1986, and Hélvio Pinheiro Lima, July 14, 1986.

111. AG, P31/615 (Cia. Brasileira Linhas p/Coser), Aug. 25, 1947.

112. AG, P3/114, May 6, 1947; AC, SESI-SP, Atas do Conselho Regional, Mar. 18, Nov. 4, 1949. A SESI council member complained that too many social educators arrived only after a strike was over.

113. Maranhão, Sindicatos, pp. 52–54.

114. AG, P79/76/553 (Sindicatos), Mar. 28, 1947.

115. Maranhão notes the role of the CGTB and the PCB in raising funds for the strikes (Sindicatos, p. 53).

116. AG, P79/76/553, Mar. 28, 1947.

117. AG, P3/114, May 6, 1947.

118. Jornal de São Caetano, Jan. 12, 1947. My thanks to John French for providing this reference.

119. AG, P3/114, Jan. 13, 1947 (two reports).

120. AG, P3/114, Aug. 2, 1948. There also seems to have been a high turnover rate in DOS's personnel.

121. French, "Workers and the Rise of Adhemarista Populism," pp. 30–31.

122. AG, P79/77, May 5, 1948; P79/83/406, Mar. 10, 1951; P79/149, Oct. 6, 1952; P79/485, July 12, 1950; P79/497, May 26, 1948. The last letter, from the president of the union for workers in the cement industry, was one of several lamenting the death of Roberto Simonsen, "dedicated friend of the workers."

123. AG, P79/77, Oct. 8, 1949.

124. AG, P79/175, Jan. 27, 1953.

125. AG, P79/488/896, Nov. 4, 1949. However, a subsequent request from this union for a very large sum of money was rejected as "simply absurd" (ibid., Sept. 24, 1951).

126. AG, P79/135/473/1647, Dec. 30, 1952.

127. AG, P79/78/1729, Sept. 20, 22, 1952.

128. AG, P79/537/892, Aug. 2, 1951. On the 1951 meatpackers' strike in Barretos, see Welch, "Rural Labor," pp. 148–49.

129. AG, P79/134/2301 (PR 20353), Sept. 15, 1954.

130. AG, P79/77 (PR 031437), Apr. 4, 1949; P79/77/880, May 7, 1951. Similarly, the president of the textile workers' union in Campinas requested funds for a May Day excursion, claiming that the trip would provide an opportunity to promote moral and Christian principles. See AG, P79/78/3304/3305, Mar. 30, 1959.

131. AG, P79/135/735/1649, Oct. 16, 1956. This negative opinion of the metalworkers' union in Mogi das Cruzes contrasts with a positive appraisal during the Dutra years (ibid.,.Aug. 14, 1948).

132. AG, P79/79/1186, Apr. 15, 16, 25, 1952. The angry regional delegate, faced with the unpleasant task of denying the union SESI funds, informed Saad that he had "exchanged ideas" with the president, who had assured him that measures would be taken to avoid the "possible *degradation* of the spectacle into a political 'meeting' as

happened in the previous year" (emphasis added). This vividly illustrates SESI's view of a proper May Day commemoration.

133. AG, P79/1142/1143, June 10, 20, 28, July 11, 1952. Osmar Rodriguez Cruz, of SESI's Serviço de Teatro, recommended a play with "moral content, which educates and morally elevates our workers." SESI also asked unions for favors, such as requesting to use the textile workers' union's playing fields for the Workers' Olympics. See AG, P79/78, Feb. 26, Mar. 12, July 6, 1951, Mar. 19, 1954.

134. AG, P79/77, Dec. 9, 1947 (letters to Saad, Simonsen, and Morvan).

135. AG, P79/77, Oct. 8, 1948 (letter of thanks for the sewing school also signed by officials of the printers' and hatters' unions in Campinas).

136. AG, P79/77, Aug. 1948; PR016640, Aug. 8, 1948.

137. AG, P79/77, PR22306, Oct. 4, 5, 1948.

138. AG, P79/77, PR-1–585, Oct. 7, 20, 1948.

139. AG, P79/77, PR-1–827, Dec. 15, 1948; PR031437, Apr. 4, 8, 25, 1949.

140. Luiz Menossi, the otherwise cooperative president of the construction workers' federation, clashed with SESI when it refused to back his campaign to allow unions to participate in the inspection of construction sites for hazardous conditions. See AG, P79/891, Nov. 23, Dec. 6, 1948, Mar. 11, 23, Apr. 5, 1949.

141. AG, P17/197, Sept. 12, 1951; P17/924/925, July 30, 1951. In 1948 Padre Horta claimed that COs in the state of São Paulo had a total membership of 90,000. See AC, SESI-SP, Atas do Conselho Regional, Feb. 16, 1948. Even if these figures are accurate, many of these members were probably not "workers" by SESI's definition.

142. AG, P17/682/1041, Oct. 17, 1950, Aug. 2, Nov. 29, 1951.

143. AC, SESI-SP, Atas do Conselho Regional, Oct. 24, Dec. 12, 1947.

144. AC, SESI-SP, Atas do Conselho Regional, Dec. 12, 1947.

145. Costa Santos became a major figure in FIESP during the 1950s, promoting industrial policies that combined support for foreign capital with protection of domestic firms. See Leopoldi, "Industrial Associations," pp. 26–64. Leopoldi places him in the "Grupo de Cadetes" that dominated FIESP after the deaths of Morvan and Simonsen.

146. AC, SESI-SP, Atas do Conselho Regional, Aug. 6, Jan. 14, 1948. DOS's share of the 15 million cruzeiro budget was over 3,300,000 cruzeiros.

147. AC, SESI-SP, Atas do Conselho Regional, Jan. 23, 28, 1948. Curiously, no one ever mentioned at council meetings that new union members were not immediately eligible to vote.

148. AC, SESI-SP, Atas do Conselho Regional, Sept. 24, 1948, Apr. 29, 1949. When SESI, SENAI, and IDORT staged a "Campaign to Increase Production," they sought the collaboration of MOP and the COs rather than the regular unions. See FIESP Circular no. 98/48, Aug. 7, 1948.

149. AC, SESI-SP, Atas do Conselho Regional, Nov. 4, 1949.

150. AC, SESI-SP, Atas do Conselho Regional, Nov. 18, Dec. 2, 1949 (closed sessions), Nov. 6, 1950.

151. AC, SESI-SP, Atas do Conselho Regional, July 14, 1950.

152. AC, SESI-SP, Atas do Conselho Regional, Sept. 11, 1951, Feb. 11, 1952.

153. AC, SESI-SP, Atas do Conselho Regional, Nov. 6, 17, 1950.

154. AC, SESI-SP, Atas do Conselho Regional, Nov. 6, 1950, Jan. 5, Apr. 9, Aug. 3, 1951, Mar. 21, Dec. 5, 1952. Saad continued to collaborate with SESI during his supposed estrangement, and the council even voted to send him to Lisbon for a conference on industrial medicine as a reward for his services.

155. Cited in Wolfe, *Working Women*, p. 162.

156. Such activities continued well into the 1950s. Robert Alexander mentions the "intelligence service" operated by DOS in São Paulo during that decade (*Labor Relations*, p. 109).

157. AC, SESI-SP, Atas do Conselho Regional, Jan. 29, 1951.

Chapter Five

1. Robert Alexander, "General Impressions of Labor-Management Relations in São Paulo," Apr. 28, 1956, p. 1, AP. For the strong coincidence in views held by industrialist and federal labor officials, see José Segadas Viana, "Problemas da Mão de Obra no Brasil," Oct. 19, 1945, Brazil, 1945–49, Roll 32, RG59, NA. Segadas Viana headed the Union Orientation Division in the Ministry of Labor.

2. Schmitter claims that industrialists in several northeastern states organized themselves into federations so that they could gain access to the funds and patronage resources SESI and SENAI offered (*Interest Conflict*, pp. 182–86).

3. Manoel da Costa Santos, who served on the regional council of SESI–São Paulo since its founding, often complained of the lack of interaction between the FIESP leadership and the "typical" factory owner. See AC, SESI-SP, Atas do Conselho Regional, Jan. 23, May 7, 1948, Dec. 13, 1949, Apr. 10, 1950.

4. The claim that SENAI (more than SESI) was founded in response to pressure from workers themselves was frequently expressed in the labor press. See "Discurso Proferido pelo Sr. Mário Sobral," *MET*, Sept. 1948, p. 4. A more militant metallurgical workers' union official, Affonso Delellis, expressed the same opinion. See interview by author with Affonso Delellis, July 18, 1986. This indicates the unions' more positive response to SENAI.

5. Alexander, "General Impressions," p. 1.

6. Ibid.

7. AC, SESI-SP, Atas do Conselho Regional, Sept. 21, 1949; AG, Processos, Correspondência c/Cia. Nitro-Química Brasileira, P34/616, Sept. 17, 1949. An earlier report by a North American observer also noted the lack of employer enthusiasm for SENAI (SESI had yet to be founded) and described the large firms as especially indifferent. See C. T. Stewart, "Report to U.S. Office of Education," July 12, 1945, pp. 14–17, Brazil, 1945–49, Roll 27, RG59, NA.

8. Simonsen, "O Problema Social," pp. 451–52.

9. Interview with Luiz Gonzaga Ferreira, Aug. 10, 1989, PM; EE, vol. 4 ("Motivos de Abandono da Escola"); Jandyra Rodríguez, "Os Pequenos Trabalhadores," *BMIDET*, no. 1 (May 1948): 20.

10. Interview with Raphael Noschese, June 25, 1990, PM; interview with Guillermo Sauer and Fred Sauer, Mar. 14, 1956, AP.

11. SIFTSP Circular no. 2,158, June 23, 1942; no. 2,216, Dec. 22, 1942; no. 2,235, Feb. 17, 1943. It is significant that all three firms consulted with IDORT member Mário Pagano, who was "in constant contact" with Mange.

12. Interview with Oswaldo de Barros Santos, July 12, 1990, PM; interview by author with Pedro Senna, July 3, 1986.

13. Interview with Gentil Palmiro, Sept. 28, 1989, PM. This account is interesting because it foregrounds the good character of SENAI graduates rather than the practical skills they acquired.

14. Probably the minority of students who completed the SENAI course were highly motivated. In 1945 SENAI-SP enrolled 5,900 students in the two-year apprenticeship program; only 3,354 remained at the end of the year. The dropout rate in the courses for adults was less dramatic: of 2,023 students enrolled, 1,354 remained at the end of the year. See PM, SENAI-SP, "Relatório do Departamento Regional de São Paulo pelo Ano 1945" (1946), p. 57.

15. Interview with Ophir Corrêa de Toledo, May 10, 1990, PM.

16. AA, SENAI, P3, June 18, 1947; EE, vol. 4.

17. PH, *Employment Bureau Annual Report* (1943), p. 24. Until the founding of SENAI, Light did not distinguish between skilled and semiskilled workers.

18. PH, Correspondência da Light, Subsérie 24 (General Orders), July 8, 1910. Light did set up smaller-scale training courses for adults in the 1930s. See AA, SENAI, P1, July 19, 1939.

19. AA, SENAI, P1, July 14, 19, 1939.

20. AA, SENAI, P1, Jan. 8, 1943. Decree-law no. 4,936 was issued on November 7, 1942, specifically placing transport enterprises within SENAI's domain.

21. AA, SENAI, P1, Jan. 13, 1943; PH, Correspondência da Light, Subsérie 24 (General Orders), Jan. 5, 1945.

22. AA, SENAI, P1, Apr. 4, 1944.

23. AA, SENAI, P1, Jan. 29, 1945.

24. AA, SENAI, P1, July 7, 1948.

25. AA, SENAI, P2, June 30, 1945, Apr. 24, 1946.

26. AA, SENAI, P2, Oct. 11, 1945; P3, Aug. 5, 1946.

27. Ibid. An apprentice who was the son of a worker hired in 1922 was discovered to be epileptic. The personnel director was advised to fire the apprentice personally and to give the boy one month's severance pay. See AA, SENAI, P3, Oct. 23, 1947.

28. AA, SENAI, P3, Mar. 1, 1948; P4, July 27, 1948.

29. AA, SENAI, P4, July 23, Nov. 8, 1948; P5, Oct. 8, 1949.

30. AA, SENAI, P5, Feb. 7, 1949.

31. AA, SENAI, P5, Aug. 8, 1951.

32. AA, SENAI, P5, Feb. 25, 1953.

33. AA, SENAI, P3, Jan. 9, 1947.

34. *O Eletricitário*, Oct.–Nov. 1962, p. 5.

35. AA, SENAI, P4, July 27, Aug. 23, 1948; *Informativo SENAI*, no. 35 (Nov. 1948): 1–3; Luiz Pereira, *Classe Operária*, pp. 105–8.

36. Interview by author with Pedro Francisco de Oliveira, June 5, 1986; interview with Sebastião da Luz, Apr. 5, 1990, PM.

37. AA, SENAI, P1, Feb. 8, 1944; P3, Aug. 14, 1946.

38. EE, 1:31–33.

39. Even within the targeted sectors, there was considerable variation. Mecânica Pesada, a French-owned firm with only 378 production workers, had 36 students (well beyond its quota) enrolled in SENAI. In contrast, the Companhia Fiação e Tecelagem São Pedro de Itú, a textile firm with over 1,000 workers, had only 2 students enrolled. See AG, Processos, P392/968, Dec. 20, 1951; P1499/3619, Sept. 21, 1959. See also Robert Alexander, "Observations on SENAI in São Paulo," Apr. 27, 1956, AP.

40. EE, 6:23–25.

41. Ibid., p. 11. For other employers' views of SENAI, see interviews with Kurt Renner, May 2, 1956; Maj. Joaquim Gonçalves Moreira, Apr. 4, 1956; Marcelo Coimbra Tavares, Mar. 27, 1956; Guillermo Sauer and Fred Sauer, Mar. 14, 1956; and Severino Mariz Filho, Aug. 6, 1965, AP; and interview by author with Onofre da Silva, June 5, 1986.

42. See Chapter 4.

43. *SESI-Jornal* ran a series entitled "Figuras Exponenciais do SESI." See *SJ*, Mar. 31, 1948, pp. 3–4 (on Simonsen and Arruda Pereira); Aug. 31, 1948, p. 3 (on Ferraz and Devisate); and May 31, 1949, p. 3 (on Rodrigues de Azevedo).

44. AC, SESI-SP, Atas do Conselho Regional, Jan. 23, May 7, 1948, Dec. 13, 1949, Apr. 10, 1950.

45. AC, SESI-SP, Atas do Conselho Regional, Oct. 24, 1947.

46. The results of another survey conducted in 1948 seem to have been suppressed, suggesting that the responses were generally negative. See AC, SESI-SP, Atas do Conselho Regional, Jan. 7, 1949.

47. *BI*, no. 31 (May 8, 1950): 23–25; *SJ*, Mar. 31, 1950, p. 11. SESI omitted the opinions of 17 percent of the companies surveyed because they were in a state of liquidation.

48. AG, Processos, P125/588 (Cia. Taubaté Industrial), Mar. 28, 1950; interview with Olavo Previatti, Apr. 27, 1956, AP.

49. AG, Processos, P34/616, Aug. 4, 1947.

50. AG, Processos, P34/616, Sept. 29, 1947 (emphasis in original).

51. The Jafet Ipiranga mill apparently installed a few services to reduce its payments. See AC, SESI-SP, Atas do Conselho Regional, Nov. 10, 1950.

52. AC, SESI-SP, Atas do Conselho Regional, Sept. 2, 21, 1949. In the case of José Ermírio, party politics may have been a factor. He was a staunch supporter of the UDN, a party promoting private investment and initiative, whereas most FIESP officials were connected to the PSD and had ties to Vargas. See Leopoldi, "Industrial Associations," p. 209.

53. AC, SESI-SP, Atas do Conselho Regional, May 20, 1949.

54. Reis, *O Serviço Social da Indústria*, p. 20. This space narrowed further since few SESI officials identified its services as a matter of workers' rights.

55. AG, Processos, P34/616, Aug. 26, 1947; "Ata da 3ª Sessao do Conselho Consultivo do DR do SESI," Oct. 21, 1946, in AA, SESI, P1, Aug. 12, 1947.

56. AG, Processos, P34/616, Sept. 17, Oct. 17, 1949.

57. AG, Processos, P142/622, July 28, 1948.

58. SENAI-SP, *Felix Guisard*.

59. AG, Processos, P125/588, May 11, 1949.

60. AC, SESI-SP, Atas do Conselho Regional, Sept. 2, 1949.

61. AA, SESI, P1, Aug. 2, 1946 (enclosure).

62. AA, SESI, P1, July 18, 1947, Jan. 22, Feb. 27, 1948.

63. AA, SESI, P1, Aug. 12, 1947, Feb. 19, 1948. Light knew it might not be able to sustain its position and ordered the personnel department to set aside funds to cover its mounting debt to SESI.

64. AG, Processos, P108/3097, Dec. 7, 1949, Dec. 3, 1952.

65. *SJ*, Feb. 28, 1950, p. 5. The Companhia Minerva Lanifícia was a subsidiary of the Companhia Guilherme Giorgi.

66. See interview by author with former SESI employee, São Paulo, Apr. 19, 1986, for the views of one of several former SESI functionaries who were dismissed for identifying with the workers' perspective.

67. *SJ*, Aug. 31, 1951, p. 6.

68. AC, SESI-SP, Atas do Conselho Regional, Dec. 13, 1949.

69. Simonsen, *As Atividades do Serviço Social da Indústria no Estado de São Paulo*, p. 24.

70. AG, Processos, P9/2573, Dec. 31, 1948.

71. AC, SESI-SP, Atas do Conselho Regional, Sept. 21, 1949. Whereas Robert Alexander in "General Impressions" speculated that smaller firms evaded the SENAI and SESI payments most often, the emphasis in the regional council meetings was on evasion by large, well-established firms.

72. AC, SESI-SP, Atas do Conselho Regional, Oct. 8, Dec. 4, 1959.

73. *BI*, no. 1 (Oct. 10, 1949): 29. By 1956, 40,000 students attended 1,800 courses, and SESI's educational division could not keep up with the growing demand. See interview with Maria Braz, Apr. 12, 1956, AP.

74. AA, SESI, P1, May 8, 1950, Jan. 22, 1954.

75. AA, SESI, P2, Apr. 26, 1960.

76. *TG*, June 1962, p. 3.

77. Dias, *História das Lutas*, pp. 212–13.

78. For a study of Brazilian labor in the 1940s and 1950s that emphasizes these issues, see Wolfe, *Working Women*, chap. 1.

79. Interview by author with João Batista Cândido, June 5, 1986.

80. Most of the statistics in this section are from SENAI; they were published either in the annual reports (*relatórios*) of SENAI–São Paulo (PM) or in the *Boletim Informativo* of FIESP.

81. Wolfe, *Working Women*, p. 83. All workers paid the union tax through a payroll deduction and were legally represented by their category's union, whether they joined or not. Joining entailed formally enrolling and paying dues.

82. The classic studies of Brazilian factory workers in the 1950s and 1960s, such as José Albertino Rodrigues, *Sindicato e Desenvolvimento*, and Juárez Rubens Brandão Lopes, *Sociedade Industrial*, reported indifference to the unions, but these studies sought to contrast the apathy of Brazilian workers to the (idealized) class-consciousness of European workers rather than to compare attitudes in the 1950s to earlier trends.

83. SENAI-SP, "Relatório" (1947), p. 4.

84. *MET*, Mar. 1947, p. 14; June 1947, p. 8; May 1948, pp. 2, 4. On metalworkers in the city of São Paulo under Dutra, see Wolfe, *Working Women*, pp. 136–45.

85. During these years, several union papers ran articles by a Professor Antônio

Cunha with titles such as "Worker: A Good and Simple Soul" that lauded cooperation between employees and employers and praised innovations associated with Frederick W. Taylor. See *MET*, Mar. 1949, p. 7. Dutra's repressive policies are discussed in Sandoval, *Social Change*, pp. 81–82.

86. *MET*, June 1951, p. 5.

87. *TT*, May 1, 1950, p. 11.

88. *TG*, Feb. 7, 1950, p. 2.

89. On unions and the project of national development, see José Albertino Rodrigues, *Sindicato e Desenvolvimento*, pp. 165–72.

90. For a discussion of metalworkers' resistance to scientific management in the United States, see Montgomery, *Fall of the House of Labor*, pp. 180–213.

91. Luiz Pereira, *Classe Operária*, pp. 47–70. For an account of a skilled worker's experiences on the shopfloor, see French, "Social Origins of Resistance."

92. Luiz Pereira, *Classe Operária*, p. 105n. Many union papers published articles about employer abuses of this sort. See *TG*, May 1956, p. 4; *MET*, Sept.–Oct. 1957, p. 3; and *TT*, Aug.–Oct. 1960, p. 7.

93. *TT*, May 1, 1950, p. 10.

94. *TG*, Mar.–Apr. 1946, p. 2; Sept.–Oct. 1946, p. 5.

95. *TG*, Jan. 1954, p. 4.

96. *TG*, Apr.–May 1954, p. 3.

97. *TT*, Jan. 1959, p. 7.

98. *TG*, Dec. 1959, p. 3; Feb. 1960, p. 6; Mar. 1960, p. 3; Mar. 1961, p. 6. In the last article, SENAI's statistics on firms in São Paulo show that, despite expansion, the number of workers declined in such sectors as the clothing industry.

99. For examples of such *desenvolvimentismo*, see "Em Defesa da Indústrial Nacional, Protestamos," *MET*, July 1957, p. 7, and "II Congresso Nacional dos Trabalhadores Metalúrgicos do Brasil," *MET*, Apr. 1959, pp. 8–9. A study of unions in this era that accepts this framework is José Albertino Rodrigues, *Sindicato e Desenvolvimento*, pp. 158–81. For a critique of the ideology of national development, see Franco, "O Tempo das Ilusões."

100. *TG*, Feb. 1960, p. 6.

101. Ibid.; *TG*, Apr. 1960, p. 3; *TT*, Jan. 1959, p. 7. For a discussion of employer opposition to job tenure for workers, see Chapter 8. Multinationals were depicted as spearheading the trend toward replacing workers with computers, but "national" firms, such as Brinquedos Estrela S.A., were also cited.

102. *MET*, Apr. 1959, p. 11.

103. *TT*, Mar. 1960, p. 3; *MET*, Apr. 1959, p. 10.

104. *A Sovela*, Sept. 1960, p. 6.

105. Luiz Pereira, *Classe Operária*, p. 128n. Government regulations required SENAI to reevaluate annually the list of jobs requiring extended training.

106. Even textile workers, who suffered a drastic shift from the skilled to the semi-skilled category, continued to praise SENAI's training courses for their category. See *TT*, Nov. 1959, p. 4.

107. *TT*, Apr. 1959, p. 11; Sept.–Oct. 1957, p. 3; Mar. 1959, p. 4; *O Trabalhador Metalúrgico*, June 1961, p. 5; *A Massa*, May 1960, p. 1; Luiz Pereira, *A Escola numa Área Metropolitana*, pp. 37–38.

108. Olavo Previatti, the conservative leader of the paper workers' federation, made a point of distinguishing SENAI (as "good" and "helpful") from SESI when he criticized the latter. See interview with Olavo Previatti, Apr. 27, 1956, AP.

109. *TG*, Aug. 1965, p. 3. See "Crise vs. Desenvolvimento," *TG*, June–July 1970, p. 11, for a somber account of automation in the printing profession between 1960 and 1970. The article called for a moratorium on training printers.

110. *BI*, no. 7 (Nov. 21, 1949): 1–2.

111. *Diário de São Paulo*, July 5, 1949, reprinted as "Vitória dos Cursos Populares," *SJ*, July 31, 1949, p. 7.

112. *SJ*, Mar. 31, 1949, p. 8.

113. Ibid., p. 7.

114. *SJ*, May 31, 1949, p. 9.

115. *MET*, Jan. 1947, p. 6. The article was oddly titled "Gallows and Ashes of Nuremberg," possibly an allusion to the fascist sympathies of federation officials.

116. *MET*, Jan. 1946, p. 6.

117. On Dutra's intervention into the metalworkers' union, see Wolfe, *Working Women*, p. 137.

118. *SJ*, Sept. 30, 1949, p. 1. The use of the term "eugenic" reflects the Brazilian vogue for linking eugenics with hygiene and sanitation. See Stepan, *"Hour of Eugenics,"* pp. 42–43.

119. *SJ*, Sept. 30, 1949, p. 12.

120. *SJ*, July 31, 1948, p. 6. The identity of the speaker is unclear; the article identifies him as Luiz Menossi, president of the textile workers' federation, but Menossi was an official of the construction workers' federation. Most likely it was Menossi, but the quote could easily have come from the lips of an official of the textile federation such as Melchiades dos Santos.

121. AC, SESI-SP, Atas do Conselho Regional, Sept. 2, 1949. Union officials participating in the first government-approved Congress of Industrial Workers in 1949 praised SESI but urged it to admit worker representatives into its advisory councils.

122. *TG*, May 25, 1948, p. 7; Aug. 1949, p. 3.

123. On May Day traditions prior to the Vargas regime's festivities during the Estado Novo, see Gomes, *A Invenção do Trabalhismo*, p. 235.

124. *MET*, May 1947, p. 1. The article did briefly refer to "respect for the Chicago martyrs"—that is, the anarchists whose deaths were traditionally commemorated on May 1.

125. *TG*, May 25, 1950, p. 9; Edgard Leuenroth, "Qual a significação do 1° de Maio?," *TG*, Apr. 1945, p. 4.

126. AC, SESI-SP, Atas do Conselho Regional, Apr. 22, 1948. The sports competitions were known as the "Jôgos Operários." "Olympics" is my term.

127. *BI*, no. 37 (Mar. 4, 1957); *VCC*, Feb. 1951, p. 4.

128. AA, SESI, P1, Mar. 1953.

129. On the Strike of the 300,000, see Wolfe, *Working Women*, pp. 176–83, and Moisés, *Greve de Massa*.

130. *MET*, Apr.–June 1958, pp. 1–2; *VCC*, May 1958.

131. *TT*, Jan. 1958, p. 5.

132. *TG*, Apr.–May 1954, pp. 1–2. "DIPS" refers to the Departamento de Informa-

ção e Propaganda Social, which organized May Day celebrations during the Vargas dictatorship.

133. Ibid.

134. Interview with Aldo Lombardi, Apr. 17, 1956, AP. Lombardi claimed that unions resorted to this because the better-financed SESI celebrations always attracted larger crowds than the union-sponsored events.

135. *A Massa*, Apr. 1962, p. 1.

136. *O Trilho*, May 1963, p. 2.

137. SESI redoubled its efforts to recruit participants for the 1954 festivities, which were part of the commemorations of the 400th anniversary of São Paulo's founding. See *SJ*, Apr. 30, 1954.

138. *SJ*, May 31, 1954, p. 1. In this detailed account of the festivities, the only representatives of organized labor mentioned were the construction workers.

139. AA, SESI, P2, May 10, 1956. Undaunted by the cold shoulder it received from labor, SESI funded even more lavish events, including a nocturnal parade in Santo André on May Day Eve, 1957.

140. By the 1960s, SESI had suspended the parade portion of its May Day festivities, citing budget constraints, overcompetitiveness, and heavy traffic on the parade route as its motives. See AC, SESI-SP, Atas do Conselho Regional, Feb. 24, Apr. 7, 1961.

141. *TG*, Nov.–Dec. 1953, p. 4; *MET*, July 1957, p. 2. STIMMMESP began offering its own course in labor law and union organization, though the material seems to have been very similar to that covered in SESI courses.

142. *TG*, May 25, 1950, p. 6.

143. *O Trabalhador em Madeira*, Oct. 1955, p. 3.

144. "Mr. Antônio Devisate, president of SESI and well-known profiteer of paulista industry, if he came to eat with us would undoubtedly clap his hand on his head and say: 'You're right, my dog gets better than this'" (*O Condutor*, Nov. 1957, p. 7).

145. Ibid., p. 9.

146. Interview by author with João Batista Cândido, June 5, 1986.

147. SESI-SP, Divisão de Alimentação, *SESI—18 Anos*, pp. 39–41.

148. *O Condutor*, Nov. 1957, p. 7.

149. For a brilliant discussion of Argentine workers' use of Peronist notions of class collaboration as fuel for social criticism, see James, *Resistance and Integration*, pp. 33–40.

150. *MET*, Dec. 1948, p. 4; May 1948, p. 1.

151. "O Imperativo," *BI*, no. 1 (Nov. 21, 1949): 1.

152. "Direitos e Deveres," *ES*, no. 1 (Jan. 1952): 11.

153. *MET*, Sept. 1947, p. 3; "Trabalhismo," *TG*, Sept. 1948, p. 1; Aug. 1949, p. 6.

154. *VCC*, Nov.–Dec. 1952, p. 7.

155. *TG*, Nov. 1951, p. 3; Nov. 1957, p. 7; Nov. 1953, p. 4.

156. "Paz Social," *MET*, Feb. 1958, p. 2.

157. "Pela Paz Social," *TG*, Feb. 1958, p. 3.

158. On the employers' view of social peace as imperative, see *BI*, no. 7 (Nov. 21, 1949): 1–2; no. 9 (Dec. 5, 1949): 24–25.

159. "Só Ambiente de Mútua Confiança pode Proporcionar a Paz Social," *O Arauto do Vendedor*, Nov. 1961, p. 4.

160. *O Trabalhador Metalúrgico*, Oct. 1961, p. 6. Andreotti may have moderated his

language for an article in the statewide federation's publication. On Andreotti, see French, *Brazilian Workers' ABC*, pp. 47–92.

161. *TT*, June–July 1960, p. 3; *MET*, June 1961, p. 3.

162. *TG*, Mar. 1962, p. 5.

163. *O Ferroviário em Marcha*, Oct.–Nov. 1963, p. 2; *A Massa*, Nov. 1962, p. 1.

164. *A Voz do Metalúrgico*, Dec. 1958, pp. 2, 7.

165. *A Massa*, June 1962, p. 2; *A Média*, June 1958, p. 1; *VCC*, Mar. 1964, p. 7. On some workers' preference for SESI services, see Juárez Rubens Brandão Lopes, *Sociedade Industrial*, p. 58.

166. Interviews with Eduardo Gabriel Saad, Apr. 13–14, 1956, AP.

Chapter Six

1. On populist rhetoric in this period, see Benevides, *O PTB*; Sampaio, *Adhemar de Barros*; and D'Araújo, *O Segundo Governo Vargas*. Ernesto Laclau in "Toward a Theory of Populism" argues that Vargas's alliances with elite groups moderated his populist rhetoric (compared to Perón); although this may be true, he nevertheless increased his emphasis on the rights and contributions of Brazil's workers in his public addresses.

2. On developmentalism, see Sikkink, *Ideas and Institutions*. Sikkink distinguishes the "national populist economic model," which emphasized smaller industries and domestic consumption, from the investment-driven developmentalist model (ibid., pp. 31–34).

3. Among the many books that explore this theme, see Carvalho, *Os Bestializados*; Célia Marinho de Azevedo, *Onda Negra*; Andrews, *Blacks and Whites*, chaps. 1–2; and Stepan, *"Hour of Eugenics,"* pp. 153–62.

4. AG, Processos, P109 (confidential letter from Cyro Berlinck to A. R. de Azevedo), Mar. 31, 1948; Jafet, quoted in Dean, *Industrialization of São Paulo*, p. 175.

5. Striking examples of this can be found in the pages of *Educador Social*, a SESI publication specifically intended for workers. In the first issue alone, see "Igualdade Democrática," and "Direitos e Deveres do Operário," *ES*, no. 1 (Jan. 1952): 11.

6. The completion rate by 1951 was 26 percent. See "Reunião da Diretoria," *BI*, no. 99 (Aug. 27, 1951): 30.

7. EE. A copy of the survey can be found in the Biblioteca do Serviço Nacional de Aprendizagem Industrial, São Paulo.

8. EE, 4:7–11.

9. EE, 1:31–33.

10. See SENAI-SP, "Inquérito entre Aprendizes do SENAI."

11. The term "pardo" is used as a synonym for "mulatto." Given the high rate of postwar migration from the northeast and the increased entry of blacks into the industrial labor market, this small percentage is surprising. On the employment of Afro-Brazilians in paulista industry, see Andrews, *Blacks and Whites*, chap. 4. If statistics from the late 1960s reflect earlier patterns, SENAI had a higher percentage of Afro-Brazilians than the state technical schools. See Castro, Assis, and Oliveira, *Ensino Técnico*, p. 242.

12. EE, 3b:7–8.

13. EE, 3b:8–9.

14. EE, 3b:16.

15. EE, 3b:17.

16. EE, 3b:2.

17. EE, 3b:5.

18. Although these researchers would probably have recoiled at the comparison, their logic is reminiscent of Eduardo Jafet's claim that workers' low standard of living was due to their low aspirations. See Dean, *Industrialization of São Paulo*, p. 175.

19. Mange, *Planejamento*, pp. 14–16.

20. Luiz Pereira argued that even a small amount of training improved a worker's job opportunities. See Luiz Pereira, *Classe Operária*, pp. 121–40, and *A Escola numa Área Metropolitana*, chap. 1; and José Carlos Pereira, *Estrutura e Expansão*, pp. 106–11.

21. *Informativo SENAI*, no. 109 (Feb. 1955): 1; Góes Filho, *Diretrizes Atuais da Aprendizagem Industrial*, p. 15. For a discussion of the shift to on-the-job training, see Chapter 7.

22. It is important to recognize that middle-class identity was neither unitary nor static. On the formation of middle-class identity in São Paulo, see Owensby, "'Stuck in the Middle.'"

23. The director of SENAI's social services expressed a similar view in *Informativo SENAI*, no. 155 (Feb. 1959): 1–3.

24. Lodi, *Positivos os Indícios*, p. 5; *Informativo SENAI*, no. 11 (Sept. 1946): 4; interview by author with José Luiz Gonçalves, June 5, 1986. Gonçalves, a SENAI graduate and SENAI instructor, eventually became president of the militant metallurgical workers' union in São José dos Campos.

25. For a critical study of SENAI that places more emphasis on the training process as the means of socialization, see Frigotto, "Fazendo pelas Mãos," pp. 38–45.

26. See, for example, "Os Acidentes de Trabalho na Indústria de São Paulo," *BI*, no. 207 (Sept. 21, 1953): 24–25, which blames the high accident rate on "ignorant" rural migrants.

27. *ES*, no. 1 (Jan. 1952): 11 (emphasis in original).

28. *ES*, no. 9 (Sept. 1952): 7; no. 3 (Mar. 1952): 2.

29. *ES*, no. 9 (Sept. 1952): 12.

30. *ES*, no. 2 (Feb. 1953): 4; no. 3 (Mar. 1953): 1; no. 4 (Apr. 1953): 1; no. 5 (May 1953): 5.

31. *ES*, no. 6 (June 1953): 1. This statement went further than usual, stressing the worker's responsibilities without making the routine reference to the worker's rights.

32. *ES*, no. 9 (Sept. 1952): 3; no. 3 (Mar. 1953): 2; SESI-SP, DOS, "Produtividade."

33. *ES*, no. 3 (Mar. 1955): 2; no. 6 (June 1955): 1; no. 7 (July 1955): 1; no. 12 (Dec. 1956): 6–7. For more on SESI's attitudes toward supervisors, see Chapter 7.

34. *SJ*, July 31, 1949, pp. 1–2.

35. Economic Commission on Latin America, *Economic Survey*, pp. 239–62; Joint Brazil–United States Economic Development Commission, *Brazilian Technical Studies*, pp. 309–83; José Carlos Pereira, *Estrutura e Expansão*, pp. 142–53. See also Cooke, *Brazil on the March*, pp. 53–86.

36. In the 1960s, this division was incorporated, as a subdivision, into the Division for the Improvement of Health.

37. The large number of females in the under-eighteen labor force was due to heavy employment of minors in textile manufacturing compared to other industrial sectors. In 1953 men outnumbered women 3 to 1 in an industrial labor force of 802,608, but in the under-eighteen category, there were 47,246 female workers compared to 41,033 male workers. See PM, SENAI-SP, "Relatório do Departamento Regional de São Paulo pelo Ano 1953" (1954), p. 9.

38. For more on the normative literature on gender roles in industrializing São Paulo, see Besse, *Reconstructing Patriarchy*, chaps. 2–4, and Barbara Weinstein, "As Mulheres Trabalhadoras."

39. *Informativo SENAI*, no. 54 (July 1950): 1–2; no. 100 (May 1954): 1.

40. SESI-SP, Divisão de Educação e Cultura, "Relatório" (1955), AP.

41. "Culto a Bandeira," *ES*, no. 1 (Jan. 1952), back cover.

42. "Sentido de Nacionalismo," *ES*, no. 10 (Oct. 1958): 12.

43. SESI-SP, *Segunda Leitura do Trabalhador*.

44. *SJ*, Feb. 28, 1955, p. 6. To honor SESI, portraits of Simonsen and Devisate were hung in the headquarters of the Associação José do Patrocínio.

45. *ES*, no. 3 (Mar. 1955): 11; no. 3 (Mar. 1960): 2.

46. For a fascinating discussion of the different images of immigrant (that is, European) workers and "national" workers, who were typically nonwhite, see Andrews, *Blacks and Whites*, chap. 3. It is interesting that SESI and SENAI rarely drew an explicit contrast between the post-1945 internal migrant wave and the earlier immigrant wave (although individuals, like Cyro Berlinck, might have done so in private). Simonsen and his acolytes tended to emphasize "environmental" factors as explaining the defects of the Brazilian working class, and thus European workers living in Brazil, even briefly, could be expected to exhibit many of the same "defects." The absence of overt racism made this approach highly compatible with the discourse of racial democracy.

47. Interview with Maria Braz, Apr. 12, 1956, AP.

48. Interview with Affonso Celso Dias, Dec. 4, 1956, AP.

49. SESI-SP, Divisão de Educação e Cultura, "Relatório" (1955), AP. Since workers could attend individual sessions as well as the entire course, SESI recorded appearances rather than the numbers of students enrolled. The number of books borrowed from SESI–São Paulo libraries is more impressive if compared with a total of 75,000 books borrowed from union libraries in all of Brazil. See Erickson, *Brazilian Corporative State*, p. 40.

50. II Seminário sôbre Problemas Educacionais do SESI (São Paulo), "Relatório," Mar. 7, 1956, AP.

51. For an interesting discussion of SESI's recreational activities, see Figueiredo, "A Produtividade do Ócio."

52. *SJ*, July 31, 1949, pp. 1–2; "Recreação do SESI," *BI*, no. 16 (Jan. 23, 1950): 25–26; *SJ*, Apr. 30, 1950, p. 11.

53. *SJ*, Dec. 31, 1951, p. 4.

54. AC, SESI-SP, Atas do Conselho Regional, May 7, Mar. 30, 1948.

55. SESI-SP, Divisão de Educação e Cultura, "Relatório" (1955), AP.

56. "O Trabalho e o Esporte," *BIT*, no. 36 (Dec. 1951): 49–50. This article praising

SESI's athletic programs also praised a noted Brazilian woman athlete who practiced thirty-five sports "without abandoning her domestic duties."

57. The young woman voted this honor in 1955 received her prize from the acting mayor, General Porphyrio da Paz. Elsewhere in Latin America, "Queen of the Workers" was a title that reflected political consciousness as well as physical beauty. See Archila, "Construction of Working-Class Identity," chap. 4.

58. *SJ*, Apr. 30, 1951, pp. 6–7; *BIT*, no. 35 (Nov. 1951): 48–49.

59. *Dona de Casa*, no. 37 (Feb. 1953): 3; *SESI-Higiene*, no. 34 (Feb. 1953): 1. By the 1960s, SESI-São Paulo had softened its critique of *carnaval* somewhat by ignoring it instead of attacking it.

60. Interviews with Cyro de Noronha Pelúcio, Apr. 12, 1956, Maria José Serra, Apr. 16, 1956, and Antônio Devisate, Apr. 12, 1956, AP.

61. "Serviço Social de Grupo," *ES*, no. 3 (Mar. 1953): 4; interview with Hugo Guimarães Malheiros, Apr. 13, 1956, AP. Malheiros claimed that the social service subdivision of SESI-São Paulo had the best corps of social workers in Brazil and was especially proud of the large number of male social workers on the staff.

62. By 1954, seven of the CADs were operating in the capital; the remaining eighteen were operating in the interior. Given the overlap in their subject matter, it is not surprising that in 1955 SESI decided to merge the two magazines under the title *SESI-Higiene*.

63. In a crude attempt to attract older women to cooking classes, a *Dona de Casa* article entitled "Agarre seu Homem!" (Hang onto your man!) argued that, after women turn forty, beauty fades and cooking becomes the means to secure a husband. See *Dona de Casa*, no. 37 (Feb. 1953): 2.

64. Interview with Maria Lourdes de Ribeiro, Apr. 16, 1956, AP.

65. *Dona de Casa*, no. 1 (Feb. 1950): 1.

66. *Dona de Casa*, no. 19 (Aug. 1951): 4.

67. For a similar argument (indeed, one probably lifted from SESI literature), see "A Educação e o Lar," *MET*, Feb. 1950, p. 4.

68. *Dona de Casa*, no. 1 (Feb. 1950): 1; *SJ*, Dec. 31, 1955, pp. 1–2, 5. Anita Devisate, FIESP's "First Lady," frequently handed out prizes such as knife sharpeners and blenders to outstanding students at graduation ceremonies.

69. Much of this material came straight from textbooks written in the United States. On these early home economics courses, see Besse, *Reconstructing Patriarchy*, chap. 5. See also Chapter 1.

70. *Dona de Casa*, no. 2 (Mar. 1950): 4. The magazine also informed current and future housewives that "the twenty-four-hour day should be divided into 'eights' in order to be better utilized" and that women needed less food than men (*Dona de Casa*, no. 3 [Apr. 1950]: 4). See also *SESI-Higiene*, no. 13 (Jan. 1956): 16. For a similar approach, see CFESP, *Noções de Higiene*.

71. In this respect, the orientation resembles that of home economics literature for working-class women in Weimar Germany. See Nolan, "'Housework Made Easy.'"

72. *Dona de Casa*, no. 4 (May 1950): 4; no. 18 (July 1951): 4; no. 34 (Nov. 1952): 3.

73. Simonsen, *Ordem Econômica*, p. 28. See also FIESP Circular no. 18/44, Feb. 14, 1944.

74. BARS, SESI-SP, "Relatório do Departamento Regional de São Paulo pelo Ano 1954" (1955), p. 36. From 1950 to 1954, SESI-SP collected 216,466 blood samples in its hunt for syphilis, describing its campaign as "the biggest blood census" ever undertaken. This intense concern with syphilis reflects the preoccupations of the earlier eugenics movement. See Stepan, *"Hour of Eugenics,"* pp. 122–28.

75. *SESI-Higiene*, no. 1 (May 1950): 2–3.

76. *SESI-Higiene*, no. 2 (June 1950): 4.

77. *SESI-Higiene*, no. 48 (May 1954): 1–4.

78. *SESI-Higiene*, no. 9 (Jan. 1951): 4; no. 28 (Aug. 1952): 2; *Dona de Casa*, no. 21 (Oct. 1951): 3. The last article, entitled "Who Knows More—The Doctor or the Godmother?," congratulated a young woman for listening to her doctor and weaning her child early instead of taking the advice of her *comadre*.

79. *SESI-Higiene*, no. 43 (Nov. 1953): 1.

80. *SESI-Higiene*, no. 39 (July 1953): 3.

81. *SESI-Higiene*, no. 2 (Feb. 1952): 4; no. 37 (May 1953): 1; *ES*, no. 8 (Aug. 1959): 8.

82. *SESI-Higiene*, no. 18 (Oct. 1951): 1.

83. *VCC*, Dec. 1961, p. 4; *SJ*, Oct. 30, 1950, p. 6. Some women may have taken the courses to improve their skills for paid domestic service, but women who became household servants usually were not the wives or daughters of factory workers.

84. For a similar analysis in a different context, see Nolan, "'Housework Made Easy.'"

85. For a description of women who chose to become "career" workers, see Veccia, "Women, Work, and Family Life." The SENAI study discussed above, while not based on "typical" working-class households, revealed that the student's mother, on average, contributed 4 percent or less of the total household income.

86. Many unions also regarded the domestic sphere as women's first concern and printed domestic advice from SESI. See *A Voz do Metalúrgico*, Dec. 1958, p. 2, and *TG*, Mar. 1960, p. 6.

87. *SESI-Higiene*, no. 13 (Jan. 1956): 16.

88. *SJ*, May 31, 1951, p. 10 (emphasis added).

89. This was also regarded as an urban problem since rural boys would be employed along with the family. See Silveira, "O Problema do Menor."

90. Isaac Mielnik, "Crianças Abandonadas," *ES*, no. 2 (Feb. 1954): 5.

91. Silveira, "O Problema do Menor," p. 44.

92. *Informativo SENAI*, no. 58 (Nov. 1950): 1–4; no. 82 (Nov. 1952): 5–8; *BI*, no. 68 (Jan. 22, 1951): 23; BCNI, Atas do Conselho Nacional do SENAI, July 13, 1954, p. 11.

93. *ES*, no. 1 (Jan. 1952): 14; no. 4 (Apr. 1952): 12; no. 4 (Apr. 1953). See also *SJ*, Sept. 30, 1951, p. 5; Feb. 29, 1952, p. 8.

94. AG, Processos, P32/377/3952/3953, May 10, 1960.

95. SESI-SP, "Relatório" (1954), p. 108.

96. *TG*, Aug. 1960, p. 8.

97. *Boletim Interno da DOS* 3 (Apr. 1953), pts. 2, 3.

98. This "failure" is particularly striking if compared to Juan and Eva Perón's highly successful use of Argentine popular cultural idioms, including themes from tango music. See James, *Resistance and Integration*, pp. 23–27.

Chapter Seven

1. AC, SESI-SP, Atas do Conselho Regional, May 7, 1954. Costa Santos delivered a vehement defense of SESI's private legal status at a FIESP directors' meeting, arguing that any alteration would turn it into a public agency, "with all the inconveniences that have been indicated in the welfare services under governmental authority" ("Reunião da Diretoria," *BI*, no. 121 [Jan. 28, 1952]: 14).

2. Schmitter, *Interest Conflict*, p. 335n; Silva and Carneiro, *Os Presidentes*, p. 104.

3. BCNI, Atas do Conselho Nacional do SENAI, July 13, 1954.

4. Interview with Oswaldo de Barros Santos, July 12, 1990, PM. Mange had good relations with FIESP and the national director of SENAI, Faria Góes, but tense relations with other figures in the national headquarters. See Stênio Lopes, *Uma Saga da Criatividade Brasileira*, p. 105.

5. Interview with Luiz Gonzaga Ferreira, Aug. 10, 1989, PM; PM, SENAI-SP, "Relatório do Departamento Regional de São Paulo pelo Ano 1946" (1947), pp. 61–70.

6. SENAI-SP, "Relatório" (1952), pp. 5–6; Góes Filho, *Diretrizes Atuais da Aprendizagem Industrial*. Mange used a 1953 apprentice survey to support his position. It showed that 96 percent of SENAI students preferred the existing system to training within industry; they cited theoretical instruction and the staff's "affection and interest" as the reasons. See SENAI-SP, "Inquérito entre Aprendizes do SENAI."

7. *BI*, no. 512 (July 29, 1959): 1330–31.

8. *Informativo SENAI*, no. 109 (Feb. 1955): 1.

9. José Carlos Pereira, *Estrutura e Expansão*, pp. 30–51; Góes Filho, *Diretrizes Atuais da Aprendizagem Industrial*; "Reunião das Diretorias," *BI*, no. 120 (Feb. 4, 1952): 30.

10. BCNI, Atas do Conselho Nacional do SENAI, Nov. 5, 1952, pp. 11–12. Faria Góes was a member of the commission that issued this executive decree, which SENAI tacitly accepted due to strong industrialist support for the measure.

11. Góes Filho, *Diretrizes Atuais da Aprendizagem Industrial*; interview with Paulo Novaes, Mar. 21, 1956, AP; Stênio Lopes, *Uma Saga da Criatividade Brasileira*, p. 101; interview with Luiz Gonzaga Ferreira, Aug. 10, 1989, PM.

12. *Informativo SENAI*, no. 53 (Apr. 1951): 1–2; Meem, "Industrial Training."

13. Joint Brazil–United States Economic Development Commission, *Brazilian Technical Studies*, p. 360. The author of this section consulted with firms in Minas Gerais, where decentralization of industry made training within the firm even more desirable.

14. One study argues that Mange underwent a shift in these years; the "thinking hand" (*braço pensante*) had become the "student worker." See PM, *De Homens e Máquinas*, p. 141.

15. SENAI-SP, "Relatório" (1954), p. 7.

16. Interviews with Oswaldo de Barros Santos, June 12, 1990, and Gentil Palmiro, Sept. 28, 1989, PM; interview by author with Pedro Senna, July 3, 1986. See also the various testimonies in Bologna, *Roberto Mange*, pp. 320–420.

17. D'Avila, *Eng*° Ítalo Bologna, pp. 1–2; *Informativo SENAI*, no. 53 (Apr. 1951): 1–2.

18. *Informativo SENAI*, no. 120 (Feb. 1956): 1–3; interview with Luiz Marcondes Nitsch, Apr. 27, 1956, AP. CBAI had already signed an agreement with the São Paulo Secretariat of Labor, circumventing SENAI, due to Mange's intransigence.

19. Various FIESP officials also called for more workplace training. See "Reunião das Diretorias," *BI*, no. 120 (Feb. 4, 1952): 30; *BI*, no. 378 (Dec. 31, 1956): 115–16.

20. Quadros, *Mensagem Apresentada pelo Governador a Assembléa Legislativa*, pp. 83–84; *Boletim do Supervisor*, no. 1 (Apr. 1956): 1.

21. SENAI-SP, "O SENAI de São Paulo," pp. 3–4 (report delivered to FIESP).

22. SENAI-SP, "Relatório" (1956), p. 25.

23. Baer, *Industrialization*, pp. 68–69. On SENAI's role in GEIA, see *Corrêio Paulistano*, Apr. 7, 1959, Apr. 15, 1960, and *BI*, no. 466 (Sept. 10, 1958): 1175; no. 120 (Feb. 4, 1952): 30.

24. Interview with Luiz Gonzaga Ferreira, Aug. 10, 1989, PM.

25. Interview by author with Onofre da Silva, June 5, 1986; *Informativo SENAI*, no. 148 (July 1958): 1–2.

26. A ten-month course to train adults as tool-and-die makers was first offered in 1962 at the Escola Roberto Simonsen. SENAI billed the course as the first of its sort in all of Latin America. See SENAI-SP, "Relatório" (1962), p. 3.

27. Interview with Luiz Gonzaga Ferreira, Aug. 10, 1989, PM.

28. In his report for 1960, the governor of São Paulo also lamented the "distortion in the wage structure" caused by fierce competition for certain skilled workers. See Pinto, *Mensagem Apresentada pelo Governador a Assembléa Legislativa*, p. 120.

29. Interview with Luiz Gonzaga Ferreira, Aug. 10, 1989, PM; PM, *O Giz e a Graxa*, pp. 72–74.

30. *BI*, no. 214 (Nov. 9, 1953): 242. Students needed an intermediate school (*ginásio*) diploma to enter the technical schools, making entry accessible only to the most comfortable segments of the working class. See D'Avila, *SENAI, 1942–62*, p. 12.

31. Visiting North American businessmen routinely lunched at the Escola Roberto Simonsen, SENAI's showplace. See "Reunião das Diretorias," *BI*, no. 120 (Feb. 4, 1952): 30.

32. *Informativo SENAI*, no. 189 (Dec. 1961): 5; Francisco Santos Lopes, "Sistema Brasileiro." The latter cited nine Latin American nations that had modeled training programs after SENAI. SENA is the Servicio Nacional de Aprendizaje (National Training Service); SENATI is the Servicio Nacional de Aprendizaje Técnico y Industrial (National Service for Technical and Industrial Training); CONET is the Consejo Nacional de Educación Técnica (National Council of Technical Education).

33. Interview with Oswaldo de Barros Santos, June 12, 1990, PM.

34. Willits, "Labor Turn-Over."

35. Edwards, *Contested Terrain*, pp. 90–140.

36. Vera Maria Cândido Pereira, *O Coração da Fabrica*, pp. 76–80.

37. SESI-SP, *Roteiro do Mestre*; Chapple, *How to Supervise People in Industry*. The SESI–São Paulo pamphlet went through at least thirteen editions.

38. FGV, CPDOC, LF/pi 42.11.09, "Relações Humanas no Trabalho"; Aldo M. Azevedo, "Em Defesa da Racionalização," *Revista IDORT*, no. 93 (Sept. 1939): 193, cited in Antonacci, "A Vitória da Razão," p. 201.

39. Hélvio M. Pinheiro Lima (SESI-DOS), *Curso de Relações Humanas*, p. 46 (emphasis in original).

40. Ibid., pp. 28–29 (emphasis in original).

41. *ES*, no. 1 (Jan. 1962): 8; illustration reprinted in *ES*, no. 183 (Mar.–Apr. 1971): 11.

42. "Problema das Relações Humanas no Trabalho," *BI*, no. 177 (Feb. 23, 1953): 235–36; *ES*, no. 7 (June 1953): 8.

43. Rudge, "O Problema das Relações Humanas," p. 9. It is significant that SESI chose this theme for the conference.

44. Hélvio M. Pinheiro Lima, "Responsabilidade do Supervisor na Indisciplina," *ES*, no. 7 (July 1955): 1; "Relações Humanas no Trabalho," *ES*, no. 6 (June 1955): 1.

45. "Relações Humanas: O Líder e o 'Mandão,'" *ES*, no. 12 (Dec. 1956): 6–7, reprinted from IDORT's *Revista de Organização Científica*.

46. "Satisfação no Trabalho," *ES*, no. 5 (May 1958): 1.

47. SESI-SP, DOS, *SESI—18 Anos*, p. 97.

48. Rudge, "O Problema das Relações Humanas," pp. 14–15. In this vein, *Educador Social* (no. 7 [July 1953]: 12) proudly described a worker confraternization party whose "guiding spirit" was a head foreman who graduated from a CSPI.

49. Interviews with Carmino Urcioli, Apr. 23, 1956, and Custódio Sobral Martins de Almeida, Apr. 5, 1956, AP.

50. Contestants for the Model Worker Contest invariably listed at least one CSPI with SESI. For more on this, see Epilogue and Conclusion and Barbara Weinstein, "The Model Worker," pp. 103–4.

51. *Boletim do Supervisor*, no. 1 (Apr. 1956): 2.

52. *ES*, no. 4 (Apr. 1959): 9. For a positive description of the SESI course in a usually critical forum, see "Relações Humanas do Trabalho," *TG*, July 1959, p. 6.

53. Mange, "Prevenção de Acidentes"; FIESP Circular no. 91/42, May 29, 1942.

54. For a description of hazards in paulista factories during this period, see Wolfe, *Working Women*, pp. 101–8.

55. The law also excluded women and minors from officially recognized "insalubrious" tasks.

56. FIESP Circular no. 62/44, May 15, 1944; no. 180/45, Sept. 19, 1945. On Cesarino Júnior's role in the Estado Novo, see Gomes, *A Invenção do Trabalhismo*, pp. 290–91.

57. FIESP Circular no. 153/45 ("Instruções sôbre Comissões Internas de Prevenção de Acidentes do Trabalho"), Aug. 17, 1945.

58. By the early 1960s, SESI was distributing 33,000 copies of each issue of *CIPA-Jornal* throughout the state of São Paulo.

59. "Rumos da Educação Social," *SJ*, July 31, 1949, pp. 1–2; Pacheco e Silva, "A Fadiga Industrial"; PH, Light, "Relatórios da Comissão Especial de Prevenção de Acidentes," 1955–60. Tables in the Light reports attributed two-thirds of workplace accidents to "fault or neglect of the victim."

60. "Da Natureza do Acidente," *Boletim SENAI*, no. 4 (July–Sept. 1945): 1–2.

61. *BIT*, no. 36 (Dec. 1951): 32–34.

62. AG, Processos, Cia. Brasileira de Artefatos de Metais, P315, Feb. 18, 1948; *SJ*, Feb. 28, 1950, p. 5. Workers at the plant cited above presented a petition to MOP denouncing hazardous conditions that "contribute to the poor movement of production."

63. AG, Processos, Soc. Paulista de Artefatos Metalúrgicos, P878/2471, June 23, 1959, Nov. 11, 1965; Ind. Metalúrgica N.S. da Aparecida, P1132/2545, Jan. 29, 1965. For an explicitly political discussion of workplace accidents, see Cohn et al., *Acidentes do Trabalho*.

64. *CIPA-Jornal*, no. 80 (Sept.–Oct. 1957): 4–5, 12; no. 81 (Nov.–Dec. 1957): 4–5; no. 84 (May–June 1958): 3; no. 86 (Sept.–Oct. 1958): 3.

65. "Fator Pessoal e Fator Material," *CIPA-Jornal*, no. 83 (Mar.–Apr. 1958): 4–6.

66. BARS, SESI-SP, "Relatório do Departamento Regional de São Paulo pelo Ano 1953" (1954), p. 37. The number of CIPAs organized increased from 79 in 1952 to 244 in 1953.

67. AC, SESI-SP, Atas do Conselho Regional, Oct. 30, 1962; "Higiene Industrial e Elevação da Produtividade," *BI*, no. 756 (Apr. 1, 1964): 13–15. The latter reprinted the text of FIESP president Raphael Noschese's speech at the 1964 Congress Americano de Medicina do Trabalho in São Paulo.

68. In the early 1950s, even some unions adopted the view that workers were largely responsible for accidents. See, for example, "Acidentes no Trabalho," *VCC*, Feb. 1953, p. 8.

69. *MET*, Sept. 1958, pp. 3, 8.

70. SESI-SP, Divisão de Assistência Social, *SESI—18 Anos*, p. 269.

71. *CIPA-Jornal*, no. 121 (July–Aug. 1964): 1; SESI-SP, DOS, *SESI—18 Anos*, p. 69.

72. *CIPA-Jornal*, no. 118 (Jan.–Feb. 1964): 7; no. 130 (Jan.–Feb. 1966): 4–5. See also "Acidentes do Trabalho em Indústrias Paulistas," *BI*, no. 498 (Apr. 23, 1959): 878–79.

73. Evidence of this can be found in the reports by SESI's social educators on firms such as Johnson & Johnson. See AG, Processos, P9/2573, Oct. 9, 1956. See also "Causas de Acidentes do Trabalho," *ES*, no. 165 (May–June 1968): 4.

74. A former union leader recalled that furnace workers, outraged over harsh conditions such as the lack of ventilation, would throw out salt pills given to them by management. See interview by author with Affonso Delellis, July 18, 1986. In a 1958 report on the chemical manufacturer EletroCloro, a social educator claimed that the firm owned the proper safety equipment but that "the employees don't like to use [it], as is common in our industries." A follow-up report noted that a new safety supervisor had convinced the workers to use protective gear. See AG, Processos, P279/3044, May 15, 1958, Nov. 4, 1960.

75. *MET*, Apr. 1959, p. 11. See also *TG*, Dec. 1959, p. 3, and *TT*, Jan. 1959, p. 7.

76. "Descuido," *CIPA-Jornal*, no. 155 (Mar.–Apr. 1970): 7.

77. A former SESI employee (interview by author, São Paulo, Apr. 19, 1986) attributed her dismissal, after eight years with SESI, to her strong support for worker-representatives in the CIPAs. I also learned of at least one other former employee allegedly dismissed for the same reason. My interviewee stressed the lack of interaction between DOS and the industrial hygiene subdivision.

78. SESI, Divisão de Assistência Social, *SESI—18 Anos*, p. 223.

79. "Os Acidentes de Trabalho na Indústria de São Paulo," *BI*, no. 207 (Sept. 21, 1953): 24–25.

80. *Resenha Jurídica* (Suplemento Mensal do *BI*), no. 1 (July 1960): 11–12. In the 1970s, the state of São Paulo created FUNDACENTRO, which became the leading institution in the field of occupational health and safety. Its discourse was virtually identical to SESI's, and it, too, lacked coercive powers.

81. Interview with Hugo Guimarães Malheiros, Apr. 13, 1956, AP.

82. Rudge, "O Problema das Relações Humanas," p. 11.

83. SESI-SP, DOS, *Manual do Estagiário*, pp. 3–4.

84. Ibid., pp. 7–36.

85. Ibid., pp. 36–38. The actual reports by *estagiários* would have been very useful, but DOS officials claimed they had been thrown out and allowed me to see only recent reports.

86. AG, Processos, Cia. Melhoramentos, P50/3151, Dec. 9, 15, 1958.

87. Interviews with Achim Fuerstenthal, Mar. 15, 1956, and Israel Sartini, Apr. 12, 1965, AP.

88. *BI*, no. 120 (Feb. 4, 1952): 30.

89. AG, Processos, P9/2573, Oct. 9, 1956.

Chapter Eight

1. *BI*, no. 71 (Feb. 12, 1951): 1–2; no. 77 (Mar. 26, 1951): 1–2. The Simonsen circle (Ferraz, Devisate, and Arruda Pereira) backed Vargas, as did some of the younger "cadets" (such as Costa Santos). But FIESP also had an anti-*getulista* UDN faction that included Raphael Noschese and José Ermírio de Moraes. See Leopoldi, "Industrial Associations," pp. 259–65.

2. *BI*, no. 71 (Feb. 12, 1951): 1–2. The icing on the cake was Vargas's appointment of Armando de Arruda Pereira as mayor of São Paulo and of paulista industrialist Horácio Lafer as finance minister.

3. *SJ*, June 30, 1951, p. 5.

4. "Importancia dos Serviços Sociais na Indústria," *SJ*, Oct. 31, 1951, pp. 4–5. This article reprinted a speech Ferraz delivered to the Santos Rotary Club.

5. *Informativo SENAI*, no. 32 (Aug. 1948): 5.

6. *ESP*, Jan. 5, 1952, reprinted in *SJ*, Jan. 31, 1952, p. 3.

7. "Indústria e os Problemas Sociais," reprinted in AC, SESI-SP, Atas do Conselho Regional, Apr. 18, 1952. The sympathetic position adopted by *O Estado de São Paulo* toward Ferraz and the FIESP leadership in these years may be linked to their earlier collaboration in IDORT. See Antonacci, "A Vitória da Razão," p. 90.

8. This antagonism dates back to Vargas's cancellation of the 1938 elections and the exile of liberal constitutionalist leader Armando de Salles Oliveira, former editor of *O Estado de São Paulo*. See Pacheco e Silva, *Armando de Salles Oliveira*.

9. "Relatório das Atividades das Diretorias em 1951," *BI*, no. 129 (Mar. 24, 1952): 32.

10. Most scholars situate this moment in the Kubitschek period, but as I will argue below, there was already tension in the late 1950s between employers and the state and the labor movement. For the alternative view, see Benevides, *O Governo Kubitschek*, chap. 2, and Miriam Limoeiro Cardoso, *Ideologia do Desenvolvimento*, pp. 227–59. For a view similar to mine, see Trevisan, *50 Anos em 5*.

11. *BI*, no. 109 (Nov. 5, 1951): 1.

12. "Intervenção Estatal no Domínio Econômico," *BI*, no. 120 (Jan. 21, 1952): 4–5.

13. On industrialists' attitudes toward foreign capital in the 1950s, see "Reunião das Diretorias," *BI*, no. 122 (Feb. 4, 1952): 30, and Leopoldi, "Industrial Associations," pp. 247–55.

14. Wolfe, *Working Women*, pp. 177–78.

15. On this strike, see *BIT*, no. 51 (Mar. 1953): 2–4; Wolfe, *Working Women*, pp. 176–83; and Moisés, *Greve de Massa*.

16. The evolving response of employers to the strike can be found in the issues of FIESP's *Boletim Informativo* (which included minutes of the meetings of FIESP's directorate). See *BI*, no. 183 (Apr. 6, 1953): 31; no. 184 (Apr. 13, 1953): 62; no. 185 (Apr. 20, 1953): 94; no. 187 (May 4, 1953): 158–59.

17. In 1954 FIESP's director of statistics called the labor courts "by nature prolabor." See interview with Carlos Borges Teixeira, July 7, 1954, AP. This was a switch from the earlier assumption that the labor courts were likely to favor employers. See Arquivo FIESP, Atas da Reunião Semanal, Apr. 14, 1943, p. 9, courtesy of Joel Wolfe.

18. On police brutality during the strike, see Wolfe, *Working Women*, p. 182. It is indicative of the collaboration between the two organizations that SESI's regional council approved funding for a DOPS dental clinic in September 1953, despite the fact that DOPS clearly fell outside of SESI's mandate. See AC, SESI-SP, Atas do Conselho Regional, Sept. 22, 1953.

19. *BI*, no. 184 (Apr. 13, 1953). Caio Plínio Barreto, a lawyer for FIESP in the 1950s, went so far as to claim that the industrialists instigated the strike as a way to reduce stocks and combat overproduction. See interview with Caio Plínio Barreto, June 17–18, 1953, AP.

20. *BMTIC*, no. 135 (Nov. 1945). Justified absences were acceptable with the appropriate documentation. On employer attitudes, see Arquivo FIESP, Atas, Sept. 29, 1943, pp. 15–17; Jan. 28, 1948, p. 21, courtesy of Joel Wolfe; FIESP Circular no. 41/46, Feb. 20, 1946; no. 39/47, Mar. 31, 1947; and PH, Correspondência da Light, Subsérie 24 (General Orders), Jan. 10, 1945, Dec. 16, 1946. In 1945 Light began granting workers Christmas bonuses, but the amount was based on each worker's attendance.

21. *BI*, no. 298 (June 20, 1955): 112; "As Omissões no Trabalho," *Revista SENAI*, no. 54 (Jan. 1950): 1–2. José Sérgio Leite Lopes sees this as a period in which many firms were trying to lower labor costs (*A Tecelagem*, pp. 287ff).

22. "Assiduidade Integral," *VCC*, Nov.–Dec. 1952, pp. 7–8; *BI*, no. 184 (Apr. 13, 1953): 62.

23. Mariano Ferraz, "Princípios de Organização Racional do Trabalho," *BI*, no. 185 (Apr. 20, 1953): 85; no. 327 (Jan. 9, 1956): 22; no. 334 (Feb. 27, 1956): 230; "As Omissões no Trabalho," *Revista SENAI*, no. 54 (Jan. 1950): 1.

24. Many managers, both foreign and Brazilian, admitted that their firms fired workers approaching tenure or examined workers before allowing them to achieve tenure. See interviews with Carmino Urcioli, Apr. 23, 1956; William Embry, Mar. 16, 1956; and Achim Fuerstenthal, Mar. 15, 1956, AP. Fuerstenthal, a psychotechnic expert, described one of his functions as evaluating workers for tenure.

25. Gomes, *A Invenção do Trabalhismo*, p. 242.

26. "Indústria e Níveis de Vida," *BI*, no. 312 (Sept. 26, 1955): 45–46.

27. SESI and SENAI also cultivated relations with U.S. officials and Brazilian military officers. The pages of *SESI-Jornal* and *Informativo SENAI* were replete with accounts of luncheons at which U.S. diplomatic personnel or military men were the honored guests. On the inclusion of SESI "technicians" in a 1953 Point Four training

program in Washington, D.C., see Welch, "Labor Internationalism," pp. 73–74.

28. SESI-SP, DOS, *SESI—18 Anos*, p. 61. A year later, SESI technicians attended a training program for labor advisers in the United States. See Welch, "Labor Internationalism," pp. 73–74.

29. Interviews with Eduardo Gabriel Saad, Apr. 13–14, 1956, AP. On SESI's approach to oratory, see SESI-SP, DOS, *Curso de Técnicas de Comunicação Verbal*.

30. SESI-SP, DOS, *O Guia dos Dirigentes Sindicais*, pp. 1–2.

31. Ibid.

32. AG, Processos, P79/77, Feb. 19, 1954.

33. "Um Líder Sindical Manifesta-se sôbre os Seminários de Legislação Trabalhista," *ES*, no. 9 (Sept. 1954): 9.

34. Interview by author with José Brasil de Castro Alves, July 18, 1986.

35. Interview by author with Hélvio Pinheiro Lima, July 14, 1986. The interviewee described these activities as reflecting Roberto Simonsen's conceptualization of the social educator's role.

36. Interviews with Eduardo Gabriel Saad, Apr. 13–14, 1956, and Antônio Devisate, Apr. 12, 1956, AP.

37. Interviews with Eduardo Gabriel Saad, Apr. 13–14, 1956, AP.

38. *Boletim Interno da DOS*, no. 12 (Mar. 1959): 17; *BI*, no. 431 (Jan. 8, 1958): 5; Trevisan, *50 Anos em 5*, p. 162. Other elite spokesmen argued that Brazilian workers' low educational level and habituation to a low standard of living would limit the spread of communism. See interview with Caio Plínio Barreto, June 17–18, 1953, AP.

39. "Labor Conditions in the São Paulo Consular District for the Second Quarter of 1953," Aug. 1953, RG84, NA, cited in Wolfe, *Working Women*, p. 184.

40. Interviews with Eduardo Gabriel Saad, Apr. 13–14, 1956, AP. Saad also expressed his belief that Brazil needed a "democratic-left" party to counteract Communist influence.

41. *SJ*, Oct. 31, 1951, p. 7.

42. "Fortalecem-se os Sindicatos Operários," *MET*, July 1953, p. 1. See also *SJ*, Jan. 31, 1954, p. 2, and Welch, "Labor Internationalism," pp. 77–79.

43. AG, Processos, P79/498, Oct. 17, 1950.

44. Interview with Olavo Previatti, Apr. 27, 1956, AP. In contrast, he praised SENAI for doing something useful for workers. See *BI*, no. 402 (June 17, 1957): 119.

45. Interview with Olavo Previatti, Apr. 27, 1956, AP; "Relatório da Diretoria: Serviço Social da Indústria do Papel, Papelão e Cortiça do Estado de São Paulo (SEP-ACO)," 1958, AP; interview by author with Mário Amato, May 6, 1986. During 1956, Previatti also spent six weeks in a U.S. training program for Latin American labor officials.

46. SESI-SP, DOS, *SESI—18 Anos*, p. 61.

47. Devisate was first elected president in late 1952 and was then reelected every two years until 1962. Leopoldi sees Devisate as performing a largely ceremonial function and having little prestige within FIESP ("Industrial Associations," p. 265), but she probably underestimates his political connections.

48. "Mensagem do Presidente da FIESP aos Trabalhadores Paulistas," *SJ*, Jan. 31, 1953, p. 3.

49. Devisate's speech at his inauguration as FIESP president praised Vargas and Labor Minister Segadas Viana, but the section on workers was entirely devoted to SENAI and SESI. See *BI*, no. 152 (Sept. 1, 1952): 185–88.

50. *SJ*, Feb. 28, 1954, p. 1. This speech was delivered at a luncheon attended by various labor federation officials.

51. D'Araújo, *O Segundo Governo Vargas*, pp. 123–25.

52. Ibid., pp. 122–26; Vargas quoted in Skidmore, *Politics in Brazil*, p. 134, and Wolfe, *Working Women*, p. 160.

53. D'Araújo, *O Segundo Governo Vargas*, p. 123. On employer opposition to the minimum wage hike, see *BI*, no. 241 (May 17, 1954): 202–3.

54. BCNI, Atas do Conselho Nacional do SENAI, July 13, 1954. At this meeting, Lodi (still president of the CNI) spoke with despair about the future of SENAI and SESI should Vargas fall. Lodi, himself, had been implicated in the plot to assassinate Vargas's arch enemy, Carlos Lacerda. See also Leopoldi, "Industrial Associations," pp. 234–35.

55. "Paz Social," *BI*, no. 247 (June 28, 1954): 11–12; no. 248 (July 5, 1954): 53; no. 259 (Sept. 20, 1954): 18.

56. Despite the emphasis on direct negotiations, a Labor Ministry representative was always present. See "Colaboração entre Empregados e Empregadores," *BI*, no. 248 (July 5, 1954): 53.

57. Ibid. On Rusticci (who was a member of the PTB but was allied with Communist union activists), see interview with J. M. Moreira de Moraes, Apr. 27, 1956, AP, and Benevides, *O PTB*, pp. 115–17. On labor relations in general during this period, see Wolfe, *Working Women*, pp. 185–86.

58. *BI*, no. 284 (Mar. 14, 1955): 113–14. For an excellent discussion of industrialists' relations with Café Filho and his influential finance minister, Eugênio Gudin, see Leopoldi, "Industrial Associations," pp. 265–73.

59. The entire text was published in *BI*, no. 325 (Dec. 26, 1955): 201–6.

60. Ibid.

61. "Harmonia Social," *BI*, no. 319 (Nov. 14, 1955): 21; Trevisan, *50 Anos em 5*, p. 104.

62. On the Instituto Superior de Estudos Brasileiros, which produced much of the literature supporting developmental nationalism, see Toledo, *ISEB*.

63. IDORT was not formally subordinated to FIESP, but the latter had an official representative on IDORT's board, and there was considerable overlap between the two organizations.

64. SESI-SP, DOS, "Produtividade," pp. 77–79.

65. *BI*, no. 378 (Dec. 31, 1956): 104; SESI-SP, DOS, "Produtividade," p. 48; interview with Affonso Campiglia, Mar. 9, 1956, AP; Trevisan, *50 Anos em 5*, pp. 178–95.

66. *BI*, no. 489 (Feb. 18, 1959): 588–89. This article described CIESP as a "seedbed for men of the elite."

67. Benevides, *O Governo Kubitschek*, pp. 87–95; Erickson, *Brazilian Corporative State*, pp. 61–62.

68. Benevides, *O Governo Kubitschek*, p. 94. For a very different interpretation of industrialists' attitudes during the Kubitschek years, see Trevisan, *50 Anos em 5*.

69. Benevides endorses this view of the labor unions as manipulated, controlled, even "anesthetized" (*O Governo Kubitschek*, p. 87), yet the degree of union autonomy was

vastly greater than in previous decades (Sandoval, *Social Change*, pp. 84–87). On labor participation in the direction of the social security institutes, see Cohn, *Previdência Social*, pp. 71–93.

70. *BI*, no. 431 (Jan. 8, 1958): 5; no. 522 (Oct. 7, 1959): 100–101; no. 527 (Nov. 11, 1959): 4–5.

71. Gottschalk was relatively liberal on the right-to-strike question. See Arquivo FIESP, Atas da Reunião Semanal, Feb. 8, 1946, courtesy of Joel Wolfe.

72. *BI*, no. 447 (Apr. 30, 1958): 548–51; "Os Efeitos Econômicos da Greve," *ES*, no. 2 (Feb. 1960): 5.

73. *BI*, no. 522 (Oct. 7, 1959): 100–101; no. 527 (Nov. 11, 1959): 4–5. The phrase "act of insanity" was quoted (approvingly) from *O Estado de São Paulo*.

74. *A Voz do Metalúrgico*, Dec. 1958, p. 7.

75. Interview with Aldo Lombardi, Apr. 17, 1956, AP.

76. "Paz Social," *MET*, Feb. 1958, p. 2; "Vitoriosa a Greve," *TG*, Nov. 1957, pp. 4–5.

77. AC, SESI-SP, Atas do Conselho Regional, Feb. 11, Mar. 11, 18, Apr. 1, 7, 22, 1960, Dec. 28, 1951. In interviews, SENAI employees noted the difficulties they encountered in pressing grievances. See interview with Sebastião da Luz, Apr. 5, 1990, PM.

78. *MET*, June 1961, p. 5. In a 1962 letter to SESI officials protesting the deal offered employees who were dismissed when SESI closed two clinics, the ASSESI president pointedly quoted a recent speech by Noschese that mentioned the importance of respecting workers' rights. See AG, Processos, P59/4413, Oct. 17, 1962.

79. *BI*, no. 474 (Nov. 5, 1958): 100–101; no. 583 (Dec. 7, 1960); Pierro, *A Indústria, o Estado e a Economia Nacional*, pp. 39–45. On "hierarchical solidarity," see Chapter 7.

80. *BI*, no. 331 (Feb. 6, 1956): 135–36.

81. Ibid. For further discussion of these issues, see Barbara Weinstein, "Industrialists, the State, and the Limits of Democratization."

82. "Opinião: A Indústria e as Forças Armadas," *BI*, no. 473 (Oct. 29, 1958): 68–69. It is revealing that SENAI apprentices were exempted from the draft. See "Aprendizes do SENAI e o Serviço Militar," *Informativo SENAI*, no. 157 (Apr. 1959): 4.

83. See Pinheiro and Hall, *A Classe Operária*, vol. 2, intro., and Wolfe, *Working Women*. For an overview, see Paoli, Sader, and Telles, "Pensando a Classe Operária."

84. For an interesting example of the extent and limits of individualized resistance, see José Sérgio Leite Lopes, "Sôbre os Trabalhadores da Grande Indústria."

85. Interviews with William Winslow, July 8, 1954; Dan Hamer, May 8, 1956; and Carmino Urcioli, Apr. 23, 1956, AP.

86. McMillan, "American Businessman," p. 69 (emphasis added).

87. Interviews with William Embry, Mar. 16, 1956, and Achim Fuerstenthal, Mar. 15, 1956, AP.

88. For a discussion of this literature, see Fausto, "Estado, Trabalhadores e Burguesia."

89. Several authors, writing from different perspectives, have chronicled these struggles. See Maranhão, *Sindicatos e Democratização*; Loyola, *Os Sindicatos e o PTB*; French, *Brazilian Workers' ABC*; and Wolfe, *Working Women*.

90. John Humphrey briefly raises the issue of employer power in the workplace to explain the weakness of shopfloor organization in this period (*Capitalist Control*, pp. 17–24).

91. This was an option that was certainly not available in the 1970s, under military rule, which helps explain the turn to shopfloor struggles. See Maroni, *A Estratégia da Recusa*, pp. 69-98.

92. "Opinião: Perspectivas Sombrias," *BI*, no. 481 (Dec. 24, 1958): 332-33. The CNI and FIESP were also unhappy with Kubitschek's 1959 decree that subjected the budgets of SENAI and SESI to review by the federal Tribunal das Contas. See interview with Luiz Gonzaga Ferreira, Sept. 22, 1989, PM.

93. Schmitter, *Interest Conflict*, p. 338. Lídio Lunardi, president of the CNI from 1956 to 1961, was chosen because he was from Minas Gerais and had a good relationship with Kubitschek.

94. Pierro, *A Indústria, o Estado e a Economia Nacional*, pp. 30-31.

95. On this scandal and the intervention in the CNI, see Leopoldi, "Industrial Associations," p. 317, and *ESP*, July 1, 1961.

96. The honored guest (along with FIESP officials) at the school's inauguration was President Goulart, who the FIESP leadership was already plotting to overthrow. See *BI*, no. 726 (Sept. 4, 1963): 6.

97. *BI*, no. 587 (Jan. 4, 1961): 149.

98. "O SENAI e a Mão-de-Obra Especializada," *Jornal do Comércio*, May 14, 1961. Enrollment in the school-based programs grew only gradually, even during the boom years after 1968.

99. *BI*, no. 568 (Aug. 24, 1960): 36-37.

100. *SJ*, July 1960, p. 1.

101. AC, SESI-SP, Atas do Conselho Regional, July 6, 1961. I found several explanations for the cancellation of the parade. Mário di Pierro criticized it as too expensive and competitive (since companies pressured SESI officials for prizes). See AC, SESI-SP, Atas do Conselho Regional, Feb. 24, Apr. 7, 1961. Saad blamed its cancellation on heavier traffic in Anhangabaú. See SESI-SP, DOS, *SESI—18 Anos*, p. 138.

102. AC, SESI-SP, Atas do Conselho Regional, Oct. 30, 1962; *BI*, no. 685 (Nov. 21, 1962): 4-5.

103. *ES*, no. 6 (June 1963): 16.

104. AC, SESI-SP, Atas do Conselho Regional, Oct. 30, 1962.

105. Ibid.; "Casa Própria para Trabalhadores," *BI*, no. 592 (Feb. 1, 1961): 288.

106. SESI-SP, Divisão de Educação Fundamental, *SESI—18 Anos*, pp. 17, 45-54.

107. "Escolas Primárias nas Emprêsas Fabris," *BI*, no. 602 (Apr. 19, 1961): 103.

108. *BI*, no. 620 (Aug. 23, 1961): 134. Even in private, SESI's regional council spoke enthusiastically about SESI's role in the primary schools. See AC, SESI-SP, Atas do Conselho Regional, July 28, 1961.

109. SESI-SP, Divisão de Educação Fundamental, *SESI—18 Anos*, p. 17.

110. Ibid., p. 54.

111. On the Goulart succession, see Skidmore, *Politics in Brazil*, pp. 205-20. The military allowed Goulart to take office only after a compromise that reduced his presidential powers.

112. FIESP officials who were Superior War College graduates included A. C. Pacheco e Silva and Mário di Pierro.

113. *BI*, no. 473 (Oct. 29, 1958): 68-69; no. 474 (Nov. 5, 1958): 100-101; *SJ*, Oct. 31, 1959, p. 2.

114. On the Forum Roberto Simonsen and industrialist politics, see Boschi, *Elites Industriais*, pp. 89–94, and Leopoldi, "Industrial Associations," p. 315n. Pacheco e Silva and new FIESP president Raphael Noschese were members of the UDN, the anti-*getulista* and anti-Goulart party. The UDNistas increased their visibility and influence in FIESP in the early 1960s.

115. *BI*, no. 654 (Apr. 18, 1962): 461–69; no. 652 (Apr. 4, 1962): 393.

116. AC, SESI-SP, Atas do Conselho Regional, Oct. 25, 1961. At this meeting, the council voted to fund a weekly page on "industrial matters" in the *Diário de São Paulo*, much of which dealt with SENAI and SESI.

117. See Chapter 5.

118. Pierro, *A Indústria, o Estado e a Economia Nacional*, pp. 13–14. A military man might be expected to view the term "captain" in a positive light. In contrast, Fernando Henrique Cardoso's contemporaneous study dubbed the more traditional and authoritarian employer a "captain of industry" and the more modern employer a "company man" (*Empresário Industrial*, pp. 133–40).

119. Pierro, *A Indústria, o Estado e a Economia Nacional*, p. 30.

120. Ibid., pp. 44–55. In Portuguese, Pierro says his social class should be truly "dirigente," which does not sound as strong as the closest reasonable translation, "ruling" class. For an early version of the "weak national bourgeoisie" argument, see Cardoso, *Empresário Industrial*, pp. 159–66.

121. *BI*, no. 531 (Dec. 9, 1959): 144–51; "Existem no País Sintomas Insurreicionais," *BI*, no. 588 (Jan. 11, 1961): 166–69.

122. *BI*, no. 623 (Sept. 13, 1961): 248; no. 624 (Sept. 20, 1961): 3.

123. Devisate did urge FIESP members to pay the "Christmas bonus" on a voluntary basis. See *BI*, no. 638 (Dec. 27, 1961): 215. On the angry response of employers in Rio to a mandatory thirteenth-month salary, see Carone, *O Centro Industrial*, pp. 162–63.

124. *BI*, no. 637 (Dec. 20, 1961): 191. In this statement, the FIESP leadership articulated positions remarkably similar to its pre-1930 attitudes: it called upon the police for support and questioned the "real" advantages of even basic social benefits.

125. "Opinião: O 'Basta' da Indústria," *BI*, no. 639 (Jan. 3, 1962): 244–45; Carone, *O Centro Industrial*, pp. 158–59.

126. *BI*, no. 641 (Jan. 17, 1962): 36–37. Even at this point, FIESP's articles did not attack Goulart directly. This reflects, in part, a traditional avoidance of personal attacks but also may be due to the influence of a cohort within FIESP that still supported the government. See Leopoldi, "Industrial Associations," pp. 314–17.

127. *BI*, no. 678 (Oct. 3, 1962): 499; no. 679 (Oct. 10, 1962): 527–35.

128. "Informativo da Presidência," *BI*, no. 698 (Feb. 20, 1963): 9.

129. AC, SESI-SP, Atas do Conselho Regional, Sept. 4, 1962; *ES*, no. 12 (Dec. 1962): 16. SESI's radio show, "Message to the Worker," culminated in a "Competition on Civic Preparation," with cash prizes.

130. Many SESI programs in this area operated parallel to, or in coordination with, the now notorious activities of the Institute for Social Research Studies, documented in Dreifuss, *1964*, pp. 305–19. In the early 1960s, SESI-SP donated 1 million cruzeiros each to the Movimento Sindical Democrático and the Movimento Universitário de Desfavelamento (a right-wing student group involved in community improvement). See AC, SESI-SP, Atas do Conselho Regional, July 28, 1961, Apr. 9, 1963. Dreifuss

focuses almost exclusively on the Institute for Social Research Studies and ignores SESI's role.

131. AC, SESI-SP, Atas do Conselho Regional, Nov. 24, 1960.

132. AC, SESI-SP, Atas do Conselho Regional, July 28, 1961; Dreifuss, *1964*, p. 312.

133. Erickson, *Brazilian Corporative State*, p. 135; Benevides, *O Governo Kubitschek*, p. 92.

134. Erickson, *Brazilian Corporative State*, p. 142.

135. *BI*, no. 694 (Jan. 23, 1963): 3.

136. See Chapter 3.

137. AG, Processos (COs), P17/2803/2804 (CO Embaré), July 27, 1962.

138. *BI*, no. 658 (May 16, 1962): 100–101. Six years earlier, the head of the Productivity Department of FIRJ (Federação das Indústrias do Rio de Janeiro) had been optimistic about Brazilian labor leaders' role in promoting rational organization. See interview with Affonso Campiglia, Mar. 9, 1956, AP.

139. See, for example, "Subdesenvolvimento Não é Destino," *ES*, no. 9 (Sept. 1961): 2; "Declaração de Princípios de Dirigentes de Emprêsa," *ES*, no. 4 (Apr. 1962): 1; "Reforma Agrária: Limitações ao Direito de Propriedade," *ES*, no. 7 (July 1962): 14.

140. *BI*, no. 702 (Mar. 20, 1963): 6–9; no. 728 (Sept. 18, 1963): 4.

141. *BI*, no. 658 (May 16, 1962): 119.

142. By far the most important and extensive study of the industrialists' role is Dreifuss, *1964*. See also Payne, *Brazilian Industrialists*, chap. 2.

143. "Opinião: A Politiquice Está Devorando o Brasil," *BI*, no. 742 (Dec. 25, 1963): 4–5. For a survey of industrialist opinion that places more emphasis on the impact of government economic policies, see Richers et al., *Impacto da Ação do Governo*.

144. Again, covert support had begun much earlier. See interview with Raphael Noschese, June 25, 1990, PM; Siekman, "When Executives Turned Revolutionaries," p. 147; and Dreifuss, *1964*.

145. Interview with Raphael Noschese, June 25, 1990, PM; *BI*, no. 755 (Mar. 25, 1964): 4–5.

146. Schmitter, *Interest Conflict*, p. 360.

147. Two accounts that give substantial weight to the role of industrialists and other business sectors are Dreifuss, *1964*, and Starling, *Os Senhores das Gerais*. Leopoldi takes a position similar to Schmitter's ("Industrial Associations," p. 319).

148. I explore the relationship between industrial social policy and industrialists' political position in "Industrialists, the State, and the Limits of Democratization."

149. *BI*, no. 757 (Apr. 8, 1964): 4–5.

150. AC, SESI-SP, Atas do Conselho Regional, July 30, 1964.

151. AC, SESI-SP, Atas do Conselho Regional, Oct. 12, 1964.

Epilogue and Conclusion

1. *Boletim Interno* (CNI), no. 38 (Apr. 17, 1964): 1.

2. Both Eduardo Saad and Raphael Noschese later claimed that "all of the people" supported the 1964 "revolution." See interview by author with Eduardo Gabriel Saad,

July 10, 1986, and interview with Raphael Noschese, June 25, 1990, PM.

3. Among the official advisers to the temporary governing board were Eduardo Saad and Mario Henrique Simonsen.

4. An authorized history recounts Bologna's appointment as reflecting the resurgence of the paulistas in SENAI's national organization. See Stênio Lopes, *Uma Saga da Criatividade Brasileira*, pp. 101–2.

5. *Boletim Interno* (CNI), no. 86 (Dec. 31, 1964): 1.

6. PH, Light, Serviços de Pessoal, "Relatório" (1964), p. 1.

7. "Nova Fase do Sindicalismo," *Unitêxtil*, July 1964, p. 1.

8. "Ano Nôvo, Novas Esperanças," *ES*, no. 6 (Nov.–Dec. 1965): 1.

9. Interview with Raphael Noschese, June 25, 1990, PM.

10. During my interview with DOS head Eduardo Gabriel Saad (July 10, 1986), he expressed indignation when my questioning implied that there was a possible incompatibility between support for democracy and support for the military coup.

11. "Ano Nôvo," *ES*, no. 6 (Nov.–Dec. 1965): 1.

12. SESI-SP, DOS, *SESI—18 Anos*, pp. 61–63, 83–84. Saad was a member of the FIESP commission that revived the Union Squad.

13. *O Trabalhador Químico*, Dec. 1972, p. 7.

14. On this contest, see Barbara Weinstein, "The Model Worker."

15. The use of the masculine pronoun is intentional; few women were nominated, even at the factory level. Ibid., pp. 101–2.

16. Ibid., pp. 103–4. The most impressive case I came across was a section head in a Brahma beer plant who, between 1961 and 1980, took eight SESI and four SENAI courses.

17. Sader, *Quando Novos Personagens*, pp. 86–87.

18. Richers et al., *Impacto da Ação*, cited in Vianna, *Liberalismo e Sindicato*, p. 277.

19. AC, SESI-SP, Atas do Conselho Regional, Feb. 23, 1967; *ES*, no. 156 (Nov.–Dec. 1966): 2–3.

20. *ES*, no. 156 (Nov.–Dec. 1966): 2–3; Vianna, *Liberalismo e Sindicato*, pp. 271–88; "O Que é a Lei 5,107," *TG*, Mar. 1967, p. 12. The latter depicted the FGTS as purely benefiting the employers and claimed that workers had no choice in the matter.

21. Vianna, *Liberalismo e Sindicato*, p. 284; *ES*, no. 156 (Nov.–Dec. 1966).

22. *Tribuna Sindical*, Aug. 1966, p. 8.

23. AG, Processos (Prefeituras), P32/377 (Santo André), May 27, 1969; P32/155 (Jundiaí), Aug. 2, 1965; AG, Processos (Sindicatos-T), P79/135/3101 (STIMME-Sorocaba).

24. *Diário Oficial da União*, Jan. 26, 1968, p. 911; AG, Processos, P79/4268/4269, July 17, 1968; P79/2463, Feb. 3, 1956. Some unions tried to evade the prohibition by making a joint request with the municipal council.

25. On difficulties in the transference of funds, see BCNI, Atas do Conselho Nacional do SENAI, Aug. 1962. On PIPMOI/PIPMO, see interview with Luiz Gonzaga Ferreira, Aug. 10, 1989, PM, and Francisco Santos Lopes, "Sistema Brasileiro."

26. PM, SENAI-SP, "Relatório do Departamento Regional de São Paulo pelo Ano 1965" (1966), pp. 1–4. SENAI–São Paulo also began receiving equipment from Alliance for Progress agencies.

27. *Revista SENAI*, no. 82 (Jan.–Mar. 1966): 1.

28. BARS, SESI-SP, "Relatório do Departamento Regional de São Paulo pelo Ano 1967" (1968), and "Relatório" (1970).

29. *Revista SENAI*, no. 82 (Jan.–Mar. 1966): 1.

30. SENAI-SP, "Quatro Décadas de História," 1960–69; *TG*, June–July 1969, p. 11; *Comunicação/SENAI*, no. 1 (Sept.–Oct. 1974): 3.

31. *Informador Sindical*, no. 2 (Mar. 1970): 28–29.

32. "Problemas do Menor," *MET*, Feb.–Mar. 1971, p. 4.

33. Tolle, *Retrospecto*, pp. 45–48.

34. Stênio Lopes, *Uma Saga da Criatividade Brasileira*, p. 191. Previous ceilings on payments, based on the minimum wage, were less restrictive.

35. PM, *O Giz e a Graxa*, pp. 84–85.

36. Tolle, *Retrospecto*, pp. 18–23; Castro, *O Ethos*, p. 7.

37. Schmitter, *Interest Conflict*, pp. 361–62.

38. Cohn, *Previdência Social*, pp. 35–93.

39. Interview with Luis Inácio Lula da Silva, Feb. 6, 1992, PM.

40. There is an extensive literature on professions and expertise in the United States. See, for example, Haskell, *Authority of Experts*. Similar studies for Brazil would have to pay considerable attention to SENAI and SESI.

41. One dramatic example would be the campaign against child labor in the United States. See Sklar, *Florence Kelley*.

42. AG, P3/114, Aug. 2, 1948.

43. Freire was innovative even as a SESI director, turning control of social centers over to labor unions. Significantly, he claimed SESI functionaries were more resistant to this idea than local industrialists. See interview with Paulo Freire, Feb. 18, 1956, AP.

44. Article from *ESP* reprinted in *SJ*, Jan. 31, 1952, p. 3.

45. Contrast this with the version of rationalization that appealed to German Social Democrats in the 1920s, discussed in Nolan, *Visions of Modernity*, pp. 30–57.

46. FIESP Circular no. 430, July 19, 1933.

47. See Chapter 3.

48. For a very insightful discussion of these stereotypes, see Andrews, *Blacks and Whites*, pp. 54–89.

49. *TG*, Aug. 1965, p. 3.

50. My thinking on this has been deeply influenced by French's study of labor and populism, *Brazilian Workers' ABC*, as well as by James's *Resistance and Integration*, a study of workers and Peronism in Argentina.

51. FIESP Circular no. 59/43, Apr. 7, 1943.

52. For discussions of access to SENAI training, see Luiz Pereira, *Classe Operária*, pp. 47–70; Castro, Assis, and Oliveira, *Ensino Técnico*, pp. 230–33; and Edfelt, "Occupational Education," pp. 384–413.

53. Castro, Assis, and Oliveira, in *Ensino Técnico*, concluded that "industrial instruction in Brazil clearly serves a masculine clientele" (pp. 226–27).

54. This should not be confused with Guillermo O'Donnell's bureaucratic-authoritarian thesis, since industrialists' concern with social peace preceded by many years the "exhaustion" of the import-substitution model. For a strong critique of O'Donnell's thesis, see Payne, *Brazilian Industrialists*, p. 153.

55. On the widespread acceptance of developmental nationalism, see Franco, "O Tempo das Ilusões."

56. Among the many studies of the new unionism, see Keck, *Workers' Party*, and Sader, *Quando Novos Personagens*.

57. Frederico, *Consciência Operária*, p. 46. This worker also noted skilled workers' greater job security. See also Humphrey, *Capitalist Control*, p. 162. On the limits of job security for skilled workers, see Sader, *Quando Novos Personagens*, pp. 86–88.

58. A former SENAI official put a different spin on this "failure," claiming that the prominence of its graduates among new union leaders proved SENAI produced the "cream" of industrial workers. See interview with Oswaldo de Barros Santos, June 12, 1990, PM.

59. Simonsen, "As Finanças e a Indústria," p. 217.

60. Sader, *Quando Novos Personagens*, p. 87.

61. Fleury, "Rotinização do Trabalho"; Springer, *Brazilian Factory Study*, chap. 2.

62. For a related view, see Isabel Ribeiro de Oliveira, *Trabalho e Política*, which diverges from the dominant interpretation of the Workers' Party as representing a sharp break with past labor discourse.

Bibliography

Primary Sources

Few of the sources for this study, published or unpublished, came from the sort of public archives or libraries in which historians are accustomed to doing research. Some sources came from "active archives," whereas others came from unlabeled closets somewhere in the precincts of Serviço Social da Indústria's São Paulo headquarters. Thus, it is especially complicated to list all of the primary sources I consulted in a way that clearly indicates the physical location of the material. To solve this problem, I have resorted to a more descriptive, and less telegraphic, mode of bibliographical citation of primary sources. What follows is a list of "locations" where I did research and the main types of material I consulted in each.

Robert Alexander Papers, Rutgers University, New Brunswick, N.J.: reports on labor relations, SENAI, and SESI; transcripts of interviews with employers, FIESP, SENAI, and SESI officials, and labor leaders conducted by Robert Alexander in the 1950s and 1960s; reports and pamphlets from SENAI and SESI, 1950s.

Arquivo da Administração, São Paulo Light & Power: correspondence between Light and SENAI and SESI, 1939–64; internal correspondence concerning SENAI apprentices and SESI services.

Arquivo do Centro dos Industriaes/Sindicato da Indústria de Fiação e Tecelagem de São Paulo: notices to members (*circulares*); other correspondence and reports of the textile manufacturers' association, 1928–47.

Arquivo do Estado, São Paulo: annual reports (*mensagens*) of governors and other state officials to the state legislative assembly, 1909–65; reports on state vocational schools; educational codes; annual publications on the state educational system.

Arquivo do Instituto de Organização Racional do Trabalho, São Paulo: minutes of general assemblies, 1931–39; annual reports; course materials; monthly periodicals.

Arquivo Edgard Leuenroth, Universidade Estadual de Campinas, Campinas: union newspapers, 1905–70.

Arquivo Geral, Serviço Social da Indústria, São Paulo: correspondence between SESI and industrial firms, labor unions, worker organizations, employer *sindicatos*, and municipal governments, 1946–70.

Assessoria de Comunicações, Serviço Social da Indústria, São Paulo: minutes (*atas*) of the regional council, SESI-SP, 1947–70; internal periodicals; dossiers of candidates for the Model-Worker Contest (Campanha Operário Padrão).

Biblioteca da Confederação Nacional da Indústria, Serviço Nacional de Aprendizagem Industrial and Serviço Social da Indústria, Rio de Janeiro: minutes of the national council of SENAI, 1944–62; monthly bulletins of CNI, SENAI; dossiers of model workers, 1964–84.

Biblioteca do Serviço Nacional de Aprendizagem Industrial, São Paulo: occasional reports; specialized monographs; internal bulletins and periodicals.

Biblioteca e Arquivo Roberto Simonsen, São Paulo: CIESP/FIESP notices (*circulares*); memoranda; correspondence; summaries of directors' meetings, 1929–49; weekly bulletins of CIESP/FIESP, 1949–64; annual reports (*relatórios*) of SESI-SP; pamphlets issued by SENAI and SESI; periodicals and monthly bulletins published by SESI.

Departamento Intersindical de Estatísticas e Estudos Sócio-Econômicos, São Paulo: union newspapers, 1950–74.

Divisão de Orientação Social, Serviço Social da Indústria, São Paulo: monthly journals; internal bulletins; course materials and manuals for social educators, supervisors, and labor leaders.

Fundação Getúlio Vargas, Centro de Pesquisa e Documentação, Rio de Janeiro: archives of Gustavo Capanema, Valdemar (Waldemar) Falcão, M. B. Lourenço Filho, and Alexandre Marcondes Filho.

National Archives and Records Administration, Washington, D.C.: Record Group 59, Brazil, 1945–49.

Patrimônio Histórico, São Paulo Light & Power: internal correspondence and "general orders" of Light, 1908–52; annual reports of the employment bureau/personnel services, 1932–70; occasional reports and bulletins.

Projeto Memória, Serviço Nacional de Aprendizagem Industrial, São Paulo: annual reports (*relatórios*), 1942–72; transcripts of interviews with former SENAI officials, instructors, and students, 1989–92; documentation of the Centro Ferroviário de Ensino e Seleção Profissional; publications of the Centro de Estudos "Roberto Mange."

Newspapers, Bulletins, and Journals

All periodicals were published in São Paulo unless otherwise indicated.

EMPLOYER ASSOCIATION AND INDUSTRY PERIODICALS

Boletim do Supervisor (São Paulo Light & Power), 1956–66
Boletim Informativo (CIESP, FIESP), 1949–64
Boletim Interno (CNI, SESI, SENAI; Rio de Janeiro), 1963–64
Boletim Interno da DOS, 1953–59
Boletim SENAI (Rio de Janeiro), 1945–47
CIPA-Jornal, 1957–70
Comunicação/SENAI, 1974
Dona de Casa, 1950–53
Educador Social, 1952–73
Informativo SENAI, 1945–62
Revista de Organização Científica, 1941–45
Revista IDORT, 1932–40

Revista SENAI (Rio de Janeiro), 1948–72
SESI-Higiene, 1950–56
SESI-Jornal, 1948–60, 1968–69
Síntese (Indústrias Reunidas Francisco Matarazzo), 1948

GOVERNMENT AND MAINSTREAM PERIODICALS

Boletim do Ministério do Trabalho, Indústria e Comércio (Rio de Janeiro), 1934–45
Boletim Informativo do Departamento Estadual do Trabalho, 1948
Boletim Informativo do Trabalho, 1951–53
Corrêio Paulistano, 1959–60
O Estado de São Paulo, 1907–67
Informador Sindical, 1969–70
Tribuna Sindical (Rio de Janeiro), 1965–69

UNION AND LABOR PERIODICALS

O Arauto do Vendedor, 1961 (salespersons)
O Condutor, 1957 (urban transport workers)
O Eletricitário, 1962–70 (electricians)
O Ferroviário em Marcha (Guanabara), 1963 (railroad workers)
A Massa, 1960–63 (bakery workers)
A Média, 1958–63 (food-processing workers)
O Metalúrgico, 1943–73 (metalworkers)
A Sovela, 1958–65 (shoe industry workers)
O Trabalhador em Madeira, 1955 (carpenters/furniture workers)
O Trabalhador Gráfico, 1905–6, 1920–69 (printers)
O Trabalhador Metalúrgico, 1961–62 (metalworkers' federation)
O Trabalhador Químico, 1970–77 (chemical workers)
O Trabalhador Têxtil, 1939–70 (textile workers)
O Trilho, 1958–63 (railroad workers)
Unitêxtil, 1964 (textile workers' federation)
A Voz da Construção Civil, 1951–64 (construction workers)
A Voz do Gráfico (Guanabara), 1959–60 (printers)
A Voz do Metalúrgico (Guanabara), 1958–61 (metalworkers)

Interviews

All interviews took place in the city of São Paulo unless otherwise indicated.

CONDUCTED BY THE AUTHOR

José Brasil de Castro Alves (shoemakers' union), July 18, 1986.
Mário Amato (president, FIESP), May 6, 1986.
João Batista Cândido (labor militant and pipe fitter), June 5, 1986, São José dos Campos.
Affonso Delellis (official, STIMMMESP, 1954–64), July 18, 1986.
José Luiz Gonçalves (union president, SENAI graduate, and former instructor), June 5, 1986, São José dos Campos.
Maria Antonieta Guerriero (social worker and technical assistant, DOS), June 10, 1986.

Hélvio Pinheiro Lima (director of public relations, SESI, and former social educator), July 14, 1986.

Lázaro Maia (general secretary, carpenters' union), July 18, 1986.

Pedro Francisco de Oliveira (lathe operator and SENAI graduate), June 5, 1986, São José dos Campos.

Eduardo Gabriel Saad (director, DOS), July 10, 1986.

Pedro Senna (assistant to regional director, SENAI, and former instructor), July 3, 1986.

Onofre da Silva (retired personnel supervisor, General Motors), June 5, 1986, São José dos Campos.

CONDUCTED BY PROJETO MEMÓRIA, SERVIÇO NACIONAL DE APRENDIZAGEM INDUSTRIAL, SÃO PAULO

Luiz Gonzaga Ferreira (assistant to regional director, SENAI), Aug. 10, Sept. 22, 1989.

Sebastião da Luz (former SENAI instructor), Apr. 5, 1990.

Ernest Mange (son of Roberto Mange), Apr. 11, June 19, 1990.

Roger Mange (son of Roberto Mange), June 3, 11, 1990.

Raphael Noschese (president, FIESP, 1962–65), June 25, 1990.

Gentil Palmiro (former technical assistant, Division of Instruction, SENAI), Sept. 28, 1989.

Oswaldo de Barros Santos (former director, Psychotechnic Testing, SENAI), June 12, July 12, 1990.

Luis Inácio Lula da Silva (labor militant, head of Workers' Party, SENAI graduate), Feb. 6, 1992.

Ophir Corrêa de Toledo (former school director, SENAI), May 10, 1990, Campinas.

CONDUCTED BY ROBERT ALEXANDER

Custódio Sobral Martins de Almeida (Fábrica Nacional de Motores), Apr. 5, 1956, Rio de Janeiro.

Caio Plínio Barreto (lawyer for FIESP), June 17–18, 1953.

Júlio Bella (director of public relations, SESI-SP), Apr. 12–13, 1956.

Maria Braz (Division of Basic Education, SESI-SP), Apr. 12, 1956.

Affonso Campiglia (director, Department of Productivity, Federação de Indústrias do Rio de Janeiro), Mar. 9, 1956, Rio de Janeiro.

Antônio Devisate (president, FIESP, SESI-SP), Apr. 12, 1956.

Affonso Celso Dias (Division of Education and Culture, SESI-SP), Dec. 4, 1956.

William Embry (Kibon), Mar. 16, 1956, Rio de Janeiro.

Paulo Freire (director, SESI-Pernambuco), Feb. 18, 1956, Recife.

Achim Fuerstenthal (psychotechnician), Mar. 15, 1956, Rio de Janeiro.

Dan Hamer (Armour), May 8, 1956, Livramento.

Aldo Lombardi (general secretary, STIMMMESP), Apr. 17, 1956.

Hugo Guimarães Malheiros (chief, Social Service Subdivision, SESI-SP), Apr. 13, 1956.

Severino Mariz Filho (Estamparia Colombo), Aug. 6, 1965, Rio de Janeiro.

J. M. Moreira de Moraes (secretary, SIFTSP), Apr. 27, 1956.

Maj. Joaquim Gonçalves Moreira (Cia. Siderúrgica Nacional), Apr. 4, 1956, Volta Redonda.

Luiz Marcondes Nitsch (head of publicity, SENAI), Apr. 27, 1956.

Paulo Novaes (subdirector, SENAI-DN), Mar. 21, 1956.

Cyro de Noronha Pelúcio (assistant director of public relations, SESI-SP), Apr. 12, 1956.

Olavo Previatti (president, Federation of Paper Industry Workers), Apr. 27, 1956.

Kurt Renner (A. J. Renner Cia.), May 2, 1956, Porto Alegre.
Maria Lourdes de Ribeiro (director, CAD, SESI), Apr. 16, 1956.
Eduardo Gabriel Saad (director, DOS), Apr. 13–14, 1956.
Israel Sartini (Artex S.A.), Apr. 12, 1965, Blumenau.
Guillermo Sauer and Fred Sauer (F. Sauer & Filhos), Mar. 14, 1956, Rio de Janeiro.
Maria José Serra (social worker, SESI-SP), Apr. 16, 1956.
Roberto Simonsen Sobrinho (director, Division of Food Supply, SESI-SP), Apr. 12, 1956.
Marcelo Coimbra Tavares (Cia. Siderúrgica Belgo-Mineira), Mar. 27, 1956, Belo Horizonte.
Carlos Borges Teixeira (Statistics Department, FIESP), July 7, 1954.
Carmino Urcioli (Ind. Reunidas F. Matarazzo), Apr. 23, 1956.
William Winslow (Winslow & Serra), July 8, 1954.

Other Sources

Albuquerque Lins, M. J. *Mensagem Enviada ao Congresso Legislativo de São Paulo pelo Presidente do Estado.* São Paulo, 1909.
Alexander, Robert J. *Labor Relations in Argentina, Brazil, and Chile.* New York: McGraw-Hill, 1962.
Alexim, João Carlos. "Origem e Concepção das Instituições Patronais de Aprendizagem e Serviço Social." M.A. thesis, IUPERJ, Rio de Janeiro, 1978.
Andrews, George Reid. "Black and White Workers: São Paulo, Brazil, 1888–1928." *Hispanic American Historical Review* 68 (Aug. 1988): 491–524.
————. *Blacks and Whites in São Paulo, Brazil, 1888–1988.* Madison: University of Wisconsin Press, 1991.
Antonacci, Maria Antonieta M. "A Vitória da Razão." Ph.D. diss., University of São Paulo, 1985.
Anuário do Ensino do Estado de São Paulo. São Paulo, 1918.
Archila, Mauricio. "The Construction of Working-Class Identity in Colombia, 1910–1945." Ph.D. diss., State University of New York at Stony Brook, 1991.
Azevedo, Aldo Mário de. "O Capital e o Trabalho, um Equívoco Tradicional." In *Quatro Discursos.* São Paulo: Revista dos Tribunaes, 1936.
————. "Discurso do A. M. de Azevedo na Ocasião da 1ª Reunião do IDORT, June 23, 1931." In *Quatro Discursos.* São Paulo: Revista dos Tribunaes, 1936.
————. "Discurso Pronunciado pelo Engº Aldo Mário de Azevedo na Sessão de 30/X/36 da Assembléia Legislativa do Estado de São Paulo." In *Quatro Discursos.* São Paulo: Revista dos Tribunaes, 1936.
————. "Na Era do Machinismo a Sociedade Mechanica." In *Quatro Discursos.* São Paulo: Revista dos Tribunaes, 1936.
————. "Uma Nova Forma de Zelar pelo Bem Estar dos Operários." *Revista de Organização Científica,* no. 126 (June 1942): 3.
————. *Quatro Discursos.* São Paulo: Revista dos Tribunaes, 1936.
Azevedo, Célia Marinho de. *Onda Negra, Mêdo Branco.* Rio de Janeiro: Paz e Terra, 1987.
Azevedo, Fernando de. *A Educação Pública em São Paulo.* São Paulo: Cia. Editora Nacional, 1937.
Baer, Werner. *Industrialization and Economic Development in Brazil.* Homewood, Ill.: Irwin Press, 1965.

Baker, Keith Michael. "A Foucauldian French Revolution?" In *Foucault and the Writing of History*, edited by Jan Goldstein, pp. 187–205. Oxford: Oxford University Press, 1994.

Benevides, Maria Victória de Mesquita. *O Governo Kubitschek*. Rio de Janeiro: Paz e Terra, 1976.

———. *O PTB e o Trabalhismo*. São Paulo: Brasiliense, 1989.

Besse, Susan K. *Restructuring Patriarchy: The Modernization of Gender Inequality in Brazil, 1914–1945*. Chapel Hill: University of North Carolina Press, 1996.

Bethell, Leslie, and Ian Roxborough. "Latin America between the Second World War and the Cold War: Some Reflections on the 1945–1948 Conjuncture." *Journal of Latin American Studies* 20 (May 1988): 167–89.

Bologna, Ítalo, ed. *Roberto Mange e Sua Obra*. Goiânia: UNIGRAF, 1980.

Borges, Vavy Pacheco. *Getúlio Vargas e a Oligarquia Paulista*. São Paulo: Brasiliense, 1979.

———. *Tenentismo e Revolução Brasileira*. São Paulo: Brasiliense, 1992.

Boschi, Renato Raúl. *Elites Industriais e Democracia*. Rio de Janeiro: Graal, 1979.

Brandes, Stuart D. *American Welfare Capitalism, 1880–1940*. Chicago: University of Chicago Press, 1970.

Braverman, Harry. *Labor and Monopoly Capital: The Degradation of Work in the Twentieth Century*. New York: Monthly Review Press, 1974.

Bresciani, Maria Stella. "Liberalismo, Ideologia e Contrôle Social." 2 vols. Ph.D. diss., University of São Paulo, 1976.

Bryan, Newton. "SENAI, Estrutura e Funcionamento." M.A. thesis, Universidade Estadual de Campinas, 1984.

Burnham, John C. *Paths into American Culture: Psychology, Medicine, and Morals*. Philadelphia: Temple University Press, 1988.

Campos, Carlos de. *Mensagem Enviada ao Congresso Legislativo de São Paulo pelo Presidente do Estado*. São Paulo, 1925.

Capelato, Maria Helena. *Os Arautos do Liberalismo*. São Paulo: Brasiliense, 1988.

———. *O Movimento de 1932: A Causa Paulista*. São Paulo: Brasiliense, 1982.

Capelato, Maria Helena, and Maria Lígia Coelho Prado. *O Bravo Matutino: Imprensa e Ideologia no Jornal "O Estado de São Paulo."* São Paulo: Alfa-Omega, 1980.

Cardoso, Fernando Henrique. *Empresário Industrial e Desenvolvimento Econômico no Brasil*. São Paulo: Difel, 1964.

Cardoso, Miriam Limoeiro. *Ideologia do Desenvolvimento—Brasil: JK, JQ*. Rio de Janeiro: Paz e Terra, 1978.

Carone, Edgard. *O Centro Industrial do Rio de Janeiro*. Rio de Janeiro: O Centro, 1978.

———, ed. *O Pensamento Industrial no Brasil, 1880–1945*. Rio de Janeiro: Difel, 1977.

———. *A Quarta República, 1945–1964*. São Paulo: Difel, 1980.

Carvalho, José Murilo de. *Os Bestializados: O Rio de Janeiro e a República que Não Foi*. São Paulo: Companhia das Letras, 1987.

Castilho de Lima, Waldomiro. *Mensagem do Gal. Waldomiro Castilho de Lima no Governo de São Paulo, como Interventor Federal no Estado*. São Paulo, 1933.

Castro, Claudio de Moura. *O Ethos da Formação Profissional*. São Paulo: SENAI-SP, 1978.

Castro, Claudio de Moura, Milton Pereira de Assis, and Sandra Furtado de Oliveira. *Ensino Técnico: Desempenho e Custos*. Rio de Janeiro: IPEA, 1972.

Centro Ferroviário de Ensino e Seleção Profissional. *Noções de Higiene—Alimentação*. São Paulo: Inspetoria Médica, 1937.

———. *Relatórios*. São Paulo: Secção de Ensino, 1931, 1933.

Chapple, Eliot D. *How to Supervise People in Industry.* Chicago: National Foremen's Institute, 1946.

Chauí, Marilena. *Cultura e Democracia.* São Paulo: Cortez, 1989.

Cohen, Lizabeth. *Making a New Deal: Industrial Workers in Chicago, 1919–1939.* Cambridge: Cambridge University Press, 1990.

Cohn, Amélia. *Previdência Social e Processo Político no Brasil.* São Paulo: Moderna, 1981.

Cohn, Amélia, Sedi Hirano, Ursula S. Karsch, and Ademar K. Sato. *Acidentes do Trabalho: Uma Forma de Violência.* São Paulo: Brasiliense/CEDEC, 1985.

Conniff, Michael L. *Urban Politics in Brazil: The Rise of Populism, 1925–1945.* Pittsburgh: University of Pittsburgh Press, 1981.

Cooke, Morris L. *Brazil on the March: A Study in International Cooperation.* New York: McGraw-Hill, 1944.

Costa Júnior, Faustino. "Roberto Mange e a Revolução Constitucionalista de 1932." In *Roberto Mange e Sua Obra,* edited by Ítalo Bologna, pp. 399–410. Goiânia: UNIGRAF, 1980.

Da Costa, Ana M. C. Infantosi. "A Educação para Trabalhadores no Estado de São Paulo." *Revista do Instituto de Estudos Brasileiros* 24 (1982), pp. 3–10.

Da Costa, Emilia Viotti. "Brazilian Workers Rediscovered." *International Labor and Working-Class History,* no. 22 (Fall 1982): 28–38.

D'Araújo, Maria Celina Soares. *O Segundo Governo Vargas.* Rio de Janeiro: Zahar, 1982.

D'Avila, Antônio. *O Código de Educação e o SENAI.* São Paulo: SENAI-SP, 1958.

―――. *Eng° Ítalo Bologna: Depositário da Ação e do Pensamento de Roberto Mange.* São Paulo: SENAI-SP, 1971.

―――. *Serviço Nacional de Aprendizagem Industrial—SENAI, 1942–1962.* São Paulo: SENAI-SP, 1962.

Dean, Warren. *The Industrialization of São Paulo, 1880–1945.* Austin: University of Texas Press, 1969.

De Decca, Edgar Salvadori. *O Silêncio dos Vencidos.* São Paulo: Brasiliense, 1981.

Dias, Everardo. *História das Lutas Sociais no Brasil.* São Paulo: Edaglit, 1962.

Diniz, Eli, and Renato Boschi. *Empresariado Nacional e Estado no Brasil.* Rio de Janeiro: Paz e Terra, 1978.

Draibe, Sônia. *Rumos e Metamorfoses: Estado e Industrialização no Brasil, 1930–1960.* Rio de Janeiro: Paz e Terra, 1985.

Dreifuss, René. *1964: A Conquista do Estado.* Petrópolis: Vozes, 1981.

Economic Commission on Latin America. *Economic Survey of Latin America in 1949.* New York: United Nations Department of Economic Affairs, 1951.

―――. *Labour Productivity of the Cotton Textile Industry in Five Latin-American Countries.* New York: United Nations Department of Economic Affairs, 1951.

Edfelt, Ralph. "Occupational Education and Training: The Role of Large Private Industry in Brazil." In *Educational Alternatives in Latin America,* edited by Thomas J. LaBelle, pp. 384–413. Los Angeles: University of California at Los Angeles Latin American Center Publications, 1975.

Edwards, Richard. *Contested Terrain: The Transformation of the Workplace in the Twentieth Century.* New York: Basic Books, 1979.

Eisenberg, Peter L. *The Sugar Industry of Pernambuco: Modernization without Change, 1840–1919.* Berkeley: University of California Press, 1974.

Erickson, Kenneth Paul. *The Brazilian Corporative State and Working-Class Politics.*

Berkeley: University of California Press, 1977.

Escola Profissional Feminina. *Relatório do Diretor*. São Paulo, 1922.

Escola Profissional Masculina. *Relatórios dos Trabalhos*. São Paulo, 1914, 1920, 1923, 1924.

Fanganiello, Helena. *Roberto Simonsen e o Desenvolvimento Econômico*. Boletim no. 60. São Paulo: FEA-USP, 1970.

Fausto, Boris. "Estado, Trabalhadores e Burguesia, 1920–1945." *Novos Estudos CEBRAP*, Mar. 1988, pp. 6–37.

———. *A Revolução de 1930: Historiografia e História*. São Paulo: Brasiliense, 1980.

———. *Trabalho Urbano e Conflito Social, 1890–1920*. São Paulo: Difel, 1977.

Ferraz, Mariano. "Princípios de Organização Racional do Trabalho." *Boletim Informativo*, no. 16 (Apr. 20, 1953): 85–88.

Ferreira, Francisco de Paula. "A Mão de Obra Juvenil e o SENAI." *Boletim SENAI*, no. 2 (May 1946): 22–24.

Figueiredo, Betânia Gonçalves. "A Produtividade do Ócio: SESI e SESC." *Revista Brasileira de História* 9 (Aug. 1989): 47–54.

Fleury, Alonso Carlos Corrêa. "Rotinização do Trabalho: O Caso das Indústrias Mecânicas." In *Organização do Trabalho*, edited by A. C. C. Fleury and Nilton Vargas, pp. 84–106. São Paulo: Atlas, 1983.

Foucault, Michel. *Discipline and Punish: The Birth of the Prison*. Translated by Alan Sheridan. New York: Pantheon, 1977.

Franco, Maria Sylvia Carvalho. "O Tempo das Ilusões." In *Ideologia e Mobilização Popular*, edited by Marilena Chauí and M. S. Carvalho Franco, pp. 151–209. Rio de Janeiro: Paz e Terra/CEDEC, 1978.

Fraser, Steve, and Gary Gerstle, eds. *The Rise and Fall of the New Deal Order, 1930–1980*. Princeton: Princeton University Press, 1989.

Frederico, Celso. *Consciência Operária no Brasil*. São Paulo: Ática, 1978.

French, John D. *The Brazilian Workers' ABC: Class Conflict and Alliances in Modern São Paulo*. Chapel Hill: University of North Carolina Press, 1992.

———. "Social Origins of Resistance in the Factory Workplace: The Not So Powerless Prevail." Unpublished manuscript, 1981.

———. "Workers and the Rise of Adhemarista Populism in São Paulo, 1945–1947." *Hispanic American Historical Review* 68 (Feb. 1988): 1–43.

Freund, Ernst. *The Police Power, Public Policy, and Constitutional Rights*. Chicago: Callaghan, 1904.

Frigotto, Gaudêncio. "Fazendo pelas Mãos a Cabeça do Trabalhador: O Trabalho como Elemento Pedagógico na Formação Profissional." *Cadernos de Pesquisa*, no. 47 (Nov. 1983): 38–45.

Gantt, Henry L. *Work, Wages, and Profits: Their Influence on the Cost of Living*. New York: Engineering Magazine, 1910.

Gerstle, Gary. *Working-Class Americanism*. Cambridge: Cambridge University Press, 1989.

Gillingham, John. "The 'Deproletarianization' of German Society: Vocational Training in the Third Reich." *Journal of Social History* 19 (Spring 1986): 423–32.

Góes Filho, Joaquim Faria. *Diretrizes Atuais da Aprendizagem Industrial*. São Paulo: SENAI-SP, 1956.

———. *O SENAI: Traços do seu Passado e Perspectivas Emergentes*. Rio de Janeiro: SENAI-DN, 1981.

Gomes, Ángela M. Castro. *Burguesia e Trabalho: Política e Legislação Social no Brasil*,

1917–1937. Rio de Janeiro: Campus, 1979.

———. *A Invenção do Trabalhismo*. Rio de Janeiro: IUPERJ/Vértice, 1988.

Gramsci, Antonio. "Americanism and Fordism." In *Selections from the Prison Notebooks*, pp. 277–318. New York: International Publishers, 1971.

Guillén, Mauro F. *Models of Management: Work, Authority, and Organization in a Comparative Perspective*. Chicago: University of Chicago Press, 1994.

Guimarães, Carlos Augusto Pereira. *Mensagem Enviada ao Congresso Legislativo de São Paulo pelo Vice-Presidente do Estado*. São Paulo, 1914.

Guzzo Decca, Maria Auxiliadora. *A Vida Fora das Fábricas: Cotidiano Operário em São Paulo, 1920–1934*. Rio de Janeiro: Paz e Terra, 1987.

Haber, Samuel. *Efficiency and Uplift: Scientific Management in the Progressive Era, 1890–1920*. Chicago: University of Chicago Press, 1964.

Haines, Gerald K. *The Americanization of Brazil*. Wilmington, Del.: Scholarly Resources, 1989.

Hall, Michael M. "Origins of Mass Immigration in Brazil." Ph.D. diss., Columbia University, 1969.

Hall, Michael M., and Marco Aurélio Garcia. "Urban Labor." In *Modern Brazil: Elites and Masses in Historical Perspective*, edited by Michael L. Conniff and Frank D. McCann, pp. 161–91. Lincoln: University of Nebraska Press, 1989.

Hamilton, Nora. *The Limits of State Autonomy: Post-Revolutionary Mexico*. Princeton: Princeton University Press, 1982.

Haskell, Thomas, ed. *The Authority of Experts*. Bloomington: Indiana University Press, 1984.

Haydu, Jeffrey. *Between Class and Craft: Skilled Workers and Factory Politics in the United States and Britain, 1890–1922*. Berkeley: University of California Press, 1988.

Hilton, Stanley E. *1932: A Guerra Civil Brasileira*. Rio de Janeiro: Nova Fronteira, 1982.

Howes, Robert W. "Progressive Conservatism in Brazil: Oliveira Vianna, Roberto Simonsen, and the Social Legislation of the Vargas Regime, 1930–1945." D.Phil. thesis, Cambridge University, 1975.

Huggins, Martha Knisely. *From Slavery to Vagrancy in Brazil: Crime and Social Control in the Third World*. New Brunswick: Rutgers University Press, 1985.

Humphrey, John. *Capitalist Control and Workers' Struggle in the Brazilian Auto Industry*. Princeton: Princeton University Press, 1982.

James, Daniel. "Rationalisation and Working-Class Response: The Context and Limits of Factory Floor Activity in Argentina." *Journal of Latin American Studies* 13 (Nov. 1981): 375–402.

———. *Resistance and Integration: Peronism and the Argentine Working Class, 1946–1976*. Cambridge: Cambridge University Press, 1988.

Joint Brazil–United States Economic Development Commission. *Brazilian Technical Studies*. Washington, D.C.: Government Printing Office, 1954.

Keck, Margaret. *The Workers' Party and Democratization in Brazil*. New Haven: Yale University Press, 1992.

Keremitsis, Eileen. "The Early Industrial Worker in Rio de Janeiro, 1870–1930." Ph.D. diss., Columbia University, 1982.

Khoury, Iara Aun. *A Greve de 1917 em São Paulo e o Processo de Organização Proletária*. São Paulo: Autores Associados, 1981.

Kowarick, Lúcio. *Trabalho e Vadiagem: A Origem do Trabalho Livre no Brasil*. São Paulo: Brasiliense, 1987.

Laclau, Ernesto. "Toward a Theory of Populism." In *Politics and Ideology in Marxist Theory*, pp. 143–200. London: Verso, 1977.

Lenharo, Alcir. *A Sacralização da Política*. Campinas: Papirus/Unicamp, 1986.

Leopoldi, M. Antonieta P. "Industrial Associations and Politics in Contemporary Brazil." D.Phil. thesis, Oxford University, 1984.

Lewin, Linda. *Politics and Parentela in Paraíba*. Princeton: Princeton University Press, 1987.

Lima, Heitor Ferreira. *História do Pensamento Econômico no Brasil*. São Paulo: Cia. Editora Nacional, 1976.

———. *Três Industrialistas Brasileiros*. São Paulo: Alfa-Omega, 1976.

Lima, Hélvio M. Pinheiro. *Curso de Relações Humanas para o Trabalhador*. São Paulo: SESI-SP, 1957.

Linhart, Robert. *Lenin, os Camponeses, Taylor*. Rio de Janeiro: Marco Zero, 1983.

Lobato, Mirta Zaída. *El "Taylorismo" en la Gran Industria Exportadora Argentina, 1907–1945*. Buenos Aires: Centro Editor de America Latina, 1988.

Lodi, Euvaldo. *Positivos os Indícios de que a Criação do SENAI foi um Ato Acertado da Indústria*. São Paulo: SENAI-SP, 1949.

Lopes, Francisco Santos. "Sistema Brasileiro de Formação Profissional para a Indústria." In *A Obra do SENAI através de "O Globo,"* pt. 2. São Paulo: SENAI-SP, 1968.

Lopes, José Sérgio Leite. "Sôbre os Trabalhadores da Grande Indústria na Pequena Cidade: Crítica e Resgate da Crise do Brasil Arcaico." In *Cultura e Identidade Operária*, edited by J. S. Leite Lopes, pp. 147–70. Rio de Janeiro: Marco Zero, 1987.

———. *A Tecelagem dos Conflitos de Classe na "Cidade das Chaminés."* São Paulo: Marco Zero, 1988.

Lopes, Juárez Rubens Brandão. *Crise do Brasil Arcaico*. São Paulo: Difel, 1967.

———. *Sociedade Industrial no Brasil*. São Paulo: Difel, 1964.

Lopes, Stênio. *Uma Saga da Criatividade Brasileira*. Rio de Janeiro: SENAI-DN, 1982.

Lourenço Filho, M. B. "Escola Nova." *Educação* 7, no. 3 (June 1929): 298–300.

Love, Joseph L. *Rio Grande do Sul and Brazilian Regionalism, 1882–1930*. Stanford: Stanford University Press, 1971.

———. *São Paulo in the Brazilian Federation, 1889–1937*. Stanford: Stanford University Press, 1980.

Loyola, Maria Andréa. *Os Sindicatos e o PTB: Estudo de um Caso em Minas Gerais*. Petrópolis: Vozes, 1980.

Luz, Nícia Vilela. *A Luta pela Industrialização do Brasil*. 2d ed. São Paulo: Alfa-Omega, 1975.

McCann, Frank D., Jr. *The Brazilian-American Alliance, 1937–1945*. Princeton: Princeton University Press, 1973.

McMillan, Claude, Jr. "The American Businessman in Brazil." *Business Topics*, no. 2 (Spring 1963): 68–80.

Maier, Charles E. "Between Taylorism and Technocracy: European Ideologies and the Vision of Industrial Productivity in the 1920s." *Journal of Contemporary History* 5 (1975): 27–61.

———. *Recasting Bourgeois Europe*. Princeton: Princeton University Press, 1975.

Manfredi, Sílvia Maria. "As Entidades Sindicais e a Educação dos Trabalhadores." *Cadernos de Pesquisa*, no. 47 (Nov. 1983): 64–77.

Mange, Roberto. "Ensino Profissional Racional no Curso de Ferroviários de Sorocaba." In *Roberto Mange e Sua Obra*, edited by Ítalo Bologna, pp. 27–58. Goiânia: UNIGRAF, 1980.

———. "Escolas Profissionaes Mecânicas." *Revista Polytechnica*, no. 8 (Oct.–Nov. 1924): 17–21.

———. *A Formação dos Técnicos para a Indústria*. São Paulo: Folha da Manhã, 1940.

———. *Lições de Psicotécnica*. São Paulo: IDORT, 1934.

———. *Missão do Serviço Nacional de Aprendizagem Industrial*. São Paulo: SENAI-SP, 1943.

———. *Planejamento e Administração Unificada da Aprendizagem Industrial no Brasil*. São Paulo: SENAI-SP, 1949.

———. "Prevenção de Acidentes na Estiva." In *Roberto Mange e Sua Obra*, edited by Ítalo Bologna, pp. 267–91. Goiânia: UNIGRAF, 1980.

Maranhão, Ricardo. *Sindicatos e Democratização: Brasil, 1945–1950*. São Paulo: Brasiliense, 1979.

Maroni, Amnéris. *A Estratégia da Recusa*. São Paulo: Brasiliense, 1982.

Martins, José de Souza. *Conde Matarazzo: O Empresário e a Empresa*. São Paulo: Hucitec, 1973.

Martins, Luciano. "Formação do Empresário Industrial." *Revista da Civilização Brasileira*, no. 13 (May 1967): 91–132.

Medeiros, Marluce Moura de. "Estradas de Ferro e Ensino Industrial: Um Estudo de Caso." M.A. thesis, Fundação Getúlio Vargas, Rio de Janeiro, 1980.

Meem, James C. "Industrial Training: A Bridge between Nations." *Bulletin of the Pan American Union*, no. 81 (Jan. 1947): 3–7.

Meyer, Stephen. *The Five Dollar Day: Labor Management and Social Control in the Ford Motor Company, 1908–1921*. Albany: State University of New York Press, 1981.

Moisés, José Alvaro. *Greve de Massa e Crise Política: Estudo da Greve dos 300 Mil em São Paulo, 1953–1954*. São Paulo: Polis, 1978.

Montgomery, David. *The Fall of the House of Labor*. Cambridge: Cambridge University Press, 1987.

———. *Workers' Control in America: Studies in the History of Work, Technology, and Labor Struggles*. Cambridge: Cambridge University Press, 1979.

Moraes, Carmen S. Vidigal. "A Socialização da Força de Trabalho: Instrução Popular e Qualificação Profissional no Estado de São Paulo, 1873–1934." Ph.D. diss., University of São Paulo, 1990.

Moraes Filho, Evaristo de. *O Problema do Sindicato Único no Brasil*. São Paulo: Alfa-Omega, 1978.

Morse, Richard M. *From Community to Metropolis: A Biography of São Paulo*. Gainesville: University of Florida Press, 1958.

Munakata, Kazumi. "Compromisso do Estado." *Revista Brasileira de História*, no. 7 (1984): 58–71.

———. *A Legislação Trabalhista no Brasil*. São Paulo: Brasiliense, 1981.

Nelson, Daniel. *Frederick W. Taylor and the Rise of Scientific Management*. Madison: University of Wisconsin Press, 1980.

Nogueira, Octávio Pupo. *A Indústria em Face das Leis do Trabalho*. São Paulo: Salesianas, 1935.

Nogueira Filho, Paulo. *Ideais e Lutas de um Burguês Progressista*. Vol. 1. São Paulo: José Olympio, 1958.

Nolan, Mary. "'Housework Made Easy': The Taylorized Housewife in Weimar Germany's Rationalized Economy." *Feminist Studies* 16 (Fall 1990): 549–77.

———. *Visions of Modernity: American Business and the Modernization of Germany*. Oxford: Oxford University Press, 1994.

Oliveira, Armando de Salles. *Mensagem Apresentado pelo Governador a Assembléa Legislativa de São Paulo*. São Paulo, 1936.

Oliveira, Clovis de. *Do CIESP à FIESP*. São Paulo: FIESP, 1969.

———. *A Indústria e o Movimento Constitucionalista de 1932*. São Paulo: FIESP, 1956.

Oliveira, Isabel Ribeiro de. *Trabalho e Política: As Origens do Partido dos Trabalhadores*. Petrópolis: Vozes, 1988.

O'Neil, Charles. "Educational Innovation and Politics in São Paulo, 1933–1934." *Luso-Brazilian Review* 8 (Summer 1971): 56–68.

Owensby, Brian P. "'Stuck in the Middle': Emergence of an Urban Middle Class in Brazil, 1850 to 1950." Ph.D. diss., Princeton University, 1993.

Pacheco e Silva, A. C. *Armando de Salles Oliveira*. São Paulo: Martins, 1966.

———. "A Fadiga Industrial." *Boletim SENAI*, no. 2 (Nov. 1946): 11–13.

Paoli, Maria Célia, Eder Sader, and Vera da Silva Telles. "Pensando a Classe Operária: Os Trabalhadores Sujeitos ao Imaginário Acadêmico." *Revista Brasileira de História*, no. 6 (1984): 129–49.

Payne, Leigh A. *Brazilian Industrialists and Democratic Change*. Baltimore: Johns Hopkins University Press, 1994.

Pereira, José Carlos. *Estrutura e Expansão da Indústria em São Paulo*. São Paulo: Cia. Editora Nacional, 1967.

Pereira, Luiz. *Classe Operária*. São Paulo: Livraria Duas Cidades, 1978.

———. *A Escola numa Área Metropolitana*. São Paulo: Pioneira, 1976.

———. *Trabalho e Desenvolvimento no Brasil*. São Paulo: Difel, 1965.

Pereira, Vera Maria Cândido. *O Coração da Fábrica*. Rio de Janeiro: Campus, 1979.

Pierro, Mário F. di. *A Indústria, o Estado e a Economia Nacional*. São Paulo: FIESP, 1962.

Pinheiro, Paulo Sérgio, and Michael Hall, eds. *A Classe Operária no Brasil, 1889–1934*. Vol. 2. São Paulo: Brasiliense, 1981.

Pinto, Carlos Alberto de Carvalho. *Mensagem Apresentada pelo Governador a Assembléa Legislativa do Estado de São Paulo*. São Paulo, 1960.

Prado, Maria Lígia Coelho. *A Democracia Ilustrada: O Partido Democrático de São Paulo, 1926–1934*. São Paulo: Ática, 1986.

Projeto Memória, Serviço Nacional de Aprendizagem Industrial, São Paulo. *De Homens e Máquinas: Roberto Mange e a Formação Profissional*. Vol. 1. São Paulo: SENAI-SP, 1991.

———. *O Giz e a Graxa: Meio Século de Educação para o Trabalho*. São Paulo: SENAI-SP, 1992.

Quadros, Jânio. *Mensagem Apresentada pelo Governador a Assembléa Legislativa do Estado de São Paulo*. São Paulo, 1957.

Rabinbach, Anson. *The Human Motor: Energy, Fatigue, and the Origins of Modernity*. New York: Basic Books, 1990.

Rago, Margareth. *Do Cabaré ao Lar: A Utopia da Cidade Disciplinar—Brazil, 1890–1930*. Rio de Janeiro: Paz e Terra, 1985.

Ramalho, José Ricardo. *Estado-Patrão e Luta Operária: O Caso FNM*. Rio de Janeiro: Paz e Terra, 1989.

Reis, Mário Goulart. *O Serviço Social da Indústria como Instituição*. Porto Alegre: SENAI, 1955.

Ribeiro, Maria Alice. "Condições de Trabalho na Indústria Têxtil Paulista, 1870–1930." M.A. thesis, Universidade Estadual de Campinas, 1980.

Richers, Raimar, et al. *Impacto da Ação do Governo sôbre as Emprêsas Brasileiras*. Rio de Janeiro, 1963.

Rodrigues, José Albertino. *Sindicato e Desenvolvimento no Brasil.* São Paulo, 1968.

Rodrigues, Leôncio Martins. *Conflito Industrial e Sindicalismo no Brasil.* São Paulo, 1966.

Rodrigues Alves, Francisco de Paula. *Mensagem Enviada ao Congresso Legislativo de São Paulo pelo Presidente do Estado.* N.p., 1912, 1915.

Roethlisberger, F. J., and William J. Dickson. *Management and the Worker.* Cambridge: Harvard University Press, 1939.

Rosenzweig, Roy. *Eight Hours For What We Will: Workers and Leisure in an Industrial City, 1870–1920.* Cambridge: Cambridge University Press, 1983.

Rowland, Robert. "Classe Operária e Estado de Compromisso: Origens Estructurais da Legislação Trabalhista e Sindical." *Estudos CEBRAP*, no. 8 (1974).

Rudge, Fernando Da Rocha Telles. "O Problema das Relações Humanas no Trabalho e a Supervisão do Pessoal na Indústria." *Boletim Interno da DOS*, no. 3 (Apr. 1953): 1–15.

Sader, Eder. *Quando Novos Personagens Entraram em Cena.* Rio de Janeiro: Paz e Terra, 1988.

Sáenz Leme, Maria. *A Ideologia dos Industriais Brasileiros, 1919–1945.* Petrópolis: Vozes, 1979.

Saes, Décio. *A Formação do Estado Burguês no Brasil.* Rio de Janeiro: Paz e Terra, 1985.

Sampiao, Regina. *Adhemar de Barros e o PSP.* São Paulo: Global, 1982.

Sandoval, Salvador A. M. *Social Change and Labor Unrest in Brazil since 1945.* Boulder: Westview Press, 1993.

Schmitter, Philippe. *Interest Conflict and Political Change in Brazil.* Stanford: Stanford University Press, 1971.

Schwartzman, Simon, Helena M. Bousquet Bomeny, and Vanda M. Ribeiro Costa. *Tempos de Capanema.* Rio de Janeiro: Paz e Terra/Edusp, 1984.

Scott, James. *Domination and the Arts of Resistance: Hidden Transcripts.* New Haven: Yale University Press, 1990.

Scott, Joan W. *Gender and the Politics of History.* New York: Columbia University Press, 1988.

———. *The Glassworkers of Carmaux.* Cambridge: Harvard University Press, 1974.

Segnini, Liliana R. P. *Ferrovia e Ferroviários.* São Paulo: Autores Associados/Cortez, 1982.

Serviço de Ensino e Seleção Profissional. *Relatório pelo Ano de 1931.* São Paulo: Secção de Ensino, 1934.

Serviço Nacional de Aprendizagem Industrial, Departamento Nacional. "Pesquisa sôbre Evasão Escolar: O Problema da Escola de Aprendizagem Industrial no Brasil." 6 vols. Rio de Janeiro: SENAI-DN, 1952.

———, São Paulo. *Curso de Aperfeiçoamento para Instrutores: Elaboração e Aplicação da SMO.* São Paulo: SENAI-SP, 1953.

———. *Curso de Aperfeiçoamento para Instrutores: Noções de Psicologia do Adolescente.* São Paulo: SENAI-SP, 1953.

———. *Felix Guisard.* Série "Grandes Figuras da Indústria." São Paulo: SENAI-SP, 1960.

———. "Inquérito entre Aprendizes do SENAI sôbre Aspectos de Sua Vida Escolar, e de Sua Situação na Indústria." São Paulo: SENAI-SP, 1953.

———. *Morvan Dias de Figueiredo.* Série "Grandes Figuras da Indústria." São Paulo: SENAI-SP, 1960.

———. "Quatro Décadas de História: Anos 1960–1969." *Comunicação/SENAI*, no. 46, Suplemento Histórico (1982).

———. "O SENAI de São Paulo no Decênio 1950–1960." São Paulo: SENAI-SP, 1961.

Serviço Social da Indústria, São Paulo. *Roteiro do Mestre.* Série Popular no. 3. São Paulo: SESI-SP, 1952.

————. *Segunda Leitura do Trabalhador*. São Paulo: SESI-SP, n.d.

————, Divisão de Abastecimento. *SESI—18 Anos*. São Paulo: SESI-SP, 1965.

————, Divisão de Alimentação. *SESI—18 Anos*. São Paulo: SESI-SP, 1965.

————, Divisão de Assistência Social. *SESI—18 Anos*. São Paulo: SESI-SP, 1965.

————, Divisão de Educação Fundamental. *SESI—18 Anos*. São Paulo: SESI-SP, 1965.

————, Divisão de Orientação Social. *Curso de Relações Humanas para o Trabalhador*. São Paulo: SESI-SP, 1957.

————. *Curso de Técnicas de Comunicação Verbal*. São Paulo: SESI-SP, 1958.

————. *O Guia dos Dirigentes Sindicais*. Série Sindical no. 2. São Paulo: SESI-SP, 1953.

————. *Manual do Estagiário*. São Paulo: SESI-SP, 1958.

————. "Produtividade." *Boletim Interno*, no. 12 (Mar. 1959): 31–84.

————. *SESI em Algarismos*. São Paulo: SESI-SP, 1960.

————. *O Voto*. Série Popular no. 6. São Paulo: SESI-SP, 1955.

Severo, Ricardo. *O Liceu de Artes e Ofícios de São Paulo, 1873–1934*. São Paulo: Typografia de "O Estado," 1935.

Siciliano Júnior, Alexandre. *Agricultura, Comércio e Indústria no Brasil*. São Paulo: CIESP, 1931.

Siegelbaum, Lewis H. *Stakhanovism and the Politics of Productivity in the USSR, 1935–1941*. Cambridge: Cambridge University Press, 1988.

Siekman, Philip. "When Executives Turned Revolutionaries." *Fortune*, no. 70 (Sept. 1964): 147–49, 214–21.

Sikkink, Kathryn. *Ideas and Institutions: Developmentalism in Brazil and Argentina*. Ithaca: Cornell University Press, 1991.

Silva, Egydio M. de Castro e. *Agua, Cerâmica, Celulose e os Homens*. São Paulo, n.d.

Silva, Hélio, and Maria Cecília Ribas Carneiro. *Os Presidentes: Getúlio Vargas, 1946–1954*. São Paulo: Grupo de Comunicação Três, 1983.

Silveira, Fajardo da. "O Problema do Menor de 14 Anos." *Boletim Interno da DOS*, no. 3 (Apr. 1953): 42–46.

Silveira, Horácio da. *O Ensino Technico-Profissional e Doméstico em São Paulo*. São Paulo, 1935.

Simão, Azis. *Sindicato e Estado*. São Paulo: Dominus, 1966.

Simonsen, Roberto. *As Atividades do Serviço Social da Indústria no Estado de São Paulo*. São Paulo: Siqueira, 1947.

————. "As Classes Produtoras do Brasil e o Partido Comunista." In *Evolução Industrial do Brasil*, pp. 455–58. São Paulo: Editora Nacional/Editora da USP, 1973.

————. "Confraternização Social." In *Ensaios Sociais, Políticos e Econômicos*, pp. 270–74. São Paulo: FIESP, 1943.

————. *A Construção dos Quartéis para o Exército*. São Paulo: São Paulo Editora, 1931.

————. "O Direito Social Brasileiro." In *Ensaios Sociais, Políticos e Econômicos*, pp. 257–59. São Paulo: FIESP, 1943.

————. *Discurso na Assembléia Nacional Constituinte em 30 de Janeiro de 1934*. São Paulo: São Paulo Editora Limitada, 1934.

————. *Ensaios Sociais, Políticos e Econômicos*. São Paulo: FIESP, 1943.

————. *Evolução Industrial do Brasil*. São Paulo: Editora Nacional/Editora da USP, 1973.

————. "As Finanças e a Indústria." In *Á Margem da Profissão*, pp. 217–60. São Paulo: São Paulo Editora, 1932.

————. *A Indústria em Face da Economia Nacional*. São Paulo: Gráfica da "Revista dos Tribunaes," 1937.

————. *Á Margem da Profissão*. São Paulo: São Paulo Editora, 1932.

————. "Os Objetivos da Engenharia Nacional." In *Ensaios Sociais, Políticos e Econômicos*, pp. 76–102. São Paulo: FIESP, 1943.

————. *Ordem Econômica, Padrão de Vida, e Algumas Realidades Brasileiras*. São Paulo: São Paulo Editora Limitada, 1934.

————. "O Problema Social no Brasil." In *Evolução Industrial do Brasil*, pp. 443–54. São Paulo: Editora Nacional/Editora da USP, 1973.

————. *Rumo à Verdade*. São Paulo: São Paulo Editora Limitada, 1933.

————. *O Trabalho Moderno*. São Paulo: Tipografia de "O Estado," 1919.

Simonsen, Roberto, and M. T. Carvalho de Britto. "Technicos para o Brasil." In *Á Margem da Profissão*, pp. 89–90. São Paulo: São Paulo Editora, 1932.

Skidmore, Thomas. *Politics in Brazil, 1930–1964*. Oxford: Oxford University Press, 1967.

Sklar, Kathryn Kish. *Florence Kelley and the Nation's Work*. New Haven: Yale University Press, 1995.

Skocpol, Theda. *Protecting Soldiers and Mothers*. Cambridge: Harvard University Press, 1992.

Springer, Joseph Frank. *A Brazilian Factory Study*. Cuaderno no. 33. Cuernavaca: CIDOC, 1966.

Starling, Heloísa Maria Murgel. *Os Senhores das Gerais*. Petrópolis: Vozes, 1986.

Stedman Jones, Gareth. "Class Expression versus Social Control?: A Critique of Recent Trends in the Social History of Leisure." *History Workshop* 4 (Fall 1977): 163–70.

Stein, Stanley. *The Brazilian Cotton Manufacture*. Cambridge: Harvard University Press, 1957.

Stepan, Nancy L. *"The Hour of Eugenics": Race, Gender, and Nation in Latin America*. Ithaca: Cornell University Press, 1991.

Suzigan, Wilson. *Indústria Brasileira: Origem e Desenvolvimento*. São Paulo: Brasiliense, 1986.

Teixeira, Palmira Petratti. *A Fábrica do Sonho: Trajetoria do Industrial Jorge Street*. Rio de Janeiro: Paz e Terra, 1990.

Telles, Jover. *O Movimento Sindical no Brasil*. Rio de Janeiro: Vitória, 1962.

Tenca, Alvaro. "Razão e Vontade Política: IDORT e a Grande Indústria." M.A. thesis, Universidade Estadual de Campinas, 1987.

Thompson, E. P. *The Making of the English Working Class*. New York: Pantheon, 1976.

Toledo, Caio Navarro de. *ISEB: Fábrica de Ideologias*. São Paulo: Ática, 1977.

Tolle, Paulo Ernest. *Retrospecto, Realizações e Problemas do Departamento Regional do SENAI de São Paulo*. Document no. 8. Rio de Janeiro: SENAI-DN, 1972.

Topik, Steven C. "Brazil's Bourgeois Revolution?" *The Americas* 48 (Oct. 1991): 245–71.

Trevisan, Maria José. *50 Anos em 5: A FIESP e o Desenvolvimentismo*. Petrópolis: Vozes, 1986.

Van Atta, Don. "Why Is There No Taylorism in the Soviet Union?" *Comparative Politics* 18 (Apr. 1986): 327–37.

Vargas, Getúlio. *A Nova Política do Brasil*. Vols. 1–2. Rio de Janeiro: José Olympio, 1938.

Veccia, Theresa R. "Women, Work, and Family Life: São Paulo Textile Workers, 1900–1950." In *The Politics of Working-Class Womanhood: New Approaches to the Study of Latin American Workers*, edited by John D. French and Daniel James. Durham: Duke University Press, forthcoming.

Versiani, Flávio R. *A Década de 20 na Industrialização Brasileira*. Rio de Janeiro: IPEA/INPES, 1987.

Vianna, Luiz Werneck. *Liberalismo e Sindicato no Brasil.* Rio de Janeiro: Paz e Terra, 1976.

Vieira, Rosa Maria. "O Pensamento Industrialista de Roberto Simonsen: Análise de Ideologia." M.A. thesis, University of São Paulo, 1987.

Von der Weid, Elisabeth, and Ana Marta R. Bastos. *O Fio da Meada.* Rio de Janeiro: FCRB-CNI, 1986.

Weffort, Francisco. "Participação e Conflito Industrial: Contagem e Osasco, 1968." *Caderno do CEBRAP* 3 (1972).

———. *O Populismo na Política Brasileira.* Rio de Janeiro: Paz e Terra, 1978.

Weinstein, Barbara. "Impressões da Elite sôbre os Movimentos da Classe Operária: A Cobertura da Greve em 'O Estado de São Paulo,' 1902–1917." In *O Bravo Matutino,* edited by M. H. Capelato and M. L. Prado, pp. 135–76. São Paulo: Alfa-Omega, 1980.

———. "Industrialists, the State, and the Limits of Democratization in Brazil, 1930–1964." In *The Social Construction of Democracy, 1870–1990,* edited by George Reid Andrews and Herrick Chapman, pp. 315–39. New York: New York University Press/Macmillan, 1995.

———. "The Model Worker of the Paulista Industrialists: The 'Campanha Operário Padrão,' 1964–1985." *Radical History Review,* no. 61 (Winter 1995): 92–123.

———. "As Mulheres Trabalhadoras em São Paulo: De Operárias Não-qualificadas a Esposas Profissionais." *Cadernos Pagu,* no. 4 (1995): 143–71.

Weinstein, James. *The Corporate Ideal in the Liberal State, 1900–1918.* Boston: Beacon Press, 1969.

Welch, Clifford A. "Labor Internationalism: U.S. Involvement in Brazilian Unions, 1945–1965." *Latin American Research Review,* no. 30 (1995): 61–89.

———. "Rural Labor and the Brazilian Revolution in São Paulo, 1930–1964." Ph.D. diss., Duke University, 1990.

Willits, J. H. "The Labor Turn-Over and the Humanizing of Industry." *Annals of the American Academy of Political and Social Science,* no. 61 (Sept. 1915): 127–37.

Winn, Peter. "A Worker's Nightmare: Taylorism and the 1962 Yarur Strike in Chile." *Radical History Review,* no. 58 (Winter 1994): 4–34.

Wolfe, Joel. *Working Women, Working Men: São Paulo and the Rise of Brazil's Industrial Working Class, 1900–1955.* Durham: Duke University Press, 1993.

Yasbek, Maria Carmelita. "A Escola de Serviço Social de São Paulo no Período de 1936 a 1945." *Cadernos PUC,* no. 6 (Dec. 1980): 11–60.

Index